MUSIC TEACHER'S Survival Guide

Practical Techniques & Materials for the Elementary Music Classroom

ROSALIE A. HARITUN

PARKER PUBLISHING COMPANY
West Nyack, New York 10995

10 9 8 7 6 5 4 3 2 1

Library of Congress Cataloging-in-Publication Data

Haritun, Rosalie A.
    Music teacher's survival guide : practical techniques & materials
for the elementary music classroom / Rosalie A. Haritun.
        p.   cm.
    ISBN 0-13-121302-4
    1. School music—Instruction and study.   I. Title.
MT1.H22 1994
372.87′044—dc20   93-43240
                                                             CIP
                                                             MN

PARKER PUBLISHING COMPANY
BUSINESS & PROFESSIONAL DIVISION
A division of Simon & Schuster
West Nyack, New York 10995

Printed in the United States of America

About the Author

Dr. Rosalie A. Haritun is the Assistant Chair and Coordinator of Music Education in the Department of Music at Indiana-Purdue University in Fort Wayne, Indiana where she holds the rank of Associate Professor. Prior to this, she was Assistant Professor of Music Education at East Carolina University in Greenville, North Carolina. Before that, she was a member of the Music Education Faculty in the School of Music at Temple University in Philadelphia.

Dr. Haritun holds a doctorate (Ed.D) and Professional Diploma from Teachers College, Columbia University in New York, and a Masters Degree in Music Education from the University of Illinois in Champagn-Urbana, Illinois. Dr. Haritun also completed a year of post-doctoral study at Teachers College, Columbia University in the area of Behavioral Modification Techniques. She earned her Bachelor's Degree from Baldwin-Wallace Conservatory of Music in Berea, Ohio.

She is an active member in a number of organizations, including Music Educators National Conference (MENC), the College Music Society, Indiana Music Educators Association (IMEA), Indiana Music Teachers Association (IMTA), Sigma Alpha Iota, and Delta Kappa Gamma. She is also a published author. Her articles have appeared in *The School Musician* and the *North Carolina Music Educators Journal*. Dr. Haritun is also actively involved as a consultant for Music Education, a presentor at state and regional conferences, and evaluator for the Southern Association Accrediting Agency for secondary schools and universities, as well as a supervisor of student teachers in both choral and instrumental music concentrations.

About This Survival Guide

The Music Teacher's Survival Guide: Practical Techniques & Materials for the Elementary Music Classroom is a down-to-earth, easy-to-use resource that will help you identify the myriad of behaviors associated with teaching each of the specialized areas of music. These behaviors range from the unobservable practices in *preparation* (such as choosing appropriate and appealing music) to the visible maneuvers in *teaching* (such as handing out and tuning guitars). Thus, this guide will be useful for experienced music teachers as well as those teachers just starting out in the music classroom.

How This Guide Is Organized

Written in a conversational style with light-hearted illustrations sprinkled throughout the text, *The Music Teacher's Survival Guide* is divided into 10 chapters. Each chapter focuses on the actual implementation of the following teaching skills and behaviors:

- verbalizing
- pacing
- response
- assessing
- sequencing
- behavior

Each chapter in this guide offers you a definition and description of the specific skill or behavior covered, its significant impact on teaching and learning, actual examples, helpful suggestions for implementation, and a concluding challenge.

A unique feature of the book is the "Less Effective" and "More Effective" contrasting scenario at the end of each section. These scenarios help you to see how the particular skill or behavior is used appropriately *and* inappropriately in realistic teaching situations.

Sample lesson plans are also included for the music specialist as well as the classroom teacher who must teach a music mini-lesson. These sample lesson plans are suggestions—or models—to help strengthen your plans already in use.

Concluding Comments

I hope you will renew your interest and concern with regard to your own teaching skills and behaviors. More than that, I hope you will want to *improve* your skills and try some of the suggestions *The Music Teacher's Survival Guide* offers.

If you're looking for help in identifying specific teaching skills, take a good look at the categories of skills. Then find the particular skill in one of the chapters and read about it in more detail.

Be sure you get the picture as to how teaching skills rate in the teaching profession. No doubt about it, the teaching profession needs to take a firmer stand on the need for good teaching behaviors, that is, good teaching skills. It was with this thought in mind that I wrote *The Music Teacher's Survival Guide*. My sincere hope is that this book will fill some small gap in strengthening the teaching skills of everyone who reads it. Good luck!

Finally, I would like to thank my illustrators, Mr. Alan White and John Hrehov, for their invaluable contribution to this text with their caricatures. My deepest appreciation also goes out to my colleagues who proofread the early drafts and provided insight for the revisions. Without their help, I could not have completed this text.

Rosalie A. Haritun

Chapter 3 BASIC VERBAL SKILLS • 99

Chapter 4 VERBAL BEHAVIORS FOR TEACHING MUSIC • 151

Preparation Skills

This chapter concentrates on preparing tasks for the general music teacher; that is, for those who teach in the classroom environment. Some of the planning and preparing practices are rather obvious. Others are less apparent but, nevertheless, equally as important. Since "planning" is generally thought of as the job of setting up a scheme, or a method, or a design, and since educators automatically associate the term with lesson planning, its meaning here will refer to the overall task of formulating the lesson plan. As for "preparing," which according to Webster means "an act or procedure undertaken in advance . . . ," the word will be understood to mean any particular action involved in the overall planning. Thus, some of the tasks will be planning tasks while others will be preparational.

There is no substitute for thorough planning and preparation. Both are keys to success in teaching. Unfortunately, many teachers are guilty of plunging into their lessons on occasion without sufficient preparation. What happens? The lesson usually self-destructs, either on the spot or little by little. And the excuses are varied. They include everything from the infamous "I forgot to . . ." to the "I just assumed . . ." to the ever popular "I simply do not have enough time." Some even gingerly

admit that they "didn't think of this or that!" But none of these excuses are acceptable. They are merely smoke screens for the real problem: insufficient preparation. What a terrible indictment! The fact is, planning and preparing are built-in responsibilities. Effective teaching depends upon both of these efforts. Moreover, they're an obligation. Teachers have an obligation to the students to be well-prepared. Thus, preparational chores rank as one of the major categories of teacher behaviors for the general music specialist.

Selecting a Variety of Suitable Activities

The selecting of activities for the general music class is the "backbone" of the planning process. It's the part of planning that demands the most time and effort—and the place where the teacher can be the most creative. But that's another preparational matter that we'll deal with later. For now, let's concentrate on the selecting of activities from the standpoint of (a) variety and (b) suitability, because these are two of the most important criteria the teacher must deal with in choosing activities and also because it's the first task that the teacher must face after determining the objectives.

Definition of Variety and Suitability

While these criteria may be understood by most general music teachers, there still may be some who need clarification. Variety in activities means that there are different experiences planned in order to help students identify the concept or skill being taught, experiences that are sometimes modified to "fit" one's class. (It's in the modifying process where the teacher can let his/her creative fancy fly! See "Adding a Creative Touch" later in this chapter.)

Look at all the different kinds of activities we have in music. There's a host of moving activities that include walking, marching, skipping, hopping, running, swaying, dancing, etc., and a number of more refined type motions such as clapping, tapping, snapping, tipping, etc. Then there's also the listening, singing, and playing activities. And look at the variety of instruments when it comes to playing; there's (a) classroom rhythm instruments, (b) pitched percussion instruments, (c) non-pitched percussion instruments, and (d) social-oriented instruments, like guitars, ukeleles, and autoharps. And don't forget reading, analyzing, and composing. In the context of musical activities then, variety means having several, or more, of these experiences in the lesson, not *just* singing, or just listening, or just playing, but a "mixture" of activities.

There's also a more refined meaning of variety that needs to be explained. It refers to the categorizing of activities. Variety in this sense means that there's a representation from three basic types of activities, namely: (1) Aural Activities, (2) Visual Activities, and (3) Performing Activities. A sampling of the kind of activities that falls into each category is given in Figure 1.1. Actually, speaking in terms of categories is a more accurate way of perceiving the term *variety*.

Category	Musical Activities
Aural Activities	Listening activities, taking dictation, following call charts, moving experiences, verbalizing responses, playing responses, etc.
Visual Activities	Following notation or themes, identifying symbols, analyzing scores, composing music, reading visual aids, etc.
Performing Activities	Playing classroom instruments or guitars, ukeleles, piano, and recorders; singing, folk dancing, conducting, etc.

Figure 1.1. Activities in the Three Categories

Now what about suitability? That simply means the activity is particularly well-suited to focusing on the concept or developing the skills. It lends itself naturally and musically to the learning material, such as (a) beating a tub drum on accented beats, (b) playing step bells on upward passages, (c) walking on tippy-toes for high sounds, or (d) strumming the autoharp to identify chord changes. These are all examples of suitable activities in that they're experiences that best accentuate the concepts when being implemented. That's what being suitable is all about—accentuating power!

Is it clear now what variety and suitability mean in terms of activities? Good! Just remember, if your activities include aural, visual, and performing experiences, they'll be varied. And if they accentuate the concepts, they'll be suitable.

Suggestions for Achieving Variety

How can you be assured of having a variety of activities each lesson? Simple. Be sure that all three categories—aural, visual, and performing—are accounted for in your activities. But don't try to plan the activities around these categories. That won't work! You'll be planning for categories rather than concepts. What you do is doublecheck **after** you've planned your activities to see if the categories are covered. If so, you know you'll have a variety. If not, you'll need to make some revisions.

Now here's the tricky part. There doesn't need to be a new activity for each category. Not at all! There wouldn't be enough class time to do this. Just deal with the three categories within the one or two activities already planned. Take, for example, a guitar lesson. Is it possible to have all three categories in a "playing" lesson? Yes, it is! While the performing category is the predominant type of activity, the visual can come in when the students are instructed to follow stroke patterns, such as /|/|/|/ or chord-patterns on the chalkboard or in their texts. And the aural experience could come from having students identify chords *before* playing them on the guitar or ukeleles. So you see, even a performance lesson can be turned into a three-dimensional activity experience.

It's even easier to achieve variety in a regular music lesson, regardless if it's a one- or two-concept lesson. Let's suppose it's a one-concept lesson dealing with upward scale-like patterns. To have all three type experiences for your students, you might have them do the following: (1) **sing** the melodic patterns with numbers and/or syllables, such as 1-2-3-4-5 and/or do-re-mi-fa-sol, when they appear in the song; (2) **play** the melodic patterns on chromatic bells while listening to the recording; and (3) **analyze** other familiar songs for upward scale patterns.

But what if you weren't aware of needing variety in your activities? In that case, all you might do for the entire lesson is have the class sing upward patterns (on "Lu" in several orchestral selections, such as "The Swan" from *Carnival of Animals* by Saint-Saëns). Compare this lesson with the one in the preceding paragraph. See how it can be transformed into a varied learning experience, and how it's possible to have variety in a one-concept lesson, as well as two? Good! The general music teacher must have the ability to plan for a variety of activities.

My suggestion for ensuring suitability is just as simple. If the activity isn't one of your tried-and-true ones, test it out yourself. See if it feels "right" with the music, if it really *does* accentuate the concept, and if it's a musical response. If your answer is "yes" to all three inquiries, then rest assured your activities are suitable. That's about all the advice I can offer. To be honest, it's the *only* advice! You'll have to be the judge after the testing. It comes down to that—your own decision.

Importance of Variety and Suitability

Why all the hoopla about variety in activities? It's obvious. Without a mix of different learning experiences, the lesson will be boring. It'll lack the excitement that comes from change. Activities need to be varied, if for no other reason than to keep the lesson from being dull and boring. Let's not assume that students in general music will have as much self-discipline to keep attending as those in the performing groups. They won't! They need variety to hold their attention.

The second reason is closely related. Without variety in the activities, there are more management problems. Discipline will always get worse when students get bored. But one of the best ways of holding onto classroom control is to keep the students challenged through a variety of planned activities.

The last reason is that variety provides more opportunity for students to develop their musical skills in order to become better consumers of music. As music educators, we dare not minimize the significance of this reason. The future of the arts, and particularly music, depends, to a large degree, upon the musical background of these consumers. We owe it to them and to our profession to provide a variety of experiences that will nurture their musical sensitivity.

The above reasons ought to convince you to vary your activities and be certain that they suitably highlight the conceptual idea. It's not just a "nice" idea or a possible suggestion, it's a definite recommendation, if your teaching is going to be successful. So give these supportive reasons serious consideration.

Concluding Challenge

Do you look for variety and suitability when selecting your activities for the classroom? You can no longer make these selections randomly. You must have an eye towards (a) providing for variety and (b) focusing on suitability. It makes a difference in maintaining interest, controlling behavior, and fostering future consumers of music. Begin now to select a variety of suitable learning experiences for your students.

LESS EFFECTIVE	MORE EFFECTIVE
Students in Ms. Minor's second-grade general music class marched and played rhythm sticks to the ongoing pulse. When they returned from marching around the room, she asked the class to stand by their seats and march in their places. "Pretend to play your imaginary drums to the same beat. But keep marching. Yes, we're going to march again! So stop grumbling," she snapped.	For the first activity, Ms. Minor asked the children to do some aerobic steps to the ongoing beat as they listened to an exercise record. When they finished, she told them that next each one was going to be a drummer in a rock band. They were to "play" the ongoing beat on high hat cymbals with their right hand and the bass drum with their right foot. The left hand would tap their desk drum. They liked this "playing."
Mr. Major's eighth-grade general music class had analyzed about five songs in regard to their phrase form, both individually and together. For the last part of the class, Mr. Major handed out a short quiz with one song to be analyzed according to its phrase form. The students groaned as the quiz was being passed out and mumbled "This is boring!"	Students were asked to call out numbers on the call chart dealing with phrase form for their first activity. When they were finished, Mr. Major praised the class. "Good work. You are beginning to recognize phrase forms quickly. Now let's turn to page 14 and, as we sing the song, hold up one finger for 'a' phrases, and two for 'b' phrases. Keep your fingers up until the end of the phrase. Then bring them down quickly. Ready."

Choosing Appropriate and Appealing Music

Teachers on all experience levels will agree that one of the most demanding aspects in lesson planning is the selecting of music. It can be time consuming and frustrating, much like the selecting of activities. (See "Choosing Appropriate and Appealing Activities" later in this chapter.) But when tackled with the idea that the music should be appropriate and also appealing, the task somehow seems less awesome! It's a matter of understanding what "appropriate" and "appealing" mean in the context of selecting music.

Definition of Appropriate

Actually, there are two facets involved in the appropriate criteria. One of the facets is that there's a clear example of the conceptual idea in the music. How can a song or recording be considered "appropriate" if it doesn't have at least one example of the concept? It can't. If the concept deals with repeated tones, then the song must have at least one, and possibly two, passages of these tones to be "appropriate" for the lesson. "Jingle Bells" is a good example, and so is "The Farmer in the Dell" with its repeated tone passages on different pitches. And don't forget Vaughn William's *March of the Kitchen Utensils*. See what I mean? To be appropriate, the music must reflect the concept. If it doesn't, it's not appropriate!

The other facet is that the conceptual material is commensurate with the class's maturity—both musically *and* chronologically. In other words, the music should be no more sophisticated or simplistic than it needs to be for the students' musical and chronological abilities. Here's a reverse example. While "Twinkle, Twinkle," "Mary Had a Little Lamb," or "Old MacDonald" might be perfectly acceptable for first graders, they would be unthinkable for upper grades. The students would call them "babyish." To be appropriate in this other sense, then, means that the music must "match" both musical **and** chronological levels of development.

The bottom line is, two aspects make for "appropriate" music: (1) presence of conceptual material, and (2) conformity of conceptual materials to students' maturity level. One without the other spells "inappropriate." There's got to be a dual conformity.

Definition of Appealing

Consider now the appealing criteria in selecting music. Specifically, it pertains to the alluring and enticing quality of the music. Selections that fall into this category have the following characteristics:

- catchy, singable tunes
- well-defined rhythms
- feelingful beat
- attractive arrangements
- suitable length

These are the characteristics that entice students to listen. Appealing music, then, is music that "draws" students and makes them **want** to respond. In a word, it's enticing music.

Reasons for Appropriate/Appealing Music

There are good reasons for stressing the use of appropriate and appealing music. Most of them you already know, but they bear repeating because they're important and they're crucial to both teaching **and** learning. Look what having appropriate music does for the teacher—it puts meaningful examples of the concept in the teacher's hand to help reinforce the concept. Being able to say, "Listen to such-and-such," is an integral part of the teaching process. Without explicit examples, the

teacher's presentation is definitely not as meaningful. Good teaching is dependent upon appropriate examples.

For the students, having music that matches their maturity levels makes it possible for them to respond more comfortably and accurately. And what better way to help facilitate the students' learning than through music that is "right" for their musical ability **and** their age level? So not only is student response strengthened by appropriate music, but student learning as well.

The reason for choosing appealing music should be as obvious as the reasons for appropriate music. When music is appealing, it holds the students' attention longer and better. One of the secrets of effective teaching is using music that has appeal. Students invariably have longer attention spans when the music is appealing.

Explicit teaching examples, better student response, and better student attentiveness are all strong reasons for making an effort to select appropriate and appealing music, so give it serious consideration.

Guidelines for Selecting Appropriate Music

How does one go about choosing music that is appropriate and appealing? By adhering to some very basic guidelines. Don't wait for a one-two-three procedure. There isn't any! But don't panic. The guidelines will help, particularly if you apply them. Note that they've been presented in relationship to each criterion, in order to make them more relevant.

If your music is going to be "right" according to the class's musical maturity, here's the first guideline. If you're just beginning to explore a particular concept, then look for music in which the concept is clear and obvious, regardless of the students' age or grade level. Remember that musical maturity and chronological maturity don't always coincide; in fact, the student's musical maturity is usually lagging behind. This is why "Danse Macabre" in *The Sorcerer's Apprentice* by Dukas, with its long, well-defined downward passage, occurring at least four times, is such a marvelous initial selection for students at **every** grade level. It's perfect, as is the distinct upward passage in Mozart's "Minuet" from *Symphony No. 73*, for showing downward movement. This is what I mean by being obvious. The conceptual idea jumps out at the students. It's so clear that they *can't* miss it! That's the first guideline: using obvious music regarding the concept.

The second one is to look for less obvious and more demanding examples as the

students' perception and understanding develop. In other words, choose music that accommodates their musical growth à la Bruner, i.e., move from the obvious to the more subtle. You will have to be careful here. There's a real danger of moving ahead too fast and selecting music that is much too subtle. When this happens, just put the selection "on ice" for a later date and find another more appropriate one.

The next guideline is in reference to appropriateness for the grade level. Exercise common sense in choosing music for each age level. For example, songs with infantile titles, babyish tunes, and childish arrangements should be avoided at all cost for older students; for younger children, avoid songs with adult-oriented words, elusive melodies, and complex arrangements. That goes for overly adultish recordings as well. It brings to mind a certain first-year kindergarten teacher who was presenting Beethoven's *Eroìca Symphony*!! When it came to the listening part, she used the heads-down-and-eyes-shut approach and then proceeded to drift into a swooning ecstasy, completely oblivious to her class. Dreadful, you say. It is, but it happens. Some teachers just need a good dose of common sense when it comes to selecting music for the various age levels.

Guidelines for Selecting Appealing Music

The guidelines here are short-and-sweet. First and foremost, be sensitive to your students' age level and special interests. Don't overlook the fact that the music is for the students, not for you! Second, use some of the popular music, or youth music—it has all the characteristics of appealing music. And some of it really **is** good music! Third, look at the new music series books. They are an excellent source for appealing songs, relevant excerpts, and interesting accompaniments. There's really no excuse for bringing dull and boring music into the classroom, not if you know what to look for and where to find it.

Concluding Challenge

How about it? Do you select appropriate music? Does it do a good job of highlighting your concepts? And does it match up with your students' musical ability and age level? If not, you need to take a close look at the guidelines. Selecting music **is** time consuming, but it has its rewards if you are successful in finding appropriate and appealing music. I challenge you to do so.

LESS EFFECTIVE	**MORE EFFECTIVE**
In trying to find a selection with an ascending stepwise passage, Ms. Bolero picked a song with silly words about farm animals for her sixth grade class. "Why aren't they singing?" she wondered. "I want everyone to sing and hand design the upward passages. I mean everyone!" she shouted. "And stop that moaning! This is a good song." With that more students rolled their eyes!	Ms. Bolero had a hard time finding the right song for today's lesson. "Guess I'll check the pop recordings too." She was excited to find one that had an obvious ascending passage, plus relevant words for sixth graders. On leaving the class, two girls told her that they liked the part of the lesson where they "sang the neat song" and raised their arms on the upward passages.
Ms. Gigue thought that Wagner's *Reingold* would be a good selection for showing slow tempo. "It's operatic music; the first graders will love it!" she commented to herself. But the class got restless and bored after a few minutes of moving like Vikings. "What's happening? Why aren't the children enjoying the activity—and this music? After all, I explained what opera was!" Finally, Ms. Gigue had to tell the class to sit down. "If you can't move correctly, we'll have to stop."	Ms. Gigue's first graders were studying slow tempo. She decided to use "Walking in the Wood" from the *Bowmar Children's Record*. She was delighted how the children glowed with excitement as they took their slow "walk" in place. They listened to the birds and watched for rabbits as they walked. The music sounded just like walking music! When Ms. Gigue said that they would take another "walk" next lesson, the children clapped with glee!

Identifying Starting Place on Recordings _____

In addition to selecting appropriate and appealing music, there is one other aspect to consider, especially with recordings. It has to do with knowing where to drop the needle. You may think this is too small a detail to be concerned with, but I can assure you that it isn't. Many a well-planned lesson falls apart for this very reason. Those who have had the experience of putting on a recording and waiting forever until the "part" comes in, know what I mean. It's panic time, isn't it? That's why determining the starting place on the recording is such an important preparational task for the teacher. It avoids the "waiting."

Problem Finding Place

What's the problem? It's a predictable one, in light of the lack of concern shown for how much listening time precedes the lesson segment. Some teachers simply ignore this planning detail. The result is that the momentum of the lesson suffers. And, worse yet, the students lose their composure.

Here's an example. I once observed a young second-grade teacher who had her children ready to "play on their imaginary triangles." But after dropping the needle, the record kept playing and playing and playing! I could tell the children were getting tired. In desperation she began shouting, "Here it comes! Here it comes!" to encourage the class to keep the triangles ready. But by the time the intended part came round, most of the triangles were on their laps or on the floor. And the children were already wiggling and squirming. The momentum was lost, all because the "waiting" part was too long.

Besides not knowing about this detail, there are others who are simply lax and, at times, too hasty in taking care of this matter. They "see" the potential difficulty, but think they can deal with it on the spot, i.e., during the lesson. But they can't. Their memory fails them, so they end up giving false cues for the class to begin and then quickly correct themselves by frantically waving their arms in criss-cross fashion and yelling, "No, not yet, not yet." Remember, relying on one's memory reaps the same havoc as not recognizing this task.

Suggestions for Finding Right Place

There really isn't any reason for long "preludes" before getting to the intended segment of the record, even when the examples are buried somewhere in the middle. This could very well happen with some of the listening excerpts in the *Adventures of Music Series* and the *Bowmar Music Series* as well.

So what can be done to avoid these long lead-ins? Play "drop" the needle? Look for another composition? Or try to remember where "that spot" was? No! Don't do any of these things! Here are two good ways of "preparing" or isolating the lesson segment. One is to record the portion you want to use on cassette tape so that your examples could be presented with a mere pressing of the "play" button. The second way is much simpler. Just mark the spot on the recording with a piece of white chalk. The chalk marking will be easy to detect and won't hurt the recording. Either of these two approaches will allow you to find the "right" spot without having those unduly long preludes that destroy a lesson.

But here's a word of caution. Lead-in lengths can be deceptive. Sometimes what seems like an acceptable duration in your preparation becomes a never-ending "intro" in your lesson. This is a perplexing yet common phenomenon. You can avoid it by using my simple formula: If there's even the slightest feeling that the lead-in part is too long, it probably is! So make adjustments—before class begins; or else make a cassette tape. Listen to that inner voice!

Rewards of Finding Right Place

It really **does** make a difference in one's teaching when this record detail is taken seriously. There are definite rewards, with one being the momentum factor. The lesson keeps its momentum better when the teacher is able to drop the needle near the right spot. Lengthy lead-ins will always bog down the momentum.

Another reward is that students' attention is better. They are "pulled into" the activity before their minds can wander off. In other words, suitable lead-ins help keep students on-task. These outcomes are both earmarks of a successful lesson, and they happen when the teacher makes certain that the "intro" portion which precedes the lesson portion is carefully considered and properly marked.

Concluding Challenge

Let me urge you to make a habit of checking and rechecking your recordings in order to avoid those lengthy "preludes" or lead-ins. This is an important preparation detail. Momentum and attention are directly affected by the planning, or lack of planning, in regard to this recording detail. It's part of your lesson preparation. If it hasn't been, what better time to start than right now?

LESS EFFECTIVE	*MORE EFFECTIVE*
Ms. Tenori had time to listen only once to the new recording. As she waited for the high register to begin, she motioned to her kindergartners to get set. "No, that wasn't it. Just wait." She didn't remember having to wait this long! When the high register part finally came, many of the children were restless. They didn't seem excited about flying like birds any more! "Guess that was a tad too long," she admitted.	Ms. Tenori knew that the high register part was in the middle of the recording, so she put it on cassette tape. She didn't want to guess where it was when she was teaching. "Everyone, get your wings ready to fly with this high register music," she instructed her kindergartners. With that she pressed the button and the music began. The children swooped like birds as they listened. When it finished, they begged to do it again!
The eighth-grade general music class was involved in a unit on Latin American music. Ms. Alto divided the class into four groups of instruments. They were all waiting for the part where they were to play the accompaniment. Ms. Alto didn't realize the record played so long before the section came in. She could tell she was losing the class's attention by the way they were holding the instruments and exchanging glances with each other.	Ms. Alto found an excellent recording for students to play an accompaniment part on Latin American instruments. In preparing for the lesson, she marked the recording with chalk in order to be able to start in the place—and avoid waiting. When the music began, there were only a few measures to wait before they were playing. Ms. Alto could see the excitement on their faces as they played. "Can we exchange instruments and do it again?" they asked when they finished.

Choosing Appropriate and Appealing Activities _____

Activities, like the music, must also be selected for the purpose of providing musical learning. Otherwise, it would be, as the saying goes, a matter of having activities "for the sake of the activities." And everyone knows what that means—not much learning goes on! Like selecting music, the job of selecting activities is time consuming and thought provoking. It's on the same par with the music when it comes to preparation, the task lies at the very heart of the planning process. Thus, activities must be selected with great care and with specific criteria.

Criteria for Choosing Activities

In order for learning to occur, there must be criteria—or certain requirements—for choosing the activities. The two that come to mind the quickest are: appropriateness and appealingness. (See the earlier section "Choosing Appropriate and Appealing Music.") Let's look at appropriateness first. There are several considerations where activities are concerned.

Appropriateness. One of the considerations is that an activity must be in line with the students' **maturity level** as well as **musical level**. In other words, both the chronological and musical aspects of maturity must be taken into account, as well as the students' musical skills. This means there are really three areas that must be considered if the activity is going to "take hold and work."

Guidelines for Matching Students' Maturity. Take the students' **musical maturity**. For an activity to be "appropriate" in this realm, it must not demand more (or less) than the students are capable of comprehending at any given point in their musical development. Thus, it would be inappropriate to have fourth graders play an autoharp accompaniment using I, IV, V7 chords without any previous background in chordal accompaniment. The problem would not be with students' ability to strum the chords, nor with the suitability of the activity itself, but rather with the students' lack of understanding in regard to changing chords. The musical demands would simply surpass the students' musical maturity.

Teachers can also underestimate musical understanding. For example, asking seventh graders to play a simple steady beat on maracas when the composition is filled with dotted rhythm patterns they recently studied, would be a frustrating experience for them. Their musical mentality would be insulted! They need to be playing some of those more exciting rhythmic and syncopated patterns like ♩. ♪♩♩ or ♪♩♩♪♩ or ♩♩♩♩. Activities must not demean students by asking less than they possess; selected activities must always match their musical maturity.

Then there's **chronological maturity**. That simply means the activities must not be too babyish or too adultish. They need to "fit" the age level. Students seem to have a built-in code of "what's right" for them. Perhaps teachers should tap into this code to be better informed, or should I say forewarned! Teachers need to have a handle on acceptable activities for the various age levels. Then you won't go around asking sixth graders to march to the beat, stretch for high pitches, or, worse yet, hold hands in a circle and walk on the slow tempo and run on the fast. You are asking for trouble if you do! Not just because the activities are so babyish, but also because the concepts are beneath the students' musical mentality. High pitches for sixth graders? Or fast and slow? Now really!

But then teachers have also been known to overestimate the age ability! Would you believe I saw a teacher ask her first graders to conduct on the "a" section of Elgar's "Fairies and Giants"? Obviously she forgot she was with little children. I also remember observing a second-grade class that was "analyzing" music by writing down the words on all the high pitches. See how ridiculous teachers can get with activities? Nothing will kill an activity quicker than "missing the mark" with age.

Matching **musical skill** is obvious. Activities need to be in-line with the students' skills. They must not demand more or less skill. Remember, all three areas—musical maturity, chronological age, *and* musical skill—must be considered if the activity is to "do the job." Suppose you planned an activity you thought was ideal for identifying the conceptual idea, but forgot to consider whether or not the students could "do" it? And suppose they couldn't? The activity would probably "bomb out!" In other words, it wouldn't be appropriate. So activities like (a) playing all the "like" phrases on the electronic keyboards, (b) sightreading the whole new song with syllables, or (c) hand designing the contour of the entire song, may well be excellent activities, but if the students aren't able to do them, they simply aren't appropriate.

A second consideration in regard to being appropriate is that the activity must lend itself to highlighting the musical concept. This means finding activities that are well-suited for responding to a particular conceptual idea. True, there *are* a myriad of activities to choose from, but only a handful will really "showcase" the concept as it needs to be for helping students to (a) initially perceive or (b) sufficiently reinforce the concept.

Guidelines for Highlighting Musical Concept. Whether the lesson centers around a single concept or several, the task is the same. The teacher needs to find the best or most suited activities for responding to a particular concept. For example, playing accented beats on tub drums would be much more apropos than simply singing the song, and conducting a 3/4 meter would be better than just listening to a recording. The point is, an activity must exist for the purpose of making the concept felt and heard. Unless it accomplishes this objective, the activity is useless for the purpose of learning. As such, it's totally inappropriate. Activities like this should have no place in the conceptual teaching process! Consider some other examples of activities in Figure 1.2 that **are** geared to highlighting conceptual ideas at various grade levels.

Appealingness. Finally, let's turn our attention to the second criterion for selecting activities. Appealingness. Do you realize that even if your activities match maturity levels and musical skills, and highlight the musical concepts, but don't appeal to the students, they'll still zonk out? It's true! You can't by-pass the appealing quality of your activities and hope to have a successful lesson. It won't happen. Let me give you some helpful guidelines.

Guidelines for Selecting Appealing Activities. How does one go about determining the appealingness of an activity? It's not as elusive as you might think. It's a matter of knowing what to consider when looking for an activity. Look for activities that are:

* interesting, not boring
* challenging, not out-of-reach
* fitting, not outmoded
* intriguing, not ordinary

Concepts	Grade Level	Highlighting Activities
Phrase Identification	4-6	–Raising "Phrase Beginning" and "Phrase Ending" cards while singing –Tapping woodblock at beginning of phrase and tremoloing at end; air tapping melodic rhythm in between –Shaking tambourine at end of each phrase while dance stepping and tapping beat throughout
Melodic Pattern with Upward 1-2-3-4-5	2-3	–Moving visual air upward pattern when it occurs and pulsating beat and visual aid in between –Playing pattern on imaginary bells when it appears while singing words of song –Swinging pattern on numbers and syllables when it appears
Melodic Rhythm (Even Rhythm)	K-1	–Tapping top of thighs with both hands together while singing song –Playing rhythm of melody on rhythm sticks and alternating in the air

Figure 1.2. Appropriate Kinds of Activities for Highlighting Conceptual Ideas

It's also a matter of knowing how to maintain this appealingness. For instance, if your activities are going to be interesting, then be sure they're always well-planned and well-paced. Don't let them bog down. Take care of the details, and make sure you take into account the active nature of children. Don't have them doing some passive response like sitting in their seats and listening to the metric rhythm when they could be standing and moving to it. See what I mean?

To maintain **challenging** activities, be sure to choose activities that stay near the edge of their musical maturity. Keep them reaching for that proverbial carrot. But be careful. Don't put it so far out that they can't reach it. The challenge comes when there's an effort involved, plus an attainable goal. Effort plus success—that's the formula for a challenging activity.

In planning for **fitting** activities, consider those more like the ones students engage in when "playing" out of school, i.e., activities that reflect the world they live in. Make your activities relevant—add a touch of reality to make them fitting. For example, use arching over phrases with freedom or brotherhood flags, raise up shuttle planes on high pitches or upward passages, and play in ensemble groups with their own names to play rhythmic accompaniments. Got the idea? Look around you for those "fitting" ideas.

To keep an **intriguing** element, add a touch of creativity or novelty. (See the next section "Adding a Creative Touch to Activities.") Don't give them an opportunity to think they know how every activity is going to go. Instead, fool them. Put a new twist here and a different angle there! Keep them guessing. Your activities will take on a more intriguing air if you take this advice to heart.

So there are some tangibles when it comes to selecting appealing activities. These are the criteria that can have a titillating effect on your students and peak their motivation.

Concluding Challenge

The next time you get ready to plan your lesson, ask yourself if your activities are appropriate and appealing in terms of the foregoing discussion. These two criteria will dictate, to a large measure, the success or failure of your lesson. They're crucial considerations that take time to think through. But you will be the winner if you succeed in making appropriate and appealing choices. It's up to you now.

LESS EFFECTIVE	MORE EFFECTIVE
"All right, this time we're going to clap the steady beat," announced Ms. Lo-Tone to her seventh graders. When the class moaned and made no attempt to get ready, she shook her head and said, "This class never wants to do anything! Can't you even clap the beat?" The students just looked at Ms. Lo-Tone without making any move. She never did anything real neat with them. That's what the students thought about Ms. Lo-Tone.	Having praised the seventh graders for responding so well to the first activity, Ms. Lo-Tone instructed the class as follows. "Now I want you to conduct the two-beat meter in the Colonel Bogey march like this, and keep a L/R marching pattern going with your feet. Let me show you. Now you try it. Ready!" The class stood up quickly and got their conducting hands in place. Ms. Lo-Tone knew they were anxious to begin.

Ms. Hi-Tone's review concept for her third-grade class dealt with melodic patterns. She planned to have the class tap the pattern on rhythm sticks. When the activity was over, Ms. Hi-Tone was surprised to find they didn't know a melodic pattern had the same rhythm *and* melody. "You need to listen better the next time we do this," she said as the class was leaving the room.

"Let's review melodic patterns, class," Ms. Hi-Tone said to her third graders. Having identified the 3-2-1 pattern after listening, she instructed the class to play the pattern on their electronic keyboards which she had prepared with yellow dots marked 3-2-1. "Let's sing the song and every time the pattern appears, play it on the keyboard. Ready!" She was pleased that the children knew a melodic pattern had the same melody *and* same rhythm. "Very good, class."

Adding a Creative Touch to Activities

One of the more challenging aspects of preparing an activity is adding the creative touch, especially with the more fundamental activities, such as clapping, tapping, marching, or playing a classroom instrument. In their natural state, these activities often seem too simplistic and not challenging enough for students. They get "old" and boring, even for younger children. Can't you remember how monotonous it was just to clap or march or beat the drum? What these overly used activities needed was a little creative touch. Teachers need to be sensitive to this situation in planning their activities.

Definition of Adding Creative Touch

Don't let the term "creative" scare you. It doesn't mean that you have to come up with something totally new; that's not the intent of the term in this case. What it **does** mean is making "mini-modifications" or slight alterations to breathe new life into these well-worn activities. Personally, I like to think of the creative touch as a freshening up or a revitalizing of an activity, or making some small change that gives the activity a new feeling. Adding a creative touch then, is simply a way of keeping those old worn-out activities alive. By the way, being creative is also part of the process for making activities appealing. (See the earlier section "Choosing Appropriate and Appealing Activities.")

Suggestion for Adding Creativity

The possibilities for modifying or altering an activity are endless. The teacher is limited only by his/her own lack of zeal to experiment, or hesitancy to add this-or-that to the activity or to change this-or-that. So, experiment with an activity.

For example, there are a myriad of ways to clap other than the usual way. Why not use the space around the body, such as right side, left side, above the head, or below the waist, etc., and then alternating these spaces? Why not clap on different parts of the body? Try clapping the outside thighs, tops of thighs, lower arms, top of head, etc., and notice the different sounds each body part makes. Try also alternating your clapping hands from right-to-left. Then clap with one, two, or three fingers on the palm of your hand, or tap the air with palms outward, with raised arms, or with arms extended outward and palms down. Why just clap when students could be doing some aerobic steps along with the clapping? Or tapping on desktops with alternate hands? Or the side of their thighs? There's nothing earth-shaking about any of

these examples. They're just different enough to make clapping more interesting and challenging, and to bring it out of the doldrums.

Now, take the rhythm sticks and experiment. Begin by trying out different ways to see if they will work. How will you know when the "new" way is right? Because it will feel comfortable and yet challenging, and you'll feel it right "down in your bones." These signs will tell you when it's a potentially good activity.

Here's one last thought to bear in mind as you experiment. Remember that creativity is not some elusive happening that blossoms out of nowhere. It has "roots" in some previous learning. These fundamental activities (clapping, tapping, marching, etc.) become our learning foundation. It's just a matter of finding some new angle or new twist, however small, to make the established activity "new." This is the crux of your creative effort in this situation.

Reasons for Creative Touch

Several reasons should come to the forefront here. Some have been alluded to in other discussions in the text and others have not.

The first, and most obvious, reason is that this creative touch puts back the element of challenge in the activity. Plain and simple, that means the activity has more substance than it did in its natural state.

The second reason is that the "new" response brings a sense of freshness to the activity, as well as to the lesson in general. Change, regardless how slight, provides for variety, and variety allows for creativity.

The third reason flows from the second, namely, that the change motivates students and captivates their interest. Activities that become dull and boring by virtue of their constant use need to be revitalized with a creative touch if they're to continue as motivators. Adding that "new" dimension is one way the teacher can regain the interest and motivation of the students.

Concluding Challenge

Do some of your activities need a touch of creativity? Do they lack a sense of challenge and motivation? If so, then it's time to take some of those tiring activities and alter the response in some small way to bring back the substance and freshness to your teaching. I urge you to "find" your own creative touch to those overworked activities.

LESS EFFECTIVE	MORE EFFECTIVE
"Everyone stand quietly and get ready to march." Ms. Con Moto put the recording on and began marching with the second graders. Some barely lifted their feet, while others were swinging their arms wildly and stomping. "What's the matter," she asked, "don't you like to march anymore?" What she didn't realize was that the students were bored with marching. When she said, "Let's try it again," the class groaned. They thought marching was for the birds!	Ms. Con Moto had her second graders stand straight like soldiers. "Now hold your gun like this and march until I give the command to play your imaginary drum. Like this. Try it with me. My commands will be 'Guns' and 'Drum.' Ready!" The class marched vigorously with their "guns" and listened carefully for the drum command. When it came, the class played rhythmically to the beat. The class alternated the two motions until the record's end. "Ahhhh, let's not stop." They liked the activity.
Ms. Piu Moso wrote the rhythmic pattern on the board and asked her sixth graders to tap it out using their palms and two tapping fingers. "Now we're going to tap the rhythm pattern every time you hear it." By the second verse, the class tapping was next to nil. Students just got bored with simple tapping. They rolled eyes at each other when Ms. Piu Moso said, "You can do better than that! One more time."	"Okay, now we're going to tap out the rhythmic pattern, with alternate hands, first on top of the right leg, then the left leg. Understand? Try it with me. Hear the different sound each leg makes? Good. Get ready for the song. Oh, be sure to begin the pattern with the right hand on the right leg and the left hand on the left leg. Ready." Ms. Piu Moso was delighted with the class's response. They liked the alternating hands bit. It was different.

Thinking Through Mechanics of Each Activity

Planning the inner workings of each activity should be a "must" on the list of every general music teacher. It's the only formula I know that puts the teacher in control of every aspect of an activity. It's the key to success with activities, especially for the inexperienced teachers who spend much of their time and energy learning to make their activities work through trial-and-error. That's why it's important to have a clear understanding of what this task really means.

Definition of Thinking Through Mechanics

The best way to deal with this phrase, "thinking through the mechanics," is to look at the word "mechanics" first. The reference here is to a sequential ordering of details, or a specific ordering of procedures **within** an activity. As for the whole phrase, I coined that years ago to see that every step of an activity is identified and addressed. The task boils down to a conscientious thinking-through process that enables the teacher to uncover potential problems before teaching and address sequential details during teaching. Simply stated, it's a matter of taking into account every sequential detail of an activity. Let's see how this can be done.

Guidelines for Mechanics

First and foremost, nothing must be taken for granted. New teachers are notorious for making assumptions. If you just assume that your activities will "work," you're being naive and foolish. Even if you're convinced that your activity is "good" from the standpoint of its matching the students' maturity levels and musical abilities, it will still give you problems unless the mechanics (or implementing details) are under control. (See the earlier section "Choosing Appropriate and Appealing Activities.") In other words, you need to be sure that every detail of the activity—from inception to dismissal—has been covered. Here are just a few of the so-called *mechanics* to be considered:

- verbiage for introducing activity
- instructions for implementing activity
- comments for assessing students
- procedures for performing on classroom instruments
- instructions for putting instrument away
- directions for moving students into groups
- plans for keeping whole class involved during individual recitations
- details for making corrections and/or improvements
- procedure for entering/exiting the class

See all the details that need your attention before you can properly implement your activity? And why the activity still may flop even if it's appropriate and appealing? You mustn't assume anything; instead, you must plan.

The second guideline is really an extension of the first, but it's significant enough to merit its own attention. Anticipate details. Nothing must be overlooked or planned haphazardly because it's the little things you didn't anticipate, or even think about, that will mess up your lesson. Haphazard preparation usually goes something like this: "First, I'll have the class play rhythm sticks and have a couple of students come up front and lead the others. (I'll ask more if there's time!) Then I'll read a call chart together with the class and . . ." Sound familiar? I'm sure it does! But let me be quick to add that for many experienced teachers, this is sufficient because they "know" what to expect. But for the not-so-experienced ones, such loose preparation is sheer suicide! None of the details have been considered, much less anticipated, like (a) what do I do if the activity needs "beefing-up" on-the-spot?; (b) how will students respond when asked to do such-and-such; or (c) what can happen when the class is being divided into two groups?

Here are some examples of situations where detailed planning and anticipation were needed but not pursued. In one instance, I recall a young teacher asked some students to go to the chalkboard. No instruction whatsoever was given as to (a) where the student should go, (b) what the student should do, or (c) what the students at their seats should do while students were at the board. What happened? Well, there was confusion galore. No one knew what to do! A potentially "good" activity turned into a fiasco all because none of the details were planned. In another class, I observed a flash card activity go down the tube when the teacher didn't tell students how to "work" the cards, and how the two teams were to face each other in separate lines. What a high price to pay for disregarding details.

Am I suggesting you write down every detail in your lesson planning? Absolutely not! Long, wordy lesson plans are useless. What I **am** suggesting is that you think through the mechanics (of each activity) before teaching. You'll be pleasantly surprised how much smoother your lesson goes when the details have been ironed out.

Reasons for Thinking Through Mechanics

There are so many rewarding reasons. The **first** has already been mentioned; namely, a smooth unfolding lesson. That's because there are fewer glitches and loose ends whenever the mechanics have been worked out. Most of the potential problems

have been circumvented, and all the maneuvering situations planned out, such as moving students from one place to another, passing out instruments, or dividing the class into groups. Is it any wonder that the lesson runs more smoothly?

The **second** reason, of course, is that the teacher has better control of the activity, and ultimately the class, when every point has been mulled over prior to teaching. It's only when this kind of thinking through the mechanics is done that the teacher can "feel" and exercise this kind of control.

The **third** reason is equally as rewarding—and noteworthy. Students are much more responsive when there is structure and organization in what they are doing. Don't forget, they like order in their lives, and expect it in their activities!

What three better rewards could you ask for? Your teaching will go smoother, you'll function more confidently, and your students will be more responsive.

Concluding Challenge

Do you take too much for granted with your activities? Do you just assume they will work without attending to any of the mechanics? If you plan off the top of your head, you've experienced glitches in your activities, haven't you? And you probably didn't get the best response from your students. What you need to start doing is start thinking through the one-two-three of your activities, so that you won't fall into the traps mentioned here, and pass up the benefits of this task. The next time you teach, I want you to think through the mechanics of each activity.

LESS EFFECTIVE	MORE EFFECTIVE
When it came time to pass out the rhythm sticks, Ms. Gong asked Bobby and Jimmy to help. She continued teaching without saying anything more to the boys. When she was ready to begin the activity with the sticks, she saw the boys were still passing them out. They were letting the other third graders pick out the color they wanted. Some children even needed to exchange their sticks for the ribbed ones. Disgusted, Ms. Gong grabbed the sticks and said, "I'll finish. You two go to your seats."	Ms. Gong asked for two volunteers. She asked Bobby to stand on the left side, and Jim, the right side. She told her helpers to hold the stick bucket and let each student take a pair quickly and move on. Then she told the class to place the sticks under their left arm pit. "I don't want to hear any clicking. Begin passing out now." By the time Ms. Gong finished her demonstration everyone had sticks. "Now take your rhythm sticks, class, like this . . ." Ms. Gong thanked Bobby and Jim for their good job.

"Now I want three people to come up to accompany the class on autoharps. Let's have John, Sue, and Mark." The fifth graders giggled nervously as they clustered behind the autoharps. "Turn to page 22, class, and sing while these three accompany us. Oh, the chords are on the board. Why aren't you playing?" asked Ms. Jingle. "Don't you know what chords to play? Just play what's on the board or I'll get someone else."

Ms. Jingle announced she needed three autoharp players. "But first let's everyone play the chord progression c-c-c-c. Good! This time sing along as you strum! I see that everyone can play the chord changes. Let's have John, Sue, and Mark come up please. John take autoharp #1; Sue, #2; and Mark #3. Watch me. Ready." The class sang and "played' their imaginary autoharps while the three up front played with confidence. "Excellent, you three. Let's have three more autoharp players now."

Trying Out New Activities

Did you realize that trying out new activities before implementing them is an integral part of your teaching preparation? It's true. The only way to really be sure that the new activities will "work" is to try them out. I mean literally try them out! Even though they may fill-the-bill as far as their being appropriate and appealing, these new experiences could still bomb out. Why? Because they sometimes have "bugs" that bog them down. These bugs, or problems, need to be discovered **before** the activities are used. That's why trying out new activities is so important; it helps the teacher find the bugs.

Definition of Trying Out

I use the term "trying out" synonymously with "doing." In other words, trying out a new activity simply means doing the activity—exactly as planned for the class—before using it in the classroom. It's not the usual procedure of working out the activities in one's head and then saying to one's self, "Yea, that oughta work!" Getting a mental image of the activity is *not* the same as getting a physical feel of it. So "trying out" in this discussion means to actually engage in the activity in order to experience how comfortable and "right" it feels before implementing it with your students. That's all there is to it—the teacher "sampling" the activity.

Implementing the Trying Out

Now let's be more specific as to how the teacher accomplishes this task, or what the ins-and-outs are of testing a new activity. In the first place, the testing is done only in connection with the *new or modified activities* that have not been previously experienced by students. Testing the tried-and-true activities would be silly. In the second place, the tryout is a literal run-through of the activity—in the confines of one's own classroom, done by one's own self. It's the moment when the activity is tried-on for size to see how it "feels" and if it's acceptable. How long is the try out? As long as it takes to make your decision. Sometimes it only takes a single run-through, sometimes more. But even then, it shouldn't take longer than a few minutes.

Third, the try out is a time for determining the shortcomings or the bugs. For example, the activity may be too busy, i.e., have too many movements to achieve an accurate response, especially with younger children, or it may have too little going on with long periods of waiting to make the response. Or the activity may just turn out to be too difficult for a particular grade level, or too uncomfortable to execute. Then, too, it simply might not "fit" the conceptual idea as well as expected, or be as practical and well-suited as you had thought. See what I mean by shortcomings?

Unless this kind of information is discovered, you can't be certain of the success for the activity. Trying out, then, is like the proverbial "test drive" for the activity.

Don't be too quick to pooh-pooh this approach. Some of you might be telling yourselves that this process isn't for you, that you know your students well enough to know what will work and what won't! But I'll bet if you looked closely, you would admit there *were* a few times when you really were taken aback by the unexpected outcome of a new activity, and it fleetingly occurred to you that perhaps you should have "done" the activity before using it in class. I suspect this happens more often than we care to admit!

The point is, neither the number of teaching years chalked up nor the extent of one's expertise can substitute for this kind of preparation. While experience can tell us what students will or will not do, or what they like or don't like, it cannot tell us whether or not an activity will work. Trying out the new activity is still the best way to find the bugs and make the final judgment call.

Resulting Realizations and Rewards

It's amazing what one discovers when trying out an activity, and what realizations result from this approach. Here are some of the realizations I have heard expressed over the years by teachers who took the time to try out their first-time activities:

- "Gee, I didn't realize this standing up and sitting down on high/low registers would be so difficult for my first graders."
- "I can see my students getting all mixed up doing such-and-such on the dotted eighths and sixteenths. Glad I tried it first!"
- "Whew! I didn't think playing the melodic patterns on the bells would be **that** hard until I tried it myself!"
- "This is a long time to be just tapping out the beat on these rhythm sticks— longer than I thought it would be. I'd better add something else to make it more challenging."

Do you see what teachers can "find out" from this hands-on try out? Many of the above realizations were made by experienced teachers, which makes it clear that teaching experience is not the answer for discovering the bugs in an activity. It's trying out the activity that does the trick! Here's one word of advice: if you have even the slightest doubt about any activity, dump it. Nine times out of ten, the problem will surface in the lesson. So, listen to your instinct!

And here is the wonderful reward for doing this simple testing: it helps the teacher avoid activity fallouts in class. In testing the activity beforehand, the teacher either (a) corrects some erroneous assumptions about the activity, or (b) finds out some unexpected glitches. Whichever the case may be, the teacher is able to ward off potential disasters and make the corrections or alterations before implementing it in the classroom. That means **the lesson** can progress more smoothly, **the students** can respond more accurately, and **the teacher** can control the activity more effectively. All in all, I would say that's a big outcome for such little effort!

Concluding Challenge

There is no getting away from trying out new activities before using them, if you want to find out the inherent bugs and if you want the new experience to be successful. If you want to feel more confident when you try something new, be sure to test drive it first and find out if there's something you didn't realize about it. Only then can you proceed to your lesson with confidence knowing you have sufficiently readied the new experience. Try "trying out!"

LESS EFFECTIVE	MORE EFFECTIVE
Ms. Largo was excited about teaching the new Christmas rote song to her children. But she was surprised to find out that they couldn't do all the gestures. There were too many. The rote song was ruined! Ms. Largo realized this as soon as she started. "Why didn't I try out the song before doing it with the children?" She promised herself this wouldn't happen again!	When Ms. Largo tried out her new Christmas song, she knew that she had better take out some of those actions. "The children won't be able to sing and do all these things," she noted to herself. When she presented the song in class, she was glad she had taken the time to revise the song. The children were able to sing and do the actions easily and excitedly! Their faces reflected their enjoyment.
Ms. Lento wrote the ostinato rhythmic pattern for the A section on the boards. "I want everyone to tap out the pattern on your desktop during the A section," she instructed, "and then conduct on the B section." She realized quickly that tapping the ostinato was boring for the seventh graders. She wished the B section would get there. To her disbelief, the conducting part lasted too long as well. She knew the students were bored-to-tears. She just assumed the activities would be fine— what she didn't realize was that the sections were too long.	When Ms. Lento tested out the ostinato pattern, she discovered that the ostinato was great for a few seconds but not for the whole A section. "Think I'll have them alternate between the ostinato pattern on the woodblocks and the metric rhythm on their books. And then we'll conduct the dynamics in the B section and make our beats small and large. Now let me try this. That works well." The activity was a success. The seventh graders loved alternating the ostinato with the rhythmic pattern and felt like real conductors in the B section.

Determining Criteria for Responses

If I had to choose which was "the" most important aspect of planning a lesson, I would have to say it was deciding my criteria for each activity. But I can almost hear some of you asking, "Aren't criteria part of the objectives?" Yes, they are; in fact, criteria are discussed in Chapter 10 on lesson plans. So why isolate criteria here? Because unless criteria are definitely established in one's planning, there's no direction to the lesson and the objectives are meaningless. Criteria must be dealt with as a separate planning issue if the objectives are to be achieved. They're the crux of the teaching effort.

Definition of Criteria

Criteria are specific terms or words that indicate how well you expect your class to respond. Or, in a figurative sense, they're "tools" that set the standards or reflect your expectations. They're the qualifiers that allow the teacher to analyze, measure, or compare the students' performance, so that **you**, the teacher, can make an intelligent decision as to continuing the lesson or reinforcing the response. Think of criteria, then, as the specific verbiage established for the purpose of achieving your objectives. (For a list of sample criteria, see Chapter 10 on lesson planning.)

Advantages of Criteria

From the teacher's perspective, look at what having criteria can do, or what they accomplish. **First**, they put teeth into your teaching. They become the guidelines for evaluating student and class responses. Here's how it happens: If class response does not "match" or coincide with your expectation, as indicated in the criterion, then you repeat the response and you tell your students why. In other words, you have a basis for your decision.

Second, criteria strengthen the teacher's confidence. Do you realize that with criteria it's you who determines how well the class will respond? That if your standard is not being met, it's you who has the right to repeat the activity? And that only with your approval can the class move on? In other words, the teacher is the standard-setter. Administrators, parents, and society have all entrusted this task in your hands. If this thought doesn't boost your confidence, I don't know what will!

But there's another reason confidence is strengthened. Having criteria allows the teacher to walk into the classroom knowing what he/she wants to hear or see. He/she is freed from worrying about how to deal with responses. There's a basis for evaluating every class response. See how criteria can affect the teacher's confidence? They're confidence builders!

And **third**, criteria help guide the learning process. Criteria "tell" students how well they must perform if it's to be accepted by the teacher. Thus, the students' interest and motivation is kindled in striving to attain these expectations. The criteria impact on the learning process by affecting students' attitude. Remember, guide the learning process in a positive way with your criteria.

These, then, are the advantages. Not only do they contribute to the teacher's confidence, but they impact on the students' learning. These are all powerful reasons for establishing—and applying—criteria.

Operating With Criteria

How does the teacher operate with criteria? What does the teacher have to do to initiate these evaluative tools? At some point before teaching a particular conceptual idea or musical skill, the teacher makes a decision as to how well the class is expected to perform in responding to the concept or skill. For example, you decide whether you want your students to respond: (a) accurately or with 100% accuracy, (b) without error, or (c) without difficulty or with a minimum of difficulty, etc. In other words, you determine the performance standard. Having made the decision, you implement activities and evaluate performances on the basis of these criteria.

Say you were using a marching activity to focus the class's attention on the steady beat. What you do, then, is observe the performance and decide whether or not it meets with your expectations, i.e., with your criterion. If it does, you can praise the class and move on. But if it doesn't, you know that it has to be repeated in order to "do it accurately." You'll no longer have to ask the class, "Did you understand?" or "Do you get the idea?" because with criteria you can "see" for yourself if the response reflects comprehension and decide confidently on the spot whether to continue or reinforce. That's how you'll operate according to your established standard.

But look at some typical illustrations of teachers who operate without criteria. As I see it, there are three categories. Some belong to, what I call, the "Bewildered Group." They're the ones who always look so baffled or tongue-tied about what to say or do once the activity is over. In their quandary, they end up asking those inane rhetorical questions like, "Did you get that?" or "Is that clear?" The question is fol-

lowed by a sweeping glance over the class and a frantic look for even the faintest uh-huh or slightest nod to convince them to move on. Confusion is rampant, and learning is nil in these situations.

Then there's the "Accommodating Group." These are the teachers who look for activities everyone can do so they can avoid evaluating the class's performance. Only those who don't want to participate or are half asleep find the activity difficult to do! Teachers in this category lack confidence in their own judgment. Their main objective is to get everyone "doing" some dull, boring activity. And to top it all off, they end up praising the performance no matter how feeble it is. As long as they "did it," everything is hunky-dory! The scenario in this situation is: no challenge and no learning.

And the third is the "Indifferent Gang." These are the robots of teaching. They simply "run through" every activity with never a thought as to what is happening. Whether the singing sounds like a murmur, or the clapping like a raucous din, or the marching turns into a shuffle-step, their goal is the same. Get through the lesson! Never mind how the students "do," just get through the lesson. Of the three groups, this is the one with least regard for standards. It's like they fuse the activity and response and "see" the response as the activity per se. They seem oblivious to the need for evaluating the response.

There you have the three groups and how they tend to operate without criteria. Hopefully, you don't find yourself in any of these categories. Understand that without criteria, you only stifle your teaching and, worse yet, curtail the learning.

Concluding Challenge

Having daily criteria for your activities is a "must." Be sure that you establish criteria in your objectives that accurately reflect your expectations. Because unless you have thought about how well you expect the class to respond, you won't assess properly or strive for the kind of participation that genuinely reflects the students' comprehension. In short, you won't teach effectively. If you need to know how to incorporate these terms in your objectives, see Chapter 10 on lesson plans. Do whatever you need to do to become proficient in teaching with criteria. It's not a choice, it's your responsibility.

LESS EFFECTIVE

"Oh, this morning we're going to tap the rhythm of the melody like this. Ready!" The class response was awful, but Mr. Presto went on. "This time let's play the melodic rhythm on the desks and tap the beat with your foot. Ready!" The class's response was much better, almost accurate, in fact, but again Mr. Presto didn't notice. He didn't even see Ryan playing his rhythm sticks in a totally creative way. "Next time we'll do some other things." The class wasn't even listening as they left the room. Mr. Presto never listened to what they did, so they didn't listen to him!

For her lesson on ABA Form, Ms. Adagio instructed the seventh graders to conduct on the A theme. "It's in three's," she said. "Try it. One, two, three, etc." Some were using their left hand, some, their right. And a few were using both. But Ms. Adagio went right on. "Let's try conducting the music now. Ready." The class got the giggles when they looked at each other. Nobody seemed to be conducting in tempo and everyone looked awkward, what with their floppy wrists and spastic beats. "That was pretty good." The students shook their heads in amazement. Before anyone could say anything, she went on to the B theme. It was all a big joke to the students. Ms. Adagio never corrected anyone. She just went from one activity to the next regardless of what they did!

MORE EFFECTIVE

"Good morning class, let's tap our rhythm sticks like this on the melodic rhythm. Try it. Tom, hold your hand farther down. Good. Get ready now." As the class tapped to the recording, Mr. Presto observed closely while participating, "I didn't see everyone alternating sticks on each phrase. Like this. Let's try it again. But practice it a few times first. Now ready." "Oh very good, class. Everyone was alternating the melodic rhythm on their sticks that time. This time we're going to tap on the desks and keep the beat with our foot. Get ready." "I am so proud of you. I saw everyone's foot going to the beat, and didn't hear one mistake on the melodic rhythm." The class beamed with pride.

"And on this A theme," explained Ms. Adagio, "we're going to conduct in three's, like this. Can we try it? Ready. Watch your wrist, David. Susan, your beat is too large. Everyone looks good. Now let's try conducting with the record." The students were serious. They corrected themselves and even tried using both hands. "Excellent! I see some good conducting. And I liked the way you kept the beat." Students smiled. "I think you are ready for the B theme. We'll do an aerobic dance step. Watch me. Let's try it. Step, swing, step, swing. Perfect! Now with the music." The class moved beautifully. "Great, you're ready to put both themes together!" A loud "all right" went up from the class. They felt ready!

Getting Materials Ready for Teaching _____

The first order of business after the lesson has been planned is to get the materials ready. The materials to be readied include texts, recordings, cassettes, equipment, and visual aids. Preparation of this nature is indispensable to successful teaching. Without it, the teacher simply invites disaster! For example, discovering that you have the wrong book or wrong recording, or finding out that the record player doesn't work in the midst of a lesson is the surest way to destroy your confidence and wreck the momentum of the lesson. Nothing is more frustrating or more embarrassing—or even more devastating. But that's what happens when materials aren't "readied" for teaching. Don't underestimate this responsibility. It's a high priority item when it comes to teacher preparation.

Definition of Getting Ready

What does the phrase "get ready" mean in regard to teaching materials? We need a clear understanding in order to get the job done. Basically, it means to prepare or to get in order. Or, to put it another way, to arrange the items needed for teaching. Then, too, consider some other phrases that connote the same meaning, such as (1) to be available, (2) to get situated, or (3) to get organized. Any one of these phrases infer a state of readiness.

But what specifically does "ready" mean when it comes to texts, recordings, equipment, or visual aids? It could mean a myriad of things. Here are some examples of what it means in a functional sense:

- arranging recordings or illustrations in order of presentation
- setting up instruments or visual aids in the classroom
- checking out the operational instructions and working order of the equipment
- marking book pages and other illustrations in order of presentation
- setting out the music series book
- writing lesson material on the board
- moving piano and record players in most appropriate place for teaching

Readying materials is simply a matter of getting them organized and/or situated, and making them available and/or accessible.

Results of Getting Ready

Can you see the impact of getting materials and equipment ready? Your teaching can profit from this kind of preparation, because several aspects of teaching are vitally affected by this readiness—and in a very positive way.

Consider, first of all, how readiness affects the momentum of the lesson. When materials and equipment are in place, there's less chance of having to stop and (a) get the rhythm sticks, (b) move the piano, or (c) arrange the illustrations, etc. All these details are handled before one teaches. That means the lesson can flow with a minimum of interruptions and the momentum can keep moving.

Another result is that the continuity, or flow, of the lesson is better. It's more apt to stay intact because the teacher doesn't chop up the lesson as much to (a) find the "right" recording, (b) look up the page numbers, or (c) write the examples on the board. None of these bloopers will happen if the teacher gets the materials ready ahead of time. The lesson can keep on going, and so can the continuity!

Then there's the positive impact readiness has on attentiveness. Students are apt to be more attentive when materials and equipment are ready-to-go, when they don't have to "wait" for the teacher to take care of this or that in the middle of the lesson. As a result, interest and motivation are apt to run higher. Of the three, this outcome probably ranks as the most significant result.

Attitudes Toward Getting Ready

Most teachers would no doubt agree that getting materials and equipment ready is an indispensable part of their preparation. Others, however, are not quite as convinced. They're more ho-hum about it. They're the ones who usually assume that everything will be "ready" without even checking. Teachers with this kind of attitude have, what I call, "Assum-itis." They assume that things are ready when they're not!

But then there's another group. They're the ones who keep forgetting to get this-and-that ready. These teachers have a good case of "Forget-itis." They can't seem to remember what needs to be done from one class to the next. As they would say, "Oh, I forgot!"

Even though both attitudes, "assum-itis" and "forget-itis", are common among some teachers, neither of them is acceptable or excusable. Plain and simple, teachers need to be committed to being ready.

Suggestions for Getting Ready

There is no denying that it takes time and effort to get the materials and equipment "ready," even when one is committed to the task. Here are some suggestions, or reminders, for getting the job done.

With regard to **recordings**, if you are using two or more in your lesson, be sure to do the following: (1) check to see that the right record is in the jacket; (2) mark the band on each recording with white chalk; and (3) arrange the recordings in order of presentation—stick a memo on each record jacket marked "1," "2," or "3" respectively.

If you're planning to use **instruments** like rhythm sticks, wood blocks, bongo drums, baritone ukeleles, first see if they're in working order and not broken. For example, check if the wood blocks aren't cracked, the drum heads aren't loose, and the ukelele strings aren't broken. In other words, be sure they're in playing order. Then decide where you'll put them for easy access. Under the chairs? On the teacher's desk? Or on the piano? Then decide how you will distribute them if they're not under the chairs. Will you use student helpers or hand them out yourself? Finally, be ready to instruct the helpers where to put the instruments until they're needed. This is all part of getting ready with instruments!

Then think about the **equipment**. Don't go into a lesson before you learn how to operate the record player. Find out how to turn it on and off. Don't laugh. A lot of teachers just assume they know—and they don't. Find out, too, how to adjust the volume, how to get the turntable working, and how to plug in patch cords to the speakers. You need to "ready" yourself to this extent if you want to avoid embarrassing situations.

For example, suppose you find the stereo deader than a doornail. Your monologue could possibly go something like this: "Uhm, let's see now. Maybe the speakers aren't hooked up. Nope, that's not it. Where's the power switch on this thing? Anybody know how to operate it? Come on up, Jim. Maybe you can figure it out. I really wanted us to hear this recording today!" If so, you need to get better acquainted with your equipment if you want to be "ready." And quickly!

And for getting **books** ready? Get book markers to put in the correct pages and to indicate the order of presentation; otherwise, you'll spend half your time flipping pages. Anything less than this with regards to recordings, equipment, or texts comes under the heading of "not being ready."

Now let me give you some so-called *salvage tactics* for dealing with disastrous moments that happen despite your readiness, when an honest oversight will be made.

The first one pertains to **recordings**. Say you do bring the wrong recording with you, accidentally, of course. Do you "cry" about it to the class? I hope not! Instead, you would briefly explain what you would have done and move on. Don't dwaddle, in other words. Keep the lesson moving, and don't go frantically looking for a recording when it's not there—even though you know you brought it! You'll waste time, and get nervous. So what should you do? Again, quickly tell what you intended to do (with the recording) and move on, unless you're absolutely certain that the recording is under this pile or that. But if you choose to move on, here's how you can fill in the time. Add on a closing activity on-the-spot using a familiar activity or action song.

The second suggestion is aimed at **visual aids**, those that seem to disappear when they're needed. Looking for them is usually a mistake because you'll give a silly grin and say, "I can't seem to find such-and-such." Then you'll start tapping spastically over the desk, or sliding your hand under every loose scrap of paper, like some mole, in hopes of "putting a hand" on the lost item. Rather than go through this charade, consider two suggestions. If you're working in the lower grades, keep in mind that children live in a world of "let's pretend," and they love pretending to be anything! Take advantage of this trait and tell them to pretend to have this visual aid. Then continue with the activity like this is the way it was supposed to be! In other words, use the vicarious approach. But if you're with older students, let them improvise and be creative. Have them take a piece of paper and quickly sketch out or write in a visual aid for themselves. So it won't be as fancy as yours! The point is, they'll have a visual aid of sorts with which to "do" the activity.

The third suggestion is for **books**, particularly when songs don't match pages. Think of the time you called out a page number and some sweet little child hesitantly whispered, "My book doesn't have that song." Or maybe it was some smart alec who shouted out, "That ain't the right page!" Then it dawned on you that there were two different editions, that you had assumed everyone had your edition! What could you do? Have students share books—that would be the easiest (except watch out for the boy-girl thing in upper elementary). Or write the words on the board quickly while engaging the class in some recitation. And, as a last resort, you can ask those with the "wrong" edition to sing along on "lu" as you accompany the class. Any of these tactics will work when page numbers don't match.

Be sure you understand that these last three suggestions pertain to those times when honest omissions happen, when stop-gap measures are needed.

Concluding Challenge

Let me encourage you to think about getting materials and equipment ready for *your* lessons. If they help, use some of the suggestions cited above. Avoid panic attacks by having salvage tactics ready. Remember, you can (1) move on to the next step in your lesson, or (2) substitute another song or activity. But the best policy is to be thoroughly prepared—check and double check materials and equipment in a meticulous manner. I challenge you to be "ready" for your next lesson. It will enhance your teaching more than you can ever imagine!

LESS EFFECTIVE	MORE EFFECTIVE
"Okay, let's turn to page, uh, page . . . Wait a minute!" Ms. Grandioso said irritatingly, "Where is it, I just saw the song!" The class watched Ms. Grandioso flip the pages back-and-forth. "I'll find it if it takes me all night," she said frantically. "It probably will," thought the students as they slumped back in their seats.	Picking up her music text, Ms. Grandioso opened it quickly to the marker. "Turn to page 54, class, and tap the rhythmic pattern for me." When the fifth graders finished the activity, Ms. Grandioso immediately turned to the second marker in the book. "Very good, class. Turn now to page 102." Ms. Grandioso was always prepared. Students knew she took care of these details!

Having introduced the motivational idea for Swww beats, Ms. Peasante looked around for her illustration. "Where is it?" she asked herself. "It's here someplace," she told the class. With that she ransacked her desk, and then ran to the piano. "It's not here either. Maybe it's in the closet." And away she went! The students thought Ms. Peasante looked silly running back-and-forth. Some couldn't help snickering at her!

"Now I want you to see these Swww beats on this illustration." Ms. Peasante pointed to the illustration which was on the stand in front of the class. "Notice the larger strong beat," she explained. "We're going to clap on the strong beats and tap on the weaker ones." When she finished, Ms. Peasante praised them as she walked towards the displayed visual aid. Pointing to the illustration, she said, "See how we were clapping and tapping on the Swww beats?"

Checking for Correct Tempo in Listening Selections

So, you have all your listening material selected for your lesson, do you? May I ask you a question? Are you sure that the tempo is suitable for each recording? You say you didn't think about tempi? You'd better because it's too late to think about it once the teaching starts. I've seen many lessons disintegrate before the teacher's eyes because of the inappropriate tempi of their recordings. The only way to be absolutely sure that the tempi are correct is to check them out **before** taking the recordings into the classroom.

Definition of Correct Tempo

It's all well-and-good to say that the tempo must be correct for each listening selection, but what exactly does this mean in terms of teaching a lesson? In general, it means that the speed of the music is suitable for the planned response, or that the students will be able to execute the activities with the recordings. That's the primary condition for being correct. More specifically, however, being correct means that the recordings are neither too fast nor too slow for the teacher's purpose, that they move at speeds that "fit" the planned activities. Now look at some of the unorthodox ways teachers deal with this task.

Identifying Approaches in Checking Tempo

Unfortunately, many teachers aren't as conscientious in checking out tempi as they should be. Some are simply willing to assume that the tempi is going to be acceptable. But they usually end up berating themselves when the crisis happens. By then, it's too late to rectify the situation. That's the price one pays when he/she is willing to operate on false assumptions.

Then there are those who depend solely upon their memory to determine how a recording "goes" instead of listening to it. They're the ones who end up saying, "I don't remember the tempo being *this slow* or *this fast* before!" No, I'm afraid we never do when we depend on memory. That's the real danger of dealing with the "right" tempo on the basis of memory. Both of these approaches are a poor substitute for the only sure way of checking tempi, namely, by listening!

Suggestions for Deciding Correct Tempo

In case there should be any doubt as to how one decides whether or not a tempo is suitable, let's discuss what should be done. It's really quite simple. If the recording has not been used for a long time or if it is new and unfamiliar, try out the planned activity **with** the recording. Do the activity—not just mentally, but physically. Because unless you, yourself, can feel your movement "fit" the tempo, you cannot be certain the students will either. Even after years of teaching on all levels, I still find this approach the most foolproof way of determining the correctness of a recording.

Sometimes I still get surprised myself to find out that what I thought would be a super record turns out to be not quite so super, that it was faster or slower than I thought it was. I always am so grateful on these occasions that I discovered this problem *before* I taught the lesson, not during. Notice I said, ". . . I thought . . ." That's the culprit act in this case. Because no matter how experienced we are, we must never assume anything when it comes to preparing the material for teaching!

Remember, it only takes a minute to put on a recording or flip on a cassette, and "road test" it to see if it's compatible with the activity. It is not necessary to do the activity for the entire selection, unless there are tempo or meter changes in the music. Then, you would want to. The same would be true if you had doubts about some portion of the music. So the only time you can omit checking out a recording or cassette is when you know the music inside out. Otherwise, check it out! Rule number one here is: Never assume.

Reasons for Checking Correct Tempo

Some of you may be thinking that this is a minor preparation suggestion. And while you agree with making your music appropriate and appealing, you aren't quite as convinced about this task. (See the earlier section "Choosing Appropriate and Appealing Music Selections.") But if you think about it, having the correct tempo is just another aspect of being appropriate. It's one of the factors that makes the music suitable for activities, such as:

- hand designing a passage to show stepwise or skywise movement in a melody
- conducting 3/4 meter in three's, not one's
- playing melodic pattern on bells
- playing chordal accompaniment to familiar song on autoharp

In each of these experiences, having the correct tempo is essential. Students cannot perform correctly if the music moves more quickly or more slowly than required for the activity. As such, checking tempo cannot be overlooked—not if you want to teach a successful lesson.

Another reason for obtaining the correct tempo is that the students' attention depends upon suitable music. It doesn't take long for the class's interest and attention to wane when the tempo is faster or slower than it should be. Attention span is tied directly to the tempi for their activities. And, of course, there's always the momentum to consider. When the tempi are appropriate for the activity, the momentum of the lesson is electrifying. It moves ahead smoothly without any unnecessary stopping. In fact, a large part of checking out the correct tempi is just for these purposes: to keep the momentum moving, for making the music more appropriate, and don't forget the students' attention span as well.

Concluding Challenge

Expend the extra effort in planning to check out the tempi of your recordings, especially for those that have not been used recently or that are less familiar to you. Make certain that your tempi are correct. Give yourself every advantage of having a successful lesson—check to see if your tempi fit the activities. Try out the activity with the recording.

LESS EFFECTIVE

"Today we're going to be elephants. Let's see how our elephants look. Very good! Can we move our elephants in place? Try it. Good. Now here we go with our music. Ready." Mr. Da Capo was surprised the music was so slow—slower than even elephants would walk. "Goodness, I don't remember it being as slow as this!" he consoled himself. "Okay, everyone sit down. No more elephants walking today."

"Now that we've learned the I and V, in G Major, follow the chart and play the chords." When Ms. Con Fuco started the tape, she knew it was too fast. After the first two measures students began to look back-and-forth at each other. Some started putting their guitars away. "It's too fast," some called out. "I didn't think it went this fast," she admitted to the class. "Guess we'd better find something else, huh!"

MORE EFFECTIVE

Mr. Da Capo listened to a number of recordings before selecting the one for the lesson. "Let me see everybody be an elephant! Very good. Get in your elephant position. Ready." The music had good heavy steady beats. They "walked" like elephants at their seats, while chanting clump, clump, clump. "Let's play follow-the-leader around the room while being elephants." The tempo is perfect for elephant walks," Mr. Da Capo said to himself."

Ms. Con Fuco listened to the recording she planned to use with her eighth graders. "This should be just right for this class," she said to herself. "Look at the chord progression on the board, class. Let's play it through at this tempo. One, two, ready, play. Great. Ready for the recording? Ms. Con Fuco was delighted to see most of the class following the progression. "I'll have to remember this song again," she reminded herself. "That tempo is just right—I'll want to use it again."

Determining Back-Up Activities

One of the best precautions the teacher can take when it comes to planning activities is to have *back-up activities* or substitutes. There are times when planned activities fall apart on the spot: (a) new activities bomb out, (b) familiar activities seem out-of-sync, or (c) the avant-garde ones seem out of line with the class's ability. Disasters such as these need to be put aside and replaced with a back-up; otherwise, the lesson will come to a halt. With back-up activities the teacher can salvage these situations.

Definition of Back-up Activities

When I say, "back-up activities," I'm talking about alternatives to the planned activities, or substitute experiences that cover the activity and highlight the same conceptual idea! This is a crucial point in selecting back-ups. Then, too, I like to think of back-ups as "reserve" activities that, figuratively speaking, are left "waiting in the wings." Actually they are stored mentally until such times, if ever, they are called upon.

Benefits of Back-up Activities

There are several benefits for having back-up activities that are invaluable to the classroom teacher. For example, with back-ups ready, the continuity of the lesson can be maintained. There doesn't have to be a total breakdown when the original activity doesn't "go." The teacher simply tables it and substitutes another, almost like it's another reinforcing activity. Hence, the lesson goes forward in a smooth fashion, many times without the students even realizing the transition! It's times like this when relief for the teacher is spelled, B-A-C-K U-P!

But not only does the continuity of the lesson stay intact, so does the momentum. The excitement of the moment need not be lost and the lesson can keep that forward move which gives the aura of something happening! There's no time to say, "Let's see, what else could we do!" when you're in the throes of a crumbling activity. If there isn't any back-up waiting "in your wings" the momentum **will** come to a halt. Here's where the back-up activity becomes a lifesaver.

And don't forget the impact on students. You can hold onto their enthusiasm and interest if there's a back-up ready. It's so easy to lose this attitude with the class when the activity starts falling apart. But when that with-it-ness is rolled over to another "workable" experience without much ado on the teacher's part, there isn't any falling away of student attention—or enthusiasm for that matter. They simply make a transfer to the back-up activity.

If you want more security in your teaching, this added preparational effort will do it for you. If, for example, you find the planned activity too boisterous for an unexpectedly hyperactive class, or too low-keyed for an unusually laid-back class, you can substitute on the spot without breaking the flow of the lesson. Or if the "new" activity proves more demanding than anticipated, it can be replaced with a minimum of confusion.

Guidelines for Back-up Activities

While there are no set procedures for establishing back-up activities, there are some guidelines that can offer help in implementing these "reserve" experiences. And they can be best handled by posing pertinent questions.

First, should your substitute procedures be written down? No! Most of the time the "substitute" is going to be one of your tried-and-true activities that you can "do" with your eyes closed. So it's just a matter of tucking it away in your mind and being ready to pull it out on a moment's notice, if you need it.

Second, how does one know when it's time to substitute? Easy! Just "read" your students. Watch the look on their faces and the signals from their bodies. Notice also their response to the activity and their attention span, or lack of attention, as the case may be! Each of these physical responses will give you a cue, and send a message—if you're looking for it. In other words, let the students themselves be your guide. And muster all the perceptivity you can in observing your students. If a teacher is sensitive toward students, and people in general, he/she will "know" when the time has come to switch to the back-up. The key word here is "perceptivity."

And third, how should this transition from one activity to another be handled? Through verbiage! The teacher needs to make comments like the following:

- "Let's put our instruments away for now and do such-and-such instead."
- "We'll come back to the activity some other time. For now I'd like us to do this."
- "I don't think this is the best time for this activity; we're going to do something else."
- "I don't think we're ready for this yet. Let's go back to such-and-such for now, okay?"
- "We still need more work on this; in the meantime, let's go on and do this."

See how smoothly this transfer can be with the right verbiage? Don't be afraid to "level" with your students. By that, I mean tell them the truth. Be upfront. Let them known when the activity isn't going well, or if it's too difficult or too easy for them. Or if you over- or underestimated their ability. They like it when the teacher "talks turkey" and is being honest with them. In fact, I've found that students always respond better when presented with the truth rather than some whitewash. I agree with Bruner in this case. He says that children can deal with any kind of information, as long as it is presented to them in terms they can understand.[1] So be ready to tell the students what's happening in a class in a clear and concise way and then get on with it!

---

[1] Jerome Bruner. *The Process of Education* (Cambridge, MA, Harvard University Press), 1965, p. 33.

Finally, what about situations where teachers don't have back-up activities ready? I can't decide whether the resulting scenarios are pathetic or hilarious! Take, for instance, the poor soul who falls back on the "let's try it again" approach out of sheer desperation. There's nothing else up-the-sleeve. He/she tries to ride out the disaster by having the students finish the activity regardless of how poorly they're responding. Then to top it all off, the teacher tells the students how awful they did— and asks them to "do it again!" So the class repeats the pitiful performance. The result? The teacher gets more baffled, and the students, more befuddled. It's a perfect formula for bedlam.

Concluding Challenge

My advice to you is always have back-up activities ready, even for those old faithful activities. Some days even these don't "go." It's the only safeguard you have to insure yourself that the lesson will continue if a planned activity fails. Too, it's the only legitimate escape, outside of dumping the activity. So get back-ups ready. You'll be happy you did!

LESS EFFECTIVE	MORE EFFECTIVE
Ms. Mezzo introduced call charts to her sixth graders. But she forgot they were slow readers. When it came time for them to call out numbers, they couldn't. Some started to fidget, while a few others made airplanes out of the charts. "Let's really try to do this," she said. There wasn't anything else she could do; she didn't have another activity! The class did even worse. They didn't even try this time. Finally, Ms. Mezzo just let them talk. "They don't want to do this anyway," she told herself.	Ms. Mezzo was anxious to do call charts today, but she had something else ready in case the call charts didn't work. She was glad she had because she could tell immediately some students couldn't read. "Let's pass the call charts forward. We'll come back to this later," she told the class. "For now, let's use our tip-clap on the 'a' phrases and step-step-stop movement on the 'b' phrases. Ready!" The class jumped into the activity without any problem. She was glad she had this old faithful activity tucked away.
"All right, let's tap out the melody in this song, class." Ms. Contralto felt sure the third graders could do it because it only had eighth and quarters. But to her surprise they couldn't! She hadn't planned anything else either! "We can do better than that! Let's try it again. Don't get silly now. Louder, I can't hear you!" She finally told the class to shut their books and sit quietly till the class was over. "They can't do anything right today," she thought. "Let them sit there."	When Ms. Contralto heard her third graders tap the song, she knew they couldn't read quarter/eighths very easily. "I see we need to work on our rhythms reading more," she said. "Let's do this instead," she suggested. "I'll show you how to read, then you repeat after me. Ready." It was a good thing she had this other activity ready! The students could do this one.

2

Personal Behaviors

This chapter focuses specifically on the personal kinds of behavior that are crucial to those who teach music in the classroom. The term "personal behaviors," as interpreted in this text, refers to that particular repertoire of physical maneuverings that can enhance the operational effectiveness of the teacher. They are also the type of individualistic acts that can promote better control of the teaching-learning process, including such behaviors as bodily gesturing, facial expressioning, physical positioning, etc. We are not talking about incidental actions—we're talking about learned behaviors, that is, behaviors that can be consciously nurtured and honed to a high level of expertise. But before personal behaviors can be developed, they must first be identified. And that's the job of this chapter: to identify the personal behaviors of teaching.

While the job of identifying behaviors in each of the chapters has been a thought-provoking process, the identification of the personal behaviors was the most elusive—and most difficult—job of all. Perhaps this is because teachers have always been a bit reluctant to share personal behaviors for fear that all teachers would be required to behave in a similar manner and, thus, curtail the use of their own operating style. But I have some comforting news for those who fear such conformity. The behaviors in this chapter have not been suggested for the purpose of undermining the teacher's own personal style. To the contrary. They've been presented primarily to give the teacher an even larger arsenal of individual maneuverings. So, teachers, you need not fear that these behaviors will, in any way, interfere with your own individuality.

The second piece of comforting news is that even though the same behavior may be practiced by hundreds of teachers, no two will execute it the same way. The truth is, there will be as many different ways of working out the behavior as there are personalities, which is as it should be! Teachers need to be their own person. What's important is that teachers will have an additional repertoire of personal behaviors that can be implemented in any way they feel comfortable. So you see, individual teaching styles will *not* be squelched. Nor will these suggested personal behaviors make teachers look like carbon copies of each other. Be sure that you understand these clarifications before going on.

Let me make a few suggestions as to the application of these personal behaviors. I strongly urge that they be implemented with the same intensity and proficiency as any of the other teaching competencies. Why? Because they carry as much weight in the overall assessment of one's teaching success, and because they make a noble contribution to the collective effectiveness of the teacher's behavior and the students' learning. Make no mistake, personal behaviors have a profound affect on teaching as well as learning.

Note that the behaviors in this chapter are not presented in any order of preference or priority. Each one is looked upon with equal value in the total scheme of personal behaviors recommended for teaching classroom music. It would not only be useless, but impossible, to prioritize them. Only you can rightly do this in light of your own needs; thus, I leave prioritizing to you.

Gesturing in a Precise Manner

When it comes to the gestures and motions a teacher makes while in the throes of (a) telling, (b) showing, or (c) giving instructions, the rule-of-thumb is that they should be done with an air of precision—and some flair! So whether you're pointing to an example, dramatizing a word, or demonstrating an activity, your gesturings ought to have a clear definition and style, and energy. And look purposeful like theatrical movements. That's the kind of gesturing students need in order to respond appropriately, and the kind teachers need to project effectively. Yes, I know this is asking a lot, especially since such behavior isn't stressed in the training of teachers. But the fact remains that precise gesturing is an integral part of being an effective teacher.

Reasons for Gesturing Precisely

There are excellent reasons for insisting that gesturing be done in a precise way, and they're all obvious. But they're worth reviewing because of the affect they have on the teaching-learning cycle. Here's the first reason. Precise gesturing results in better class responses. It's true! Students aren't as confused about what to do or where to look. They have more direction, so they can imitate more accurately, follow instructions more easily, and focus on some example more quickly. In other words, they can participate better—and more willingly! If you're already in the habit of gesturing precisely, you know what I'm talking about here, and you know the affect it has on the teacher too! There's even more effort to be precise, isn't there? So your teaching gets better. That's the second reason. Precise gesturing simply inspires better teaching. It feeds on itself, so to speak. And the added bonus is that precise gesturing makes the teacher look more "with-it" when teaching.

See how the teaching learning cycle is set into motion? In a nutshell, the cycle works like this: Precise input (by teacher) *reaps* better output (by students); better output (by students *inspires* better input (by teacher), etc. Notice how the complete cycle looks and works in Figure 2.1.

The third reason for advocating precise gestures is that it helps pacing go more smoothly because the teacher doesn't have to keep stopping. Careless gesturing invariably leads to a stop-and-start syndrome which plagues many teachers. Vague motions almost always have to be done over. I often have the urge to ask the teacher who is gesturing haphazardly if he/she thinks this is normal teacher behavior, or if he/she feels that the first gesture attempt doesn't count. If so, the teacher is wrong. Gestures *don't* have to be done twice, and neither does pacing have to suffer from this stopping-and-starting syndrome. Not if gesturing is done precisely the first time. So here's the formula: The more precise the gesturing, the smoother the pacing. It's so simple, and yet so true.

Perhaps now you can understand why I'm so adamant about teachers gesturing in a precise way. Not only will it smooth out pacing, but will perk up the students—

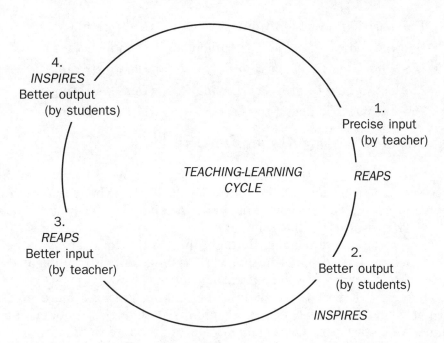

Figure 2.1. Teaching-Learning Cycle Initiated by Teacher's Precise Gesturings.

and improve one's teaching to boot! What three better reasons could there be for insisting upon gesturing in a precise manner.

Definition of Precise Gesturing

Some of you may still not be clear about the concept of *precise gesturing*, and would like it explained a bit more. Just think of it as being specific motions, or well-defined movements exercised in the process of (a) telling, (b) showing, or (c) giving instructions. Say you're going to demonstrate how to raise your arms for a particular activity. Here's what you need to consider to be precise. When raising your arms, will your palms be facing each other or facing outward? What about your fingers? Will they be together or spread out? How high will you raise your arms? All the way? Or half way? When will the arms come down? Go up again? See what I mean? Being precise is accounting for all the details of the movement while "doing" the gesture. Precise gesturing then is making well-defined motions.

But there's one other characteristic that clarifies the preciseness. It's the element of polish and finesse. By that I mean there's a theatrical aura about precise gesturing. It's eye-catching. It's done with style and character, and gracefulness. There's a sense of finish about the gesture. It also means that it's natural-looking. The teacher looks comfortable and at ease doing the gesture. In addition to specificity, then, it's the poise and finesse that makes for precise gestures.

Here's a sampling of some teaching tasks that call for precise gesturings:

- Pointing to a particular student   (Instructing)
- Sectioning off rows in the classroom   (Instructing)
- Selecting students to come forward   (Instructing)
- Calling attention to book example   (Instructing)
- Dramatizing a descriptive word   (Informing)
- Referring to a specific object   (Informing)

- Emphasizing an action word   (Informing)
- Showing how to hold an instrument   (Demonstrating)
- Modeling a particular activity   (Demonstrating)
- Motioning how to drop jaw in singing   (Demonstrating)
- Presenting action song to class   (Demonstrating)

Suggestions for Making Gestures Precise

A good cue comes from the basic premise that gesturing happens, either consciously or unconsciously, because of the desire to clarify (a) what's expected of students or (b) what's being said to them. Note the objective: To clarify some activity or information. That desire is what stipulates the criteria as to how gesturings should be done. These criteria differ slightly according to the task, i.e., whether they're done in conjunction with demonstrating, with telling, or with giving instructions. Let's look at what's needed for demonstrating first.

There are at least three criteria for making gestures more precise for demonstrating. They must be (1) large enough, (2) theatrical enough, and (3) realistic enough. We'll start with *large enough*. You're probably wondering how large is large, right? You can get some insight from the fact that students generally give back *less than half* of what they hear or see. So if your demonstrating gestures aren't as large as they should be, the class's response will be next to nil. The best way to interpret "large enough," then, is to view it as being as overt and expansive as *you* need to be to get the desired response. And only *you* can be the judge of your own overtness and know whether or not it's your best extended effort. So my advice is to make your demonstrating motions as large as needed—large enough so that you are confident the class will respond according to your expectations. Practice in front of a mirror, or put yourself on video-tape so you can see yourself as the students see you. In other words, put yourself in *their* place. Then ask yourself how *you* would respond if *you* were a student. If you'll be honest, you'll see where larger gesturing is needed and make the necessary adjustment. And that, dear teacher, is when your gesturing will start being large enough—when *you* begin to recognize what "large" means for *you*. That answers how large is large.

Here's one more piece of advice. Stop feeling self-conscious or silly when you're making large gestures. Start thinking like a teacher. Remember that you're making your gestures for the students' sake, not for yours! So rather than catering to your feelings and excusing your efforts, concentrate on developing your gesturings and deciding upon what you can do to improve. That's a more constructive approach. Let me suggest role playing when you practice—and really getting "into" it. The more realistic you can be in front of the mirror, the less self-conscious you'll begin to feel in the classroom. Try it and see. You need to feel comfortable if you're going to gesture effectively when you're demonstrating.

The second criterion for precise demonstrating gestures is to see that they are *theatrical enough*. You really can't be precise enough without being somewhat dramatic. Demonstrating gestures need a good dose of showmanship, or a sense of realism. If there's any one criterion that can make gestures more definitive, it's making them realistic. Only when motions are being done like the real thing do they have all the elements of form and flair. Precision goes hand-in-hand with realism. So do your demonstrating actions like the real thing, and with as much conviction as a skillful mime so that the students will be chomping at the bit to try them with you. Timpson and Tobin were right when they said that teaching is a whole lot like acting when it comes to demonstrating.[1] If you're serious about being more precise in your demonstrating gestures, try being more theatrical and realistic. In fact, why not take a theater workshop or theater class? It'll do wonders for your gesturing skills!

The third criterion is being *energetic enough*. Your gesturings may well be large enough and done with all the theatrical flair you can muster, but if they lack energy, they'll still fall flat and look wimpy. Precise movement requires energy. It simply takes a lot more steam to (a) initiate precise movement, (b) sustain precise movement, and (c) release it in a precise way, than it does to make a dozen vague motions. Energy and precision are the two ingredients that captivate students' attention and entice them to emulate the teacher. Plain and simple, energy must be expended to beget energy. So dig down deep and cough up every ounce of energy you have if you want a precise edge to your gestures—and an energetic response from your class.

It would be wonderful if all demonstrating gestures were done with these three criteria. But they usually aren't. Too often they're limp, miniaturized replicas of what they ought to be! I always think of one teacher in particular in this case. She was demonstrating a hand designing activity for the class—at least that's what she said she was doing! But her hand designing was floppy. She also designed the entire major scale between the second and third buttons of her blouse. That gives you some idea how small those scale degrees were! And to top it all off, the designing was lifeless. I honestly didn't think she'd make it up the scale! If it weren't so pitiful, it would have been hilarious. When the students' turn came, it was a disaster! Had her hand designing had been more energetic and realistic, the results would have been totally different!

Now what about the criteria for precise gesturing when it comes to telling, explaining, or giving instructions? Actually the criteria are the same: gesturings need to be (a) extended more, (b) aimed better, and (c) sustained longer. It's impossible to have precise gestures, when explaining or instructing, without these stipulations. So let's talk about each one.

More extension? That simply means to get the gesture away from your body. Use all the space in front of you as far as your arms will reach, especially when pointing to someone in the back of the room or something on the front chalkboard. Why teachers insist on doing all their gesturing two inches away from the body, I'll never know. It's not only more difficult to make gestures large in this position, but also visible. Stop hugging your elbows to your sides, and try positioning them where they would be if you were starting to lift up your arms. Go ahead; try it. See where the elbows go and how they automatically move away from the body? Not only do you have more operating space with elbows in this position, but also more freedom to move. If you want to be more precise-looking with your gestures, then get those elbows out! That's a "must."

Then there's exercising better aim with gestures, especially when referring to an example on the board or directing instructions to a particular student or group of students. Gestures like this need to be right on target, not some aimless waving in the general direction or some nebulous nodding. For example, when pointing to something, the finger needs to be directly on-line with the subject and so pinpointed that there is no question whatsoever as to which example, which person(s), or what "thing" the teacher is talking about. See what I'm saying? Whether you point, nod, or motion in some other way, the gesture must be accurately aimed. And here's what

[1]William Timpson and David Tobin. *Teaching as Performing* (Prentice-Hall, Inc., Englewood Cliffs, NJ, 1982), p. vii.

puts the finishing touch on a well-aimed gesture. It's the definite stop, or halting point at the end of the gesture. That's the feature which gives definition to so-called "aiming" gestures. So practice "stopping" with your pointing or nodding. In fact, go back to role playing in front of a mirror. It's still the best way I know of to discipline yourself. And remember, being accurate with your aim is one of the simplest, and quickest, ways of making gestures look more precise.

The third criterion for creating more precise-looking gestures when in the act of telling or instructing is being sure that they're *momentarily sustained*—frozen for a split second after making them or before they're released. Obvious as it may seem, most teachers don't do this. Instead, they let go, or "drop," their gestures as soon as they do them, or let them fizzle out! Either way, the gestures look awkward. And they're "gone" or "over" even before they can make an impact or project a definite image. But by holding onto the gesture for a moment, like soloists do with their bodily stance after singing or playing the last note, this wouldn't happen! The teacher would lock in, or preserve, the form of the gesture and project the intended message with more polish and poise. Let me warn you, however. You'll need to discipline yourself firmly if you're not accustomed to this sustaining thing. But be patient. As you become more consistent, you'll notice a marked difference in your gestures. Not only will they *look* more precise, but also *feel* more precise. That's what this sustaining bit does. Try it and see!

Have enough suggestions now? Good. Let's recap them then. In a nutshell, gesturings need to be (a) properly extended, (b) accurately aimed, and (c) momentarily sustained when used in conjunction with telling and explaining. If they are, they'll definitely be more precise than they were.

Concluding Challenge

Now what about your gesturing? Do you make them large and theatrical when you demonstrate? And energetic looking? When you're explaining something or giving instructions, do you extend your arms? Sustain your gestures momentarily? Point accurately? If not, start now. Not only will you perfect your gesturing, but upgrade your teaching—and even improve the response of your students! Sound exciting? It is! Try it and reap the benefits.

LESS EFFECTIVE	**MORE EFFECTIVE**
Mr. Tonality asked his sixth graders to watch as he demonstrated accented beats on rhythm. Half-heartedly, he picked up the sticks and began tapping the strong-weak beats so lethargically that students could hardly tell which were accented. Those in the back couldn't see his demonstration because the sticks were too low. What's more, he was holding them so close to his stomach that students were waiting for him to hit himself—and to bust out laughing. When he instructed the class to play, he got annoyed at their poor performance. "No, not like that. Play like I showed you," he bellowed. The sad truth was, they were.	In demonstrating accented beats for his sixth-grade class, Mr. Tonality held his rhythm sticks chest high and kept his left one parallel to the floor and the right one poised over the left. Holding this readiness pose for a moment, he proceeded to tap the strong beats with vigorous, well-defined taps and the weaker beats with softer taps. Then he chanted "strong-weak" as he tapped. "Notice where I tapped the strong beats, class. Now try it with me. Ready." When the class finished, Mr. Tonality let out an enthusiastic "Bravo. I heard every strong beat!"

Ms. Texture introduced the new concept of quarter and eighth notes by asking the students to look at the examples on the board. She stood behind her desk as she explained and waved her arm back-and-forth in the air in the direction of the examples like she was whitewashing a barn. Expecting her to point out which-was-which, the students began looking from one-to-another and shrugging their shoulders to indicate their confusion. But Ms. Texture kept right on talking, although she did switch to pointing which amounted to the same aimless motion. Then she concluded by saying, "Now, does everyone understand about quarter and eighth notes?" The students just looked at her in total confusion—and frustration.

"Okay, class, let's talk about eighth and quarter notes today, shall we?" announced Ms. Texture. She was standing next to the chart which showed examples of each. "Now, the quarter notes represent our long sounds," she said while pointing to the quarter note. As she continued talking and showing the class how quarters sound, she would place her pointer finger under the note from time to time. When she asked the class to read the accompanying exercise, she made sure that she pointed to each note as the class clapped. "Very good, class, you read that perfectly." Pointing now to the eighth note, she began questioning the class about eighth notes. Students knew exactly what she was referring to as she talked. There was no confusion.

Exercising Mobility in the Classroom

Have you ever thought of teacher mobility as being a personal behavior? If not, you should! Circulating is one of the most personal—and most rewarding—things a teacher can do in the classroom. But it's unfortunate that many teachers don't think of mobility as being a teaching behavior—much less a personal competency. It's probably because mobility seems like such an ordinary kind of behavior, and a far cry from anything special. But the truth is that when it's properly and prudently used, mobility is anything but an ordinary behavior. It's actually a very personal, and professional, way of (a) responding to students and (b) coping with teaching. Not only is mobility underestimated, it's also misunderstood. A lot of teachers simply don't understand what it means. So the first order of business is to make sure that there's a better understanding of mobility as it applies to the classroom.

Definition of Teacher Mobility

Let's begin by defining the concept of *mobility* as it applies to teaching. In a nutshell, it's the capacity for moving one's self about in the classroom, or the tendency to circulate from one place to another as the lesson progresses. It's the opposite of immobility, which implies a tendency to stand in one place for an entire lesson with locked knees and braced heels, or to sit behind a desk for the whole time. Mobility, on the other hand, implies motion. It's not a matter of sitting down or standing still.

And here's what else it's not! It's not a continuous back-and-forth pacing. The teacher should not look like a caged animal! Neither should mobility be a constant trekking up one aisle and down the next. That's nothing but nervous flittering that only distracts the students' attention and destroys the teacher's poise. Nor must it be thought of as a non-stop circling round the classroom. That's simply an abuse of the behavior! Mobility is none of these antics—not a perpetual pacing, an interminal trekking, or a continual circling. Be sure you're clear about these no-no's before going on.

Another matter that needs to be understood is that there are two types of teacher mobility: (1) focused mobility and (2) non-focused mobility—and both are

exercised by the classroom music teacher. That's what causes so much misunderstanding and confusion. Let's look at focused mobility first.

Focused mobility is easier to understand and to spot! It takes in all the intentional treks a teacher makes toward a specific student for a specific reason, like for reprimanding, assisting, or encouraging. You can also think of it as a deliberate jaunt with a determined stride and a definite direction. The teacher already knows where he/she is going even before the first step is taken in the direction of the so-called "victim." In other words, there's a focus, an objective. See why we understand focused mobility better? It's so easy to label and to justify. But we also need to acknowledge non-focused mobility if the potential of the behavior is to be fully understood and not underestimated.

Non-focused mobility is more difficult to describe and to justify because there's usually no other reason for making a move other than for the sake of moving; or, at the very most, to avoid standing in one spot for the whole lesson. It looks like aimless meandering or mindless shuffling. It's usually accomplished in two different ways: (1) by meandering around the room from time to time, or (2) by stepping away from a spot every now and then. We'll look at each of these approaches.

The occasional *meandering* is just what it says—an on-and-off strolling around that doesn't have any particular destination. You've seen teachers do this; in fact, you've probably done it yourself! It's that slow, hesitant—and even zig-zag—stepping off teachers do while teaching. Like they aren't even thinking! And you know what? Most of the time, they aren't. Not when they're moving just for the sake of moving. And where do teachers move to in this purposeless kind of roaming? Lots of places. Sometimes it's (a) from the front of the room to the back, (b) from across one side to the other, or (c) up one aisle and down the next. And consider the time-frame of such meandering. Sometimes the move from one spot to another is made in one fell swoop, and sometimes it's done in short jaunts with plenty of pauses. But whether it's done all at one time or in short spurts, aimless meandering happens only when the teacher "feels" like meandering, or when he/she is so inclined. That's what makes non-focused mobility such a personalized behavior. It's done on the teacher's own terms—with the how and when of it being up to the teacher. Now look at the stepping approach.

Stepping off occasionally is still another way the teacher achieves a sense of mobility. Here's how it's done. Every now and then, the teacher takes a step or two, or maybe more, (a) backwards, (b) forwards, or (c) sidewards. Sometimes the teacher takes one step at a time over a period of several minutes, and sometimes several steps at a time. It doesn't matter. What matters is that the teacher doesn't stay in the same spot forever. Does he/she move back to the original spot? Sometimes yes, sometimes no. That isn't important. What's important is that the teacher moves whenever his/her intuition "says" it's time to move. While it's a more confined and subtle way of creating a sense of mobility, it is, nevertheless, equally as effective!

So, in terms of teaching, *mobility* refers to the teacher's capacity to move about in the classroom. And when there's a need, that mobility takes on direction and purpose—in relationship to the student(s), of course. That's focused mobility. But when left up to the teacher's whim, it becomes an aimless meandering or a mindless stepping. That's non-focused mobility. Clear! Good! Let me give you some guidelines now as to how mobility needs to be executed to have the most impact.

Guidelines for Executing Mobility

You need to have definite criteria for moving around in the classroom, and unless the criteria are applied in a conscientious way, your mobility will have little or no affect on the students.

For Focused Mobility. To be most effective, at least four criteria should be considered when exercising focused mobility: (1) a set stride, (2) a speedy route, (3) some bodily gesturing, and (4) eye contact. Think about these for a moment. With regard to a set stride, there should be no dilly-dallying. The teacher's gait should quicken—sometimes even in the midst of a normal gait. Quite literally, swift steps are needed to get to the student(s) who needs the attention. The second criterion is that the teacher needs to take the speediest route to the student(s) in need. This is not the time to meander or go the long way around. It's the time to get from points A to B in the most direct way possible. Or, to put it in the vernacular, to make a bee-line dive in the right direction. How does the teacher do this? By mentally mapping out the route as soon as the situation is perceived—and then following that route with those quickened steps. In a way, the first two criteria are really one. The third criterion is especially important. It's using some kind of bodily gesture while heading in the direction, like tilting one's head toward the student(s), pointing a finger at the student(s), or placing a finger on one's lips to indicate no talking while moving closer to the person. Such gestures indicate that (a) you are heading the student's way, (b) you see that student doing this-or-that, or (c) you want some activity to stop before you get to the person(s). In other words, the gesturing adds impact to your mobility. And the last criterion is to make eye contact with the student(s) while in motion. This isn't the time to be scanning. It's the time to be connecting with the individual(s) with the eyes! Students need to know who's got your attention and that you are on your way to either stop the problem or offer assistance. Whichever the case, eye contact enroute is an excellent way of reinforcing the impact of a purposeful trek. Take these four criteria to heart if you want to be more effective with your focused mobility.

For Non-Focused Mobility. Now look at the four criteria for non-focused mobility. Even though there isn't a specific reason for moving, there still needs to be some criteria to make it a viable behavior, like having: (1) an aimless appearance, (2) a leisurely spirit, (3) an unobtrusive manner, and (4) an intuitive response. Take the aimless appearance. Movement that doesn't have a purpose or a focus *should* look aimless, like it's being done without any premeditated thought as to which direction to go or which aisle to pursue. In other words, it shouldn't appear to have any set course. As for the leisurely spirit, the movement needs to reflect a relaxed attitude, a laid-back feeling that makes it obvious there isn't any rush to be anywhere. Too, there should be an air of nonchalantness that says to the students you are totally at ease—and comfortable—in moving this way. And being unobtrusive? That simply means the movement must be done in such a low-key manner that it's no more distracting and no more disturbing to the students than erasing the chalkboard, announcing a page number, or passing out some papers. It also means that it's exercised often enough so that the students are accustomed to seeing this kind of meandering. But probably the most important criterion for non-focused mobility is that non-focused mobility be an intuitive response—not a regimented happening. The teacher should move only when he/she "feels" like moving. So whether it's wandering slowly to the back of the room, taking a few steps forward in the direction of the responding student, or stepping back a step or two from the first row, the move is made only when the teacher's intuition says it's time. No sooner, no later. That's a crucial ingredient in making a non-focused move!

For Both Types of Mobility. Here's one final guideline that applies to both types of mobility. Mobility should be exercised just as freely with a whole class as with several students. The number of students should not be the deciding factor; neither should the type of class. Mobility must be governed by either (a) a perceived need or (b) an intuitive feeling, regardless if there are two or twenty-two students! Remember that the next time you get ready to exercise mobility.

Opportunities Presented by Mobility

Why make so much of teacher mobility? Because the results of this behavior should be of interest to every classroom music teacher. Here they are: (a) better control of classroom behavior, (b) more variety in classroom environment, and (c) closer proximity to students needing help or praise. Yes, they do result in both types of mobility.

First, there's better classroom control. Make no mistake, circulating around the room is an excellent way of coping with students engaged in disruptive behavior. The mere fact that you are able to position yourself close to the student(s) means that you become a deterrent to the disruption. It's really amazing, or should I say amusing, how angelic the student(s) can become when the teacher is approaching, or how quickly the chatter stops when the teacher is in the vicinity. I just love to plop myself between two note-writers, or two gigglers, or even two or three whisperers. It bursts their bubble in a flash! And the look on their faces is worth a million. Then, if you add the element of physical touch, when appropriate, you become even more potent in controlling discipline. For example, placing a finger on the student's hand or tapping a student's shoulder does wonders for stopping a problem on the spot. Believe

me, there's nothing like teacher mobility, and an appropriately timed touch, to squelch some annoying or disturbing behavior. That's the first reason for advocating mobility—it's good for discipline.

The **second** result is that it creates an environmental contrast for students. By moving to a different part of the room or by taking a few steps this way or that way, the teacher is able to change the scenery. Facing the front of the room, the teacher's desk, or the front chalkboard for the whole lesson can get monotonous. Students could probably tell the teacher how many cracks there are in the above wall, or how many thumbtacks there are in the adjacent bulletin board, or even how many letters there are in the sign over the teacher's head! Don't laugh. Students get bored with the same scenery day after day, and class after class. But, by being mobile, the teacher has the power to vary the setting. In essence, mobility accomplishes the same purpose as changing the bulletin board or varying the lunch menu. It provides variety! Isn't variety the "spice of life"? Mobility, then, is one way of adding a fresh breath of change to the classroom setting.

The third outcome is that the teacher is able to get closer to the students who need encouragement and/or praise. Teachers who stay in one place miss out on establishing rapport with their students. But those who make the effort to be near student(s) in time of need are the ones who make it clear they care. By placing an encouraging hand on a shoulder, sharing an understanding smile, or whispering an encouraging word, the teacher further reinforces his/her concern. Teacher nearness is often the difference between success and failure for a lot of students who need this kind of support. For those who need praise, being near allows the teacher to give that special look of appreciation. It's a priceless moment for both teacher and student. And what about the times when a student has just received an award? Being able to (a) reach out an acknowledging hand, (b) express a commending thought in the student's ear, or (c) display a congratulatory smile while approaching the student are all responses the student will long remember. These are the kinds of gestures the teacher can bestow on students when mobility is an integral part of the teacher's personal behavior—and the kind of rapport that can be nurtured in the process.

Concluding Challenge

Do you see that it's necessary to exercise mobility in the classroom? While it seems like such an ordinary behavior, it's really a powerful tool. But let me caution you again. Don't travel over every inch of floor space, or march up and down every aisle three times before the lesson is over. That isn't necessary. Rather, use it wisely. And don't forget to apply the guidelines. I guarantee you'll enjoy the rewards.

LESS EFFECTIVE	MORE EFFECTIVE
As soon as the fourth-grade lesson began, Ms. Tutti saw Sarah and Jane giggling. She glared at them from her front desk with her arms folded. When the girls continued to giggle, Ms. Tutti yelled out, "Stop that giggling this minute!" Everyone turned to look at Sarah and Jane, who couldn't stop giggling. One look at the teacher staring at them made them giggle even harder. Ms. Tutti kept on glaring. Finally she said, "Leave! I can't have any of that in here." The two could hardly contain themselves as they left.	Ms. Tutti watched Sarah and Jane giggling for several minutes. She cast a number of glances in their direction and shook her head at them at least five times. But they still continued to giggle. Slowly, while continuing to teach, Ms. Tutti made her way up the third aisle until she was standing between them while giving the directions for the next activity. The girls stopped giggling immediately and began participating. Ms. Tutti gave each girl an appreciative smile when they looked up.

Mr. Solo's seventh-grade class sang quite well with syllables. A few had some problems, however. Bob was one. When it came his turn, he faltered in the second measure. Mr. Solo waited at the piano and then asked him to start again. When he stopped at the same spot, Mr. Solo said that he needed to try harder. Bob still could not sing the passage! Mr. Solo sighed impatiently from the piano and went on to Sally. Bob slumped down in his seat.

Mr. Solo's seventh graders were candidates for the eighth-grade chorus! But some, like Bob, still had trouble singing with syllables. So, when it came to Bob's turn, Mr. Solo made sure he was standing next to Bob's seat. Whenever Bob sang a syllable incorrectly, he leaned down and got Bob back on pitch before he could stop. Then Mr. Solo let Bob continue on his own. When he finished, Mr. Solo gave Bob a soft tap on the shoulder and a thumbs up sign! Bob grinned. He was proud of getting through the exercise.

Mirroring Class's Movements

So many of the activities used in the general music classroom involve body movement. For example, there's clapping, playing, marching, swaying, etc., all of which call for bodily motion to a greater or lesser degree. When using such activities, the teacher generally demonstrates for the class and then participates *with* the class. It's during these particular times that teacher mirroring is indispensable. Notice, I said "teacher" mirroring and not student mirroring. This distinction is crucial to mirroring behavior.

Definition of Teacher Mirroring

In a word, *mirroring* is synonymous with "modeling." It's nothing more than an imitating ritual, or an intentional aping process. But here's the catch. In "teacher" modeling, it's the teacher who imitates the class, or the teacher who does the activity opposite to what the students have been instructed. In other words, the teacher uses the same hand or moves in the same direction as the students. Why? To avoid confusion. We'll talk about that later. For now, let me give you some examples.

If the teacher instructs the students to turn right, the teacher will turn left. If

the class is told to start marching on the left foot, the teacher begins on the right foot. If the teacher indicates that the students are to hold the tambourine with the left hand and tap with the right, then the teacher must hold it with the right and tap with the left. What teacher mirroring does, then, is to give students the same impression, or sensation, as watching themselves in a mirror. That is, to "see" the teacher as their own image, moving with the same hand, same foot, or turning in the same direction. Mirroring is the teacher imitating the class by reversing his/her own movements or directions.

Significance of Mirroring Students

I know that some of you think this is a minor detail in the overall act of teaching, that it's "icing on the cake" when it comes to presenting an activity. But it isn't. Mirroring is one of those subtle teacher "ways" that separate the master teacher from the average teacher. It belongs to a higher order of teacher behaviors that adds a touch of class to one's teaching. Here's how. Mirroring elicits a more accurate and more uniform response from students the *first time around*. When the teacher is doing exactly what the students are doing with the "same" hand, foot, or instrument, the class's response is noticeably more unified, more precise! Because there's an ongoing model, students can see exactly what to do. So the response is better on the first try!

But even more rewarding is the impact of mirroring on one's own pacing. It can virtually put an end to the start-and-stop syndrome; in other words, your momentum can be streamlined. You don't have to go back and explain or demonstrate a second time. Students can watch the teacher and see what they should be doing. Of course, there are times when activities *need* to be reinforced, or repeated, because they are more challenging. That kind of stopping-and-starting is a necessary part of the teaching process. But I'm not talking about necessary repetition. I'm talking about the needless stops-and-starts that result from not mirroring. These are the ones that can destroy your pacing. But just think! You can remedy this problem if you will just use teacher mirroring. It works like a charm!

Problem With Teacher Mirroring

The problem, however, is that teacher mirroring is often overlooked. The most logical reason is that teachers concentrate more on the obvious demands of demonstrating, like being deliberate, energetic, and precise. They often aren't even aware of the need for teacher mirroring. That's why I call it the "hidden behavior." It's easy to overlook. And when it is overlooked, it's often the culprit that unravels the whole activity. There's always confusion when students do one thing and see the teacher doing another.

Here's one vivid example of a non-mirroring situation that has stayed with me over the years. A young teacher in her second year of teaching was beginning to show prospects of being a super general music specialist. Her big problem, however, was getting her fourth graders to do an activity without confusion. They constantly imitated what she was doing rather than doing what she instructed. She thought this was just one of those occupational hazards that plagued every beginning teacher. Consequently, her lessons sputtered along with one stop-and-start episode after another to reprimand the students. When she finally discovered teacher mirroring, her lessons were immediately transformed. They became smooth operations. I can still hear her exact words the day she tried teacher mirroring. "It's so simple," she beamed. "All I needed to do was imitate what the class would be doing!" A few months later she was still "on cloud nine" when she reported, "It works every time."

Teachers need to bear in mind that students will generally "do" what they see, rather than what they hear, when it comes to activities. That's why you need to be savvy about mirroring. And be prepared to reverse *your* actions on every instruction. Don't let mirroring be your problem.

Helpful Hints for Teacher Mirroring

But let's talk about how mirroring must be done to have the greatest impact on students. Above all, teacher mirroring, like teacher demonstrations, must be done in a very precise and theatrical-like manner that totally captivates the class's attention and makes them want to "do" what the teacher is doing. That precise, theatrical, and yes, energetic kind of mirroring is what gives the teacher that marvelous, almost mysterious, feeling of being able to "draw out" the kind of response desired. If you've ever experienced this charismatic power over your class as a result of your own mirroring skill, you know what I'm talking about. That's how persuasive and precise your mirroring needs to be, if it's going to do the job.

Ah, but I can just hear those who are skeptical about mirroring say this is a misleading way of dealing with students. Is it? I don't think so. Most of the students won't even notice—or care, for that matter—that you're mirroring. But if you think they will, then simply tell them what you will be doing and why. It's been my experience that children are more flexible and accepting than adults, particularly when they know the reason(s) for something. So don't let this notion stop you from mirroring. Just tell it like it is.

The more logical concern, I would think would be how difficult mirroring will be for the teacher. Can it be confusing? Initially, probably so. But if you begin planning for it and disciplining yourself to raise the opposite arm, tap with the opposite hand, or turn in the opposite direction you instructed the class, it will soon become second nature. In the meantime, you might want to take a few seconds before each demonstration to get your proper mind-set. Pretty soon you'll find yourself mirroring your instructions automatically. Trust me, you will!

I get a charge out of those who persist on handling this situation with the infamous "Turn Around" approach. You've probably seen this stunt a hundred times too! It goes like this. Following the instruction, the teacher whips around so that his/her

back is to the class and while raising his/her right hand says, "Raise your right hand with me—that's this one—and wiggle it just like this." So everyone raises the right hand and goes wiggle, wiggle, wiggle. But as soon as the teacher turns around, you know what happens—boom. Half the class quickly snatches down the right hand and shoots up the left. Wondering what went wrong and scolding the children to listen, the teacher repeats the silly process. Thus begins a series of useless stops-and-starts. The solution? Chuck the turn-your-back stint. It's time-consuming and silly. Substitute teacher mirroring. It's more efficient and more sensible.

Concluding Challenge

Is it clear that the secret to better class responses is teacher mirroring? Good! Because if you mirror your class's action when you demonstrate or participate, you will be able to lean back and enjoy a few moments of teaching bliss you didn't think possible. Just remember, as the great Sherlock Holmes would say, "It's all in the mirroring, my dear Watson. It's all in the mirroring!"

LESS EFFECTIVE	MORE EFFECTIVE
Ms. Clef's second-grade class was listening for high sounds in the recording. She instructed the children as follows: "And when you hear the high register, I want you to hold up your high card with your right hand like this." (Ms. Clef used her right hand.) "Now let's get ready. Listen." Some raised their right hand like Ms. Clef instructed, while others raised their left hand—like Ms. Clef. "No, no. Your right hand," she shouted as she waved her right hand back-and-forth. Some of the children still looked puzzled.	Ms. Clef instructed her second-grade children carefully concerning the listening activity. "We're going to test our listening ears today. When you hear the high-sounding register, I'd like to see our high cards come up with your right arm, like this." (Ms. Clef raised the card straight up with her *left* arm.) "Now you show me. Good! Hold your cards in front with both hands." Ms. Clef was pleased when everyone raised his/her card up with the right hand each time the high section played. It helped to have Ms. Clef do the activity like they were doing.
For the next activity, Ms. Goodtone anxiously announced, "We're going to march to the beat with this recording class. Let me show you how we are going to march. Notice that I begin on the left foot." (Ms. Goodtone pointed to her left foot as she lifted it and began to march.) "Now, you try marching. Get ready! Stand tall like a soldier. Ready. Left, right, left—wait, stop. I saw some of you starting to march on your right foot. Didn't you hear me say left?" she blurted out while stomping her left foot against the floor. "Okay, let's try it once again!"	Ms. Goodtone continued by saying, "Let's see if we can make our feet march to the beat with our record, okay? Watch how I march and on what foot I begin marching." (Ms. Goodtone pointed to the right foot and began marching with a high step while chanting, left, right, left, etc.). "Did you see what foot I began with? Good. The left. Everyone point to your left foot. Show me how you will lift your foot. Great. Let's get ready to march. Ready?" When the recording began everyone started to march on the left foot while she started on the right. "Very good, class. We all began on the correct marching foot."

Maintaining Eye Contact From the Piano ⎯⎯⎯⎯⎯⎯⎯⎯⎯⎯⎯⎯

The general music teacher spends a lot of time at the piano, especially in the upper grades. Some teachers sit when playing; some stand. It really doesn't matter. It's what the teacher feels most comfortable doing. What does matter, however, is whether or not the teacher can exercise eye contact regardless of standing or sitting. You see, eye contact is just as important from the piano as from any other place in the classroom. And, in many cases, even more. So let's take a minute to discuss this behavior. It definitely merits our attention.

Definition of Maintaining Eye Contact

Contrary to what some think, maintaining eye contact does not mean to watch constantly, or stare permanently in one direction, or at one student. If you've ever tried to stare at your class while playing, you know that constant eyeballing is not only impossible, but impractical, especially if you're using music. It's also unnecessary! So what does *eye contact* mean then? It means to glance up frequently—for two or three beats (or approximately a half a measure)—during which time the teacher either (a) scans the class with one broad sweep from right-to-left or left-to-right, or (b) zeros-in momentarily on the disrupting or faltering one(s). That's the essence of eye contact, whether at the piano or elsewhere—frequent glances. Actually it's more like "snatching" a quick look here or doing a brief scan there. It's the only practical way to have eye contact at the piano, particularly when music is being used.

Implication for Eye Contact at Piano

There's a definite implication when it comes to maintaining eye contact at the piano. You've probably already guessed it—and you're right! Eye contact implies that the teacher must have functional competency at the keyboard. Basically, functional competency means having the ability to (a) sight read any of the simplified accompaniments in the music series texts, (b) edit or simplify the written accompaniment when it's too difficult, and (c) improvise an accompaniment when none is available or when the given one is not suitable. In other words, it's being able to function at the keyboard as a result of having a working knowledge of harmony and chordal accompaniments. Keyboard competency is a prerequisite for having good eye contact at the piano.

Suggestions for Exercising Eye Contact at Piano

Since keyboard competency is the key to eye contact, my suggestions here focus primarily on the keyboard. That's where the problem lies. I can already hear some of you saying that you just don't play well enough to look up, no matter how much you simplify or how well you improvise. I say hogwash! Whether you're all thumbs or a bundle-of-nerves, you still need do-able options that can make you competent at whatever level your proficiency may be!

My first suggestion is this: edit the accompaniment to the bare bone. By that I mean play just the melody in the right hand and block chords—in closed position—in the left hand. Play the chords on the first and third beats of each measure, or just on the first beat if no chord change is needed. In other words, analyze the chord (or chords) in each measure and play them in block style rather than what's written. And one more thing, write in the fingerings for the melody. If necessary, get help. You'll be surprised how much easier it is to play with correct fingerings! Also write in the chords for each measure, either by number or letter name. Then all you need to do is read the chords. Better yet, memorize the progression so that you don't have to look at the accompaniment. In short, simplify the music so that even *you* can have eye contact at the piano.

The second suggestion is to improvise your own accompaniment. Now wait; don't panic. Let me show you how easy this can be—and how much fun! You can either (a) simplify the chordal progression by substituting other chords and using simple chording styles, or you can (b) compose your own accompaniment using only the I, IV, and V7 chords with simple chording styles. You don't have to use what's written. Most of the songs in the basic series texts can be accompanied with the I, IV, and V7 chords, so use primary chords almost exclusively—with some dominant sevenths and minor chords thrown in for those who are able. See how easy it is to improve?

But let's say a word about chording styles. For those who fret about their keyboard ability, use any of the following styles:

a. Block Chord Style (Left Hand)	In closed position on first and third beats of the measure, or first beat only, if no chord is needed.
b. Broken Block Style (Left Hand)	$\begin{matrix} & 1 & 1 & 1 \\ 5 & 3 & 3 & 3 \end{matrix}$ (in 4/4) $\begin{matrix} & 1 & 1 \\ 5 & 3 & 3 \end{matrix}$ (in 3/4)
c. Arpeggiated Chord Style	5-1-3-5 in 4/4 and 2/4 5-3-1 in 3/4 and 6/8, or
d. Root-Block Chord Style	Root (in octaves)-chord-chord-chord in 4/4 Root (in octaves)-chord-chord in 3/4

If you need to stay with block chord style, fine. Otherwise, select the chording style that sounds the most appealing for each song. It will vary. Mind you, there's no short-cut here. You'll just have to try out each style. And, whichever you choose, you'll discover that your eye contact will improve; you won't have to keep your eyes glued to the music as much. By the way, if your class knows the melody well enough, you can just vamp or play a chordal accompaniment with the root of the chord in the left hand and the block chords in the right hand.

Beyond these two suggestions, the only other one I have for improving eye contact would be to beg, borrow, or steal an autoharp. But even then, you'll need to have eye contact. So why not try editing the piano accompaniment or improvising your own? In my opinion, these are your best solutions.

Reasons for Eye Contact at Piano

The need for eye contact at the piano is obvious. First of all, it is necessary for classroom management. Without visual monitoring, it's only a matter of seconds before the mayhem monsters realize that you're not going to "see" them. Talking about eye contact always brings to mind the amusing scenario of a teacher sitting behind the piano with only the top of her bobbing head showing and the whites of her wide eyes popping up now and then like some jack-in-the-box. You're laughing but this happens. Some teachers get so caught up in singing and/or playing that they completely forget their classes. I guess they just assume that students get turned on too. But they don't. Some of the little darlings start doing their "own thing" as soon as they see the teacher isn't looking. It never fails. Classroom deportment always goes down the tube when there's little or no eye contact at the keyboard.

There are two other classic scenarios of overly engrossed teachers at the piano that must be mentioned, and both are a detriment to discipline. I'm thinking about those who lean back and sway from side-to-side with their eyes pinched shut, and the ones who bend forward 'til their noses touch the ivories and then lean back 'til their faces are parallel to the ceiling. These latter ones are a picture of aesthetic bliss! But,

oh, what bedlam results! There's giggling here, punching there, and mumbling everywhere. But listen. Accompanying in the classroom is not the time for personal ecstasy. It's the time for visual surveillance. Classroom control depends on it!

Then, too, visual monitoring is desperately needed for assessing responses. Unless the teacher is able to glance up periodically, it's impossible to provide the appropriate assessment. Remember, the act of teaching is a three-pronged process involving (a) observing, (b) assessing, and (c) instructing. Without assessment, the process comes to a halt! There's no instructing without first assessing, and no assessing without observing. Eye contact is crucial for feedback. Look what happens without feedback. The quality of their performance declines rapidly—no one is watching to see if the students are doing it "right." In short, they slough off. Students need to be assessed in order to challenge them to perform at their best and to provide a viable learning experience for them. See how important eye contact is for a quality response? And how vital it is to the task of assessing? It's all the more reason to be functionally competent at the keyboard.

Still another reason for eye contact at the piano is that it allows the teacher to communicate better with students. A lot can be gleaned from a glance if one is observant. The way a student is sitting, looking, or participating are all cues as to how the student is feeling, and indicative of his/her attitude. If "read" correctly, these cues can help (a) catch a floundering child, (b) motivate a dwindling response, or even (c) discourage a potential prankster. Any of these reactions on the part of the teacher goes a long way toward building communication—and strengthening the bond between teacher and student(s). For rapport purposes, students need to have confidence in the teacher to "spot" predicaments, as well as achievements, and handle them in an appropriate way.

I know what some of you are mumbling about here. You're saying that you can't see everyone from your piano, that it's not possible to establish this communication with every student. So why not rearrange the classroom? Or move the piano? If you don't you'll never be able to make visual contact with those on the periphery of your scanning range. And they'll continue to fidget around and get bored because they feel left out. And they are—visually speaking! What you need to do is change the seating arrangement or the position of the piano so that you can see everyone. A new classroom arrangement may be the remedy for your eye contact and the solution for better communication.

Concluding Challenge

Are you negligent in exercising eye contact at the piano? Or just lax in glancing up even though you have keyboard skill galore? If so, then start disciplining yourself. If you can't because you're struggling with the accompaniments, then start simplifying or improvising. It's the only way to improve your eye contact, and the only way to have better classroom control, class assessment, and student rapport. So develop your functional proficiency. It's the key to eye contact at the piano!

LESS EFFECTIVE

The two boys in the middle of the front row began elbowing each other as soon as the teacher started playing. They knew Ms. Legato never looked up from the piano. But as soon as Ms. Legato stopped playing, they would quit and wait until she started again. The other third graders kept hoping that Ms. Legato would see them. But she never did. So the two continued to jab and snicker throughout the whole lesson and disturbed those around them.

Ms. Staccato asked her fifth graders to clap the melodic rhythm of the song while she accompanied them. Some were clapping incorrectly but she couldn't tear her eyes away from the music. So she stopped playing and had the class clap without the piano. "Now see if you can clap the same way when I play." But she heard the same mistakes again. "Who is having the trouble?" she asked. Frustrated, Ms. Staccato wondered what she could do since she couldn't look up. "Well, let's try it again," she said, "and watch that place where the uneven rhythm appears." Students rolled their eyes.

MORE EFFECTIVE

As soon as the third-grade class began singing, Ms. Legato noticed Frank and Bill who were sitting towards the end of the semi-circle on the right. Each time she glanced up she saw them elbowing one another. The next time she glanced up, Ms. Legato stared at the boys. They felt her stare, looked up sheepishly, and stopped elbowing immediately. Ms. Legato nodded approvingly. Glancing up later, she noticed Frank and Bill were now singing along with the class.

When the fifth-grade class began to clap the melodic rhythm, Ms. Staccato heard some incorrect clapping. She scanned the class until she finally located the ones having a problem. "I think it would help you, Stan and Jackie, to have a clapping partner. Let's try clapping without the piano." Immediately the two clapped the exercise correctly. When she added the accompaniment Ms. Staccato saw that Stan and Jackie were not only clapping accurately but more confidently. On the next scan, Stan and Jackie gave her that "I've done it" look.

Getting Class's Attention Before Teaching _____

Know what the teacher's first task is at the beginning of each class? I mean the very first task—even before the opening salutation? It's getting the class's attention. If there's to be a proper frame of mind for learning, the teacher must, first of all, establish an attentive environment. That's the first order of business in any situation, and especially the classroom. So don't take this responsibility for granted. It won't happen, if you don't attend to it.

Definition of Getting Class's Attention

There's really more to this task than meets the eye. To be exact, three different happenings occur when getting the class's attention. The teacher (a) monitors the behavior, (b) establishes the atmosphere, and (c) focuses the attention. Take the *monitoring of attention*. That means there's an immediate curtailing of unacceptable behavior, and no disruptive doings are allowed from the very outset. The *establishing of atmosphere* is a matter of immediately creating an aura that is conducive to learning. It's like spreading an air of expectation that emanates from the teacher's whole being and pervades the entire classroom. It's the task of setting the tone of the class. That's the most elusive, yet most important, task of the three. Then there's the *focusing of attention* that entails an immediate directing of eyes, ears, and mind to the particular material or concept being considered, whether it be on the board or in the text. Mind you, all three of these entities must happen; if not simultaneously, then surely in a quick succession, if the teacher is to claim the class's attention. Only when these three conditions or tasks have been secured are the students in a true state of readiness. Actually getting the class's attention is synonymous with achieving the class's readiness. See what's involved? It's no small task, is it?

Problem in Getting Class's Attention

But here's what happens to a lot of teachers, experienced or inexperienced, when it comes to getting attention at the beginning of class—or any other time for that matter. They start to teach before the class is settled down or before anyone is paying attention. They make no effort to get the attention, or use any language—spoken or unspoken—to indicate what they expect. Instead, they proceed to talk over the hubbub thinking that sooner or later the students will settle down. And it's usually later! The scenario looks something like this. There's loud talking across the room, mad dashes to the pencil sharpener, brittle crunching of notebook paper, and a constant scraping of desk chairs happening everywhere. Oh sure, some teachers get upset enough to quit talking, and others look like they're even going to burst into tears or else throw their hands up in exasperation. But then there's always those who attempt to out-shout the situation.

But wait! Did you ever notice what these teachers do when they realize they've "lost the battle"? Or what poses they assume? I have. And it's really hilarious! They either fold their arms over their chest, stare straight ahead, put hands on hips, or lean with one hand on the desk or piano. What I can't figure out is why they don't realize they're doing their theatrical number after-the-fact? They're letting the cart come before the horse. You see, their charades are too late! That's the bad news. The good news is that the solution is simple and effective. It's all in the timing. If you're interested, continue reading.

Solution for Getting Class's Attention

Stop and think now. Wouldn't it be more effective to do one's charades at the very beginning—that is, the minute class begins? Of course it would! That's precisely the "right" time for such theatrics as:

- the arms folded, wide-eyed, and stare straight ahead stance
- the hands-on-hip, tilted head, and pursed lips stance
- the sit-at-desk, folded hands, and fixed stare stance
- the lowered head, folded arms, and stare-at-floor stance
- the palms-on-desk, eyes squinted, and stare-at-clock stance

You see, assuming that your theatrics are up-to-par, any one of these stances or poses has the potential to curb the commotion and set the tone of the class. Without a word uttered, you can create a state of readiness just by using body language at the right moment. I'm taking for granted, of course, that you have already established your own repertoire of poses, including some of those described above. If you haven't, start right now. Get in front of a mirror and experiment. Start with your face. Find out how to manipulate your lips, your eyes, and your eyebrows in order to convey the message that it's time to begin class. Then try out different body stances with these expressions. The key is to find the pose that works best for *you* in capturing attention. That discovery is essential if you're going to be successful. Then it's just a matter of casting your theatrics upon the class and watching the outcome!

Significance of Getting Class's Attention

Don't underestimate the importance of this task. It's indispensable to the whole scheme of teaching. One reason is that it leaves more time for actual teaching. With only 20 to 40 minutes per week for general music, depending on grade level, the teacher needs every minute he/she can get. And if his/her repertoire of poses and expressions is ready, the students can be seated and started on the opening activity in a matter of *seconds*. That's all it should take if your stances and expressions are convincing.

The second reason for getting the class's attention at the outset is that it establishes classroom protocol. You see, when body language does the job of clearly communicating your expectations, you can rest assured that students soon learn that the first order of business in your classroom is to be attentive. The truth is, students like structure. And they like to know what's expected of them. So by demanding attentiveness at the very beginning of class, the teacher sets into motion a mutually accepted routine that is satisfying to both students and teacher alike.

The third reason it's important to get students' attention quickly is that it immediately establishes the proper frame of mind for learning. The students' attention is being channeled at the same moment the classroom environment is being nurtured. In other words, all the factors that promote a proper mind-set for learning are being addressed. Thus, the environment gets settled and the attention gets focused almost immediately. That's what makes the students "ready" to begin—and puts them in the "right" frame of mind.

There are three good reasons for pursuing this task. It leads to more teaching time, better classroom protocol, and a proper mind-set for learning. Don't lose sight of these outcomes; they're invaluable to good teaching.

Concluding Challenge

Now what about you? Do you get your class's attention before you start to teach? If not, you're losing all the rewards. You need a repertoire of body stances and facial expressions to get the job done. You'll be surprised how well poses and expressions work in getting the class's attention at the very outset.

LESS EFFECTIVE	MORE EFFECTIVE
The third graders were still talking noisily when Ms. Barline was ready to begin. "I can't hear myself talk," she shouted. "Today, we're going to learn about . . . . . . I can't hear myself," she shouted even louder. "Will you stop talking. STOP TALKING! This instant." Looking totally frustrated, Ms. Barline folded her arms and stared at the clock. After a while, the class finally stopped talking. But Ms. Barline was steaming by that time. "This is the noisiest class I have," she told the children.	Ms. Barline noticed that the third graders were still excited and talking loudly when the class was ready to start. Ms. Barline put her pointer finger to her lips and gave a soft "ssh-hhhh" as she made eye contact with each child. Immediately the children realized they were talking and that she was ready to begin. Some of them imitated Ms. Barline and put their fingers to their lips too. "Very good, children," Ms. Barline said while smiling and nodding. "I like the way you got quiet so quickly."
"Okay, turn to page ten," Mr. Lownote instructed his fifth graders. But when he saw that they were still cutting-up, he yelled out, "Are we ready? Page ten. Ready, sing." The class was still fooling around, however. "I'm waiting. Everyone isn't ready to start. I'm waiting," he said louder. When he tried to start again, some students continued to talk. "That's it. Everyone gets a zero today unless the talking stops right now. Little by little, the talking stopped. But not before five minutes had gone by. Mr. Lownote just kept tapping his finger on the piano and glaring at the class.	Mr. Lownote was surprised that his fifth graders were so talkative today. As soon as they were seated, he assumed a leaning position against the piano and stared down at the floor. He was waiting for them to quiet down. In a few seconds, the loud talking stopped. Then he took a deep breath, lifted his eyes slowly, and looked at the clock. The class knew what that meant. It meant that they would have detention after school for talking when Mr. Lownote was ready to start. "Thank you for stopping so quickly, but we still lost three minutes. Can we begin now?" The class nodded sheepishly.

Using Only Gestures and Expressions

Teachers need to be as competent in the nonverbal realm as in the verbal because there are times when it is better to communicate solely with body language and facial expressions, and times when gestures and expressions are indispensable as reinforcing tools. The truth is, there are just as many opportunities for teachers to communicate in a nonverbal way as there are verbal, and maybe even more. I'm not saying that verbal skills are ineffective. Not at all! Verbalizing is the teacher's mainstay in communicating with students, and, in some cases, the teacher's salvation. What I *am* saying is that verbalizing is not always enough by itself, regardless of how articulate it may be! It often needs to be reinforced and even replaced on occasion with the nonverbal way. It's to the teacher's advantage, then, to have the nonverbal skills ready.

Problem Affecting Nonverbal Behavior

But there's a problem when it comes to responding in a nonverbal manner, at least for some teachers. They have a tendency to talk too much and rely too heavily on their words. Most likely, it's because knowledge of subject matter has always received more emphasis in our teacher training institutions than the delivery of subject matter. That's what Timpson and Tobin think.[2] And so do I! It's unfortunate that teach-

---

[2]Timpson and Tobin, p. 4.

ers aren't groomed more intensely in the art of nonverbal behavior at the preservice level, especially since it's so important. But revamping the teacher training program is not our concern here. Rather, it's learning *how* to become more nonverbal. Teachers need to be skillful in nonverbal behaviors in order to function proficiently in the classroom. They should not rely totally on their speech. That's where the problem comes in.

Definition of Nonverbal Behavior

Let's define nonverbal behavior before going on. To put it simply, it's a complete gesturing response without any speaking, a total reliance upon (a) bodily stances, (b) hand/arm actions, or (c) facial expressions as a way of communicating. Many times it's a combination of all three! Galloway describes this kind of communicating as operating in time and space without the spoken word.[3] I like that definition. It identifies two important aspects of nonverbal behavior: time and space, both of which are indispensable to nonverbal behavior.

But there's another point that helps put nonverbal behavior in its proper perspective, namely, its placement in the total communication spectrum. To the extreme right we have total verbal communication, void of any body gestures or facial expressions whatsoever. To the extreme left, the total nonverbal approach without any verbiage. This left position is the one we are concerned with now. In the middle though, we have what Goodall and Kachur call the "Total Communication Process" which is made up of both verbal and nonverbal efforts.[4] The middle position is really the most explicit way of communicating we have as teachers. It's the spoken word illuminated by our gestures and expressions. But it's the most difficult of the three to implement. Some teachers look silly and awkward communicating this way unless the verbal and nonverbal responses are "in sync." (See the Spectrum of Communicating Behaviors in Figure 2.2.)

Come back now to the nonverbal way of communicating, or the extreme left position in the spectrum. It includes such responses as giving a reassuring smile,

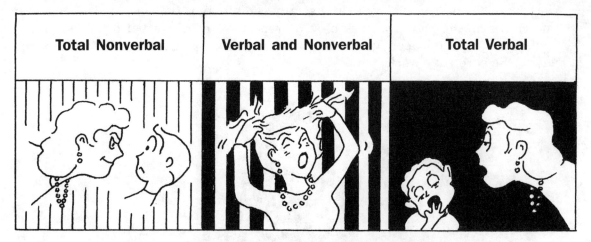

Total Nonverbal	Verbal and Nonverbal	Total Verbal

Figure 2.2. Spectrum of Communicating Behaviors.

---

[3]Charles M. Galloway. "Improving Non-Verbal Communication," *Proceedings of the Association of Teacher Education Summer Workshops*, DeKalb, IL, Northern Illinois University Press, 1979, p. 18.

[4]Robert Goodall and Donald Kachur. "Non-Verbal Communication: Implications for the Classroom Teacher," *Proceedings for ATE Summer Workshops*, DeKalb, IL, Northern Illinois University Press, 1979, p. 22.

touching a student's arm, tapping a student's head, or even shaking a finger at someone. Get the idea? Any one of these behaviors can easily communicate the teacher's message! But that's only a sampling of non-verbal behavior. There's a host of nonverbal responses at the teacher's fingertips. Perhaps the best way to present these would be to cite some of the responses in regard to the specific parts of the body. Look at the possibilities in Figure 2.3.

Remember, these are just some of the nonverbal responses at your own disposal. No doubt you have some of your own. If you do, add them to the list. Don't forget, you can also combine these bodily gestures and facial expressions to get another whole group of nonverbal behaviors. Here's just a sampling of such combined behaviors:

- Look inquisitive with outstretched palms to "ask" if you can help or if there is a problem.
- Nod head and smile while giving thumbs-up sign to "tell" student that he has done well.
- Shake head or finger in no-no way while glaring at student to "say" you want that put away.
- Look disgusted with tilted head and point finger to indicate you've had enough.
- Pull imaginary zipper over mouth while frowning to "instruct" students to stop mumbling.

The collection of responses is almost inexhaustible when you start combining facial expressions and body gestures! You can speak without actually saying a word, and the marvelous part is that you can use any combination that feels most comfortable and convincing to *you*. That means your repertoire of nonverbal behaviors is up to you! It all depends upon your own ingenuity—and personality. But one word of advice: Be sure they work.

Head	Facial Expressions	Fingers
Nodding Head	Frowning Look	Pointing Finger
Shaking Head	Questioning Look	Making Circle for OK
Tilting Head	Surprised Look	Thumbs Up
Looking Up	Can I Help Look	Shaking Finger
Looking Down	Not Again Look	Tapping Finger
Staring Ahead	That Was Good Look	Snapping Fingers
Staring at Student	Puzzled Look	Placing Over Lips
Raising Head Slowly	Disgusted Look	Pointing in Book
		Placing Pointer
		Finger on Cheek

Mouth	Eyes	Eyebrows
Pursed Lips	Wide Open	Arched High
Open Mouth	Squinting	Raised Slightly
Pulled to One Side	Glaring/Staring	One Arched
Corners Pulled Back	Look Over Glasses	Both Drawn
Dropped Jaw	Lower	
Smile	Flutter	
Smirk	Squeeze Shut	
Oooh Shape	Roll	
Aw Shape		

Hand	Body Postures
Touching Student's Arm/Hand/Shoulder	Lifting Shoulder(s) Up
Placing Over Student's Hand/Arm/Shoulder	Slumping Shoulders Down
Grasping Edges of Desk	Leaning Forward on Desk
Clasping Hands Together	Standing with Arms Folded
Clapping Hands	Sitting with Hands Clasped
Placing on Hip(s)	Freezing Present Position
Holding Palms Towards Class	Leaning on Student's Desk
Holding Palms Upward	Standing Over Student
Pulling Zipper Over Mouth	Standing in Front of Student

Figure 2.3. Nonverbal Behaviors for Specific Body Parts.

Reasons for Cultivating Nonverbal Behavior

Why am I so adamant about nonverbal behavior? There are definite reasons, all of which cry out loud and clear for a repertoire of body gestures and facial expressions. The **first reason** is obvious: nonverbal behavior works. As Timpson and Tobin noted, it's a very successful, and even eloquent, way of communicating.[5] Research by Goodall and Kachur confirms this success by stating that combinations of gestures and expressions usually do the trick.[6] If you have ever experienced the impact of nonverbal behavior either as a giver or a receiver, you know that it works too! Is there any doubt, then, that students could "read" the teacher's intention in the examples given earlier? There shouldn't be! You see, communication experts tell us that much of what students receive in the communication process comes from these nonverbal cues anyway, and that the estimates run from 55% to as high as 93%. That's how successful nonverbal behaviors can be in communicating with students. Isn't that reason enough to cultivate your nonverbal behaviors?

[5]Timpson and Tobin, p. 42.
[6]Goodall and Kachur, p. 24.

But there's also a **second reason**, namely, that nonverbal behaviors are readily available. There is no waiting or researching. The teacher has all the necessary tools at his/her disposal. Think about it. There's (a) the face for putting on expressions, (b) the hands and fingers for making gestures, and (c) the body for displaying stances. And the most exciting part of it all is that these so-called *tools* can be combined to make up a myriad of behaviors. That's why Timpson and Tobin refer to nonverbal behaviors as one of the teacher's most abundant and accessible resources for communicating.[7]

The choice is limited only by the teacher's own lack of skill and perhaps sensitivity to situations better suited to the nonverbal responses. Regardless of one's limitations, however, the fact remains that nonverbal behaviors are a readily available resource!

The **third reason** for cultivating nonverbal behaviors is that they are all-purposeful. Look what you can do without even saying a word. You can: (a) reinforce correct responses, (b) encourage faltering responses, (c) curb disruptive behavior, and (d) control classroom climate. There's nothing like a beaming smile or a patting touch from the teacher to encourage a child and make him/her feel "like a million bucks." It's these small, compassionate gestures that often help students the most to excel or persevere. And what about the effect it has on curbing unwanted behavior? Striking a particular bodily pose, like pointing a finger while frowning and pursing one's lips, can bring a disturbance to a halt in a minute without going on a verbal tirade. In fact, many disturbances can be handled silently like this. That means there's better control of the classroom climate. Quite literally, nonverbal behavior becomes a silent mender. Take, for instance, a facial exchange between the teacher and student. It's obviously a more preferable approach than shouting over students' heads. It allows the teacher to reprove the student without breaking the concentration of the entire class. See why teachers need a stock of nonverbal behaviors? You can handle a lot of your classroom disturbances just by using body language and facial expressions—and offer meaningful encouragement along the line as well.

Suggestions for Developing Nonverbal Behavior

For those of you who feel uncomfortable by using facial expressions or bodily gestures, here are some suggestions. Begin by experimenting with each nonverbal "tool" individually. Start with facial expressions, then hand/arm gestures, followed by finger gestures. Finally, explore your body movements and postures. Build a repertoire of responses in each of these areas, like those listed in Figure 3.3, which can be practiced on a daily basis. Yes, practiced. These expressions and gestures must be so well-rehearsed that they look natural, which is the only way they'll "work" for you. Take your facial expressions for starters, and get in front of a mirror. You need to see yourself and know what you look like. Now make up expressions that show disappointment, uncertainty, appreciation, inquiry, impatience, confusion, and a host of other reactions you would need in the classroom. (See the repertoire of expressions in Figure 2.4.) Find out how your eyebrows and forehead can move, how your eyes look, and what your mouth can do when you put on these expressions. Your eyes could squint when you're uncertain or be wide-eyed when you're disturbed, or cast downward when disappointed. And what about your mouth when you're upset? Do you purse your lips? Drop your jaw? Pull back both corners? You need to know your face and how each part can convey your intended expressions. Only when you know this information about yourself are you ready to practice your list systematically.

---

[7]Timpson and Tobin, p. 42.

Figure 2.4. Repertoire of Facial Expressions.

Let's move on to hand/arm gestures, then finger gestures, and end with body postures. Check the list of examples under each category in Figure 3.3. Then practice the gestures you find most comfortable and effective for yourself. Next, make up a list of classroom situations to which you can react. This final step is crucial. Don't be surprised if you start adding your own gestures as you role play. When this happens, you'll know that you're on your way to becoming an expert in body language.

Finally, begin combining gestures with expressions, stances with expressions, or gestures and expressions with stances. Follow through here by taking your list of classroom situations and reacting to them using the various combinations. Get to the point where you can do all three automatically. As you develop your repertoire and your ability to apply it, notice that you're talking less and gesturing more—and even communicating better with your students!

Concluding Challenge

Now it's up to you. Your nonverbal behavior can be a viable addition to your verbal behavior, and a significant supplement to your communication process. But these behaviors must be cultivated. It will take time and effort to develop gestures and expressions. But if you are persistent, you will enrich your teaching behavior beyond your expectations!

LESS EFFECTIVE	*MORE EFFECTIVE*
When the fourth-grade class was seated, Ms. Softer noticed that Henry was chewing gum. From the front of the room she shouted out, "Henry, take that gum out of your mouth this minute and throw it in the trash can." Students started snickering here and there. "Stop that," Ms. Softer screamed. She warned them that they would not be in the school program if they didn't stop. Little by little the giggling stopped.	As the fourth graders entered the room, Ms. Softer saw Henry chewing gum as he came in. When he reached his seat, Ms. Softer caught Henry's eye and made a chewing gesture and pointed to the basket while others were still taking their seats. Henry removed his gum immediately and whispered "I forgot" to Ms. Softer as he dropped it into the basket. Ms. Softer gave Henry a big smile and mouthed, "Thank you."

Mrs. Louder looked up from the chalkboard to see Marsha and Janie passing notes again. "How many times must I tell you girls that you are not to write notes in this class. Would you like to stand up and read the note, Marsha?" Immediately a "whoaaaa" rose up from the class. Mrs. Louder shouted, "Stop it!" When the class settled down, she told Marsha to put the note on her desk. In the same breath, she said she would lower everyone's grade if the whoaaaaing happened again. She knew that would stop them!

As she scanned the class from the chalkboard, Mrs. Louder saw Marsha and Janie passing notes again. She stepped to her right to get in line with the girls' vision. Looking disgustedly at the girls, she tilted her head and folded her arms until the girls looked up. Immediately, Janie put the note away and mouthed, "We're sorry!" Mrs. Louder smiled and shook her head in a manner that said, "I know you are" and walked back to the chalkboard.

Attending to Personal Appearance

You can't talk about the personal behaviors without mentioning personal appearance. It's high on the list of essential ways of handling one's self in the classroom, and it has a direct bearing on how students perceive the teacher. Just notice your own reaction towards people sometime. You might be surprised to discover that even your impressions are based largely on appearance! So it's important that we discuss the teacher's personal appearance. Let's take a closer look at the term "personal appearance."

Definition of Personal Appearance

What do we really mean by one's so-called *personal appearance*? It's a difficult trait to define, but if we think of it as a collection of ingredients rather than an overall description, it will be easier to grasp. Look at the specific so-called ingredients I'm talking about:

- bodily carriage
- bodily gait
- personal attire
- personal grooming

These are the components of personal appearance, or traits that create the impressions students have of teachers. Making a positive impression usually means that the teacher has (a) a proper bodily carriage or bearing, (b) a natural gait or stride, (c) an attractive personal attire, and (d) a careful grooming or caring of one's person and one's clothes. This is the essence of a positive personal appearance.

But look at some appearances that make a poor impression on students. Take the hanging skirt hems or the dangling hair strands. Such "loose ends" make the teacher look harried in the students' eyes, as if the teacher can't get his/her act together. Or how about paper sticking out of every pocket or a crumpled-looking blouse or shirt? One glance and students know they have a scatterbrain on their hands! What about shuffling feet and worn-down heels? Slumping shoulders and a gawking neck? Students put these teachers in the wimp category! Needless to say, they have a heyday mimicking these teachers. Enough said? Teacher appearance does make an impression—and if it's not a positive one, it'll be negative.

Reasons for Neglecting Personal Appearance

So why is personal appearance so low on the totem pole for some teachers? There are a number of reasons. For some, it's because they just aren't aware of their appearance. They don't take the time to look at themselves carefully. For others, it's because they just don't know what professional, personal appearance means. They've never been told. Still others just don't care. Their personal appearance isn't important to them. And for a few others, it's because no one has ever approached them about improving their appearance. Whatever the reason, it really isn't important. What's more important is that these teachers start taking note of personal appearance right now! There are some basic suggestions that can help improve one's appearance almost overnight.

Suggestions for Improving Personal Appearance

Consider body carriage first. *Proper carriage* calls for a body stance in which the shoulders are pulled back and the head is held high. You can achieve this stance by pulling yourself upward to your full height. Try raising your arms straight up over your head. Feel those shoulders go back and your head perk up? It should remind you how you used to stand against the wall during gym class. What you were doing then was stretching to your proper height by pulling back your shoulders and head! Try it now. You might be surprised to see how far your shoulders are from the wall. Start doing it everyday until you feel comfortable with your shoulders back. And why not go to an aerobics class? It's an excellent way to rebuild posture and keep in good shape.

Then, too, attractive bearing also implies a *natural looking gait*, or a presentable manner of walking. That means feet don't shuffle, drag, or slap the floor. You don't look like you're doing the goose-step or taking little itty-bitty steps like a robot. If

you're self-conscious about your walk, critique yourself in a mirror or with a video-tape. Do your steps need to be smaller? Or larger? Should you swing your arms more? Or less? Do you need to look up rather than down? Do you need to walk faster? Or slower? Why not ask a friend to give you some constructive criticism? But whether *you* do the critiquing, or a friend, try and find a gait that (a) feels comfortable and (b) looks presentable. The correction may feel awkward at first, but knowing that it will improve your personal appearance should make it bearable. And here's a little secret. When you make your body do what *you* want it to do, the mind activates the adrenaline and gives you a new surge of energy to keep on trying!

As for *attire and grooming*, the rule-of-thumb is: be appropriately attired and neatly groomed. Take appropriate attire first. Oh, I know that dress is a touchy subject with teachers and I have no intention of dictating garb. That's the teacher's prerogative. But I do think that teachers ought to have enough sense to know they need to look professional. That's precisely the intent of the adjective *appropriately* in this case. To be professionally clothed. But let me say a bit more about attire. Ever notice how "unteacher-ish" some teachers look in their tennis shoes and casual outfits? How rumpled and crumpled others look? Well, if *you* don't, the students do! In fact, they talk about Ms. or Mr. So-and-So's appearance. That's right, they gossip about the teacher. My advice is simple: assess yourself honestly day-by-day. That's the easiest, and surest, way I know to achieve appropriate dress on a daily basis. Most teachers know when they're dressed professionally; it's just a matter of being honest with one's self.

My advice for grooming is just as simple: check yourself carefully in a mirror. Check (a) your clothes, (b) your hair, and (c) your hands and face. With your clothes,

be sure nothing is wrinkled, nothing is showing, and nothing is missing. As for your hair, see that it's clean, well kept, and attractively styled. Check those fingernails; be sure they're trimmed and clean. Keep them freshly polished if you use nail polish. If you wear make-up, be sure it is appropriately applied; don't overdo it! Good grooming takes time. There's no short cut to checking yourself carefully everyday.

Importance of Personal Appearance

All the fuss about teacher appearance is necessary because personal appearance has a lot to do with overall teacher presence.[8] Appearance can either build up or tear down the teacher's image. If appearance is negative, the teacher loses much of the respect and admiration of his/her students. Inevitably that means the teacher is stripped of some much needed clout. On a larger scale, it means that the teacher process is hindered. Why? Because students simply are not as responsive to teachers without presence—or clout. The fact is, a professional presence is very important to students and extremely rewarding for teachers. It goes hand-in-hand with an attractive appearance. Attending to personal appearance, then, not only strengthens the teacher's image, but draws the students' respect. To be even more precise, it commands authority and influences presence.

Concluding Challenge

What about *your* personal appearance? Do you dress appropriately? Do you have good carriage and walk with a natural gait? Good. It's the teacher's responsibility, as well as an obligation, to maintain this kind of appearance. After all, the teacher is the students' model in *all* respects, including teacher appearance!

LESS EFFECTIVE

Ms. Crescendo was one of the teachers all the students imitated behind her back because she walked with big steps and made such loud noises with her heels. Strands of hair also hung out from the bun on the top of her head. Students spent more time imitating her than paying attention. They didn't take Ms. Crescendo very seriously. That was obvious.

When Mr. Decrescendo shuffled into the class, some students moaned and some started to laugh. He dragged his heels so that they were always worn down. And he had a funny way of looking up quickly and then looking down that students imitated all the time—even in front of him. Students didn't think much of his personal appearance, so his classes were always noisy and disorderly.

MORE EFFECTIVE

Mrs. Crescendo's students heard her sprite clicking steps even before she arrived. She always carried her shoulders so straight; the students wondered if she practiced standing against a wall! Not only did she walk spritely and stand straight, Ms. Crescendo was also neat looking. Students wondered if she went to a hairdresser every day. They liked the way she looked.

Mr. Decrescendo was known as a real "neat" teacher. Students liked him but they knew not to mess around in his classes. He stood straight and walked with a definite stride that sent the message, "Look out, here I come!" His hair was never out of place and his shoes were shined to the hilt. He always looked like he had everything under control. Students looked up to him for that reason.

---

[8]Kenneth E. Eble, *The Aims of College Teaching* (San Francisco: Jossey-Bass Publishers, 1983), p. 9.

Avoiding the Dead Spots in Teaching

Ever experience one of those deadly silent moments in your teaching that you hadn't anticipated? When everything came to a standstill? When the only sound was the pitter-patter of your footsteps as you walked to the piano? Most teachers have at one time or another. These silent moments are what I call *dead spots*. Believe me, they need to be avoided like the plague! They can be scary and bewildering. Some of you know what I mean, don't you? But do you also know the reasons for these dead spots? What causes them? It's important to know this information in order to avoid them. Let's take a look at the two most common reasons.

Reasons for Dead Spots

There are really only two reasons for having dead spots in one's teaching. You may not like the reasons, but nevertheless, here they are. Most of the dead spots can be attributed to (1) what the teacher *does* or (2) what the teacher *doesn't* do. For example, remember when you simply didn't know what to say at one point, so you decided to say nothing? Remember that it got so quiet you could hear a pin drop? What about the time(s) you simply didn't realize you needed to say or do something until it got deathly still? Remember how uncomfortable it felt and how shook you were to discover this was happening? There's really no good excuse for not knowing what to say or what to do. But, be that as it may, these are the two reasons for dead spots in your teaching.

Situations Conducive to Dead Spots

The question now is *when* are these dead spots most likely to occur? You experienced teachers already know, don't you? You know your own habits and idiosyncrasies. But for those who aren't quite as experienced or quite as in touch with their own teaching habits, let me pinpoint some of the more likely times when dead spots can happen.

Perhaps the most vulnerable time is when the teacher is moving from one spot to another: when you're moving from the chalkboard to the record player, or from the record player to the piano, or from the front of the room to the back, etc. For some strange, unknown reason, the distance from one point to another becomes like a demilitarized zone—everything stops! The teacher suddenly clams up or else appears to go blank while making the trek.

These self-initiated silences are a no-no. They are responsible for (a) disrupting the flow of thought, (b) interrupting the momentum of the lesson, and (c) providing the opportunity for daydreaming and mayhem. From a practical standpoint, this "dead" time is a waste of precious moments that could be used more advantageously for both teacher *and* students. One word of warning is needed here: do not confuse deliberate pauses with dead spots. They're not the same. Deliberate pauses are moments of *intentional* silences executed for the purpose of emphasizing a word or making an impact. Dead spots, on the other hand, are moments of *unintentional* silence, or awkward stops, that become brief lapses of embarrassment.

Another likely time for dead spots is when passing out materials or instruments. Some teachers get so absorbed in counting out or putting down materials that they automatically stop talking or paying attention to what's going on around them. Students usually stay quiet for about three seconds and then cut loose. To them, it's their "golden opportunity"! And what's so ironical is that the teacher is usually appalled by the class's behavior, without ever realizing that he/she was the cause. Still another prime time for succumbing to a dead spot is during waiting times, such as when students are:

- coming forward for an activity
- going to the board for an assignment
- passing work to the front
- waiting for the class to end

You know what I'm talking about, don't you? I can hear you chuckling! You've probably experienced a dead spot or two where you and your class just gawked at a student who was getting to where he/she was going. Not only are precious teaching moments wasted, but attention spans lost as well. What about times when teachers go mum while waiting for some student to finish something? This is usually an embarrassing moment for the student(s). I have a hard time excusing the teacher for this one! Teachers ought to be more perceptive and sensitive in these situations. It's a simple matter of keeping the other students busy. The same advice applies when a student is coming to the front or going to the board—the teacher should keep the class occupied until the students have arrived. Students' traveling time must not become empty time. Suffice it to say, waiting situations are notorious places for dead spots.

Tactics for Avoiding Dead Spots

Stop and think for a moment. These dead spots can actually become valuable teaching moments. It's a matter of seeing them as opportunities rather than pauses. Look what can be accomplished while traipsing across the room, waiting for a student to come forward, or walking to the piano. You have a choice of:

a. reinforcing instructions by either questioning the class or repeating the instructions

b. requesting verbal or behavioral response from students regarding the upcoming activity

c. reviewing the lesson material by asking questions of the class or individual students

d. passing out books, materials, or instruments with student helpers

e. asking for questions or comments students may have concerning the lesson or the activity

See how dead spots can be eliminated in your teaching? Clearly then, in light of all these possible solutions, there should be no reason for you to entertain dead spots. All you need to do is plug in the tactic that best fits your needs at the moment.

But wait! Do you know what you would say when using these approaches? Suppose you're getting ready to hike over to the piano, to the record player, or run to the chalkboard. Here is what you might want to say *while* you are moving (or

waiting, as the case may be). In other words, you're going to talk as you walk, or talk as you wait. Like this:

a. *For Reinforcing Instructions* say, "So what are you going to do, class, every time you hear the 'I' chord? That's right! Hold up your pointer finger. Ready?"

b. *For Requesting Behavioral Evidence* say, "I want to see everyone in playing position with the recorder in the mouth and correct fingering for 'G' before we start to play."

c. *For Reviewing Conceptual Idea* say, "Mary, what did we call our phrases that sound just like the first phrase? Very good, like phrases is correct." (Notice the individual approach!)

d. *For Passing Out Materials* say, "Tom and Bob, would you please pass out the call charts to the first person in each row on your side of the room while I get the record."

Notice that these are nothing more than straightforward, to-the-point instructional statements. Nothing elaborate or witty; they simply do the job of keeping students occupied and momentum moving.

Incentives for Avoiding Dead Spots

What happens when the teacher makes a conscious effort to avoid dead spots and apply the suggested tactics? Plenty. Potential dead spots turn into bonus times. Here's why. Class momentum can be maintained as you move from one place to another, and you can keep students occupied while waiting for an individual student or another group. Don't overlook the fact that you can use these waiting situations to elicit individual responses as indicated in the third suggestion above. What marvelous opportunities to achieve a better balance between class and individual responses! Questions with short answers are great for these occasions because momentum doesn't have to come to a halt. There are plenty of ways to avoid those dead spots—and lots of incentives!

Concluding Challenge

Do you see how simple it is to convert idle moments into active interludes? It's a matter of being on-your-toes to seize the opportunity. Whether walking to the piano or waiting for a student, you can be reinforcing, requesting, reviewing, or passing out materials. That's how to avoid those dreadful dead spots that can mar your teaching. It's up to you now to incorporate the above suggestions.

LESS EFFECTIVE	MORE EFFECTIVE
Having announced the rote song to her first graders, Ms. Stretto turned to the piano without saying another word! Her heels echoed clickety-click. By the time Ms. Stretto reached the piano, she noticed that many of the boys and girls were squirming and wiggling in their seats. "I don't think some of us are ready to sing," she said! "Let's set up now and sit still."	When the first graders were seated, Ms. Stretto said, "Let's sing 'Rudolph, the Red Nose Reindeer,' okay?" As she started for the piano, she asked "I wonder how many of you remember the words? Good! Let's say them together. Ready! Rudolph . . ." By the time they finished the words, Ms. Stretto had reached the piano. "Excellent! Now let's sing 'Rudolph.'"
When Mr. Maestoso finished explaining Binary Form to his sixth-grade general music class, he said, "I want to see if you can distinguish the A and B themes in this recording." With that, Mr. Maestoso excused himself and proceeded to walk back to the record player without saying another word. The students slumped back in their seats. The low mumbling turned into giggles and snickers. Mr. Maestoso wheeled around and shouted, "Can't you behave yourselves even for one minute?"	After discussing Binary Form, Mr. Maestoso asked the sixth graders for questions. Before going to the record player, he asked if everyone had his/her A and B cards. As he began walking back he asked, "Now show me how you'll move your card and with which hand when you hear the A theme. Very good. The B theme? Excellent." By this time Mr. Maestoso reached the record player. "Now get your cards ready. Which card will go up first? Right, the A card. Ready?"

Using the Teacher Voice

One of the least acknowledged and most under-rated teacher behaviors in the classroom is that of using the teacher voice. Maybe it's because everyone takes for granted that teachers automatically assume a teacher voice. But that isn't always true. Many teachers don't. In fact, many aren't even aware that teachers have two kinds of speaking voices. So let's take a look at the teacher voice versus the social voice and find out why the teacher voice is best for teaching.

Definition of Teacher Voice Vs. Social Voice

Let's talk about the social-sounding voice first. The easiest way to describe the so-called *social voice* is to say that it's your conversational voice, or your normal way of talking in a social setting. As such, it's not as projected and authoritative sounding. It's really your one-on-one style, which means it isn't the most conducive voice for teaching.

Take a look now at the *teacher voice*. If it's a bona fide teacher voice, it will encompass a core of qualities that clearly make it better suited for the classroom. I'm talking about the kind of speaking voice that has:

- sufficient projection
- effective inflection
- convincing expression
- dynamic contrast
- proper modulation
- appropriate pace

See what I mean by a teacher voice and why it's such an essential behavioral tool for the teacher? It is obviously the more qualified voice for teaching. Let's examine these qualities more closely.

Characteristics of Teacher Voice

The first characteristic is *sufficient projection*, which means the voice has enough breath support to be heard in the farthest corners of the room and by every student. Sufficient breath support is the secret. Another way of describing projection is to say that it's a full, strong sounding voice—*not* a shouting voice. Projection uses the lower end of the loud range, not the upper end! Some teachers, however, make a habit of speaking with soft breathy tones because they think they're saving their voices. But that's a myth. Using a soft, breathy voice does not save the speaking voice. It's healthier for the voice and better for breath resonance to have more breath support.[9] By the way, projection also implies that the head is up—and not buried in the book or the music—so that the sound can radiate outward.

A second characteristic of the teacher voice is *effective inflection*. This has to do with vocal intonation. It's the way a teacher emphasizes certain words, syllables, or phrases with higher or lower pitches in order to be more expressive and explicit. In a sense, intonation is the teacher's verbal way of displaying emotions and convic-

[9]Pearl Shinn Wormhoudt. "The Voice, Its Enrichment and Care," *The Bulletin*, Delta Kappa Gamma, Winter/Spring 1986, Volume 522-2, p. 47.

tions. It's a contrast in pitches that adds variety to one's speaking voice. Those who lack even a smattering of vocal intonation are in danger of being monotones.[10] And nothing is more deadly than a monotone teacher!

A third characteristic is *convincing expression*, which refers to the believable tone of the voice. It's one that leaves no doubt in students' minds that you mean what you say. It's that authoritative quality, a tone of voice that (a) ends sentences on a final sounding note rather than a questioning note, (b) delivers instructions in a convincing, not imploring manner, and (c) announces information with assurance rather than with hesitancy. Convincing expression, then, is synonymous with being persuasive.

With *dynamic contrast*, the voice has moments of loudness and softness. The quality is closely linked to vocal inflection in that dynamics play a large role in the stressing and subduing of syllables, words, and phrases. But in the larger sense, a dynamically contrasted voice is one that raises or lowers the volume over a longer stretch of words in order to establish a mood, create an impression, or control a situation. It's that quality in the voice that makes the teacher's speech more expressive and interesting.

A fifth characteristic is that the teacher voice is *properly modulated*, which means the voice is correctly placed. It's neither too strident nor too grating; neither too nasal nor too guttural; neither too choked nor too breathy. Young women teachers often have a problem of speaking with an overly high-pitched voice that is not only demanding on the students' ears, but hard on the teacher's vocal chords. The fact is, whenever the voice is improperly placed and extensively used, there is always a possibility of getting nodes on the vocal chords. These are little knots that cause continual hoarseness and scratchiness in the voice, which usually have to be removed surgically. So a properly modulated voice is not just a matter of obtaining a pleasant sounding voice, but, more important, a matter of protecting the speaking voice.

As for being *appropriately paced*, this means that the teacher's speaking voice moves at an acceptable rate the students can track. In short, it's the speed of the speaking voice. There are no bursts of rapid words or string of drawn-out phrases. The properly paced voice has a more even tempo. Indeed, teachers who spit out words like a machine gun are every bit as annoying as those who drag out their words. Even though the teacher's voice may have proper projection and inflection with magnificent dynamic contrasts, if the speaking rate is too fast or too slow the voice will lose much of its expressiveness. That's the power of pacing in the teacher's voice!

Suggestions for Developing Teacher Voice

If students ask you, "Whad ja say?" a hundred times a day, then you need some help with your teacher voice. Here are some ideas that will be of help to you.

To get better vocal projection, try emulating the way you would speak to a friend across the street or a long distance from you. Notice the way you fill your lungs before calling, and how you pushed out the air when you're calling out. See how your vowels opened up with your breath support? How much easier it was to project your voice? Well, that's how to project in the classroom as well. It's the same principle. Take in air, push out, and direct your voice to the back of the room. Not only will you be heard better, but you'll also get rid of that breathy quality and increase your vowel resonance! So fill those lungs and speak out! Start doing some breathing exercises to help you use your diaphragm properly when you breath in and out.

---

[10]Timpson and Tobin, p. 54.

To improve vocal inflection and dynamic contrast in your teacher voice, try to recall the last time you got excited.[11] Do you remember how your voice rose in pitch on some words and dipped on others? Did you notice how much dynamic contrast and vocal inflection you were using? That's how much expressiveness you need in the classroom, too! Here's what you do. Make up a list of as many classroom situations as you can in regard to talking, giggling, fighting, etc., and practice responding to these situations extemporaneously. If you have trouble improvising, write a script. Tape record yourself to hear how much inflection and dynamics you're using. Or get a friend, a speech therapist, or a drama coach who will give you honest feedback. That's the only way you're going to improve your vocal inflection and dynamic contrast in your speaking.

Want to know whether or not your voice is properly modulated? Try doing this. Have someone ask you a question that requires an excited "uh-huh." Use any question like, "Do you love your dog?" "Do you like Christmas time?" "Do you like chocolate cake?" Notice where the "huh" part falls when you answer. This is roughly where your normal speaking pitch should be.[12] Do it several times to be sure. If you need to lower your speaking voice, try this. Put your right or left hand just above your head with the palm facing the floor. Then, using the "ahh" or "oooh" sound, bring your voice down to the "huh" level while moving your hand down—go slowly now. If you need to raise your speaking voice, reverse the above process. It's a very simple test, but amazingly accurate. You might also want to check with a voice teacher or speech specialist to see if your analysis is correct. Then it's up to you to begin speaking with your more modulated voice.

As for speaking too fast or too slow, it's a matter of your being more self-aware and more self-disciplined. Only *you* can make the difference. It's a slow and arduous process, but it can be done. **First**, get a baseline of your present pace by tape recording yourself in order to find out how much you need to alter your speech rate. **Second**, make a tape recording of how you want to sound, i.e., tape record a model for yourself—someone who you think speaks well—and listen to it. **Third**, strive to emulate the model until you get your pacing "right." The key is to have the pacing model clearly established in your thinking, otherwise you will be fighting a losing battle. Follow the formula: analyze, then discipline—in that order.

Reasons for Using Teacher Voice

Why all the hoopla about using the teacher voice? Is it that important? Yes, it is because it's one of those personal behaviors that can clearly establish the teacher's credibility in the eyes of the students. It's only when the voice exhibits the kind of traits just discussed that the teacher can command the attention of the students and sound authoritative enough to have an impact on such matters as:

- classroom behavior
- student attention
- student motivation
- classroom attitudes

Students simply don't respond as readily, or attend as willingly, or behave as commendably without a teacher-sounding voice. It's the authoritative quality that helps

---

[11]Timpson and Tobin, p. 57.
[12]Wormhoudt, pp. 46–47.

get the job done. Much of the teacher's success is related directly to this learned behavior.

Concluding Challenge

Let me urge you to cultivate your teacher-voice if you haven't already. Make sure that it's properly projected, appropriately inflected, and dynamically contrasted. Keep it well modulated and moderately paced. Most important, be sure that it's switched on when you step into the classroom. You need it to be more convincing and motivating. Remember, the teacher voice has a strong bearing on how you are perceived as a teacher.

LESS EFFECTIVE	*MORE EFFECTIVE*
Ms. Singing always had to ask her students to do something at least two or three times. They never seemed to listen. Much of her class time was spent getting students ready to do an activity. What Ms. Singing didn't realize was that her instructions always sounded like she was asking students' permission and wasn't sure what she wanted the class to do. Thus, the children never listened.	Students in Ms. Singing's music classes were always ready to respond when instructed. They knew by the tone of her voice and the way she spoke that they were supposed to do this or that. There was no mistaking that she expected them to be ready for an activity. She not only commanded the attention of the younger children, but the older ones as well. She made instructions clear by accenting important words.
Nothing Ms. Humming said ever sounded like she was excited. She just went on-and-on-and-on in a bland tone of voice. Sometimes it was difficult even for the older students to tell when she was done with one idea and beginning another. The sixth graders called her "the droner." She never used any vocal inflection. She bored her students to death! They hated music and turned her off as soon as the lesson began.	Students enjoyed Ms. Humming's music classes. She was always so interesting to listen to because of the way she raised and lowered her voice to make the information clearer. She could make students feel like singing or playing just by the way she talked! Students kept their eyes and ears glued to her; they didn't want to miss a word!

Exhibiting Poise and Composure

This is one of those hard-to-nail-down behaviors teachers don't like to talk about, or even mention, for that matter! It's too personal and too touchy to deal with, they say. Yet, despite the reluctance to discuss it, most classroom teachers would quickly admit that they need to be paragons of poise and composure! So let's put aside the personal fears and professional inhibitions and deal with the matter of poise and composure openly, okay?

Definition of Poised Behavior

Consider poise first. Webster says that *poise* is a bearing of dignity and self-assurance. For the teacher this definition translates into having a refined and stately carriage that exudes an air of confidence. In other words, every move and every gesture should be cultured, not crude; gracious, not gruff; and calming, not skittish. There should be no personal idiosyncrasies or distracting habits or mannerisms. These

don't belong in a poised posture because they strip the teacher of dignity and detract from the teaching—to say nothing of the distraction to students' learning. Idiosyncrasies can do more to mar teacher poise than almost any other aspect of teaching. Here are some of the more notorious idiosyncrasies:

- Toying with button
- Pulling ear lobe
- Twirling strand of hair
- Twitching mouth
- Swaying side to side
- Clearing throat
- Blowing nose
- Tapping fingernails
- Scratching head

- Clicking pen
- Pushing up glasses
- Opening-closing locket
- Saying "uhm" or "uh-huh"
- Fiddling with necklace
- Jingling bracelet
- Rocking back and forth
- Rattling change in pocket

Idiosyncrasies like the above really do happen! And here's the most worrisome part of these habits. Most of the time, the teacher isn't even aware of doing this quirk. It's done without even thinking. The other unfortunate happening is that students start mimicking the teacher's mannerism. That's the bad part about idiosyncrasies. But students *do* get distracted, or else annoyed, with teachers' quirks. Sometimes they even get embarrassed, particularly when the mannerism is something personal, like toying with a blouse button or a belt-buckle, or clearing one's throat. Habits like these can hardly be called refined! To the contrary! They're undignified and they detract from the teacher's poise.

I always think of one particular teacher when it comes to idiosyncrasies. Her little foible was to twirl keys on a long chain, like a lasso. The keys spun around without even jingling! Only her hand was circling. I knew it was time for the twirling act every time she reached for her keys. One time she twirled up to a count of 110! I think every kid in the school could imitate Ms. Twirly-Keys; she was infamous for her twirling!

But idiosyncrasies aren't the only behaviors that annoy students. There are some sporadic antics that happen only once or twice, but they have the same undig-

nifying effect. Some common examples would be teachers (a) blowing bubble gum, (b) biting fingernails, or (c) using slang language. Not only do these antics make a teacher look foolish, but they also destroy some of the teacher's stature in the eyes of the students. They're unbecoming. They have no place in a poised teacher's behavior—not even on isolated occasions.

Definition of Composed Behavior

Then there's composure. *Composure* is the trait that reflects a stable frame of mind. The slang term kids use for it is "being cool." If ever teachers needed to be cool and exercise an aura of composure, it's in today's classrooms. But sometimes the teacher blows his/her cool. Here are some of the unstable kinds of things teachers do when this happens?

- Pouting with students
- Smacking ruler on desk
- Yelling at students
- Stomping of feet
- Crying in class
- Running out of room
- Insulting students
- Clenching fists
- Throwing books down
- Shaking student
- Striking student
- Hiding face in hands
- Refusing to answer
- Arguing with students(s)
- Making angry faces
- Berating student
- Slamming door/drawers
- Kicking wastebasket

Obviously, none of these childish stunts contribute to the teacher's stature or stability. My advice is to avoid doing any of them. The consequence is just too costly. They totally destroy the teacher's credibility as a stable-minded individual. The truth is, students don't like to see teachers doing these sorts of things. They feel uncomfortable and even get embarrassed. But the most significant fact is that they simply don't expect such shenanigans. And those who do blow their cool in these ways, quickly get tagged as being "childish." Not a very good reputation for a teacher, is it?

Suggestions for Poise and Composure

Let's consider how to be poised and composed. Remember what Webster said about poise? He labeled it as a bearing of dignity and self-control. How does one act with dignity? By acting professional and mature. When a concentrated effort is made to behave in a mature and professional way, you are automatically (a) more courteous, (b) more proper, and (c) more dignified—as well as more proficient. Note that these are all the responses that characterize a composed person! As your bearing becomes more dignified little by little, you soon discover that some of your personal idiosyncrasies and unrefined behaviors will occur less and less. But it won't be easy. You will need to exercise self-discipline in order to act professional and mature. But the reward will be worth it, however; you become a more poised individual.

As for your composure, you must be constantly aware of your own stability. That means, first of all, knowing in your heart that you *are* a stable-minded individual. This conviction is integral to exhibiting a state of well-being. Moreover, it means that you also know you are a (a) patient, (b) understanding, and (c) reliable person. You are able to act in a sensible and knowledgeable manner during troublesome times. See what I'm getting at? You need to know yourself—like a book. I want to repeat that. You must know yourself. Know your attitudes, your values, and your beliefs—as well as your own strengths and weaknesses.[13] Only then will you be able to display the kind of quiet composure and convincing presence you need as a teacher. The key to composure is self-awareness. Know thyself. That was Socrates' advice—and my advice as well.

Importance of Poise and Composure

Let's talk now about the importance of being poised and composed. Two reasons come to mind immediately. One is that this poise and composure foster a healthy respect in the eyes of the students, who sense this aura of dignity and self control. The other is that it nurtures credibility. Students witness the teacher's stability and develop a trust and respect for the way the teacher operates in the classroom.

But there's a third outcome that is so obvious it's almost overlooked. It's the overall presence created by poise and composure. Eble[14] notes that presence has more to do with how a person acts than how one looks, as important as appearance is to presence. More specifically, it's what a person *is* that ultimately establishes presence. Thus, those who know who they are, and who are able to give that same assurance to others, are the ones who radiate the greatest presence.[15] "Knowing thyself" is the key to being poised and composed.

---

[13]Shirley F. Heck and Ray C. Williams. *The Complex Roles of a Teacher* (New York: Teachers College Press, Columbia University, 1984), p. 2.

[14]Eble, p. 9.

[15]Ibid, p. 6.

Concluding Challenge

Now, that wasn't so difficult to deal with, was it? Just bear in mind that it's your personal awareness and common sense that dictate poise and composure. That means it's possible to have control of your bearing when you teach. Isn't that exciting? You can be more poised and composed if you would just make a conscious effort to apply the suggestions. They really work!

LESS EFFECTIVE	MORE EFFECTIVE
"Okay, let's stop the talking," Ms. Unity shouted at her fifth graders. The talking continued. "I said quiet!" When she went to close the classroom door, they still continued to talk. So she slammed the door. Then she began slamming her desk drawers. The students were embarrassed for her. Slam! Slam! Slam! They rolled their eyes at each other and watched in disbelief.	Ms. Unity noticed that the fifth graders were noisy as they came in. When they were seated, she folded her arms and stood at her desk. She stared at each of the students. When the students looked up, they stopped talking immediately. The students could tell that Ms. Unity was waiting and that she was not pleased with the class's behavior. But she got their attention quickly by using an "I'm waiting" stance.
Every time the class stopped singing, Ms. Variety would start toying with her dangling earring. She pulled it, tapped it, and even jiggled it while she was talking. Some of the junior high students would play a game of seeing how many times she would toy with her earring during the class. Even the younger children mimicked her gesture.	Ms. Variety always wore the big, dangling earrings. She told the students that they were her "trademark." But Ms. Variety never toyed with her jewelry. Her hands were always being used in some other way as she talked. That's what made her an interesting teacher—her hands and voice "worked together." At least that's how the students put it!

Displaying a Sense of Humor

Can you laugh easily when something funny happens? Can you laugh at yourself? Can you see humor in situations? Good, because you need a sense of humor in teaching. It's one of those personal qualities that every teacher must have in order to survive in the classroom, and, more important, to be effective. Let's take a closer look at what it means to have a sense of humor.

Definition of a Sense of Humor

A sense of humor actually means being able to do three things: (1) perceive humor, (2) express humor, and (3) enjoy humor. It takes all three of these efforts to be a humorous person. *Perceiving humor* translates into recognizing humorous happenings, or attending to them as they happen. More specifically, it involves taking time to acknowledge and respond to comical situations, comical people, and comical material, both written as well as spoken. In short, perceiving is a matter of being "open" to humor. And *expressing humor*? That's the job of actually verbalizing and/or displaying humor one's self, and demonstrating a quick-witted and whimsical ability to joke, tease, or mimic. To me, expressing humor is synonymous with "making" humor or being funny! But perhaps the most important aspect of having a sense of humor is being able to enjoy it. That means having the capacity to release the response in a pleasing and healthy way to the body, like through laughing, giggling, or guffawing. That's what having a sense of humor means—being able to perceive, express, and enjoy the funny things in life.

Ways of Expressing Humor

Describing a sense of humor is easy; it's the prescribing that's difficult. I'm not sure it's even possible! How do you tell someone to be humorous? You can't make someone laugh if he/she doesn't want to. Neither can you insist that he/she recognize humor when it happens. What is possible, however, is to suggest some basic ways of being able to *express* humor. Here are some of these suggestions:

- telling about personal humorous experiences
- making witty comments when appropriate
- throwing out funny one-liners (at appropriate times)
- joking about some humorous situation
- getting tickled, not embarrassed, with your own doings
- returning whimsical rather than ordinary answers
- recalling hilarious happenings

You see, you *can* learn how to express humor more comfortably just by doing some of the above things. Don't be afraid to let out a hearty laugh when something funny happens or to make a witty remark when it's at the tip-of-your-tongue or to giggle when a funny joke is told. These are the things that make people humorous!

Precautions in Expressing Humor

There *are*, however, some precautions for the classroom teacher when it comes to expressing humor. The **first** is that humor should not be confused with silliness. So often it is! Not all teachers know how to express humor properly, even though they can perceive it and enjoy it properly. Some interpret it as a license to be a clown, a smart-aleck, or worse yet, a joker. They constantly banter, tease, or crack jokes. In short, they act like simpletons. They are either very naive or very foolish—and, most likely, very insecure. Expressing humor is definitely not a barrage of bantering, teasing, or wise-cracking. Rather, it's being appropriately witty and genuinely funny. It's a momentary act of true mirth, not a show of buffoonery.

A **second** precaution is that humor must be exercised with discernment. One is in knowing which classroom happenings should be acknowledged, and which should be ignored. Not everything deserves a humorous response. Some situations *must* be ignored, while others need to be reprimanded rather than laughed at. In order to exercise this discernment, teachers must recognize certain facts when it comes to classroom humor, such as: (1) students are always ready, willing, and able to laugh at almost anything in the classroom setting, (2) students generally over-react to non-humorous situations that are acknowledged by the teacher, (3) younger children are generally amused at just about everything they do or say, (4) older students are excellent mimickers and pranksters—and, as a result, a bigger challenge in knowing what to acknowledge and what to ignore, and (5) some students will try anything to get the teacher's attention. This information should help in knowing what to expect and how to cope with humor in the classroom.

But there's one other piece of advice I need to give you, and it's probably the most crucial! It concerns the teacher's maturity and self-assurance. Both traits must be firmly in place in order to have proper discernment in dealing with classroom humor. Acknowledgment of humor must be on the basis of merit, and not on the basis of fear of displeasing the students. Knowing *what* to acknowledge, then, is the first discernment teachers need.

The other discernment is knowing when to be humorous as a teacher. It's not an easy answer. The teacher must be keenly in tune with the attitude of the class, as well as intuitively convinced that the moment is ripe for a bit of humor. If you've ever felt that conviction, you know what I'm talking about. It's a feeling of rightness and control of the situation at that moment and a strong inclination that it's all right to respond to this thing now. On the other hand, it's also a matter of exercising control when the "vibes" say no; of listening to that inner voice, or to your own intuition, that the time isn't right. The best rule here is: when in doubt, don't.

Coming back to precautions, the **third** one is to be sure to pull back the class immediately following a humorous reaction. You see, students will usually take a mile when given an inch. That's particularly true when they see the teacher laugh. It's like giving them the okay to go overboard. If you don't corral their outburst quickly, the results will be disastrous. Let me give you a good illustration. I observed a teacher once who started laughing when one of her little first graders dropped the box of triangles and jingle clogs. It was the loud clash of clinging and ringing that "got" to her. When the other children saw the teacher, they broke out in giggles and squeals, and began jumping up and down like jack rabbits. And when she started to crawl around and pick up the instruments, the giggling and squealing got even louder. By the time she had all the instruments, the noise was unbearable! The children were well on their way to being hysterical. That's what happens when the class isn't controlled immediately.

Here are suggestions to bring a class back from a laughing spree. One of the best ways is to get back to the activity immediately. Simply announce something like this in your best projected teacher voice:

- "All right, let's begin such-and-such again. Ready?"
- "Turn back to page so-and-so and put your finger on the first note."
- "Instruments up. One-two-ready-play."
- "Everyone stand up quietly and get ready to conduct in two's."

You squelch the outburst by getting the students immediately back on track. It works every time! The noise dissipates within a matter of seconds, and your lesson is on its way again. Another tactic is to assume some bodily stance with a facial expression that "tells" the students you are ready to continue. Such stances are:

- placing hands on hips while staring at the floor
- holding hands behind back and looking out the window
- shaking head back-and-forth with finger on lips and hand on hip
- sitting down at desk with head cupped in palm while staring at clock

These are just a few of the stances and expressions you could display to get the message across without having to shout over the class. Remember, actions *can* speak as loud as words. Just be sure to do these theatrics with conviction, flair, and definition; otherwise, they won't do the trick.

Reasons for Exercising Sense of Humor

We can't close this discussion without acknowledging why a sense of humor is such an important personal trait for a teacher. **First,** a sense of humor is crucial to the teacher's sanity. You've heard teachers say, "If I couldn't laugh at things in the classroom, I'd go crazy." What teachers mean is that if they weren't able to chuckle at the shenanigans, see the brighter side, or snicker at their own bloopers, they wouldn't be able to survive! While a bit exaggerated, the expression "I'd go crazy" is a good indication of how important humor is in maintaining a stable frame of mind. Humor provides the classroom teacher with a moment of levity—or fleeting frivolity—in a normally serious setting. It's like a breath of fresh air! **Second,** a sense of humor helps to release built-up tensions, like a pressure valve. It's part of the tension-and-release phenomenon in the rhythm of life, and one of the personal behaviors that helps keep the teacher on an even keel. Believe me, humor is vital to the teacher's productivity on a daily basis.

Third, think about the teacher's personal well being or state of wellness. Laughter has long been recognized as good medicine for the body. It's an antidote for anger, an outlet for stress, and an expression for enjoyment. Some medical authorities even go so far as to say that it's a deterrent for major disease; they claim that it relieves stress, which can lead to illnesses. Whether or not this particular claim is true, there is one which *is* true: a sense of humor makes for a better balanced personality in the classroom and a healthier mental state. The teacher who is always somber and stone-faced and has difficulty expressing humor does not have a balanced temperament. Teachers need to be able to giggle as well as glare, mock as well as model, and quip as well as comment. It makes for a more personable classroom teacher.

And **four,** a sense of humor is important because it builds a rapport between teacher and students. Think about that for a moment. Laughter is a shared experience in which everyone is equal. It's the laughing with the laughees, not the teacher with students! It's a moment of togetherness, a time of mutual enjoyment when teacher and student bond through laughter. Highet referred to that togetherness as a "feeling of unity" resulting from a shared experience like laughter.[16] Then, too, rapport is strengthened even more when students get a glimpse of the teacher's humorous side. Whether it be sharing one's personal experiences, being witty with words, or responsive to amusing happenings, the teacher endears himself/herself to the students. That's how a closer rapport blossoms between the teacher and student. They learn that the teacher is human, that he/she is affected by the same silly situations, and responds to funny things in the same manner—by laughing, giggling, or chuckling.

Concluding Challenge

Let me repeat a word of advice. Share your humorous personality with your students. Don't hide it. Not only will you have a better rapport with your students, but you'll also have a much better frame of mind about yourself. Teachers need moments of release through laughter and wit. Your sense of humor is a precious commodity, so use it often, but use it wisely. If you have difficulty showing your humorous side, try some of the above suggestions. They'll get you started the right way!

---

[16]Gilbert Highet. *The Art of Teaching* (New York: Alfred Knopf, 1950), p. 63.

LESS EFFECTIVE	**MORE EFFECTIVE**
When one of the strings broke on Ms. Strum-strum's ukelele, it made a twanging sound as it popped up. The fourth graders tried to stop their snickering but couldn't. Ms. Strum-strum glared at the class and continued playing. But the dangling string made the students even more giggly. Ms. Strum-strum stopped playing. "I see that you can't behave yourselves, so we won't continue." With that, she walked back to her desk.	While the class was singing, one of the strings suddenly broke on Ms. Strum-strum's ukelele. It made a funny pinging sound which made everyone laugh. Even Ms. Strum-strum began to laugh. When one of the students pointed to the dangling string, everyone began laughing even harder. "Okay, class, let's finish our song before another string breaks. Ready." The class began singing as she continued with her three strings.
When the singing stopped, one of Ms. Tom-tom's little first graders let out a huge hiccup. Tommy looked surprised for a moment and then started to giggle along with the other children. They pointed their fingers at Tommy and tittered with delight. "Children, turn around and stop laughing. That wasn't funny," Ms. Tom-tom said. "Tommy, you need to apologize to the class." Ms. Tom-tom never laughed at anything. The look on Ms. Tom-tom's face made the children stop their giggling immediately. They were afraid to continue.	The first graders had just finished singing their favorite rote song when Tommy let out a big hiccup. The whole class started giggling with delight. Tommy slapped his hand over his mouth and looked at Ms. Tom-tom with his big eyes. She smiled at Tommy and said in a loud voice, "That was a new ending to our song. Tommy, would you like to get a drink of water?" Ms. Tom-tom was still smiling at Tommy as he walked over to the drinking fountain. "Okay, class, let's continue." Immediately the class was back to normal with smiles on their faces.

Projecting a Firm Attitude

Besides using a teacher voice, maintaining eye contact, and displaying personal poise, etc., projecting a firm attitude is yet another personal behavior that teachers need in the classroom. A firm disposition is essential to good teacher performance.

Definition of Firmness

The simplest and clearest description of a firm disposition is given by Kounin. He describes it as the "I mean it" factor in one's disposition.[17] It gets to the heart of the matter and implies a convincing manner, one which says, "I mean what I say and I say what I mean." It might also be thought of as a more business-like manner, one that makes the teacher "ready for teaching" in the eyes of the students. But let's go one step further and nail down some of the more specific traits that characterize a firm disposition. They include the following:

- using a "teacher voice"
- projecting a business-like expression
- displaying a confident bodily carriage
- maintaining eye contact

[17]Jacob Kounin. *Discipline and Group Management in Classrooms* (New York: Holt, Rinehart, and Winston, Inc., 1970), p. 66.

- speaking confidently and articulately
- exuding an expectancy regarding student participation

These are the behavioral ingredients, you might say, of a firm disposition. They're the qualities that describe a self-assured teacher.

Misconceptions Regarding Disposition

The most common misconception about a firm disposition is that it's the same as a tough disposition. It's not! Ranting and raving must not be confused with firmness; neither should roughness nor unreasonableness, or a lack of sensitivity. Teachers who behave in this manner are big bullies. Students obey out of fear rather than respect, which breeds more dissention than participation.[18] So let's not equate a firm disposition with a tough one. It's not necessary to be tough in order to be firm. It's a matter of having the necessary personal qualities as cited in the above definition.

Another misconception is that a firm disposition automatically outlaws a sense of humor. That isn't true! The two responses aren't mutually exclusive. It's not only permissible, but even advisable, to interject humor into a business-like disposition— and to savor it as well. The problem comes in knowing how to get the students back once the humorous response has started—that's the hard part, but it can be done. If you need some suggestions, refer to the earlier section, "Displaying a Sense of Humor." The point is, don't squelch the opportunities for humorous responses; they help to liven up a firm disposition. They make students more responsive when they discover the teacher can be humorous as well as firm. So, sprinkle your firm disposition with a sense of humor—the two complement each other.

Outcomes of a Firm Disposition

There are at least two convincing reasons for maintaining a firm disposition. One has already been mentioned above: firmness commands a better response. For example, students are more apt to (a) participate as instructed and (b) straighten up as requested. That's because there's an "I mean it" quality to the teacher's voice and an appropriate facial expression—and possibly even some gesture—to reinforce the verbiage. But then watch a wimpish-dispositioned teacher when it comes to getting the students to obey. It's rather pitiful. Students just don't respond well to weak dispositions. They do better with the stronger, more business-like teachers because it's clear from all the personal traits that the teacher (a) means business, (b) expects participation, and (c) won't be swayed. Platoon leaders in combat are good examples of firm leadership; it's their confidence and expectation that make soldiers want to follow them and fight. Teachers are like platoon leaders. They motivate students when they manifest a firm, confident disposition.

The second outcome is that there's better classroom management because a firm disposition resembles a more professional disposition that students come to respect. The teacher sounds more like a teacher, looks more like a teacher, and acts more like a teacher. Classroom control is almost impossible without this kind of disposition. That's why it's so important to nurture a firm demeanor. But let me warn you. You'll have to earn your chevrons because the students will put you through the mill! You will have to be persistent; but in the end, you will reap the joys of better classroom control.

---

[18]Johanna K. Lemlech. *Class Management* (New York: Harper and Row, 1979), p. 19.

Tactics for Executing Firmness

Here are tactics for displaying firmness. One is to make sure all comments and instructions are made with the teacher voice. Another way is to use body stances and body language. Still another is to use a repertoire of facial expressions. And, one of the most important is to apply the established consequences consistently when rules are broken.

Look at verbalizing comments with a teacher voice. Whether you are asking for participation or settling a disturbance, your teacher voice is an essential tool for revealing a firm attitude. It tells the student what you expect right now! Here are some typical remarks you probably voiced a hundred times while teaching:

- "Sit down this minute!"
- "Bob, will you go to the chalkboard and write out a C Major Chord?"
- "Susan! Beth! Stop that giggling!"
- "Everyone stand up and march to the beat."

But, in what tone of voice did you deliver these commands? Did the students immediately respond upon your request? If not, chances are you weren't using your teacher voice. You were using your social voice. Let me explain the difference. Your teacher voice is a more projected, more inflected, and more articulated voice. It also has better contrasted dynamic contrasts (See the earlier section "Using the Teacher Voice.") On the other hand, your social voice is your normal conversational tone. It's more informal sounding and not always projected. It really doesn't carry as much clout. So speak with your teacher voice. It's one of the best signs of a firm disposition.

Firmness is also conveyed by body language and body gesturings. Placing hand on hip, folding arms, shaking a finger, or putting your hand over the student's are just a few of the gestures at your disposal. You can let a student know that you're displeased with his/her behavior just by what you do—not just by what you say. (See the earlier section "Using Gestures Without Verbalizing.") Develop your own gestures and body stances that feel comfortable to *you* and that are best for your own personality. Then be sure to execute them with conviction. In short, make sure they do the job for you; otherwise, you might look silly! Half-hearted efforts always do!

Then there are facial expressions. Believe me, they're indispensable in conveying a firm demeanor! After all, your face is what students look at 99% of the time! Read the section on using facial expression to find out how you can develop a repertoire of expressions. For instance, you can "say" the following thoughts just with your face:

- "I'm surprised at you!"
- "May I help you?"
- "Are you doing that again?"
- "Stop that!"

And when "What are you doing?" expressions are coordinated with speech or gestures, you can have dozens of ways to convey your intentions. Words and gestures will simply reinforce the facial expression. Take, for example, your "I'm surprised" look. If you put your hands on your hips and call out the student's name in conjunction with the look, you will get results—and fast! You can communicate anything you want through facial expressions, and be as convincing as you wish. It's a matter of refining your repertoire of facial expressions. (See the earlier section "Using Facial Expressions.")

The last is the application of the consequences to your classroom rules. I'm assuming you and your students will establish rules—together—and that they will understand why rules exist. That's the best way to insure the students' cooperation. But please don't set rules down and fail to carry them out, not unless you have stated in your rules that the first offense is a warning. Students will size you up in a minute by how you deal with disciplinary measures. Let the students know that you are ready to follow through on your consequences; that you are fair, but consistent, when it comes to disciplining. This is not being strict or mean—not if there are rules. Rather, it's being steadfast and prudent! One last piece of advice: be sure to make your consequences reasonable.

Concluding Challenge

Okay, so now you have some techniques to fall back on for displaying a more firm disposition. The responsibility is in your corner. It's up to you to (a) analyze your own personal behaviors that affect a firm disposition and (b) work on any or all of the techniques cited above. If you do these two tasks, you will be surprised and pleased how much better your classroom management is. Take this discussion to heart. Teachers need a firm disposition in the classroom.

LESS EFFECTIVE	MORE EFFECTIVE
When one of the students in Ms. B-Flat's sixth-grade class threw a paper plane across the room, she called out his name and reminded him of the rules. "Now, Robert, you know we don't throw things in here. I won't make you write a report this time, but you'd better not let me catch you doing that again." Robert smirked at his buddy. He knew she wouldn't do anything—and so did the rest of the class!	Out of the corner of her eye Ms. B-Flat saw Robert shoot the paper plane. She turned to Robert and said, "Would you go over and pick up that paper airplane and bring it to me?" When Robert brought the plane, Ms. B-Flat simply said, "You know the rule about throwing things, don't you? That means you'll have to write an extra report by Friday. Take your seat." Robert knew that Ms. B-Flat meant what she said.
Ms. C-Sharp's teacher voice wasn't very good. Even the little kindergarten children didn't listen very well. She would sort of point to a student and either tell him or her to stop in a half-baked way or else use an asking-tone of voice. She acted like she really didn't expect anyone to listen. Students thought Ms. C-Sharp was a real push-over!	One thing about Ms. C-Sharp was that you knew you had to listen. Just the way she spoke let you know that she thought what she was saying was important. But she was interesting to listen to because of her vocal inflections and dynamic contrasts. And if you misbehaved, you got called on. Ms. C-Sharp didn't mince words. Students knew she meant what she said.

Using Facial Expressions

If there's one place where facial expressions are needed, it's in the classroom. No one should set foot inside the classroom unless he/she is able to display a whole stock of expressions so that the teacher can communicate his/her thoughts more effectively. Teachers ought to want students to be able to "read" their expressions and decipher their thinking on occasions! The truth is, facial expressions need to be a vital part of the teacher's personal behavior. There should be a repertoire of facial expressions in the proverbial hip pocket of every classroom music teacher.

Definition of Facial Expressions

The concept of *facial expressions* is difficult to define. I see it as a collection of looks that one intentionally does to reflect a particular thought or specific feeling. Technically speaking, they're deliberate manipulations of one's facial features, such as the eyes, the eyebrows, the mouth, the lips, and the forehead, for the purpose of conveying a particular thought. Even the head itself becomes part of the facial expression in the way it's tilted, turned, or raised and lowered. Figuratively speaking, however, facial expressions are avenues of communication, or facial portrayals of the teacher's thoughts or feelings arising from surrounding circumstances. But the simplest way to define facial expressions is to call them "facial looks." That's what they really are!

Repertoire of Facial Expressions

Yes, there are a lot of facial expressions possible! But let's identify some of the more common expressions used by the classroom teacher. One of the most helpful ways to go about doing this task is to label a facial expression as a particular "look." It's a good way to think about facial expressions and "work" on them. Here are some of the different "looks" teachers can cast in the classroom:

- "Can I help you?" Look
- "I don't believe it!" Look
- "Are you doing that again?" Look
- "I'm surprised at you!" Look
- "Stop that!" Look
- "Shhhh" Look
- "I've had it!" Look
- "Is that what I think it is?" Look
- "Oh, I'm so sorry" Look
- "Oh, come off it!" Look
- "Gee, that was dumb!" Look
- "I'll wait" Look
- "I know you didn't mean it" Look
- "That's enough!" Look
- "Aw, you're pouting" Look
- "That's very good!" Look
- "Did you say something?" Look
- "Aw, how cute!" Look
- "Oooh, how nice!" Look
- "I'm not so sure" Look

See all the possibilities and all the particular situations to which they can relate? The interesting thing about these looks is that each one reflects a particular emotion as well as intent. For example, the "Can I help you" look is motivated by an inquisitive emotion, and the "I don't believe it!" one by disgust or surprise. Then there's the "Stop it" look, the "I've had it" look, or "That's enough" look, all of which convey a feeling of displeasure. Now, you go through the list and identify the related emotion(s) and indicate, if you can, what might be the provoking situation(s). Remember, some looks have more than one emotional tag. Then make up some of your own "looks" or expressions. Think of specific situations in your own teaching. Your personal list of expressions can be as numerous as your imagination. Timpson and Tobin feel that facial expressions are one of the teacher's most abundant and accessible resources for communicating in that they live within the teacher![19]

---

[19]Timpson and Tobin, p. 42.

Need for Facial Expressions

Teachers need facial expressions for many reasons. One is that facial expressions make the teacher more dynamic and interesting. They complement and even reinforce the teacher's verbiage. Another reason is that they offer a more sensible solution in some instances. Giving a particular look is often much more effective, and less disruptive, than making a comment. Promoting a better rapport between teacher and students is a third reason. Facial expressions can convey a world of emotions, and they can help seal the bonding between the two more effectively at times than the spoken word. The fourth reason is that facial expressions are essential tools for classroom management. Let's consider each of these reasons more closely.

Becoming a More Dynamic Teacher. Facial expressions are one of the keys to being a dynamic teacher. Not just in disciplinary situations, but with your teaching as well. Look what they can do. They can (a) reinforce the impact of certain words, (b) imply a different meaning intentionally, or (c) enhance the tenor of the whole conversation. Think about this for a minute! If you were stressing a certain word (or words), isn't it natural to display an expression to match that word? For example, when talking about a forte passage, the eyes usually get big as saucers, and the eyebrows arch up almost to one's hairline! Even the head rears back slightly.

Then think about the expression the teacher uses when he/she wants to be coy or impish in suggesting something other than what is being said. The eyeballs either roll upward or sideward while the mouth is pursed off to one side like an overdone smirk. Or maybe the teacher gives a wink accompanied by a "We know better!" look. These are good rapport-building tactics that acknowledge the students' with-it-ness.

As for enhancing the tenor of one's conversation, look how easily this happens when talking about soft music. The teacher can make a gentle-looking face with shushing lips that he/she taps lightly with pointer finger. Or a scary face when telling about a spooky song. See how facial expressions can "up" the teacher's ratings for being dynamic? And, oh yes, be sure your expressions are definite—half-baked ones won't work! Practice in front of a mirror, if necessary.

Providing a More Sensible Solution. There are times when a facial expression is ten times better than the spoken word. **First**, it's less disturbing for the rest of the class, especially when students are working individually, because speaking out tends to break their concentration. It's really more considerate at such times to foist a "look" rather than make a comment. **Second**, it's less embarrassing for the students involved in cheating, gesturing, or hanky-panky. Such situations are best handled discreetly with a facial expression followed by private conference. **Third**, it's a more sensible alternative when dealing with students who constantly seek attention. Subjecting the whole class to a constant barrage of reprimands isn't fair. Nor is it advisable to give these students that much attention. A surprised look like, "Are you doing that again," or a quick "Cut it out" look will do the job quickly and quietly. **Fourth**, facial expressions are less time-consuming than verbal comments. They can be made without even interrupting the lesson. You can keep right on clapping, playing, or marching, even if Billy *is* busy whacking Bobby over the head with a rhythm stick. If the expression is explicit, Bobby will quit! You won't have to stop the lesson. That's when facial expressions save teaching time—they cut down on verbalizing time.

Creating a Better Rapport with Students. So often facial expressions are thought of only in terms of maintaining classroom discipline, but there's another important application as well. They help build better rapport between teacher and student. Facial expressions have the power to encourage, praise, or motivate the student(s). They create a special bonding with students by providing tangible evidence that the teacher recognizes his/her particular (a) effort, (b) achievement, or even (c) predicament. Facial expressions also tell the student(s) that the teacher is genuinely concerned and really interested in his/her welfare. Here are some specific expressions or "looks" that can create the bonding:

- "Oooh, that was good" Look
- "Verrry nice, indeed" Look
- "I'm proud of you!" Look
- "See, I knew you could do it!" Look
- "Good, keep going!" Look
- "Well, look what you did!" Look

Whether directed towards the whole class or to one individual, the results will be the same, and eventually a feeling of trust and respect will develop that contributes to a more conducive teaching/learning environment. Positive-looking facial expressions are an important aspect of one's teaching style. They draw the teacher closer to the students and make the students more responsive towards the teacher.

Improving the Classroom Management. It's impossible to be an effective disciplinarian without a repertoire of facial expressions. While they aren't the only factor for controlling discipline, they're, nevertheless, one of the most effective! A convincing, well-delivered "look" is capable of squelching most disruptions just as quickly and effectively as the spoken word. I'm talking about looking puzzled at something, appearing displeased with someone, displaying disappointment with a student, looking tired of something, or being surprised. Will students be able to read these expressions? Yes, especially if they are deliberately delivered. Students should get the message loud and clear that (a) what they are doing is unacceptable, (b) that it must be stopped—immediately, and (c) that they must return to the task at hand. That's why facial expressions are called a "communicative tool."

Developing a Repertoire of Facial Expressions

Many teachers feel awkward displaying facial expressions, while others just aren't sure which expressions they should use. But the situation can be remedied; you *can* learn to use facial expressions. It's a matter of knowing your own face and how each feature or component can operate. You'll recall that your features include the eyes and eyebrows, the lips and the mouth, the forehead, and the head. Take each feature and discover all the ways it can be manipulated. Take the eyes, for example. You can (a) open wide, (b) lower lids, (c) squint, (d) flutter, (e) squeeze shut, (f) stare ahead, and (g) even roll your eyes. Do each of these in front of a mirror in order to find out exactly how you look when doing these things. See which responses work the best for you or make the best impression. Then tackle the eyebrows, followed by the lips, the mouth, then the forehead, and finally the head. (For a listing of ways to manipulate each feature, turn to Figure 3.3.) Once you feel comfortable with each feature, try making your expressions more exaggerated. The more obvious and well-defined your expressions, the better students will respond.

Now comes the fun part. Make up a list of as many classroom situations as you can think of, or as many as you have recently encountered. Then write down the "look" or "looks" you might use for each of these situations, and the particular emotion it evokes. Here's a sampling of what your list might look like:

Punching Each Other

"I don't believe it!" Look (disgust)

"Cut it out!" Look (irritation)

"I'm surprised at you!" Look (surprise)

"Not again" Look (tired of)

Throwing Paper Across Room

"I saw that!" Look (anger)

"Did I see what I think I saw?" Look (disbelief)

"Here we go again!" Look (disgust)

Giggling

"Are you at it again?" Look (tired of)

"I'll wait!" Look (disgusted)

"That's enough of that!" Look (mad)

Singing in Two Parts Correctly

"You did it!" Look (pleased)

"That was just great!" Look (excited)

"I didn't think you could do it!" Look (surprised)

Most likely each list of looks will be totally different. That's fine. Put down the ones *you* want. After all, you're the one who knows which expressions work best for *you*. Now go ahead and practice these looks in front of a mirror until they feel comfortable. Identify the ones you can start using immediately. See how expressive you can be once you know (a) the different ways to manipulate facial features and (b) the different kinds of "looks" to show various emotions. By the way, if you find yourself using gestures along with these expressions, that's terrific! It's almost impossible to do these expressions without gesturing.

Let me tell you quickly about Timpson and Tobin's suggestion for developing facial expression. It's a more general approach involving a reaction to certain words, such as tall, short, long, proud, humble, shy, embarrassed, and cagey, to mention just a few. Their point is that if you respond to the conceptual idea behind each of these terms, you'll naturally make some kind of facial expression. Then, if you look in a mirror, you can discover what each facial feature is doing.[20] If this approach works for you, use it!

Concluding Challenge

Your facial expressions need to be part of your personal behavior. They'll contribute to (a) making you a more dynamic teacher, (b) providing more sensible teacher responses, (c) establishing a better rapport with your students, and (d) controlling your classroom discipline. If you don't already have a repertoire of well-defined facial expressions, get started on it!

---

[20]Timpson and Tobin, p. 44.

LESS EFFECTIVE	MORE EFFECTIVE
When Beth was finally able to march correctly to the on-going beat, Ms. Acappella breathed a sigh of relief. "It's about time," she said to herself. At that moment, Beth looked up at her. Ms. Acappella nodded and pursed her lips tighter. "Keep listening to the beat," she shouted out at Beth. Big tears welled up in Beth's eyes.	Ms. Acappella had worked hard to get Beth to feel the beat. The day she saw Beth finally march in-step she was so excited that she almost ran up and hugged her. Instead, she gave Beth one of her "You did it!" looks. Beth smiled back with a big toothless grin and kept on marching.
Once again Bonnie and Marsha were passing notes. Ms. L'Accompaniment glared at the two sixth graders. "Would you like to read that note, Bonnie?" Bonnie's face got red. "Well, would you? Then put it away!" By this time all the other sixth-grade students were looking at Bonnie and Marsha and snickering. The class thought Ms. L'Accompaniment was an old meanie for doing this.	Ms. L'Accompaniment saw Bonnie and Marsha passing notes again. While reciting the letter names of the notes with the class, Ms. L'Accompaniment gave a disgusted "Are you doing that again?" look. Both girls looked guilty and embarrassed. They whispered an "I'm sorry." On the way out Bonnie and Marsha apologized. "We know you must be tired of us; we won't do it again. We promise, Ms. L'Accompaniment!" "She's a neat teacher," Marsha said to Bonnie as they left class.

Exercising Teacher Proximity

Probably the least talked about behavior a teacher exercises, or should exercise, is that of positioning himself/herself nearer the students on occasions. It's such an instinctive response—almost like an intuitive beckoning—that it's easy to overlook as being a specific behavior. But teachers do it often enough for us to recognize it as definite teacher response. This positioning of one's self closer to students is known as *teacher proximity*. And it has its rewards. But before we discuss the rewards, let's be sure we have a clear understanding of proximity.

Definition of Proximity

Very simply, proximity is the state of being nearer, or closer, or next to something or someone. In this case, it's the students. More precisely, you could say that it's an *intentional* closeness to the students: (a) in front of the student, (b) beside the student, (c) behind the student, d) in the middle of the student's aisle, or else (e) across in the adjacent aisle. Note that all the positions are near by, that the close positioning is deliberate on the teacher's part. And why do teachers occasionally want to get nearer to the students? To either reinforce their own teaching or to impact on students' learning. Or perhaps both! So now we have the what, where, and why of exercising proximity. (We'll talk about the why aspect later.) For now, let's continue with the when issue.

The easiest answer for knowing when to use proximity is to say not all the time! Proximity does not imply a constant hovering; that would be nerve-racking for the students and absurd for the teacher—and even impossible! There are times when the teacher *must* be at the chalkboard, by the desk, or behind the piano. When should proximity be exercised then? Whenever the teacher senses or realizes that his/her presence would be best served, at that moment, by being nearer the student than farther away. That's about as specific as I can get. Only *you* can decipher when it's right to get nearer. Your own intuition will have to call the shots, especially if you are a beginning teacher. But for the more experienced teacher, the move will be based on a learned perceptivity that comes only with experience. In other words, experience will "tell" the veteran teacher when it's more expedient to move in. But make no mistake, intuition still plays a large part in even the experienced teacher's decision.

Perhaps it would be best to make a distinction between mobility and proximity. There's a difference. *Mobility* refers to physical movement from one place to another during the act of teaching. It focuses on the teacher's sporadic movement. (See "Exercising Mobility in the Classroom" at the beginning of this chapter.) *Proximity*, on the other hand, is a stationary placement or a specific positioning achieved as a result of mobility. Obviously, the teacher needs to move in order to get to a particular place. So the emphasis is on placement, i.e., where the teacher is *standing*, and not on *movement*. It's important to understand this distinction.

Teaching Without Proximity

What happens when proximity isn't part of the teacher's behavior? Here are some typical examples of how they cope. Some teachers get behind anything that resembles a blockade, like their desk, their chair, a music stand, or even a mounted visual aid—and stay there. They're trying to barricade themselves against the students. There they stand, not daring to move one inch this way or that. The blockade becomes their security blanket. They can't seem to deal with getting close to the students. Proximity is out of the question for these teachers!

Then there's the crowd that hides behind the piano and becomes acrobats. Some practically drape themselves over the piano while others resort to a more reserved position like leaning on the lid with both elbows. Yet they never step out. Still oth-

ers get more daring by leaning against the side of the piano with one elbow resting on the lid. They look like they're standing at the gate of the OK Corral! How about those who grab the edges with outstretched arms like campaigning politicians or revved-up preachers? The real culprits, however, are the ones who rest their backside on the keyboard when they get tired of standing and create ripples of tones when they stand up.

But my favorite ones are the teachers who fear proximity so much they invariably start backing up little by little until they bump into the wall or the chalkboard.

Some try to keep pushing back, while others try to cling to the board like a vine. Some even look like they're being plastered back by a giant fan! How about the ones who start taking little bitsy steps this way or that way? They look like they're doing a two-step!

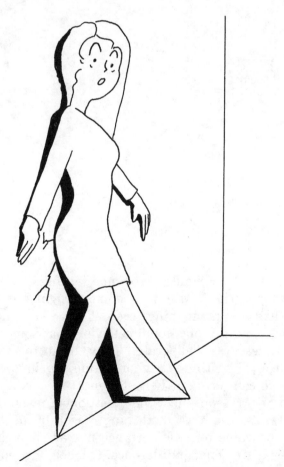

While each of the scenarios above are comical, they're sad as well. They describe teachers who feel uncomfortable with proximity and prefer being as far away as possible from the class. There are several reasons for feeling this way about proximity. Let me share them with you.

Reasons for Fearing Proximity

One of the most obvious reasons, especially among those with less experience, is that they are intimidated by the students. They tend to see the class as a whole—as an overpowering mass—rather than as individuals, especially when they teach. They let their imaginations play funny tricks on them. For example, with each step backward they take, the more intimidated the class becomes. It feels like a tidal wave or a herd of buffalo is coming at them! And after making a bee-line dive for their desks or some other fortified place, they start fussing nervously with something. That's the way they deal with their anxieties. Intimidation is a real problem for some teachers where proximity is concerned.

Another reason is ignorance. Some teachers simply aren't aware of the proximity phenomenon. That's why they don't recognize it when they see it happening! It just seems like a natural thing to do. They don't understand that in the classroom proximity becomes a professional behavior, that sometimes it may be an intuitive act, but most times, it's deliberate. They need to be told this—and even shown. Otherwise, they'll continue to ignore using proximity and never experience the effect close presence can have on their students.

One other reason must be mentioned, even though it's not as prevalent. Nevertheless, it's the most disturbing reason of all. It's the indifference of teachers who know the value of a close stance but are not concerned enough to exercise it. But whether it's teacher indifference, teacher burnout, or personal entrenchment, it doesn't matter; none of these is excusable. Teachers in this state of mind should not be teaching.

Rewards for Proximity

Why insist on practicing proximity? Because the rewards are so significant. Probably the most appealing reason, especially for the beginning teacher, is that it instills a feeling of control, of having a hand on the situation. Here's why. When you get close to the class or a student, you assume an offensive rather than defensive role. Your mere physical presence in an upright position gives you this advantage. While you look down, the students must look up, and even more so when you are standing close. Your position of leadership and authority is probably never more imposing in the eyes of your students than when you exercise proximity. You not only have a professional advantage, but a positional advantage! That's why I encourage all those who suffer from the tidal-wave or buffalo syndrome to begin utilizing proximity. It does wonders for building confidence and projecting authority—and for maintaining classroom control.

Then there's the positive effect on student responsiveness. It's amazing how much more ambitious and motivated students become when the teacher is standing a few feet away, or how much more attentive the back rowers become when the teacher is behind them. The teacher can keep better tabs on the students from this closer vantage point. And the students, in turn, learn to stay with it better because they fear the teacher might pop-up beside them at any time. An enticing reward, isn't it?

A third reward is the strengthening of rapport between teacher and students. The teacher makes two things clear by going into the trenches occasionally: (1) he/she is approachable, and (2) he/she wants to be near them. The teacher's closeness helps to create a feeling of camaraderie in the students' mind and to dispel the notion that the teacher wants them an arm's length away. Proximity breaks down all these barriers and establishes the kind of warm rapport teacher and students need in order to work together in a positive way.

Last, but not the least, is that proximity puts a lid on disruptive behavior. It's simply more difficult to whisper, pass notes, giggle, chew gum, or throw paper planes when the teacher is close by or right in front. It's even more impossible to continue misbehaving when the teacher is moving in the student's direction. The marvelous part of this moving tactic is that the teacher can keep on teaching without even interrupting the lesson! As Callahan and Clark[21] noted, by the time the teacher reaches the student, the devilment has usually stopped. So proximity is a good thwarter of disruptive behavior, which should be an appealing consequence for any teacher!

Executing Proximity

There's really no particular formula or procedure in exercising proximity. Neither is there any spot or specific aisle to which the teacher must be committed. It's simply a matter of moving in the direction of student(s) as soon as the behavior is spotted,[22] and then staying in that spot for as long as the situation warrants or however long the teacher thinks necessary. Remember, intuition plays a big role in initiating and terminating proximity. One final point. Please don't stay glued to one spot once you

---

[21]Joseph F. Callahan and Leonard H. Clark. *Teaching in the Elementary School* (New York: Macmillan Publishing Co., 1977), p. 116.

[22]Ibid, p. 116.

get there. Exercise your proximity wisely, not absurdly. Here's the rule: Go only **when** it's conducive and **where** it's conducive; in other words, only when and where it's the most advantageous to position yourself at that moment.

Concluding Challenge

Want to experience the thrill of feeling in command, getting better class response, or building a stronger rapport with your students? Then get away from behind your desk or your piano, and make an occasional effort to walk the aisles or stand closer to your class or to your students. That's what proximity is all about—utilizing bodily presence to glean greater results!

LESS EFFECTIVE

Ms. Fugue was one of those teachers who stayed plastered to the chalkboard. Students just expected to see her with arms outstretched on both sides and hands clutching the chalkboard tray like her life depended on it. She never moved from this spot! Not unless she had to play the piano. So there was always some talking going on because the students in the back got away with murder. To them, Ms. Fugue was just an oddball. Her nickname was "Fuge-on-the-board."

Ms. Minuetto's class wondered why she always stayed by the windows. Sometimes she would be leaning on an elbow and slumped over on the window sill; other times, both elbows would be on the sill. Occasionally she would perch herself up on the window sill, which always surprised the students. Ms. Minuetto knew that her teaching was hampered by her fear of moving around the class and that her class control suffered as well. But she excused herself constantly. "I just can't help it." So her classes continued to be noisy and disruptive.

MORE EFFECTIVE

Students in Ms. Fugue's music classes knew they had to be on their toes. They never knew where she would turn up! Sometimes she would be standing in the back of the room, sometimes in the middle of an aisle. You just weren't sure where she would be. One thing you did know was that you had better pay attention because she had her eye on everyone. But they could tell Ms. Fugue really liked them by the way she smiled and spoke to them. They thought she was a neat teacher.

When Ms. Minuetto finished the opening song at the piano, she went immediately to stand in front of the second row. When the activity ended, she moved to the middle of the third row—Judy and Sandy were always whispering. After introducing the next activity, Ms. Minuetto saw that Jack was having trouble tapping the syncopation pattern, so she slowly made her way to be near him. When the class ended, Ms. Minuetto was back in front of the class. A good portion of the time she was stationed here and there throughout the room. The students liked Ms. Minuetto. She was always around when you needed her, and she kept her classes under control because she just didn't stay in front.

3

Basic Verbal Skills

Verbalizing skills play a major role in the act of teaching. In fact, they're the backbone of the teaching process. A lot of the teacher's time and energy is spent in such tasks as:

- explaining
- instructing
- questioning
- discussing
- challenging
- encouraging
- praising
- correcting
- reprimanding
- motivating

Yet so little time is spent in analyzing these tasks and determining how to deliver them more effectively. This chapter does just that. It discusses many of the above skills, plus others not listed, then goes on to mention a number of suggestions, guidelines, or, in some cases, steps for carrying out these tasks. First, let's take a minute to consider the reasons why good verbal skills are so important.

Good verbal skills, such as giving specific directions, emphasizing important ideas, using correct grammar, applying timely pauses, etc., facilitate the teaching process. Plain and simple, they go hand-in-hand with "good" teaching. While most of these skills are just common-sense behaviors, they do wonders for expediting the job of teaching and making the teacher more competent. That's one of the best reasons for having good verbal skills.

The second reason is that effective verbal skills improve the ongoing momentum. The momentum is always better when instructions are clear, assessing is precise, verbiage is appropriate because these skills help students understand what's being said. The pacing doesn't bog down as often, which means the momentum can keep moving.

The third reason has to do with learning, namely, that good verbal skills expedite the act of learning. Students "get" conceptual ideas a lot easier and a lot quicker when correct terminology is used, precise explanations are given, and pedantic verbiage is avoided. In addition, their attention is better whenever tactics like verbal bridging, timely pausing, and honest feedback are used.

Speaking Correctly and Distinctly

If there's one verbal skill every teacher needs it's being able to speak in a correct and distinct manner. Actually, these are two separate skills. The "correct" part refers

99

to **speaking properly**. Good grammar is a "must"; so are the right words—not just because the teacher is the model, but because teachers are *supposed* to speak correctly. It's one of the trademarks of being a teacher.

The "distinct" part is a plea for **speaking with good diction**. You've got to speak correctly, as well as distinctly, when you're a teacher.

Speaking correctly and distinctly, then, isn't just an option or a suggestion—it's a high priority.

Definition of Correct and Distinct Speaking

The best place to start with this skill is to get a clear definition of what each aspect means and what each requires. "Correct speaking" is verbalizing with the proper parts of speech, or talking in such a way that:

- Verbs agree with their subjects
- Verbs are modified with adverbs
- Nouns are modified with adjectives
- Pronouns can be used as subjects or objects of verbs
- Pronouns are correct after prepositions
- Verbs reflect right tenses

It's a matter of having good command of the English language, learning to talk with good grammar and correct terminology.

"Speaking distinctly," on the other hand, has to do with the proper delivery of vowels and consonants. It's speaking in such a way that all your **vowels** are enunciated with the right sound and proper clarity,[1] and each a, e, i, o, and u is given its rightful pronunciation. It also means that your **consonants** are delivered with the right speed and force when they're being formed.[2] In a nutshell, then, speaking distinctly involves (a) enunciating the vowels and (b) articulating the consonants.[3] Or simply having good diction.

Significance of Speaking Correctly/Distinctly

No one would dispute the fact that speaking correctly and distinctly is important. At the same time, many teachers would do their share of hemming-and-hawing when it came to giving their reasons for not speaking correctly and distinctly. There are, however, important rationale that every classroom teacher ought to know about, and value highly, if correct and distinct speaking is to be taken seriously.

The first is that the **teacher projects greater credibility**. Think about it! When you speak correctly and distinctly, you give parents ample evidence of being sufficiently trained.[4] The fact is, parents **want** teachers to "sound" like teachers—and even **expect** them to sound teacherish! By doing so, you bolster your own credibility in the parents' eyes.

But don't forget the students, because the way you speak has a powerful impact

---

[1]Christy, Van A. *Foundations in Singing* (Dubuque, IA: William C. Brown Company Publishers, 1965), p. 59.

[2]*Ibid.*, p. 59.

[3]*Ibid.*, p. 59.

[4]Rich, John Martin. "Reducing Teacher Incompetence." *Planning and Changing*, Vol. 19, No. 2, Summer 1988, p. 119.

on them, too! They may not be able to tell you in so many words why you sound like a teacher, but I can assure you they **do** have opinions as to the way you speak, especially those in the upper grades! It's only when you have that "teacherish" way of speaking that they start to "see" you as the teacher and, more important, that your own credibility as a teacher begins to take shape.

The second reason correct speaking is so important is that **it serves as a suitable model**. Teachers are modelers for everything, including speech. So when you make a conscious effort to use good grammar and precise terminology, you are actually setting an example and providing an opportunity for students to hear proper speaking. Believe me, they need all the modeling they can get, especially in a society that has gone batty over buzzwords and slang. The teacher may well be the last vestige of hope students have to hear the correct use of the English language!

A third reason for speaking correctly is that **it leads to a better response** because students aren't as confused. They don't have to ask as many questions to clarify instructions or explanations when (a) terminology is precise, (b) grammar is correct, and (c) diction is good. They can follow the lesson more easily and feel more confident in participating; thus, the response is better.

The last reason is that the **momentum moves more smoothly**. When there's less confusion and more comprehension, the lesson doesn't get interrupted as much because students don't have as many questions. They understand what you're saying—and know what you want. That means the momentum can keep moving.

Suggestions for Speaking Correctly/Clearly

Let's take correct speaking first. You begin by becoming aware of what's right and what's wrong. The **first guideline**, then, is: Learn your English grammar. At the very least that means acquiring a "working" knowledge of the six basic rules identified in Figure 3.1. For example:

1. **Make Verbs Agree With Nouns/Pronouns**. While you won't have any problem with the normal singular and plural words, like cats, boys, or kites, you'll need to watch out for irregularities such as:

   a. Singular nouns with plural connotations, such as group, family, jury, or crowd, that call for singular verbs;

   b. Plural nouns having singular meanings, like news, sports, or dynamics, that must have singular verbs, e.g., sports **is** next; and

   c. Indefinite pronouns like everybody, anybody, or nobody, that also require the singular verb, e.g., nobody is here or everybody wants some.

2. **Modify Verbs with Adverbs**. With adverbs, most of the abuse comes with the ones modifying verbs. Make an effort to end adverbs which tell how the action is being done with "ly." That means saying slowly, quickly, or frequently after the verb, like this:

   He ran slowly.

   She came quickly.

   It rains frequently.

   The "ly" is a "must" when an adverb follows a verb. Other adverbial usages aren't as tricky, like the ones that modify another adverb, such as **very** slowly or **more** accurately. Or the ones modifying adjectives, like a **very** good book.

When Using	Say This	Instead of This
Plural nouns needing singular verbs	• Mathematics comes later. • Ethics *has* suffered a blow.	• Mathematics come later. • Ethics have suffered a blow.
Collective nouns needing singular verbs	• The jury *is* still out. • The team *has* been losing. • His family *lives* in New York.	• The jury are out. • The team have been losing. • His family live in New York.
Adjectives to modify nouns	• That's a piercing sound. • What an appealing song. • It's a perfect day.	• That's a bad sound. • What a good song. • It's a nice day.
Adverbs to modify verbs	• Let's sing the song *slowly.* • He did *poorly* on the exam. • The band played *loudly.*	• Let's sing the song slow. • He did poor on the exam. • The band played loud.
Pronouns with preposition	• The secret is between *you* and *me.* • It's for *him* and *her.* • Keep it between *us* girls.	• The secret is between you. • It's for he and she. • Keep it between we girls.
Pronouns as subjects or objects	• You and I should know. • It's *he* who said it. • Neither of them saw *his* mistake.	• You and me should know. • It's him who said it. • Neither of them saw their mistake.

Figure 3.1. Correct and Incorrect Ways of Using Parts of Speech.

3. **Modify Nouns with Adjectives**. What you need to do here is use more descriptive adjectives. There's a tendency to use the same adjectives over and over, or else rely on those trite, overworked modifiers, such as nice, good, or pretty, all of which lessen the impact of what's been said. Use a thesaurus to find some new and more appropriate adjectives. That's the quickest solution in this case.

4. **Use Pronouns as Subjects or Objectives**. The pronoun can spell trouble if you don't know whether you're using it as a subject or an object. You need to know which ones are subject pronouns and which are object. Here's a list of pronouns as subjects and objects:

PRONOUNS AS SUBJECTS	PRONOUNS AS OBJECTS
You and I	You and me
He and I, or she and I	Him and me, or her and me
He, she, or I	Him, her
We, they	Us, them
Who	Whom

If you're going to use a pronoun as a subject, use he, she, it, or I; otherwise, it's him, her, and me. In addition, get "who" and "whom" straight! If you're not sure, test it by substituting "him." For example, if you ask "who/whom should I call?", simply reverse it and say, "I shall call 'him.'" Thus, for this sentence, it's "whom."

5. **Use Proper Pronoun After Prepositional Phrase**. The rule of thumb is: Pronouns automatically take the objective form in prepositional phrases. So, you would say: ... to **me**, or ... for **them**, or ... with **him**, and watch out especially for ... between **you** and **me**. So often I hear the subject pronoun, I, being used after "between," which is incorrect.

6. **Use the Right Verb Tenses**. The problem here is using the past and past perfect tenses incorrectly with certain verbs, like go, sing, or drink to name but a few of the more common offenders. The best advice is to learn the tenses.

PRESENT	PAST	PAST PERFECT
Go	Went	Has or have gone
Sing	Sang	Has or have sung
Drink	Drank	Has or have drunk
See	Saw	Has or have seen

That way you'll know when to say ... has gone instead of has went, or ... he sang rather than he sung, or ... he drank and not he drunk. Or ... he saw him as opposed to he seen him. Another option would be to get a colleague or friend to monitor your use of tenses. There's no short-cut here. It's going to take some effort on your part to learn the right verbs.

So the first guideline is to learn the grammar. The **second guideline** is: Listen to yourself. If you know your grammar, you should be able to hear your errors. That gets you ready for the **third guideline**, which is: Correct yourself—immediately, and not by making a mental note. You need to correct yourself out loud. Just say, "Excuse me, I should have said such-and-such," and go right on. In other words, start being your own teacher! That way your progress will be much faster.

The **fourth guideline** is this: Avoid using slang. Don't be fooled into thinking you've got to use the students' lingo in order to communicate with them. Students don't need your pseudo slang—they have friends who use it naturally. Your job is to use the most grammatically accurate speech you can. Remember, students need correct modeling; they hear enough of the other stuff without you chiming in!

The **fifth guideline** is: Use precise words. If you don't, you won't be very articulate. Your choice of words has to be specific. It's a matter of saying (a) "Melodies move upward" instead of "Music moves up," (b) "Tap your rhythm sticks" rather than "Hit your sticks," or (c) "Construct a chord" and not "write out a chord." To speak correctly, you've got to use precise verbiage.

Now let's get some suggestions for speaking distinctly, or with good diction. With regard to **consonants**, be sure that you pronounce:

- "d" and "t" endings (bird, hand, chart)
- "er" and "ed" endings (recorder, softer, marched)
- "ing" and "est" endings (singing, playing, loudest)

As for vowels, you need to: (1) formulate them properly, (2) pronounce the diphthongs correctly, and (3) support the breath sufficiently. To formulate vowels properly, be sure there's proper resonating space in the mouth when using words with a, i, or o; like boy, tie, and old. Vowels need that cavity space to get pronounced properly. Exercise lip formation when you use your a, e, i, o, and u's. The vowels have to be formulated properly if you're going to speak distinctly.

Let's not forget the **diphthongs**. These are syllables that have two vowel sounds, such as:

- ie as in vie, die, tie
- oy as in boy, toy, soy
- ow as in vow, now, cow
- ou as in thou, our, sour

What you've got to do is pronounce both vowels, but put more emphasis on the first one and let the second one vanish or fade. For example:

- vie should sound like vah-ee
- boy should sound like bow-ee
- vow should sound like vah-oo
- thou should sound like thah-oo

Notice that the jaw, and often the lips, work twice on these diphthongs because you've got to move your mouth in order for the diphthongs to sound properly.[5] So zero-in on those diphthongs and be sure you pronounce both vowels.

Concluding Challenge

Are you concerned about your own speaking and feel you really ought to have better command of the language? Learn the basic rules and then begin correcting yourself as you speak. You can be your own teacher. And if you want to speak more distinctly, take a look at how you're pronouncing your vowels and consonants. You'll improve quickly if you follow the suggestions.

LESS EFFECTIVE

"Okay, let's get to our seats quick now and get ready to leave," shouted Mr. Len Tissimo. "You always move so slow and take so long to put back the ukeleles!" When they got back to their seats, he told them in no uncertain terms that he expected them to line up "real quiet." But no one was listening. Mr. Len Tissimo was always telling them to do something faster, or quicker, or quieter. No wonder the students called him "Ole Groucho!"

Noticing that one of the students didn't have a partner for the folk dance, Ms. Lib Retto asked, "Who did you pick?" Without waiting for the student to answer, she pointed to a nearby student and said, "You and her can be partners, okay? Everyone get in place now." With that Ms. Lib Retto switched on the CD.

MORE EFFECTIVE

"We need to move more quickly, class, if we're going to be ready to leave." Mr. Len Tissimo nodded approvingly as the students hurried to return the ukeleles. "I appreciate how quickly and quietly you got back to your seats," he told them. "I can always depend upon this class to follow my instructions correctly. Thank you." As they filed out the door, the students grinned and waved good-bye to Mr. Len Tissimo. They thought he was neat!

When Ms. Lib Retto saw that one student was without a partner for the folk dance, she asked the girl, "Whom did you select?" When the student answered, Ms. Lib Retto smiled and said, "Why don't you and she be partners today since your original partner is absent?" The student agreed immediately. When the new partner was in place, Ms. Lib Retto asked everyone to get ready.

---

[5]Christy, Van A., p. 71.

Giving Specific Directions

If there's one verbal skill that every teacher would say was necessary for teaching, it would probably be this one. You can't really teach effectively without clear-cut instructions. And even though some of you less-experienced teachers may think that specific instructions will automatically pop out when you teach, let me be the first to tell you it's not so. To be good at giving directions, you've got to work at it, even when you're an old hand at the task. At the very least, you've got to keep evaluating yourself. So whether you're a more experienced or less experienced teacher, this skill deserves your attention.

Clarifying the Definition

There's no need to define "specific directions" per se; everyone knows what it means. But there's more to it than just being precise. There are some salient points that don't always get mentioned.

One of these points is that specific directions involve **proper terminology**—or giving the proper name for a task, an object, or a concept. (See the earlier section, "Using Correct Terminology," in this chapter.) This is an important aspect of the definition and is probably the one that has the most bearing on whether or not the instruction is specific. A more accurate definition, then, would be to say that specific directions are precise commands involving precise terminology.

Another salient feature is that specific instructions are **to the point**. Just the term itself ought to tell you that conciseness is crucial, and that directions need to be "lean and clean" to convey only *what's expected*— and *no more*.

There's one more point that's seldom mentioned: **visual contact**, or looking directly at the student(s) when delivering the instruction. Being "specific" is also a visual effort. You've got to establish eye contact so there's no doubt whatsoever in the student(s)' mind as to whom you're speaking. That's an essential condition when it comes to specific instructions.

Importance of Specific Directions

Specific instructions are one of the keys to successful teaching for several reasons. First, the **flow of the lesson is better** when instructions are specific. The lesson doesn't bog down *as much*, which is the crux of the matter. When you have to keep stopping to explain your instructions, the lesson doesn't flow as smoothly. Also, flow is usually the first thing "to go" when instructions get too wordy, so put it down. The lesson always flows more smoothly when instructions are lean and clean.

Second, the **students' attention is better**. Nothing is more frustrating for students, especially the sharper ones, than stopping and starting all the time because of muddy instructions. They get bored—and distracted. But when instructions are precise and to the point, students "stay" with you and they're more alert.

And better attention implies better control. When students are more attentive, you can move more smoothly and more quickly from one activity to the next. You don't have to worry about disruptions. Thus, good classroom management is perpetuated by specific instructions. It's sad that more teachers don't make this connection.

Finally, the **daily objectives are achieved more quickly**. If the lesson is flowing, the students are listening, and the management is working, you've got all the ingredients for a successful lesson. That means you have a better chance of accomplishing your objectives in a shorter period of time, and getting more done.

Problem Concerning Specific Directions

It isn't difficult to figure out the problem. Directions (or instructions) simply aren't stated precisely enough. Let's dig a little deeper, though, to find out what that means in terms of the delivery.

First of all, it means that a lot of teachers get **too wordy** and say too much. They make their instructions so long that students are completely befuddled by the time they've said it! What happens is teachers keep adding information to the instruction while delivering it. For some reason they feel the need to say more to "make it clearer." (Perish the thought!) Saying too much is just as deadly as saying too little. (The solution for this will be covered in the Suggestions section.)

In addition to being too wordy, many teachers are **too vague**. The biggest offender for making an instruction vague is the terminology. Some teachers use terminology that really doesn't "say" what they intend it to say, which is why they get the blank looks and loud "huhs?" It's so easy to get in the habit of using vague terminology, but it causes havoc with the class's response.

There's one other problem: being **too general**. It has to do with speaking in broad terms, or not saying exactly what you want to say. The expression for it is "beating around the bush." Sometimes it's compounded by being too wordy as well, or too vague because of the terminology—or *both*!

Suggestions for Specific Instructions

Here are some suggestions you'll find helpful in being more specific with instructions. But let me warn you: you'll need a good dose of stick-to-itness; otherwise, the suggestions won't work.

Wordiness. If you need some help with being too wordy, here are three approaches that really do the job. See which one(s) you can use.

1. Write out your instructional statements in your lesson plan—verbatim.
2. Monitor your own instructional statements as you speak.
3. Tape yourself or ask a fellow teacher to evaluate your instructional statements.

The most time-consuming suggestion is writing out the instructions, but I heartily recommend it. It makes you think through your instructions **before** you teach. But writing out is only half the job; getting them in your head is the other half. You can't just write down instructions and forget about them. You've got to do both tasks: (1) write them out and (2) assimilate them.

Don't let writing the instructions scare you because it isn't as big a chore as you think, not if you use the verbal bridging technique. (See "Using Verbal Bridges" later in this chapter.) All you have to do is prepare an (a) assessment and (b) instruction after each class response. You'll be amazed at how quickly you'll get accustomed to saying only what's necessary. For example:

Verbal Bridge #1

Assessment—"Your folk dancing was excellent, class. I saw everyone keeping step with 3/4 meter."

Instruction—"Now, take your seats quietly and this time let's conduct in 3's, like this."

Verbal Bridge #2

Assessment—"Very good, boys and girls. Everyone tapped the ongoing beat perfectly."

Instruction—"Do you think this next time we can march *and* tap to the ongoing beat, like this?"

Notice that the instructional part makes reference to the next activity and the selected concept—and that's all! Occasionally you might want to add an adverb, like quickly, quietly, slowly, etc., to indicate how to carry out the activity. But, in general, you can pattern your instructions after these examples.

The second suggestion is self-explanatory, but a few words of advice. First, remember that this is a self-improvement chore. As such, you need to be honest and hard-nosed about the progress you make. Don't excuse anything or rationalize anything. Be a demanding taskmaster on yourself; otherwise, you won't get better. If you're not willing to be your own worst critic, don't use this approach. One more thing: Keep a record of what, when, and where so you can track your improvement.

The same advice applies to the third suggestion where you call on a fellow teacher to monitor your instructions. The crucial factor here is finding someone who will be honest and demanding, someone whom you trust and respect—someone with integrity and compassion. If you know anyone like this, you'll have an ideal arrangement. But, remember, you'll need to be ready for each visit! And, don't forget to have your evaluator keep an accurate record of your progress. That's a "must."

Vague. The solution for being too vague is to discipline yourself to use correct terminology. (Refer back to the section, "Using Correct Terminology," earlier in this chapter.) It's going to take all the self-discipline you can muster to start calling "things" by their correct name. You'll need a system, so check out those suggestions in the terminology section.

Unfocused. Here are two simple suggestions to help keep your instructions focused. They work if you follow them exactly.

1. Ask yourself what you want students to do, then say exactly that—and no more, **and**
2. Think through your instructions prior to teaching the lesson.

The first suggestion works like a charm. You'll say just **exactly** what you want *to yourself*, but you'll get too long-winded when you say it *out loud*. So, discipline yourself to say just what you said to yourself—*and no more*. Whenever my teacher-trainees start to get off-track, I stop them and ask, "What exactly do you want the students to do?" And without any hesitation, they blurt it out—plain and simple, and to the point.

Here's an illustration. When one of my teachers-trainees got long-winded in telling the class to stand, I asked my usual question. Her immediate response was, "I want them to stand up quietly." I could tell it sounded simple and clear to her, too. I smiled and said, "Then that's all you need to say." Moral of the story: listen to what you tell yourself and say only that—and no more.

The second suggestion is a matter of preparing your instructions and thinking through each one to be sure it's specific enough. You'll still need to keep close tabs on yourself when you teach and make on-the-spot corrections; however, there's no substitute for thorough preparation.

Whatever your problem when it comes to giving specific instructions, you should be able to find something here to help you. But let me warn you again. In the final analysis, improvement will depend on self-discipline.

Concluding Challenge

Are you too wordy? Or too vague? Or not focused enough? If so, you're robbing yourself of some good rewards, and also hindering yourself from being a more effective teacher. Specific instructions are vital—even indispensable—to both teaching as well as learning. The bottom line is, you need to be competent in giving specific directions!

LESS EFFECTIVE

When Ms. Clara Net's fourth graders entered the room, she instructed them to "Get seated and do what's on the board." As she walked back to her desk, she scolded some of them for not following her instructions. "Some children never listen," she said to herself. "It says as plain as day to find the phrases on page 33." Disgustedly she offered to read the directions. "I don't know why they can't read for themselves," she grumbled under her breath.

Ms. Vi Linn's kindergarteners were exceptionally noisy during music time, so she played a recording. "Sit down over here and leave your things there." The children came running to get seated. Some still had their rhythm sticks. "Didn't I say leave those back there? And don't squeeze into one spot," she shouted. "Billy, Sharon, Robert, give me your rhythm sticks. You didn't listen, did you?" It was days like this that she wondered if it was worth trying to teach the children anything!

MORE EFFECTIVE

While the fourth graders were filing into the room, Ms. Clara Net directed their attention to the board. When they were all seated, she said to them, "If you'd turn to page 33, I'd like you to identify the like and contrasting phrases in this song. Remember to compare every phrase with the first phrase." Ms. Clara Net floated up and down the aisles giving smiling approval. In no time the students were finished, and ready to move on.

The kindergarteners were restless today. "Better change my lesson," Ms. Vi Linn told herself. With that, she instructed the class to put their rhythm sticks under their chairs. "Thank you, children. You put them away so quietly. Now I'd like these six people to come and sit right there (she pointed to the spot) and six more, right here, etc." In short order, Ms. Vi Linn had the children seated properly around the record player. She praised the boys and girls and then continued with *Peter and the Wolf.*

Talking on Students' Level

You're probably wondering if this is a legitimate skill, aren't you? It is! It belongs right up there with the "biggies" such as speaking correctly, using proper terminology, and giving specific directions. I've seen many teachers who had the other skills "down pat," but forgot about speaking on the students' level. Talk about fiascos! You can't teach if you don't talk to students on their own level. It's as simple as that.

Definition of Talking on Students' Level

The simplest definition for "talking on the students' level" is to say it means speaking in a manner commensurate with the age and maturity of the students. That so-called "manner" of speaking implies several conditions that help insure the right level.

First, it implies that the vocabulary is appropriate for the age level, meaning that the teacher talks to first graders like they were first graders and to high schoolers like they were high schoolers. The vocabulary is fit for the intellectual level as well. If talking is going to be on "the students' level," it's got to be expressed in terms of their own understanding. That's one of the important conditions for the "right" manner.

The second condition is that there's a proper tone of voice involved. The sing-song tone of voice we use with early elementary children sounds ludicrous with upper-level students. It's not appropriate voice for older children; and neither is an adult-sounding voice appropriate for younger children. So, in order for the manner of speaking to be "right" for the age level, there must be a proper tone to it.

Importance of Talking on Students' Level

Rapport. This skill is crucial when it comes to establishing and maintaining rapport with students.

Rapport is dependent upon communication. You can't have good rapport without good communication. As Durenfield explained, "Words are the tools which transfer ideas from one to another."[6] Unless these words mean the same thing to both teacher *and* student, there won't be much communication—and even less rapport.

For example, if you talk to your high schoolers in the same childish way you talk to your elementary kids, you'll turn them off in a minute, and even faster if you use that sing-song tone of voice teachers use with young children! You can't establish rapport if no one is listening. So talk on an adult-like level with your high schoolers. Make that your first rule for building rapport on the upper level.

Your manner of speaking is probably even more crucial at the elementary level. If you use an overly adult-sounding voice, you'll alienate the children. But if you speak in child-like terms and with an appealing tone of voice, the rapport will blossom. Children will seek out ways to speak with you. Rapport, then, is the primary reason for talking on the child's level in the early elementary grades.

Management. When there's a good rapport between teacher and students, there's generally good classroom discipline. The two outcomes go hand-in-hand. Students are more obedient when there's mutual trust and respect, and when they feel comfortable communicating with the teacher. This is the idyllic situation we all strive for as teachers. We'd all like to have such good rapport with our students that classroom management was no longer a problem. So, just talk to your students on their own level. It has a profound affect on the management of your classroom discipline.

Problems with Talking on Students' Level

We need to look at both the upper and lower grades in this case because there are different problems on each level. Take the junior and senior high levels (grades 7–12) first. Here's where many teachers have a tendency to talk down to students. They use that placating tone of voice and simple language that drives older students crazy! It's really inexcusable, yet some teachers talk like that. The upshot is that students

---

[6]Durenfield, Richard. *Learning to Teach* (Century Twenty-One Publishers, Saratoga, CA, 1981), p. 73.

start losing respect for the teacher and, even worse, start mimicking the teacher. Mimicking is hard to stop once it begins, so talk to your junior and senior high students on their own level; otherwise, you'll reap their wrath.

Switch your thinking now to the elementary level. Oddly enough, I see both problems here: teachers talking too babyish and too adultish. Some kindergarten and first-grade teachers revert to baby-talk with their children, or talk in a high-pitched voice that swoops up at the end of every sentence or question. They then use that sing-song effect as well. Children don't need this kind of coddling, especially not in this day and age! Most of them already talk fairly adultish when they come to kindergarten or first grade.

But then other elementary teachers seem to have a problem of talking too adultish to children. They can't seem to get that warm tone of voice and have a hard time "getting down" to the students' level with their verbiage. In a nutshell, they talk over the children's heads, which means communication goes out the window.

Guidelines for Talking on Students' Level

Below the Students' Level. Let's deal first with talking below the students' level. This problem can be remedied more quickly than talking above the students. But before you look at any of the suggestions, first identify your own problem(s).

Use an Adult Tone of Voice

Replace the childish-sounding voice with a mature-sounding voice, particularly at the upper level. That means activate the "adult voice" by:

- Using your diaphragm to inhale and exhale;
- Projecting your speaking voice;
- Lowering your speaking pitch; and
- Maintaining your breath support to the end of the sentence.

The resulting adult voice will make older students feel like they're being treated as adults. Whether you're giving instructions, handing out reprimands, or sharing banters, you need to use an adult tone of voice, even in your opening salutation!

Remember the Age Level

Keep reminding yourself, particularly with junior and senior high schoolers, that these are young adults. They hear adult-level talk all around them and have the capacity to communicate on an adult level. My advice is: Consider students from fourth grade up to be "little people," and seventh graders on up, "young adults" and talk to them as though they were grown-ups. Society started doing this a long time ago, so students expect it. Remember, in many ways, the students today are more adult-like, than child-like.

Use an Adult Vocabulary

Communicate with the appropriate words, phrases, and sentences, "appropriate" meaning that your vocabulary is on par with the students' intellectual level and verbal comprehension. In other words, use verbiage that "fits" your students. If that means adjusting your communicating style, then so be it. You may need to use more challenging word choices, more sophisticated sentence structures, or perhaps more substantive class presentations. Whatever your weak niche is, deal with it. You can correct this problem almost 100 percent.

Above the Students' Level. Now let's see what can be done about talking **above the students' level**. This is the tougher problem. It's not as easy to say, "Do this-and-do-that." The suggestions are harder to nail down, but here are some of the more concrete ones.

Sequence Your Teaching Material

Break down your information into smaller, logical steps. In other words, sequence your ideas. This is probably the most valuable suggestion I can give you because it's the one thing teachers with this problem **don't do**. But, listen! You've got to get down to the most basic, fundamental idea of the concept you're teaching and build on that idea step by step. The information must be unfolded in a **logical**, **cumulative fashion** such that one idea leads to the next. When you start in mid-sequence, you get into trouble "talking above the students' heads." It doesn't mean that you're more demanding; it just means that you haven't figured out how to sequence your material! And that is a problem. Yes, it will take more initial planning on your part, but once you've disciplined yourself to plan and teach sequentially, you won't be talking above your students anymore and getting those blank looks.

Inflect Your Speaking Voice

Inject variation in your speech pattern, some differentiation in the high and low ranges of your voice to give more meaning to what's being said. Many times those of you who don't inflect your voices in the upper grades make it worse by talking in a monotone voice, so you sound even *more* boring! You've got to use the right inflection to connect with upper-level students, but you can't overdo it—not even at the lower level! How much is enough? The best answer I can give you is use enough so you can hold the students' interest without sounding phony. You'll need to experiment to find the proper amount for you. Just remember, the right amount of inflection is vital to communicating with students on their own level.

Question Your Students Periodically

Throw in some questions as you teach to give yourself immediate feedback. That way you can tell on the spot if you're reaching them. This means, of course, you must be able to turn information into a question and also paraphrase a question several ways to help students answer it. Work on this competency if you aren't comfortable with it. It's an excellent way to see if you're talking on the students' level.

Concluding Challenge

If this is one of your verbal deficiencies, you've got a job on your hands. It doesn't matter how competent you are in giving clear instructions, using correct terminology, or speaking good English, you'll still have bedlam if you talk down to your students; or, turn them off if you talk over their heads. So learn to speak to students on their own level if you want better control and better rapport.

LESS EFFECTIVE	MORE EFFECTIVE
When Ms. Bea Thoven introduced melodic rhythm to her first graders, she told them that they were going to learn about the long and short duration of various notation values in the melodies of familiar songs. "These children don't respond to anything," she grumbled to herself. "I know you're going to enjoy this. So sit up and look this way." Mrs. Bea Thoven wondered if the class even heard her. "Guess I'd better tell them again," she sputtered under her breath.	Ms. Bea Thoven was ready to introduce the concept of melodic rhythm to her first-grade class. "Today, children, let's learn about the rhythmic sound of a melody without its pitches. Suppose we make our hands sing 'Jingle Bells.' Ready." The children tapped "Jingle Bells" perfectly. "Did you hear the rhythm of the 'Jingle Bells' tune?" The children nodded their heads vigorously. "Now we know that a melody can have its own rhythm, can't it?" The class answered "Yes!" immediately.
Mr. Monte Verdi's eighth graders slumped further down in their seats when he turned around to explain cut-time. "Do you think we could remember to cut every note in half? Let's try. If a whole note gets four beats in 4/4, how many beats would it get in 2/2?" Mr. Monte Verdi wondered why the class was acting so bored. As he turned to the chalkboard, two boys started mimicking his explanation. "What's all the giggling about?" he snapped out. "Everyone should be counting!"	The eighth graders in Mr. Monte Verdi's music class leaned forward to hear his explanation of cut-time. They liked the way he explained things. "Here's the easiest way I know to understand cut-time. Simply cut 4/4 in half, which means all the notes will get half their value. Got it? Look at the example on the board. The half notes are worth what? Yes, one beat. And the quarter notes? Good, a half a beat, like an eighth note. Let's see if we can count and clap the example. Ready! Excellent. You're on the ball."

Using Verbal Bridges

The "verbal bridge" is my own technique and appears for the first time in print.

Definition of Verbal Bridge

A "verbal bridge" is a communicating tool used **after** each class (or individual) response involving (a) an **assessment** of the previous activity and (b) an **instruction** for the new activity. In short, it's a verbal mechanism for assessing and instructing students. (Figure 3.2 should clarify the concept for you.)

The verbal bridge **has a definite place** in the scheme of a lesson—immediately following class responses. Another point is that verbal bridging **is a recurring phenomenon**; it comes after every class or individual response.

The third point has to do with the two tasks involved. You need to understand that verbal bridging **is simply a two-step process**. The first step is evaluating (what's been done) and the second step, instructing (what will be done). That's all verbal bridging is—a procedure for assessing and instructing.

Let's translate verbal bridging into a skill. To put it simply, it's the act of assessing and instructing after each class response throughout the lesson. Be sure you understand this before you use verbal bridging; otherwise, you won't do it properly.

Value of Verbal Bridges

Verbal bridging **gives structure** to the lesson. If you look at Figure 3.2 again, you'll notice that the verbal bridge is implemented as soon as the activity (or response) is

finished. Boom! You immediately assess what the class (or the student) did and immediately instruct what to do next. You don't have to hem and haw while you figure out what to do next. Verbal bridging gives you a plan of action: Activity–Verbal Bridge–Activity–Verbal Bridge, etc. It doesn't matter if it's a class activity or an individual response, you just plug-in the verbal bridge (See Figure 3.3).

The second advantage is that verbal bridging **makes provision for assessments** throughout the lesson. So many times teachers omit the assessments in order to have more "teaching" time, but with verbal bridging, you can't omit them or push them aside. Assessing is part of the verbal bridge technique, and that's good because assessing lies at the very heart of both teaching and learning. It accomplishes two objectives: (1) it identifies the performance standard for students, and (2) it provides the necessary feedback for growth. These are crucial to the educational process and must happen!

Here's another advantage. Verbal bridging **improves momentum** in the lesson. The logical structure resulting from the application of verbal bridging makes it possible to move through a lesson more swiftly and more smoothly. You know exactly what you need to do after each response. That's why it has such an impact on pacing. There's a feeling of structure and stability, which is crucial in maintaining momentum.

One other incentive is worth noting, namely, that verbal bridging **builds**

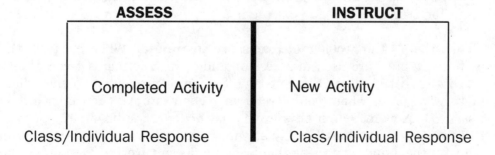

ASSESS	**INSTRUCT**
Completed Activity	New Activity
Class/Individual Response	Class/Individual Response

Figure 3.2. Example of Verbal Bridge (Two-Pronged Communicating Tool).

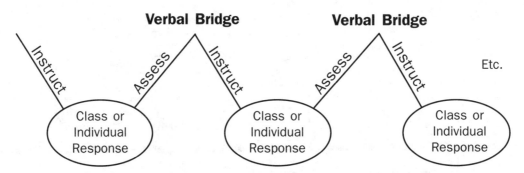

Figure 3.3. Lesson Structure Resulting from Verbal Bridging.

teacher confidence. Having a set procedure (to begin and end activities) makes you feel more secure and gradually increases the faith in your own teaching ability. You can see the results of verbal bridging before your very eyes! There's nothing like success to build confidence. If this reason doesn't "sell" you on verbal bridging, nothing will!

Problems with Verbal Bridges

There are some pitfalls connected with verbal bridging, any one of which can cause you to question its effectiveness.

A **flip attitude** is the worst. It stems primarily from not believing in verbal bridging. Those who have this attitude simply go through the motions and do it half-heartedly. They make the verbal bridging sound simple and pedantic, and give the impression they're just tolerating the whole thing. To these brash souls, I say, "Don't do it." It won't work with that kind of an attitude. Unfortunately, it's usually those with little or no teaching experience who feel this way. Too bad because they're missing out on a marvelous teaching tool!

Another problem is a **pedantic delivery**, or a very stilted and unimaginative presentation. Some teachers seem to fall into this pedantic manner more easily than others. They use that flat tone of voice and "this first" and "that next" verbiage. It's not only dull sounding, but boring as well and so predictable, like saying, for example, "That was good. Now let's go on." Then, to add insult to injury, sometimes there isn't any vocal inflection either, so the verbal bridge sounds monotonish.

Repetitive verbiage is another problem. It's the same assessment over and over, such as "You did this-and-that very well," or "I like the way everyone did so-and-so," and the same instructions, "Now let's do . . . next," or "This time we're going to . . . ." What happens is that bridging gets old very quickly, and starts sounding trite, superficial, and even mechanical. I don't know whether repetition is the result of laziness or indifference or both, but better preparation would help. After all, verbal bridging is a skill, which means you have to work at it and get a variety of verbiage for assessing and for instructing, or else you'll run the risk of repeating yourself.

Then there's the problem of **excessive pronouns**. When a lot of "that, them, they, those, it, etc." are used in assessing and/or instructing, the verbal bridge loses its pizzazz and its impact. Students don't analyze pronouns, so they don't always know to what or to whom you're referring. For example, "You did **that** perfectly" (*assessment*) "Now let's do it **this** way" (*instruction*). See how many pronouns there are? Students will just look blankly at you, and you'll stand there wondering what's wrong with them and why the verbal bridging doesn't work. If you don't want to get frustrated, quit using so many pronouns.

Suggestions for Verbal Bridging

Over the years I found myself making the same suggestions when it came to verbal bridging. If I wasn't recommending more supportive gesturing, then it was encouraging the teachers to use more emphatic inflection, or more proper nouns rather than pronouns, or else prodding them to prepare more creative comments. These suggestions make all the difference!

Use Supportive Gesturing. While this suggestion applies to speaking in general, it's a "must" for verbal bridging. I tell my teachers all the time to "talk with your hands" because it reinforces the assessment and makes it more convincing. It also clarifies the instructions. Gesturing gives the impression that you really mean what you're saying. I often ask teachers who don't use gesturing, "Don't you want to be convincing? And exciting?" Gesturing is a fantastic way of being both. Remember, you need to be as convincing and appealing as possible in your verbal bridges. Identify the gestures you use in your social life and then transfer them to your verbal bridging, but be sure you do them with more flair and precision. Sustain them momentarily; don't let them drop so quickly. That's one of the secrets of effective gesturing.

Exercise Emphatic Inflection. Use those high and low pitches, and that loud and soft volume to emphasize certain words or phrases. That's how students can tell if you're sincere. It also makes you more appealing, interesting, and "alive" in the classroom. Sometimes I have to drag out from students what they really want to say in order to get them to emphasize their words; maybe you need someone to drag it out of you, too! Better, though, that you think through the verbal bridges yourself and see what you want to emphasize. The point is, verbal bridges mustn't sound flat or monotonish. They've got to have inflection and emphasis.

Insert Proper Terms. Don't use pronouns in place of proper terms, especially in the assessment. Give the activity or object its **rightful name**. All the its, thats, those, and thems water down the intent of the assessment. Whenever I hear someone say "That was good, class," I immediately ask, "What was good?" Or after the umpteenth time, just "What's 'that'?" I said this so often to one pre-service teacher that she started doing her own correcting. She'd thrust out her hand like a police officer at an intersection and blurt out, "No, I meant to say blankety-blank." Then she'd smile at me and go on. What a time we had getting rid of the pronouns, to say nothing about the police officer gesture! But she finally got rid of both.

You've got to use proper terms in your instructions, too. Pronouns just make things confusing and unclear. So avoid giving hackneyed instruction with pronouns. Here are some of the more common culprits. See if you recognize any:

- "Let's do **that** again."
- "We'll do **it** one more time."
- "Look at **it** on the board."
- "Say **that** for me a little louder."
- "Turn to page . . . and look at **it**."
- "See **them** on that table?"

- "Go back **there** and begin with . . ."
- "Everyone, look at **these** with me."
- "Do **that** a little slower."
- "See how **it's** done?"

If your instructions are going to be explicit enough so that they can be followed on the first hearing, you've got to replace the pronouns. You may think you're being redundant, but your students won't. From their side of the fence, the instructions will make more sense and you'll sound more articulate!

Plan Varied Statements. Saying the same verbiage every time is deadly! In the first place, there isn't any excuse for it and second, it can be corrected very quickly with proper preparation or some legitimate planning beforehand as to what to say when you assess or instruct. It takes discipline to build up a repertoire of statements you can "pull out" without having to prepare them each time and to avoid repeating yourself. Look at some of the suggestions for more creative comments in Figure 3.4. Notice that both the "don't" and "do" statements are saying the same thing, but that the "do" ones are more appealing and creative and if you add just the right inflection, the statements come alive! It does take a little planning initially to develop the knack for verbal bridging, but don't discard it because of your own indifference or laziness. Give it your best shot first.

FOR ASSESSING

DON'T SAY:	BUT RATHER:
"You did . . . perfectly."	"Your clapping was excellent, class."
"I like the way you did . . ."	"I'm so proud of the way you did . . . ."
"Everyone did . . . so well."	"I saw everyone doing . . . so beautifully."
"That was very good."	"The singing was exceptionally good that time."

FOR INSTRUCTING

DON'T SAY:	BUT RATHER:
"Let's do . . . this time."	"We're going to do . . . this time!"
"Now we'll go on to page . . ."	"Do you think we can do . . . ? Let's try"
"All right, I want you to . . ."	"This time I've got something special for you."

Figure 3.4. Examples of Varied Expressions in Assessing and Instructing.

Concluding Challenge

Verbal bridging is a marvelous technique for moving from one event to the next in your lesson. Don't discard it, though, if it doesn't go well the first few times. Most likely you're doing something you shouldn't, like making repetitive statements or commenting in a pedantic way. Or, maybe it's what you're not doing, like not using any gestures or proper names. Verbal bridging works magnificently if it's done right.

LESS EFFECTIVE	**MORE EFFECTIVE**
When Mr. Otto Harp noticed the sixth graders were finished with their compositions, he looked at the clock, shoved his hands in his pockets, and shuffled back to his desk. "Okay, I see you're finished with your compositions," he mumbled while yanking at his desk drawer. "We'll listen to them tomorrow," he yelled out as the bell rang. "Well, that's gratitude for you! They didn't even hear me!" Needless to say, these weren't Mr. Otto Harp's favorite sixth graders!	As he roamed from group to group, Mr. Otto Harp saw that each group had finished their compositions. Immediately, he praised the students. "I really like what I saw of your compositions. Good work, class." He used a sweeping gesture to include everyone. "I'd like each group to play its composition for the others next class. Now take your seats quietly before the bell rings." Mr. Otto Harp was proud of the way the sixth graders followed directions.
"That wasn't too good," Ms. Cora Net snapped at her second graders. "We're going to do it again." When the children clapped the melodic rhythm the same way, she shouted, "No, not that way. I wanted you to do it this way." Then she told them they needed to listen better. "How many times do I have to tell them what to do?" she wondered. "I spoke English, didn't I?"	Ms. Cora Net wasn't pleased with her second graders' clapping of the tune for "Jingle Bells." "I didn't see everyone's hands clapping correctly that time. Let's try clapping softer with two fingers, okay?" This time the children did it perfectly! Ms. Cora Net praised them for listening more closely and clapping better. She learned long ago that using specific labels helped children respond better.

Projecting Voice When Reciting With Class ───────────

This isn't one of the verbal skills you hear talked about very much because it's never been recognized as a skill! But that doesn't alter the fact that projecting the teacher voice during class recitations is a specific skill. It belongs to that select group (of skills) that helps to refine the act of teaching.

Definition of Projecting Voice

"Projecting" is raising the dynamic level of your speaking voice when reciting jointly with students so that you can "lead" them with your voice, especially on the first few tries. This helps the students respond better right off the bat and gives them more confidence because there's someone to follow. If you want a simpler explanation, think of it as turning up the volume and using more belly-breath so that you can be heard over the class.

You've got to be innately aware, however, of the need to project your voice, especially when the class is (a) learning new words, (b) reciting from the board or book, or (c) chanting an exercise. That's the key to this task—sensing when and where to project it. Without that gut reaction, it doesn't happen. You won't just "do it" on the spot, not unless you sense the need.

There's one other point. I'm not saying project your voice on every response; that would be counterproductive. You use this "leading" tactic only on initial responses—on first tries, not every try.

Reasons for Projecting Voice

The first reason will surprise you, but it's probably the most convincing reason of all. Projecting your voice on initial responses **motivates the students**. The energy, the inflection, and the expressions you display are all powerful stimulators. They get

the students "going" like nothing else, which is worth noting because students aren't always ready and willing to go on the first try, are they? By projecting your voice, you have an effective way of getting them started and motivating them.

Another good reason is that it **nurtures confidence in students**, almost immediately. As soon as they hear the teacher's voice, their insecurity and their fear of failing start to wilt. They feel more like jumping in and trying when they can follow the teacher, and not sit back and watch. But probably the most important happening is that they feel able and confident.

The third reason is that projecting your voice during class recitations **sharpens participation**. Granted, it's an obvious outcome, but it's still worth noting. Students always respond better when they have a model, particularly when it comes to verbalizing. They'll try to imitate, follow your inflection and your enunciation, and sound just like you! They'll recite more accurately and more enthusiastically. A good teacher model is the key to sharper participation.

The last reason is the clincher! A projected voice **reflects expectations**, the teacher's expectations, that is. Your voice sets the standard for the students. It "says" to them, by example, "This is what I expect from you—or this is the correct way to do it." How else are students supposed to know what you want if they can't hear you? Unless your voice projects (on those initial responses) and models the standard, the class response will be puny.

Projecting the voice, then, is essential for the classroom teacher in reciting situations, especially on the first go-round. You can (a) generate motivation, (b) instill confidence, (c) sharpen participation, and (d) set expectations, just by being the lead.

Problems With Projecting Voice

There are some problems, though, with projecting the voice. To have any success with this skill, you've got to be aware of the pitfalls, and savvy enough to avoid them so you don't become a victim.

Being unaware is by far the most serious pitfall. It's amazing how many teachers have never heard of doing this! They've never felt inclined to do it instinctively, especially when they model in almost every other activity, like marching, tapping, playing, etc. No wonder I get confused looks when I ask teachers to project more when they're reciting with their class; they don't know what I'm talking about!

This reminds me of the time I brought up the subject with a defensive teacher after watching her fourth-grade music lesson. When I suggested she might want to try projecting her voice to get the class to respond better, she inhaled a stream of air through flaring nostrils and glared at me with bulging eyes. "But I don't want to shout at my students. I want them to say it by themselves!" she snorted. You'd think she was sitting in the electric chair the way she was clutching the arms and pushing herself back. What a time I had explaining the technique to her and convincing her to use it! But she's not alone; a lot of teachers don't know about projecting the voice during class recitations.

The other pitfalls have to do with the way the projecting is done. **Lack of proper projection** comes first. I have said to many teachers, "Project more. The students can't hear you." The response I usually get back is, "But I thought I was talking loud enough!" It doesn't matter what the teachers hear, but what the *students* hear. That's the key! Plus using enough breath. Lack of breath support is a chronic problem when it comes to reciting with the class.

Another problem is the **misplacement of the speaking pitch**. Many times the pitch isn't high or low enough when reciting with students. You can't tell the teacher's voice from the students', even when the teacher's is more projected. There's no difference in the pitch level. The voices blend together. This is a costly pitfall because the whole effort goes up in smoke. The students can't hear the teacher, and the teacher, sorry to say, can't "lead" the students.

Guidelines for Projecting

Whether you're having trouble projecting your voice, or if you're not sure projecting really "works," check out these suggestions.

Do the Projecting Immediately. Don't wait or hesitate, or forget. You've got to project your voice as soon as the students start reacting. They need that initial jolt to get them going and to know what you expect, so be ready!

Project Your Voice Sufficiently. You've got to raise the volume of your voice enough so that the students can hear you above the class. The whole point of projecting is to provide an immediate model they can hear in order to recite in a more acceptable manner to meet your objectives.

Exert Verbal Energy Consistently. You need to verbalize with vim and vigor, and be enthusiastic. That's crucial for motivating students. Your voice can't sound flat and lifeless. It's got to be energetic to be effective.

Adjust the Voice Level Properly. Be sure the pitch level of your voice doesn't "mix in" with the students'. If it does, raise it or lower it. Your voice needs to be audible and distinct, not just in volume, but in pitch. If it isn't, it can't "lead" or be a model.

Use Facial Expressions Appropriately. Your expressions make or break the projecting effort. Your face must genuinely reflect what you're saying and what you're doing. It's an essential part of the projecting. Use your eyes, eyebrows, mouth, and head to reinforce your verbiage.

Use Verbal Projection Instinctively. You need to "feel" those times when you can lower your voice and let the students "go" on their own, and when you need to jump in, especially on the outset of the recitation. That's when the skill is really working—when you can jump in and out of projecting your voice. But you've got to be tuned-in to the way students are responding.

Concluding Challenge

You may still be skeptical about this skill, especially if it's new to you. But start projecting your voice during recitations and follow the suggestions. See what a difference it makes in the way the class responds.

For those of you who are ready to toss it aside, give it another try. But this time, make sure you cover all the bases with the guidelines. Projecting your voice in class recitations is too important to ignore.

LESS EFFECTIVE	MORE EFFECTIVE
"I want everyone to march to the beat," Ms. P. Ano said to her kindergarteners. "And say 'march, march' while we're marching." When the children started to march in place, Ms. P. Ano marched with them and mumbled "march, march" under her breath. "I can't hear you saying 'march,'" she yelled out. "Let's try it again so I can hear you." But this time she was so concerned about the children that she forgot to chant herself. "We don't chant and march too well, do we?" she grumbled.	When Ms. P. Ano instructed her kindergarten children to march in place and chant "march, march," she reminded them to listen and watch her. As soon as the recording started, Ms. P. Ano chanted loudly so that the children could follow. Since her voice was lower than the students', she had no trouble being heard. The children joined in immediately. Soon they were marching and chanting as vigorously as Ms. P. Ano. "You marched and chanted to the beat just like soldiers. I'm proud of you."

Mr. O. Beau planned to do rhythmic counting with his sixth graders. After the instructions, he gave a "Ready, count" and started counting with the class, but not so anyone beyond the first row could hear him. "What's going on here? I can hardly hear you. Can't you count?" Even the second time around, he didn't project his voice. Students started snickering as the counting trailed off and got less after the third or fourth measure. "You're never going to learn how to count if you don't stop laughing," he bellowed out. "What's the problem?" Nobody said a word!

When the sixth graders were ready to do the rhythmic counting, Mr. O. Beau cautioned them to listen and read carefully. When they started, he counted with them loud enough so that everyone could hear, even those in the back. Mr. O. Beau's voice was much lower sounding than the class's so that it was easy for the students to hear him. Their counting was crisp and clear, and just as rhythmic as Mr. O. Beau's counting. As the class continued, Mr. O. Beau pulled back with his voice. "They're doing fine on their own," he said to himself. "I don't need to chant so loudly now."

Emphasizing Important Words and Ideas

Another high-priority skill is that you **must** be able to emphasize important words and ideas when you teach. That's one of the essential ways of communicating with your students and getting them to listen. Emphasizing words is every bit as important in teaching as speaking distinctly or assessing precisely. Unless you can stress words and ideas comfortably and competently, you won't communicate as effectively or impact as strongly.

Definition of Emphasizing

Webster defines "emphasizing" as the act of making something prominent, or stressing some concept or thought deemed important. Both definitions hit the nail on the head.

To emphasize some word or idea while in the throes of teaching means that the teacher makes that thought more prominent, or obvious, than other verbiage. The teacher stresses it more to indicate it has greater weight.

The definition implies that the person emphasizing must know what to emphasize. It seems obvious, but usually teachers don't emphasize properly because they *don't know* what to emphasize!

Problems With Emphasizing

The worst problem is **not emphasizing at all**. You don't have to look too hard or too long to find teachers who don't emphasize any of their words. These teachers are not just boring, they're ineffective! They don't give any clue as to what's important—which means they make learning more difficult and less interesting. Either they're not sure of what's important or else not secure with the technique.

In the middle of the spectrum is the **half-hearted emphasizing**, or those half-baked efforts where the inflection is turned up just enough for the students to notice but not "hear." It's not that there's no attempt to emphasize; the problem is that it's not convincing enough!

Then there's the problem of **emphasizing too much**. Some teachers just get carried away. They think everything they're saying is important. These teachers lean on every other word and reinforce them by nodding their heads. Students just tune out when this happens; it's too overwhelming for students when too many words have too much intensity. They can't tell what's important and what's not.

But the problem isn't always emphasizing too many words; sometimes it's **emphasizing with too much gusto**. It makes the teacher sound melodramatic and even overbearing, like an umpire calling "out" all the time. I remember a teacher who was always belting out the word(s) she thought were important to the point that it was obnoxious! For example, the day she was teaching the concept of loud, she nearly jumped out of her skin every time she used the word "loud." Emphasizing was never meant to be a shouting match, and when it is, it's no longer a teaching tool.

Another problem is **emphasizing without any gestures or expressions**. The teachers look like zombies. They don't use one bit of gesturing or even the slightest expression. Unless some gestures and expressions are used, emphasizing loses its punch and looks ridiculous.

Suggestions for Emphasizing

Let's start with the different ways you can emphasize important ideas. Some suggestions are for those of you who aren't in the habit of emphasizing; others are for those who just want some help.

Use Inflection. Try raising or lowering the pitch of your voice on those important words or ideas. Change the speed of your words, and be a little theatrical sounding, too. Getting the "right" pitch and speed will depend upon the particular word or idea. You'll know exactly what to do if you follow your instincts—and don't get "cold feet."

Try Repetition. Repeat the important word or thought. In fact, repeat it several times and pause slightly in between. But *never* repeat the same way. Change the inflection, the dynamic level, or the speed—make it different the second time. Change your gesture and expression as well. It'll make your point.

Rephrase. Reword a phrase or a thought when you say it again. Paraphrasing can strengthen the original idea and even clarify. Do the same for a specific word by using another term or several terms. You'll have to work at this one because it takes a bit of doing to rephrase ideas on the spot and to build up a working vocabulary. It's worth the effort, though. Here are some examples:

ORIGINAL STATEMENT	*REPHRASED STATEMENT*
"If you listen carefully, you can hear the accented beats."	"You can't whisper or talk if you want to hear the strong beats!"
"When there's an opening theme followed by a different second theme, you have a two-part form."	"A two-part form in music has an opening A theme and a contrasting B theme."
"A rhythm pattern with a short-long-short sound (♪ ♩ ♪) is called a 'syncopated pattern.' "	"Remember, a syncopated pattern has a short-long-short sound, doesn't it?"

Use Questioning. Turn a statement into a question. Phrase it so that it only needs a one- or two-word response. You can do this with an individual student or the whole class. But remember, repeat the answer if it's from an individual, and if you ask the whole class, coordinate the collective response by taking in a prep breath and giving a slight nod. In other words, "conduct" the class's response. See the following examples:

ORIGINAL STATEMENT	*REPHRASED QUESTION*
"Within a melody we have musical sentences that are referred to as 'phrases.' "	"What do we call the musical sentences we hear in a melody?" (*Answer*: phrases)
"The dotted quarter (♩.) gets one full beat plus half the next beat or a beat-and-a half."	"How many beats do we give to a dotted quarter note?" (*Answer*: one-and-a-half)
"In some songs we sing, part of the melody moves in an upward direction, like an escalator!"	"In what direction can a part of a melody move in some songs?" (*Answer*: upward)

Let's say you **do** use all these tactics, but you're still not very effective. You don't feel you make an impact or get your point across. If so, consider the following tips:

Use Proper Stressing. You really have to "lean" on the words or phrases you want to emphasize and use more "oomph" on them; otherwise, they won't sound emphatic enough. Push down more too, so you feel inside that downward pull the moment you exert the oomph. Don't be afraid of force! You've got to have the right amount of stress on words to make the emphasizing obvious.

Apply Appropriate Inflecting. You need to put those dips and peaks in the pitch of your voice when you're emphasizing, like scooping up on one thought and sliding down on another, or drawing out the pitch as when you say "sloow" and "looow." Also change the speed of your words. Drag out a word here, and speed up a few there. Don't speak at the same rate when you're trying to emphasize some idea. Vary the speed as well as the pitch on the words you're emphasizing.[7]

Maintain Visual Monitoring. You simply must keep your eyes on the class when you're emphasizing something. Don't look down at the floor, in the book, or at the board. Look at the students and make eye contact as you scan the class. It may well be that you **do** stress and inflect to the max, but if you don't keep that eyeball contact with the students, you'll checkmate your own effort. You need that visual bonding to put a convincing touch on what you're saying.

Exercise Suitable Expressions/Gesturing. You'll want to use the "right" facial expressions and bodily gestures when you emphasize your ideas to put the finishing touches on the task. If you haven't already, work on a repertoire of facial expressions. Learn how to change your eyes, mouth, and eyebrows to express surprise, pleasure, disappointment, etc. (See "Using Facial Expressions" in Chapter 2.) When working on your gesturing, stick with the ones you normally use. Role play in front of a mirror to be sure your gesturing is larger and more definitive for teaching. And be a bit theatrical—add a little flair to your gesturing.

Exert Careful Planning. The best way to avoid getting tongue-tied or muddle-headed when you emphasize something is to prepare. There's no short-cut in learning to emphasize. You've got to select your concept(s) and/or skills, and then decide *what* you need to emphasize in your procedures and *how* you'll emphasize this information. Careful planning is the only way to success when it comes to emphasizing.

Reasons for Emphasizing

Emphasizing is the primary way of letting students know which ideas are important and what they need to know.

It's simply not enough to state an important idea only once or to say it just in passing. You've got to **reinforce** the ideas and make it **obvious**.

Another reason is that emphasizing helps to **maintain the student's attention**. It gives you that little extra edge in keeping them on-task and keeping them "with you" longer, especially when the emphasizing is done effectively.

Concluding Challenge

How good are you at emphasizing your words? Do you do it automatically? If not, you should. You'd be so much more effective as a teacher. Don't hide behind the excuse that you don't know what to emphasize because by planning more carefully, you'll know what to stress.

---

[7]Highet, Gilbert. *The Art of Teaching* (New York: Alfred A. Knopf Publishers, 1950), p. 115.

LESS EFFECTIVE	**MORE EFFECTIVE**
When she was reviewing quarter and eighth notes with her second graders, Ms. Brahms vaguely reminded the children that quarter notes were longer than eighth notes. And that in the next lesson they would hear more quarters and eighths. None of them seemed to care what she said as she lined up the children to leave. "They aren't very alert," Ms. Brahms thought to herself.	Ms. Brahms finished her lesson with a review. Holding up the quarter and eighth note cards, she emphasized that the quarter note was LONGER. When she said "longer," Ms. Brahms raised up the quarter-note card. "Which note is longer?" she asked. The children responded quickly. "That's right, the quarter note. We'll continue with our quarter and eighth notes tomorrow."
Mr. Shubert's fifth-grade class followed their call charts dealing with like and contrasting phrases while listening to the tape. "We can call the like phrases 'A' phrases, and the contrasting ones, 'B'. That's another way of identifying the form of the song. All songs have a form." With that, he asked the class to follow the call chart again. He was puzzled a short time later when the class didn't know what to call a "like" phrase.	After Mr. Shubert's class finished reading the call chart with the tape, he told the class that the like phrases were called "A" and the contrasting, "B". Then he reworded it. "Like and contrasting phrases can be given letter names, so that like phrases are 'A' phrases and contrasting phrases 'B' phrases." He paused a moment and then instructed the class to listen and mark down the "A" and "B" phrases.

Applying Timely Pauses

One of the best ways to punctuate your speech, besides emphasizing words verbally, is to use timely pauses. Silence can be even more powerful than words.[8] Unfortunately, there's a lot of teachers who don't know how to pause. They feel uncomfortable stopping, even for a moment, primarily because they haven't been taught how to use pausing. But that's starting to change. Educational leaders are beginning to study the act of pausing as a verbal skill,[9] and teachers are starting to recognize the power of pausing in their own teaching.

Description of Pausing

Probably the best description is the one that calls pausing "planned silence."[10] Pausing is an intentional stillness, a premeditated quietness; in other words, a deliberate act. Talking is stopped purposely for the sake of letting the silence impact on the spoken words.

Shostak referred to timely silences as "pregnant pauses."[11] It says that a pause can feel like a heavy silence, a suspenseful moment, or a thoughtful hesitation. It's a moment filled with the essence of what's just been said. That perceived essence is an important part of the pausing concept.

There's one more expression that has to do with the length of the pause, or what we call the "duration of pausing." There's no specific time limit given. In some cases, the duration is longer; sometimes it's shorter depending on the nature of the

---

[8]Highet, Gilbert. *The Art of Teaching* (New York: Alfred A. Knopf Publishers, 1950), p. 118.
[9]Shostak, Robert. *Lesson Presentation Skills* (Lexington, MA: D. C. Heath Co., 1977), p. 139.
[10]*Ibid.*, p. 139.
[11]*Ibid.*, p. 139.

thought. The decision rests solely in the hands of the one who is pausing. It's an intuitive duration.

Thus, if you're going to use pausing effectively, you've got to keep in mind that it involves (a) a deliberate effort, (b) an impactful moment, and (c) an intuitive duration.

Reasons for Pausing

There are good reasons for using the pause as one of your communicating tactics. By using timely pauses you can[12]:

Emphasize Important Items. Pausing briefly after an important point allows students to concentrate on that point. The last idea you express just before pausing is usually the idea students ponder upon during the pause. That's why a timely placed silence is such an excellent reinforcing tool.

Give Students Prep Time. By taking time to pause momentarily after a question, you give students some thinking space, or some breathing room to answer. Likewise, when you wait a few seconds after an instruction, it gives students a digesting period—or time to take in the directions—and gets them mentally prepared for the event. Pauses often make the difference between a mediocre response and a great response.

Capture Students' Attention. An appropriately timed pause can "grab" the attention of drifting students and retrieve their concentration. It's an excellent substitute for reprimanding or changing the lesson. A moment of silence can jolt the student's curiosity like nothing else! Pausing is golden when it comes to capturing attention.

Create Aura in the Classroom. The power of a timely pause is awesome in generating excitement, building suspense, or filling the air with expectation. A whole new aura can be created by a moment of silence after a challenging remark! The fact that it's a readily available tool makes it all the more appealing for generating an aura.

Show Disapproval for Unwanted Behavior. The pause is your best ally in thwarting unwanted behavior. There's no better way to register disapproval than to suddenly stop talking. It's mightier than the spoken word! Not only is your displeasure transmitted swiftly and silently, but without any confrontation. Pausing is a marvelous management tool.

Separate Information for Understanding. Pausing is also a logical way for breaking down information, separating it, and making it easier to grasp and clearer to understand. Pausing makes it obvious that you've completed a particular concept.[13] At the same time, it helps structure your presentation.

Problems With Pausing

Duration heads the list of problems. Pauses are either too long or too short. It all comes down to intuitive sense, plus experience. But initially it's with intuition and not being able to sense the "right" length. Sometimes it's because the teacher is new

---

[12]*Ibid.*, p. 139.
[13]Highet, *The Art of Teaching*, p. 118.

and concentrating on too many other "things." Other times it's due to a lack of confidence in one's own judgment. Either way, it creates a problem.

Placement is another problem. Some teachers just don't have a feel for pausing, so they stop at the weirdest times. They pause for the sake of pausing, which makes the pause sound forced and contrived. The question I always ask is, "Do you know what you want to emphasize?" Most times, they don't. So the problem is not enough preparation or not thinking out beforehand what needs to be stressed where. Without planning, pausing will always be a problem. The sad part is it doesn't need to be!

Content of the pause is a problem. Teachers often pause when nothing of earth-shattering importance has been said to merit the silence or no instruction has been given. Instead of making certain there's something to emphasize, they pause at the drop of a hat and waste a gesture. What you have is pausing abuse.

Omission, of course, is the obvious problem. Too many teachers avoid pausing altogether. Some just don't know how to pause, in which case, they need some instruction. Others, like the beginning teachers, are simply afraid of what will happen if they stop talking![14]

Suggestions for Pausing

The following "how-to" tips include some practical advice for almost everyone: (a) those who don't know how to pause, (b) those who are too afraid to even try, and (c) those who want to know how to do it more effectively.

Identify Important Ideas Beforehand. What you've got to do before you get up to teach is decide what information you want to emphasize. That means you have to plan ahead. It's the only way you're going to know for sure what needs to be stressed. So do your homework and be prepared—down to the nitty-gritty of knowing when and where. Also practice in front of a mirror. This can do a lot towards making you feel more capable, more effective, and less fearful. Preparation is your first priority!

Keep Duration of Pause Fitting. It's hard to say how long you should hold a pause. Three or four seconds might be fine after a comment, but not for a question. In either case, seconds last an eternity when you're pausing. You'll need to depend on both your experience and your intuition. Duration generally boils down to instinct time anyway, so don't fret if you haven't used pausing before. But let's suppose that you need to be more confident about your instinct. Then try the following. Observe closely how much you rely on intuition in your private life, and how you respond to it, such as when something "tells" you to wait one more minute, call right now, or turn left here! Then loosen up and try to respond the same way in the classroom. Your instinct will "tell" you.

I always tell a particular story when I'm talking about duration in pausing. I had just finished conferencing with a student-teacher about her long pauses and telling her that I wanted to see some improvement on my next visit. When I returned, she came flying up and blurted out all excitedly, "I've got it! I figured out how to get my pauses shorter." Naturally I was curious. But I wasn't ready for what I saw. She would suddenly freeze in her tracks, clamp her mouth shut, and stare out in space like she was a statue. Then pow! She'd jump in like nothing happened. Even

---

[14]Shostak, *Lesson Presentation Skills*, p. 139.

the students were stupefied. Know what she was doing in that trance? She was counting up to six. Why six? Because it "felt right," she said. I'll admit her pausing was shorter, but it was also off the wall—and I told her so.

Maintain Eye Contact Throughout. Part of the mystique of pausing is the eyeballing that goes with it. You've got to keep your eyes on the students. Not on the floor, the window, the chalkboard, or on one student—not unless the pause is for reprimanding. Keep that eye contact going the whole time. And one more thing: look at faces, not the tops of heads or the noses, but right in the eyes. Then scan the whole class. Run your eyes up one row and down the next, or make a slow sweeping glance from side to side while still maintaining contact. The impact of eyeballing, together with the silence, is what makes pausing so effective. If eyeballing is hard for you, practice it in your social life, and read what the professional literature says about eye contact. You've got to be good at eyeballing when you pause!

Use Expressive Tactics Appropriately. You need to accentuate your pauses with expressiveness. You just can't stand there. You've got to use facial expressions—sometimes subtle ones and other times, conspicuous ones. For example, at times all you need to do is raise your eyebrows; or purse your lips or pull them to one side; or tilt your head forward, backward, to the right or the left; or squint your eyes or open them wide, like saucers. Sometimes a combination of these is needed. Other times, you may feel the need to use a full-fledged expression to create the effect you want. Use the full gamut of facial ploys with your pausing, depending, of course, on what you're saying.

It's the same with gesturings. With some pausings, you can simply (a) extend an upward palm, (b) raise a shoulder—with an extended palm, or (c) point a finger. But don't forget the facial touch. With other pauses, you'll need to be more dramatic and use larger, more theatrical-looking gestures. Also, sustain your gestures momentarily to give them a chance to have an effect. Remember, expressive tactics need to be done properly.

Execute In-Between Pauses Correctly. If you're going to fragment information with pauses, you'll have to pause at the right times, be sure the material is organized into small complete ideas, and make it clear that you have finished an idea.[15] That requires: (1) knowing your material cold, and (2) planning mentally or in writing how you'll fragment the information and where you'll pause. I like Highet's formula: " . . . Pause only after you have uttered a fragment of thought big enough to be understood and examined by itself."[16] Thus, a good yardstick for pausing is make it a clear-cut signal for a completed idea.

Use Pausing Ploy Sparingly. You'll need to be careful not to overuse the pause. It can become "old hat" stuff very quickly. Think of it as a special effect, and use it only for stressing something very important. That doesn't mean you can't pause after asking a question, seeing a disturbance, or completing an idea. These are utilitarian uses that have an obvious purpose—even to the students. Use them as needed, but save the "real" pausing ploy for those important declarations.

Concluding Challenge

Do you use the pause in your own teaching? Are you good at it? If not, do you want to improve? You can if you consider these suggestions. For those of you who don't feel comfortable with pausing or don't know how to get started, study the guidelines. There are enough do's and don'ts there to steer you in the right direction. You need to work at it so that pausing becomes a vital part of your verbalizing skills.

---

[15]Highet, *The Art of Teaching*, p. 110.
[16]*Ibid.*, p. 105.

LESS EFFECTIVE

"Class, listen now for the long and short sounds in this melody." Walking over to the tape player, Ms. Rossini commented over her shoulder, "All melodies are composed of long sounds and short sounds." And without turning around, she started the music. "I shouldn't be hearing any talking," she barked out as she adjusted the volume. "You're not going to hear the long-short sounds."

Mr. Scarlotti was ready to introduce chord construction to his fifth graders. Looking at the chord card he was holding, he pointed to the notes and mumbled, "See how chords are built by taking every other note?" Then he constructed a chord at the board and, without looking at the class, said, "That's how a chord is built. See that?" Without waiting he went right on to another chord.

MORE EFFECTIVE

Ms. Rossini continued, "Now let's listen to the long and short sounds in this song, children." Then she said in a very deliberate tone of voice, "All our melodies have long and short sounds." With that, Ms. Rossini tilted her head back and paused for a moment while scanning the faces. Still keeping her eyes on the children, she took a few steps backward and said, "Now listen and watch me." Then she started the tape and began to demonstrate.

"We're ready to talk about chord construction," Mr. Scarlotti told his excited fifth graders. Holding a chord card, he looked at the class and said very slowly, "Chords are built by taking every other note above the bottom note." Quickly he outlined the tones with a pointer. Then, he paused and scanned the class. "Let's build a chord together," he continued while keeping his eyes on the class.

Speaking Fluently

When it comes to verbal skills, speaking fluently is probably the one that teachers value the most—and need the most. Fluent speech is the **epitome** of verbal proficiency—the final product. Those who can speak in a fluent manner are held in high esteem. But, it shouldn't come as any shock to learn that many teachers don't speak as fluently as they should! That's why we need to examine this important verbal skill.

Definition of Fluent Speaking

To "speak fluently" simply means to express yourself in a smooth, flowing manner; to speak in an articulate way without any hesitation or any misuse of grammar or vague vocabulary. It's a proficient speaking style.

But there's more to fluent speaking than what's been said; there are other skills that go into it as well, including:

- proper sentence structure
- clear connected thoughts
- recognizable explanatory expressions
- appropriate age-level vocabulary
- right choice of words[17]
- suitable speaking pace

---

[17]McIntyre, Donald, Gordon MacLeod, and Roy Griffiths, eds. *Investigation of Microteaching* (London, England: Croom Helm Publishers, 1977), pp. 50–51.

- rational pausing technique
- correct English grammar

Significance of Fluent Speaking

First, fluent speech **indicates that the teacher is more competent** in a host of verbal skills. You can't speak in a smooth, comfortable manner without using the other tactics that contribute to the fluency: (a) a good command of English grammar, (b) a large repertoire of needful words, and (c) a knowledgeable application of expressiveness. In short, it requires expertise—not just in one, but a whole batch of skills. That's why fluency is a valid measure of your own verbal ability.

Another reason fluency is important is that smooth speech **holds the class's attention better**. There's a steady flow in the verbiage that makes the lesson easy to follow, as well as a precise selection of words that makes it simpler to understand. Plus, there's usually an appealing application of expressive gesturing that makes the presentation even more enjoyable. Too, there usually aren't any idiosyncrasies.

There's a third reason: fluent speaking **achieves the objectives more easily**. Most of the time, fluent speech goes hand in hand with a clear presentation. Thoughts are more connected, verbiage is more precise, and the emphasizing is more pronounced. Even the tempo of one's talking is more suitable. These are the crucial factors that clarify a presentation and make it possible for students to "get" the information quicker and easier. The upshot is that the objectives are achieved more readily.

Pitfalls in Fluent Speech

Unfortunately, not every teacher speaks fluently. That's the obvious problem. There are pitfalls galore to keep a teacher from speaking fluently. Some foul up the work in a second; others become an ongoing distraction. It doesn't matter which, both disrupt fluency with equal success. Let's take a look at some of the pitfalls and the remedies.

Too Many "Ers" and "Uhs". Ending sentences with meaningless "ers" and "uhs" is one of the major pitfalls in speaking more fluently. It not only breaks the flow of verbiage, but can drive students crazy as well. What's even worse, some teachers think that "ers" and "uhs" give the impression that they're "thinking on their feet." What it really does is make them sound fuddy-duddy[18] and look silly. **Remedy: Omit "ers" and "uhs."** You've got a job here! It's hard to stop "ering" and "uhing," so you'll have to discipline yourself. Use a tape recorder or fellow teacher to monitor your speech. Then accept the results. Don't rationalize them; otherwise, you won't make an effort to stop. You stop by anticipating omissions and by being ready to stop the "ering" or "uhing" before you say it.

Too Many Unfinished Sentences. Letting unfinished sentences hang in mid-air and reformulating them halfway through puts a wrench in the works every time.[19] Still, a lot of teachers are guilty of this. They wreck their own fluency by not finishing their thoughts. **Remedy: Finish Sentences**. There's only one way to make yourself do this: keep tabs on yourself. Start making a conscious effort to complete every sentence you begin. In other words, use some willpower, not excuses like (a) "I

---

[18]Highet, *The Art of Teaching*, p. 104.
[19]McIntyre, MacLeod, and Griffiths, *Investigations of Microteaching*, p. 50.

ER, AH, UH...

think faster than I talk," (b) "I get better ideas on the spot," (c) "I just can't get back to finish a sentence; I think of too much to say in between." These won't wash. You've got to put demands on yourself and keep the pressure on until you've got the problem licked.

Too Many Untimely Pauses. Taking *unnecessary* pauses is another stumbling block. It creates an embarrassing gap, interrupts the flow, and chops the presentation into small, unorganized pieces. Sooner or later these pauses become a source of irritation and disruption. **Remedy: Pause Wisely.** You've got to pause in the right places and at the right time to make it "work." *Plan* before you teach, particularly if you're having problems with pausing. Here's a simple formula: **First**, determine what information you want to stress; **second**, decide which ideas deserve a pause; and **third**, settle upon when and where to apply the pause(s). As your technique gets better, let your instincts help out. Both preparation and intuition are necessary for pausing wisely. (See the previous section, "Applying Timely Pauses.")

Not Enough Link Verbiage. Excluding words or phrases that lead naturally to an explanation is another reason for a lack of fluency. When you leave out such words as "because," "so that," or "in order to" (which lead to the reason for some statement or question), you destroy the train of thought and the logical flow of the idea.[20] To put it bluntly, you short circuit your fluency. **Remedy: Remember Link Verbiage**. Preparation is a wasted effort if you don't remember to use "link words":

---

[20]McIntyre, MacLeod, and Griffiths, *Investigations of Microteaching*, p. 51.

- Because . . .
- The result of . . .
- The cause of . . .
- By . . .
- Therefore . . .

- So that . . .
- The purpose of . . .
- The consequence is . . .
- The reason is . . .
- Here's why . . .[21]

You simply must remember to use them! If you can't remember, give yourself some help by using note cards with the words written out. Select just one or two until you get better at it. In other words, train yourself!

Too Many Vague Words or Expressions. Using vague words or expressions is probably the most common problem of all! Words and expressions such as "about," "a lot of," and "nice" lack precise meaning.[22] As a result, they rob your speech of its clarity—and without clarity there's no fluency. **Remedy: Use Specific Words or Expressions**. The solution is obvious: avoid vague verbiage. Whenever possible, use specific wording that (a) utilizes the proper names for any material, activity, or equipment (calling it by its rightful name), (b) selects the most appropriate adjectives and adverbs, and (c) gives the precise descriptors in your expressions, such as saying "a large percentage of . . ." instead of "a whole lot of . . . ." Use a dictionary and thesaurus, if necessary, and be sure the verbiage you choose is age-level appropriate as well.[23]

Not Enough Expressiveness. This is the most understated problem of the lot. Without appropriate expressions and gestures, words sound dull. Sometimes it's nothing more than this dullness or lack of expression that kills the flow, so you can't ignore expressions and gestures and expect to sound fluent. **Remedy: More Expressive Action**. You need a plan of action because expressiveness is hard to cultivate. It can be done, though, if you're patient and persistent. **First**, videotape yourself to get a baseline on your own expressiveness. See what facial expressions and bodily gesturings you do effectively, and which new ones you could add. **Second**, practice being expressive. Get in front of a mirror or camera and role play until the expressions and gestures start to feel natural and begin to come without your having to think. That won't happen overnight; but stick with it. **Third**, observe the students' reaction. If you can keep their attention and maintain the momentum, you'll know you've been successful. **Four**, reevaluate yourself periodically so that you don't get complacent. Keep a close check on yourself. Every so often, add new expressions and gestures to your repertoire.

Concluding Challenge

If you're not a fluent speaker, isn't it time you were? It will take time and effort, but the rewards are worth it. When you've succeeded, you can take pleasure in knowing that you are, indeed, a more articulate and effective teacher.

---

[21]*Ibid.*

[22]McIntyre, MacLeod, and Griffiths, *Investigations of Microteaching*, p. 51.

[23]*Ibid.*

LESS EFFECTIVE	MORE EFFECTIVE
"The meter in any piece of music—uh—can change, which means that—uh—the music has—uh—shifting meter," explained Mr. Al Toe to the sixth graders. "Uhhh, let's say the song starts in 2/3 and—uh—changes to 3/4—uh—in the chorus." The buzzing got louder as he spoke. "I'm tired of this class never listening while I'm talking," he chided. "I'm not going to—uhm—say it again." With that, the class started to clap. Mr. Al Toe was taken aback. "How come they're clapping?" he wondered.	To introduce shifting meters, Mr. Al Toe told the sixth graders, "Any musical selection can have two (or more) different meters. The meter can shift, in other words." Walking to the board, he gave an illustration. "Suppose a song begins in 2/4 so that the metric rhythm has a strong-weak, strong-weak, etc., sound, and then switches to 3/4 or strong-weak-weak sound." Mr. Al Toe pointed to the example and paused. He noticed that every eye was on the board. He complimented the class and continued.
"Okay, class, we'll start our . . . , just look quickly at the board first." Then Ms. Sue ZaPhone glanced up at the class. "We're going to clap the rhythm and . . . Don't rush now. Keep the beat steady." When the class clapped incorrectly, she waved it to a halt. "You didn't hold the dotted quarter—I mean you've got to hold this note a beat-and-a-half. Remember? We'll try it again to . . . ready?" Ms. Sue ZaPhone was annoyed because the class looked so confused.	Ms. Sue ZaPhone opened the fourth-grade lesson by saying, "Let's begin with a rhythmic round; look at the pattern on the board." Then she told the class, "I'd like you to clap the two-bar figure and be sure to hold the dotted quarter for a beat-and-a-half. Like this." After demonstrating, she said, "Now you try it. Ready." When the class clapped it correctly, Ms. Sue ZaPhone praised the response. "You're on the ball today! That was great."

Eliciting Responses by Telling, Not Asking

Beginning teachers, here's a skill you've just got to use. Telling, rather than asking, when it comes to eliciting student participation is a crucial teaching tactic. The teacher has to be "the boss" in the classroom, and the one who "gets the ball rolling." That's why you need to be competent in the art of telling, especially if you want to control your class and keep it rolling.

Definition of "Telling" Approach

The "telling approach" is used in the process of initiating participation and comes right before the students' response.

There's no hidden meaning here; I'm simply making a distinction between **informing** students and **asking** students when it comes to their participation. With the telling approach, you announce (or inform) what the students will be doing. It's not a matter of asking if they want to; it's a matter of telling them.

Actually, the telling is nothing more than an instructional statement, the instructional part of the verbal bridge. (See "Using Verbal Bridges" earlier in this chapter.) Thus, telling is just another word for announcing or informing; the meaning is straightforward.

Reasons for "Telling" Approach

There are five good reasons why it is so important to use a "telling" approach. See if they don't convince you to do more telling (rather than asking) when you're eliciting class participation.

Better Control of Your Class. Telling students what they're going to do is much akin to giving a command. It isn't open to any discussion, rebuttal, or refusal. The response is an expected happening, a foregoing conclusion on the part of both teacher and students. In a nutshell, students know they're supposed to do what they've been told. So they do it—good or bad as their response may be! You avoid any unnecessary commotion when you "tell." That's what gives you the "upper hand"—and more control—with this approach.

Better Control of the Momentum. These first two outcomes always go together: better control always means better momentum. There's less chance for disruptive remarks and negative comments, so the momentum has a better chance of moving more smoothly. This is one of the main reasons for using more telling when you're dealing with class participation. It's also one of the easiest ways to maintain a flowing momentum.

More Authority as the Teacher. This is true especially when the telling is done with the right tone of voice. Don't misunderstand me now—I'm *not* saying to use the telling ploy to gain power. Rather, it's a way to project an authoritative image. There *is* a difference. Telling establishes the teacher as the person in-charge, the authority figure.

More Excitement in the Lesson. Even though this proposal depends largely on the delivery, it needs to be included. When the telling is delivered in the right tone of voice, with the "right" choice of words, and with the proper dose of enthusiasm, you bring an aura of excitement to the lesson.

More Credibility as the Teacher. You may not know it, but students **do** have preconceived notions as to how a teacher should "teach," and one of these is that they feel teachers should "lead." When you assume the responsibility of telling, not asking, you not only satisfy their expectation, you also strengthen your own credibility as "the teacher." It matters how you deliver the invitation for student participation, especially in terms of establishing yourself as "the teacher" in the eyes of your students.

Tendency Regarding "Telling" Approach

The tendency, particularly among newer teachers, is to initiate participation by asking rather than telling, most likely because no one ever called it to their attention before or they've never been taught to do otherwise. No wonder you hear such willy-nilly instructions as:

- "Would you like to do . . .?"
- "Do you want to do . . . with this song?"
- "Can we try doing . . . this time?"
- "Is this something you'd like to try?"
- "How would you like doing . . . next?"

The real problem, however, is the disruptive response the teacher gets from "asking." Some students get very vocal, even though the question is intended to be moot, while others get very passive and just sit and wait. So much for the class control and momentum. Here's a prime example. I recall a particular class where the teacher's favorite question before every activity was "Do you think you'd like to do such-and-such?" Even though she had all the pep and energy of a bouncing cheerleader, she always got an instantaneous bellowing of "Nooo's" and a whining of "We don't want to's!"

Suggestions for "Telling" Approach

Here are a few tips for initiating participation by "telling."

Tip #1. Remember that "telling," in this case, refers to instructing or informing. In other words, it's an announcing task, not a polling stint. Your sole purpose is to communicate what the students **will** do, not determine what they **want** to do. It's the instructional part of the verbal bridge.

Tip #2. Keep in mind that "telling" needs to be expressed as a statement, not a question. That's not to say questions can't be used; they can, if it's for the right reason. (See Tip #7.) However, most of the time, the "telling" is done in the form of a directive. Here are some typical statements:

- "We're going to do . . . this time."
- "Let's see if we can . . . to this recording."
- "Now we'll try doing . . . this way."
- "Here's what we'll do the next time. We'll . . . ."
- "I'd like you to try doing . . . as you listen."
- "Let's do . . . this time around."

Tip #3. Use an appealing **tone of voice** when you're telling (or instructing). Sound up-beat and positive, and be sure you've got enough vocal inflection so that students can sense your interest and anticipation. Unless the intonation of the voice is genuinely motivated and excited, you won't entice the students one iota! Intonation and inflection are crucial.

Tip #4. You've got to use the **right words** and the most appropriate wording. For the lower grades, use figurative expressions—like marching feet, tapping fingers, or clapping hands. (See "Using Figurative Language" earlier in this chapter.) Whether lower or upper grades, use precise terminology for actions, objects, and materials, i.e., the proper names, as well as specific adjectives and adverbs for the actual response, such as telling students to stand quietly, clap softly, or take smaller steps. In a word, be articulate!

Tip #5. You mustn't overlook **facial expression** in this task. Even if your tone of voice is appealing and your choice of words is correct, you still need the appropriate facial expression to do an effective job of communicating. Remember, students aren't just listening, they're also looking at your face! So your expressions need to complement and even reinforce the "telling." (See "Using Facial Expressions" in Chapter 2.)

Tip #6. You also need a good shot of **enthusiasm**! Look and sound alive, and be energetic! Everything about you—your face, your voice, your stance, and your attitude—must reflect your enthusiasm. It's the most potent ingredient you can bring to the job of telling.

Tip #7. When you want to add a challenge, throw out a **question**. This isn't a contradiction; it's an alternative, especially when you're reinforcing or modifying an activity in some way. It's a marvelous way to motivate students. Instead of the usual statement, ask a question that makes the students anxious to prove themselves and "show you" they can do it. For example:

- "Do you think we could . . . all the way through?"
- "How many think we can . . . better this time?"
- "Can we improve our performances if we do it again?"
- "I wonder if we could add . . . this time around?"
- "Would it be too difficult if we changed our . . . to . . .?"

Tip #8. Don't forget your **gesturing motions** when you do your "telling" or instructing. They not only reinforce your words, but also make you look more convincing. The key is to use the gestures that are most natural to you. Just make sure you get them away from your body (use your air space) and sustain the gestures a second or two (instead of dropping them quickly) for greater impact. You can get started by modeling your own social gestures. (See "Using Only Gestures and Expressions" in Chapter 2.)

Concluding Challenge

Don't get in the habit of asking students if they would like to do this or that every time they participate. That can be disastrous. What you need to do is discipline yourself to make soft-sounding commands, like "This time I'd like you to do such-and-such." Or "Let's all take our . . . and play . . . together." Get accustomed to simply announcing what the class will do, instead of asking; that way, you can have more control of the lesson. If you're uncomfortable telling, take a closer look at the tips and use the examples.

LESS EFFECTIVE	*MORE EFFECTIVE*
Ms. Dee Major's first graders were using their roller-coaster hands for up and down passages. After relating the ups-and-downs of their hands to a melody, Ms. Major asked the class, "Would you like to hand design this melody with me?" Half the class shook their heads, while others let out a loud "Uh-uh!" "Let's settle down now. I've had enough of this nonsense," Ms. Major shouted. "I don't know what your problem is today!"	After showing the children how the up-and-down roller coaster resembled the directions in a melody, Ms. Dee Major and her first graders move their roller-coaster hands. "I like the way everyone's hands moved up and down like a roller coaster," she told them. "Now let's take our up/down cards and move up and down with the melody like this." Immediately the children put their cards in position. Ms. Major smiled at the children as they moved their cards.
In reviewing the concept of metric rhythm in 3's, Ms. Bea Minor asked, "Fifth graders, who would like to conduct a three-pattern to our song? It goes down-out-up, like a triangle. Want to try it?" After a few seconds of loud mumbling, someone blurted out "Do we have-to?" Ms. Minor frowned at the students. "You don't want to conduct?" she asked. "All right,	The review concept in Ms. Bea Minor's fifth-grade class was metric rhythm in 3's. After the opening exercise she announced what they would do next. "What we're going to do now," she said, "is conduct a three-beat pattern that goes down-out-up, like a triangle. Like this." After her demonstration, Ms. Minor prepped the class and positioned them to

we'll put it away and try something else. What about some aerobic movements?" Again there were loud moanings across the room. "That's it," she shouted. "We'll just sit then." Ms. Minor was fuming. "This class doesn't ever want to do anything!" she said to herself.

begin. She was delighted with their performance and praised them warmly. "This time we're going to tap the rhythm sticks on 'one' and your laps on 'two and three.' Try it." Once again, the class responded as Ms. Minor had hoped.

Giving Appropriate Feedback

Giving feedback is the first task most teachers think of when it comes to verbalizing, and for good reasons. Feedback is a significant part of the act of teaching—an indispensable part, to be exact. It's also a crucial step in the process of learning. Teachers can't teach without giving it, and students can't learn without getting it. That means you've got to be good at giving feedback and know what to say, and when and where to say it.

Definition of Appropriate Feedback

Feedback refers to the teacher's response that can be (a) an **evaluation**, either positive or negative, (b) a **recitation**, in the form of an explanation, or (c) an **instruction**. But that's only part of the meaning where teaching is concerned.

What's missing is the part about being appropriate. The definition needs to state clearly that feedback is "appropriate"—that it's viable and understandable. Viable in the sense that the response is honest and accurate, whether it be an appraisal, an explanation, or just an answer to a question. And understandable in the sense that the response is easily grasped by the students. Otherwise, feedback can't be of any consequence.

Importance of Giving Feedback

Feedback is important and should be kept fresh and challenging to avoid getting in a rut with the same expressions. Here are four good reasons for giving feedback.

The most obvious reason is that feedback is an **ideal tool for establishing communication**. You can say what you're thinking and share what you're feeling. It's like having a direct line for "airing" your thoughts and ideas. If communication is one of the key ingredients for successful teaching, then feedback is a powerful communicating tool—probably the most powerful one you have as a teacher.

A second reason is that it's an **ideal tactic for building rapport**. It creates a bonding with the students because you're more likely to be yourself during feedback than at any other moment in your teaching. Your wit, humor, and sentiments come through. Students get a peek at the "real" you, and it's those little peeks that whet their respect and admiration for you as a teacher, and ultimately lead to a closer relationship.

Third, feedback is the **ideal way to inform students**. It lets students know (a) the results of their participation, (b) the answer to their question, or (c) the reason(s) for their problems. Students need this information, which is germane to learning. Students don't learn as quickly or as easily without it, and there's no faster or easier way to keep them informed and to insure their learning.

The fourth reason is that feedback is an **effective ploy for improving performance**, an assessing tool. You have a chance to say what was good and what wasn't good, and more important, how to make it better. Feedback paves the way for a better performance the second time around and raises the participation level. This is the best reason of all for giving feedback.

Although you don't need any more reasons than these, some of you will think of others, such as feedback being good for instilling confidence, nurturing self-esteem, clarifying information, improving momentum, etc., and that's good because these things *do* happen. They just strengthen my point that feedback is a vital procedure for both teaching as well as learning.

Pitfalls/Solutions for Feedback

There are plenty of pitfalls when it comes to teacher feedback. Here is a list of some of them:

- being overly negative
- giving exaggerated praise
- using "asking" tone of voice
- making generalized assessments
- using "in" expressions
- delivering lengthy responses
- displaying expressionless face
- neglecting bodily gestures
- ignoring individual attention
- delaying assessing comments

Being Overly Negative (in Evaluative Feedback). The problem here is using more "don'ts than do's"[24] or more "didn'ts than did's." After a while, the students get discouraged. Some even begin to think they can't do anything right, so they quit trying. Others get the impression that all you do is criticize. It's easy to get overly critical like this. But avoid it because all that does is chip away at the students' self-esteem.

Suggestions:

- Concentrate on what students do right, not wrong.
- Use more "do's and did's" than "don'ts and didn'ts."
- Praise students individually and collectively.
- State positive aspects before the negative.
- Use pleasant tone of voice, even with corrective feedback.

Giving Exaggerated Praise (in Evaluative Feedback). The trap a lot of teachers fall into when evaluating students is going overboard with their praise, to the point that it doesn't sound sincere or natural but fake—and put on.[25] The praise then loses its impact. What's even worse, these teachers actually think they're conning the students. But not so! It's the students who are conning the teacher. Kids

---

[24]Seefeldt, Carol. *Teaching Young Children* (Englewood Cliffs, NJ: Prentice-Hall, Inc., 1980), p. 166.
[25]Lemlech, Johanna. *Class Management* (New York: Harper and Row Publishers, 1979), p. 17.

know when praise is exaggerated. Here's a perfect illustration. I recall a junior high teacher who, in my opinion, was the queen of exaggeration. She pontificated on virtually everything the students did—good or bad. This was "super," that was "outstanding," and someone else was "just wonderful." After twenty minutes, I couldn't take it any longer; evidently one of the students couldn't either, because from the back of the room a fed-up sounding voice blurted out, "Hey, teach, why you lying to us again?"

Suggestions:

- Establish realistic criterion for each activity.
- Keep criteria in mind during the lesson.
- Temper praise in accordance to established criterion.
- Withhold ultimate praise for achievement of objective.
- Compile list of appropriate comments for achievement, such as:

  – "Great! Everyone did . . . perfectly. I'm proud of you!"
  – "Bravo for you, class. We did . . . without making a mistake."
  – "You were able to . . . exactly right that time. Congratulations!"
  – "I am proud of you! That was the best you've ever . . ."

Using Asking Tone of Voice (in Instructional Feedback). Many teachers make the mistake of using an asking, rather than telling, tone of voice when they give instructions. They use the questioning inflection that goes up at the end of the instruction so that it sounds more like a plea than a prescription. The voice doesn't have that expectant tone—or that "I mean it" quality which tells students the teacher is really expecting a response.[26] There's the problem! An asking tone of voice doesn't say "do it!"; it's too wimpish for instructing purposes.

---

[26]Seefeldt, Carol. *Teaching Young Children*, p. 106.

Suggestions:

- Be able to distinguish between your asking and telling tones.
- Be sure vocal inflection goes down, not up, at the end of statements.
- Use proper breath support for better vocal projection.
- Write out all instructions if necessary.
- Practice instructions with telling tone of voice.
- Record and evaluate yourself.

Making Generalized Comments (in Evaluative Feedback). Probably the most common pitfall when it comes to giving evaluative feedback is not being specific enough. For example, I constantly hear teachers say, "**That** was good," "**This** is correct," or "Do **it** better this time." If you notice, they don't identify the activity; instead, they use a pronoun—in fact, too many pronouns most of the time, such as *this* and *that*, *them* and *those*, and a lot of *its*. So it's not always clear what they mean. The teachers also rarely mention the concept or skill involved. Without reference to the concept and activity, feedback isn't specific enough to be meaningful or helpful.

Suggestions:

- Use the proper name for the activity, not the pronoun (this, that, those, them, these, it).
- Refer to the concept involved for reinforcement purposes.
- Give clear-cut evaluation of class's response.
- Make a complete statement by referring to the name of the activity and the concept after the assessment, such as:
  - "Very good! Everyone changed the I, V chords correctly on your keyboard." *Instead of*: "That was good."
  - "Excellent! The whole class tapped the melodic rhythm without a mistake." *Instead of*: "You did it right that time."
  - "Not quite. I didn't see some of you playing your bells on every upward passage." *Instead of*: "That wasn't good."
  - "You didn't play the figure accurately on your recorders." *Instead of*: "You did it wrong."

Using "In" Expressions (in All Feedback). Some teachers think it's "cool" to use the latest slang expressions and words in their feedback, such as "hang loose," "to the max," "real bad," "awesome," and "heavy." They think they're really being "with it," but the effect is just the opposite. They sound foolish and look foolish. Worse yet, they undermine their own stature.

Suggestions:

- Tape record yourself for self-evaluation purposes.
- Make a conscious effort to use teacher, not student, verbiage.
- Review teacher words/expressions mentally prior to teaching.
- Correct yourself on the spot when necessary.

• Seek assistance of other teachers/supervisors/consultants.

Delivering Lengthy Responses. The problem here is being long-winded, going on-and-on-and-on when assessing or explaining—and not knowing when to quit! The same thing happens when giving instructions. Some teachers keep adding stuff between the "do this's" and "do that's" until the instruction gets too cumbersome! What's scary is these teachers don't even know they're yakking too much, or that the students are getting antsy and the lesson is bogging down. They just keep on talking and sabotaging their own feedback.

Suggestions:

• Prepare verbal bridges for assessing/instructing.
• Discipline yourself to implement verbal bridging (assess/instruct) immediately after response.
• Outline presentations to avoid getting "off track."
• Set time limit on your presentations/explanations.
• Watch students' body language, facial expression, and attention span.

Displaying Expressionless Face. You might think giving feedback without facial expression is picayune, but it isn't! Too many teachers have this problem. It doesn't matter if they're praising or punishing, being serious or humorous, or feeling excited or disappointed; their expression never changes—eyebrows never lift, lips never purse, eyes never get wider, etc. The pity is that their feedback loses its steam.

Suggestions:

• Explore facial expressions in a mirror.
• Practice assessing/instructing with a mirror or videotape.
• Recognize the need to exaggerate expressions for noticeable results.
• Make concerted effort to apply facial expressions in teaching.
• Videotape yourself for self-evaluation purposes.

Neglecting Bodily Gestures (in All Feedback). What happens here is that a lot of teachers forget to use gesturing with feedback, so there's no motioning, mimicking, or posturing to reinforce their assessments or to clarify their instructions or explanations. It's almost like they're inhibited and think they'll look silly if they use gesturings. What they don't understand is that they look a whole lot sillier—and less confident—without them!

Suggestions:

• Study your own gesturing habits in social situations.
• Practice applying gestures to assessing/instructing response.
• Make gesturing large and precise, and away from body.
• Sustain bodily gestures momentarily—don't drop them suddenly.
• Recognize need to exaggerate gestures for best results.

Ignoring Individual Assistance (in Evaluative/Instructional Feedback). Some teachers have a tendency to slight individual students when they're instructing or assessing the class. They have trouble focusing on one student, or directing remarks to one person. Instead, they constantly speak to the class as a whole and rarely personalize their attention by offering individual assistance or personal correction. This causes problems because after a while, some students just stop listening and responding, and others start driving you crazy!

Suggestions:

- Discipline yourself to zero-in on the students, not yourself.
- Anticipate feedback comments in order to focus on students.
- Be committed to achieving objectives with every student.
- Scan class constantly, focusing on individuals when necessary.
- Watch for tell-tale body language, facial expressions, or annoying behaviors to identify student(s) with problems.

Delaying Assessing Comments (in Evaluative Feedback). The last shortcoming has to do with waiting too long to give feedback. What happens is that some teachers start talking or explaining before assessing—and they talk too long. When they finally do give the feedback, it doesn't mean much and loses its impact! Many teachers are guilty of delaying their feedback, which is too bad because the students are the losers in this case.

Suggestions:

- Discipline yourself to assess/instruct immediately.
- Be more sensitive to the flow of the lesson when assessing is delayed.
- Follow the lesson plan to-a-tee, especially with verbal bridging.
- Invite a fellow teacher or supervisor to observe your progress.
- Take a closer note of students' attentiveness and enthusiasm.

Concluding Challenge

Would you say your feedback technique was effective most of the time? And understandable? What about the pitfalls? See any you recognize? It just might be that you do exaggerate your praise sometimes, or you don't use enough gesturing, or you really are guilty of using slang. If so, take stock of your feedback and get going on some of these suggestions.

LESS EFFECTIVE	MORE EFFECTIVE
Mr. Rock Moninoff considered himself a "with-it" type of guy. So when his sixth graders clapped the suggested rhythm without a single mistake, he praised them with his "in" lingo. "Right on, man! You really swing on that one. Now don't chill out on this next exercise." Rock felt he was making a connection with students this way. But when he turned to the board, the students gave each other that "Gee, he sounds dumb" look. "Cool it," he snapped.	The upper elementary kids thought Mr. Rock Moninoff was a neat teacher. They liked the way he made them feel good when they did something right, such as when they clapped the syncopated exercise correctly. Immediately he told them, "Good for you! I didn't hear anyone make a mistake. You're ready to go on to the next exercise!" The students glanced at each other with a look of pride. Mr. Rock Moninoff really knew how to make a class feel good—that was the feeling as they smiled back.
"Quiet down," Ms. Della Joyo yelled. "I'm tired of yelling at this class all the time." When she finally got the fourth graders to play their recorders, she kept shouting out, "You missed the C♯ again!" Ms. Joyo was obviously annoyed. "Jim, Susan, Bill, Peter, you people still don't know your fingering. Why is it that you're always the last ones to learn your notes? Just about everybody played the dotted quarter note wrong, too! Let's do it again. No, no! Can't we even get the right starting note?" By then, the students weren't even trying. They were thinking, "She'll only yell at us!" And they were right!	"I know you're all excited about playing your recorders, but we'll get to it quicker if you're quieter." With that, the class settled down. "Watch out for that C♯ in the third measure," Ms. Della Joyo warned the fourth graders. She was pleased how well they played the song. "I still see a few people who need help. If it's a fingering problem, please ask your neighbor quickly and quietly. Okay, let's try it one more time." That time she heard the dotted quarter being butchered! "Let's work on the dotted quarter/eighth measures, okay? Now you've got it! Let's try it one last time, okay?" The students felt encouraged by Ms.

Delivering the Opening Salutation

Although you probably never hear much about it or read anything about it, the salutation really is important. It isn't just a frivolous gesture or some meaningless chatter—and it *does* take skill to do it right.

Definition of Opening Salutation

The salutation means exactly what you think: an **initial greeting**, or someone's opening words, as Webster puts it. In this case, it's the teacher's opening words.

Think of it as a **word of welcome**, such as when the teacher says, "Good morning! It's nice to see your smiling faces again!" Or, "I'm glad that you're here today. I've been looking forward to seeing you!"

But there's another interpretation. You could also think of it as a **personalized greeting**, or one's own individual way of saying "How do you do" and "It's nice to see you." The emphasis is on the personal touch.

Significance of Opening Salutation

Delivering an opening salutation *is* a skill. Here are some concrete reasons for giving attention to the salutation.

Provides a Greeting Mechanism. The salutation is an established protocol. You don't have to invent a new approach every time you greet students because it's already in place. You also can be certain that the students are "tuned into" this gesture. The point is, you have a ready-made greeting mechanism at your disposal, which is an excellent reason for the salutation.

Acknowledges the Students' Presence. In essence, the salutation rightfully recognizes students. It tells them they are worthy of your attention, and it makes them feel important. In turn, that heightens their self-esteem—and their self-respect; and that, in turn, nurtures their emotional well-being. By acknowledging the students, then, you promote their feeling of self-worth.

Sets the Tone of the Lesson. This is probably the most immediate justification. In short, the salutation establishes the mood. When the greeting is upbeat and encouraging, it establishes a positive tone for the lesson and starts it off on the right foot. But when the salutation is downbeat and discouraging, it puts a damper on the lesson and defeats the whole purpose of a salutation, which is to create an uplifting mood.

Indicates the Start of Class. Here's the most practical reason of all. The salutation is a tactful way of saying, "It's time to begin and start paying attention." Even kindergarten children know it's the signal to begin.

Pitfall Regarding Opening Salutation

The salutation doesn't get much attention, it's virtually an after thought or one of those details teachers improvise at the last minute. Thus, the biggest pitfall is that it's not taken seriously enough.

The most disastrous consequence of such thinking is that it **discourages proper preparation**. The general consensus is that you can just get up and do it, and say whatever comes to mind. But that's precisely why most salutations sound so sim-

ple and even silly. They're not properly thought out.

Here's a good illustration of this. I can still see this teacher standing dutifully by the door until the last student came in. I remember, too, how quickly she ran to her desk, flashed a smile from ear to ear, and chirped out a short, high pitched "Hi!" In the same breath, she fluttered her eyelids and asked in a cutesy-sounding voice, "How's everyone feeling today? Good?" She sounded dumb, like she didn't know what else to say. Even the students didn't bother answering. It was an awkward moment, to say the least.

The second consequence is that it **makes for an irrelevant effort**. In other words, it results in saying something that doesn't mean anything to students and sounds trite. Students automatically tune out when this happens. Here are some classic examples:

- "So, everybody doing all right today. Yes?"
- "What's up? Anything interesting happen lately?"
- "What's happening with everyone today?"
- "Everybody feeling okay this morning? You are?"
- "What do you think about all the snow? (or rain? or fog?)"

The third consequence is that it **undermines an effective impact** and sets a negative tone because the comment or question usually sounds patronizing and simple. The teacher loses a perfect opportunity to establish an upbeat atmosphere.

Notice that one consequence leads to another—that without preparation, there's no substance; and without substance, there's no impact. That's the bad news. The good news is, you can avoid these glitches.

Suggestions for Opening Salutations

The following is a simple five-step plan you can start doing immediately.

Step 1: Recognize the Value. You've got to identify the reasons(s) for giving a salutation and then believe in them with your whole heart. Unless you're convinced the salutation is important, you won't even try to improve.

Step 2: Observe the Task. Observe other teachers. Listen to what they say and how they say it. Then note those comments or questions that catch your attention and make a favorable impression. In other words, get yourself some good examples—and good role models.

Step 3: Establish a Repertoire. Initially, you need some good "working" statements at your fingertips, so make up a list from your observations. You'll save a lot of time and energy if you do, and you'll experience the success you need to nurture your expertise. Look for salutations that have the following characteristics:

- **A Personal Touch**: "Good morning, class! It's good to see all your bright, cheerful faces. I can see you're ready to begin!"
- **A Relevant Topic**: "I see you all got back from your field trip to the planetarium yesterday. Did you enjoy it?"
- **A Positive Tone**: "Bravo! I'm so proud of you. Everyone came into the room in such a quiet and orderly way. Thank you."

- **A Newsworthy Twist**. "Greetings! How did you feel watching the space shuttle take off this morning? It's unbelievable, isn't it?"

Step 4: Practice the Delivery. Practice, not because you need to remember what you'll say, but because the delivery requires skill. You've got to be ready to articulate and gesticulate in such a way that you immediately project a positive and uplifting attitude. Until you can respond like this automatically, you've got to practice. Here are some delivery tips to keep in mind:

- Use appropriate vocal inflection.
- Establish eye contact with whole class.
- Project energy and enthusiasm.
- Utilize reinforcing gestures.
- Apply appealing facial expression.
- Keep a positive tone.

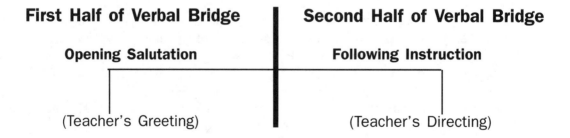

Figure 3.5. Diagram of Verbal Bridge with Opening Salutation (Where Salutation Happens in Verbal Bridge).

Step 5: Include in Lesson Planning. Whether you make a written plan or mental outline, be sure the salutation is included. Think of it as the first part of the opening verbal bridge, which is normally an assessment, and then follow it with an instructional statement. (See Figure 3.5 for a diagram of the verbal bridge.)

Concluding Challenge

Do you say anything off the cuff? Or do you give the salutation some serious thought beforehand? It's important that your salutation sets the tone of the lesson, and that it has a personal touch, a relevant interest, or a newsworthy twist. That's the only way it will make an impact. If it doesn't, try the five-step plan.

LESS EFFECTIVE	MORE EFFECTIVE
Mr. Mel O. Deez's sixth graders quieted down when he played a loud chord on the piano. "Do I have to get your attention like this every time? You're the noisiest class of sixth graders I've ever had!" With that, he stomped off to his desk. The students sprawled back in their seats and dropped their heads. "At least sit up and look alive," he scolded. "We need to get started." But nobody moved!	By the time the last sixth grader was seated, Mr. Mel O. Deez was at the board ready to start the lesson. Students liked the pleasant way he always looked at them. "You certainly know how to make my day," he said. "You came in so quickly and quietly, I hardly had time to get to the board. You're great!" The class grinned at Mr. Mel O. Deez and sat up tall in their seats eager to begin.
As usual, Mr. Harmon Eez was sitting at his desk as the fourth graders came dashing into the music room. When everyone was seated, he looked up and began to mumble about the unit coming to an end. "We only have two, or is it three, lessons left in this unit. So you'll need to stay with it, okay!" But no one was listening. Students just waited until he announced a page number. They couldn't care less about the unit or anything else. It didn't interest them one bit!	Mr. Harmon Eez was standing at the doorway when the fourth-grade class arrived. As soon as they were seated, he came to the front of the class and said, "I heard something very nice about this class. I heard that you had the highest class average in the school these past six weeks! That's wonderful. I congratulate each one of you." Every student was listening to every word Mr. Harmon Eez was saying. They were excited that he was congratulating them and anxious to begin the lesson.

4

Verbal Behaviors for Teaching Music

Using Correct Terminology

When it comes to identifying verbal skills needed for teaching, we can't leave out correct terminology. Using the "right" verbiage makes the teacher's speech more lucid and more articulate. The fact is, successful teaching demands this kind of clarity and rationality; so does successful learning, for that matter.

Definition of Correct Terminology

"Correct terminology" is simply the "right" professional word (or name) for whatever you're talking about. It is calling something by its rightful name whether it be (a) a concept, (b) an activity, (c) a response, or (d) any object, like an instrument, a visual aid, a book, etc.

But let's look at what it doesn't mean for a moment, because sometimes a negative perspective is more helpful than a positive one. For instance, correct terminology isn't a nebulous synonym or a common cliché, like saying "hit" instead of "tap" or "Ready, go" instead of "Ready, play." Correct terminology rules out these generic expressions. Instead, it focuses on the legitimate professional jargon. That's what correct terminology is all about—**proper jargon**.

Significance of Correct Terminology

Besides the obvious reason that it makes you more articulate, there are at least three other good reasons for using correct terminology. If you're talking about a specific activity, calling it by its rightful name **facilitates the activity**. It lets the students know precisely what you want them to do. For example, don't tell your students to "hit" their drums or "hit" their rhythm sticks. The word "hit" isn't even a musical term! What you really want is for the students to tap the sticks in a light bouncy manner, and not bang them to death! So why not say "tap" in the first place? It would convey the style immediately and help children respond correctly—even on the first try, which means you can handle the activity more quickly.

Here's the second reason. Using the proper name **reinforces a conceptual**

idea. Students begin to connect the sound of the concept with the name. In other words, a bonding of sound and label starts to happen. For example, say you're teaching an uneven rhythmic pattern. By calling ♩.♪♩.♪♪ an "uneven rhythmic pattern" rather than a "tum-ta-tum-ta-tum part" you help solidify the students' perception of the concept and establish proper perspective. The same holds true for every concept you teach. That's why correct terminology is so crucial in conceptual teaching.

The third reason is it **improves the pacing**. Whenever you use proper names for your concepts and activities, the pacing will always move more smoothly and with less interruptions because there's less ambiguity as to what you're teaching and what you expect. If you use correct terminology in your instructions and with your materials, your pacing will go even *more* smoothly. Pacing improves dramatically just by using proper terminology for everything: for activities, concepts, instructions, materials, etc. It's one of the keys to good pacing!

Problem With Correct Terminology

You probably already know the problem. It's lack of awareness. For some reason, a lot of teachers are oblivious to correct terminology.

But the problem goes deeper than just being oblivious, because obliviousness creates a whole set of other problems. One is that it leads to a **lack of clarity**. Without correct names for concepts, activities, materials, or instructions, it's impossible to be explicit and clear. You simply aren't as coherent without correct terminology!

Another problem stemming from being oblivious is a **shifting of blame**—to the students. This happens again and again, particularly with activities. Instead of calling an activity by its proper name, teachers give it some other generic label that really doesn't "tell" students what they're supposed to do. Specifically, when teachers tell students "to move" instead of "to march" and then berate them when they don't march!

And here's one more problem. There's usually a **dip in pacing**. Without the "right" labels the teacher has to keep stopping either to (a) re-explain the activity, or else (b) redefine the concept, such as when he/she instructs the students to "Mark your call chart," instead of telling them to "Circle the correct answer for like or contrasting phrases as you listen." See how much more specific the second statement is?

I still remember the teacher who was totally flabbergasted when she noticed her sixth graders doing everything from underlining to x-ing out the answers on their call charts. She threw up her arms and ran down the aisle shouting, "Stop! Stop!" She couldn't believe they didn't know they were supposed to circle the answer! But all she told the class was, "Let's do our call charts." The verb "do" simply didn't "say" to circle, so the students did their "own thing" and the teacher went bananas! Nebulous terminology fouls up the works every time and wrecks the pacing.

The same thing happens with concepts. Calling accented and unaccented beats "loud and soft" instead of "strong and weak" will confuse students. You'll have to stop—you can bet on it!—and there goes the pacing.

Suggestions for Correct Terminology

Now that you know it's important to use correct terminology, you're probably asking yourself what you can do. That's good because you've got to have a plan of action if you're serious about this. It's not enough just to say, "I'll do it!" You need a do-able strategy. Here are three simple steps:

Step One: Analyze Your Terminology. First, you need to "sit back" and take a long, hard look to see if you're using the "right" names for concepts, activities, materials, etc. In other words, get a baseline as to how precise you are. Where are you consistent and not consistent? Is it with activities? Concepts? Instructions? Where? You've got to have a clear picture of your present performance before you can start tracking your improvement. The first step, then, is self-analysis.

Step Two: Plan Your Strategy. Once you've evaluated your performance, you're ready to do something about it. For example, you could make up a list of all the incorrect words (and/or expressions) you found yourself saying, and then compose another list of what you should be saying. See a sample listing in Figure 4.1. Notice the list is divided into categories of activities, concepts, and instructions. By dividing the list, you can concentrate on each category for a set period of time or

	Incorrect Expressions	**Correct Expressions**
<u>Activities</u>	"Hit sticks"	"Tap sticks"
	"Move this way"	"March/sway/skip this way"
	"Do this on the strong beats and this on the weak beats"	"Slap thighs on the strong beats and tap fingers on weak beats"
<u>Concepts</u>	"Loud/soft beats"	"Strong/weak beats"
	"Up parts"	"Upward passages"
	"Repeating rhythm"	"Rhythmic pattern"
	"High music"	"High range music"
<u>Instructions</u>	"Ready, go"	"Ready play, march," etc.
	"Say with me"	"Chant with me"
	"Mark the answer"	"Circle the answer"
	"Begin with this hand"	"Begin with the right hand"

Figure 4.1. Examples of Incorrect and Correct Terminology for Classroom Teaching.

until you make sufficient progress. Then you can move on to the next category, and then the next. This is one way of dealing with the problem. Or, you could work on a particular expression from each category for a certain length of time. The point is, the more organized you are in dealing with the problem, the quicker you'll conquer it. So get organized! But be patient; don't expect a miracle overnight!

Step Three: Evaluate Your Feedback. You've got to have feedback if you're going to get better, so use a tape recorder. If you feel more comfortable asking a fellow teacher to observe you, then ask; or, better still, set up a video tape in your room.

It really doesn't matter what tool you use. The important thing is that you get the feedback you need to improve; and when you do, you'll hear the difference and get excited about it. That's what makes feedback so valuable. It provides the incentive for improvement.

So there's the three-point plan. You've got to (1) analyze your terminology, (2) plan your strategy, and (3) evaluate your feedback. Actually, it's nothing more than a monitoring process. But it really works!

Concluding Challenge

The question now is, how precise is your terminology? And how consistent? If you want to speak more clearly and sound more articulate, examine yourself. See if you're calling activities, concepts, and materials by their proper names. Set up a plan of action as soon as possible. You'll like the results.

LESS EFFECTIVE

During her lesson dealing with meter in 3's, Ms. Chopini kept urging her second graders to "Listen how the music moves." When she asked them to step-snap-snap to one of their favorite recordings, she urged the children to listen more carefully so they could "move correctly to the music." When the music ended, she let out a sigh and said, "We all know that music can move in 3's now. Right?" When she saw the blank stares, Ms. Chopini was puzzled. "Didn't they understand the lesson?" she asked herself. "What's wrong with them? I told them to listen to how the music moved!"

In preparing the sixth-grade class for the next activity, Mr. Berliozo yelled out, "Okay, now I want you to step off on the like-phrases and conduct on the contrasting phrases. Like this. Let's try that together. Ready." The class's response was a disaster! "Didn't you see what I did?" he shouted. "Step like this and conduct the beat like this. Try it again." Mr. Berliozo pointed to Mark, "Take smaller steps, and go the other way." He growled at Susan and Michelle because they weren't "keeping the beat" the right way. "I don't know why it takes this class so long to get an activity right. We waste so much time!" With that he stalked off to the record player.

MORE EFFECTIVE

Ms. Chopini's second grade lesson was on meter in 3's. She was careful to stress that the children needed to listen for the grouping of the beat. So when she gave the instructions for the clap-clap-snap activity, Ms. Chopini urged her children to "Listen to the grouping of the beat." She very quickly reminded them that the beat would have a strong-weak-weak sound, with the strong beat being beat "one." After the activity Ms. Chopini praised the children and then asked, "So in some songs and recordings, the beat can move in groups of what? Yes, groups of three! Excellent, class!"

Mr. Berliozo enjoyed his sixth graders. They always responded so well. His lesson was on like-and-contrasting phrases. In the first activity, he told them "On the like phrases, let's do a waltz step. Like this. Take a step forward with the right foot, followed by L/R step, and then a step backward with the left foot followed by R/L. And repeat. Let's try it. Ready." Mr. Berliozo chanted the dance steps, while the class did the stepping. "Excellent! Your steps were perfect. For the contrasting (or 'b' phrases) we're going to conduct in three's, like this. Down, out, up—like a triangle. Ready." Mr. Berliozo was impressed. "Great conducting. We're ready to waltz and conduct with the music!"

Using Figurative Language in Lower Grades

Here's a skill you might not recognize at first, but don't worry; I labeled it myself. It's time that figurative language is recognized as a legitimate skill, especially at the lower elementary level (grades K–2) where it's most appropriate. Young children thrive on vivid imageries and creative metaphors.

Definition of Figurative Language

"Figurative language" is a term for more imaginative wording in place of the ordinary way of saying something. It's using more creative expressions to make activities and objects come alive, such as telling young children to use their "marching feet" instead of just asking them "to march," or to play their "tapping sticks" rather than their plain rhythm sticks.

It is a metaphorical exercise as well, likening one object or event to another, such as telling children to "stand straight and tall like soldiers." Think of it as verbal representation, not a literal transformation.

If you're an early elementary music teacher, you need figurative verbiage for

spicing up your speech, for creating more imaginative expressions and creative metaphors, and, most of all, for making the "doing" more fun for children by letting them "be like something else" for a moment. Young children love to pretend.

Reasons for Using Figurative Language

The first reason is figurative speaking **accommodates the learning style more effectively**. Children in grades K–2 "feed on" illustrative wordings and creative likenings with their activities, their materials, and with themselves. It helps them pretend more easily, which is the way children learn at this age. Figurative language obliges the children's learning style by furnishing them with the kind of illustrative verbiage they need, and want, in order to pretend.

The second reason for using figurative language is that it **makes the learning experience more interesting** and more appealing. Children love it when you make reference to their "tapping hands," "marching feet," or their "listening ears." It makes the experience more exciting because it's one of the high-order skills, one of the refining tools in the art of verbalizing. Figurative language is a marvelous tool for enticing young children because it (a) utilizes verbiage on their own level and (b) relates the verbiage to their own little world.

The third reason is that figurative speech **helps activities move more smoothly**. When you use a teaching tactic that coincides with the way children learn and, at the same time, makes their learning more enjoyable, you create the ideal condition for a smooth-moving activity. Children become much more attentive and more responsive.

But this third outcome can happen only because figurative speech (a) accommodates the children's learning style and (b) stimulates their interest.

Problem With Figurative Language

All you've got to do is look around and see that most elementary teachers don't use figurative verbiage, either because they don't know about it or because they just don't remember to use it.

Many teachers have the "What's the big deal?" attitude. Of course you don't have to use figurative language and you can *still* teach successfully, but you're missing a lot when you don't use figurative verbiage.

First, you **miss a golden opportunity to inject more finesse in your speech**. Figurative verbiage gives your speech a professional ring and makes it sound more polished because figurative verbiage is more fitting for young children.

Another consequence is that you **miss a chance to communicate in a more meaningful way**. When you purposely omit or carelessly forget to use figurative verbiage, you miss the opportunity to have your students respond more enthusiastically to imaginative language. You forfeit your chances of having a closer rapport and getting a better response. That's a big price to pay for by-passing such a little task.

The third consequence is that you **jeopardize your chances to obtain a smoother momentum**. When you don't use figurative speech, children don't respond as readily or as enthusiastically and usually not as accurately either. You end up doing more coaxing and stopping-and-starting, which means the momentum begins to sputter. So does the flow of the lesson. This is the most damaging consequence of the three.

You don't realize what you're missing when you're indifferent towards figurative speech! You jeopardize three important aspects of your teaching: (1) your verbal finesse, (2) your communicating skill, and (3) your ongoing momentum. So don't let indifference, forgetfulness, or especially ignorance stop you from using figurative language.

Guidelines for Figurative Language

Use at Early Elementary Level Only. Figurative speech is only for grades K–2. You'll be in trouble if you try it with older students because the verbiage is too babyish. Here's an illustration. I recall very clearly a particular music teacher who kept telling her sixth-grade class to get their "promenading feet" in place and "clapping hands" ready when they were learning to square dance. You could tell how embarrassed the students were by the look on their faces. The girls had that "how gross" attitude and took to pouting and rolling their eyes while the guys just stood around shuffling their feet. It didn't take a genius to see that they were completely turned off.

Use with Bodily Movement. The best occasion for figurative verbiage is when you're doing activities with bodily movements, specifically, when you're (1) introducing the activity, (2) prepping the activity, or (3) positioning the children to begin the activity. It doesn't matter if it's a large movement, like swaying or marching, or a more refined action, like tapping, or tipping, or snapping. Figurative verbiage works beautifully with both. For example, you could refer to "marching feet" or "tapping fingers" with equal success. Both would be more meaningful—and more interesting—to children than the usual "Let's march" or "Let's tap."

Here's a simple rule for formulating figurative expressions with regard to movement: Use the participial form of the activity to modify the body part. If the activity is to tap the beat, simply change the verb (or the activity) to its participle form (tapping) and tack on the body part (hands). Thus, you've got "**tapping hands**." Grammatically speaking, it's a participial phrase—a participle being the "ing" form of a verb that modifies a noun. Here's another illustration. Suppose you want the children to snap the accents. Using the formula, you would tell them to use their "**snapping fingers**." (See Figure 4.2 for more figurative verbiage for bodily movement.)

Use with Instrument Activities. Another built-in opportunity for figurative verbiage occurs when children are using classroom instruments. Use it to (1) intro-

duce, (2) prep, or (3) position the children, like with bodily movements. Whether it's rhythm sticks, sand blocks, tambourines, maracas, or triangles, the formula for figurative expression stays the same; only now the participle form of the verb will modify the instrument, not the body part. The participle refers to the specific way children are to play. For instance, if you're having children tap the strong-weak beats on their rhythm sticks, you'd tell them to play their "**tapping sticks**." If you want them to tremolo on triangles at the end of phrases, just ask them to play their "**tremoloing triangles**." This verbiage is much more appealing for young children. (Check out Figure 4.2 for more figurative expressions with instruments.) Lest you think that children don't learn the proper names of instruments this way, what you do is introduce the instruments before you make any figurative remarks. That way there's no chance of their not learning the proper names.

Use with Teaching Materials. There's one other ideal time for applying figurative verbiage: when you're using visual aids or concrete objects. There are several ways to express the figurative remark. One, you can use your conceptual idea as the modifying agent, such that cards, drawings, or objects can be called by the concept they're supposed to represent. For example, 5″ × 8″ index cards with "Phrase Ending" written on them could be called "phrase cards"; cut-outs of colored leaves can be referred to as "down leaves" when focusing on the downward direction (↘); and a basketball, as an "accent ball" when accented beats are involved. The formula is so simple, yet so effective. Two, you can modify an item with an appropriate participial verb, like referring to the above examples as the children's "phrasing cards," their "falling leaves," or their "accenting basketball." In other words, you could call a handout or an object by its functional use. (See Figure 4.2 for more examples.)

So these are the four guidelines to help you with figurative language. Remember, the most logical times for using such verbiage would be when you're: (1) introducing an activity, (2) preparing an activity, or (3) positioning the class to begin. If you

WITH BODY MOVEMENT	**WITH INSTRUMENT PLAYING**	**WITH VISUAL AIDS/OBJECTS**
•Tapping Fingers	•Tapping Sticks	•Up or Down Card
•Dotting Fingers	•Dotting Sticks	•Swww or Sww Card
•Pointing Fingers	•Shaking Maracas	•"a" circle phrases
		•"b" square phrases
•Snapping Fingers	•Tapping Maracas	
•Clapping Hands	•Rattling Tambourine	•Long/Short Bibs
•Tapping Hands	•Tapping Tambourine	•Eighth/Quarter Signs
•Designing Hand	•Knocking Woodblock	•Falling Leaves (down)
•Swinging Arms	•Tick-Tocking Woodblock	•Ascending/Descending (up/down)
•Lifting Arms	•Ringing Triangle	•Sailing Boat (across)
•Walking Feet	•Dingling Triangle	•Booming Drum (loud)
•Stepping Feet	•Tremoloing Bells	•Tinkling Bell (soft)
•Marching Feet	•Singing Bells	•High Star/Balloon (high register)
•Dancing Feet	•Rubbing Sandblocks	•Accenting Bell (strong beats)
•Tapping Foot	•Tapping Sandblocks	•Thumping Rabbit (beat)
•Sliding Foot	•Beating Drum	•Choo-Choo Train (SWW)

Figure 4.2. Examples of Figurative Language When Using Body Movement, Instrument Playing, and Visual Aids.

understand the so-called "rules" and use the right verbiage like that shown in Figure 4.2, you should be in business.

Concluding Challenge

If you're not using figurative language in your own teaching, you need to start right now because you're missing out on the joy of relating in a more effective way with your children and making their learning more appealing. You've got to think of figurative language as a "must," especially if you're at the lower elementary level. Don't use "I don't know how" as an excuse. If you need more help, check out the guidelines.

LESS EFFECTIVE	**MORE EFFECTIVE**
Ms. Dy Namics was teaching her kindergartners the words to "Twinkle, Twinkle." When they came to the last line she said, "Now raise your arms again because this last line is just like the first line." Slowly the arms went up. "We won't be able to learn the rest of Twinkle, if we don't get those arms up," she chided. "Don't you like this song? I thought you'd like raising your arms like stars. But maybe you don't."	The kindergartners were learning "Twinkle, Twinkle." After ". . . like a diamond . . .," Ms. Dy Namics told the children the last line was exactly like the first. "So put your 'Twinkle Hands' up high in the sky," she instructed excitedly. Immediately arms shot up and fingers began to twinkle. "Good, I see everyone's 'Twinkle Hands' up. Let's say the last line now. Ready. Twinkle, Twinkle . . ."

Ms. Timbre's first graders were tapping the strong beats on their laps and tapping the weak beats with their fingers. After prepping them for the activity, she told them to "get your hands ready." Some placed their hands over their laps, but most just put them anywhere. "Hands over laps," she snapped. "We can't start if you're not ready." Ms. Timbre shook her head disgustedly. "These children just don't listen!" she said to herself.

"We're going to tap the strong beats on our laps and tap our weak beats with our fingertips, like this," Ms. Timbre instructed her first-grade class. She prepped the children carefully and then positioned them to begin. "Very good. Now let's see your tapping hands over your laps. Excellent! I see all the tapping hands in place and everyone sitting up tall." The children were eager to begin. "Here we go. Tapping hands, ready!"

Articulating Concept/Environmental Similarity

This task may sound more like a procedure than a tactic, but it *is* a verbal skill involving the ability to verbalize clearly and concisely that a particular environmental phenomenon is a good "likeness" of the musical concept (when the concept is new, of course). It helps students "get" the concept more quickly. If you've never used this approach, this is the time to get acquainted with it; if you do use it, it might be worthwhile to check out the guidelines. In either case, you've got to articulate the relationship clearly in order for it to "work."

Definition of Articulating Similarity

This is the technique of actually saying (to the class) that this concept is like this-or-that phenomenon around us! You literally make the statement that there's a definite likeness between the two phenomena. It's **relating a relationship**.

Be sure you understand that such a statement is made in conjunction with the motivational idea, or the environmental idea. (See "Using the Motivational Idea" in Chapter 6.) It comes after the relationship has been discussed, almost like a summary. For example, suppose the new concept is upward stepwise passages and an UP escalator is your environmental "picture." After discussing escalators with the children, you might close the motivational exercise by saying any of the following:

"Did you know that melodies (or tunes) have passages that go up in steps like escalators?"

"Well, melodies (or tunes) can have passages that move up in steps like an escalator, too."

"See how the escalator goes up by steps? Some passages in the melody can move the same way."

It's a matter of spelling out "this-is-like-that" in the form of a question, a statement, or a combination of both, as in the last example above.

Significance of Articulating Similarity

The most important reason for articulating a relationship between concept and environment is that it **establishes a familiar frame of reference**. It relates the new idea to something familiar in the students' own environment—something they already know about. It gives students a mental "picture" of the new concept, or an idea of what to expect.

A second reason is that verbalizing the relationship **expedites the initial grasp of the concept**. Students identify with the idea. It resembles something they already know, so they make the connection immediately! They don't need a long-winded explanation, so it speeds up the learning time.

The third reason is just as important. The relating statement **gives a cohesive touch to the lesson**. It pulls the motivational discussion together and puts a finishing touch on the discussion, especially when it's said with the proper emphasis. It brings the motivational part of the lesson to a smooth close, and demonstrates your expertise as a teacher.

Problems with Articulating Similarity

The most obvious problem when it comes to this task is that most **teachers don't do it**, mostly because they've never heard of it and don't feel comfortable doing what they've never done! Of course, there are always those who think it's just someone else's gimmick and that it's not for them. An attitude like that is hard to change.

On the other hand, some of you do use this technique, so you know there are some problems. The most common ones are (1) not using enough specific conceptual terminology, and (2) not being emphatic and deliberate enough in the delivery. Let's look at each problem separately.

It may not seem like such a big deal if specific terminology isn't used, but it is! Teachers who use general terminology and indefinite pronouns (e.g., this, that, it) aren't very articulate. I don't know how many times I've heard vague comments like, "... such-and-such happens in music too." Or, "Music has the same thing as this," whatever "thing" is supposed to mean! Or, "That's just like what we have in music." Such vague wording ("... in the music," and "... the same thing") makes the comments too ambiguous to be meaningful. But here's the zinger. Because the verbiage is so wishy-washy, students miss the connection!

The other problem is the delivery. It usually isn't emphatic and deliberate enough. What teachers do is make the relating statement in such a passing sort of way that students don't even notice it, let alone "see" it—even when the correct terminology is used. There isn't enough stress on the right words or enough deliberateness in the speech. Instead, they use a ho-hum tone of voice where nothing sounds important.

Guidelines for Articulating Similarity

Here are some tips for articulating the similarity—*and doing it right.*

Select Appropriate Phenomenon. Be sure the "like" idea really gives a clear picture of the concept. If it doesn't, all the talking in the world won't make a difference. It's got to be something you know will do the job.

Establish Comment List. Help yourself by making a list of sample statements—not more than three or four. That way you won't have to flounder or trip over your own words when it's time to use it. Too, you can concentrate on the delivery. Here are some examples:

- "Know what? Melodies in music have the same (long/short sounds) as (environmental idea)."
- "The ongoing beat in music also has (strong/weak beats) just like (environmental idea)."

- "Did you know that there are sentences in music just like in English? We call them phrases."

Use Correct Terminology. You've got to refer to the aesthetic element. Don't say ". . . in music" when you mean ". . . in the melody." You've got to give an activity its proper name. Don't tell students "to play their rhythm sticks" when you want them "to tap." Avoid pronouns like *it, this, that, them, those,* etc.; use the proper nouns instead. Correct verbiage is a "must."

Emphasize Important Words. Stress the important words/phrases. Use vocal inflection, different dynamic levels, or repeat the word/phrase. Make the statement sufficiently pronounced so that the students hear it. Be emphatic and enthusiastic—and practice! Tape yourself, if necessary. Do whatever it takes!

Use Deliberate Tempo. Don't rush through the comment. Make a point of **speaking slower** as you emphasize the relationship, like saying one word at a time in places. Changing tempo also gets the attention every time! Stretching out certain words is another way. Remember, don't rush. Be deliberate.

Add Facial Expressions. Remember to speak with your face, too! Your face needs to reinforce your words, generate enthusiasm, and help get the message across that what you're saying is important.

Use Appropriate Gesturing. Talk with your hands as well as your face. Get in the habit of dramatizing words (up/down, high/low, loud/soft, etc.) to reinforce the relationship even more, plus capture the students' attention. Copy your social gestures to get started, but do them more precisely and with more flair.

Use Intentional Pause. Make yourself wait a moment or two after the statement is made. Give it time to sink in. Say it and then scan the faces. Slowly. Maybe say it again—more deliberately. The point is, don't rush ahead; pausing helps the students solidify the relationship.

A Scenario

Let's come back to one point. Are you sure you know where to make this statement? I said earlier it comes immediately after the motivational discussion. But that probably doesn't mean very much unless you see it in the context of a lesson, so here's a scenario. Let's say you just finished an activity for the review concept, and you're ready to start a new concept. To make a smooth transition, use a verbal bridge to assess the review activity and then instruct for the new. In other words, you instigate the motivational discussion in the instruction part of the verbal bridge. The relating statement would come at the close of the motivational discussion. (See Figure 4.3 for a diagram of the situation.)

Concluding Challenge

Do you use this approach? Do you tell students that a new concept is like some environmental phenomenon? It's a marvelous way to give students an immediate "idea" of the new concept. Make sure, though, that you articulate the statement in such a way that it makes an impact.

LESS EFFECTIVE

When he introduced meter in 4's, Mr. Barry Tone kept talking about four-leaf clovers. "Clovers don't always have four leaves, but they're there! You gotta look hard. They're like 4/4 time in music. You just don't have one bigger leaf. Interesting, huh? See if you can hum the four beats in this next piece. Sit up and listen, or else you won't hear it." No one looked up or even attempted to sit up as the music started to play.

Mr. Ty Note told his fourth graders they were ready to learn about the long-short sounds in melody. "How many of you know Morse Code?" he asked. "No one? It sounds like this." Then he tapped out several requests and told a few war stories about the Code. "See how important Morse Code is? And how it's based on long-short sounds, like dot, dot, dash? See? Just like in music." But the class was still thinking about Morse Code. They didn't even hear the music part.

MORE EFFECTIVE

Mr. Barry Tone held up a four-leaf clover when he introduced meter in 4's. "What do you notice immediately? That's right, the clover has four leaves!" The class talked excitedly about clovers. At the right moment, Mr. Barry Tone said, "So clovers can have four leaves, can't they?" He paused. "Beats in music can move in groups of four also." Eyes lit up as the connection sunk in. "Listen to this selection and see if you can hear the meter moving in 4's."

"We're going to learn about long-short sounds in the melody today," Mr. Ty Note told his fourth graders. "Let's talk about long-short sounds, okay." The class was fascinated with the Morse Code discussion. They even learned a short message. Then, in a very deliberate tone of voice, Mr. Ty Note said, "Listen! We have long-and-short sounds in the melody, just like the dot, dot, dashes in Morse Code." A ripple of "Oh yeahs!" went across the room. Mr. Ty Note could tell they got the idea.

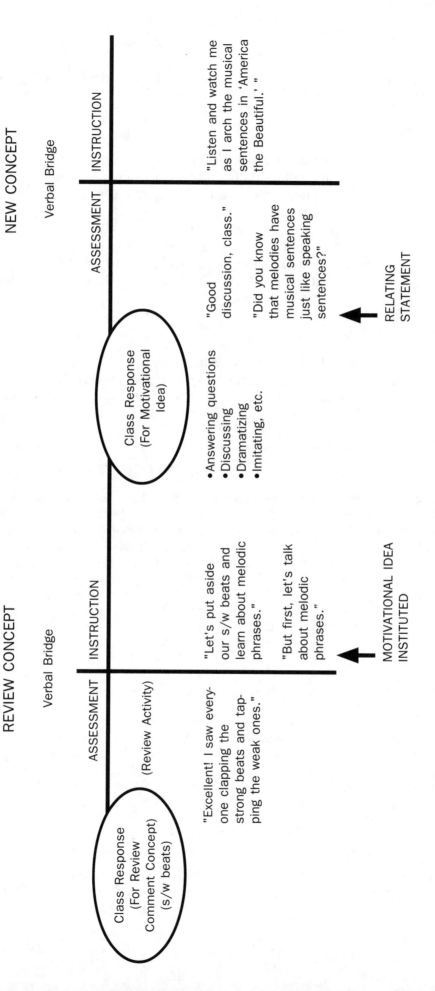

Figure 4.3. Placement of Relating Statement in the Context of Verbal Bridging.

Closing Concepts in Lesson

Another tactic you should know about is *clearly and concisely* bringing one concept to a close before starting another. It doesn't happen automatically, so you've got to make a conscious effort to do it. That means you need some know-how and then some expertise.

Definition of Closing Concepts

First of all, I'm talking about lessons with two, or maybe three concepts, where you need to bring the first concept to a close before you start the second. If there's a third, the second one is closed before you introduce the third one.

More specifically, though, the term refers to a verbal announcement, or a specific comment to the effect that the class is "done" (for today) with one concept and ready for the next. For example, "Let's put aside our melodic rhythm concept about long-and-short sounds and get ready for a new concept called such-and-such." It's an instructional statement announcing the end of one idea and the start of another.

Reasons for Closing Concepts

Closing each concept in a multiple-concept lesson is crucial to good teaching. Here's why.

First, it **gives the lesson more structure**. This is one of the easiest, and most effective, ways to make your lesson more organized. When you bring each concept to a close, you automatically organize the lesson into smaller, logical segments which make for a more orderly presentation. Concepts aren't left hanging in the air; instead the lesson takes on shape—or structure.

Second, it **makes the students more attentive**. The more structured the lesson, the better the students stay with you. By putting a clear-cut ending (and beginning) to each concept, you help the students follow the lessons better—and you make them feel part of the process. More important, you keep them on your own wavelength so they "know" what's happening; they're better informed!

Third, it **makes your teaching more polished**. Closing a concept is a high-level competency. It puts a finishing touch on your teaching because the lesson moves more smoothly from one concept to the next. In essence, you're demonstrating one of the distinguishing trademarks of a master teacher.

Guidelines for Closing Concepts

Here are some guidelines with regard to (a) where the closing statement is made, (b) what the closing statement entails, and (c) how the closing statement is delivered.

Where Closing Statement is Made. There's an ideal spot in your lesson for the statement no matter what your procedures are: in the instructional part of the verbal bridge. The verbal bridge is a communicating tool that can be used after any class (or individual) response involving (1) an assessment of the previous activity, and (2) an instruction for the next. In this case, the statement comes in the instructional part following the final activity for the concept. (See Figure 4.4, which diagrams the closing statement in the context of a verbal bridge.) What's so great about verbal bridging (for this task) is that it gives you an organized way to close each concept while still maintaining your own style of teaching. The best place, then, to close a concept is in the instruction part of the verbal bridge, after the assessment.

Verbal Bridge

Closing Statement for "Ending" Concept

Class Response (or activity)	**Assessment**	**Instruction**	Class Response (or activity)
(Final Activity for Concluding Concept)	"Excellent, class! I saw everyone tapping their rhythm sticks on the eighth notes and sliding on the quarter notes."	"Let's stop our rhythmic reading for today—we'll continue next lesson. Let's move on to like-contrasting phrases."	(First Activity for Next Concept)

Figure 4.4. Example of Closing Statement in the Instruction as Part of the Verbal Bridge.

What Closing Statement Entails. The statement must be to the point; the more concise, the better. All you need to do is make reference to three items in the statement:

1. the impending action
2. the closing concept
3. the starting concept

And, most of the time, in that order too. This is neither the time nor the place to get flowery or wordy. You need to state your intention in the most articulate way you can and move on. Below are several examples. Notice (1) that each example contains the three criteria, (2) that each one is a clear-cut, definitive statement that neatly ties up one idea and opens up another, and (3) that each is an instructional statement (which comes after the assessment) in the verbal bridge.

- "We're going to put away our high/low pitches now and work more on loud and soft sounds."
- "I'd like to stop working on Rondo form for today and introduce a new rhythmic concept called Syncopation."
- "Let's shut off our keyboards and continue our I-V$_7$ accompaniment next time. We have to move on to intervals."
- "That's it for melodic patterns, class. If there are no questions, let's deal with phrases for the rest of the class."
- "We'd better call it quits with rhythmic reading for today, class. We need time now for sight singing."
- "Let's put away our high-low call charts, boys and girls, and get ready to work on accented beats next."

These are simple two-part directives that end one concept and announce another. Let me share a story with you of one teacher who really struggled with loose ends. I could never tell where one concept ended and another began; neither could the kids. Take her lesson on rhythmic patterns and phrase form (ABAB). When the last rhythmic activity was over, she said something like, "You got that rhythm pattern every time. Great! A lot of music has a rhythmic pattern. And a phrase form, too! Did you know that?" Just when the phrasing activity was about to begin, some confused-sounding student piped up wanting to know, "Are we supposed to do the pattern stuff too?" A bunch of "yeahs" went up everywhere. The poor teacher came unglued! But the day she finally decided to try clear-cut closings, the light went on! She couldn't believe how much better students followed her. Moral of the story? Know how to make closings as clear as possible.

How Closing Statement Is Delivered. The skill and expertise comes in delivering the statement effectively. Here are basic delivery techniques that will make your statement more meaningful and give it more punch!

Be Deliberate and Emphatic

Slow down your speech in the statement and speak in a more deliberate and authoritative tone of voice. Be emphatic and emphasize the conceptual terms and the instructional phrases, such as, put aside, move on, etc. Use your most persuasive manner of speaking in the closing statement.

Maintain Eye Contact

Look directly at the class when you make the statement. Slowly scan from side to side and front to back. Make actual eye contact with as many students as possible while you're giving out the comment. Don't talk to the chalkboard or the floorboards! Eye contact is essential in communicating effectively.

Use Timely Pauses

Stop talking for a moment to create an effect or make an impact. You could pause (a) right before, (b) right after, or (c) anywhere in between, as you see fit. But use it sparingly. The key is being sensitive to the right moment.

Add Appropriate Gestures

Use your hands to reinforce the statement and make it more appealing. Dramatize phrases like setting aside, putting away, or sitting down. My favorite gesture is packaging the concept by "tying the bow" before putting it aside. You can dramatize concepts, too, such as high-low, up-down, loud-soft, etc. But, don't be self-conscious; do the actions with a confident, theatrical flair so that they appeal to the students.

Repeat When Necessary

Say something again if you feel you need to, whether it be a single word, a particular clause, or the whole statement. You can do it several ways, like (a) pausing momentarily before repeating, (b) repeating immediately with more emphasis, or (c) indicating you'll repeat by saying, "Let me repeat that," "I'll repeat," or "I'll say that again." But don't get repeat-happy; use it wisely, especially in the closing comments.

Concluding Challenge

If you're not used to giving a closing statement, try it a few times so you can see how well it works and how easily it can fit into your own procedures. See what a sensible and effective step it is for structuring your lesson and refining your teaching.

LESS EFFECTIVE

"Okay," Mr. Ron Doe said after the fifth-grade class finished its tone row melody. "Here's a handout on Schoenberg, the twelve-tone composer. We've got to listen how meter shifts from 2/4 to 3/4 in this tone row composition." When the selection ended, Mr. Ron Doe asked if they heard the meter change. "What change? Weren't we listening for the tone row?" Mr. Ron Doe wondered why the class was so confused. "Get with it," he chided.

"Put your rhythm sticks under your chairs, class," Ms. Sara Nade instructed. Incidentally-like she added, "And we'll work on high-low pitches." But the children weren't listening. "Look up here, not out the window," she snapped. "Tommy, leave your sticks alone!" She made a mental note to work on their listening skills. "Then pay attention to me," she said more irritably.

MORE EFFECTIVE

"Great tone row you composed," Mr. Ron Doe said to his fifth graders. "Let me give you this handout about Schoenberg, the twelve-tone composer." Then he paused briefly and said, "Right now, we need to set aside our composition and turn our attention to a review of shifting meter from 2/4 to 3/4." With that he prepared the class and then instructed them to listen for the meter change. When the selection was over, Mr. Ron Doe praised the class. No one seemed confused.

When the activity was over, Ms. Sara Nade told the children how pleased she was. Then pausing for a moment, she smiled and said in a more deliberate voice, "We'll stop our accented beats for today, class. Let's go on to high-low pitches." Ms. Sara Nade stretched up and reached low when she said that. The children nodded excitedly and kept their attention glued to Ms. Sara Nade as she held up some visual aids. "I appreciate your attention," she said.

Referring to Motivational Idea in Summary

You should bring back the motivational idea when you summarize a new concept in a lesson because it's a good way to pull the concept together after it's been introduced and experienced through the activities, particularly when the motivational idea was used to introduce the new concept. (See "Using Motivational Idea" in Chapter 3.)

Clarification of Referring to Motivational Idea

The word "referring" here means just what it says—**actually making reference to the motivational idea**. It's telling the class one more time how the new concept is "like" such-and-such, and, if some visual aid is used, consciously displaying that item in the summary as well. The point is, the referring is literal, not figurative.

Significance of Referring Back

This might seem like an insignificant detail at first glance, but it isn't. Here are several reasons to show why it's not. Referring back to the motivational idea (in the summary) is more than a small detail because it:

Adds a Finishing Touch to the Lesson. The truth is, so many of the refining tactics of teaching seem like little details—and, in a sense, they are. They deal with a higher order of tasks that are executed for the purpose of refining one's teaching, not enabling it. That's what referring back does! It adds that touch of finesse to the lesson, or that finishing touch, if you will.

Why be concerned with high-order tasks, when some enabling tasks—such as giving specific instructions, maintaining effective pacing, or managing classroom behavior—might still need attention? Because it's possible to have pockets of finesse in your lessons, even while some of the enabling skills still need attention.

Gives a Unified Feeling to the Lesson. By bringing back the motivational idea in the summary and reminding students how it resembles the new concept, you establish a feeling of unity in the lesson. You help "tie" the lesson together, or "pull" it together, so that the lesson has a more cohesive feeling. But the best part of it is that the students "catch" this effect!

Provides a Closing Sensation for the Lesson. There's a definite sense of the lesson coming to a close with this tactic. Students get a clear indication that the teacher is wrapping it up. Students need to feel this sense of closure, which is why it's so important to have a satisfying close to the lesson. Referring back to the motivational idea is an ideal way of achieving this closing sensation.

Reinforces the New Concept in the Lesson. Making reference to the motivational idea in the summary helps to solidify the new idea in the students' minds. It comes immediately on the heels of their hands-on experiences—while the concept is still fresh. Reiterating the relationship strengthens the concept even more and makes it clearer to the students. This is probably the most obvious reason for using this approach, but it's still significant nonetheless. In short, it's a reinforcing gimmick.

Stimulates the Students' Thinking During the Lesson. There's a subtle difference here between reinforcing the conceptual material and stimulating the students' thinking. Both have to do with the learning process, but with a slight distinction. Reinforcing "nails down" the concept, while stimulating "opens up" the concept to other ideas. It gets students thinking and asking questions about the similarities between the motivational idea and the concept. Referring back to the motivational idea, then, becomes a stimulus. It keeps the students alert and motivates their thinking.

Problem With Referring Back

I don't know why the motivational concept is ignored so often, or why more teachers don't use it. Relating the new idea to something familiar seems like such an obvious thing to do! The tactic is **revealing**, especially when you're introducing a concept, and it's **reinforcing** when you're summarizing it.

But I'm even more perplexed by those who **do use a motivational idea** to introduce a new concept, but then forget to bring it back in the summary. What a waste—particularly when a lot of time and energy is spent preparing a visual aid for the motivational idea, and it ends up leaning against the desk or laying on the floor after the initial presentation. What's even worse is that the motivational idea doesn't get used to its full potential. It can't become that (a) finishing touch, (b) unifying factor, or (c) closing indicator. This is an unfortunate oversight for more teachers than you think!

Here's the situation: a lot of teachers don't refer back to the motivational idea because they don't use a motivational idea. That's one problem. The other problem is, some teachers just forget about it, even after using it to introduce the concept. Hopefully, you don't have either problem. But if you do, check out the following suggestions.

Suggestions for Referring to Motivational Idea

These suggestions will give you some idea how to handle the task and what to say. It always feels awkward when you're trying something new (like referring back to one's motivational idea) or when you're changing something. It's easier, however, when you have a few "rules" to give you direction.

Display Visual Aid Properly. If you've got a visual aid of some sort with your motivational idea, be sure to display it **in a conspicuous spot** when you're done with it in the introduction. If it's a drawing, a poster, or a sign, put it on a tripod, hang it on the chalkboard clips, or stand it in the chalk tray. If it's an object, like a stuffed animal, an historical artifact, or a homemade replica of something, then set it on the piano, your desk, or a table. That way you (1) keep the item in view as a **constant reminder** of the concept, and (2) make it readily available for **reference purposes** in the summary. Unless it's accessible, you won't use the visual aid. That's why the proper display is so important.

Verbalize Relationship Articulately. Keep in mind this is a verbal task, which means its success depends on how well you articulate the relationship and how you bring it forward in the summary. There isn't any pat formula or set script, but a rule-of-thumb will help; namely, indicate how "this" is like "that" or "that" is like "this." Then preface this statement with a question, such as "Did you know that . . . ?" Or, "Do you remember that . . . ?" You've verbalized the relationship! Here are some examples of this rule-of-thumb in the summary:

- "Remember our *motivational idea*? See how it's like our new concept about ....?"
- "Can you see how our *motivational idea* resembles the new concept we've just learned?"
- "And what did we say our new concept was like? That's right! Like this *motivational idea.*"
- "We talked earlier in the lesson that our new concept about .... is just like what? Good! Like the *motivational idea.*"

But wait. You still need to "get into" this statement. You can't just start summarizing by saying "This is like that." What you do is make this comment within the context of a verbal bridge. (See "Using Verbal Bridges" in Chapter 3.) That means you **assess the activity** just completed, then **instruct for the review**. "Let's review what we learned today," or "I'd like to review the lesson now." Now you're ready for the relationship comment as shown in Figure 4.5 below.

Focus on Visual Aid Directly. Here's the key to this tactic: Direct the students' attention back to the visual aid **while you're making the comment**. Actually (a) point to it, (b) pick it up, or (c) set it closer to the class. This helps to clinch the students' perception of the new concept, especially in the light of the activities they just did. **Be very deliberate** about focusing on the visual aid as you reinforce the fact that "this" is like "that." It's one of those little touches that refines your lesson and distinguishes the master teacher.

Comment on Motivational Idea Briefly (Optional). Do you need to say anything more about the motivational idea after making the review comment? Sometimes yes, sometimes no. Sometimes all you need to do is make the comment. My advice is to play it by ear. It's not how much you say, but what you say. The comment itself may be enough!

Concluding Challenge

Take a brief inventory now. Do you refer back to the motivational idea when you summarize a new concept? Do you even use a motivational idea? If you don't, I encourage you to start because it's an effective tool when you're introducing a new concept. If all you need, however, is a little tip or gentle reminder to come back to the motivational idea in the summary, then consider yourself nudged. You don't want to overlook this tactic. It has too many rewards.

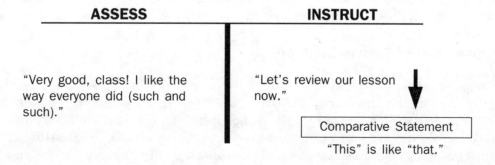

Figure 4.5. Placement of Relationship Comment Within Context of Verbal Bridge.

LESS EFFECTIVE	MORE EFFECTIVE
"Let's review now," Ms. Tap-a-Tap said to her first graders. "What did we learn about loud sounds? Does tiptoeing make a loud sound? No. Does stomping? Yes! And what did we do to sound loud? Yes, we clapped our hands. And played our drums. Very good. I can tell you know what loud sounds are. In our next lesson we'll listen to more loud music. And we'll clap some more. Okay? You aren't listening to me, class. Look up here. (They're ready to leave!)" she mumbled to herself!	"Can we review our lesson before we leave?" Ms. Tap-a-Tap asked. Picking up a picture, she reminded the first graders that "Animals make loud sounds too. Just like music! What kind of a sound does this lion make? Yes! A loud roar. And what about this hippopotamus? Very good. A loud sound too! And what did we do to show our music was loud? That's right, we clapped and played drums. We were loud like the animals, weren't we?" The children shook their heads excitely.
"That's it for today, class. We've been concentrating on melodic patterns today, haven't we?" Ms. Ring-a-Ling told the class. "Let's review what we learned. Jim, what's a melodic pattern? Not quite. Sally? Who can sing the melodic pattern in our song we used today. Thank you, Jane. How many times did you hear it, class? And what did we do to emphasize the pattern? Pay attention!" By the time Ms. Ring-a-Ling finished reviewing, the fifth graders were fidgeting and talking. "You didn't pay attention very well in our review," she scolded. "I'm disappointed in you." The class looked glum as they filed out. Ms. Ring-a-Ling frowned at them and shook her head disgustedly.	"Okay, let's go back and pull together what we've learned today. We've been dealing with what? Yes. Melodic patterns." Then Ms. Ring-a-Ling picked up the patch quilt on her desk and held it up for the fifth graders. "Remember how we said that this quilt resembled our melodic patterns? How so?" Hands flew up everywhere. "Yes, Jason? The light green patch keeps showing up, you say. Good. Mary? That's right! It's like our melodic patterns because certain patterns can be seen a number of times. Not just once. And does the pattern always look the same? Yes, just like our melodic pattern. Good review, class. But it's time to go." The class moaned. "Do we have to?" Ms. Ring-a-Ling smiled and nodded.

Summarizing With Short-Answer Questions

Summarizing is the most under-rated verbal skill there is! That's a "heavy" statement, I know, but there's more truth to it than meets the eye. That's a pity because summarizing is such an integral part of teaching a lesson. It's crucial that you are able to "conduct" a meaningful summary and, more specifically, that you know how to ask questions that have short answers. Why? So you can get **feedback from the students**. That's the whole crux of asking questions. It's also the reason why you need to be skillful in the art of asking questions, especially the short-answer kind.

Explanation of Summarizing

Everyone understands what a short-answer question is, so we don't need to define it. But we do need to clarify the principle involved: **responding versus telling**.

Summarizing a lesson by asking the class (or individual students) questions that need only one- or two-word answers, or possibly three, is a **student-oriented approach**. It places emphasis on the feedback from students and on assessment of learning, as well as involvement of students. In short, it's a responsive approach that focuses on the student.

Here's what it's not. It's not summarizing by way of "telling," or regurgitating for the class "what we learned today is . . . ." That's a **teacher-oriented approach**, where the teacher does all the "telling" and the students, all the "listening." This is not what happens in the questioning approach—students do the "telling" instead.

The key to summarizing with short-answer questions, then, is involvement. Students have an opportunity to speak in the summary, not just listen to it.

Problems With Summarizing

There are two problems when it comes to using the questioning technique in the summary.

The **first one** is the more common. It's simply that the questioning tactic isn't used by a lot of teachers when they summarize because they think that a "summary" needs to be a recitation, or a recap of what the class did. In fact, they think of the summary in terms of "telling" the students they learned this and that. Some "telling" turns into a blow-by-blow account that turns off students. Other "tellings" are over before they begin. It's too bad that so many teachers have this false notion about summarizing. They get into the habit of "telling," and it's hard to break.

Let me share an illustration of one of those blow-by-blow summaries. I remember thinking that it was a good lesson, and that the teacher had some good activities for the fourth graders. Then it was time to wrap it up. I thought I had seen and heard it all when it came to "telling" summaries, but this one took the cake! She started with, "First we did . . . . Then we did . . . Remember how we . . . ? After that Sally and Janet came up front to . . ." and on-and-on-and-on, etc. I could see she was taking great pride in remembering every last detail. The kids were basket cases by the time she finished—and so was I! I was anxious for our conference! *THE SUMMARY* was at the top of my list.

The **second problem** is that some teachers have problems phrasing their questions to get short answers. What happens is that they (a) hem-and-haw, (b) miss-the-mark (and ask a long-answer question), or (c) get all tongue-tied trying to ask the question. It's a difficult skill to develop, but it can be done! You've got to start from scratch and think through your questions beforehand *in your planning*. Then write them out—and memorize them, if you have to at first. After a while, you'll start asking short-answer questions automatically. So instead of asking, "Why do we call this an upward passage?" you would ask, "This is an upward passage because all the tones are moving how?" (*Answer*: Upward!)

Suggestions Regarding Summarizing

Asking short-answer questions isn't easy. Inexperienced teachers are always quite shocked to find out just how difficult it is, and how awkward and tongue-tied you can feel initially. The fact is, you've got to work at it. It helps to have some suggestions to guide you. The following are very basic, yet very instructive.

Prepare Questions Beforehand. The only way to be ready for this task is to prepare your questions before teaching the lesson. Actually write them down. That way you can discipline yourself to think through a series of sequential questions—in light of the outline for the lesson, that is. Formulate questions that require only one or two words for the answer. The summary is not the place for long answers. You should ask questions about (a) the motivational idea, (b) the planned activities, (c) the selected concept, (d) the musical examples, etc. Remember, preparation is first!

Practice Questions Out Loud. After you get the questions written down, practice them out loud in front of a mirror. Concentrate on two objectives when you practice: (1) getting the questions firmly established in your mind, and (2) improving the delivery of the questions with regard to inflection, projection, and dynamic differentiation. Remember, the practicing must be done out loud. You need to hear yourself speak, and know how your voice sounds so that there aren't any surprises when you teach.

Rephrase Questions as Needed. What are you going to do about those questions the student(s) can't answer? You can't keep repeating the same question, so you've got to rephrase the question. If you can't do it on the spot, then it's back to the drawing board, writing out the rephrased questions, and then practicing them. Your rephrasing skill will come more easily as you go along, but you've got to work at it. One word of caution, though: You might need to **make the rephrased question simpler** and easier to answer, especially if the original question was a bit over the heads of the students.

Conduct Class's Response. You want to have the class answer the questions together whether it's one word or two. You do this by "conducting" the class's response, just like you would a choral group. Here's what you do—immediately after the question:

- Take a prep breath through slightly open mouth.
- Bring head back simultaneously with the intake of breath.
- Drop head and bring to a stop with a slight bounce, or ictus. (Class comes in on ictus.)
- *Optional*: Bring right hand up in sync with the head on inhaled breath, and back down. (Class comes in on the ictus.)

By using a gesture with the head, the hand, or both, you can "coordinate" the response and have the class answer together. Work on your head downbeat. You really need to "conduct" the class response to have control of the question-answer technique.

Have Class/Individual Responses. You can ask individual students to answer as well. You don't have to limit yourself to just class responses. In fact, you can and should intersperse the class questions with individual responses. For example, you can go from, "Class, what do we call this symbol?" to "Jim, remember how many sharps for D Major?" Getting a mix of responses keeps the students on their toes and makes the summarizing more interesting!

Assess Students' Responses. Finally, use some immediate feedback sign with the student(s). You need to indicate that they answered the question correctly. For example, you could do any of the following kinds of things:

- Nod your head and smile
- Give thumbs up and smile
- Clap your hands and smile
- Say "good," "yes," or "that's correct"
- Pat student on back or shoulder

• Wink at student and smile

Notice that many of these signs can be given without stopping the flow of questions. They're done silently, with the exception of the verbal ones, of course. But even those can be given with a minimum of interruption. What's important here is that you give immediate approval of each response. You'll get a lot of mileage out of this recognition—students will respond better when they know they'll be stroked. By the way, that "smile" gesture means putting on a pleasant face. It's important to look pleased as well. Remember, then, to give immediate feedback with a pleasant face.

Reasons for Summarizing With Questions

There are several professional reasons why I prefer questioning to "telling." Let me share them with you.

Involves the Students in the Summary. The questioning technique keeps the students "in" the lesson right to the end. They don't suddenly become passive participators while the teacher "tells" them what they've just learned. The hands-on approach is vital because it holds their attention. If you don't believe me, watch the class carefully the next time you end up "telling." Can you see them "turn off"? No matter what age level you're teaching, if you don't keep them "with you," they'll leave you! **Involvement is the key here.**

Assesses the Students in the Summary. There's immediate feedback for both parties! You, as the teacher, get on-the-spot satisfaction because you accomplished your objectives and because the students really learned the conceptual idea. It's always a rewarding feeling when the questioning goes well, more than when you just tell the students "what we learned today."

But look what the question-answer approach does **for the students**. By virtue of the fact that they can answer the questions—collectively or individually—they get immediate approval, and have a greater sense of pride in themselves. You can even see it on their faces and read it in their body language. Notice this when you try the questioning technique.

So both teacher and students feel the positive impact of the short-answer approach. Questioning is a perfect on-the-spot assessment tool.

Provides the Enjoyment in the Summary. You can't argue with this reason once you've seen the students' reaction. They're more alive, more with-it, and more turned-on when the questioning is going on. It holds their interest, as opposed to the telling. The telling technique gets boring and dull very quickly, especially if you don't use any inflection, dynamics, or gestures when you speak. But with question-and-answer, you can make it more enjoyable just because you're involving the students.

Concluding Challenge

What approach do you use to summarize a lesson? Do you do a telling job? Do you say, "Today we learned about . . . ?" Or, do you summarize the lesson by asking? If you do ask questions, do you use short-answer questions? I hope you can say "yes" to both of these last questions because it's time that teachers become more skillful in the art of summarizing a lesson through questioning. If you need some help, consider the suggestions. The truth is, you've got to work at developing this skill.

LESS EFFECTIVE

"Today we've been dealing with accented beats," Mr. Ernie Block said to his third graders. "What's an accented beat? No one? Hmm. Guess I'll have to tell you what we learned today about accented beats. I want everyone to write down this definition. No talking. Maybe next time you'll listen better during the lesson, and you won't have to write anything." Mr. Ernie Block could tell the class was bored, and that they didn't want to write down the definition. "Sit up and get ready."

When the last activity was over, Mr. Johnny Cage started to summarize the lesson on ABA Form. Closing his book, he said to the sixth graders, "Let's review what we did today. We began by discussing the shape of the White House, didn't we? Remember that we discovered it had an ABA shape, like this? A B A And after that we marched and clapped on the A sections, and swayed on the B section. And then we . . . etc." Someone let out a sigh while others yawned and looked bored. "Sit up, everyone, and listen," he scolded.

MORE EFFECTIVE

"Let's see how much you remembered today," Mr. Ernie Block said to his third graders. "What kind of beats were we talking about today? Bill? Yes, accented beats. Are accented beats the stronger or weaker beats, class? Good, the stronger beats. And what did we compare these strong beats to earlier? Pete? Very good. The first loud CHOO on a steam engine. And do we usually have two accented beats following each other? Class? No! That's right. What kind of beats follow an accented beat then? Everyone. Terrific! Unaccented beats. You're on-the-ball today!"

Mr. Johnny Cage praised the class for their performance in the last activity. "Let's see what we've learned today. What do we call our three-part form? Yes, ABA. What's another name for it? Jim? Great! Ternary Form. Are these parts called sections or phrases? That's right, sections. And how do we know when B starts? Michelle? Sure, it sounds different." The class was alert and ready to answer. "Good review, class. You answered everything perfectly. I'm proud of you."

Specifying Specific Movements for Activities

Preparing students properly for an activity involves specifying specific actions during the prep step, before the activity actually starts. Students need to know which arm to raise, on which foot to begin, or in which direction to turn; otherwise, the activity won't be executed accurately. You can't leave these details to chance and think that students will do them on their own—they won't. You have to tell them. That's why specifying the specific movements is such an important step in the prepping of an activity. It insures a more accurate response.

Clarification of Specifying Specific Movements

Let's first clarify the distinction between the **activity movements** versus the **specific movements**.

I use the term "activity movements" to refer to the generic response of the activity itself, like marching, singing, or playing (rhythm sticks, maracas, or tambourines). It's the particular experiences called for in the lesson plan—not the specifics, just the type of activity. The "specific movements," on the other hand, are those detail actions within the generic response. They have to do with matters about left or right, fast or slow, or loud or soft. Here are some examples:

- Turning to the left or right (**specific**) while marching (**general**)
- Tapping softly (**specific**) while playing melodic rhythm woodblocks (**general**)

- Starting on left foot (**specific**) with marching/clapping (**general**)
- Swaying to the right, then left (**specific**) while tapping/snapping (**general**)

Notice that the "specifics" are observed simultaneously with the main activity. Here's the important fact: They can either make or break an activity, depending upon whether or not they're addressed by the teacher.

Reasons for Specifying Specific Movements

If your activity has some specific movements, such as turning, bending, or motioning, you need to deal with it. The results below should be enough to convince you it's the right thing to do. Take a look at these results. They're strong reasons for dealing with specific movements **prior to the actual activity**.

More Accurate Class Response. When you take care of these movement details beforehand, you won't get umpteen different responses. Everyone will do the detail actions the same way—and the *correct* way—because you've informed them to turn left, or raise their right hand, or to tap softly, not loudly. When you make certain that students are properly instructed, you set the stage for a more accurate response when the activity begins. This should be reason enough for taking care of those details in the activity. Remember, the better the preparation, the better the response!

Better Ongoing Classroom Pace. You won't have to stop and start as much when you take care of details beforehand. The lesson can flow more smoothly. Just the opposite happens when you overlook the details. The pacing starts to sputter. No sooner does the activity begin than it has to stop because students aren't doing it right. Some turn right, some left, some raise the left hand instead of the right, and some play with mallets in their left, not right hand. The point is, there's confusion and disarray with the activity. You have to stop and give the specific instructions after the fact. In the meantime, the pacing bogs down. With proper preparation, though, you avoid this situation. You can keep the lesson flowing because the students know what to do.

More Available Classroom Time. Going hand-in-hand with better pacing is the fact that there's **extra teaching time** in the lesson, extra minutes you would have lost with stopping and starting. When you take time to prevent problems **before** the lesson, you reward yourself with more teaching time **during** the lesson— even if it's only two or three minutes.

More Positive Class Attitude. Don't overlook this aspect because it has too much bearing on the activity, as well as the whole lesson. When you genuinely demonstrate a pleased and satisfied response with regard to the class's performance, you establish a comfortable classroom aura. You give students a sense of accomplishment and self-worth. They feel rewarded for their efforts, and more willing to stay "with it" and participate again. All of the outcomes mentioned are vital, but this one is indispensable. So **cherish the positive attitude**. It makes teaching, as well as learning, a more pleasant experience for everyone involved.

Problem Regarding Specifying Specific Movements

The major problem in dealing with the detail movements is assuming too much— assuming that the students will do the turning, or the lifting, or the bending in the right direction, or with the right hand, or at the right speed—without any instruction. You can't take anything for granted in teaching, especially with an activity. It leads to too many problems.

Wastes Class Time. Whenever you start an activity without attending to the details, you better plan on stopping and starting, and squandering valuable teaching time. You'll be doing the job twice. No matter how you look at it, that's a waste of time.

Interrupts Class Momentum. Any time you have to stop and start an activity to make a correction (that should have been done beforehand), you disrupt the momentum and stop the flow of the lesson—to say nothing about destroying the continuity! Unfortunately, when you make the assumption that students will "get it" on their own, you sacrifice the momentum.

Destroys Class Enthusiasm. You dampen students' spirits when you have them go back and do something they should have done the first time—if they had been told! Students quickly figure this out. Enthusiasm goes downhill fast when there's too much backtracking, especially when it's preventable.

Hinders Class's Response. Instead of helping to make the class response better, you make it worse by what you don't do—omission of proper preparation. You're really guilty of not doing all you could have done to help the class do the activity the right way.

Suggestions for Specifying Specific Movements

The questions here probably run the gamut, all the way from how to determine the specific movements to how to get the job done—and when. Here are three basic guidelines or suggestions. Read and study them carefully. Then try putting them into practice.

Anticipate Necessary Movements. There's no substitute for careful forethought—or planning—of what's involved. Let me give you a quick one-two-three approach for preparing:

- **Step 1**: Select the appropriate activities (age-appropriate and level-appropriate).
- **Step 2**: Try the activity, literally, to determine the specific movements.
- **Step 3**: Think through the implementation and/or practice the prep step to hear yourself verbalize the instructions.

Careful planning is the key to "knowing." Don't shortchange yourself here. You can't specify the specifics if you don't know what they are. If planning is something you need to do, then do it.

Follow Proper Procedures. For those who need some guidance in how and where to implement this task, here's another three-step "Activity Readiness" procedure you might find helpful. It's a game plan for getting at the specifics.

- **Step 1: Give Teacher Demo**. This is where you model the activity. Get into it by means of an instructional comment, such as "Now listen and watch me as I . . . ." Then do the activity exactly how you want students to do it. How long? No more than three times or five or six seconds, whichever is more suitable.

- **Step 2**: **Conduct Class Prep**. This is the class prep step where you're going to specify the details. As soon as you finish your demo, give a simple command like "With me," or "Together," or "Everyone now." That way the class knows they're supposed to try it with you. But just before trying it, give the brief instructions for the details, such as "Start on your left foot," or "Turn towards the door," or "Hold up the card in your right hand," etc. It'll only take a few seconds to give these instructions. Then get right to the try out or the mini-drill. Prep students just before you drill them. It's such a simple step, but what a lifesaver!

- **Step 3**: **Assume Starting Position**. As soon as the mini-drill is over, immediately get the class in the starting position. Keep them focused by snapping out, "Hands in starting position," or "Mallets up," or "Rhythm sticks." Also, assess the drill ("Good tapping, class") just before they assume the starting position.

Provide Verbal Reminders. Once the actual activity is underway, all you need to do is throw out verbal reminders just before an action is about to happen. That way, you make sure the students remember to turn left, play softly, or stand instead of sit. It won't get in the way of the music or distract the students, not if it's a one- or two-word comment such as "Sit," "Turn left," or "Right hand up" etc.

Concluding Challenge

How do you handle these detail movements in your activities? Are you aware of these details and have a plan of action? If you've never thought of focusing on these detail actions, then it's time you did. I've given you reasons for pursuing the task and specific suggestions. If you begin with careful planning, everything else will fall in place. Try it and see.

LESS EFFECTIVE

"We're going to do an easy line dance today. It goes like this. Watch me," Mr. Rock Music said to the sixth graders. "We'll try it first. Good job. Now let's do it with music." "They're not stepping over with the left foot," he said to himself, "but they'll get it!" But when they tried dancing with the music, it was a bomb. They were turning the wrong way and not stepping over with the right foot. "That was horrible!" Mr. Rock Music blurted out. "Let's see if we can get our turns better this time. And watch what foot you're using. Let's get it right."

MORE EFFECTIVE

When Mr. Rock Music told his sixth graders they were going to line dance today, they ooooed excitedly. "Let me show you a few simple steps. See how I turn here. Now watch how I step over with my left foot. Try it with me. Ready. Turn now. Good. Step-over. Very good. Think we can do it with the music? Okay, let's try. Straight line, please." Mr. Rock Music watched closely as he danced along. "Turn left here. Good. Left foot over. Uh-huh. Left again! I'm impressed! That's the best line dance I've seen yet! We'll get a new step next time." He gave them a thumbs up.

Ms. Dixie Land-Music was about to demonstrate the Hi-Lo activity with cards. "Look up here. When the music sounds hi, raise up this card. When it's low, this card. You try it now. Good. With the music now." Ms. Dixie Land-Music was surprised when the first graders got their cards mixed up. "High card in right. Right hand. Not left. Raise card above your head. Not on your head, Charles, above it." "They can't do this," she said to herself! "They're all mixed up."

"Let me demonstrate how we'll use our Hi-Lo Cards. Notice I hold Hi card in my right hand. And Lo card, in my left hand. See how high I hold it. Pretend you have cards and try it. Hi card in right hand. Hold it up high. Lo card, left hand. Left hand. Good. Let's do it with the music. Ready." Ms. Dixie Land Music smiled. "Hold it high. Left hand, Harold." She nodded approvingly. "Lo card down, Jake." "They did that better than I expected," she said to herself. "Super job today, class!"

Keeping Class Informed

Making an effort to keep the students **on your same wavelength** might not be a familiar concept to some of you. Nevertheless, it's still a crucial happening because the more the students can "follow you" in the lesson and know why they are doing this or doing that, the more attentive they'll be. Being in-the-know shouldn't be just a teacher-thing; it needs to be a student-thing as well. Students need to feel like they're important in the student-teacher relationship, and that the teacher cares enough to share. But it can't be done unless there's a confident-minded teacher at the helm, someone who knows the value of keeping the students informed. Let's examine this task more closely.

Explanation of Keeping Class Informed

I need to explain further about "keeping the class informed." Don't think it means sharing everything with the students—that would be absurd, and even improper. "Keeping informed" is in reference to the lesson. It's letting students know what's happening as the lesson progresses. That's as far as the "knowing" goes in this case.

Now that we've got the "everything" part settled, let's make sure we know what "keeping informed" really means. There isn't any hidden agenda here. It means just what it says. Namely, to put students in-the-know throughout the lesson in regard to such matters as:

- Why you're using this activity or that
- When you're bringing an old concept to a close
- When you're starting a new concept
- Why you're asking the class to do this or that
- Why you've selected this or that piece of music

Informing students simply means letting them know what's happening, when it happens. In a figurative sense, it means keeping the students on your own wavelength. Literally, however, it means keeping the students abreast of what's happening.

Reasons for Keeping Students Informed

Here are some of the reasons why informing students is such a valuable ploy.

Makes Students More Attentive. When students can follow what's happening, they're more attentive. They know what's going on and don't feel left out. No doubt about it, students tend to pay attention better and stay with-it longer when they know what's happening. The task is worth it for this reason alone.

Makes Participation More Meaningful. When students are told why they will be doing this activity or that activity, they're more willing to participate. The activities have a purpose; they aren't just doing for the sake of doing or for the teacher's sake. They're participating because they know the reason for it. In this situation, a little knowledge is a good thing!

Builds Rapport More Quickly. If you want to build rapport, or perhaps strengthen your rapport, this is the way to go. Keeping the students appraised of what's going on is a marvelous way to nurture a lasting rapport between teacher and student because students can sense the teacher's desire to "reach out" and draw them closer through sharing rather than telling. These factors contribute in a large way towards nurturing the rapport between teacher and student.

Develops Self-Esteem More Noticeably. By keeping the students informed, you make it clear that you think they're important and have self-worth. Sooner or later, they start believing it; and when they do, their self-esteem starts going up as well.

Problem With Keeping Students Informed

Most teachers just don't use this tactic due to three main reasons. **One**, many teachers don't feel the need to share their procedures. They say it takes too much time, and that it doesn't make a difference with students. Personally, I think they just don't want to be accountable to the students.

Two, a lot of teachers just don't know about the approach. Nobody has ever told them or showed them how it works. They don't use it, because they don't know about it!

And **three**, some simply don't agree with this approach. Their point is that students have no basis for knowing what's appropriate and what's not. So why spend time telling them? One of their other complaints is that it involves too much talking on the teacher's part and that it dilutes the lesson.

These are the most common reasons why teachers don't keep students informed. Whether or not you agree with these positions isn't the point. The point is that they shouldn't be used as excuses. Every teacher should at least try this approach to see how it works.

Suggestions for Keeping Students Informed

Here are a few suggestions for those of you who use this tactic, and for those who would like to start. Read each suggestion carefully. Then decide which one(s) will help you the most.

Have a Clear Understanding of Purpose. Before you even try to use this tactic, be sure you're clear about the purpose in your own mind. Keeping the students informed is not done for corrobative reasons; in other words, not for obtaining students' approval of your procedures. Rather, it's done for informative reasons, for keeping the students enlightened with regard to the unfolding of the lesson. Once you're clear about the purpose, you'll feel more comfortable and motivated to use this tactic.

Settle on Appropriate Place for Information. What you need to decide upon next is, when do you give out this information. The best time is usually right **after the activity** or procedure has been announced, or right **before the teacher demonstration**. That's the most logical place. Stay with this "rule" until you start feeling comfortable giving your rationale. After that you can give out the information whenever, and wherever, you wish. Remember, the best place is just after the announcement. For example:

(*INSTRUCTION*)	"This time we're going to swing and snap to the metric rhythm in 3's."
(*INFORMATION*) (*the "WHY"*)	"It's a good activity to feel the S and W beats." because we swing on the strong beats and cluck on the weak beats.

By the way, that announcement is really the instructional part of the previous verbal bridge. What's important here is that there's really a logical place for the rationale if you use verbal bridges in your teaching. (See "Using Verbal Bridges" in Chapter 3.)

Give a Short Rationale for Activity. Keep your rationale statements short. You don't need to say a whole lot, nor *should* you say a lot. You'll need to work on being brief and to-the-point. Here are some examples:

- "We're using 'Drummer Boy' because it has such a clear-cut rhythmic pattern."
- "Call charts are good for developing our listening ears."
- "We'll go faster this time. I want to see if you can keep your eye a measure ahead."

The secret is to keep the rationale short and to the point. One other helpful tidbit. Use key phrases on terminology, like the following:

- "It's a good song for . . ."
- "You can hear the . . . clearly here."
- "This activity is good because . . ."
- "Let's put aside our . . ."
- "This is a good review song. . . ."

Get a repertoire of these generic phrases so that you can pull them up in a moment's notice. You can add other verbiage after you get more settled in keeping students informed.

Concluding Challenge

Do you keep students informed in your classes? Or do you ignore this task and think it's a waste of time? I hope you do use this sharing tactic and that you make your rationale short-and-sweet.

But, if you don't keep your students informed, you're missing the boat. The reasons should help convince you. Then focus on the suggestions, and you'll be ready to go. The ball's in your court now. Run with it.

LESS EFFECTIVE	MORE EFFECTIVE
"We'll begin today with some rhythmic readings. Page 12, please. Here's your beat." Ms. Accenta made some corrections and turned to the next page. "We're getting better," she told them. "Let's listen to this CD next and see if you can hear the large form. Yes. It's ABA. I'm passing out call charts now. Let's be ready to listen and circle what you hear. No talking." "This time we'll call out the numbers together. Ready." "Coming along. Good!"	We're going to continue working on our rhythm reading with ♩♩.♪. Watch out for the ♩.♪ figure." Ms. Accenta gave the count off. "Very good. Just some rushing of the beat. Go over to the next page. I'm still concerned about the ♩.♪. Ready? That was excellent. You clapped every ♩.♪ correctly. Bravo! Let's put our rhythmic reading aside and talk about large form. Remember what form we learned last time? Yes, ABA. Let's listen to this call chart. It really spells out the form in the Sousa March. Circle your answers. Can we call out the numbers together this time? Let's try. Excellent job!"
"Take your seats quickly and put on your listening ears. Let's see how well you can march to this music. I don't see everyone marching," Ms. Tempoe said to her first graders. "Let's try it again. Much better. This time can we tap our rhythm sticks. Very good, class. Sit down quietly. Now I want you to look at this picture and tell me what you see. Yes, birds, trees, an airplane. Let's listen to this recording and pretend to be birds. Ready. Don't hit Randy," Ms. Tempoe said to Sue. "Let's try it again. Reach way up high. Ready."	"I like the way you came in so quietly. Thank you. Let's put on our listening ears. We're going to listen to a march that has a strong beat and make our feet march to the beat. Ready. Very good! Can you play the beat on your rhythm sticks this time? Excellent. Let's put away our steady beat now. I've got a new musical idea for you. Let's look at this picture. Tell me what you see. Yes, birds, clouds, and an airplane. These are all high things. Well, we have high pitches in music too. Let's be a bird now and pretend we're flying high in the sky. Bird wings ready. Hear the high sounding music?"

Giving Directions for Dividing Class

Because so many activities in classroom music involve dividing the class, you've got to have the ability to give clear-cut instructions for this task so that you can avoid any disruption. I'm always amazed at how many teachers unconsciously believe that students will naturally move in the quickest and easiest way possible when they're being divided. That just isn't so. Unless you instruct students specifically, you can bank on the fact that they will either meander slowly to the designated area or else make a mad dash for it. Either way, the lesson is disrupted. Teachers need to develop the skill of giving specific instructions when it comes to dividing the class into groups.

Explanation of Directions for Dividing Class

Teachers tend to limit the meaning to a verbal exercise. Yes, it is a verbal exercise, but that's not all. It's also a gesturing exercise. That means you need to think in terms of both words and gestures when using the phrase "specific instructions" and realize that both the words and the gestures need to be specific when it comes to dividing the students in the classroom.

It's crucial that you have the meaning of the term "specific directions" straight before attempting to divide a class because it takes the combined effort to do the job competently.

Reasons for Specific Directions for Dividing Class

The reasons why this task is so important are obvious. The lesson can fall apart in a split second if dividing isn't done in a competent and organized manner. Also lost are the continuity and the students' attention.

The most important reason for specific directions is that they **avoid confusion**. You can get the job done more quickly, more efficiently, and more orderly. There isn't that frantic scramble where one minute there's order-in-the-court and the next, there's chaos. With specific directions, you can prevent confusion and create an aura of orderliness. All the qualities, in other words, we look for in a properly managed classroom.

The second reason is closely related, yet important enough to be mentioned separately. You also **prevent disruption** when instructions are specific. You maintain the continuity because there isn't any delay (in the lesson) while you deal with the chaos and confusion. The dividing becomes an orderly part of the lesson, so that no extra time is taken for the dividing chore, and no precious time is lost for the confusion.

A third reason for needing specific instructions is that they **maintain momentum**. They allow you to keep the flow of the lesson. When there isn't any disruption, the momentum can continue. The lesson can move along as planned because the dividing is handled in such an orderly manner. Without disruption, there's better momentum. It's that simple.

The fourth reason why specific instructions are so valuable is that they **provide control**. Good classroom management depends upon clear-cut instructions that students can follow easily. You avoid potential problems when your dividing instructions are clear and concise. Students don't have time to start fooling around. As a result, you have better control of the classroom.

Problem Regarding Specific Instructions

Of course, the most common problem teachers have is that they just aren't specific enough when they divide their classes. How many times have you heard directions like these?

- "That row, go stand over there."
- "You, you, and you come up front."
- "Go over by the chalkboard, you two."
- "Can I have all of you go back there."
- "These two rows go somewhere by the piano."

We're all guilty of giving instructions like these—but then we all know the results too! Vague instructions result in bedlam.

Let's look at some of the gesturing that usually accompanies these vague instructions. You've seen teachers do things like:

- Wave their hand fleetingly over some rows (like a fairy godmother) or in some direction
- Point their finger nebulously at a supposed group or designated area
- Nod their head quickly in the direction of some area or several rows of students

These are the kind of gestures that detract from one's decisiveness. They're all so vague that all they do is confuse, rather than help. You just can't have nebulous gestures and expect students to follow your directions!

Suggestions for Specific Directions

To be successful in dividing the class into groups, you need to be specific with your instructions and with your gestures. Here are suggestions as to how you can be more specific with verbiage and gestures respectively:

Verbiage	*Gestures*
• Indicate specific rows	• Straight pointed finger
–Rows 1 and 2	• Blocking off hands (for rows)
–Rows 2 and 4 and 6	–Out-stretched arms
• Indicate students' names	–Fingers closed
in each group	–Palms facing inward
• Identify designated area	• Nodding head at specific student
–In front of piano	• Outstretched arms (to encompass group)
–Behind teacher's desk	
–In right corner of classroom, etc.	

Here are descriptive illustrations of teachers giving specific directions. You can see how some of these specifics fit.

- Let's suppose Ms. X wants a group to stand in front of the chalkboard. Here's what she might say, "Everyone in the first row please stand quietly (*hand conduct standing motion*). Walk single file to the front chalkboard (*point to front chalkboard*). Charles, move down to the farthest end so everyone has room (*point to farthest end*).

- Let's say Mr. Y wants to divide the class into three groups in order to sing a round. Don't just wave an arm over the rows as you call out. Instead, Mr. Y would block off each group (*with outstretched arms, fingers straight and closed, palms facing inward*) and say, "Rows one and two will be Group one; Rows three and five, Group two," etc.

Concluding Challenge

Are you one of those people whose directions aren't very specific when you're dividing a class? Is it your verbiage? Do you need to make reference to specific names or rows, rather than saying "you, you, you, and you"? Or is it your gestures? Do you look wimpish? Put a video camera on yourself. The camera won't lie. Then you can begin to make corrections. Keep in mind that "specific directions" refer to both verbiage and gestures.

LESS EFFECTIVE

Mr. Bart Tok called four fifth graders to play the maracas and tambourines. "Get them from my desk," he said. All four made a dash to get an instrument. They were all bunched up in front of the desk arguing who would get what instrument. "Get your instrument and go to your seat," Mr. Bart Tok yelled. "And stop that talking." They shook the instruments all the way back to their seats. "Stop that playing! Now!" he shouted.

"Let's divide the class in two groups. Like this." Mr. Mac Dowell made a squiggly motion with his hand down the middle of the rows. Immediately the third graders started asking, "Am I group one? Am I group two?" "Settle down, now," Mr. Mac Dowell told them. "This side is group one. Go get the rhythm sticks." The children practically flew out of their seats. "Walk," he shouted. "Hurry up! Group two, you get the maracas. Wait for group one. Wait, I said." Both groups were still running back and forth when Mr. Mac Dowell yelled out, "That's it. No more instruments today. Put them under your seats." The students look bewildered! Mr. Mac Dowell was mad.

MORE EFFECTIVE

"I'd like a group of four people to play the tambourines and maracas for the accompaniment." As he selected each student, Mr. Bart Tok told the student to go quietly to his desk and select an instrument. (He pointed to his desk.) When all four had an instrument, Mr. Bart Tok asked the group to come up front. He pointed to the exact spot for each person. Quickly he assigned parts for maracas and tambourines and rehearsed each part as the class joined in vicariously. When they finished, Mr. Bart Tok instructed them to return the instruments on his desk and take their seats quietly.

Mr. Mac Dowell told his third graders he was going to divide the class in two parts. He stretched his right arm out with palm sideward and very carefully drew in the "magic" line. "This side will be group one, and this side, group two," he pointed to each group as he spoke. "Now group one will go quietly in single file to the shelf and get your instruments in single file! Quickly." In less than a minute the students were back with their sticks. "Put your instruments on your desk and don't play. Group two, you can get your instruments. No playing. Very good." Then Mr. Mac Dowell prepped each group for a few minutes. "Playing position, everyone. Ready." Mr. Mac Dowell was pleased with the class.

5

Activity-Related Teaching Behaviors

This chapter is concerned with those behaviors that are directly related to the actual job of teaching, especially those associated with classroom activities. I refer to behaviors of this sort as "activity-related" actions, as opposed to those that are not related. We'll discuss the non-related ones in the following chapter. As far as the activity-related "doings" are concerned, they include some of the most important behaviors in the act of teaching. More specifically, they're the kind of responses that lie at the very heart of the teaching process—the kind integral to teaching and crucial to learning. Moreover, they are the "things" a teacher must be able to do to function effectively in the classroom.

Another reason these activity-related behaviors are so important is that they impact on the quality of teaching. Much of the bumbling and sputtering that goes on in presenting activities in many instances need not happen, if the strategies in this chapter were put into practice. They include many of the nitty-gritty responsibilities that often get lost in the shuffle of preparing procedures or else overlooked in the hustle and bustle of implementing them. Whatever the reason, however, the outcome is the same; the quality of one's teaching is affected. Without activity-related behaviors, it may not be possible to achieve the level of expertise required in effective teaching. For this reason, you should cultivate the kind of behaviors discussed in this chapter.

A number of activity-related behaviors have been selected for this text. For the more experienced teachers, they can serve as a checklist or a list for comparison, and for those with less experience, as an "awareness" list. As stated in the Introduction, the text has been written as a teaching resource for classroom music teachers on all levels of experience. So for many of you, the behaviors will simply confirm your expertise, and give you a feeling of satisfaction in knowing that you already do many of these suggestions. If so, bravo for you. However, should you be one who finds that a good portion of these behavioral tasks are foreign to your own teaching, take the time to find out which one(s) you think would be most helpful to you. But let me warn you. Don't try to incorporate too many suggestions all at once! Take one at a time and you'll have better success. Select the one you feel is urgently needed at the moment, that is, the one that would have the greatest impact on your teaching right now. Then get that behavior locked in place before adding another. Start reading the chapter and making up your list. You should notice the results very quickly with many of these suggestions. Here, then, is a potpourri of activity-related teaching behaviors.

Engaging Whole Class in Opening Activity

One of the best ways to get the lesson "rolling" at the very outset is to involve the whole class in the opening activity. Let's quickly define "opening activity" in case there's any question. Most general music teachers generally understand it to mean the initial happening in the lesson, or the very first activity. Sometimes it's related to the lesson, and sometimes it's not. That's not the issue here; rather, it's a matter of deciding whether or not the opening activity should involve the whole class or just a select handful. The fact is, it needs to be a class experience, rather than an individual affair, if it's going to do the job of getting the lesson started on the right foot. There are some other important reasons as well.

Reasons for Engaging Whole Class

I can think of three good reasons for engaging the whole class in the opening activity. The **first reason** is obvious. The teacher can **corral the whole class's attention**, not just two or three individuals'. Everyone becomes an immediate participator, with no one left sitting and watching. It's unfortunate that some teachers lose sight of the fact that the opening activity works best as a class event, and that it serves as an ideal occasion for getting **everyone's** attention at the very outset. The opening activity is probably the one place in the lesson where only a group experience will suffice for getting everybody's attention.

The **second reason** for engaging everyone is that the teacher can **capture the students' enthusiasm**. The opening activity becomes the bait and "catches" the enthusiasm the students bring with them. Notice this phenomenon the next time you involve your whole class in the opening activity. Notice also how eager they are to continue when everyone has participated in the opening exercise. Don't lose sight of the fact that students are full of energy and enthusiasm, and that by involving everybody in the opening exercise, you simply cash in on this wonderful quality.

The **third reason** is that the teacher can **focus the class's thinking** on music. Let me make a distinction between getting the class's attention versus focusing the class's thinking. Getting the class's attention means to secure the students' eyes and ears or to obtain their concentration. On the other hand, focusing the students' thinking refers to directing their thoughts towards something specific, like music. The opening activity does this by blotting other happenings. We've all seen students come to class looking angry, upset, or distracted. But by the end of the opening activity, their feelings are usually soothed and they're in the mood for music. In a very real sense, then, the opening activity is instrumental in focusing the class's thinking.

If you're not in the habit of engaging the whole class in the opening activity, you're missing out on some valuable rewards. You can get the attention, capture the enthusiasm, and focus the thinking of the whole class in one fell swoop!

Problem in Engaging Whole Class

So what's the problem, you ask? Mostly one of omission. Some teachers don't use this strategy. Instead, they seem more inclined to open the lesson by calling on individual students right off the bat. Not only does this approach put an immediate damper on the class's enthusiasm, but, in most instances, it also disperses the attention. Unless the individual approach is an attention-getter, the class gets "blah" very quickly. And everyone knows how difficult it is to recapture interest and enthusiasm once it's lost. So don't create a pitfall for yourself. Prepare opening activities that involve the whole class, and you'll minimize your chances of losing the class's interest and enthusiasm for the rest of the lesson.

How do individual openers stifle the class? Let me show you. Picture, if you will, a second-grade class coming down the hall to your music room in that half-walk, half-run gait that only children seem capable of doing. See how their eyes sparkle and their bodies gyrate with energy? You can almost feel their excitement and hear them asking, "What are we going to do today, Mr. So-and-so?" Then, in the midst of all this energy and enthusiasm, the teacher begins by calling on individuals. That's when the enthusiasm starts to go—when these individuals start to hem-and-haw or wiggle and squirm through the ordeal. Here are some typical examples of how the dialogue goes in these individual episodes:

a. Bobby, can you remember the words to our new Thanksgiving song? (Class ooohs and waves hands.) No, let Bobby try. (Pause). Hurry, Bobby. Yes, that's the first line. What comes next? Think hard. (Ooohing and hand waving start again.) Hands, down. I want Bobby to do it. (Pause). We're waiting, Bobby.

b. Okay, Jane and Sally, will you come up and show us the square dance steps we learned last week? Jane? Sally? Yes, I know you all want to do these steps, but let's have Jane and Sally show us. Stop giggling, girls. (Pause, pause). Everyone watch! No, that's not right. It's like this. Let me show you. Now try it again. And stop that giggling. (Pause).

c. I would like to have someone tap the rhythm of the melody on "Jingle Bells." Who would like to try? (A dozen "I woulds" ring out.) Let's see. Billy, you try it. Here's your introduction. Ready! You almost got it. Once again. Better! Try it one more time. Shhh class! We'll wait till you're ready to listen. Ready, Billy?

See how devastating these individual antics can be for opening events? In a matter of minutes, the class can get lethargic and bored. Why does a teacher operate like this? Usually it's because of one (or more) of the following reasons.

One, some teachers just aren't aware of the class's attitudes. They don't sense the dwindling enthusiasm or, for that matter, the initial interest and enthusiasm. Teachers need to be more sensitive to the mood of the class, especially when it comes to the opening activity.

Two, some others aren't willing or, worse yet, able to change their teaching habits. You'd be surprised how many teachers do what they "do" in the opening activity because that's what they've always done. Teachers must learn how to be flexible and open to new suggestions, especially those that can improve their teaching.

And **three**, there are those who naively believe that the students who watch will get mentally involved. But this rarely happens with adults, much less with students! Students get involved by **doing**, not by watching, and while they may be patient for a while, sooner or later their enthusiasm will fizzle. It's inevitable, especially in the opening exercise.

You really can't afford to be insensitive to the class's attitude or hesitant to change an ineffective strategy when it comes to enthusiasm. Yes, I'm well aware of the fact that it takes more than an opening exercise to capture interest and enthusiasm. But a dragged-out individual approach will make the task even more difficult, if not impossible. That's why I say stay away from one-on-one openers unless you can move quickly and effectively from one student to the next. Don't complain how dull this class or that class was if you opened the lesson with a one-on-one exercise. None of these reasons can excuse teachers who insist on doing this, especially when they know that a group effort works best for opening activities.

Suggestions for Engaging Whole Class

Now that you know more about the merits of including the whole class in the opening activity—and the pitfalls with using just a few—let's consider the kinds of activities that qualify as "class" openers.

Singing experiences are particularly good for children in the lower grades. I'm talking about a favorite action song or singing game the children know from memory or which they are just learning. And don't forget, any song can become an "action" song simply by putting suitable motions to the words. Just don't get too many actions in any one phrase; young children don't have full control of small movements, so they can't move quickly or precisely. Don't forget this! In the upper grades, try using partner songs, rounds and canons, or songs with simple ostinatos or descents. You say that older kids won't sing? Just select appealing enough songs and they will. Use some of the rock music and make up simple ostinatos or descents. Rock music lends itself well to this tactic because of the repetitious harmony. And there's a lot of those partner songs that are fun to sing at any age. The trick here is to be sure each group knows "its" song before putting the two together. The same goes for rounds and canons. Familiarity is one of the chief factors in making the singing experience so enjoyable. You might even get to the point where the class can open with an easy two-part song the students enjoyed learning. In fact, a sight-singing exercise often makes for a great opening activity, too. See all the options you have with singing?

Another suggestion would be playing **instrumental accompaniments**, regardless if you only have a few instruments at your disposal. Students can always clap or tap the rhythm on their bodies or some other surface, such as the desk. Latin American accompaniments are always interesting because of the different instruments used, such as congo drums, maracas, guiros, and wood blocks, and also because of the catchy rhythms. If you only have one or two pairs of maracas, or one congo drum, let the other students clap the particular rhythm—but not in the conventional way. Have the students clap their laps, their thighs, or their chest to get varying sounds. Or why not tap on the desktop, on books, or with pencils? See how you can have everyone "playing" even though you have just a few instruments? You can make the rhythmic accompaniments as simple or sophisticated as needed for the grade level involved. Don't forget that young children love to pretend, so they'll enjoy "playing" vicariously.

Still another good opening activity for the whole class is a rhythmic reading exercise using specific note values, such as eighths, quarters, dotted quarters and eighths, and half notes. Students could sight read any exercise on the board or on the screen or select any song in the music text. For example, suppose the following rhythmic line was on the board:

Students would then chant quarter, eighth-eighth, eighth-eighth, quarter, half-note, quarter, quarter within the context of an established beat. In fact, there could be two or three of these lines on the board that could be chanted and clapped at varying tempi or row by row. You could take the activity one step further and have students read the words to fit the note values. This is an especially good opening activity for upper-level students, but should only be used if there is sufficient evidence that they are reading note values accurately. It'll challenge their rhythmic understanding.

And what about **rhythmic rapping**? You could make up raps for the whole class. Older students could read them and younger ones could learn them by rote, providing there's enough repetition. Why not put a few step movements and clapping with the rap? You say you want to get everyone involved? Well, this opener will do just that because it's such a popular performance medium.

Then consider all the movement-type activities the class can do together—whether it's responding to the (a) ongoing beat, (b) accented beats, (c) melodic rhythm, or even (d) metric rhythm. Movements can vary from the most rudimentary swaying, stepping, bending, or stretching to the more sophisticated gestures of conducting or aerobics. The market is flooded with marvelous aerobic recordings that can be adapted to the classroom. Believe me, students of all ages—even those moody junior highers—will get "into" a twisting-and-turning in the opening exercise.

Let's not forget **echo clapping** and echo singing. You can be as simplistic or as challenging as you need to be here. For kindergarten and first grade, stick with even-sounding patterns—only one measure in length. You can increase the length as the children's skill increases. Make the echo clapping more difficult and longer at the upper level to really challenge the students' rhythmic memory. Like this, for instance:

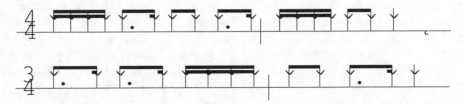

You can even turn echo-clapping into a game. Set up an ongoing tempo from teacher-to-student that must not be interrupted. That's the rule. Then ask everyone to stand and go up and down each aisle with each student echo-clapping the teacher.

Whoever makes a mistake in the echo or who breaks the beat sits down. The "game" moves quickly, and students really get excited about being a winner. They thrive on healthy competition, and, it's an excellent ploy to get them listening.

Here's one last suggestion. Use **call charts**. The new editions of the music texts are jammed full of attractive and interesting charts. You could have the class "read" the call numbers or have them raise their hands as each conceptual idea appears. For that matter you could assign call numbers to individual students while the rest of the class responds rhythmically or vocally to each number, or else just monitor the responses of those "calling out." The beauty of this exercise is that you can use both familiar and not-so-familiar music. It's an excellent opening activity for the whole class.

Concluding Challenge

See how you can involve your whole class in the opening exercise? The suggestions above are just a sampling of what can be done with everyone. Hopefully, they will trigger some other ideas you might have as well.

LESS EFFECTIVE	MORE EFFECTIVE
When the class was seated, Ms. Skipwise asked the students to turn to page 45. "Who can give me the title of this song? Billy? What's the time signature, Sallie? And what does it mean? Put your hands down class; I want Sallie to answer. Sallie? No, that's not what the top number means. Think again. All right, Jane, tell her. We can't wait any longer. What is the key? Jim? Yes! And how can you tell? Remember the rule for sharp keys, Jim. Say it for me. Not quite. How far do you count down? Think now." Ms. Skipwise noticed that the class was getting restless. "The students are awful today!" Ms. Skipwise said to herself. "I wonder what's wrong with them?"	As soon as she seated her class, Ms. Skipwise asked students to raise their hands when they found page 45. "Good. Now let's answer some questions about this song. What's the title? Together. And the time signature? Right, 3/4. Three means the beat does what? Great! What's the key signature? Yes, G Major. Let's say the rule for finding sharp keys together. Ready? Very good. Do you think we can read the note values in rhythm? One, ready, read. Excellent, class. This time I'd like rows one, three, and five to read the first two phrases, and rows two, four, and six, the last two phrases. Super. I saw everyone reading the note values." Ms. Skipwise could feel the class's enthusiasm.
For the opening activity with her third graders, Ms. Stepwise instructed Alan, Marsha, and Judy to fill in the letter names of the notes at the board. "Let's watch and check their work." After a few minutes, Ms. Stepwise said, "I don't see everyone checking the boardwork. David, turn around. Rick, stop talking." When the three were finished, she checked the letter names and called three other students to the board. "I want that talking to stop. Your eyes should be on the board. This class doesn't pay attention very well. Everyone look up here," she scolded.	Ms. Stepwise knew that her third graders enjoyed identifying the letter names of notes. So she asked everyone to look up at the front board where she had written a string of notes. "I want everyone to identify the letter names silently. Then we'll identify them together." After a few moments, she asked the class to "follow my finger. Excellent! Since you're getting so good, let's sing 'Peter Cottontail' with letter names. Okay." The children ooohed with excitement. "Here's your first pitch. You are really getting good at reading letter names, class."

Allotting Appropriate Time for Activity _____

Have you ever been in a class where the activity seemed to go on and on, and you found yourself wondering why the teacher didn't bring it to an end? I've seen students start out like gangbusters and then wilt—the activity simply went way beyond its effective time limit. It lost its impact; but impact can also be lost when an activity is cut short or when it doesn't last long enough for students to relate to the concept. Both situations need the right amount of time for an activity. It's an important task in the act of teaching, and it needs to be implemented in a competent way by classroom music teachers.

Definition of Appropriate Time

Let's take a moment to define the term "appropriate time" as it applies to classroom activities. Basically, it refers to having the "right" duration for an activity, or the suitable length of time—no more or no less. Notice that these descriptions imply a time limit. But, mind you, it's not in terms of minutes. The fact is, sometimes the appropriate time is longer, and sometimes it's shorter. It doesn't hinge on "x" amount of time. So what **does** determine the so-called "right" time limit? The class's response. That's the key. The way students respond will tell you whether or not the activity has gone **beyond** its effective time, or whether it has been called off **before** it's had time to be effective. If it has gone beyond or been stopped before, then the appropriate time has not been allotted. It's a matter of running the activity for the "right" length of time in terms of how the class is responding.

Problem With Appropriate Time

A lot of teachers struggle with knowing how long to "run" an activity. As a result they either (a) carry it out too long or (b) cut it off too soon. Take the first problem. Over-extending an activity happens daily in many music classrooms. The reason is that some teachers are oblivious to the class's response and insensitive to the fact the students have been kept participating long after they have responded successfully to the concept or skill. So there's a real danger of letting the activity last too long and wearing out its usefulness. Invariably, students lose their enthusiasm. Many good activities have gone down the drain because of prolonging them beyond their time.

   One quick clarification must be made. We're not talking now about those times when activities are purposefully prolonged as a result of (a) students thoroughly enjoying the activity and (b) the teacher having leeway, timewise, to extend the activity. These are acceptable exceptions; they're intentional. The problem above is accidental. That's a big difference, so be sure you make the distinction.

   The other problem is the reverse of the first, but it's just as detrimental. It's ending the activity too quickly. The teacher fails to recognize that the students need more hands-on experience with it, that they have not bonded with the concept, or had enough time to grasp it—and that it's too soon to end it. Almost always there's an unfinished feeling in the air, and even a bit of a let-down that affects the students as well as the teacher.

So there are two problems when it comes to the appropriate time limit. Sometimes the activity is "run" beyond its time of impact, and other times, it gets cut short. In either case, the activity is not being given its so-called *appropriate time*. But there are suggestions that can help.

Suggestions for Allotting Appropriate Time

How can you be assured of allotting the "right" time for your activities and not letting them go on and on, or stopping them too soon? By following some simple suggestions as far as practicality goes, but significant in terms of results.

The **first**, and most important, suggestion is this: assess the class's response according to your criteria. This means, of course, that you have a set criterion for each activity, or a definable standard that indicates **how well** you expect your students to respond. (See "Determining Criteria for Responses" in Chapter 1.) Look how criteria expedite this task for you. Once you have determined your standards, such as, correctly, accurately, easily, or without error, you can initiate a purposeful watch for, what I call, the *vital signs of achievement*. By vital signs I mean those particular kinds of reactions that "tell" you the class is "getting it!" Look for three "signs": (1) an improving response, in line with the criterion, (2) a heightened confidence, and (3) a growing sense of enjoyment. These are clear-cut indicators that the activity is going well, and that it has lasted the "right" amount of time; or that it's not going well when they're absent, meaning the activity needs to continue until the "right" time arrives. In either case, however, it's the criteria that make the signs a reality in determining the appropriate time. All the teacher has to do once the criteria are determined is assess what's being done. The class's response will tell the rest. So put down your criteria and start assessing your way to the "right" length of time for all your activities.

Here's the **second suggestions**. Consider the class's ability and their musical skill. As the general music specialist, you're responsible for knowing this information and for having reasonable expectations as to how well each class will perform. So, anticipate activity times on the basis of the class's ability—it's a good way to get a "ballpark" estimation. For example, suppose you have a class you know responds quickly to most activities. The implication here is that you would plan a shorter span of time for each activity and be ready to move on before it can get tiresome and boring. But what about those classes that take longer to assimilate information and skills? You would anticipate a longer participation time to avoid frustration. See how you can anticipate performance times more closely? Having this suggestion under your belt should help you be a better judge of appropriate times for your activities.

The **third suggestion** for insuring the "right" time is: Be ready to augment or alter the activity if necessary. There are times when it's the activity that needs to be doctored-up if the appropriate time is to be spent on it. Sometimes you'll misjudge an activity, and it'll turn out to be too easy or too difficult—often to your own surprise. In situations like this, be ready to either (a) beef-up the activity or else (b) pare it down, as the case may be. Unless you're prepared for these kinds of adjustments, it's useless to talk about having the proper time with the activity. My advice? Always be ready to adjust.

The **fourth suggestion** concerns those activities that use recordings or cas-

settes. Make the music subject to response, not vice versa. A lot of teachers seem to think they need to wait for the end of a section or the end of the band on the record before stopping an activity. But that's nonsense. You can stop the recording or the cassette player anywhere. Simply lift the needle, manually if necessary, on the first obvious cadence you come to after deciding it's time to stop. Don't let the music "run your show"; let the class's response "call the shots." You won't prolong your activities, if you do.

These four suggestions should help you considerably. Give them a try and you'll see!

Rewards for Appropriate Time

All the discussion about running an activity for the "right" length of time has been for a purpose, and it's not because teachers have problems with it, although that's true. Rather, it's because there are some very genuine and satisfying rewards when activity times are appropriate. Look what happens: (1) The lesson moves along more smoothly without the disruption of needlessly prolonged activities or the confusion of carelessly shortened ones; (2) The class with-it-ness runs higher because students are neither bored by the overextended events nor blighted by the abbreviated ones; and (3) You have better control of the teacher-learning process because the class's ability and the selected criteria have all been seriously considered. The teacher is much like a puppeteer in that by successfully controlling the "time strings" of each activity, he/she can make rewards, like those above, come to fruition.

Concluding Challenge

Now what about you? Do you have the ability to "run" an activity for the "right" length of time? Do you know when the activity is going on longer or shorter than it should be to properly accommodate the learning process? If not, you need to cultivate this ability. How well do you know your students in each class? Well enough to be able to approximate the time needed for each activity? Hopefully you do! And one last challenge. Strive to become a master evaluator; it's the key to appropriate activity times.

LESS EFFECTIVE

Mr. Sharp instructed his kindergartners to tap the beat on their rhythm sticks. Because they were an accelerated class, they responded quickly and accurately. As the tapping continued, some of the children got bored and stopped. "Children, children, let's continue until the record stops!" Mr. Sharp was relieved when the recording ended because many of the children were no longer tapping or even listening. "That wasn't very good. Some of you didn't keep on tapping! Put your sticks down."

Ms. Flat's sixth graders were learning a partner song. First, the class sang each song individually. Then, she divided the class. By the second verse, the class was singing as well as she had expected. And better. "Let's do all four verses," she announced. By the third verse, some horsing around started among the guys and some giggling among the girls. Ms. Flat scowled at the students from the piano. When the fourth verse ended, it sounded worse than the first time they sang it! "Goodness, what's happened! They sound awful," Ms. Flat exclaimed to herself.

MORE EFFECTIVE

When Mr. Sharp's accelerated kindergarten class was asked to tap the ongoing beat with their rhythm sticks, he knew they would have no problem responding. And they didn't! It was obvious they could hear the beat. At the next cadence in the recording, Mr. Sharp lifted the needle and stopped the activity. "I'm so pleased with you! Everyone was tapping right on the beat with their rhythm sticks. We're ready to go on to our next activity." Mr. Sharp couldn't help noticing how pleased the children were with themselves, and how excited they were to continue.

Ms. Flat informed her sixth-grade class that one simple kind of harmony was created by pulling two songs together. "I'd like us to sing each of these songs a few times. They're partner songs. Excellent. Now let's divide the class and sing them together." By the end of the first verse, they were sounding beautiful and she stopped to tell them. "Aren't we going to sing the other verses?" the class asked. When they finished the third verse, Ms. Flat praised them again. "I'd like to call the principal, so he could hear you. Shall I?" Ms. Flat felt proud as her class sang two verses for him.

Calling on Students to Participate Up Front

One of the most common tactics used in classroom teaching, including music classes, is having students come forward to engage in some task related to the lesson. But although it's wisely used, it's rarely thought of as a task or a teacher behavior. That's unfortunate, because it **is** a task and it **does** require skill and expertise, as well as a relaxed and untraumatic delivery. These are crucial requirements when asking the student to do any of the following assignments:

- Write out an exercise on the board.
- Identify some item on a visual aid.
- Display some object to the class.
- Recite some learned material.
- Present a prepared report.
- Engage in an organized presentation.
- Perform on a classroom instrument.

So let's examine this strategy more closely to see what's involved in implementing it with skill.

Problem in Calling Students Up Front

Many lessons come apart at the point where students are asked to come forward, and it's usually because it's not handled in an adept manner. Little or no thought is given to the task once it's been selected. It's like teachers think they have no part in it—like it will just happen—or that the students will just "be" there. The upshot is the students get called upon without any warning and, thus, react in the typical time-consuming ways, like (a) freezing momentarily in their seats, (b) slinking out slowly from their desks, (c) swaggering lazily up to the front, or (d) giggling nervously before going forward. An uncooperative response, then, is one problem.

Another problem is losing the class's attention when the student is up front because too much time is spent telling the student what he/she will do, while the class is left twiddling its thumbs. Invariably the attention span goes out the window and the class gets noisy—and sometimes even rowdy! Then there's the out-of-hand "whooooing" that often starts when the student is coming forward as a way of releasing the class's apprehension of the unknown.

You can expect problems, then, with (a) the student coming forward and (b) the rest of the class if you don't know how to properly handle the task. Here are some guidelines.

Guidelines for Calling Students Up Front

There are several suggestions to help you carry out this tactic in an orderly and efficient way. To be specific, there are two. I like to call them *rules* because that gives them more clout and makes them easier to remember.

Rule Number One is: Inform the student what's expected before he/she comes forward. No matter what the task, how obvious, or how mundane it may seem, tell the student what he/she will do ahead of time. Do this by first informing the class that you would like a volunteer to do this-or-that, or that you will be selecting someone to do such-and-such. Believe me, you'll eliminate a lot of the fear and hesitancy students have about coming forward. They'll be more cooperative, and the rest of the class won't tease as much. Let me give you an example.

Suppose you want a student to come up and put in the bar lines for an exercise on the board. Rather than calling on a student out-of-the-blue without any time to get mentally set, you make this announcement:

> "Look at the example on the board, class. Let's take a few minutes to fill in the bar lines at your seats. Then I'd like a volunteer to come up and write them in."
>
> *OR*
>
> "Everyone, fill in the bar lines for the first example on the board and then I'm going to call on someone to write them in. We'll go on to the second exercise after we check the first one."

Can you see that the student isn't as vulnerable with this approach? That he/she doesn't have to wonder what the teacher wants? Or if he/she will be able to do what's asked or look like a fool? Rule Number One helps avoid those surprise requests and hesitant responses. It removes a lot of the fear and anxiety of coming forward.

Rule Number Two is: Prepare the student for the task before he/she comes forward by preparing, or readying, the whole class. Do this by following three simple steps:

- First, indicate whether you want a volunteer or draftee.
- Second, tell the class what the person will do.
- Third, have the whole class play the exercise or execute the task together several times.

Here's an example of the three-step procedure. Say you want a volunteer to come up and play a 1-5-1-5-6-7-1-3-1 ostinato on the bass xylophone. You announce (a) whom you'll ask and (b) what you want, as simple as this: "I'd like a volunteer to play an ostinato on the xylophone." Then ask the class to play it together. In other words, drill the class briefly so that everyone is ready. Be creative here. You could have the class "play" on photostated replicas of the xylophone with the pitch numbers written on the bars, as shown in Figure 5.1, and use pencils as mallets.

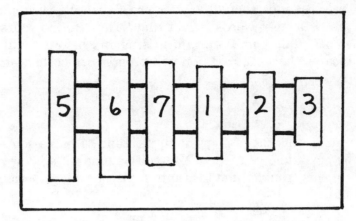

Figure 5.1. Xylophone Replica With Numbered Pitches.

Preparing the whole class is an excellent way of implementing Rule Number Two in that it gets everyone ready to do the task and does away with having to turn your back to the class for a private instruction session.

But, not every task performed by a student up front needs preparation. Some assignments are simply on-the-spot assists or helpful deeds that only need instructions, such as (a) holding up a visual aid, (b) turning pages for someone, or (c) being an example for something. No preparation is needed for these particular activities, so be sure to determine which tasks need both instruction and preparation before the student comes forward.

Just in case you're wondering how these two rules work when more than one student is asked to come forward, here's your answer: the same way! You simply tell the class how many students you want to select or draft, what you want them to do, together or individually, and then prepare the task(s), if it's necessary. The rules work just as well with two or more. Just be sure you properly prepare each task if the assignments are different. Otherwise, it'll be a fiasco!

Here's one last piece of advice that applies to every situation where students come forward. If there are specific instructions involved as to where to stand, how to hold, when to speak, or when to play, give these **just before** the students come up. These so-called specs are important because they help the student(s) do the assigned task more accurately—and independently.

So whether you're asking one student or four to come forward, use the same rules. And give out the needed specs, if you want to be more skillful in handling this task.

Reward for Calling Students Up Front Properly

While calling students forward may seem like an insignificant teaching responsibility, it really is a giant factor in the outcome of a lesson. Particularly when it's handled according to the two rules. The rewards are immediate and obvious.

The **first** is, you will have fewer interruptions and slowdowns in the momentum of the lesson. Students won't be as hesitant to come forward. They'll have less fear and trepidation and won't take as long to get out of their seats. Too, there will be fewer disruptive tauntings from the class in that their own apprehension is reduced by the class preparation.

And the **second** is, you'll experience more willingness on the students' part to come forward. You won't have to prod as much, and hands will shoot up more frequently to volunteer or be selected as a result of the students feeling more prepared.

In fact, the raised hands should be your proof that the class preparation worked!

These are enticing rewards, aren't they? They can be yours just by applying the rules. Remember, Rule One is to inform students before coming forward, and Rule Two also prepares them. Your lesson will progress smoother, and students will cooperate better.

Concluding Challenge

If you have taken this task for granted, it's time to make some changes. Follow the two rules the next time you teach. You will be amazed at how these two procedures can transform this troublesome task into a pleasurable experience, both for you and your students.

LESS EFFECTIVE

Mrs. Wholenote was teaching the letter names of the lines and spaces. Without further ado after explaining to them, she asked for a volunteer to go to the big staff on the board. Billy dashed up and stood by Mrs. Wholenote. "Not here. By the staff, Billy. Face the board and pick up the pointer. Now be quiet, class, while I tell Billy what to do." Placing her arm around him, Mrs. Wholenote began explaining what she wanted. Soon she whirled around and shouted, "Stop that talking; I can't even hear myself think! Can't you see I'm getting Billy ready?"

Ms. Halfnote needed help to hold up the chart. So she called Bobby and Larry. "You come on this side, Larry, and, Bobby, on that side. Hold it higher, Larry. Bobby, step back. No, not you, Larry, just Bobby. Wait a minute. Now you're holding it crooked. Larry, raise it up a bit." While Ms. Halfnote continued, the class began to snicker and giggle. Soon Bobby and Larry were giggling too. "All right, put the chart down and take your seats. Everyone fold your hands on your desk and stop snickering. Next time I won't use the chart since you can't behave yourselves."

MORE EFFECTIVE

When Ms. Wholenote finished explaining the letter names of the lines and spaces, she said, "I'll be looking for some volunteers to come to the board and identify the names of the lines and spaces after we recite them together. Ready! Very good! Now do I have some volunteers?" Almost every hand went up. "How about Mark first, Sally second, and James third. Here's what you'll do. Take the pointer from the chalk tray and hold it with your right hand. Then stand to the left of the staff—that's the side closer to the flat—and name each line as you point to it. Are you ready, Mark? And class, say the letter names to yourself."

When the time came for Ms. Halfnote to use the chart, she selected Mary and Mike. "I'd like Mary to hold it on this side just like I'm holding it, and Mike, you hold it on that side. Be sure to stand off to the side so that everyone can see. Mary, would you stand right here. And Mike, over here. One more thing, please hold the chart about eye level. That's right. Good. Can everyone see?" The class nodded. Mary and Mark held the chart exactly as instructed, and the class eagerly participated. When it was over, Ms. Halfnote thanked Mary and Mike, and praised the class for their good response.

Evaluating Student Responses Correctly

It's impossible to talk about teaching responsibilities without mentioning the evaluation process. Evaluating is part-and-parcel of the act of teaching. Whether it's evaluating the collective response of the class or the individual performance of the student, it's a crucial responsibility. It's the "other half" of the teaching process—

implementing is useless without evaluating. It's like doing something for the sake of doing, and doesn't result in any learning. Do you see the implication here and realize how important it is that you be able to evaluate properly and competently? Expertise in evaluating is essential where teaching skills are concerned.

Problem With Evaluating Students

I'm always puzzled by those teachers who seem to avoid making an honest and accurate assessment of the students' participation. Is it because they're afraid of hurting the students' feelings? Fearful that the students won't like them anymore? Or is it because they just don't care enough to exert the effort? At times I even think it's because some don't know how to evaluate! Any one of these reasons could be the culprit, or maybe a smattering of all of them.

Let me give you two examples. They're classic cases of evaluating irresponsibly. The first example involved a class of sixth graders that was getting ready to sing and accompany a familiar song on guitars and autoharps with I-V$_7$ chords. Well, the result was pitiful. The students weren't changing the chords correctly, strumming on the beat, or playing in tempo. And to top it off, they weren't singing on pitch either! Know what the teacher said when they finished? She said, "That was pretty good." I practically fell off my chair! Everything that **could** be wrong, **was** wrong—and she just ignored it. What was her problem? I don't know. Your guess would be as good as mine.

The second example was just as incredible. A third-grade class was going to tap out the melodic rhythm of a familiar song on rhythm sticks. Well, it turned into a free-for-all. Everybody seemed to be doing his or her own thing! There wasn't even a semblance of the correct rhythm, only a conglomeration of clickings! How anyone could listen to that "noise" and not try to correct it, I'll never know, but that's what this teacher did—nothing!

Both these examples smack of the desperate need for an honest evaluation. If more teachers had a definite approach to evaluating, they would do a better job. Know-how is probably one of the missing ingredients, so let's get some help here.

Suggestions for Evaluating Properly

Because the whole teaching-learning process hinges to a large degree on how well you can evaluate the student input, I'd like to suggest a **four-step** procedure for evaluating in a more proficient way.

Step One. Establish your criteria. The accurate and honest assessment of every class or individual response depends upon the selected standards you intend to achieve. It's not enough to have criteria, you must also have the drive to achieve them. And it's just as foolish to have the drive without any criteria. While there's hope for the ones without criteria, my advice to those without drive or desire is, shape up or ship out! (See "Determining Criteria for Responses" in Chapter 1 for more detailed discussion.) In short, first decide how well you want students to perform. Accurately? Easily? Completely? What will it be?

Step Two. Make an overall judgment; that is, assess the response as a total entity or as a whole. Ask yourself if the students did what you expected for the most part. Don't get distracted by every detail or by some facet not specifically spelled out in the objective. Let these infractions pass. Look at the total response. You'll know in a flash whether it's acceptable or not, if you're committed to the criterion. If it is, move on. If not, it's on to the next step.

Step Three. Focus on the problem, and determine what needs fixing or correcting. Actually, this starts to happen in Step Two when the performance is being judged. You begin to notice what the students aren't doing in accordance with the criteria. For example, the sixth graders in the accompaniment example weren't playing the chords "accurately" (on the instruments) or "correctly" (with the music). The teacher should have caught these problems. Criteria will illuminate the problem(s). All you need to do is put your finger on what the class, or the student, isn't doing to comply with your criterion. See how criteria help you focus on the problem(s) and determine what needs fixing? That's the beauty of having criteria!

Let me say a word about verbalizing the problem once you identify it. You need to know what to say when the students don't respond up to snuff. The best advice is, be up front. Don't beat around the bush or hem and haw. Tell it like it is, with tact, of course. Here are some examples:

a. "I liked the way you played the chords on the beat, but some of you weren't fingering the V_7 chord correctly. Let's review the V_7 or G_7 fingering again before playing the song again."

b. "We almost played the accompaniment perfectly that time except for rushing the tempo! Let's try it once again to see if we can keep the tempo steadier. It'll help if you tap the beat with your foot. Ready."

c. "I didn't see everyone's feet marching correctly to the beat that time, children. Get into your soldier position and let's try making our feet march right on the beat this time. Be sure you listen closely to the music."

Get the idea? Just tell students exactly what the problem is—and how to "do it better." That's the best formula, and the best clue for the last step.

Step Four. Provide a solution. Students won't do better just because they've heard what's wrong. That's not enough. They need to know how to do it better, and that means you must have a solution ready that will either (a) correct the response, or (b) improve it to some degree. This is the crux of the evaluative process—obtaining the desired response—and the ultimate outcome of the fourth step. You need a repertoire of solutions in order to evaluate students properly, but it takes years to build a repertoire. You can start yours now by:

- talking with other teachers
- going to music workshops/conventions
- reading the professional journals
- exploring the current music texts
- engaging in brainstorming sessions
- consulting pertinent research studies
- observing other teachers in action
- studying demonstrations on videotape

In a nutshell, the four-step procedure is as follows:

Step One: Establish the Criteria
Step Two: Make the Overall Judgment
Step Three: Focus on the Problem(s)
Step Four: Provide the Solution(s)

Try the procedure if you want more expertise in evaluating your students. It'll give you the necessary know-how, and the desired results.

Reasons for Evaluating Responses Properly

To those who are successful in obtaining high-level responses through proper evaluation, I say bravo! You are the ones who put excitement back into teaching and learning. Look at some of the other reasons for evaluating student responses with honesty.

First, more learning goes on because students are challenged to perform more precisely and more accurately. Approximating is not acceptable. Neither is faking. What happens is that the student response is elevated to a level that promotes learning, and even motivates it—many times in spite of a student's resistive attitude. High-level responses are avenues of the learning.

Second, more interest is generated. The better the response, the more with-it the students become. It's like what happens in a crack marching unit; the esprit de corps fires up the individual members. Likewise, the precise, unified performance by the class is what turns on individual students, even the disinterested ones. Students are genuinely more enthusiastic about participating when the class response is good.

And **third**, more expertise is nurtured. In pursuing your high-level responses, you are not only ensuring student learning, but developing your own evaluative skills as well. The keen observations and the prepared solutions are all part of the process that nurtures your expertise. As the old saying goes, we learn best by doing; and that's what you do each time you evaluate in a responsible manner—you nurture your skill.

Concluding Challenge

What about your evaluating? Do you have the skill to evaluate effectively? If not, consider the four-step procedure. Just determine your criteria and follow the steps. They'll help you exercise more accuracy and integrity, and make your teaching more effective. It's exciting!

LESS EFFECTIVE

Mrs. Strongbeat planned to have her fourth graders sing a familiar song with an ostinato for their harmonic experience. Thinking about her next class, she didn't notice the obnoxious chest voice some students were using, or see the ones holding their ears to block out the other part. When she finally tuned-in, she was shocked! Not only was the singing awful, but the ostinato was getting faster. "Guess I'll just let them finish. I'll never get them to do that ostinato part! And what am I going to do with that awful singing?" Actually, Mrs. Strongbeat didn't even know what to do. So she just said, "Fine" when it ended.

Ms. Weakbeat never worried too much about criteria in her lesson plan or how the class was going to respond. But when her sixth graders did the rhythmic reading exercise, she was at a loss as to how to begin correcting it. "Maybe they'll do it better if they repeat it." So she had the class do it again. "It's just as bad this time! Now what do I do?" she asked herself. "Better go on to the next activity." Ms. Weakbeat felt frustrated by not knowing what to do.

MORE EFFECTIVE

As the fourth graders sang, Mrs. Strongbeat cringed on hearing the blaring chest voice in the ostinato and got annoyed with the rushing that told her they weren't listening. Soon there was more belting out with chest voice. "This is ridiculous," she said under her breath and stopped the class. "It's impossible to hear the harmonic effect when we're singing so poorly. Let's work on our head voice for a minute." Mrs. Strongbeat helped the class "find" the head voice again before instructing, "Okay, now let's try it again." She was delighted this time. The class was using its head voice and the ostinato part wasn't rushing.

When Ms. Weakbeat selected the rhythmic reading exercise for the sixth graders, she remembered that they had difficulty with the skill. So she indicated improvement, not perfection, with her criterion. When the class began reading, she spotted the problem immediately. "You're rushing the second eighth note, class. Let's tap and chant eighth notes like this. Eighty-eighty, etc. And be sure the second eighth comes on the upbeat. Ready. Now let's go back and read it according to the down-up beats. Much better!" Ms. Weakbeat felt rewarded by the class's improved response.

Switching Activities That Don't Work

One teaching behavior not talked about very much is knowing when to switch an activity that isn't working, or is coming apart before your very eyes, even though it was selected with great care, like being sure it was suitable for the age level, appropriate for the musical ability, and right for the conceptual idea, etc. (See "Choosing Appropriate and Appealing Activities" in Chapter 1.) We're not talking about salvageable activities now. Be sure you understand that. We're talking about the real "bombs," the ones that just don't "go" perhaps because of (a) an unforeseen attitude, (b) misjudged ability, or (c) overlooked facility. What about those activities in which the response surprises even the most experienced teachers? These are the ones you must be ready to handle, and have sufficient skill to keep the class from falling apart. So let's not forget this switching responsibility. It needs your attention.

Tendency When Activity Doesn't Work

What a lot of teachers do when they're caught in this predicament—whether they are really caught off-guard or else have their pre-conceived fears confirmed—is opt to ride out the disaster and keep it going right to the end. Why? Mostly because they feel trapped. They think that if they don't have any back-up activity up their sleeve, they've got to go on. So they put themselves and their students through misery, just because they don't know what else to do. That's one common tendency.

Here's the other one. Some teachers are prone to criticizing the class. In their frustration with the response and with not knowing what to do, they start blaming the students. They insist that this is wrong, that's not right, such-and-such isn't done that way but this way. It isn't very long before the class quits trying and just pouts, while the teacher keeps on harping. Talk about an unhealthy class environment!

Obviously, neither of these reactions is acceptable. Opting to continue or choosing to criticize only leads to more problems. But there is a better way to deal with a fizzling activity.

Suggestion When Activity Doesn't Work

The best advice I can give you is this: drop it and move on. It's the only intelligent thing to do. Time is too valuable to waste, unless, of course, you have another activity ready. Then you would pull that one out. But if not, drop it. How does one just "drop" an activity in progress? By stopping it and verbalizing the situation to the class. We'll use an illustration to make the point. Suppose your sixth graders were singing a song in two parts to hear the harmonic sound of thirds and sixths. Even though they had previously worked on thirds and sixths, the song fell apart. Yes, you could work on each part individually, but this would negate the objective. Furthermore, your inner voice is probably telling you, "This is not going to work!" So rather than doing the parts over and over, you choose to verbalize something like this:

- "We're certainly having our trouble singing in parts today. Let's move on to something else right now and come back to this in our next lesson."
- "I can see we're not quite ready to tackle this song. We'll work on the parts later. For now, let's turn to page so-and-so and sing this song in thirds. Ready."
- "This song isn't going well today, is it? Why don't we put it aside and work on the individual parts in our next lesson. Right now let's do such-and-such."

You simply tell the class that the activity isn't working and that you need to move to something that does work. There's nothing wrong with the plain truth, besides, the students know when the lesson isn't going well. So what you say isn't going to shock them, I can assure you! Be up front—that's always the best policy.

That's how you drop an activity that isn't working. But what would you do if you didn't have something to replace it? Plenty! There are a number of things you could do:

- Pull out a tried-and-true opening activity.
- Review a concept and activity from last lesson.

- Return to the previous activity with slight alteration.
- Backtrack to a less-challenging activity for the concept.
- Work on some performance skill.
- Initiate a short question-and-answer session on the concept.

If you know what options you have when these no-go situations happen, you won't feel as trapped to continue or criticize the class. The fact is, you do have alternatives, and you don't have to stay chained to a lost cause. Know your options.

I know some of you are wondering if you'll lose face by dropping an activity. Absolutely not! Every good captain knows when it's time to abandon ship. Moreover, it's the wise captain who will issue the order to save the shipmates. The teacher is very much like the captain. By dropping an activity to rescue the students, you exhibit the quality of a wise leader. Think about this for a moment. It's an awesome thought.

Reasons for Switching an Activity

Let's consider the reasons for dropping or switching an activity that isn't working. The **first reason** is that it avoids an unpleasant, unproductive classroom environment. The class doesn't get bored or discouraged; neither does the teacher. By replacing the activity, you help maintain a healthier, more productive learning environment. This reason alone should justify the action.

The **second reason** switching is important is that it keeps the momentum from bogging down. The pacing can continue without the class coming to a halt. The replaced activity regains the students' interest so that the teacher doesn't have to keep stopping to reprimand. In short, the momentum is salvaged.

The **third reason** is that it allows for better class control. Students don't have a chance to cut loose when you're ready with an alternative, and you don't have to lose control by continuing with an activity that isn't working. You can keep on task and focus the students' attention with any of the alternative suggestions mentioned earlier, and, thus, have better control of your classes.

The **fourth reason** is that it provides yet one more way to acquire credibility in the eyes of the students. Your actions let them know that you are capable of adjusting on the spot and that you are on top of the situation all the time. As indicated earlier, you establish yourself as a true leader. In so doing, you increase your stature in the students' eyes.

Concluding Challenge

Are you convinced that this is an important teaching responsibility? If so, then take the time to evaluate your own ability to switch activities that aren't working. Consider also the various alternative activities at your disposal, and, more important, learn how to apply them. Start cultivating this skill right now.

LESS EFFECTIVE	MORE EFFECTIVE
Ms. Rotesong was excited about her activity for the third graders. "They'll love doing this call chart." But to her complete surprise, the activity was flopping! "What's happening? Why isn't this working? What'll I do?" she asked herself. "I'll just let them finish it. What else can I do? Wonder what's wrong with this class today. They're so noisy." "Quiet, class, and listen to the music." "That's the last time I do call charts," she vowed to herself.	Ms. Rotesong planned a call chart for her third-grade class. She was anxious to see how they would respond. To her amazement, the call charts just didn't go. "This is awful," she commented to herself. So she stopped the class and said, "I think we'll do something else and come back to the call charts another time, okay? Let's review our strong-weak beats from our last lesson." Soon the whole class was marching and tapping to the beats. Ms. Rotesong was glad she had switched.
Ms. Singsong wasn't too sure about her next activity. It might go, and then it might flop. Well, flop it did! "I didn't think it would be **this** bad. I don't think the students are really trying," she said to herself. "All right, let's try it again and **this** time I want everybody participating. No, not like that, like this. Straighten up, now. We can do this better if everyone tries hard." The students rolled their eyes and began to get silly. "Stop being so silly. Let's do it one more time. And try to tap the melody softer—and listen!" Ms. Singsong was annoyed. "They're getting worse instead of better" she said to herself. "We'll just keep doing it until they do it right."	Although Ms. Singsong didn't feel confident about her next activity for the fourth graders, she decided to try. She wasn't surprised when it fell flat. "Why don't we put this activity aside for now and go back to the activity we just did. But this time, let's add the long-short sounds to the rhythmic patterns by chanting as we play. Like this, short-short, short-short, long. Try it with me before we put on the record. Good. Now let's try it with the recording." Ms. Singsong was pleased with the class's clapping/chanting. They perked up immediately when she switched back to their previous activity. "It's a good thing I dumped that listening activity," she said to herself.

Using the Vicarious Experience With Activities

Do you engage your students in a vicarious, or imitative, experience when you implement your activities? If not, you should, especially when using classroom instruments because it's a marvelous teaching tactic and an essential responsibility when it comes to classroom activities. You can use it to (a) prepare your students for the planned activity, or to (b) keep them involved when individuals are performing. But it does require some know-how and some skill if it's going to be handled effectively. Let's take a closer look at using the vicarious experience.

Definition of Vicarious Experience

Vicarious experience is just a fancy name for imitative participation. It is a make-believe exercise, more commonly called "let's pretend," when used with younger children. In the classroom, it means having students imitate the real "thing," like assuming the strumming motion of a guitar, in order to get them prepared or else occupied while others are responding. For students, then, the vicarious experience is a pretend exercise, but for the teacher, it's a teaching technique.

Reasons for Using the Vicarious Experience

There are five convincing reasons for using the vicarious experience.

The **first reason** is that the vicarious approach **saves class time**, particularly when it's used as a preparation tool. By having the students simulate the actions before doing the actual activity, you "ready" the class for the experience. That means you don't have to keep stopping to help students once the activity begins, or waste time instructing the ones who come forward. (See the earlier section, "Preparing Students to Come Forward.") The students already know what to do and understand what's expected. This readiness is what saves time when implementing an activity.

The **second reason** is closely related to the first, namely, that vicarious preparation, particularly with instruments, **helps class momentum**. There's less stopping and starting because students know what's happening. You can go from the vicarious exercise right into the actual activity without any major interruptions or without bogging down in the activity. In other words, the momentum of the lesson can keep moving.

Reason number **three** is that the vicarious exercise **prepares every student** to play the real instrument. By being involved in a simulated preparation, the students are able to make an immediate and automatic application to the real instrument. It simply is a matter of taking the instrument and doing what they've already practiced, so any student is capable of performing on the actual instrument without any further instructions. And you can feel free to call on **any** student!

The **fourth reason** for supporting the vicarious experience is that it **keeps everyone involved**. Whenever there aren't enough instruments for everyone, or whenever just a few students are selected to participate, you can still involve the whole class and turn each student into an active rather than passive participator. In fact, you can get the students to "play" along in such an authentic manner that they experience the same musical learning as those having the real instruments. That's the beauty of the vicarious experience. But the point is, it keeps everyone busy.

And the **fifth reason**? It, too, is linked to the previous one. Keeping the class vicariously involved **improves classroom behavior**. The students' attention is focused on "doing" rather than watching. They don't have time to get into trouble. Moreover, there's less chance of needing to work individually with some students and ignoring the others; you can concentrate on the whole class and keep better control because everyone is "doing" the activity, either legitimately or vicariously. The vicarious approach definitely improves classroom behavior.

Why use the vicarious experience in your teaching? Because, in a nutshell, it results in the following outcomes:

- saves teaching time
- sustains class momentum
- provides class involvement
- improves classroom behavior
- prepares every student

Problem Concerning the Vicarious Experience

The main problem is that many teachers are not in the habit of using a vicarious, or pretend, experience in preparing an activity, especially not with those involving classroom instruments. So what do they do to get students "ready"? Very little beyond the stereotype saying, "Now let's do such-and-such." They just jump right in with such antics as:

- Giving out instruments without any instructions as students come in.
- Passing out instruments while announcing the activity.
- Asking for volunteers to play an instrument without specific directions.
- Selecting student(s) to come forward before telling them what to do.
- Instructing students to get an instrument before announcing the instructions.

Whichever tactic is used, the teacher is guilty of putting instruments into the students' hands without any preparation. I call this the "kamikaze approach" because the results are almost always devastating. Some students mutilate the instruments even before the instructions are given, while others continue banging, clicking, or jingling until the activity begins. Then there's all the hullabaloo that breaks loose when the one-on-one routine is used to instruct the students who come forward, or when the teacher descends upon a student at his/her desk like Count Dracula. These are the kinds of things that happen when the teacher isn't in the habit of using a vicarious experience with classroom instruments.

As for using a vicarious experience to involve the whole class when only a few instruments are available, a lot of teachers don't worry about doing this. That's the problem. It doesn't bother them that most of the class is just sitting and watching, missing a musical experience, and probably losing enthusiasm. But it's all part of the problem when vicarious involvement is ignored.

When it comes to the vicarious experience, then, for preparation or involvement purposes, a lot of teachers simply aren't accustomed to using it. So they don't!

Procedures for Using the Vicarious Experience

Having discussed how teachers operate without the vicarious experience, let's make a quick comparison with teachers who do use the vicarious approach. The best way to do this would be to show how the experience is implemented.

Consider the preparation procedure. Following the teacher demonstration, you would **ask everyone to "do" the playing** with you. Pretend, that is, without any instrument. How long? Only as long as it takes for the students to appear secure and comfortable. Probably a minute or two; not much more. The secret here is to be sure that the students participate in a realistic and convincing manner to ensure the proper results.

Then you're ready to **assign the instruments**. You can do this in a number of ways, such as:

- Ask for volunteers in their seats.
- Select students to come forward.
- Pass out in random fashion.
- Put under chairs before class.
- Assign students to pass out.
- Ask students to pick up on shelf.

Any one of these approaches will work; it just depends on which one would be the most feasible for your situation. The fact is, once the class has had its simulation exercise, you can put an instrument into the student's hands any way you wish. And here's the best part. You can choose any student because everyone is equally prepared!

All that's left now is to **involve the whole class** vicariously while those assigned to real instruments perform. Whether the selected students are up front with their instruments or at their seats, they're ready to go. They don't need any extra coaching. Just ask your class to continue to realistically imitate the playing, be it strumming chords, playing an ostinato, or fingering a melody. There you have it— three simple steps to obtain all the rewards mentioned above.

Before closing, let me comment on having instruments for everyone. Lest you think that the whole purpose of the vicarious experience is to compensate for not having enough instruments, I can assure you it isn't! That's only part of it. The other part is to provide a more meaningful experience than 25 rhythm sticks clicking at the same time. It isn't necessary for every student to have an instrument in order to have a meaningful experience. Here's why.

Children are great pretenders and love to imitate. They'll "play" imaginary instruments without one thought of being deprived. That's because it's the process, not the instrument, that nurtures the feelingful response. Then, too, a class full of sandblocks, triangles, or maracas generally drowns out the recording or the piano, no matter how soft the students try to play! Here's where an instrument for every child becomes counterproductive. So you see, few instruments are often better for a more musical experience.

Concluding Challenge

If you've never used the vicarious approach, why not try it in your next lesson? (Even if you do have 25 pairs of rhythm sticks in your room!) Just follow the three steps outlined in the procedures, and be sure the students imitate in a realistic manner.

Use it to prepare the students for playing or keep them involved while others play the real instruments. You'll like the results.

LESS EFFECTIVE

"Okay, today we're going to learn how to accompany ourselves on autoharps," Mr. Strum-strum announced. When no volunteers came forward, he called Bob and Judy to come up. "Let me show you what you do." With that Mr. Strum-strum turned his back to the class and began to explain. After several minutes, he whipped around and told the class they were being rude. Finally, he announced that Bob and Judy were ready. "Now let's try to be a good audience for them. Stop that fidgeting and listen." "Wonder what's wrong with them today? They've been so talkative."

Ms. Bang-bang planned to have her third graders play a repeated rhythm pattern on wood blocks. Quickly placing the three instruments in front of students, she told the class what they would do next. "Stop that tapping while I'm talking." Then she went on to talk about rhythmic patterns. "Let me show you what to do," she said to the wood block players. Then she went from one to the other explaining! When she finally finished, the class was practically swinging from the rafters. Ms. Bang-bang glared at the students. "I'm surprised at you! I thought you would listen while I explained to these students. Do you think you could sit quietly enough to listen to these students play along with the recording? Let's try." But as soon as the record started, the class got noisy again. "That's it. We'll just sit for the rest of the period, if you can't listen."

MORE EFFECTIVE

When he told the class they were going to learn how to accompany themselves, Mr. Strum-strum asked that everyone pretend to have an autoharp. After demonstrating how to press the chord buttons and strum, Mr. Strum-strum asked the class to "play" with him. "Very good. Now let's strum our F chord on every beat while we sing. Here's your pitch. Ready? That was good singing and accompanying. Now who'd like to come up and play on the real McCoy?" Bob and Judy were there in a flash! They knew exactly what to do. "Let's accompany on our silent autoharps while Bob and Judy play and sing."

When she continued the lesson on rhythmic pattern, Ms. Bang-bang announced that there would be a woodblock activity. "First, let's all imagine we're holding a woodblock in our left hand, like this, and use our right hand pointer finger as a mallet, okay? Now listen to the pattern, and repeat after me. Listen. Very good. Can we try 'playing' with the record? Just play when you hear the pattern; otherwise, tap the beat in the air. Like this." Ms. Bang-bang smiled, "I like the way everyone heard those patterns. I'm going to pass out three woodblocks today, and if we have time, we'll pass them on to three others, okay?" She was delighted that all three woodblockers picked up their instruments correctly. "Now let's play along with the record. Great. We played on all the patterns and tapped the beat other times. Great. Let's pass on the woodblocks."

Using Secondary Response Between Conceptual Responses

One of the tasks not usually mentioned in presenting an activity is establishing a secondary response for the "waiting" times between the conceptual responses. We tend to forget that with a lot of activities, we need to be concerned about the times when students are **not** responding to the concept; that is, when they are waiting for it to reappear each time, like with contrasting phrases, melodic patterns, or downward passages. In activities of this nature where there are longer or more frequent waiting periods, students tend to get bored and even off task. There's not enough to keep them occupied **throughout** the activity. But by adding a filler, or secondary, response, you can alleviate this situation and keep the students involved—from start to finish. So don't forget this task; it can really help beef-up your activities.

Definition of Secondary Response

While you may be clear as to the rationale for secondary responses, you may be still confused about the meaning. I use the term "secondary response" to refer to a filler exercise earmarked for the waiting times between responses. It's really a bonus activity that focuses on another ongoing concept in the music, like the steady beat, the metric rhythm, or the melodic rhythm.

For example, suppose your primary activity for identifying the rhythmic pattern was to have students play the pattern on their desks, using alternating strokes with the rhythm sticks. Then you instruct them to tap the beat between each pattern to keep them more involved. What you did was to use a secondary response. Thus, a secondary response is nothing more than a separate, unrelated exercise set aside for the empty time between conceptual responses.

Problem with Using Secondary Response

The problem with using secondary responses is that it's not a common practice among general music teachers. It's not even given much thought. For some reason, many teachers seem content with activities that have more waiting than "doing" time.

Here's a typical example. I can vividly remember a particular fifth-grade class that was waiting for an eternity, it seemed, to hold up the crescendo card during a listening lesson. They sat patiently, and idly, for almost two or three minutes. When they finally got to raise their cards, I wasn't surprised in the least to see that some cards looked like they had gone through a paper shredder! Neither was I shocked by the silly way students held up their cards despite the instructions. Some put the card on their faces like a Lone Ranger mask, while others perched it on their heads as if it were a crown, or tucked it under their chins like a bib. It didn't take a genius to figure out that the students had "had it" with the waiting!

Funny, you say? It would be except for the fact that it exposed the teacher's oblivion to the use of secondary responses, and also a lack of concern for the stu-

dents' learning experience. Again, you must not ignore situations that cry out for a secondary response. It's time to deal with the problem.

Suggestions for Using Secondary Response

Implementing a secondary response is as simple as one-two-three. **First**, you instruct the class clearly regarding the filler or secondary response. **Second**, demonstrate the activity with the secondary response. By the way, don't forget to use mirroring in your demonstration. (See "Mirroring Class's Movement" in Chapter 2.) And **third**, you participate in the activity with the class and anticipate each secondary response for the class. The implementing is actually very simple; routine, really.

But there are several suggestions to ensure success. **First**, be sure to select an obvious, or well-defined, concept for your secondary response. One that the students "can't miss," as the saying goes. Remember, the secondary response will focus on a different concept than the one for the activity. Stay away from the more subtle concepts. Secondary responses work best when the concepts involved are clear cut. If you need to, listen to the music beforehand in order to make the "right" selection.

Second, be sure that the students are familiar with the secondary concept, that they can respond to it easily—and even enjoyably, being that it is familiar. Keep in mind that a secondary response is only a "fill-in" exercise. As such, the concept must not be more challenging than the one for the activity. It should be "old hat" stuff.

Third, see that the students can do the activity in the secondary response without any problem. It really should be something they could do in their sleep, but still be something that's fun to do! They must be able to move in-and-out smoothly and easily from the activity response to the secondary response—several times over. So make sure it's manageable if you want the response to work.

And **fourth**, whatever you do, don't forget to try out the secondary response yourself. Be sure it works before using it! In fact, try the planned activity with both the primary and secondary responses, just like the class would do. Does the filler activity feel comfortable? Can you switch back-and-forth easily? Do you have any doubt about it? If so, change it. Doubtful situations have an uncanny way of coming to fruition in the lesson. Be absolutely sure the secondary response is "right," that it can be executed easily and switched smoothly, and that the concept involved is a familiar one. Don't be guilty of the "I thought it would work" syndrome. (See "Trying Out New Activities" in Chapter 1.)

Here are a few examples for these suggestions. Suppose the new concept for your third-grade lesson is the 3-2-1, or MI-RE-DO, melodic pattern and you want the students to play the pattern on their imaginary step bells each time they hear it. Since it appears only three times, you decide upon a secondary response. So you look for another concept. Is there a good steady beat? Or does it move too fast? Or too slow? What about the accented beats? Are they clear cut and easy to hear? Or would the melodic rhythm be better? If you go with the steady beat, you could have the students tap the beat on their thighs with closed fingertips. Or if you choose the melodic rhythm, why not ask them to clap with just two fingers on each hand?

In another example, let's say you're concentrating on phrase identification with your sixth graders. You want them to clap at the beginning of each phrase and snap at the end, but you know this isn't enough to keep them involved. What do you do? You select another prevalent concept, and a suitable activity, like having the students "conduct" the beat, or do some aerobic movements to the metric rhythm, or tap out the melodic rhythm with two fingers in the palm of hand. Are you beginning to see what's involved in selecting a secondary response? It's really a challenge to make them "fit" smoothly with the primary response.

Reasons for Using Secondary Responses

You already know a few of the reasons for using secondary responses. But here are some others:

- They remove idle times.
- They reinforce previous learning.
- They make activities challenging.

The **primary reason**, of course, is that the idle times are removed. Too much waiting time between conceptual responses leads to daydreaming, restlessness, and boredom. The secondary response makes it possible to fill in the idle times with profitable, as well as enjoyable, experiences for the students. So, keeping them involved is the first reason.

The **second reason** is that previous learnings can be reinforced. In other words, this is a good time to get some reviewing done—particularly with those concepts that lend themselves to an ongoing response, like the pulse, the accented beats, and the melodic rhythm. While responding to the newer concept, then, students can be strengthening previous learnings. Old and new learning can happen simultaneously.

The **third reason** is that activities become more challenging, and appealing as well. Students must listen more carefully in order to be able to change from the secondary to the primary response, and vice versa. Not only must they listen carefully, but respond accurately as well. Students love this kind of challenge, so don't hesitate to use secondary responses. And remember, don't make the secondary response more challenging than the primary response.

Concluding Challenge

Can you recall those times in your teaching when you needed a secondary response? When an activity you were presenting needed to be "doctored up" to make it more challenging and appealing? But you didn't quite know what to do? If so, now you have the know-how and the teaching tool to cope with these occasions. Don't let your students sit and wait between conceptual responses—keep them occupied. Give them a "filler" exercise, and yourself a teaching treat!

LESS EFFECTIVE

Mr. Largo instructed his first graders to raise their hands and wiggle their fingers every time they heard high pitches. When the recording started, the children were all sitting with their hands ready. Finally, the high pitches were heard and up went their hands with a wiggle-wiggle. Then it was back to waiting. When the children started talking and fidgeting, Mr. Largo was disappointed. "This was such a lovely recording, I wonder why they didn't like it? They seemed bored."

MORE EFFECTIVE

Mr. Largo's first-grade class was learning about high pitches. In readying the class, he told the children, "When you hear the high pitches, raise both hands high above your head, like this." Knowing that the high-pitch passages were spread out, he continued his instructions. "And while we're listening, let's quietly march to the beat with our marching hands on our laps." The children moved easily from one activity to the other. He could tell they were listening. When the recording ended, they begged to do it again.

Ms. Vivace's seventh graders were going to play chords on the resonator bells today. "We'll play the chords at the end of each. Those having the I chord will play only on that chord. Same with V_7. And let's sing along as we play." As the activity continued, the students started getting silly and began playing the chords at the wrong times. Purposely! "That's enough," she called. "Play the chords where they should go." "Wonder what's gotten into them? I thought they would like playing the chords. Guess I was wrong!" "Do we have to do it again?" they asked. "Let's not."

"I think you will enjoy playing chords on resonator bells with the triple mallets," Ms. Vivace told the class. "All those playing the I chord, raise your hands. V_7 chord? Let's tremolo, like this, when we play our chords. And while we are waiting for our chords at the end of each phrase, I'd like each of you to snap and tap the metric rhythm in three's with your left hand. Let's practice the first two phrases. Ready. Very good. Think we can do the whole song?" "They're snapping and tapping right on the beat and tremoling the chords beautifully." "Excellent, class!" "Can we do it again?" the students asked. "That was fun."

Using Visual Aids Effectively

Do you use visual aids in your teaching, such as when you're introducing or reinforcing a concept? You probably do. Just about everyone who teaches general music in the classroom uses visual aids, whether it be pictures, posters, slides, or any other object, such as a doll, a ball, or a drum. It's one of the most common tactics in teaching, and one of the most effective! You can't talk about the essential tasks of a lesson without mentioning visual aids. They're too vital! That's why it's important you be able to handle visual aids skillfully, be familiar with the pitfalls, and have some guidelines for utilizing visual aids in an effective way.

Definition of Visual Aids

Even though everyone basically knows what visual aids are, let's get a specific definition for purposes of this discussion. I like Broadwell's description. He says that a visual is simply anything used in a classroom that helps one teach by means of showing; that is, by appealing to the students' sight.[1] By definition, then, all of the following items are visual aids:

- pictures
- posters
- charts
- drawings
- photographs
- film strips
- slides
- movies
- cut-outs
- hand-held objects
- chalkboard markings
- audio-visual tapes
- people/animals
- toy replicas

Be sure you understand, however, that not every visual aid is good just because it's a visual aid. As Broadwell warns, not every visual aid is worth a thousand words. Sometimes it's best to use a few good words, rather than a poor visual aid.[2] And one that doesn't "fit the bill."

---

[1]Broadwell, Martin M. *The Supervisor as an Instructor*, 4th ed. (Reading, MA: Addison-Wesley Publishing Co.), 1984, p. 99.

[2]Broadwell, p. 100.

Pitfalls in Using Visual Aids

How can there be any pitfalls with such a simple task? After all, what's so difficult about lifting up or plopping down some visual, or relating its relevance? Nothing! The procedure is as easy as one-two-three. The pitfalls come with the implementation, or with the handling of these procedures. There are four pitfalls that contribute to the ineffective handling of visual aids:

- poor planning for placement
- nebulous gesturing for reference
- sloppy modeling for reinforcement
- inarticulate verbalizing for clarification

Let's talk about the **placement**. The pitfall is not planning beforehand where to "put" the visual aid once it's been whipped out. No big deal? But it is! The upshot is that there's always a mad scramble from pillar-to-post to find a "good place" to set it down. First, it's to the chalk tray where pictures and posters always buckle, and then to the piano rack, where everything flops over like a wilted flower. Next, to some desk to frantically stack books to lean the picture or poster against. See how you lose the impact of the visual aid when there's no planning for placement and how the momentum suffers? A third repercussion is that the hand-held objects never get properly displayed for further reference. They're just thoughtlessly tossed aside once they're used. Not having a display spot is definitely one of the pitfalls.

Nebulous gesturing is another. I call it the "magic wand syndrome." There's a tendency to "wave" the hand over the visual aid in some vague, circular motion when making reference to it, or to sweep back and forth a dozen times without the pointer finger ever landing on the specific part or place in question. By the way, did you ever notice the pointer finger? For a lot of teachers, it's always slightly curved—never straight. And never directly over anything, which adds to the students' confusion as to what the teacher is talking about. Then, too, some of these wand wavers or hand sweepers never look at the visual aid to get a bearing. Or get on-target! But it's the ones who gesture from across the room that take the cake! They motion in the general direction of the visual aid while referring to something specific. That's the epitome of nebulousness! They might as well be motioning to the moon. Students have no idea to what they are referring. There definitely is a problem with vague gesturing when it comes to visual aids.

Still another pitfall is the **sloppy modeling** with visual aids in the demonstration and/or the activity. The effort is often so half-hearted that it defeats the purpose of the visual aid, which is to highlight the concept. There's a lack of energy and enthusiasm and no theatrics. For instance, the hands-on objects aren't positioned precisely, moved realistically, or mirrored accurately. There's no attempt to make the visual aid depict the concept. If prioritizing these pitfalls was necessary, this one would have to rank as number one. It has direct bearing on how the students respond and how well they grasp the concept. So be sure that your modeling manner with the visual aids isn't sloppy.

Then there's the **verbalizing pitfall**. I'm sure many of you are modeling aces and gesturing specialists with your visual aids. But because you aren't articulate in verbalizing the (a) introduction, (b) the purpose or the relationship, (c) the implementation, and (d) the summary, your effort somehow "falls flat." Most of the time, there's little thought given to the verbiage surrounding a visual aid presentation. What do you say when presenting the visual? "Uhm, here's the ____." Do you have

key phrases prepared for the purpose? The relationship to the concept? How clear are your instructions for handling the visual aid? Your summary? You see, verbiage really affects the use of visual aids.

Be sure that you are well-acquainted with these four hazards, and that you critique your own teaching for these pitfalls.

Guidelines for Using Visual Aids

There are definite guidelines that can help you avoid the foregoing pitfalls and make you feel more confident in handling visual aids. Read through each of the guidelines below and select the one(s) you feel would help you the most.

Plan for Placement. As part of your lesson preparation, decide where the poster or chart will be placed once it's been brought forward. Don't leave it to chance. It takes just a few minutes to put masking tape on the backside of posters and charts so that they can be "put" on the chalkboard, the wall, or even the door. Or get those clips that hook to the molding of the chalkboard. Or be extravagant and get your own tripod. When you're dealing with hand-held visual aids, know exactly where you want to set it down so that it can be properly displayed for further use and be readily available.

Gesture for Specificity. Take time to point directly to your visual aid. Don't just wave your hand in the general direction, and be sure your pointing finger is straight and firm with the other fingers folded into the palm, and the thumb resting on the middle finger. Don't let it curve. That makes you look wimpish and strips you of your bodily authority. If you're referring to something specific on the visual aid, point precisely to that item—not around it, over it, below it, or on it! By being precise with your pointing gesture, you can get students to focus better.

Model with Precision. You need to maneuver the visual aid in a very accurate and even theatrical manner if it's going to reflect the concept. You can tell if you're being accurate by rehearsing in front of a mirror or the audio-visual camera. You need to see yourself as the students will see you and gauge your actions in terms of the "beholder." You may not be doing what you think you're doing! If the visual handout is supposed to move in a downward direction by steps, then you must position the handout, in mirroring fashion, slightly above the head on the right side and move down in precise equidistant steps **with** the passage. There's no room for approximation where visual aids are concerned, not if you want students to respond as accurately as possible. So get in front of a mirror or camera and see how precise you are.

Speak with Clarity. There's no secret to being articulate; it simply takes preparation and practice. You need to think through each step and determine what needs to be said. Then it's just a matter of practicing the verbiage—out loud, if necessary. Here are some examples of the kinds of comments you need to be ready to articulate with your visual aids:

- **Introduction**

   "What's this? Yes, a basketball to help us with strong-weak beats."

   "And here's a grandfather clock for our lesson on steady beats."

- **Relationship**

   "Let's listen to hear the strong bounces and weak bounces just like in our beats."

   "Did you know that our grandfather clock has tick-tocks that sound just like our steady beat?"

- **Summary**

   "So our basketball has strong-weak bounces just like our what?"

   "And what do the tick-tocks in our grandfather clock sound like? Yes, the steady beat."

See how articulate your verbiage needs to be? How both the manual aid and the concept are articulated as proper nouns, not pronouns? Only when verbiage is this articulate can you help to clarify the concept for the students.

Reasons for Using Visual Aids

Visual aids are a marvelous teaching tool for many reasons, most of which you already know. Let me share some of the more important ones with you.

First, using visual aids **helps students** learn faster because of their appeal to the eye. They seem to grasp the meaning of concepts better. The visuals somehow clarify the idea. I've seen so many marvelous visual aids over the years; each one seems to make the concept crystal clear—almost in a flash. The drawings of a big drum with big upper-case letters for *B O O M* and three little drums with smaller lower-case letters for *b o o m* were always one of my favorites. It was fantastic for clarifying strong-and-weak beats. Then there was the staircase outlined on the tile floor with white chalk to picture the concept of stepwise movement. Children grasped the concept in a split second after walking up and down the stairs with the music. Is there any doubt that visual aids help children learn and clarify musical concepts in a jiffy? I think not!

Second, visual aids also **reinforce concepts** as well. You don't need to limit visual aids to introductory situations. They can be equally effective as reinforcing tools for more familiar concepts.[3] For example, older students enjoy using "phrase ending" cards they hold up at the end of each phrase while tapping the melodic rhythm throughout the phrase with their other free hand. You could do the same with a "phrase beginning" card. Send it up at the beginning and down at the end. In between, have the students respond to the ongoing beat, the accented beats, or the melodic rhythm. Phrase cards are great reinforcers; so are a host of other visual aids that can reinforce high-low registers, up-down direction, etc., for younger children.

And **third**, visual aids **generate interest** and enthusiasm. Not only do they provide a legitimate hands-on experience for the students, they also offer a change in the type of activity used in the classroom. I vividly remember one kindergarten class that was holding up their brightly colored leaves, and each time they sang, "Down, down, yellow and brown . . ." to the tune of a descending major scale, they would let their leaves go floating downward. The children bubbled over with excitement. It was delightful to see them scoop up the leaves again and again and wait for that downward passage. Were these leaves generating some interest and enthusiasm? You bet they were! And that's what visual aids can do best—generate interest.

Concluding Challenge

Have you been examining your own efforts with visual aids as you read this task? Are you guilty of any of the pitfalls? Do you always plan for the placement and use definitive pointing gestures? Do you model precisely and verbalize articulately? If not, take heed of some of the guidelines if you want to be more effective with visual aids. It's up to you now!

---

[3]Broadwell, p. 100.

LESS EFFECTIVE	MORE EFFECTIVE
Mr. Round had a great poster ready for his kindergartners. It showed various objectives that made loud and soft sounds. "Guess I'll lean it against the back of the chair. That should work." But the poster couldn't stay on the chair. It kept sliding off. Disgusted, he whisked it up and marched to the chalkboard. "There, that ought to work!" When it fell over three times, the class started to snicker. "That's it! We won't use it," he snapped.	When Mr. Round finished with his poster showing environmental objects having loud and soft sounds, he got the masking tape and put some on each corner. He proceeded directly to the board and put the poster up where everyone could see it. Mr. Round made several references to the poster during the lesson. "I'm going to leave the poster on the board. It's the best place for it." And the children enjoyed it so much.
Mr. Canon demonstrated the action song with his visual aid. He ran through the actions quickly and told the class to watch him. "When the music goes high, put your bluebird up here." He waved the bluebird off to one side. "But be sure to put it over your head, okay? Put it over here when the high part is over." He flopped the bluebird by his side. "Are we ready? Get those birds up high. Like this. Harold, not like that!" "What's wrong with these students today? They're not doing anything right."	Mr. Canon positioned his bluebird in front of him before he demonstrated the song for his class. He carefully performed all the actions and then called attention to the bluebird. "Watch me again and you'll see how I hold up the bluebird over my head, like this, on the high sounding part. And when the high part is over, put your bird by your side." Immediately he put the bird down against his leg. "Got it? Let's try it." When the high part came, the class put their bluebirds high over their heads. "You did that so well. I'm proud of you!"

Singing When Recording/Tape Is Too Fast

As a classroom music teacher, you must be ready to sing your songs in place of the record (or tape) when the tempo is too fast for the activity. If you don't, the lesson will come to a halt. Students can't do the activity when the tempo is too fast. Something has to be done—and quickly! In this case, singing is the most logical, and expedient, way of handling the matter. Here's why. **First**, the voice is readily available—you don't have to go after it! **Second**, the "right" tempo can be established immediately without further delay. And **third**, the students can adjust quickly—they're accustomed to hearing your voice. So sing in place of the record (or tape) when the tempo moves too fast for the activity.

Situation Responsible for Fast Tempo

This can happen even when activities are checked out faithfully before the lesson. (See "Trying Out New Activities" in Chapter 1.) Generally, it's an honest mistake. You simply forget about the students' body tempo and judge the recording (or tape) in light of your own. Thus, when the recording is played in class, you're totally surprised that the tempo is so fast! It's an oversight that can happen to anyone—and usually does! But it need not be disastrous if you're ready to jump in and sing the song yourself. You can salvage both song **and** activity.

Let me tell you about a beginning kindergarten teacher who epitomized this situation. She had just finished demonstrating the stretching and bending activity, and I could tell by her stricken expression and huffing-and-puffing that it suddenly dawned on her that the recording was too fast! She froze in her tracks. When she dropped the needle for the children, I know she didn't have any strategy up her sleeve. Needless to say, the activity was a hodge-podge! The children who liked the stretching kept on stretching without ever bending, and those who were fascinated with the bending just stayed bent and giggled to the others in this same position. One child even got so mesmerized by a fly on the ceiling that she stayed stretched for the whole activity! I left the class speechless! She obviously had not listened to the song before the lesson, or else was completely unaware of the children's body tempo. Whichever the case, it was a fiasco!

Significant Outcomes from Singing

If you're thinking that this isn't a real significant responsibility with regard to activities, I can assure you it is! There are two important outcomes. The **first** is that by being ready to sing at a more appropriate tempo, you can continue with the same selection. You don't have to put it aside or use a substitute recording, or even change the activity.

The **second** outcome is that the lesson can continue without interruption. You won't go into a tizzy if the tempo does take you by surprise, or enact one of those silly charades where your head suddenly whips back in the direction of the record or cassette player and, in two giant leaps, you're hovering over the recording like a witch over a cauldron. You might even start spinning your head round-and-round with the record like you're trying to read the label. I hate to admit it, but I've done this once or twice myself. It was my way of blaming the record and saying "Hey, it's not me!" I felt betrayed. But since I didn't know what else to do, I stayed with the recording, and the class came unglued! If I would have shut off the recording and sung the song myself, I could have avoided the disaster.

Do you see why this task is so important? It gives you the edge in keeping your lesson afloat, and relieves the anxiety of coping with inappropriate tempi. But, like other tasks, it needs to be implemented effectively, and that calls for some guidelines.

Guidelines for Singing

There are several guidelines to consider if this singing substitution is to work. The **first guideline** is that you need to be well-acquainted with the song before the lesson begins from the standpoint of its (a) beginning pitch, (b) meter signature, (c) key signature, (d) written text, and (e) appropriate tempi. Don't even attempt to sing the song unless you have this information down pat! Get it from your music text; most of your recordings will probably be coming from your music series anyway, so you should know these songs—from memory. The smooth switch from the recording to your singing depends upon your competence in assimilating the above items.

The **second guideline** is that you need a working knowledge of the singing voice. I'm assuming that you can sing with (a) good tone, (b) proper breathing, (c) correct diction, (d) accurate pitches, and (e) correct intonation. (This is not asking too much!) Students must always have an accurate and appealing rendition of the music, regardless of grade level; that means even the early elementary children also need to hear proper singing. If you don't feel confident about your singing voice, then consider using back-up recordings. But be sure to bring them with you. If we're going to develop perception and discrimination, as Bugelski notes, we must give students high caliber presentations.[4] That's why I'm suggesting you have a working knowledge of the singing voice.

The **third guideline** for being ready to sing is that you select song(s) you can handle. This is the key to success in this task. In fact, this should really be the first guideline. In a nutshell, the rule is: Choose songs **you** know **you** can sing. Songs must lie within your own ability level if you're going to feel comfortable, and confident, singing them. If you forget this criterion, you'll be booby-trapping your own efforts. Believe me, it relieves a lot of the pressure to know that you can "do" your songs—if you had to!

A **fourth guideline** is that you think through the strategy for the transition. Have you ever actually planned what you would do or say? If not, let's walk through the process. First, go to the record or cassette player and lift the needle or press the stop button. That's right. Stop it! You don't need to stand there and stare at the machine, adjust the dials, or scratch your head. Then, as you're walking back to the class, instruct the students what to do, that is, use walking time as instructing time. You might say something like this:

- "Since the tempo is so fast on the record, let me sing the song for you as we . . ."
- "That recording is too fast for us, isn't it? So why don't I sing and play for us? Ready!"
- "That tempo moves too fast for this activity. Let's continue . . . while I sing the song, okay?"

See how easy the transition can be made? Once you've delivered the instructions, then the rest depends upon your own state of readiness, as described in the first guideline. By the way, the sample statements are simply verbal bridges with a comment (about the tempo) followed by an instruction. (See "Using Verbal Bridges" in Chapter 3.)

Here are a few more reminders. **One**, get the right starting pitch from the piano or autoharp. Don't sing in another key because it destroys the tenor of the activity. **Two**, be sure to emphasize the conceptual idea like in the recording. The students must be able to hear the concept in order to respond. If the concept is the 3-2-1 melodic pattern, then sing the pattern in a very deliberate and accurate manner whenever it appears; or "lean" on the accented beats as you sing or play, if an accompaniment is being used. Remember, you're responsible now for communicating the

---

[4] Bugelski, B. R. *Some Practical Laws of Learning*, The Phi Delta Kappa Educational Foundation, Bloomington, Indiana, 1970, p. 18.

concept. And **three**, be animated and enthusiastic as you sing. Project the same spirit as the record or cassettes; otherwise, you'll bore the students.

These reminders will help you "pull off" the task. So don't ignore them. They're the hands-on stuff that can make the difference between a mediocre and an effective effort.

Here's one last reminder. Suppose you want the class to sing along with you. What you do is apply the procedures for group singing. (See "Establishing Pitch and Tempo" in Chapter 8.) Basically, the procedure is this: (1) Sing beginning pitch on "lu"; (2) Ask class to match "lu" pitch; (3) Use counterclockwise conducting gesture to cut off when class "has it"; and (4) Sing "Ready, sing" on the beginning pitch followed by a prep breath with a down beat and/or nod of head, which tells students when to start singing. Just be sure your head tilts back slightly when taking the prep breath. Your nod will be more definite if you do. Don't forget the ictus on the downbeat either!

But whether the class sings with you or you sing yourself, you need some strategy. To be without a plan of action is like being up a creek without a paddle.

Concluding Challenge

Is this one of those responsibilities you avoid? If so, this challenge is for you. Check and recheck your recordings before teaching, unless you're using one of your tried-and-true songs you **know** will work. Be sure that the tempo is right and be ready to sing your songs. I know this will take more time and effort, but you will be ever grateful to yourself on those occasions when the tempo surprises you! If you want to add another ounce of class to your teaching, learn to rely on your own singing when recordings are too fast.

LESS EFFECTIVE

Ms. Mozart had checked her recording before class. That's why she was so shocked when she heard it in class. "Why is it going so fast? The children won't be able to clap the melodic rhythm at that tempo! But I don't know what else to do." As soon as the activity started, she knew she was in trouble. One-by-one the first graders dropped out. By the end of the song, most of the class was doing something else—either looking out the window, talking, or squirming in their seats. "Guess I can't use that song again." "All right, let's get quiet. We'll do something else since our clapping didn't go so well today! I'll try to find a better song next time."

When Mr. Bach realized that the tempo of the recording was too fast for his fifth graders to play the ascending penta-scale, he turned it off. "That's too fast for us. We can't do this activity. Nothing else to do but forget that recording and go on," he announced. When the lesson ended six minutes early, he felt a bit hurt that the class had let him down. "I certainly hope we won't have to put aside too many more of our activities. Maybe we need to listen more closely next time. Okay, get out your books and study until it's time to go."

MORE EFFECTIVE

When Ms. Mozart readied her class for the activity, she turned on the record player. She was excited about the activity because she had tried it out with the record before the lesson. So she was totally surprised when she heard how fast it sounded in class. It hit her that she hadn't even thought about the children's body tempo. So she immediately turned off the recording and said to the children, "We would have to make our hands clap very fast with that record, wouldn't we? So let me sing the song." With that she gave herself the pitch on the autoharp and began singing the song. "I'm glad I learned this song!" she said to herself. The children clapped the melodic rhythm vigorously as Ms. Mozart sang. "Excellent, class. Everyone was clapping the melody with me, even with my singing. I'm proud of you."

Mr. Bach was anxious to see how well his fifth graders could play the ascending penta-scale. But, as soon as the recording started, he knew the tempo was too fast. "I forgot you weren't little Mozarts! Suppose I sing the song for you." By then he was at the piano and playing the intro. Because he had maneuvered the transition so smoothly, the class was hardly aware of the need for a change in the presentation. Mr. Bach slowed the tempo down as he played and sang, and the class continued with the activity. "Thank goodness I took the time to learn this song," he said to himself.

Insisting on Musically Performed Activities

Here's one task every music teacher knows about! It's making sure that the activities in your lesson are executed in a musical way. So whether it's singing, playing, or moving, all need to be done within the context of a **musical** response because activities not performed musically are nothing more than noisy recreation and don't contribute to a musical experience. See how crucial it is to insist upon musically performed activities? You dare not take this responsibility lightly; or, worse yet, be hesitant about reinforcing it. It's one task that epitomizes the essence of teaching for musical growth, and one that desperately needs your expertise.

Problem for Musically Performed Activities

Unfortunately, the problem is an obvious one. Just visit some music classes and you'll discover that there's not a lot of persistence to see that activities are performed in a musical fashion. The truth is, the activities are often done so raggedly, raucously, or anemically that they lose their impact.

Let's look at some examples of non-musical responses. Take **clapping exercises**. They usually get so loud that they drown out the recording! Why? Because the whole class starts clapping in the conventional way without being given any instructions as to how to make the clapping more musical, a hand-smacking free-for-all. You can hardly call hand bashing a musical experience, can you? Clapping must conform to the character of the music in every sense—and be subservient to the dynamic level—to be musical; otherwise, it's unmusical.

Singing activities are usually the most blatant examples of non-musical participation you can find due largely to the "sing-louder syndrome." Listen sometime when children are being coaxed to "sing out." You'll hear them oblige by shouting out in their chest voices, and converting their singing into yelling. Instead of having them sing with their light head voice, they're encouraged to use their heavier chest voice, and to constantly "sing louder" and force the voice. What a travesty to mishandle the singing voice and rob the children of having musical experiences through singing.

Moving activities also have a high rate of being non-musical. A lot of times it looks like the students are getting rid of energy, rather than responding to music. Their marching, swaying, dancing, or pulsating is so vigorous they no longer hear the music. They would be better off on the playground doing exercise than in the classroom doing music. There must be a conscious effort on the part of the student to move "with" or "to" the music, if the moving is to look musical and be musical. A play-like response that isn't "with" the music will not look musical.

Then there are the **playing activities**. I don't know how many times I've seen wood blocks, drums and rhythm sticks beat to death during an activity. But it was enough times to know that instruments are almost always played too loudly and uncontrollably. All that booming, banging, and clicking make it nearly impossible to hear the music. These occasions hardly qualify as musical experiences.

The bad news is that the above examples are not uncommon; they happen all too often! But here's the good news. You can insist on musical responses if you have the know-how.

Procedure for Musical Responses

A simple formula for obtaining musical responses with your activities is a straightforward one-two-three approach. But if you follow it, you'll get those musical responses.

First, determine the performance criteria for each activity. In other words, decide how well you want the students to respond. Accurately? Easily? Without error? Without stopping? It's up to you. Ask yourself, "How must the students respond in order to have a musical experience?" If the tub drum must be played softly and lightly to the ongoing beat of a certain recording or if the singing must be in tune, then this is what you strive for with your students. The class's musical performance starts with your criterion.

Second, demonstrate the activity for the class. Students need to be shown how to respond musically rather than recreationally. Their musical growth depends upon this awareness; but be sure to demonstrate very precisely. Tap the rhythm sticks lightly, march quietly, and do action songs realistically. Then have the students imitate your demonstration with you, to-a-tee, before doing the activity with music. This way you can check out their response and correct any problems. But don't drag out this "prep session." Do it just long enough to see that the class is ready. The second step, then, is demonstrating in accordance with the criteria.

Third, assess the response of the students throughout the activity. If you see that the class isn't performing up to the criterion levels, isn't listening to the music, or isn't following the instructions, then stop the activity. And plug in a *verbal bridge* or a dual statement composed of (a) an assessment and (2) an instruction. In other words, you tell the students what needs fixing or correcting, and then you give instructions whether to continue or repeat the activity. Thereafter, the assessment goes on throughout the activity. It's a matter of correcting responses and showing students how to perform in a more musical manner.

If you set your criteria, demonstrate activities, and assess responses throughout your lesson, you'll begin to experience success.

Reasons for Musical Responses

While the reasons are probably obvious to everyone, let's briefly reiterate them for a matter of record, and share them with those who might not know why it's important to pursue musical responses.

First and foremost, musical responses are crucial to the students' aesthetic development. They help titillate this feelingful nature. Don't forget that the nurturing of aesthetic sensitivity is the primary goal of the music experience. There's no stronger reason for stressing the importance of **musical** responses.

Second, musically achieved performances are good motivating tools. Students like to be successful and enjoy being a part of a satisfying experience. Participating in a musical response provides the opportunity of experiencing both of these needs. In short, students get motivated and inspired when they "do"' activities in a musical way.

Third, musical responses affect classroom control. Students can sense very quickly when the class is just going through the motions of an activity. When this happens, discipline goes out the window and students get bored. But when they're challenged to respond in a more accurate and musical fashion, their attention is drawn to the activity, so classroom discipline gets better.

You couldn't have more impressive reasons for acknowledging the importance of this task. It contributes to aesthetic growth, motivates the class's interest, and improves classroom discipline.

Concluding Challenge

If you've not been very demanding about getting a musical response from your students, hopefully you will be now. Don't falter in this responsibility. The student's aesthetic development depends upon this task to a large degree. Too, obtaining musical responses is one of the earmarks of an effective teacher, not only for the above reason, but for other discipline and motivation reasons as well. Follow the three-step procedure and change your whole outlook on your teaching.

LESS EFFECTIVE	*MORE EFFECTIVE*
Mr. Tension instructed his fourth-grade class to clap the accented beats over their heads and the unaccented on their laps. After he demonstrated, he jumped into the activity. "They don't need to practice." "Ready?" But when the activity started the clapping got louder and louder. Then the tapping started to rush. "Maybe it'll get better. I'll keep on going," he said to himself. He saw some girls roll their eyes as the activity came to an end. "Well, at least they got through it." Most of the class wasn't even doing the clapping/tapping when the activity ended.	"I'd like us to clap the strong beat above our heads, like this, and tap the weaker ones on our laps. Let me show you. Try it with me. Very good. Be sure your clapping doesn't get too loud because you won't hear the music." But they did start rushing. So Mr. Tension stopped and told them they were rushing and clapping too loudly. "Let's try it again. What a difference!" They were clapping better because now they were listening. He could tell the class was enjoying the activity by their response and the look on their faces. "That was a big improvement. Your clapping was done so well."
As soon as Ms. Release started the marching activity with her first graders, she remembered that she forgot to tell them how to march on their feet. So some were stomping loudly while others were barely lifting each foot. "Oh well, let them continue this time. I'll correct them later." But then the loud stompers started getting silly. "Don't stomp that hard, boys. March on your toes." She breathed a sigh of relief when the recording was over because the marching was getting out of hand! You could hardly hear the music. "We'll try to march better next time, won't we?" But no one was listening! "Let's get settled down now."	When Ms. Release finished demonstrating how to march for her first graders, she asked the class to "practice" before they marched with the music. "Jimmy, be sure to march on the front part of your foot. Like this. Very good. Now, let's see if you can march just like you did with our music. Ready!" She was so pleased to see everyone marching lightly. "Excellent," she remarked as they marched. "I especially like how Mark and Susan are marching. You too, Billy." When they finished, Ms. Release praised them again. "You listened so well and marched right with the beat." Then she instructed them. "You know what? We're ready to tap the beat with our rhythm sticks this time. Watch me first." The children ooohed with excitement.

Adopting a Student's Version of Activity

You may not have thought of this action as being a teaching task, but it is. Remember the times you saw a student doing something a bit different during an activity and how you immediately sensed that the student's version was much better than your own activity? And how glad you were that you switched to the student's way? You were actually doing this very task; in fact, you were using one of the higher-level tactics in the process of teaching. I say higher level because it goes beyond the basic responsibilities needed in implementing an activity. It adds that touch of finesse that earmarks the master teacher. As such, it takes skillful handling, and a keen, sensitive attitude toward students. Even so, it's an option all classroom music teachers must be ready and willing to exercise where activities are concerned.

Significant Rewards for Adopting

Why all the concern for tuning-in to the student's version—especially when it's not one of the more basic teaching tasks? Because the rewards are so significant for both teacher and student.

For the teacher, taking the student's version leads to a more exciting activity because it comes from the "horse's mouth." The adopted version emanates from one who has the same likes and dislikes as the rest of the class. That's why it usually "works"! I cherish the times I made the switch because they resulted in some of the most exciting experiences I ever had in the classroom! It was like a breath of fresh air coming out of nowhere. So don't be so full of pride that you miss the beauty of what the student is offering.

That paves the way for the second reward: keeping an open mind also means that you can learn more about the students. For example, you can discover (a) hidden abilities, (b) typical responses, (c) favorite activities, and (d) special interests, all of which can help you plan your own activities more effectively. However, you will need to be keenly discerning as to which variations merit your recognition, an issue we'll talk about later.

Perhaps the most significant reward, however, is the one students receive. There's an immediate surge of self-respect and self-worth. Ever notice how students respond when you acknowledge "their" version? They stand two inches taller and radiate an inner glow. You can almost see the welling-up of pride and self-respect happening before your eyes. You really can't put a price tag on this outcome; it's one of those intangibles that makes this practice so rewarding. And you have the privilege of nurturing the student's feelings of self-worth and self-respect just by being alert.

You can see why I feel so adamant about this effort, and why I urge every teacher to be on the lookout for student ingenuity during an activity. The rewards are significant. The teacher's success and the students' well-being are both affected.

Problem With Adopting a Student's Version

The difficulty when it comes to adopting the student's variation boils down to an attitude problem. A lot of teachers tend to "see" deviant responses from the planned activity as being either (a) more effective or (b) less effective. But each position taken by itself is dangerous and requires a word of warning.

The pitfall of seeing everything the students do—apart from instructed response—as "better" must not happen. Every different wiggle and squirm will not be better! In fact, most of it will need correction to tell the student to "straighten up." But that doesn't mean you'll never have a truly "better" response. There **will** be times when you will be surprised, and even amazed, at what you see the student doing, times when you actually like the student's version better than yours. You'll recognize these times too. The point is, don't be fooled into thinking that every variation you see is better.

The opposite attitude is just as confining. It's the notion that **none** of the deviating behavior is any good—that it's all fooling around or goofing off, and needs to be reprimanded or, at the very least, frowned upon and even ignored. But that just isn't true! Not all deviant responses are mischievous and inconsequential. Some actu-

ally *are* more effective versions of the activity. In other words, sometimes kids do come up with better actions to our activities, and when they do, use them.

So don't be guilty of thinking every deviating response will be either better or worse than your own. It won't. But when it is, you'd better be able to do the switching. If you need a procedure, continue reading.

Procedure for Opting Student's Version

Let's say you've spotted a student doing something a little different with the activity and you liked it. How would you actually go about switching to the student's version? Just follow the **three-step procedure** outlined here:

- **Step One**: Spot student's version
- **Step Two**: Assess student's version
- **Step Three**: Announce student's version

The **first step** should be no problem; after all, you're constantly scanning the class anyway. It should be easy to spot the student who is doing his/her own version of the instructed activity. No judgment call is made in that initial moment. Only a singling out that can happen at any point in the activity.

The **second step** is the one that requires discrimination. It involves the assessment of the student's version and it happens almost instantaneously after the "spotting." The decision as to whether the variation the student is doing is more appealing and appropriate than what the class is doing, is usually made in the twinkling-of-an-eye—after the student is spotted.

The basis for this decision is actually a combination of your keen awareness of what's effective and your own innate conviction. Put more succinctly, it's your learned judgment plus professional instinct that gives you the confidence to make these decisions. And trust your own judgment. That's the basis for your decision-making.

In the **third step**, you recognize the version publicly; that is, you tell the class about it and then instruct them what to do. The best way to do this is to stop the activity so that everyone can hear you. Here are some examples of how you could verbalize this kind of information.

- "Jimmy, I like what you were doing with your hands. Can you show the class your version? Very good. Let's all try Jimmy's way, class. Good! Now let's try it with the music."
- "I stopped you because I wanted you to see what Jimmy was doing. He's added a different hand motion. Show us, Jimmy. Would you mind if we all did it your way? Come up front and help me lead the class, Jimmy."
- "Everyone was doing . . . so well, but I saw Jimmy doing something special to make it even more challenging. Jimmy, would you show the class your way? Now try it with Jimmy. Ready."

Statements like these will allow you to handle the process smoothly and orderly. When you do see a worthy variation, you can graciously acknowledge the student, quickly implement the variation, and anxiously wait for the exciting results.

I can almost hear some of the questions and concerns you have about this task. Let's see if I can answer a few. No, your taking the student's version **will not** dilute your stature in any way. To the contrary, it will show students that you are an open and flexible individual, and willing to recognize a student's ideas. If anything, you will elevate your leadership role. Will the altering of an activity bother the students? No, not if you handle it as suggested above. And no, you will not have students calling out, "Hey, look what I'm doing." Students will do an activity your way most of the time, so don't worry needlessly. You won't have variations on an activity every lesson!

But wait! Suppose **you** have a sudden brainstorm? Would you keep going with your planned activity or switch? My advice is, switch only if you feel strongly that your brainstorm is better. But don't get the idea that you can change your activity every time you "feel" like it. You don't have that liberty. Use your brainstorm only when your learned judgment and professional instinct say, "Yes, the new idea is better than the old." That's your measuring rod!

Concluding Challenge

How often do you recognize and utilize a student's version of your activities? It's an exciting and vital part of the teaching process. Most times students will be goofing off, but on occasions the variation will be good. When it is, be ready to use it. Look for those "gifts." They'll come at the most unexpected times and bring a moment of sunshine into your lesson.

LESS EFFECTIVE	MORE EFFECTIVE
"We're going to march to the beat of every phrase and at the end of the phrase we're going to kick our foot forward like this," Ms. Tonic instructed the fourth graders. "Try it. Good. Now with the record." Out of the corner of her eye she saw Tony throwing out his arms with his foot. "Stop that, Tony." She glared at him until he stopped. "I can't have any of that in here," she said to Tony after the activity. "But that wasn't such a bad idea though," she thought later.	When Ms. Tonic finished telling her fourth graders that they would be marching and kicking at the end of each phrase, she had them try it. "Very good, class. Let's see if we can do it with the music." She saw Tony kicking out his arms with his foot. Ms. Tonic stopped the class at the end of the next phrase. "I like what you were doing, Tony. Would you show the class? Can everyone try this? Tony, you be our leader. Ready." "I'm glad I spotted him. His way really is better than mine!"

The next activity was to tap out the melodic rhythm by alternating hands and using two fingers on the desktop. When the activity began, Ms. Dominant spotted Mark switch from one side of the desk to the other for each phrase. "Mark," she called out and shook her head. "That's not what I asked you to do." "Can't have everyone doing his/her own thing here," she said to herself. "That Mark is always trying something new!"

Ms. Dominant demonstrated how she wanted the class to tap out on their desktops with two fingers of each hand. As the activity got underway, she saw Mark doing something clever. He was alternating the melodic rhythm of each phrase from one side of the desk to another. She stopped the activity and asked the class to watch Mark. "Would you please show the class what you were doing? Can we all tap Mark's way?" "Yeah, that's neat!" they said. The class loved Mark's way of playing the melodic rhythm.

Demonstrating in Deliberate Manner

While much has been said about teacher demonstrations throughout this chapter, nothing has been mentioned concerning the deliberate manner with which demonstrations must be executed. This is an indispensable aspect of teacher demonstrations and must not be underestimated. True, there **are** other criteria for demonstrating effectively, such as being precise, overt, and a bit theatrical, but even these are affected in one way or the other by the degree of deliberateness in the teacher's demonstration. If you're not familiar with these other criteria, read the section "Providing Teacher Demonstrations" in Chapter 6. It's up to the teacher, then, to be sure that his/her demonstrations are done in an intentionally obvious way.

Description of Deliberate Manner

To demonstrate in a deliberate manner means that the teacher executes the modeling in two specific ways: (1) intentionally slower and (a) increasingly exaggerated. It's slower from the standpoint that the teacher doesn't hurry through it before the students can blink their eyes. Slower also in the sense that it's done in a purposely slower tempo than normally used in order to be more obvious.

As for being more exaggerated, the actions are intentionally magnified, or made greater in size, in order for students to grasp the details. The deliberateness is a calculated criteria or contemplated happening. The teacher should be totally aware of doing demonstrations slower and more exaggerated, that is, not hurried or underplayed and concentrating on the precision, the size, and the theatrics. Deliberateness is the quality that highlights the other criteria, and the quality that makes a demonstration effective! You now have the formula for demonstrating in a deliberate manner.

Problem Regarding Deliberateness

The problem is that teachers don't always do their demonstrations in a deliberate manner. Much of the time they rush through them—almost absentmindedly and even lethargically, whether it be a rote song, a rhythmic exercise, or some playing example. But it's not just the rushing that causes the problem, it's the attitude that goes with it! It seems that teachers try to do the demonstration in the fastest way possible, like it's a bother or a demeaning chore they feel awkward or put-upon doing. There's little or no comprehension of how important the demonstration is to the students. Instead of slowing down and exaggerating, they do the demonstration in a hurried, slough-off manner that limits the impact.

I get especially annoyed with teachers doing a new rote song. Do they ever look in the mirror when they're preparing the song? If they did, they would shock even themselves! Here's what I'm talking about. This particular person was teaching "Six Little Ducks," the one that tells about the fat ones, skinny ones, and the one with the feather on its back. When it came to doing the actions, she whizzed through the fat and skinny gestures, then turned quickly and put her thumbs somewhat on her lower back and wiggled her fingers for the "feather on his back" part. On the quack-quack-quacks she made some kind of unduckly sound I haven't been able to imitate to this day! Her demonstration was over before I knew what happened. And the children? They just sat there with mouths open! Then she had the nerve to ask them if they would like to do the song with her. The children, of course, were baffled. So was I. Nothing was slow and exaggerated.

Reasons for Not Being Deliberate

The illustration above is common. It happens all the time in other demonstrations as well; teachers just aren't mindful of being deliberate mainly for **two reasons**. One pertains mostly to the younger teachers—they are usually **scared and a bit embarrassed**. This is particularly true for those who are insecure about their own singing voice and must sing during the demonstration. Their primary objective is to get through as quickly as they can. They have no desire to prolong and exaggerate the demonstration. Nerves really *can* affect a teacher's performance in a rote song demonstration.

But then nerves can also get in the way during instrumental demonstrations, when all the teacher has to do is go click-click on the rhythm sticks or ding-ding on the triangle. Here's the scenario. The teacher usually starts playing the beat pattern or melodic rhythm when the instrument is barely in his/her hands or just being picked up. By the time the instrument is in the proper playing position, the demonstration is over and the teacher is saying, "Now let's play that together!" The nervous rushing and lack of deliberateness will kill a demonstration every time. Whenever I question a teacher about his or her rushing and lack of deliberateness, the individual usually tosses out a hand or flips the bottom of her hair and says, "But I was so nervous!" To which I answer, "Well, you'll just have to conquer your nerves because your demonstrations aren't doing the job!" It's a matter of getting control of one's self through careful preparation and thinking more about the children than one's self! We'll talk more about that later.

The other reason for not executing a demonstration in a deliberate manner is the same reason given for many other things. Namely, a **lack of awareness**. Many teachers simply do not know they must be very deliberate. They have never been videotaped, personally informed, or professionally instructed to notice this response in other teachers. I suppose there are some who have had these experiences but have chosen to ignore them. To these I say, reconsider the responsibility—it's vital to your modeling efforts. But wouldn't teaching experience make the need more evident? Not necessarily. It's amazing how many teaching skills can be overlooked even when the solution is really quite obvious—much like being deliberate in teaching demonstrations. So for those who have not given much thought to demonstrating in a slow and thoughtful manner, let me urge you to become more deliberate.

Need for Deliberateness

The need for being deliberate is obvious. In the first place, you would probably cite the fact that the **student response will be better**. And you're absolutely right! That's because in being deliberate you're providing an easy-to-follow model. More important, you're showing students how they should strive to respond. We know that unless effort is exerted, students will not have a clear grasp of what you expect. But sometimes that's the problem. Teachers don't really know what they expect themselves. They don't have any criteria or set standards. And, if they don't, all this talk about demonstrating in a deliberate manner is useless.

The first step, then, must be to determine how well you want the student to respond. (See the section "Establishing Criteria" in Chapter 1.) Once you have determined what you expect from the class, then you are ready for the second step, which is to determine how well you need to respond in your demonstrations, i.e., what expectations you have for yourself! That's where the deliberateness comes in; you must do your part well if you expect your students to respond well! The more deliberately **you** do your demonstration, the more deliberate **your students** are likely to respond and the more deliberateness you can demand. Remember, the quality of your class response is in exact proportion to your own deliberate performance.

In the second place, **teaching time is saved**. You won't have to stop the class and ask them to watch you again, and you won't have to wonder what's the matter with them. Students will respond more confidently and more accurately. However, when the teachers aren't deliberate on the first time, it always seems that they respond a bit more obviously the second time. It must be out of sheer necessity at that point. I always wonder why teachers can't be deliberate the first time around. Why is it necessary to say, "No, you didn't watch" (Watch what?) or "You didn't do what I did" (What **did** you do?). You can save yourself a whole lot of time—and aggravation—if you would just plan on being deliberate the first time. With only thirty minutes per week with each class, saving lesson time should be a prime consideration. Demonstrating in a deliberate manner is a "must" in your teaching.

Practice Suggestions

Here's some advice on how to become more deliberate in your teaching demonstrations. I've already pinpointed why teachers overlook this aspect in their demonstrations. It's nerves. I won't even pretend to tell you how to get rid of your nerves, but I can make some suggestions that will help you be more deliberate and, in so doing, less nervous.

My **first suggestion** is to **be well-prepared**; that is, know exactly what you are going to do for your demonstration. Rehearse if you need to! **Second, demonstrate for yourself** in front of a mirror. It's the only way to get an honest picture of how you actually look. You can see if your demonstration possesses all the other requirements, including (a) precision, (b) overtness, (c) exaggeration, and (d) a bit theatrical in nature. If it does, then you are ready to move on to the third suggestion. **It's checking to see that you're doing the demonstration slowly and exaggerated**. If you can, move on to my final suggestion. It's the most difficult one, but the one that does the trick! **Get totally absorbed in assessing your demonstration** from the students' point of view, rather than from your point of view.

There's the secret: to become more concerned with what the students will see than with what you feel. Yes, you can learn to acquire this kind of an attitude. But you need to be aware of having to cultivate it—to work at it in a conscious way. Let's discuss it further.

A student-oriented attitude is nothing more than having the good of the students foremost in your mind rather than your own nervousness. And how do you go about cultivating this concern in the privacy of your own preparational period? By becoming critical of your performance in the mirror—critical of your precision, overtness, exaggeration, and theatrical qualities. Once you are satisfied with these aspects, then zero-in on (a) slowing down and (b) exaggerating more as indicated above. Keep doing your demonstration and asking yourself if you were a student, would you be able to imitate yourself? In other words, put yourself in your students' shoes and keep this frame of mind until you feel you're ready to demonstrate. When you actually get in front of your class, you'll find that two things happen. One, you'll feel less self-conscious of your own demonstration, and two, you'll be thinking more of the students and how they are responding to the demonstration. This does happen! It won't happen overnight, but you will notice a drastic difference the first time you prepare in this manner. And by the second and third times, you'll find that it's no longer yourself but the students who have your sole attention during your demonstration. You'll be saying to yourself, "Let me be sure I do this-or-that," or "Slowly now, don't go too fast," or "Put that hand way up just like you want them to do!" When you find yourself in this state of mind, you will also find that you have said "good-bye" to your nerves and "hello" to better class responses!

Concluding Challenge

Now you know about a deliberately delivered demonstration. You no longer have any excuse. You know that basically you must slow down and intentionally exaggerate your motions if you expect your students to imitate more easily and more accurately. You must cultivate this skill, particularly if you want to provide effective teacher demonstrations, and if you want to get away from your own nervousness.

LESS EFFECTIVE	MORE EFFECTIVE
"Listen now while I clap this ostinato," Ms. Woodwind instructed her fifth graders. The next thing the class knew, she was through with her clap, clap, clap-a-clap, clap. Ms. Woodwind was rather annoyed when the students couldn't clap it. "All right, listen again." This time she clapped more deliberately. "Well, that's more like it," she commented to herself when the class clapped back without any trouble! "They should have done that before!"	When Ms. Woodwind told her class to listen carefully as she clapped the ostinato pattern, she made a special effort to slow down the tempo and clap the uneven parts in an exaggerated way. "Now, do you think we could clap it together?" The fifth graders nodded with confidence. "Listen to it again." Once more she clapped the pattern deliberately. When the class responded without any difficulty, she beamed at them and said, "That was great!" Ms. Woodwind's classes always responded well because of her deliberate demonstrations.

Mr. Brassytone's sixth graders were going to accompany a song with the I and V7 chords for the first time. "Okay, listen and watch me as I sing," instructed Mr. Brassytone. The students looked at each other as he raced through the song. They knew how to play the chords, but they weren't quite sure they could play them that fast. "Okay, let's try it," Mr. Brassytone announced. "What's the problem? You know the chords!" While he slowed it down somewhat, Mr. Brassytone still didn't do the chord changes in an exaggerated way. The class got silly when they couldn't do it any better. "That's it," shouted Mr. Brassytone, "if you can't take this seriously, then we won't do it at all!"

The sixth graders were excited about playing the ukeleles. They had learned the I and V7 chords and were going to accompany themselves today. Mr. Brassytone asked the class to listen and watch. He strummed at a slower tempo and leaned forward every time a chord changed. Some students were pretending to strum along with him. "Okay, do you think we are ready to try it?" An excited "Yesss" went up. The class played the slower time which gave them time to change the chords. Mr. Brassytone smiled to himself. When they finished, he complimented them on their performance. "Let's do it one more time," begged the class!

Participating in Class Activities

What are **you** doing while the class is doing the activity? Do you stand there with your arms folded like some Indian chief? Scoot around the room like a referee in a boxing ring? Or, do you jump right in and do the activity **with** the class? I hope you do the latter, because participating with students in the activities is an integral part of the act of teaching. You can't just stand there; otherwise, you miss a golden opportunity to set an example for the students and help them respond better. Your activities will be more meaningful for students, if you join them.

Clarification of Participating

"Participating" is the conscious **act of doing** an activity with the students after it's been demonstrated. Thus, "participating" refers to a deliberate effort on the teacher's part to "do" an activity with the class.

Reasons for Participating

Your participating with the class is vital to the teaching-learning process for three good reasons.

First, and foremost, the teacher's participation **provides an ongoing model** for the students, a continual example of how to do the activity properly. It's a silent way of saying, "Like this," "Do it this way," or "That's it! Like this!" You'd be surprised how many students really depend on the teacher to keep them "on task" and how much influence the teacher's participation has on obtaining a better response.

The second reason is that the teacher's participation **serves as a motivating agent** for the students. You might not realize it, but your participation has the power to get students "going" and inspire them to get involved to do the activity like you! This is assuming, of course, that your own performance is energetic and enthusiastic. That's the only way you're going to get them "going." Just watch some pop or rock-and-roll singers sometime. See all the energy they exert? You get all perked up, because some of the energy has rubbed off on you. Teacher participation can have the same effect on students. It can be an energizer and a motivator!

The third reason is that teacher participation in activities **results in helping opportunities**. For example, on occasions the teacher may find it beneficial to call out "Strong-weak-weak, Strong-weak-weak" while doing a stepping activity in order to help some students feel the accented versus unaccented beats better. Other times, the teacher's helping hand may be something as simple as giving a signal to alert those who are having difficulty hearing the concept, such as saying, "Listen now," or "Here it comes," or raising your hand, or holding up a finger.

Then, too, there are times when exaggerating some movement or action really helps. Let's say you're using the "Dagger Dance" by Victor Herbert in *Adventures of Music*, Grade Three, Volume One, for strong-weak beats (SWWW). Suppose you notice several children having trouble feeling the strong beats. Wouldn't you, almost instinctively, make some large gesture on the accented beats? With your whole body? Of course you would! So, participating in the activity provides the perfect opportunity to **help students in either a verbal or physical way** to "get" the concept.

Situation Regarding Participation

Despite all the justifiable reasons mentioned in the previous section for participating in the activities, there are still some teachers who prefer to "watch" rather than "do." No matter how attentive they try to look, or how encouraging they try to sound, they don't do justice to the activity because they aren't modeling the activity, motivating the students, or meeting the needs. They just stand there and watch—and wait for the activity to end. How boring that must be for them!

Sure, some will jump in for a minute or two, and then stop. But whether this little spurt of energy is done out of boredom or out of guilt, it's a meaningless gesture. Students don't even notice it.

Guidelines Regarding Participating

Let's take a look at the following suggestions.

Make Actions Precise and a Bit Theatrical. Display the same exactness and showiness you used in your demonstration. Remember, it's the precision and flair that attract the students, so don't let up on these two qualities while you're participating. Be just as precise and just as showy because students will watch you just as closely **during** the activity, as they did **in the demo**. Maybe even more!

Exude Large Dose of Energy and Enthusiasm. You get students inspired and motivated by participating with zest and exuberance. The more enthusiasm the teacher shows, the more enthusiastic the students are apt to be, and the better they're apt to respond—which, in turn, excites the teacher—which in turn, motivates the students, etc. See what happens? The **cycle of good teaching** is set into motion, and it all starts with the energetic, enthusiastic response of the teacher.

Exercise Competent Perceptivity and Preparedness. Perceptivity, or keen awareness, is one of your most valuable attributes, especially when you are in the throes of participating in the activity. It's important that you be able to "spot" the students needing help—while you're doing the activity. That's a "must." But, even as important as this assessing is, it's still not enough. You must also have a solution ready. **Perception** and **preparedness** go hand-in-hand where teacher participation is concerned.

You get prepared by anticipating problems in your planning. Ask yourself, "What if such-and-such happens? What would I do?" Covering all the "What if's" in your planning is the best preparation there is! But not every teacher follows this advice.

Here's a good illustration. I distinctly remember one beginning teacher who would bomb out every time it came to dealing with a problem. She never seemed to have a good solution. On this particular day her children were tapping out the melodic rhythm to "Old MacDonald." I was impressed with the way she was tapping along with the class, until someone's tapping got off. She froze. I don't think it ever entered her mind that this could happen. She just glared at the poor student. When that didn't work, she began shaking her head no-no non-stop! It never dawned on her to sing "Short-short-short-short-long" on the e-i-e-i-o part, or to make exaggerated dot-dashes with her hand(s). She just kept glaring at the student and shaking her head. Right then and there I knew I had to have a heart-to-heart talk with this teacher, who was then tickled pink to get some suggestions about anticipating problems and solutions.

Concluding Challenge

Do you participate in activities with your students? If so, great! You're contributing in a meaningful way to the teaching-learning process in your classroom. But if you don't, why not begin in your next lesson? It really does make a difference in the way the students respond. They'll be more precise and more enthusiastic, especially if you follow the guidelines discussed earlier.

LESS EFFECTIVE

"We're going to move to the SWWW beats in our Indian dance," Ms. Drummer told her second graders. After she demonstrated the dance, she turned on the CD and then sat down on the corner of the desk. She fiddled with her pearls and periodically yelled out, "Listen, listen!" Sometimes she pointed a finger at a child and told him/her, "You aren't listening!" When the music finished, Ms. Drummer jumped off the desk and told the children, "We weren't all good Indian dancers today. You'll have to listen more carefully next time." The class pouted as they left the room.

Ms. Mallet paced back and forth as she listened to several sixth graders call out the numbers on the call chart. Every time she heard a mistake, she would wince, let out a sigh, and look up at the ceiling. Then she called on another student. She leaned against the chalkboard and tapped her fingers on the book she was holding when the student made a mistake. "Get it right, we don't have all day," she snapped. "I'll have to ask Bill and Sharon, if you can't read it right." With that, Ms. Mallet shook her head disgustedly and leaned back against the board.

MORE EFFECTIVE

When Ms. Drummer finished demonstrating the Indian dance, she asked the children to practice the dance before the music began. "Good," she said, "now let's get in starting position." As soon as the CD started, Ms. Drummer scooted up front and began doing the dance with the class. At one point, she got a drum and played the SWWW beats while getting closer to the ones having problems. She smiled and gave a "victory" wink when they began to feel the S-W beats. When they finished, Ms. Drummer told the class that everyone had been excellent Indian dancers. The children beamed at her!

Ms. Mallet's sixth graders got out their call charts on phrase form. When the CD started, she came back to the front of the room. As the class called out the numbers, Ms. Mallet mouthed the numbers silently with the class. "Very good, class. Now how about you three doing the honors this time!" Because call charts were relatively new, Ms. Mallet nodded slightly on each number as the students called out. She smiled each time they called the number correctly. "Good job, you guys. How about Bill and Sharon this time." She gave them an encouraging smile as they began.

6

Teaching Responsibilities Not Related to Activities

While Chapter 5 concentrated solely on behaviors related to the implementation of activities, this chapter will focus on the non-related behaviors. By that I mean, those efforts that are a normal part of the teaching process, regardless of the activity. These include such teacher behaviors as:

- learning students' names
- executing student-oriented lessons
- doing teacher demonstrations
- conducting when not accompanying
- maintaining effective pace
- seating/standing students quietly

These behaviors go hand in hand with the act of teaching. It doesn't matter what the activity is or when it's being implemented; behaviors like these are ongoing and are a normal part of the teaching process.

The reason I make this distinction between behaviors connected with the implementing of activities and those that aren't, is that I feel strongly about emphasizing the so-called *non-related behaviors*. It's important to identify those efforts inherent to the act of teaching and distinct from the ones associated with an activity. While both are essential for successful teaching, those in the non-related category need to be of special concern in that they deal with some of the more basic tasks of teaching.

Should these non-related behaviors be of interest to you? Absolutely! Not just because they're basic teaching tasks, but also because of some other reasons. One is that they help expedite the teaching procedures, and take out the possible glitches. Remember, these are the normal routines, such as knowing names, maintaining pace, doing demonstrations, seating students, etc., that can make or break a lesson if they aren't handled properly.

The other reason these behaviors should be of interest to you is that they perk up the learning environment. Keeping students informed, using motivational ideas, and preparing student-oriented lessons are just a few of the tasks that make this outcome possible. If you're going to be successful in energizing the classroom environment, you'll need to be familiar with this category of behaviors. Activity skills alone won't do it!

These behaviors deserve your serious consideration. Your teaching ability will move up a notch or two with these kinds of teaching behaviors under your belt. If you want some suggestions on how to go about implementing a particular task, go to the "suggestions" part of each identified task. Don't write-off these routines. They're by no means incidental in the total scheme of teaching! They're very consequential, so take a closer look at them.

Learning Students' Names

One of the most taxing efforts the classroom music teacher faces at the outset of each new year is the learning of names. Whether the classes are large or small makes little difference; it's still a nagging effort. Students want to be addressed by their given names, so you need to tackle the job immediately.

To be honest, however, the task is more pressing for (a) the beginning teacher and (b) the teacher taking on a new position. They're the ones who need to learn every Tom, Dick, and Harry from scratch! Those of you who enjoy the luxury of teaching in a particular situation for several years have the advantage of carry over. You know students from previous years, which means only the kindergartners' and the new incoming students' names have to be learned. Not so with the first-year teachers and those in new jobs—they're the ones who really need the help! If you fall in either of these two groups, continue reading.

Approaches for Learning Names

There are several good ways to help yourself learn names—and alleviate some of the frustration and pressure.

Use Name Tags. This is especially good for the lower grades. Tags may be attached to the child's clothing with some kind of tape, or else strung on a string and hung on the child's neck. Of course, there are obvious problems with each of these tactics. Children will lose the taped-on names no matter what kind of adhesive is used! And I hesitate to use straight pins for fear that someone will inadvertently get hurt. As for hanging the name tags from the student's neck, it never fails the tag gets turned over just when you need to see it! Can you ask the classroom teachers to make the tags? Why not? Most will be happy to oblige. Some classes will come in with tags already made. When this happens, be happy for small favors in life! Consider, then, the name tags.

Put Names on Desks. This is a marvelous tactic if you're a floating music teacher and go from room to room. Simply ask the classroom teacher to have the students put their name plates on their desks before you come, or make the "plates" yourself and give them to the teachers, if you have to! In most cases, the teacher will beat you to the draw and have names already taped on the desk or else displayed on the desktop. You'll want to shout "Hallelujah" when they do! By the way, putting tags on chairs or desks won't work if you have your own music room. You would spend all your time passing out tags and collecting them with each class, so don't try it!

Make Seating Charts. Yes, I know they take time, but once you get them made, they'll be a lifesaver. You can just whip out your chart and keep it handy when

calling on students. I admit this is an impersonal way of dealing with students, but when you have back-to-back classes and none of the students have name tags, what other choice do you have? You can't keep calling students "you and you." You'll start learning the names from the chart soon enough. In the meantime, be patient. Your students will wait while you are in the throes of learning their names.

Come back a moment to this impersonal matter. Don't dismiss seating charts because you think they make you impersonal. They don't. No seating chart can rob you of relating to your students. It's what you do apart from the seating chart that establishes your rapport. You'll have plenty of time to demonstrate your personableness while you're teaching—and you won't be tied to the seating chart forever!

Have Students Give Name. This is a good approach for the upper grades. Ask students to give their first names before responding when they're called upon. I like this tactic because it gives you a chance to look momentarily at the student and see him/her as a person. Some little gesture or mannerism may help you remember the student and, more important, relate to the person. If you're concerned about rapport, this is one of the best ways of opening up those lines of communication!

Actually, two revelations are happening when the student gives his/her name:

1. The names are being impressed upon your mind.
2. The personalities are being revealed in some small way.

Will it take more time to do this? No! How long can it take to speak one's name? A half a second? Now if you were using this approach with younger students, you would have cause for concern. Some children just take forever to say their name, while others just freeze! So don't use this approach with kindergartners or first graders; you'll get frustrated if you do!

Call Students Alphabetically. I call this, *the gradebook way*. It's a matter of going down your roster of students in the gradebook in alphabetical order and calling on the first five students one day, the next five the next, etc. It's just following a systematic approach to remembering students. Some teachers go so far as to assign seating in alphabetical order, too! The only trouble with this plan is that compatibility goes out the window. The alphabetical order often takes precedence over student personalities. If you use the gradebook way, don't forget about compatibility; try to be flexible where personalities are concerned.

Any one of these suggestions will work, depending upon the grade level, of course. The trick is to have an approach ready. Make up your own system if none of the above appeal to you or "work" for you. The fact is, you need to get those names learned as quickly as possible.

Reasons for Learning Names

Learning the names of students in the classroom setting is a necessary task—or curse, as some would say! It's not only important that teachers have the students' names at the tip of their tongues, but that students know the teacher recognizes them by name.

One reason for knowing names is that calling out a name **helps build rapport** between teacher and student. There's something very personal about one's name, and when a teacher is able to call out the student's name, especially at the beginning of the school year, it says to the student that the teacher "sees" him/her and cares. A feeling of personal worth wells up in the student and a personal warmth towards the teacher. Often that's the beginning of a special camaraderie. If there's any one teacher effort that can draw teacher and student closer together in the first few weeks of school, it's having the teacher speak the student's name. It's more meaningful than being a teacher's helper, getting a good grade, or being patted on the head. You want better communication with your students? Better rapport? Then learn their names—no matter how many students you have. Find a way to learn them.

A second reason learning names is necessary is that it **helps control classroom discipline**. It's amazing what effect the calling out of a name has on stopping a disturbance. When combined with some facial expression and/or body gesture, the name calling becomes even more effective. (See Chapter 2.) But even without these other facets, the calling out of a name will do the trick. Be sure, however, the name is said in a short clipped way that clearly says to the student, "Stop that!" You can make your voice convey any thought you want just by using the proper inflection and duration with the name. So learn those names so you can have a better handle on the discipline.

A third reason for learning names is that it **saves teaching time** in the classroom. Having to point and say, "Let's have you, you, and you come to the chalkboard," can be troublesome as well as time consuming. You know what students will do, don't you? They'll point to themselves and say, "Who, me?" Then you have to stop and say, "Yes, I mean you. No, not you, him." In the meantime, the rest of the class is either snickering or else mimicking the one pulling your leg. See how time is lost? Don't put it past your class to "give you the business" when they sense you're not sure of their names. They'll pull the "Who me" stunt just to get you.

Here's a typical example of one teacher who never bothered to learn names. One day he called on "Henry" only to discover he had the wrong name. By the student's sly grin, I knew something was coming. "I'm not Henry. He is!" he blurted out. The one he pointed to shook his head and said, "Uh, uhn! I ain't Henry. I'm Mike. He's Henry." Well, it was like watching a basketball being tossed from one player to the other. The boys were having a good joke at the expense of the teacher. When he finally caught on to what was happening, the whole class was rocking with laughter. He would have been better off to apologize to the student, get the right name, and move on. But instead, he wasted all that time—and got embarrassed as well—just because he didn't know the students' names! That's learning the hard way.

Common Problem in Learning Names

There's a problem when it comes to learning names, however. It's not that teachers don't learn the names—they do. The problem is they don't learn the names soon enough in most cases. They learn three or four names this week, a couple more next week, and hopefully the rest in the following weeks. Sure, everyone would like to learn all the names in the first two weeks, but the argument is that there's too much to do in the opening weeks. So learning names gets pushed way down on the to-do list, especially with classroom music teachers who meet their classes only once a week.

While it's true that you do have a lot to do at the beginning of the year, you must not let these responsibilities keep you from learning the students' names. Knowing names is crucial in those first few weeks of school. Make every effort to help yourself learn those names. Don't be guilty of dragging your feet on this responsibility.

Concluding Challenge

Do you learn your students' names quickly or do you string out the job over a period of months? If you're guilty of the latter, find a way to help yourself. Use name tags, seating charts, or name signs. It may be that you need to use one approach with the older students and another with the younger ones. If so, do it. You'll have better rapport and control if you do!

LESS EFFECTIVE

Mr. Oom-pah wanted three children to come to the board. "Let's have Sharon, (giggle, giggle from the class) Michael, and—wait just one minute! What's all that giggling about?" "You called Marsha 'Sharon,'" said one of the gigglers. With that the whole class started to giggle. "Okay, so it's Marsha. Let's go back to the lesson." But the class giggled even more. Mr. Oom-pah folded his arms and glared at the class. "This is ridiculous; they've been giggling for three minutes already!"

"Okay, I want you two guys in the third row to clap the next line," Mr. Ding-a-ling said. Bob and Billy looked at each other and shrugged. "No, he means us," shouted Jim and Jack. "I pointed to these two," Mr. Ding-a-ling snapped as he walked closer. "But I thought you pointed to me," Jim said disappointedly. "Well, I didn't. So let's continue, shall we?" Mr. Ding-a-ling instructed. "Ha, he wanted us, not you," Bob teased. "All right, that's enough of that. Turn around, Bob. And stop pouting, Jim. You'll get your turn later. Now where were we?"

MORE EFFECTIVE

Mr. Oom-pah checked his seating chart before the class came in. He wanted to be sure to know the names. When it came time to pick children to go to the board, Mr. Oom-pah picked up his seating chart and called out the children who raised their hands. "Let's have Steven, Martha, and Harold!" As they came forward, he smiled at each student. He knew that the children liked to be called by their right name and that they would get silly if he called them by someone else's name. "Thank you, Steven, Martha, and Harold. Can I have three more people now?"

Mr. Ding-a-ling wanted Bob and Billy to clap the melodic rhythm of the next line. He looked carefully at their name tags and called out their names. "Bob, Billy. Will you please read the next line? Yes, I see your hand, John. I'll get to you next time, okay?" Mr. Ding-a-ling knew that if he called out the wrong names, the class would start to laugh. "Very good, Bob and Billy. Now, John, how about you doing the next line! And Steven too." He was glad he had taken the time to make the name tags. It sure saved a lot of time during the lesson.

Keeping a Neat, Attractive Room

Surprised to see this chore here? Well, don't be! Keeping the classroom neat and attractive is every bit as important as doing the activity-related chores in Chapter 5 or any other non-related ones in this chapter. In fact, few chores, if any, have as much lasting impact on students or such an immediate reward for teachers as this one. That's the reason it ranks so high on my list of responsibilities in this chapter. Take note, however, that there's a distinction between (a) keeping the classroom neat, and (b) making it attractive. Let's discuss them separately in order to do justice to each task.

Keeping a Classroom Neat

There's probably no other chore in all of teaching that is more mundane and tedious as cleaning up the classroom. I say *mundane* because it's so routinish. It's the same picking up and putting back every day! That's why it's so tedious! But the worst of it all is that the effort isn't always appreciated. Students don't seem to notice—or even care—if the classroom is neat or sloppy. Yet, most teachers would agree that cleaning up is one of the more self-satisfying efforts of teaching.

Describing a Neat Classroom. What qualifies as a neat-looking classroom? There are as many ideas as there are teachers! But I think everyone would agree that the following are necessary:

- chairs/desks arranged orderly
- textbooks shelved neatly
- materials stacked neatly
- instruments stored orderly
- chalkboard washed cleanly
- recordings/tapes arranged orderly
- teacher's desk straightened neatly
- equipment placed appropriately
- bookcases organized suitably
- floors picked up cleanly
- posters/signs hung properly
- students' work displayed neatly

In essence, then, a neat-looking classroom is one in which everything (furniture, equipment, books, and instruments) is in its rightful place and carefully arranged or placed. Too, it's a room that has an orderly appearance and tidy look. Yes, it does take extra effort to keep the room looking shipshape, but it's worth it. Let's see why.

Results of a Neat Classroom. One of the most valuable rewards for being exposed to a neat classroom is that students acquire a healthier **respect for orderliness**. It doesn't happen overnight, mind you, or even over a period of weeks. It happens little by little. At some point, unbeknownst to either teacher or student, there's a dawning awareness of the orderliness—almost like an inner awakening. Sometime later, the student has fleeting moments of appreciation when he/she actually notices, and even admires, the neat surroundings, but never voices these thoughts. When's the last time you had a student tell you the classroom "looks nice"?

Finally, somewhere down-the-pike when that student is no longer with you, a healthy respect emerges for an orderly environment. So you see, your classroom may well be the place where the concern for orderliness begins.

The second result is an outgrowth of the first. Students begin to acquire a **sense of responsibility** towards property. What happens is that the growing respect for an orderly environment begins to spill over on the instruments, the equipment, the furniture, and even the textbooks. As a result, students become more mindful of how they handle these items. They take greater care not to bend, fold, or mutilate; to get chairs or desks out of place; or to shelve textbooks out of order. They begin to "see" the need to do their part in keeping the classroom property neat and orderly. Quite a life-long impact, wouldn't you say?

The third outcome concerns teachers. Plain and simple, a neat classroom **saves time and energy**. When textbooks, instruments, or other materials are shelved in a neat and organized way, they can be removed and returned quickly and efficiently. I know of one teacher who has her bookcase next to the classroom door. Students reach for a text as they pass the bookcase and move on to their seats. What's so neat is that the books on the lower shelves are for the lower grades and the higher shelves, for upper grades. When they leave, they just return them to the same shelf before going out the door. The teacher never takes class time for passing out books or wastes her energy with the task. And you know what? Students love this responsibility.

You can save even more time if your tapes and recordings are organized by title and/or composer, so that you could pull them out without having to go "looking" when an emergency arises. Too, make a practice of keeping your chairs or desks straightened and eliciting the students' help. Then you won't have to go hustling between classes or use class time to do any straightening.

Problem in Keeping a Classroom Neat. Even with all the potential outcomes, there's still too much negligence in keeping a neat classroom. A lot of teachers just don't feel that the condition of the room is a prerequisite for good teaching. They say that other responsibilities are more important, like handling discipline, preparing lessons, or gathering materials. True, these are important tasks, but not any more important than keeping a neat, orderly room. Don't underestimate this responsibility.

I must share with you one situation I saw some years ago. I can still remember how bowled-over I was! There the teacher was, sitting behind an old upright piled high with junk. I expected it to go toppling over any minute! Then I noticed the windowsill. It was littered with textbooks, worksheets, and broken autoharps, plus two dried-up flowers. And her desk? It looked like an oversized bird's nest with loose papers, torn music, and broken instruments sticking out on all sides. The bulletin board behind the desk looked like it had been up for the last five years. All the reds, blues, and greens had faded into that dull purplish color. The room was a disaster. I couldn't wait to leave!

Ignoring the orderliness of your classroom is a serious matter. Sooner or later you'll lose valuable time looking for something and waste your energy as well. But, even worse, you'll rob your students of learning (a) respect for an orderly environment and (b) responsibility for someone else's property. The consequences are just too costly! Let's set some suggestions for being orderly.

Suggestions for Keeping a Classroom Neat. There isn't any one particular "way" to keep a neat-looking classroom; there are only helpful tips. Besides, everyone usually has his/her own way. But in case you don't, here's an approach that works for me and it may help you, too.

First, clean up your classroom. I know the custodians mop the floors and empty the trash each night, but I'm talking about real cleaning—cleaning where you roll up your sleeves (after school hours) and get busy:

- dusting bookcases/chairs/desks/sills
- washing down chalkboards/desks/chairs/sills
- picking up books/materials
- straightening up teacher's desktop
- putting back instruments/equipment
- filing materials not being used
- adjusting and/or replacing posters

Second, organize your classroom. Much of this organizing can go hand-in-hand with the cleaning, like straightening up the bookcase or your desktop after dusting it. But then there are times when you'll just have to make a special effort to organize such items as:

- desk drawers
- filing cabinets
- closets or storage corners
- wall shelves/windowsills
- recordings/tapes
- classroom instruments

But let me warn you. Organizing is a tough job, so allow yourself enough time to get it done. Set up a work schedule over a period of weeks, if necessary, and don't get discouraged. Just keep thinking how great it's going to look when everything's organized and clean!

Third, inform your students. The fact is, students need to be told about their neat surroundings. Don't expect them to notice it on their own because they won't! That means literally call attention to the straightened chairs, the clean floor, the organized bookshelf, etc. If neatness and orderliness are to have any impact, students must be made aware of these things. Awareness always precedes response, so tell the students what's neat and orderly. It makes all the difference in getting their cooperation.

Fourth, indicate your expectations. In other words, let them know what you expect from them and how you want them to respond when they come into a neat, organized room. You can do this right on-the-heels of the suggestion above, or even in the same breath. Be specific; for example, some of your rules might read like this:

- Throw paper in trash can, not on floor.
- Return books in upright position.
- Leave chair in same position.
- Keep instrument under the chair.

If you follow this sequence of telling them (a) what to notice and then (b) what to do, students will have a better idea of what you're trying to accomplish with your ground rules, and be more apt to pitch in!

My **final suggestion** is be consistent—and persistent. Take consistent first. It's imperative that your students follow the rules in the same way each day, and that you don't let them do something less today than they did yesterday or ask them for something more. In other words, don't keep changing the ground rules. Students need to know that your expectations stay the same. If you expect chairs to be put back in the same orderly way after every lesson, then see to it that students straighten the chairs before they leave. Every time. That's being consistent!

Be persistent in the sense that you keep after the students day after day to straighten those chairs, pick up that litter, or return the instrument to the same shelf. It's the only way students are going to know you mean business. You've got to persevere, but in an appreciative, yet firm, way. That means praise them in the same breath you instruct them. Like this:

a. "Check to see that your chair is straightened when you stand to leave. The chairs look great."

b. "Is your chair straightened? Good! I appreciate your help in keeping the chairs in order."

Not only will students try harder when you praise them, but they'll also develop a sense of pride in helping to keep the room orderly. Your praise will soften your persistence.

Thus, the system for keeping a neat, orderly classroom is a matter of (1) cleaning the room, (2) organizing the materials, (3) telling the students, (4) setting the guidelines, and (5) being consistent as well as persistent.

Making a Classroom Attractive

Making your classroom attractive looking is a more enjoyable chore, isn't it? And, more satisfying too! The catch is that it takes a lot of time and effort, but those of you who have attractive rooms know it's worth it. Actually, it's the creative part of this responsibility, and also an essential aspect of the teaching process. As such, it deserves a closer look.

Describing an Attractive Classroom. We need to know what's meant by a so-called *attractive-looking room*. Let's describe it as a room that is aesthetically appealing to both teacher and students from the following standpoints:

- appealing display on bulletin board
- tasteful arrangement of furniture/equipment
- vibrant coloring on posters/signs
- enhancing placement of plants/posters

That should be an acceptable description because the criteria encompass the elements of shape, color, form, line, etc.—all of which go into making a room appealing and pleasing. But even the aesthetic elements can't make the classroom attractive looking if it's not, first of all, neat and orderly. Remember, the classroom needs to be neat before it can be attractive!

Problem With Making a Room Attractive. The problem is that many teachers stop with the cleaning up and ignore the creative part of the task. The result is that a lot of classrooms have a stripped-down, drab-looking appearance. Oh, there's always a few faded pictures of Beethoven, Bach, and Mozart hanging around, and, of course, those old faithful instrument posters tacked up on some wall. But other than that, there's little else to spruce up the room.

The excuses run all the way from "I'm just too busy to decorate" to "I'm not an interior decorator; I don't know what to do." I have a strong hunch teachers in this boat don't believe an attractive classroom is necessary. They argue that it's more important to spend time on the lesson, and that an attractive-looking room doesn't make them teach any better. But they're missing the boat; making the room attractive is just as important as keeping it neat.

Significance of an Attractive Room. In a nutshell, an attractive room is a more pleasant and more motivating place to teach—and learn. Ever walk into a classroom with battleship grey walls and no colorful posters or displays? Did you notice the effect it had on your attitude and emotions? Be honest now. You felt blah and depressed, didn't you? That's what an unappealing room can do to you! But an attractive, colorful classroom can give you a psychological boost, make the class come alive, and be more motivated to "work." So don't shrug off making your classroom more attractive. It's a marvelous motivational tool.

Suggestions for Making a Room Attractive. You can make your classroom more attractive by focusing on these three tasks and following the suggestions:

1. **Brighten the Room**. If your room is dark because of poor lighting, lack of windows, or dark wall paint, correct it. Ask for brighter lights, or warmer colors like tan, peach, beige, or yellow, especially if you're on the cool side of the building. (If you're on the sunny side, opt for the cool blues and greens.) The point is, lighten up your room with better lighting or brighter paint, or both!

2. **Rearrange the Room**. Move desks around if they aren't bolted down. Try (a) facing them in a different direction, (b) spacing them closer or farther apart, or (c) grouping them in various ways. Then see where your desk can go to give the room more pizazz. Move it from one side to the other, or from the front to the back, or else catty-corner. Do the same with the piano and

record player, if you're not limited to where they can go. Play with it until you land on an arrangement that strikes your fancy.

3. **Decorate the Walls**. Now comes the fun part. Put up colorful bulletin boards and posters. Use stencils if you're writing out something. Then arrange some interesting displays of students' work. Decorate with attractive, colorful props on special days; for instance, use real pumpkins and paper fold-out witches and black cats at Halloween. Be as creative as you can be. Remember, decorating is like putting on the finishing touch! It really makes a difference!

Concluding Challenge

Is your classroom neat and organized? Are you cultivating a respect for orderliness and a sense of responsibility? If not, start making your room neat and attractive. But don't expect any pat on the back because you won't get it! You will, however, reap the rewards.

LESS EFFECTIVE

The chairs in Mr. A'Note's room were never in a straightened order. So when the fourth graders came in, they moved the chairs around even more. When Mr. A'Note asked the class to get their books from under their chairs, some of the boys yelled out, "I don't have a book." What happened was that the books got kicked under other chairs. "Here's one," said Jim as he kicked the book towards Ed. "Don't kick that book, Jim. Get that book over there, Mike. No, don't throw it, Alan! Everyone have a book now? Let's have no more kicking books."

The students always dreaded coming to the music room. Ms. E'Note never made the room look inviting. "Let's look alive today. After all, it's Halloween. Sit up now. What kinds of things do you expect to see on Halloween?" No one answered. "Let's get some enthusiasm here," Ms. E'Note chided. "Wonder what's wrong with these children? They're not very excited. They don't even want to sing the Halloween song!"

MORE EFFECTIVE

Mr. A'Note always has his classes straighten their chairs and be sure the book was under the chair before leaving. So when the fourth graders came in, Mr. A'Note reminded them to keep the chairs as they were. "Let's get out our books from under the chairs and turn to page ten." Since the chairs were left in a straightened position, the students found the books under each of their chairs. Mr. A'Note felt a sense of pride as he watched the class handle the books with care. "I'm really proud of the careful way you're treating your books, class."

It was Halloween and Ms. E'Note had her bulletin board and all the Halloween decorations up. When the students came into the room, they oohed with excitement. "Since today is Halloween, let's talk about all the Halloween items you see in this room." Hands flew up. Everyone wanted to answer. "What an excellent discussion, class. I can tell you're all excited to sing our Halloween song now."

Presenting Student-Oriented Lesson

It's important that you concentrate on getting students to respond **throughout** the lesson and that your primary concern be to keep them involved as much as possible. After all, students learn by doing! Whenever you make a conscious effort to "run" a lesson with student input uppermost on your mind, you are involved in what's known as a *student-oriented lesson*. You really need to operate with this frame of mind; it's vital to your effectiveness as a teacher.

Comparing Student-Oriented vs. Teacher-Oriented Lesson

Know the difference between a student-oriented lesson and a teacher-oriented one? In a student-oriented lesson, the teacher makes every effort to get as much verbal and performance participation from the students as possible—in addition to the class activities, that is! In other words, it's an approach where students are continually being asked "to do" something as a group or individually.

In the teacher-oriented lesson, it's just the opposite. The teacher tries to do it all—the telling, the showing, and the explaining! All the students do is sit, listen, and watch, except when they're doing an activity. It's a passive situation. There's little involvement because the teacher is "hogging the show."

Here's an example of a *teacher-oriented lesson*. Let's say the new concept is a large ternary or ABA Form. Here's how the teacher-focused lesson would probably go:

- The **teacher** begins by **relating** some environmental idea that has a three-part shape, like the White House, and **pointing out** the "A" parts and the "B" part.

- Next, the teacher begins **comparing** the White House shape to the musical selection and **explaining** the "A" and "B" themes.

- Sometimes the teacher embellishes by **singing** the themes for the class (pssst! you'll usually see some eyes rolling back there) or else **playing** them on piano.

- Then you'll see the teacher prance over to the record player and start **telling** the class what to listen for in the music.

The irony of it all is that the teacher will then stand and grin like a Cheshire cat thinking, "Isn't this a swell lesson!" But it isn't. The students are out of the picture completely.

But look at the flip side. Here's how a **student-oriented lesson** would go if it were focusing on rhythmic patterns:

- The **students** would be **identifying** environmental examples that have a "patterned" look or sound, like a school bell between classes.
- Next, the students would be **answering** questions about the bell, such as: How many rings at one time? (three) How often does it ring? (after each class) How long? (three short rings) What likeness? (same rhythm—short, short, short)
- Then the students would engage in **defining** a rhythmic pattern after answering the above questions.
- Then they participate in **chanting** the rhythm pattern ♪♪♪♩ from "Oh Susannah" with note values, like eighth-eighth, eighth-eighth, quarter, followed by **chanting and clapping**.
- On the first activity, the students would stand up and **play** the pattern on rhythm sticks while singing along with the recording.
- In the reinforcing activity, the students would be further challenged by **tapping** the pattern with their feet while **singing the note values** every time it appears.

See how involved the students are in this lesson and how the teacher constantly has the class doing something? That's because student involvement is the teacher's primary consideration.

Problem With Teacher-Oriented Lesson

Teachers who don't have a student-oriented lesson seem to suffer from an overdose of self-preoccupation, and think only in terms of what they will be doing. In a way, they're almost immune to the students and insensitive to their reactions.

But there are some other reasons why the teacher-oriented approach is so dangerous. First of all, it's a **self-deceiving effort**. It'll give you the false impression that the students are just as involved as you are. But they aren't! They're just sitting and watching! That's why I'm warning you about doing all the "doing." You can get "caught up" in your own talking, moving, and demonstrating, and be convinced that the class is experiencing the same involvement. And the frightening thing is that you won't even be aware of it happening. The best advice I can give you is, avoid teacher-oriented lessons.

The second reason it's so dangerous is that it's a **limiting effort**. As long as you continue to monopolize the class with your own tellings and doings, you will be robbing the students of their time to participate and to learn. Students need all the opportunities they can get to reinforce the concepts and skills. They can't internalize the learning without participation. So when you gobble up all the time yourself, you literally take away the students' time. It's a frightening prospect, don't you think?

While the problem is easy to diagnose, the consequences aren't quite as evident. Teacher-oriented lessons can lull you into a false impression that the students are just as involved as you, and also usurp all their learning time. They can even make you immune to their reactions. See the problem?

Suggestions for Student-Oriented Lesson

Here are a few suggestions to help you get started with a student-oriented lesson.

One, get students to verbalize more. Verbal participation is an important part of a student-oriented lesson. Look at the different ways you can get students to verbalize:

- through answering questions as a group or an individual—short-answer questions good for class response
- through class discussion
- through chanting exercises as a class or individually
- through repeating words or phrases after the teacher
- through presenting a report or debate

Find as many ways as you can to get the students verbalizing. It's a marvelous tactic for achieving student with-it-ness, especially between activities. In fact, it is one of the distinguishing facets of a student-oriented teacher.

Two, select appropriate activities. Plan learning experiences that work best for revealing, reinforcing, or challenging the concept. In other words, choose activities that follow a logical or sequential presentation in line with the class's ability. Move from the more simplistic to the more challenging within the context of the lesson or the unit, and be sure your activities are appealing. In other words, use your activities as your "big guns" to keep students interested. Well-planned activities make the difference when it comes to student-oriented teaching.

Three, make effective use of visual aids. Any teacher who has the students' best interest at heart knows that visual materials are great teaching tools, whether they

be posters, drawings, or some chalkboard example. They can help clarify a concept when used with the motivational idea for a new concept; or can reinforce the idea by putting some item in the hands of the students during the activity, such as using a geometric triangle for like phrases and a geometric square for contrasting ones. Visual aids are a mainstay in student-oriented lessons. (See "Using Visual Aids Effectively" in Chapter 5.)

If you follow these three suggestions: (1) eliciting verbal participation, (2) selecting appropriate activities, and (3) using visual aids, you'll transform your lessons almost immediately into student-oriented experiences. Try it and see.

Rewards of Student-Oriented Lesson

Here are the virtues of student-oriented lessons as opposed to teacher-oriented ones:

- **First**, it provides more opportunities for student input and participation because the focus is on the students. This hands-on way is the most effective approach we have in teaching.

- **Second**, it presents an effective way for keeping students "with you," that is, on your same wave length because the activities are sequential. They can "move" through the lesson without any confusion, and stay with it because the activities are also appealing.

- **Third**, it makes the learning experience more enjoyable because the students are constantly "doing" something throughout the lesson. Their attention is focused either on some activity or some verbalizing.

- **Fourth**, it allows for more accurate assessment of the students' participation because the teacher's attention is consciously focused on the students.

Concluding Challenge

Can you identify in which of the two camps you belong? If you're not functioning like a student-oriented teacher, the discussion above should persuade you to do so. Once you begin operating in this way, I know you'll be "sold" and become a more effective teacher.

LESS EFFECTIVE	MORE EFFECTIVE
Ms. Jingle-Clog presented the poster for her third-grade lesson on like-contrasting phrases. "Look at the first line, class. See the series of ducks and sailboats? Now look at the second line. Here we see another line of ducks and sailboats. See? So you can see that those two lines will sound the same. Right? But look at the third line. It has cats and dogs. It's different from the first two lines, isn't it? We're going to call this third line a 'contrasting line,' okay? Now look at the last line" . . . blah, blah . . .	When Ms. Jingle-Clog mounted her poster on like-contrasting phrases, she immediately asked, "How many lines do you see, class? That's right, six. What objects do you see on the first line? Mark? Good. Ducks and sailboats. Remember, now, this first line becomes our model for the rest of the lines. What about the second line? Class? Sure, it has the same objects. So what kind of phrase would our second line be then? Mary? Super! A, 'like phrase'. Who else knew this answer? Wow, everybody! Let's look at the third line. What objects do you see now? Yes, dogs and cats. Would this be a 'like phrase'? That's right. It wouldn't. It would be a what? Great! A 'contrasting phrase' ". . . .

In summarizing the lesson on loud-soft with her kindergartners, Ms. Sand-Block began by saying, "Today we have learned about loud and soft sounds. Whenever we hear a fire engine, we now know that's a loud sound. But if a kitty cries, that's going to be a soft sound. Understand? Remember how we held up our soft cards when we listened to soft music? And when we heard the symbol crash we held up our loud card? Well, now we know . . . sit still and listen!"

When the lesson was finished, Ms. Sand-Block reviewed the new concept of loud and soft with her kindergartners. "What kind of sounds did we learn about today, children? Yes, loud sounds (she stretched out her arms) and soft sounds (she made a ssshhing gesture). And what kind of a sound does a fire engine make?" Ms. Sand-Block used her outstretched gesture indicating she wanted everyone to do likewise when answering. "Yes, it's loud. And what about our little kitty?" The whole class followed her sshhing as they whispered "soft." "Very good."

Conducting When Not Accompanying

While it's true that conducting is not used to the same extent in the classroom as on the podium, it's, nevertheless, a useful tactic in teaching general music—primarily, when the classroom teacher isn't accompanying, as in the upper elementary and junior high levels where students are more accustomed to a cappella experiences and do more singing with recordings. In other words, there are opportunities to conduct at the upper elementary and middle school levels, and those of you who teach in these grades ought to be ready for these times—for the students' sake. If you're one who shies away from conducting, read this section carefully.

Opportunities for Conducting

When do these opportunities occur, or, more specifically, when should the teacher be conducting when he/she isn't? In the main, it's during the times when an accompaniment (a) isn't necessary and/or (b) isn't desired. There are three very specific situations that fall into one or both of these categories and become marvelous situations for some conducting, namely:

- when the class is singing with a recording
- when the class is singing a cappella with a familiar song, round, or canon
- when the class is performing on recorders, guitars, or rhythm instruments

Obviously, there's no need to accompany with a recording or with a cappella singing, and it's optional with instrumental situations. So conducting could be an effective alternative in all these situations. However, I am not saying that the teacher should always conduct at one of these times. Here's the key: conduct when the time feels right; that is, when you think it would be the most beneficial thing to do at the moment. There's no magic formula, just use your professional instincts. That's about as close as I can come to telling you **when** you should conduct; what I can be more definite about is **why** it's important to conduct on occasions.

Reasons for Conducting

One of the most compelling reasons for conducting occasionally is that it **exposes students to ensemble skills**. Look what you can teach through your conducting:

- how to come in together
- how to keep a steady tempo and not rush or slow down
- how to carry through on phrases
- how to cut off together

I know that most of your students aren't going to be music majors, or that your class isn't a choral ensemble. But that's not the point. The point is that these are fundamental skills for group singing. As such, every student should have the opportunity to cultivate them in classroom music; don't forget, your students are future members of church choirs and community choruses. But you say these skills aren't your responsibility and they should be taught in the performance groups? They are—and many more, but only a small percentage of your students are in chorus or band. Where will the others get these skills if they don't experience them with you? So you see, you do need to conduct occasionally so that these kinds of skills can be nurtured.

The second reason is an outgrowth of the first. Conducting **helps improve classroom performance**. When students are taught to watch a conductor, they generally are better in maintaining a steady tempo, singing or playing through a phrase, and starting and stopping together. In other words, they begin executing the kinds of responses that will make their singing better. Skills like these are best gleaned through the medium of conducting. Let me illustrate. To get a clean entrance, the most effective approach is through a preparatory breath with a downbeat, not a lecture. And if you want the class to sing without breaking a phrase, or to hold the last note, a pulling up or out will do the job better than any marking of the music. See what I mean? Conducting provides the best solution for cultivating some of these kinds of skills. That's why classroom music teachers need to make an effort to conduct on occasions. If you don't, students may never obtain these skills—and your class singing may never improve.

The third reason is a more personal motive. Conducting **offers the teacher an appropriate behavior** for those times when there is little else to do but stand back and watch—and feel awkward. Believe me, it's much more comfortable to conduct than just stand there, even if it's nothing more than pulsating up and down with the beat. You'll feel more in control and more involved, and if you can throw in a cut-off or fermata, so much the better! Conducting is a good "filler" activity whenever there's nothing to do but stand and watch. These are strong arguments for using conducting gestures more often in the classroom.

Suggested Conducting Gestures

Before discussing the particular gestures, a word needs to be said first of all about the conducting ability of the teacher. Some of you are anxious to know just how well you'll need to conduct. Here's the bottom line. You don't have to conduct as though you were in front of the New York Philharmonic or Boston Pops—nothing quite as lowbrow as that, I assure you. You just need to be comfortable with the kinds of gestures you can execute. If you want some specific suggestions, here are four basic gestures recommended for the classroom conductor:

- conduct the beat
- give a preparatory beat
- execute cut-offs
- use sustaining gestures

Let's discuss each of these briefly.

Conducting the Beat. Notice that I didn't say you should conduct the beat patterns for 3/4, 4/4, etc. It's really more practical for you to conduct a clearly defined beat, that is, a simple down-up-down-up 2/4 gesture, like so: . You can do this with one hand or both hands. If you do it with both, the right hand does a slight curl to the right, and the left, a curl to the left—opposite directions, in other words. You don't need any fancy twirls or large sweeps—not in the classroom. A well-defined down-up pattern is more practical.

If you feel awkward even doing this, here are some quick suggestions. Get in front of a mirror and stand so that you look and feel comfortable. Spread your feet about a foot apart, with one foot slightly ahead of the other. Next, let your hands dangle by your sides. Then, bring them up naturally about chest high. Notice the position of your palms. Are they facing inward? Downward? Or at an angle? Whichever way they come up is your natural hand position for conducting. Don't let your elbows hug your sides; they should come out naturally when you bring up your arms. Now start conducting—down-up-down-up, etc. And one last thing—don't curl your fingers back. Keep them extended and slightly separated with the pointer finger a bit straighter than the other fingers. Practice until you look comfortable and feel competent; otherwise, you won't want to conduct in the classroom.

Giving a Preparatory Beat. When you get ready to start the class, don't just drop your hands like dead weights and expect the students to come in. They won't.

They need a preparatory beat. The "prep" beat is nothing more than a little upbeat, coordinated with the intake of breath, coming just before the downbeat. Here's how it's done. Put your hands in conducting position. Now, as you take a big breath through open lips, bring your hands up simultaneously with the in-take. Go up about six or seven inches. Then given the downbeat. Practice by counting one-two-three-four-prep breath-one-two, etc. Do it in rhythm. Be sure to give an ictus or little stopping bounce at the end of the curl on the downbeat. That's what actually "tells" the class when to come in. For more information about the ictus, read "Establishing Pitch and Tempo for Songs" in Chapter 7. Now all you need to say is "Ready, sing" in tempo right before the prep beat, and your class will start singing. Like this: One-two-ready-sing-(prep beat.)

Executing the Cut-Offs. You'll want to be sure you can give a cut-off. Very simply, it's done like this. Bring your hands up in conducting position. Next, make a counterclockwise circle with your right hand and a clockwise circle with the left—about the size of a basketball. Do both hands at the same time. The circles will move in opposite directions. To cut off the circles, bring your pointer finger together with your thumb. The cut-off usually comes near the point where the circles began. You'll need the cut-off gesture for the last note of a song and for fermata signs. You can use both hands or one hand. It doesn't matter. The important thing is that you do it!

Using Sustaining Gestures. There are times when you'll want to sustain a note or be sure that the phrase isn't broken. For these times, you'll need a sustaining gesture. You have several choices. One is to pull outward in opposite directions as though you had a piece of taffy or you were stretching a strong rubber band. Feel the "pull" happening? That's the feeling you want to convey to your class. Another gesture is to raise one or both hands upward with the same taffy-pulling feeling. The pull would be done slowly, of course, just like the outward pull. Gestures like this will get results. Students will hold a note or sing the phrase as you dictate.

These, then, are the basic kinds of gestures you need for the classroom. Practice in front of a mirror and analyze yourself. Don't worry if you look different from someone else; conducting styles vary from one person to the next. The only criterion you need is that you look and feel good while conducting. If you do, you'll use it. If you don't, you won't. It's that simple.

Problem Regarding Classroom Conducting

Many classroom teachers don't take advantage of conducting opportunities because a lot of them don't feel comfortable conducting. They say they aren't able to conduct—never could and never will. So they don't! Others just don't **like** to conduct. They want no part of it. And those who feel it isn't necessary, never even try. It's an attitudinal thing more than anything else.

Ever notice what teachers do when they just stand and watch? I have! Some teachers settle themselves against anything that will support them—the desk, the radiator, a table—and proceed to daydream out the window. I remember one teacher who used to get totally absorbed in her cuticles every time the class sang along with a recording! Students began to imitate her. How about those who begin correcting papers or checking their grades while the class sings the round for the umpteenth time? What marvelous opportunities they miss—all because they thought they couldn't conduct. What a pity!

Concluding Challenge

Don't let yourself think you can't conduct or you don't need to conduct in the classroom. What you need to do is practice so that you can develop your skills to the point where you don't hesitate when the opportunity arises. Students should be accustomed to seeing you conduct occasionally, and experience your conducting for their own musical growth. Try to conduct the next time you aren't accompanying.

LESS EFFECTIVE

When it came time to sing the round, Ms. Chromatica divided the class and then started the first group with a nod of the head and a loud "go." For the second group, Ms. Chromatica shook her head. Then she folded her arms and walked back and forth as the class sang. She didn't tell the class how many times to sing the round and group one petered out. "I didn't tell you to stop. Keep going!" she yelled. "You too," she snapped at the other group. She gave a disgusted look and walked back to her desk.

Mr. Diatonica's sixth-grade class liked to sing along with a recording. When the recording started, he raised his eyebrows at the class in a questioning way because everyone still wasn't singing. Then he went to the chalkboard and started to write out the music for the next activity while the class sang. "I can't hear everyone singing," he scolded. "That's better! And sing the next verse." Every now and then Mr. Diatonica would peek over his shoulder to see that the students were behaving. "Keep singing!"

MORE EFFECTIVE

After Ms. Chromatica divided the class for the round, she brought the first group in with a prep beat and downbeat. She did the same for the next group. While the class was singing, Ms. Chromatica conducted. She cut off the first group when it finished the first time and gave them the downbeat to sing it a second time. When the first group came to the ending the second time, Ms. Chromatica gave them a big cut off. Then she cut off the second group. "That was wonderful, class! Everyone came in and ended together."

For the opening activity, Mr. Diatonica selected a familiar song the class liked to sing with the record. "Everyone ready?" he asked. When the intro was over Mr. Diatonica conducted the song with a bouncy beat as the class sang. It was always so much fun to start and end together when Mr. Diatonica conducted. When the song was softer, he conducted smaller. And when it came time for the fermata at the end of the song, Mr. Diatonica held out both hands and held the note to the very last second before the class's breath gave out. They loved it when he conducted.

Providing Teacher Demonstrations

Is there a classroom music teacher who doesn't know about demonstrating? I doubt it. Demonstrating is a natural happening in the realm of teaching. I'd even go so far as to say that teaching per se is dependent upon teacher demonstrations, and that you really can't teach, at least not effectively, without doing some kind of teacher demonstration every now and then. Demonstrating is the ultimate teacher effort that needs to be done in a competent manner, and not sloughed off.

Definition of Teacher Demonstrations

The term *teacher demonstrations* means to model or to show. In classroom lingo that translates into showing students how to do something in relationship to the lesson. For example, it might be showing them how to:

- perform a class activity
- complete a written exercise

- execute the given instructions
- correct an inappropriate response

For you, then, demonstrating is simply a short showing session during which you literally go through the motions of what you want done. And for students, it is a specific example of what the teacher expects.

Reasons for Demonstrations

Teacher demonstrations are important because they do a **better job of "telling"** than explaining. How many times have you heard that actions speak louder than words? Probably dozens of times, and it's true! Teacher demonstrations "speak" loud and clear to students—not audibly, but visibly. They actually help the students see what you want. It doesn't mean, however, that you can't ever do any instructing. It just means that showing is a more powerful way of informing students than explaining, and that one demonstration is worth a thousand words. That's the first reason.

The second reason is equally important. Demonstrations **set the performance standard** or establish your expectations. Unless the student sees what you want, and what the student should want for himself/herself, the student may be content to stop with a response that is only "pretty good" or just "good enough to get by."[1] The demonstration indicates the performance level and "tells" the student what he/she must do to achieve a "good" performance. The fact that standards can be obtained should make demonstrating an exciting facet of your teaching.

The third reason is obvious, but still significant. Demonstrations **become actual models**, and the teacher, the chief modeler. In fact, **you** become the built-in model to show students:

- how to respond
- what to emulate
- what to improve
- what to repeat
- what to alter

Without this modeling, students have nothing to imitate, and nothing with which to compare themselves. When this happens, Bugelski notes that students' responses are generally more inferior and they usually give more wrong answers.[2] That says it all, doesn't it? With demonstrations, you provide the specific examples students need to make better responses.

The fourth reason is that demonstrations **help motivate and challenge students**, especially when they're done in such an appealing way that students sit up and take note. They get excited about what the teacher is doing, and even jump in before the demonstration is finished. Your demonstrations can become motivational tools for you, too, if they're done "right."

Thus, demonstrations are effective for (a) telling students, (b) setting standards, (c) providing models, and (d) motivating students. While other reasons could be mentioned, these carry the most weight. They're the reasons I urge you to give this task your utmost attention. It's worth the effort.

---

[1]Bugelski, B. R. *Some Practical Laws of Learning*. The Phi Delta Kappa Educational Foundation, Bloomington, Indiana, 1970, p. 18.

[2]Bugelski, p. 16.

Problems Regarding Demonstrations

There are three common problems when it comes to doing teacher demonstrations. Let's identify them so you can avoid these problems. The fact is, demonstrating is usually done:

- too sparingly
- too sloppily
- too hurriedly

Sound familiar? They do for a lot of teachers. Any one of these can stifle the student's motivation and lessen the impact of your teaching. Let's talk briefly about each problem.

Demonstrating **too sparingly** seems to stem from one or two incorrect assumptions. One is that teachers think students will be able to figure out for themselves how they should respond, and, the other, that demonstrations encourage more mimicry than mastery. That first assumption is all wet! Students **do** need teacher demonstrations to know what the teacher wants. If you don't demonstrate, you keep your students in the dark as to what constitutes a good response, and that's a travesty because then they never respond up to par.

And the second assumption? Many teachers think that students are just mimicking. No, they're modeling. There's a difference. Mimicking is mindless aping, while modeling is a conscientious imitation or an accepted challenge. So if you're one who doesn't do much demonstrating because you think it's just an aping process, think again. It's a modeling tactic that establishes a performance standard. That means there needs to be **more** demonstrating, not less.

The second problem is the one that concerns me even more. I'm baffled why some teachers get so **careless and sloppy** in their demonstrating. Their gestures are too confined and often too flippant. Whether they are showing students how to (a) march in place, (b) hold a book, (c) play a drum, or (d) tap the rhythm sticks, their "showing" effort always looks like it's done off the cuff, without much forethought, and without any conviction. The result is that they fail miserably in setting performance standards and motivating students. It's crucial that you display the kind of motions worthy of being emulated. There's no place for sloppy demonstrating in teaching.

The third problem is that of doing demonstrations in a **hurried manner**. Rushing almost always takes the edge off the precision and definition of your motions. It also gives the impression that demonstrations aren't very important or really necessary! I often wonder why sloppy demonstrators even bother. Their motions are simply a rough approximation of what's expected. Nothing is clear cut and well defined, and then it's over! Is it any wonder that the class response is poor? Modeling must never be done in a hurried manner! It defeats the purpose.

If you have a tendency to (a) model sparingly, (b) demonstrate sloppily, or (c) present hurriedly, consider some of the following suggestions.

Suggestions for Demonstrations

Regardless of what your problem(s) might be when it comes to demonstrating, my advice, first of all, is to **get a clear-cut picture of the steps involved**. I like the procedure outlined by Good and Brophy. Here are their four steps:

1. Tell students what they will be doing.

2. Inform them you will be demonstrating by saying something like:
   - "Listen and watch as I . . ."
   - "Let me show you how we will . . ."
   - "Here's how we will be doing . . ."
   - "This is how such-and-such is done . . ."
   - "Now watch me as I do such-and-such."
3. Execute the demonstration step-by-step.
4. Ask students to repeat the demonstration.[3]

Now here's the catch. You may very well execute these four steps to-a-tee, but still flop because of the **manner** in which you demonstrate. You need to do these steps (a) deliberately, (b) precisely, (c) accurately, and even (d) theatrically. Unless you demonstrate in a deliberate, somewhat exaggerated, manner and a bit of flair, your demonstration won't "work." If you adhere to these criteria, you'll have your students watching your every move. And if you're not accustomed to demonstrating, you, too, can get-in-the-swing by following the four steps.

There's one other suggestion. You need to know where these steps come within the verbal bridge, the commentary used after each class or individual response. It includes (a) an assessment and (b) an instruction. (See "Using Verbal Bridges" in Chapter 3.)

Teacher demonstrations occur in the instructional part of the verbal bridge. (See Figure 6.1.) Notice that this instructional part now has five steps:

- Step One - telling students what they will do
- Step Two - informing them teacher will demonstrate
- Step Three - executing teacher demonstration
- Step Four - instructing class to imitate demonstration
- Step Five - obtaining class ready position

Figure 6.1 should make it clear where these steps occur. To be specific, the steps begin immediately with an instructional statement as to what the student(s) will do next. This is Step One. In Step Two, you tell the class that you will demonstrate your instructions for them, using such verbiage as:

- "Listen and watch as I . . ."
- "Let me show you how we will do . . ."
- "Here's how we'll be doing . . ."
- "This is how such-and-such will be done . . ."
- "Now watch me as I do such-and-such . . ."

Any of these comments will pave the way for the actual demonstration, which is Step Three. Don't forget the behavioral criteria when you demonstrate, or else it won't "go." Then have the class match your modeling briefly to determine if they "have it." That's Step Four. Finally, in Step Five, get the students in a "ready" position to start the movement.

---

[3]Good, Thomas and Jere Brophy, *Teachers Make a Difference* (New York: Holt, Rinehart, and Winston Publishers, 1975), pp. 125–126.

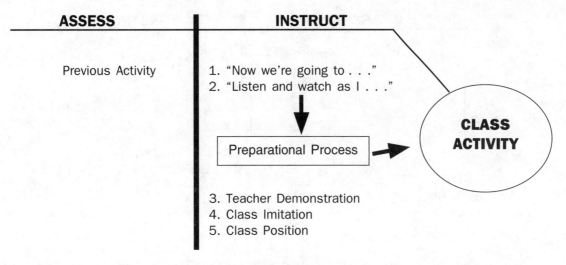

Figure 6.1. Placement of Teacher Demonstration Steps Within the Verbal Bridging.

Let's see what needs to be done when demonstrating for correction purposes, or when students need to be shown a more accurate way of doing something. The only difference here is that the demonstrating happens during what I call the *Fix-it Procedure,* which has five steps:

- Hearing the problem
- Verbalizing the problem
- Demonstrating the correction
- Drilling the correction
- Returning the correction

Look at this procedure for a minute. You've got to hear or see what's wrong first. That's a "must." Then you need to tell your students about it so they know what needs to be fixed and why you're demonstrating for them; otherwise, your demonstration is meaningless. As soon as you finish demonstrating, have the class do the correct way with you. Then you can return the corrected response and continue.

The Fix-it Procedure happens in the assessment part of the verbal bridge. If there's a problem, it starts immediately with the hearing or seeing. The verbalizing, or the assessment, might go something like this:

- "I didn't see everyone doing . . ."
- "Everyone wasn't doing such-and-such . . ."
- "Some of us weren't doing such-and-such."
- "Such-and-such wasn't very good, was it?"

Remember, verbalizing the problem is the second step of the Fix-it Procedure. Move right into your demonstration with the same kind of verbiage used in the demonstration procedure discussed earlier. If the corrected response is noticeably improved **after** the drilling, then this comment would be the second part of the assessment, or the "b" part, with the initial fix-it assessment as the "a" part. (See Figure 6.2.) The "b" assessment may be expressed as follows:

- "Very good. Now everyone is doing such-and-such right . . ."

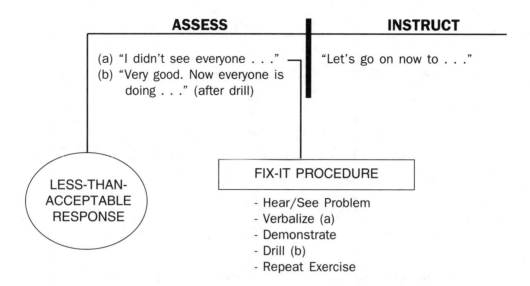

Figure 6.2. Demonstrating Step in the Fix-It Procedure of the Verbal Bridge.

- "I like the way everyone was doing . . . that time."
- "So much better, class. I saw everybody . . ."
- "You're doing such-and-such a hundred percent better."
- "Now you've got it. So much better, class."

Let's get back to demonstrating style. The fix-it demonstration won't work unless it's done (a) slowly, (b) deliberately, (c) precisely, and with (d) flair. I cannot stress style enough. Unless your demonstrating is done with these criteria in mind, it won't work and it'll go sour—guaranteed!

Concluding Challenge

Examine your demonstrating efforts. If you find that you're doing them any old way or rushing through them, it's time to mend your ways. If you feel awkward about demonstrating, I say grow up and start thinking of your students instead of yourself. Be sure also that you demonstrate deliberately, precisely, and theatrically. Remember, you're the model. Your behavior must be worth emulating[4] and capable of motivating and upgrading the class's response. That's how effective your demonstrating must be!

---

[4]Seafeldt, Carol. *Teaching Young Children* (Prentice-Hall, Inc., Englewood Cliffs, NJ, 1980), p. 154.

LESS EFFECTIVE

Ms. Cymbaliné instructed her sixth graders to clap a rhythmic ostinato to a Latin American recording. "Okay, you're going to clap like this." Then she proceeded to slap out the pattern on the board with her left hand. "See how it goes? Get ready." When she put on the recording, Ms. Cymbaliné kept frowning. "That was awful," she growled after the activity ended. "Do it right this time or we'll go on to something else." With that, she stalked off to the record player. The students rolled their eyes at each other.

Ms. Tambouriné was teaching her first graders "Six Little Ducks." While their words were correct, their actions were terrible! Ms. Tambouriné kept shouting, "Watch me, watch me." But none of her actions were precise. Not her six fingers, her fat and skinny ducks, or her little tail. Most of the children weren't doing anything. "Don't you like this song?" she asked. "You aren't doing your actions." Some children said "Uh huh," while others just looked at her with a blank face. "Sit down. Maybe you'll do better next time."

MORE EFFECTIVE

Ms. Cymbaliné asked her sixth-grade class to "watch and listen" as she clapped an ostinato pattern. Extending her arms from her body, she clapped slowly and precisely. "Listen again," she instructed. She clapped in a precise, exaggerated manner again. "Now you try it with me," she said to the class. "Excellent, class. I believe you're ready. Get into clapping position," she said as she walked over to the record player. "They're clapping very accurately," she commented to herself. When they finished, the class asked to do it one more time. "Let's do," she said.

Ms. Tambouriné was anxious to teach her first graders "Six Little Ducks." When she did her actions, she was very careful to hold out her six fingers on "six little ducks." When she came to "fat ones, skinny ones, fair ones too," she stretched out her arms for the fat ones, stood tall with her arms pinned against her sides for the skinny ones, and smiled prettily while framing her face with her hands for the fair ones. When the class joined her, she was delighted to see them imitate her so well. They giggled with delight as they did their actions.

Getting Class to Stand/Sit in Orderly Way

One of the more routinish responsibilities connected with teaching music in the classroom is having to stand or sit the students throughout the lesson. You're forever asking the class to stand up for this-or-that activity, to sit down when it's over, and to stand again when it's time to leave. Regardless of how many times the request is made, it must always be carried out in an orderly and efficient way, whether it be made:

- in the regular classroom with only desks
- in the music classroom where only chairs are used
- in any room space where children are sitting on the floor

This may seem like a trite task in light of all your other responsibilities related to teaching, but it isn't. It's vital to good teaching. Let's look at what's involved.

Definition of Orderly Standing/Sitting

By an "orderly" approach to standing and sitting students, I simply mean that you get the students to stand up or sit down:

- quickly
- quietly
- systematically

Get them up or down as quickly as possible, and as quietly—but systematically as well. That means with a semblance of unity or togetherness, like a unit. That's the essence of an orderly approach. You get the class to stand or sit quickly, quietly, and methodically. But, look at what *usually* happens.

Tendency in Handling Standing/Sitting

The tendency with this task is to ignore it. Many teachers act like this chore isn't a part of their teaching job, as if it's something the kids do on their own and it's nothing for them to worry about. These teachers either wait for the chaos to come to an end, or else engage in some dilly-dallying, like erasing the board or checking the record, for however long the students twaddle. During these few moments, the class is usually in a state of confusion.

Why do some teachers renege on this responsibility? Most likely because they have the wrong attitude and don't understand its place in the overall teaching process. As a result, there's an appearance of being:

- immune to the responsibility
- oblivious to the situation
- indifferent to the happening

Let's look more closely at these three postures. They shed some light on the problem.

Those who seem **immune** to the students' rowdy way of standing or sitting are the ones who no longer allow themselves to be bothered by it. They do this by mentally tuning it out and becoming calloused to the situation. Their philosophy is that ignoring is the best policy for their own peace of mind. Even experienced teachers become immune on occasions, as well as the beginning teachers who are often at a loss in handling the standing and sitting. For these teachers, blocking out is the only way of dealing with this ordeal.

As for those who appear **oblivious**, they can usually be numbered among the less experienced. They are genuinely unaware of the need to correct the disorderly response, so they tolerate the mayhem and even accept it. I think I know why. Beginning teachers are too caught up in their own teaching. They're engrossed in the procedures (What do I do next?), the pacing (What do I do if the lesson ends too soon?), or the activities (What if the students can't do them?). They're too involved with themselves to notice how the students are standing up or sitting down.

But the **indifferent** teachers are the ones who pose the biggest problem. They're the ones who simply don't care if the students fly-out-the-window or sit-on-a-tack when they stand or sit, or if they're as quiet as church mice. It's all the same. Indifference like this usually stems from (a) teacher burnout, (b) professional disillusionment, or (c) personal displeasure with family, peers, or administration. Whatever the reason, indifference is an unacceptable way of handling this task. Thus, the problem is that too many teachers don't follow through on standing and sitting students, and their reactions usually mean they don't have a set way of doing this routine. Unless they do, they open themselves to some unwelcome happenings. Let's look at some of these incidents.

Class Response Without Any Approach

When given carte blanche to "stand" or "sit," without any instructions, students are quick to do their own thing—and it's usually not the most desirable response either!

Let's take the music teacher going into the classroom. The biggest nuisance here is the chair. When students stand, there's usually a deafening racket of screeches and shudders. If the floors are wooden, the chairs make that low thudding sound; but if there's linoleum, they screech and squeal on all pitch levels and timbres. The noise level is incredible for those few seconds! And while there's much less pushing back of chairs in the music room, one or two inevitably get shoved back with the same ear-piercing results.

Then there's the occasional splat or smack of chairs being knocked over. These incidents never fail to twist heads. Sometimes the knocker-over swells with pride at making the "loudest" noise, or else grins from ear to ear. If the culprit is one of the hyper or wiry kids, he'll start climbing up or jumping over the chair before it can be uprighted. Oh yes, don't forget the macho kid who'll lift the back of his chair while shoving out the front and then let the back legs drop with a sharp crack or loud bang. It always scares everyone half to death. Think these antics don't happen? They do, especially when there isn't any orderly approach.

Look what happens in the music room. If chairs are too close, the older kids get into pushing and shoving on the way up. The younger ones will get silly and start giggling if they get too close to each other. Another gimmick the kids in the upper grades try is finding ways to lift themselves off their chairs very slowly or as if they've been shot out of a cannon. These situations can get out of hand if the kid is a show-off and can get the class "oohing" at the antic. Students will do all these things, and more, if you don't have any order in standing and sitting them.

What happens when students sit down? Especially when there's nothing more than a simple "sit down" thrown out? All I can say is you'd better be ready! If students are participating at a distance from their chairs and there's no orderly way of getting back, they'll go racing back with all the finesse of a bull in a china shop! If they're standing in front or in back of their chairs, you can count on the usual din of screeches and squawks before they get seated. Another happening when chairs are too close is that students will try sitting down on their neighbors' chairs or in their neighbor's lap—purposely. The older boys will sometimes jostle for their seats with the kid next to them. It's all in good fun, but still disturbing. Things can really get out of hand if you don't have order and control with this task.

Approach for Standing/Sitting

There's really no master plan for getting students to stand or sit in an orderly way. But if there were, it would be this: Make it part of your activity, that is, start thinking of this task as one of the procedures in your activity.

Think of doing this task in three steps wherever it appears in the procedures:

1. Instruct the class to stand or sit.
2. "Conduct" the class to stand or sit.
3. Assess the class for standing or sitting.

The first step is to **instruct the class**. All you need to do is state a simple command to either sit or stand. Just say exactly what you want the students to do—no more or no less. If you say more, you babble; if less, you baffle. My advice is: keep instructions lean and clean. Then just add a criterion, or a single adverb or short clause that tells students **how** you want them to stand or sit. For example:

SINGLE ADVERBS	SHORT CLAUSES
• quickly	• without talking
• quietly	• without giggling
• silently	• without pushing
• carefully	• without moving chairs
• immediately	• without any noise

Slip in this criterion (a) at the end of the instruction, (b) at the beginning, or (c) somewhere in the middle. Here are some examples of lean and clean instructions with criteria:

- "Would everyone stand **quietly**."
- "Let's stand **quickly**."
- "I'd like everyone to sit without **making a sound**."
- "**Quickly**, take your seats."
- "Let me see how **silently** we can stand!"
- "Stand, please, **without any talking**."
- "Sit **without moving** your chair."

Did you notice the little challenge in some of the instructions? That's a good technique. Students like being challenged. So don't forget to keep your instructions lean and clean, and put in your criterion. That's how orderliness starts.

The second step is to **"conduct" the class** as they stand or sit. I'm adamant about this step because it's the key to getting students to stand or sit in an orderly way. Here's what you do.

As soon as you have given the instructions, take a big preparatory breath through an open mouth. Then quickly extend your hands a little above the waist with palms facing the ceiling and, with a slight scooping motion, raise your hands slowly as the class rises. You are literally "conducting" the students to stand. To get them seated, bring the hands up about shoulder high with your palms facing the floor. Then bring them down slowly as the class sits.

But listen! Be sure to "conduct" up or down at the same speed at which the students are standing or sitting. Don't go faster or slower. If you do, your "conducting" won't work. The students will pop up at different times just like they always did. Conduct in the **same tempo** they're standing or sitting.

Here's one final piece of advice. Let your facial expressions help you, too. For example, use a "Shhh-ing" look with your upward or downward gesture to get students to stand or sit quietly; or a wide-eyed "oooh-ing" expression to get them to stand up quickly. Get the idea? It's using your facial expressions to reinforce your instruction. If you need more assistance with conducting, refer to "Conducting When Not Accompanying" earlier in this chapter.

The third step is to **assess the class** as to how well they accomplished their standing or sitting. It is necessary to assess just about every time. If you want the class to keep on doing "right," you'll need to keep rewarding them—not with candy, but with words. Your assessment can be as brief and simple as "Very good" or "Great!" or "Thank you," particularly when the class has been standing and sitting a number of times. When it's not happening as frequently, it's best to be more specific as follows:

- "Very good. I like the way everyone stood up so quietly."
- "I saw everyone sitting down without making a sound. I'm proud of you."
- "That was the quietest you have ever been when standing up. Bravo!"
- "Thank you for not talking as you sat down."

The point is, students need to know that you recognize their effort and that you appreciate it. They also like to be praised. Who doesn't? So acknowledge your students when they've done what you've asked.

And when they don't stand or sit as you instructed? You still assess them, but in an honest and corrective way, like this:

- "You were very noisy standing up. Let's try standing again."
- "I heard too many chairs and desks being shoved back. We can sit down better than that, can't we?"
- "It's taking us too long to get up from our seats. One more time."

A fair and accurate assessment is crucial in dealing with this routine task. Be forthright, but tactful, in your comments. That's a large part of achieving orderliness.

So there you have the three-step formula. It's really a simple operation that can be used at any point in your procedures. Plan on instructing, conducting, and assessing whenever your class stands or sits. That's what it takes to get an orderly response.

Reasons for Orderly Standing/Sitting

You should be concerned with getting students to stand or sit in a responsible manner for three good reasons. **First**, it facilitates the flow of the lesson by reducing the number of interruptions. You don't have to keep stopping to correct the commotion. Let's face it—all the shuffling and scraping that goes on when students are given free rein is disruptive! But when the task is handled in a quiet, methodical way as part of the activity, you promote a smoother flowing lesson. It's a good reason for supporting this task, isn't it? Believe me, it'll make your teaching a more pleasant job!

Second, it saves teaching time. Doing this task in a proper way is less time consuming than doing it improperly. You don't have to hustle to get the students under control again, or wait for everyone to finally stand up or sit down. You don't have to waste all this valuable time when there's an orderly approach. You can save time for more worthwhile purposes in the lesson. That's the second reason.

And **three**, an orderly approach improves classroom control. Think of it as a preventive measure—like an unspoken rule. If there's a set way, or an established procedure, students are more apt to do their standing or sitting like this rather than some other way. That will automatically result in a noticeable improvement in classroom control. Everyone isn't doing his/her "own thing." This should entice you to do this task in an orderly way.

All of the reasons above are essential criteria for effective teaching. That's what should make this task a "must" with your students. If you do, you'll improve your pacing, conserve your time, and increase your control of the classroom.

Concluding Challenge

If you have been amiss about standing and sitting your students, take a close look at the three-step approach and use it. It's an easy plan you can implement immediately. You'll be amazed at the results.

LESS EFFECTIVE

When the fifth graders finished the partner song, Ms. Half-Rest went to the board. Looking over her shoulder, she nonchalantly said, "Okay, sit down." With that, there was an immediate uproar of shoving, shuffling, and chair screeching. "Whooooha! What's going on? Can't I even turn my back for one second? What are you doing over there, Mark? And how did that chair get way over there?" By the time Ms. Half-Rest got the class settled down, at least three minutes went by. "I don't want any of that again. Hear me? Or else we'll just sit for the whole lesson." Ms. Half-Rest glared at the class.

As he continued to search for the chalk at his desk, Mr. Whole-Rest asked his class to stand, sort of under his breath. Some heard it, and some didn't. Nick, the class clown, saw that Mr. Whole-Rest wasn't looking so he put his hands under himself and began lifting his body off the chair. When the others saw him, they started "yahing" before Mr. Whole-Rest knew what was happening. "Cut that out, Nick. Everyone get back to your own seats. Go on! I'm waiting. Jim, get back. Nick, you see me after class." Immediately a "whoooh" broke out. "That's enough of that! Look how much time we're wasting," Mr. Whole-Rest blared out. Five minutes of class time had already gone by!

MORE EFFECTIVE

As soon as Ms. Half-Rest's fifth graders ended the partner song, she instructed them to sit down. "Let's be seated now—very quietly." She hunched her shoulders, squinted her eyes, and used outstretched hands with palms down to seat the class. "Excellent, class. I really appreciate the way you sat down so quietly." Ms. Half-Rest learned a long time ago that if you wanted students to stand up or sit down, you needed to do something to make this happen. She found that using facial expressions and bodily gestures worked the best. "It's worth the effort," she said to herself with a smile.

When it was time for the class to stand, Mr. Whole-Rest came around to the front of his desk and instructed the class carefully. "I'd like everyone to stand up quickly and quietly." He raised his hands slowly with the class. "Thank you, that was great. You follow directions so well in this class!" Mr. Whole-Rest was always precise in telling his class how he wanted them to stand up or sit down. He always "conducted" them and the students always knew what he expected. There never was any fooling around or wasting time in Mr. Whole-Rest's classes. It wasn't any big deal. You just stood up or sat down in a quiet orderly way. That was the way you did it in Mr. Whole-Rest's class!

Handing Out and Tuning Guitars/Ukeleles Efficiently _____

On those occasions when you want to use guitars and/or baritone ukeleles for the class activity, the job of distributing them and tuning them will be no small feat! The sheer size of the guitar or baritone ukelele (preferred because it more closely resembles the guitar) makes the handling process more difficult than any other classroom instrument. If you've ever tried putting a guitar under a chair, you know what I mean. It's just about as impossible as having students hold the instrument on their laps. It's a matter of logistics that must be worked out **before** you teach your class.

Then there's the matter of getting the instruments tuned—in each class! This isn't a normal task with other classroom instruments—bells, drums, triangles, etc., don't have to be tuned. But with guitar and baritone ukelele, it's a necessity, which means you need to have some sort of tuning system ready in which students can participate.

So, if you're going to use guitars and baritone ukeleles, you will need to have the know-how and the skill to carry out the distributing and the tuning. This discussion will provide some insight and suggestions on distributing and tuning, and offer several suggestions.

Problem With Distributing/Tuning

The problem is that the handing out and tuning of guitars and/or baritone ukeleles isn't always done in an orderly or efficient manner. To the contrary. A lot of teachers carry out these two chores in such a slip-shod way that the lesson momentarily goes to pot. Ever notice that when there isn't a set procedure, students start taking matters into their own hands and that the momentum of the lesson starts to fall apart? It happens when teachers let students come running up for an instrument like scurrying little mice, or when they let them "tune" on their own.

Here's a typical example of what happens when students go about "tuning" without any systematic approach. A few students will gather together in a small group and try to match their strings, while two or three others will have an ear glued to their finger board trying to "hear" the notes amidst all the other plucking and

strumming. But most of the students will probably be busy doing their Elvis Presley impersonation rather than tuning. Where's the teacher? Usually up front yelling out, "Get it tuned! Get it tuned!" Or else at the piano banging out the string notes to which no one is listening.

There's no way these students can tune quickly or correctly, not under the conditions described! And teachers who go through the motions of "hearing" the so-called *tuned strings*, after the students have done the tuning themselves, are just wasting their time and carrying out a farce. Most of the guitars will still be out of tune!

Then there is the problem of students having difficulty singing when the instrument isn't tuned properly. It's hard enough for most students to sing when the guitar and/or ukelele is in tune, let alone when it isn't. So, not only does the lesson fall apart when the instruments aren't handed out in an orderly way, but, even more serious, the students can't have a musical experience when the tuning process is botched.

Approach for Handing Out/Tuning

The only way to rectify the problem of being slipshod and avoiding all the repercussions is to have a definite approach.

Handing Out Guitars/Ukeleles. Let's deal with some ways to hand out instruments first. There are several options:

Pick Up from Rack

If you're fortunate to have a built-in rack in your classroom where the instruments could be "hung up," all you need to do is have students file up row by row, take an instrument, and return quickly and quietly to their seats. You would also have to tell the students what to do with the instruments when they got to their seats, that is, where to put them or how to hold them until everybody had his/her guitar/ukelele. That way you don't have to put up with the occasional plinking or strumming sounds escaping. This approach is quick and orderly.

Pick Up from Central Location

If you don't have a hanging rack, then consider putting the instruments in a centralized location for pick up, such as:

- lining up against a wall
- laying down on the floor
- Stacking up on your desk (if they're in styrofoam boxes)

Then have the students come in an orderly way and pick up an instrument. By the way, this pick-up procedure should take no more than two or three minutes maximum, even with a large class. All you have to do is get the instruments lined up, laid out, or stacked so that they are in pick-up position. Then insist on "no playing" during the pick-up time. If someone does, carry out your consequence. That's the only way you'll make an impression on the class that you want the pick up done **quickly and quietly**!

I can almost hear some of you sputtering that this pick-up procedure wouldn't work with your crew. Yes, it will, but you need to lay down the rules and carry through with them. Students really want things to be orderly. More important, they really expect you to do things the "right" way. Don't worry about your students; they'll do their part, if you do yours.

Give to Worthy Students

Suppose you only have four or five guitars or ukeleles. You could do several things:

- Pass out instruments yourself to deserving students.
- Select students to come forward to play instruments.

Before you pass out any instruments or call any students forward, you need to "rehearse" or prepare the whole class briefly first. This *class preparation*, as I call it, accomplishes two things. **First**, it keeps everyone's attention in that each student is hoping to be selected or given an instrument. **Second**, it avoids any one-on-one instruction, at the expense of the others, when the student gets the instrument. This class preparation is actually a step in the preparational procedure used for an activity. (See "Implementing Prep Procedure for Class Activity" in Chapter 7.)

I know some of you are wondering what the students do who aren't selected or who don't get an instrument. Do they just sit and watch? No! Have them "play" vicariously in a very realistic way; in other words, imitative playing. You could also give them a replica made out of sturdy cardboard. These vicarious experiences work beautifully if they're presented as viable options for involvement as opposed to sitting and watching. Too, the success with older students will depend largely on the teacher's business-like attitude. It won't work if it's suggested in an off-the-cuff, embarrassed manner. It all depends upon how professional and realistic you make the experience.

Disburse to Students in Pairs

A variation of giving to worthy students would be distributing to pairs of students or partners. I often refer to one of these students as the back-up person or the "understudy" who participates vicariously with the other student. You could have them change off so that the understudy would also have a chance to play the real instrument.

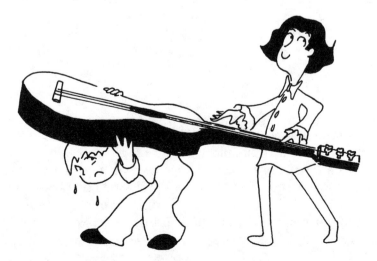

In fact, you can distribute to pairs of students even if you choose the passing-out approach. Simply have the students on one side or both sides of the individual getting the instrument be the back-up. That way if there were only four guitars or ukeleles, you could have from eight to twelve students taking a shot at the real thing within a few minutes.

Divide Students into Groups

The most obvious approach would be to divide the class into groups of four or five and give an instrument to one person while the others "play" vicariously. Then the instrument would be passed to the next student for an equal length of playing time. If possible, it would be best to select the student who would provide a good example for the others in each group.

All of these approaches are designed to bring order and control to the distributing of your instruments. You may even have your own procedures. If so, great! What matters most is that you are able to hand out instruments in an orderly and efficient way.

Tuning Guitars/Ukeleles. Now look at the job of getting the instruments tuned. Even if you yourself tuned each instrument before the first class arrived, you know that some of the pegs will invariably slip. That means some of the instruments will need re-tuning despite your own efforts; and after the first class, you know the instruments will need tuning for the next class. There's no way to get around the need for re-tuning, and it will need to be done **by the students** if there's to be any time left for the lesson in each case.

Here's one way to get this tuning done that is simple, yet effective. Go to the piano and play the lowest string ("E" on guitar and "ˆD" on baritone ukelele) while the class tunes just that string. Be sure you have talked about being sharp or flat and how to correct the problem before students take on the tuning task themselves. When the student gets that low string in tune, have the student nod his/her head and wait for the others to finish tuning, or else help someone having difficulty.

- Instruct students to loosen the peg and start re-tuning if they get confused.
- Then go on to the next string and follow the same process.

- When all the strings have been tuned, play the string sequence slowly while students make one last check.

While you might think the process would be too time consuming, you'll be surprised as to how quickly students learn to tune when it's done like this. The whole procedure should take no longer than three to five minutes, and less as the students get better. Notice that this is an individual effort within a class context, and that students are tuning themselves and then bowing out to let others hear better and helping those who are struggling. If you're looking for a way to get your students tuned, try this approach. It really works.

Once the students get more experienced at tuning, you might want to use group leaders who can tune themselves in a matter of seconds and then help tune a small group. This is a great time-saving approach, especially if your "leaders" have the ability to get the job done.

Another way is to have **tuning-partners**, that is, teaming up a stronger tuning student with a weaker one. Not only does this method give more individual attention to those having problems tuning, but it also adds a measure of self-respect and pride to the ones providing the assistance.

Getting any ideas for your situation? Hopefully, you can use some of the above suggestions if you don't have any set way of tuning at the present time. Any of these approaches will make your tuning effort more orderly and efficient.

Reasons for Handing Out/Tuning Orderly

Most of the reasons for dwelling on an orderly approach for this task have already been inferred, but they're important enough to restate. An orderly and efficient manner makes for a smoother paced lesson. You won't have to keep stopping and starting to deal with individual problems or with goofing-off situations. In other words, the flow of the lesson won't disintegrate before it even starts. Getting those instruments properly tuned will help to keep the lesson flowing.

Then, too, precious class time isn't wasted on time-consuming procedures that simply add to the confusion of class tuning. I'm always so amazed to see students go running up one by one with their instrument, and the teacher allowing such antics!

As with handing out instruments, a controlled tuning approach gives you better control of your class. It allows you to feel "in control" because **you're** the one who's running the show, not the students. That's one of the real perks in having an orderly procedure ready for tuning those guitars and ukeleles.

Give these reasons some serious thought. They can make a difference in your effectiveness as a teacher.

Concluding Challenge

How do you handle your distribution and tune-up procedures? Is it orderly? If not, your planned experiences will suffer because of your poor handling procedures. Take the suggestions above to heart, and find the one(s) you feel will "work" for you. It's time you start putting order and efficiency into handing out and tuning your guitars and/or ukeleles.

LESS EFFECTIVE	*MORE EFFECTIVE*
Ms. In-Tune had a ukelele lesson planned for her sixth graders. She walked over to the shelves where the ukeleles were stacked and said, "Okay, let's get our instruments. First row." With that, all six students stampeded forward. "Stop pushing. Don't take that instrument, Mark. I'll give it to you. And don't take the instrument out of the case just yet!" she yelled at the students returning to their desks. When Ms. In-Tune called the second row forward, the room was ringing with strums. "Stop that strumming until we all start. And stop pushing, second row. If we can't behave better than this," she warned, "we'll put the ukeleles away." Ms. In-Tune was at her wit's end!	Last week, Ms. In-Tune told the sixth-grade class they would be playing the ukeleles today. They came in all excited. "Now, let me tell you how we're going to get our ukeleles. I'm going to give each one an instrument from the shelf. You will take it and go directly to your seat. You'll put the case down on the right side of your chair and wait until everyone has a ukelele. Do not open the case. Understand? I'll call each row. Any questions? Let's start." The students came up quickly row by row, got the ukeleles, and took their seats quietly. "I'm very proud of you, class. You got your ukeleles in two-and-one-half minutes. That's a record!"
When everyone picked up his/her guitar from the rack, Ms. Out-of-Tune asked the class to stop plucking the string and get ready to tune. "Everyone, tune to this low E. That's still sharp, Jason. You're sharp, Mary. Let's go on. Here's your 'A.' " Someone yelled, "Wait. I don't have the E yet." So Ms. Out-of-Tune played the low E again. The rest of the class began to groan and plink at their instruments. "I can't hear. Stop that plinking! We'll never get done tuning if you don't stop. Now who needs that A again? Hurry, class, it's taking you too long."	"I liked the way everyone picked up his/her guitar so quickly, class. Now let's get ready to tune." Since Ms. Out-of-Tune had established the "no playing" rules before tuning, the class was ready. She divided the students into five groups and picked out the leaders. It took only a matter of seconds to get the leaders tuned. "Get back to your groups now and help tune each student in your group." The group who gets tuned correctly the fastest will get an A! Immediately the leaders started tuning string by string with their groups, while Ms. Out-of-Tune circulated. She was delighted with the business-like approach of her leaders, and how quickly they were tuning.

Pacing the Lesson Effectively

Of all the behaviors involved in the act of good teaching, none is more essential and more complex than that of pacing. Pacing is affected by every other teacher behavior. If sequencing of procedures is off, delivery of instructions is vague, selection of materials is inappropriate, or preparation of the lesson is ignored, your pacing will sputter along. Pacing, then, demands a great deal of understanding and skill, and a lot of attention. It's too important to skip over lightly.

Definition of Pacing

For such a crucial task in the overall teaching process, there's a lot of confusion as to the meaning of pacing. Actually, it's nothing more than the speed of one's teaching or the rate at which one moves through a lesson. To use the jargon, it's the on-going momentum established (by the teacher) throughout the procedures, and particularly during the activities. In a nutshell, then, pacing is one's momentum.

Let's clarify the meaning even more. There are three important principles connected with pacing. The teacher is responsible for setting the pace—not the students. That's the first principle to recognize. The second is that pacing is really a twofold operation: (1) **establishing** the "right" momentum and (2) **maintaining** that momentum. It's the maintaining part that makes pacing such a challenge—and, more important, that determines its effectiveness. Let me repeat. It's the sustaining of the "right" pacing that indicates its effectiveness. Sustaining it is the key to good pacing, and the third principle as well.

But go back to the term "right" in the establishing part. Be sure there isn't any confusion here. "Right" doesn't refer to some arbitrarily selected momentum. It's a teaching tempo that best suits a particular class or activity, or the one that "fits" both. For the class, that means a pace that is in-line with the students' mental, musical, and even physical abilities—one that doesn't go any faster or slower than the class is capable of going. For the activity, it's the most accommodating speed—the one that doesn't go too fast for reading letter names of notes or for tapping out the melodic rhythm of a song, or too slow for getting students situated for an activity or for singing an action song. Thus, the "right" momentum is simply the most accommodating momentum for the situation.

How do you establish and/or maintain this "right" momentum? We'll discuss some suggestions later. What's important right now is that you have a clear concept of the pacing task, that you recognize its dual nature and accept it as the teacher's responsibility. These concepts are crucial to the understanding of effective pacing. The fact is, effective pacing promotes effective teaching.

Outcomes of Effective Pacing

There are at least three significant ways that effective pacing promotes effective teaching. The first is that pacing helps to **stimulate the classroom climate**—as well as stimulate the students. The second is that it helps to **capture the class's attention**. Third, it helps to **reduce discipline problems**. If these results sound a bit pompous and overly optimistic, let me assure you they aren't. They really happen when the pacing is "right." You experienced teachers can vouch for what I'm saying. But let's take a closer look for you skeptics.

In regard to **stimulating the climate**, the truth is that momentum plays a powerful role in generating classroom excitement—that is, in breathing life into the class milieu. Just get the "right" momentum going and notice what begins to happen. Students start to come alive, the air begins to tingle, and the lesson starts to click! Almost in that order! That's when you say to yourself, "This is exciting!" And it is, because you're experiencing the things teachers dream about. You're reaping the rewards of a stimulated environment, and good pacing is a classroom stimulator!

With the **capturing of attention**, we're dealing with the most immediate outcome of an effective pace and one that contributes mightily to stimulating the environment as discussed above. Ever notice how quickly students start heeding (or attending) when the pacing is "right"? How their minds don't go wandering off as easily? How they stay with it so much better? With-it-ness and pacing go hand-in-hand. Then, at some point in the lesson this with-it-ness blossoms into a genuine interest or a motivated awakening on the part of the student(s). You can almost feel it happen. It's the moment when you can tell the class is really "with you"; when teacher and students seem to be operating on the same wavelength, and the activity begins to flow like a well-oiled machine. Do you see how pacing first impacts on attention span? Then how it stimulates the students and influences the activity? Attentiveness happens first. That's the logical order of these two outcomes.

As for the **curbing of discipline**, this should be an obvious consequence, especially if students are attending. The fact is there isn't any time—nor the inclination—to whisper to one's neighbor, throw an eraser, or punch the other fellow. Students don't want to miss anything when they're caught up in the momentum. But probably the most overlooked reason for discipline getting better is that there's a sense of pride in keeping up with the class. Don't underestimate the impact of group participation. Look what esprit de corps does for a marching unit or a baseball team! That same spirit of pride and accomplishment happens in the classroom, too. That's when participation becomes more important than diversion. If there were no other outcome than the curbing of discipline, that would be sufficient enough to encourage proper pacing.

Unfortunately, some of you have never reaped the benefit of reducing disciplinary problems with your pacing, and even more who have never collected on any of the outcomes. Let's find out why.

Reasons for Pacing Problems

It isn't that some teachers don't want to pace properly, or that they don't try, or that they purposely let their pacing get slower or faster. Any of these would be like sabotaging one's own teaching. So what's the problem then? There are two: the more perplexing one is that some teachers aren't sensitive enough to their own pacing, and the other more correctable one is that there's a definite lack of pacing know-how. Take insensitivity first.

It's difficult to understand how anyone could not notice when momentum starts to slow down or speed up, but some teachers don't! It doesn't seem to register that the wiggling, the daydreaming, and the whispering are all signs of a slow pace. Nor does it dawn on them that the pacing is too fast when students sit back and quit responding. It's as if the teachers are immune to pacing, as if it's something they're supposed to ignore. Haven't they heard about pacing, you ask? Of course they have, but as most would admit, they didn't understand it before they taught, and don't understand it now. But that's a poor excuse for continuing in oblivion, especially when there's so much material currently available on the subject of pacing. The more knowledgeable you are, the less insensitive you will be!

The second problem is the more common one and the easier to correct. It's not having enough experience to cope with one's pacing, or enough strategies up-one's-sleeve once the pacing starts to slow down or speed up, or enough know-how to get the "right" pace started at the beginning of the lesson. See how handicapped a teacher is by not knowing what to do? If you have ever been in this spot, you know how uncomfortable and frustrating it can be. Unless there's a mentor teacher, a helpful supervisor, or a teacher's guide around, most of these teachers simply continue to struggle and excuse themselves for their ineptness. The most sensible and immediate solution, apart from attending workshops or classes, is to research the literature for practical suggestions, like the ones that follow. In other words, learn to help yourself.

But before discussing these suggestions, let's look quickly at the two pacing scenarios that inevitably result from the above pacing problems. In a nutshell, the pacing either gets (1) too slow or (2) too fast. Although teachers speak frequently about fast- and slow-paced lessons, I wonder how many could recognize the factors that cause them. Let's identify some of these factors.

Suppose the pacing is going too slow. Why? What's making it slow? A number of things! It could be that the teacher is:

- speaking too slowly or too deliberately
- talking with too many pauses

- making explanations too long
- not talking while walking (see "Avoiding the Dead Spots in Teaching" in Chapter 2)
- Being too wordy in the verbal bridging (See "Using Verbal Bridges" in Chapter 3)

See all the possible reasons? Any one, or a combination, of these teaching flaws could cause the pacing to slow down.

I've got to tell you about the teacher who had a habit of grinning after everything she said or did—for at least three or four seconds. If she told the class to "open to page so-and-so," she grinned. If she trotted over to the piano, she looked up and grinned. If she erased the chalkboard, she would look over her shoulder and grin as though she were posing for a picture. I finally had to tell her to "can the grinning." She fussed at first, but then agreed. Her pacing improved immediately, and her students were overjoyed to be rid of her grinning!

What makes the pacing get faster? It could be that the teacher is:

- speaking too fast
- talking without any pauses
- moving from one activity to another without assessing
- rushing through an activity
- starting before everyone is ready
- explaining things too quickly
- showing visual aids too fast

But enough about what makes pacing too fast or too slow. Let's move on to some suggestions for effective pacing.

Suggestions for Effective Pacing

There are many suggestions for helping the teacher establish and/or maintain the "right" pace. Some of those cited here will be **preventive strategies**, that is, those efforts used to keep pacing from slowing down or speeding up. Others will be **corrective tactics** for those times when the pace has already slowed down or speeded up. Whether you're looking to expand your pacing strategies or to find out more about pacing per se, you will be able to find suggestions to help with your particular pacing need(s).

Observe Students Closely. One of the best strategies for sustaining a good pace is to keep a close, sharp eye on students to know when the pacing needs to be altered. There's no better pacing index than the students! They'll be bad when it's wrong and good when it's right. As simple as it may sound, it's true! Students will start to act up when pacing is off. When they do, here's how to respond. Zero-in immediately on your pacing. If it's too fast, slow it down; or if it's slowing down, speed it up. Use observing as your corrective tool.

Some teachers are blessed with a sixth sense, or an intuitiveness, for sensing when the pace needs altering. For these individuals, observing become a preventive exercise.[5] Most teachers, however, aren't quite as intuitive. They tend to rely on what they see rather than what they sense with their pacing.

---

[5]Lemlech, Johanna K. *Class Management* (New York: Harper and Row Publishers, 1979), p. 25.

But whether one operates more on intuition or on observation, there are two stipulations that must be adhered to in order to get the best results from observing: (1) keep constantly attuned to the students' behavior, and (2) be well acquainted with the behaviors associated with ineffective pacing.

The **first stipulation** requires the teacher to take note at all times of how the students are behaving—in conjunction with the ongoing momentum. To ignore behavior for even the shortest time is to give one's pacing the green light to speed up or slow down. A keenful watch is crucial to this strategy whether it be for corrective or for preventive purposes.

The **second stipulation** requires the teacher to be knowledgeable in the ways students respond when pacing is "off." Knowing that when they start fidgeting in their seats, toying with their pencils, teasing another student, daydreaming into space, or whispering with a neighbor, the pacing is probably moving too slow. Or knowing that it's going too fast when students begin shouting out the answers rather than raising hands, sitting back and watching instead of leaning forward and participating, or hopping up and down to get a chance to respond.[6] See what I mean about knowing the behavioral antics? Without this information, this suggestion is useless.

If you're adhering to these two stipulations, then you're well prepared to gauge your own pacing, determine when it needs adjusting, and better able to nurture your own sensitivity as well. Become an astute observer if you're serious about your pacing. Moreover, know the kinds of behaviors to expect and, on those occasions when your sixth sense is working, enjoy the warning!

Execute Other Skills Competently. Another sensible way of maintaining effective momentum is being sure that all other teaching skills are executed in a competent manner. As stated earlier, every other teaching skill affects pacing. It makes a difference how well the teacher can verbalize instructions, guide class responses, implement activities, distribute instruments, seat the class, pass out materials, etc. The list of skills could go on and on, but you get the picture. The more competently each is discharged, the more likely you will be able to sustain an effective momentum. Competency is an excellent preventive tool. In fact, it is an insurance policy for good pacing!

What you need to do in order to benefit from this suggestion is to constantly evaluate your teaching skills and identify the specific tasks that have a tendency to bog down or speed up. If you can't put your finger on the problem(s), why not ask your mentor or music supervisor to observe you? Or videotape yourself? Do whatever it takes to find out what's hindering your momentum. Let me help you get started.

See if any of the following pacing traps sound familiar to you. It may be that you don't use talking time wisely, that you use it only for traveling. If so, why not use your traveling time for instructing as well?[7] Could it be that you take too long to pass out materials? Then you don't have a system for passing out things. Why not get student helpers and have materials ready to be distributed? Is it you don't use multiple instructions on appropriate occasions? Why can't you, for example, instruct the class as follows: (a) Find page so-and-so, (b) Put your finger on such-and-such when you find the page, and (c) Raise your hand when you've done so. This is a great way of keeping the momentum rolling; and if you're worried about the students, don't be. They're capable of handling triple requests. Try it and see!

---

[6]Small, Ann R. "Pace Yourself," *Music Educators Journal*, May 1979, p. 32.
[7]Small, p. 33.

Once you've discovered your problem(s) and put a name tag on them, determine how they can be corrected or improved. Unless you submit yourself to this kind of scrutiny and discipline, your pacing will continue to plague you.

Use Opening Activities Purposefully. A good suggestion for setting the "right" momentum at the beginning of your lesson is to use your opening activity as a pace setter and not just an interest-getter. Your opening activity can set the pacing tone and heighten the interest level at the same time. But teachers tend to concentrate on capturing the interest—that's been the long-standing reason for using opening activities. It's time, however, that you recognize the potential in opening activities for establishing the pace.

Here's why opening activities are good for establishing momentum. **First** of all, they're usually familiar events that students have experienced many times before. They know what to do without any explanation. **Second**, they're experiences the students can perform easily by virtue of their repeated encounters. In other words, students don't have difficulty doing the activity. **Third**, they're experiences that students enjoy doing. You don't have to twist any arms to get students to participate. They jump right in! And, **four**, opening activities generally need little or no instructions other than a "Ready, sing" or a "Ready, play." They can be implemented in a split-second. Is it any wonder that opening activities can set the "right" pace?

But let's talk about the teacher's role in the opening activity. It's not enough for the activity to be familiar or for students to be eager. Neither the activity nor the students can set the pace; only the teacher can by being dynamic and enthusiastic in his/her own involvement in the activity. Whether the opening exercise be (a) rhythmic readying, (b) ethnic dancing, (c) instrumental accompanying, or (d) singing with partner songs, it's the teacher who must take the reins in defining the momentum by the way he/she executes the activity for the class and with the class. The opening activity is not the time for the teacher to be laid back, half-hearted, or willy-nilly. Rather, it's the time to be enthusiastic, energetic, and motivating. It takes hard work to get the students responsive to your pacing, but that's how pacing is established—through inspiration (by the teacher) and imitation (of the teacher).

The secret (for setting the pace) with opening activities, then, is a matter of (1) knowing that the opening exercise is capable of establishing the pace of the lesson, and (2) exerting the kind of energetic and enthusiastic momentum that inspires students to follow suit—with the same momentum. Now it's up to you!

Execute Verbal Bridges Proficiently. One place in the lesson where pacing almost always comes unglued is in the verbalizing between activities. It happens to teachers on all experience levels. This verbalizing segment of the lesson is the *verbal bridging*. In actuality, it involves two specific tasks: (1) **assessing** the activity just completed by the class or an individual, and (2) **instructing** for the next planned activity. (See "Using Verbal Bridges" in Chapter 3.) If you're serious about keeping the momentum going between activities, learn to articulate succinctly and accurately when you assess and instruct. Make your language precise and to the point. Comment only on how well or not so well the class (or individual) responded and what you expect the student(s) to do next—no more and no less. For example, suppose your class has just finished playing the melodic rhythm of some song perfectly on rhythm sticks. An articulate verbal bridge might sound like this:

> "Excellent, class. I liked the way everyone played the rhythm of the melody without making a single mistake. (*assessment*) We're ready now to chant the words to that rhythm (*instruction*) like this . . . Ready, read."

See how lean-and-clean this verbal bridge is—how the assessment speaks to the very thing the class did well and how the instruction tells very simply what the class will do next. This is how you can move from one activity to the next without losing momentum. Should your assessment be negative, such as, "Almost, we didn't quite get the rhythm correct in the last two measures," you would simply demonstrate the correction and then instruct them to play these two measures once more. The trick is in saying specifically what you liked or didn't like and then indicating what will be done next. To say anything more slows down the pacing—and to say less, necessitates clarification.

Let me say a word about verbalizing habits in the bridging segment. Sometimes your assessments, or your instructions, or both, for that matter, can get (a) too wordy, (b) too repetitive, (c) too vague, or even (d) too irrelevant. Any of these verbal vices will take its toll on the pacing. Wordy and repetitive assessments will slow down the pacing in a minute, and so will vague irrelevant instructions because they have to be repeated. Take my advice: be articulate and concise. It's the only way to prevent the momentum from going amuck in your verbal bridges.

Another suggestion is to try doing part of your verbal bridging without speaking; in other words, silently. Or do all of it without speaking by using your bodily gestures and facial expressions. For example, you can nod your head repeatedly, give a smile, or clap your hands to show your approval or to give positive assessment. Then you could either verbalize the instructions or else use another kind of gesture to indicate what to do next. Suppose you weren't pleased with the class's performance. You could shake your head from side to side (as if you were saying "no") along with an "I'm surprised" look and then quickly point to the first note on the board to indicate doing it over. All you need to say, then, is "Ready, play." This silent bridging could be done in a matter of seconds! On the right occasions, it's more effective than the spoken bridge.

Here are two quick tips. **One**, assess with sincerity and enthusiasm. Mean what you say, and then say it with gusto. Otherwise, you'll lose the students no matter how articulate and concise you might be. **Two**, avoid long pauses between the assessment and the instructions. You'll break the flow of the pace if you do. It'll also detract from the articulateness of your verbiage. Move right into your instructions with just a bit of emphasis on the first few words to make it clear that it's a new thought, such as:

(*Assessment*) . . . "Now let's go on to. . . ."

(*Assessment*) . . . "This time we're going to. . . ."

(*Assessment*) . . . "We'll do it one more time, like this. . . ."

(*Assessment*) . . . "Here's what we'll do this time . . ."

This verbal emphasis might seem like an insignificant point, but it's one of those little teaching details that make the verbal bridge even more effective. Remember, too, to keep those verbal bridges lean and clean.

Plan Lesson Thoroughly. This is such an obvious suggestion that I hesitate to mention it, but I must. In fact, I would probably cite it as one of my first priorities, if the suggestions here had to be prioritized, because it's so often the problem behind poor pacing. Pacing is literally at the mercy of the teacher's preparation. In order to have any assurance of keeping an ongoing momentum, here's what the teacher needs to do before teaching:

- *Sequence Overall Procedures.* Outline each step of the lesson from opening activity to the closing activity and arrange learning experiences in order of difficulty for each concept when necessary.
- *Attend to Verbal Bridges.* Think through the assessment and instructions between each activity so that they can be expressed in an articulate and concise manner.
- *Choose Appropriate Activities.* Select activities that highlight the concept(s) for the lesson and match the students' musical and maturity levels.
- *Work Out Details of Each Activity.* Go step by step through each activity and determine how the activity will be implemented from start to finish to avoid any surprises, i.e., from the beginning instructions to the closing assessment.
- *Choose Appropriate Music.* Look for music with interesting melody, catchy rhythm, and appealing words. Make sure the song or recording clearly highlights the concept.
- *Structure Presentation of New Concept.* Arrange the information in a logical order for the clearest presentation beginning with motivational idea to the instructions for the initial activity.
- *Organize Materials to Be Used.* Get all books, recordings, and visual aids assembled and placed for easy access when teaching; put page markers in books and chalk markings on recording bands.
- *Check Out Equipment and Instruments.* Be sure the record player is working before teaching and that all the instruments are available and in working order.
- *Set Up Classroom in Orderly Way.* Arrange room in a neat and orderly way that best suits your lesson needs. Put instruments and/or books under chairs if this is the procedure you use. Make provisions for visual aids.
- *Prepare Summary for Lesson.* Be ready to pull together the review concept(s) before going on to new concept (if you have one). Then summarize new concept by using the motivational idea and referring to activities used. Bring each conceptual idea to a clear-cut close before going on to next idea.

These, then, are the facets of a lesson that must be worked out before teaching. Otherwise, the teacher invariably succumbs to such pacing no-nos as (a) pausing too frequently to think, (b) delivering vague and/or wordy instructions, (c) stopping to ready materials, (d) saying too much in the verbal bridges between activities, (e) interrupting the lesson to fix the equipment, (f) floundering through a new concept presentation, (g) looking for the visual aid poster, and many other no-nos that could be mentioned. For the most experienced teacher, planning is generally more of a mental exercise, of running through the procedures in one's mind except for the checking out of equipment and the assembling of materials. But for those with less experience, preparation should entail a written plan with the details of every activity and the wording of every verbal bridge spelled out until the time when such detailed planning is no longer necessary.

But whether one is experienced or not-so-experienced, there is no room for winging it, that is, going in unprepared. Sooner or later the lack of preparation catches up and, when it does, it's the pacing that invariably suffers. You can't maintain an effective momentum without procedures being clearly defined and activities carefully worked out. Don't jeopardize your own pacing. Do the smart thing and plan your lessons thoroughly. As the old saying goes: an ounce of prevention is worth a pound of success.

Keep Students Focused Constantly. One of the most challenging tactics for sustaining a good pace is to keep students focusing on something at all times—not just during the activity, but before and after as well. You see, unless students are focusing on some specific item or information, they lose their with-it-ness and do their own thing, like flipping through a magazine, snickering with a neighbor, or daydreaming out the window. That's when you resort to (a) calling out a name, (b) asking the student to stop, or (c) making some comment. Or all three! Perhaps you even stop to address the student(s). But if students **are** kept focused on something specific at all times, they won't lose their with-it-ness, and you won't have to interrupt your pacing.

Something specific could be any one of the following items:

- conceptual idea (during activity)
- information on chalkboard
- musical theme on chart or board
- visual aid or teaching prop
- handout materials
- teacher demonstration
- verbal instructions
- reinforcing strategy (by teacher)
- music textbook
- anticipated actions (by teacher)
- teacher explanation

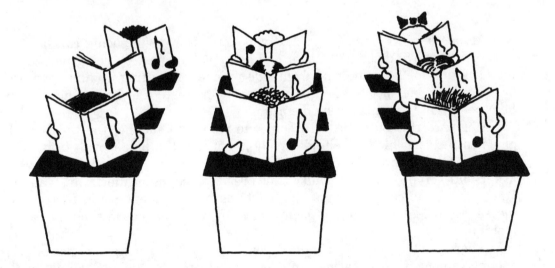

It really is possible to keep students focusing on something specific at every point in the lesson, whether it be when (a) reviewing a concept, (b) delivering instructions, (c) explaining a problem, (d) introducing a new idea, or (e) implementing an activity. Let's find out how to accomplish the job.

Getting the students to focus is not a problem when the students are involved in the activity. The activity itself will keep the students on task; but not so between activities. It takes more effort to get students to zero-in when you're explaining, asking questions, or giving instructions. More than just saying "Look here" or "Listen to this," it takes a personal touch, or some individual effort, such as:

- facial expressions
- eye contact
- bodily gestures
- vocal inflection
- vocal projection
- pauses (at opportune times)

- varying speech tempi
- dynamic differentiation
- repeating words/question
- bodily mobility
- bodily proximity
- definite pointing

Without this personal input it's practically impossible to get students to focus. The teacher's actions do the actual job of "wooing"—of drawing students' attention; but they need to be executed in a very precise and theatrical manner in order to accomplish the task. Here are some examples.

Besides using a projected voice, you also need to do such things as: (a) pointing specifically to the word(s) or note(s) on the chalkboard rather than circling vaguely above, (b) speaking with vocal inflection and dynamic variation instead of a drone-like voice, (c) utilizing bodily gestures and bodily movements as opposed to standing in one spot, and (d) using facial expressions and vocal pauses to be more emphatic in expressing yourself. A whole lot of one's self goes into keeping students focused. To be honest, you need to be a bit of a "ham" in order to make this suggestion work.

When the focusing isn't consistent and the personal mannerisms aren't convincing, the pacing goes up and down like a yo-yo. One minute the students are focusing and the momentum moving; the next minute, the momentum is floundering and students are dangling. Pacing like this is hard on students; it's emotionally draining—and tiring as well. To avoid the yo-yo syndrome, be sure to (1) maintain a constant focus on something specific at all times for your students, and (2) check out your personal actions. This could very well be the strategy that helps your pacing the most.

Move Around Regularly. Did you know that your pacing can be affected by occasionally moving about? That it can be kept alive just by being mobile? By walking back and forth, sauntering from side to side, or drifting up and down the aisles, or even from one spot to another, you can help create a feeling of motion, and even help perpetuate an ongoing momentum.

Compare this outcome with someone who isn't mobile, the teacher who stays glued to the seat, hidden behind a piano, or planted in one spot in front of the desk or by the chalkboard. Besides being a hindrance to the momentum, these teachers also create an air of predictability that breeds a feeling of inertia instead of energy.[8] You see, it's difficult to conjure up a feeling of movement when the teacher never moves. Many lessons go to pot pacing-wise for no other reason than a lack of teacher mobility.

There's one other way mobility promotes effective pacing, one not often thought about. Namely, it puts teachers in a position to touch students. A tap on the head, pat on the shoulder, ruffling of hair, or laying a hand over the student's become ways of speaking to individual students without having to stop the lesson. Momentum can continue whether the teacher is reprimanding for disruptive behavior or praising for exemplary participation.[9] So you see, mobility helps to perpetuate momentum by giving you opportunities to touch and do the job of speaking for you.

---

[8]Small, p. 33.
[9]Small, p. 33.

Mobility should be executed in a seemingly spontaneous and relaxed manner. It shouldn't be a deliberate stalk or a routine route; nor should it be a spastic jump in any one direction. Mobility must be a very casual, almost aimless effort, incorporating only short distances—not grand hikes from one corner of the room to the other. Too, it should be like an intuitive wandering that gives the lesson a sense of motion when motion is needed. Using hand and arm gestures while talking—and a lot of facial expressions and upper body movement—can also be helpful in creating a feeling of movement.

If you're looking for an effective, yet comfortable, way of maintaining your pace, try moving more. Mobility is a marvelous strategy for manipulating momentum.

Change Activity Quickly. Here's a common solution for handling the pacing when it gets too fast or too slow for the activity in progress and you aren't able to turn it around. Just change the activity. It may be that the experience is (a) not compatible with the class's ability, that it's too babyish or too adultish, that you under- or over-estimated your students; (b) not appropriate for the class's immediate disposition, that it's too energetic or too low-keyed for students' present temperament; or (c) not suitable for exposure reasons. Perhaps it's been overused and the students are too saturated with it, or maybe it's not familiar enough and they're too leery of it. The fact is, any one of these reasons could affect the way students respond.

So, if the pacing is doing a slow death with the present activity, then chuck it—immediately—and substitute another activity on the spot. Do the same when the pacing is running away and getting out of control. Yes, it is tricky to know exactly when to change. While it's often an instinctive decision for some teachers,[10] it's more often a matter of being able to assess for most other teachers. Ideally, it takes both a touch of intuitiveness and a lot of learning to know when it's right to change.

If you're not quite sure how to make this switch, here are some guidelines. **First**, have a back-up activity ready, especially for those that aren't from your tried-and-true list. Be prepared to substitute, if necessary. Take the back-up activities from your oldy-but-goldy collection. You need something to get your pacing back on track quickly. **Second**, switch the activity immediately once you sense and/or see that it's hindering the momentum. Don't hesitate; the longer you wait, the worse it will get! Trust your own insight as well as instinct! The big hang-up then comes in knowing what to say once the class is stopped. And **three**, simply indicate what to do and why the students are doing it. Think of it as a two-part statement including: (1) instruction to put aside the present activity, and (2) instruction for the substitute activity. Be sure also to include a brief comment as to the reason for this action. Here are some examples of verbiage that might be used in switching an activity:

- "Let's put this activity aside for today and do such-and-such like this . . . We need to get more perked up, don't we?"
- "Please put the rhythm sticks under your chairs and sit down quietly. We'll do this activity some other time when we're less hyper. Right now, we're going to . . ."
- "Close your books quietly. We'll continue with that activity when we're not quite so restless. For now, let's do . . . in this way."

See how the teacher first tells the class to put aside the first activity; and then tells what the class will do instead and why? The "why" part concerns the fourth guide-

---

[10]Lemlech, Johanna K., p. 191.

line: be forthright about your decision to change. Students can handle forthrightness. In fact, they often "see" more than the teacher realizes. But more important, they'll respond better when they know why they are having to change and have more respect for a teacher who tackles a situation rather than ignores it. So let your students know why you're switching the activity.

The next time your activity is holding back or speeding up your pacing, be ready to make a switch. You'll have no problem if you (1) prepare a back-up activity, (2) implement it without hesitating, (3) verbalize the instructions, and (4) exercise forthrightness with the students. It'll do the trick—providing the activity is the problem.

Use Group Responses Frequently. Probably one of the least thought of ways for sustaining one's momentum in the classroom is to utilize a group-to-individual approach when it comes to eliciting verbal responses. This is not to say that individual responses aren't as valid or as necessary. Rather, for pacing purposes, it seems to work best if the teacher goes from the class-to-individual rather than vice-versa because by working the class first, the teacher is able to (a) keep the whole class involved, (b) keep the momentum moving, and (c) set the stage for individual responses. That means when the individual is called upon after the class, there's a greater possibility that the students will respond more quickly and keep the momentum going.

When individual responses are pursued first, to the exclusion of class responses, this is what happens. The momentum comes to an abrupt halt while teacher and class wait for the answer, and if there's a lengthy prodding period with the individual student, the class's attention goes down the tube as well. You see, there's a right time and a wrong time for individual response, and calling for individual answers (a) at the opening of a lesson, (b) at the beginning of a review session, or (c) before any group drill or preparation has been attempted by the teacher, is the surest way to cause havoc with one's pacing. That's why working from the group to the individual can prevent pacing havoc.

Here's how going from the group-to-individual works. Ask a question that requires a short-answer response. Address it to the class by prefacing the question with such verbiage as: "Class," "Boys and girls," "Everyone now," or "All together." Then state your question. To get a better coordinated response, don't forget your conducting principles. That is, immediately after the question, take a prep breath while the head is going back, and then give the ictus with the head or the hand, or both, which tells the class when to respond. In other words, do what you would do if you were conducting a band or chorus. If you're not pleased with the response because of its feebleness or raggedness, make your assessment and repeat the question. Recognize the verbal bridging here? Getting an accurate, confident response is essential to the strategy. It's preparing the class for the individual questions that come afterwards.

The most advantageous time for individual questions would be immediately after the class response. Whether it be about the motivational idea just discussed, the old concept just reviewed, or the new idea just explained, the student will answer better because of verbalizing out loud with the others, and also because the class's response was approved by the teacher. Believe me, you'll get a better individual response when you have class recitations first.

So instead of opening up your lesson with individual questions, reviewing one-on-one, or asking only two or three students, have the whole class recite together before asking for individual responses. Not only will you be more pleased with the quality of the individual responses, but with the momentum of the lesson as well. Going from the group-to-the individual works wonders for pacing.

Concluding Challenge

You should be able to find some suggestions here for your own pacing needs. Whatever your problem is, it **can** be rectified. It doesn't matter if your pacing has a tendency to speed up or slow down, or if it's naturally on the slow side or the fast side. Start applying the preventive or corrective measures that seem most applicable to you. As you become more skillful in dealing with your pace, you'll become more sensitive and flexible in your own timing as a teacher, and that's significant because effective pacing is crucial to effective teaching.

LESS EFFECTIVE	*MORE EFFECTIVE*
Mr. Berny Stein instructed his sixth graders to listen to the CD. He had the themes written on the board, but didn't tell the class to follow them. When some boys began fooling around, he stopped the music and glared at them. "I want everyone listening," he snapped. Even after that, he forgot to focus attention on the themes. A little while later, he had to stop again to say, "Cut it out" to some giggling girls. Problem was, the students got bored just listening. In fact, one of the students told him so. "We're never going to hear all of this music if I have to keep stopping to yell at you," Mr. Stein said disgustedly. The lesson had bogged down completely.	Before Mr. Berny Stein turned on the CD player, he called the class's attention to the themes on the board. "I want you to follow these themes as you listen, and raise your right hand every time you hear an upward passage. Any questions?" Everyone understood because the class was doing a unit on ascending/descending passages. All eyes were on the board. Mr. Berny Stein liked the way the class was listening and watching. When the ascending passage sounded, every hand shot up. Mr. Stein gave the class a big smile and a thumbs up sign. When the music stopped, the class wanted to hear it again. "Certainly," Mr. Berny Stein said. It was a good lesson—It was moving smoothly.
"Okay, let's hand design the melodic pattern this time," Mr. Mac Dowall told the fourth grade class. "Stop that moaning right now." He was thoroughly annoyed with this class today. "Get your hands in position." Then he instructed them to tap the beat until they heard the melodic pattern. "I don't see everyone's hands in starting position. Mike and Sean, get your hands ready." When the music started, the class got silly and started clapping the beat and twirling fingers on the pattern. "What's going on here?" Mr. Mac Dowall yelled. "Stop this silliness. Let's try it again." But the class got even sillier. "Sit down. Everyone!" shouted Mr. Dowall. "We can't even get through one activity today. I don't know what's wrong with everyone today!"	"This time, class, we're going to hand design the melodic pattern every time we hear it. In between times, we'll tap the ongoing beat, like this. Mr. Mac Dowall could sense that the class wasn't too thrilled about designing. "Let's try it, okay? Hands in starting position." But when the music started, some of the students started to get a little silly. Especially the boys. Immediately, Mr. Mac Dowall instructed the class over the music to follow him. "Take your pencils and tap out the rhythm of the pattern. Watch me." He demonstrated the next time the pattern appeared. Without having to stop the music, the class joined right in. Mr. Mac Dowall could tell the class liked this activity better. They participated better. When the music ended, he praised the fourth graders for being so flexible. "Good job! We kept the class moving."

Using the Motivational Idea

Introducing a new conceptual idea by relating it to a familiar situation or phenomenon ought to be a common practice for classroom music teachers. Those of you who already do this can vouch for its effectiveness. The motivational item really helps students connect with the new idea quickly. But the catch is that the motivation example needs to be enough "like" the concept and accurately related for the students to get the idea. That calls for skillful know-how in selecting and presenting motivational ideas.

Definition of Motivational Idea

I think of a motivational idea as some familiar item in the class's environment that is similar in looks, or function, or sound to the new concept being introduced, such as:

- a person
- an object

Items with STEADY BEAT

- windshield wipers
  (*swish-swish-swish*)
- pendulum in clock
  (*tick-tock-tick-tock*)
- bass drum in parade
  (*boom-boom-boom-boom*)
- ringing church bell
  (*ring-ring-ring-ring*)

Items with ACCENTED BEATS

- railroad train chooing
  (*CHOO-choo-choo*)
- basketball bouncing
  (*BOUNCE-bounce-bounce*)
- Indian drum beating
  (*BEAT-beat-beat-beat*)
- fire engine bell
  (*DING-ding-DING-ding*)

Items with Own Sound MELODIC RHYTHM

- trail wheels
  (*Clickety-Clack clickety-clack*)
- rooster crowing
  (*cock-a-doodle-do, cock-a-doodle-do*)
- word pronouncing
  (*hamburger, Jello*™*, Baltimore*)
- robin singing
  (*chirp-a-chirp-a-chirp*)

Items With UPWARD DIRECTION

- escalator going up
- airplane taking off
- going up stair steps
- climbing mountain

Items Having DOWNWARD DIRECTION

- escalator going down
- airplane landing
- sliding down slide
- riding down roller coaster

Items With ABA LARGE FORM

- White House
- city street with buildings
- arrangement of objects:
  cat, dog, cat
  boy, girl, boy
  square, circle, square
- Oreo™ cookie:
  cookie, cream, cookie

Items with MELODIC PATTERNS

- color recurring on clothing
- patch reappearing on quilt
- bell ringing between classes
- tile design on floor

Figure 6.3. Examples of Motivational Ideas for Musical Concepts.

- a condition
- a phenomenon

Figure 6.3 gives you a sampling of motivational ideas for the following concepts.

Do you notice how each of these examples depicts objects that move upward or downward? Have a natural strong-weak beat? Possess their own rhythmic sound? Each one is an obvious image, or clear illustration, of a particular concept with which students can easily identify. That's what makes for a good motivational idea—something familiar that clarifies the new concept.

Significance of Motivational Idea

After years of teaching, I am convinced that using a motivational idea is still one of the most effective strategies in teaching for the following reasons:

One, the motivational idea gives an immediate impression of the concept. What it says to students is, "This is what the concept is like!" Right away, there's an awareness of the new idea; that is, some inkling of what such-and-such is about and what they should be listening for in the music. In other words, there's an immediate tuning-in to the idea. You can't really begin to appreciate this outcome unless you've tried introducing a new concept without a motivational idea!

Two, the motivational idea saves teaching time in the lesson. The immediate awareness that happens as a result of using a similar idea in the students' environment definitely speeds up the learning process. You don't have to do as much explaining about the concept, especially if you use a visual aid in presenting the motivational idea, such as a drawing of a grandfather clock for the steady beat, having a basketball for the accented-unaccented beats, or bringing a quilt to show the patch pattern. Students grasp the meaning of the new concept in a flash when a concrete example from their own environment is used. That's the beauty of this strategy—it helps lock in the new idea in short order, with very little being said other than some key statements, and gives you more teaching time for the rest of the lesson.

Three, the motivational idea captures the class's attention at the outset without fail! Using a familiar idea with a prop does wonders to "grab" the students' attention. Not only does the motivational item get their attention, but it also generates a whole lot of interest that carries over into the activities.

You couldn't ask for any better reasons than these. Illuminating the concept, conserving the time, and generating the interest are heavy outcomes that should "sell" this approach to anyone who teaches music in the classroom.

Guidelines for Motivational Ideas

To get the most out of this strategy, you need to adhere to some guidelines because your motivational idea won't work as well without them. If you're not having the success you'd like with your motivational ideas, perhaps you can get some help from the following guidelines.

Guideline #1. Prepare an introductory statement; in other words, know how you're going to "get into" the motivational idea smoothly. Do it informatively so that the class knows what's happening. You can use some key statements, after announcing the new concept, like the following:

- "Let's see how the steady beat is like. . ."
- "I'd like us to compare the melodic rhythm with . . ."

- "First, let's discuss upward direction in melody with . . ."
- "We can get a better idea about rhythmic patterns if we look at . . ."

See how these kinds of statements set you up for the motivational idea? Now you're ready to deal with it.

Guideline #2. Plan the class approach. Decide on how you will present the motivational idea with the class. There are several ways you could go here, depending upon the grade level and the particular concept. You could use any combination of the following approaches:

- class discussion
- question/answer
- class imitation
- prop presentation

Conducting an interesting discussion is always a good approach with older students. They can "discover" the similarities through their own comments, and the question-answer technique can be used effectively at all grade levels! But have your questions prepared—don't try to wing it. You'll need to ask the "right" questions to make your point. The imitation simply means that the class vicariously experiences the idea to get a better "feel" for the concept, such as moving the hands like windshield wipers, imitating train wheels for strong-weak beats, or "walking" up the stairs for dealing with upward direction in melodies. (This kind of movement is especially good for the younger children.) Props in the form of pictures, objects, or handouts "work" with any age group and with any of the other tactics as well.

Guideline #3. Consider the allotted time. You've got to remember that the motivational idea is not the whole lesson, so you've got to have time for your activities. That means you better put a time limit on how long your motivational presentation can last. In a thirty-minute lesson, you really can't afford more than three or four minutes. That's the reason for guidelines 1 and 2. You need to be well prepared in order to get to the main order of the day—your activities. You move in and out of the motivational idea without belaboring the discussion or the imitating.

Guideline #4. Prepare a summarizing statement, a crucial step in doing your motivational idea. It solidifies the relationship and says, "This is like this." Students need to hear that kind of statement from you. It pulls the motivational episode together and gives it a real purpose in the eyes of the student. Consider any of the following typical summarizing statements:

- "Did you know that the steady beat has accented beats just like . . ."
- "And listen to this. We have upward passages in music that move just like an upward escalator."
- "Here's the interesting part now. Our listening selections can have an ABA structure just like the White House."
- "Now then, the melody in music also has its own rhythmic sound that we've been discovering in our words."

This summary statement is what clinches the motivational idea and is really all that needs to be said once an idea has been presented. Use any statements you wish. Just be sure to tell the students that the same phenomenon happens in music, either in the melody, the rhythm, or the form.

So there you have it! Take these guidelines to heart because they really make the difference. But if this strategy is going to do its job, you'll need to be prepared. That means planning the introductory and summary statements, the specific time limit, and the presentation strategy.

Concluding Challenge

Is the motivational strategy part of your teaching procedures? If it isn't, it's not too late. Reread those outcomes again, and get a grasp of what really happens with a motivational idea, that is, what the outcomes are. Then select one class where you will try out your motivational idea. Take your new conceptual idea, and subject it to the four guidelines. You can use some of the same verbal examples, if you want. Then just plan your strategy, and you're ready. You'll like the results, especially when the students grasp the new idea so readily as a result of the familiar example. Try it and see.

LESS EFFECTIVE

Ms. Choo-choo used the idea of broom sweeping to introduce the new concept of steady beat to her first graders. The children talked about sweeping, pretended to sweep themselves, and watched others do the sweeping. When they finished the motivational idea, Ms. Choo-choo told the children to sit down. "Now I want you to listen to this recording and we're going to do our sweeping, okay? Stand up again." The first graders looked confused at each other, but, nevertheless, they stood up. "What's wrong with them?" Ms Choo-choo wondered.

Mr. Ding-dong's new concept for today's lesson dealt with similar phrases. He referred to a suit of clothing for his motivational idea, and showed the class how it can be changed slightly and still be the same outfit. After a lovely question-and-answer session, Mr. Ding-dong continued by saying, "This is what happens in musical phrases. Listen to this song." Then he sat down and had the class sit and listen. When the song was over, he announced to his yawning eighth graders that they had just listened to a good example of similar phrases. By that time, the class really didn't care!

MORE EFFECTIVE

Ms. Choo-choo's first graders enjoyed talking about how they sweep the floor at home. They pretended to sweep in earnest and watched each other sweep. When they finished talking about how steady their sweeping was instead of jerky, Ms. Choo-choo said to the class, "Did you know that we have steady, ongoing beats in our music, just like the steady back-and-forth movement of our broom? We're going to hear this steady beat in the recording. Let's stand quietly and get our brooms ready to sweep on the steady beat. Ready?" Ms. Choo-choo could tell they were excited about "sweeping" to the beat.

In preparing for the introduction of the new concept on similar phrases, Mr. Ding-dong guided the eighth graders through discussion using his own suit of clothing as an example. The class discovered how his suit could be changed slightly to look different, yet still be the same outfit. When the discussion ended, he said to the class, "Do you know that we can apply this same principle to our musical phrases? We can change them slightly so that they're almost the same but not quite. We call these 'similar phrases.' Let's follow along with call-charts as we listen to this song on the recording." Mr. Ding-dong was pleased with their attention.

7

Teaching Behaviors for More Complicated Tasks

This chapter will concentrate on teaching tasks that require a series of sequential steps; in other words, multiple-step tasks, especially the ones used in the classroom by the music specialist or the elementary teacher. The reason these skills have been singled out from others is not because they're more important, but because they're more involved. Any task that requires a series of actions for completion is generally more demanding in terms of concentration and skill, and the ones discussed in this chapter are no exception. They call for insight and ability.

In that light, I've dedicated this chapter to helping classroom teachers cope with these complicated tasks. Both the music and non-music teacher must be able to implement sequential steps competently, even skillfully, in order to provide rewarding musical experiences. These tasks include such responsibilities as passing out classroom instruments, dealing with singing problems, preparing students to participate in an activity, and many others. Each of the tasks presented will include clear-cut guidelines or procedures, and sometimes, a chart or diagram to further clarify these procedures. Keep in mind, however, that regardless of the effort here to organize and simplify the steps, they are still very demanding responsibilities that require all the competency a teacher can muster.

Therefore, all you general music teachers and elementary classroom teachers who teach your own music should study these tasks—and even commit the suggested steps to memory, if you don't already have a set procedure in place. One other step, particularly for you pre-service people and beginning teachers: practice these sequenced steps, literally. Stand in front of a mirror and talk-out-loud until you can execute the actions and verbiage consistently and automatically. As for you experienced teachers, you, too, can add yet another touch of finesse to your teaching by incorporating some of these procedures, even if you already have a "system" of your own for most of these tasks.

Passing Out Classroom Instruments

Ever try distributing classroom instruments for some activity in the lesson without having a strategy up your sleeve? If not, let me tell you what happens. Bedlam! Sheer bedlam! Within seconds! Sooner, rather than later, you find yourself shouting "Stop it!" to save your sanity and restore order. Believe me, it isn't worth all the chaos to be without a plan. You've simply got to have an orderly approach for handing out instruments if you want to keep the lesson moving and avoid any confusion. Let's take a closer look at what goes on when you don't have a strategy.

Situation Without a Strategy

There's not another teaching task in teaching music that can turn into a fiasco as quickly as this one, mostly because kids on all levels are fascinated by classroom instruments. Just the thought of having an instrument—any instrument—in their hands gets them higher than a kite. So when instruments are handed out in some haphazard way, you can expect pandemonium. Little children will start "Oohing" and jumping up and down like a jackrabbit, or grabbing out just for a touch of an instrument. And if they get their hands on one, they'll start clicking, banging, or shaking the thing until the noise drives you mad.

And what happens with older kids? The same nonsense. Not as babyish, but just as nervewracking. You won't get the "Oohing" effect, you'll get the smart wisecracks, the jeering, and the loud imitating of some rock star that only the kids recognize.

So here are the consequences—whether it's at the lower level or the upper level. If there's no strategy, you can bet that:

a. **Class Control Goes Out the Window**. Students will do their own "thing" without ground rules, and most of the time it will be disruptive. Unless the passing out is done in an orderly and efficient way, you will lose control of the class, to a greater or lesser degree, and stop the smooth flow of the lesson.

b. **Conceptual Progress Stops in its Track**. Teaching stops when the class gets out of control. More specifically, the conceptual progressions come to a halt because the students' attention gets diverted by the sloppy procedures. Naturally, everything comes to a screeching halt until the instruments get distributed and the class is under control again.

c. **Teaching Time Gets Short-End-of-Stick**. Teachers rob themselves of their own teaching time when they don't have a strategy, especially when there's only a minimal amount of time allotted per week for music. It's like shooting themselves in the foot! It's a costly oversight (or blunder) on the teacher's part to goof up in this area!

That's the picture, or should I say "problems," that you create for yourself by not having a modus operandi. Here's the point: there are enough "things" that can and do happen, even with a planned strategy, without laying yourself open to these predictable handicaps. So start exploring some approaches if you don't already have one. Three are given to you in the next section.

Suggested Approaches for Passing Out Instruments

Here are three approaches that accommodate any classroom setting and that "work," whether you have two or twenty instruments.

1. Place instruments under chairs BEFORE the lesson.
2. Pass out instruments DURING the lesson (by selected students).
3. Select students to play instrument up front DURING the lesson (while rest of class continues "playing" vicariously).

Let's look at each of these individually.

Approach #1: Placing Instruments Under Chairs BEFORE the Lesson.

I'm assuming you have your own room for this approach, and that you'll have time before school to get the instruments in place. (Why not get a student helper?) Here's what you do. After each class uses the instruments, instruct the students to put them back under the chairs so that they'll be in place for the next class. That way you won't have to scramble around! But let me warn you. You'll need to instruct each class not to touch the instruments until you tell them—and abide by your consequences. If you don't you'll have some wise guys messing around and ringing, rattling, or clicking the instruments until you're ready to scream. The best time to tell students "Hands off" is at the very beginning, right after the greeting. That doesn't mean you won't have to tell them again; repeating instructions goes with the territory in this case. Some students won't listen just because you told them. You'll need to **keep** telling them.

Now about the matter of every student having an instrument. That's always an issue. Do you put an instrument under every chair? Or just some? It's not necessary to give everyone an instrument, especially young children, because they're pretenders. They love playing "let's pretend." Even if you did have 25 pairs of rhythm sticks, you might not want to use all of them; they can get too loud and overpower the music, and the children aren't able to hear in order to respond correctly. That's why I like more pretending and less instruments at the lower level; however, if you do use all 25 sticks, then be adamant about children playing **softly**. It **can** be done.

Soft playing applies at the upper level, too, if everyone has an instrument, that is. But even with the older kids you don't need an instrument for everyone. They can participate by imitating. Just be sure that the imitating is done in a realistic and serious way. Not silly and babyish. That's the key right there!

Whether you put instruments under the chairs of a few or everyone, it's still an excellent approach, especially if you have your own music room or classroom. It's also the most time-saving approach of the three; plus, there are fewer interruptions when the instructions are followed.

Approach #2: Passing Out Instruments DURING the Lesson (by selected students). The second approach uses student helpers to pass out instruments during the lesson. It's an effective strategy, but I've got to warn you, its success is contingent upon several steps. **First**, you've got to have definite **guidelines for the passing out** the *very first time* you use helpers. That way everybody gets to hear what's expected, regardless of who is passing out the instruments. The instructions have to be explicit. For example, you need to say that so-and-so will take rows one and two, and so-and-so, rows three and four, etc. Or that helper number one will take the right half of the semicircle up to Jim, and helper number two, the other half from Jim on. And that you want the helpers to put the instruments on the students' desk, or in their laps, or on the floor. By spelling out the guidelines at the outset, in front of the whole class, you avoid having to repeat the same instructions for each new helper. Will students forget? Not on your life! They'll take great pride in remembering how the teacher "wants it done!"

Second, you need a definite **procedure for selecting helpers**. Should you always use the same people? Or choose different ones from lesson to lesson? This is your decision. Personally, I prefer using different students because it gives me an opportunity to do some simplified behavior modification. I use it as a "reward" for good behavior—and it works! You'd be surprised how hard students will try to be "good" just to be chosen for "teacher's helper." Not teacher's pet, now. There's a difference. Even students know that. To be a "helper" is a compliment, not a stigma.

But, having permanent helpers has its advantages too. Generally speaking, they do a better job because they're usually the more mature kids who take pride in doing something without having to be told, and who enjoy the recognition and the status. What's more, they're dependable. They'll always be there and get the job done—without fuss or muss.

The choice is yours. You can get the instruments out with either arrangement.

The secret is to explain the procedures the first time instruments are used. Then you can decide how you will select your helpers.

Approach #3: Selecting Students to Come Up Front to Play Instrument DURING the Lesson. This third approach requires the most input on the teacher's part. It involves selecting qualified students from the class (to come forward) to play the real instruments while the others "play" vicariously or pretend. It's a good choice when there's just a limited number of instruments. But you need some guidelines.

The **first guideline** is be sure that the selected **students are ready to come forward** and that they know exactly what's expected of them. Most important, they should be prepared *before* they come forward. You do this by prepping the whole class before selecting the students. Simply tell them you'll be looking for some good players for the real instruments before the prepping starts. Watch how quickly they straighten up and try to impress you. Trust me, it's real easy to pick out the one(s) who would be good models. Not only that, it's a good way to avoid those disastrous one-on-one "do this" sessions where the teacher goes rushing up to "tutor" the students in hushed tones with his/her back to the class. It always reminds me of a boxing trainer hovering over the boxer in the ring. You mustn't do this, though; it's poor teaching. Prep the whole class instead. That way everybody knows what to do if he/she is selected. It'll save time in the long run and help keep everyone more involved as well.

Here's the **second guideline**. Be sure that the selected **students are told what to do** once they get up front, i.e., where to stand, what direction to face, when to start, when to stop, etc. The best time to give this information is immediately after the class prep and just before selecting the student(s). That's when everyone will be listening to your every word in hopes of being chosen.

If, for example, you want to select a student to play the I-V7 accompaniment on the real autoharp, and there's only one, prep the whole class first by having them play their imaginary autoharps on the desktops. (Of course, you'd tell the class beforehand that you're looking for someone.) When the prep is over, immediately give instructions like:

> "... come to my desk, please, stand directly behind the autoharp, and play the same accompaniment we've just rehearsed. Remember, you have to use pressure when you strum."

Then all you need to do is call out a name, and the student will come up and do it—without any private tête-à-tête.

The **third guideline** is to be sure **instruments are in place beforehand**. In other words, have the instruments laid out (a) on the floor, (b) on your desk, or (c) on the chairs so that the procedure will go more smoothly, and students will know where to go after being told and shown. Here's an illustration. Suppose you're using an activity with rhythm sticks, but you only have three pairs. Don't fret. Remember, everyone doesn't have to have "real" sticks. Let the students pretend or imitate. What I like to do is put the sticks on the floor at an equal distance somewhere up front. Then, just before the students are called up, I say to the class "... the first person will stand behind the first pair (pointing to the spot), the second person, behind the second pair, etc." Then I call the students up. And bingo! They "go to it" without my having to say a word.

You'll like this tactic once you try it. But you'll have to prep students carefully and place the instruments properly. That's the only way it will work! Remember, you have more say-so in this approach. That's what makes it so challenging. Try it and see.

Concluding Challenge

There shouldn't be any question about the need for an orderly system in distributing classroom instruments, or for being competent in carrying out the mechanics. But how about you? Do you have your own system? Does it work? Does it get the job done smoothly and quickly? Or do you need some help?

If you don't have a procedure, why not try one (or all!) of the approaches? They all work! It's just a matter of finding which one fits your particular teaching style and classroom setting the best. Don't waste any more teaching time or lose control of your class every time instruments are passed out. Get a procedure, and see the difference.

LESS EFFECTIVE	MORE EFFECTIVE
"Jim, John, will you get the rhythm sticks for everyone?" Ms. Tempoz asked. Soon she heard giggling, dropping of sticks, and bickering. "Just give everyone two sticks. Never mind the color," she shouted. "Jimmy, start on this side of the room." It wasn't long before she had to yell at the children for grabbing sticks from Jim and John. "I should have passed the sticks out myself," she moaned. "Aren't you finished yet? We don't have all day for passing out rhythm sticks!"	When it was time for the rhythm sticks, Ms. Tempoz asked Mike and Susan to help. "Susan, you take the first three rows, and Mike, the last three. Give everyone two sticks and put them in the pencil slot, not their hands. And do it quickly and quietly!" By the time she finished her demo, everyone had rhythm sticks. "Thank you, Susan and Mike, for doing such a good job." She was thankful she had set up her passing-out procedure early. Even so, she still had to remind them like she did today.
Mr. DaCapoz said, "I want Sharon, Bill, and Jack to come up and play the tambourines. Stand here, not over there, Jack. Come get the tambourines. Sharon, you'll play like this." Then he moved on to Bill. Meanwhile the mumbling got louder. "That's enough," he shouted. "Can't you see I'm busy? Jack, pick up that tambourine!" By the time he finished with Jack, the class was out of control. "That's the last time I'll let anyone come up and play instruments," Mr. DaCapoz said as he snatched up the tambourines. "Take your seats."	"Today we're going to play a rhythmic accompaniment on tambourines. Let's practice it together first, and then I'll select three people to come up and play the real tambourines." After several practices, Mr. DaCapoz said, "When I call your name, take your place behind the tambourine I'm pointing to and wait until I tell you to pick it up." With that, he called three students who promptly took their places. On cue, they picked up the tambourines and stood ready to play. They tapped the ostinato perfectly.

Applying Fix-It Process to Singing

One thing you can count on happening in classroom music is having singing problems. The singing usually isn't that good, which means you've got to have some way of dealing with it or some sort of fix-it procedure for the problems. Here's the bottom line. If classroom singing is going to get better, you must have a way of correcting it or improving it. That makes the fixing process a vital tool for singing problems.

Importance of Fix-It Procedure

Let's be sure we really understand the importance of handling singing problems in the classroom, whether it be the pitches, intonation, or both. What we all rattle off is that fixing makes the singing sound better. And it does! But as commendable, and practical, as this reason may be, that's only part of the answer.

The other important reason we just take for granted is that specific problems are addressed. You see, unless the problems are corrected or improved, the students continue to sing out of tune or with wrong pitches, and to reinforce their mistakes so that they never "do" the song right. But the greater tragedy is this: students are robbed of the pleasurable and uplifting experience that comes from group singing when they can't sing in a reasonably accurate way themselves. This mustn't happen. The joy of singing together is an integral part of the students' musical heritage in school music. Yes, fixing is obviously needed to improve the class's singing, but don't lose sight of the fact that it's equally important for preserving the joy of singing as well. So continue to work on those problems. The better they can sing, the more they'll enjoy singing together.

Situation Without Fix-It Procedure

I won't dwell on the point. We all know how awful classroom singing can get, especially if nothing is done to correct the pitches or improve the intonation, and if the only instruction is to "sing louder!" That just lends to out-of-tune yelling, not singing. But enough about the poor singing; it's the teachers I want to talk about now.

I don't know why some teachers tolerate poor singing, nor can I figure out why they don't find a fix-it routine. Maybe they're just burned-out and don't feel like tackling the problems. Or maybe they honestly think that's the way students are "supposed to sing!" That kind of thinking really scares me. But then how many of you are just stumped and don't know what to do? I suspect there are more in this last group than we'd all care to admit. So, if you're looking for some help, here's a procedure.

Suggested Fix-It Approach

Check out the following "fix-it" approach. It's simple and sequential in that it moves logically from one step to the next.

- Step 1: Identify the Problem
- Step 2: Relate the Problem (to the Class)
- Step 3: Demonstrate the Problem (for the Class)
- Step 4: Drill the Correction (with the Class)
- Step 5: Reinstate the Correction

Step 1: Identify the Problem(s). To begin with, you've got to hear the deficiencies as they happen. Or "spot" them. Specifically, that means being able to put your finger on the exact word(s), pitch(es), or measure(s) where the problems occur and ascertain the particular shortcomings.

Actually, it's a two-pronged operation. **First**, you recognize the problem, or decide **what** it is, and **second**, you register the place, or determine **where** it is. That doesn't mean you do these one at a time; rather, both operations happen almost **simultaneously**, not separately. That's what must happen when you "identify" the problem, or else you can't correct it.

This identification happens preferably the moment the infraction occurs—on-the-spot; otherwise, you fall into the "let's do it again" syndrome where the class repeats the whole song just so you can hear what you missed the first time. That's a waste of time! You've got to identify the problem the class is singing.

Look what you accomplish when you isolate the problem. For one thing, you identify what's broken. For another, you pinpoint the location of the problem in your mind, and third, you get to the problem(s) more quickly. That's because you know what and where it is even before the class stops singing. Do yourself a favor and cultivate this skill. It's essential for teaching music.

Step 2: Relate the Problem. This is the place where you let the students know that they didn't do right, or what needs to be done better. Positive reinforcement is important, too, but it's not relevant to this fixing discussion. What's relevant here is the timing. You need to tell students **immediately** after they stop singing or when the song ends.

Attitude is also important. Keep in mind that this isn't a soapbox situation where you browbeat the class for its singing bloopers. Rather, it's a sharing time when students learn what their problem(s) are and what needs to be improved. No more or no less. In other words, don't embellish or abbreviate. You say that students won't understand what you're saying? Rubbish! Bruner[1] said children can understand any subject as long as it's expressed in an intellectually honest way which they can comprehend.

Let's talk now about **what you would say**, which is always a tricky part for some. But if you've identified the problem(s) accurately, it's a piece of cake. You've got all the information, you know what and where. So, if the sixth graders sing wrong pitches on the "tis of thee," you'd simply say, "Very good. You sang all the correct pitches, except on the words such-and-such." Or, "We're singing flat, or under pitch, on those high notes." See how easy? Just say what you've heard, and be straightforward and precise. You can't miss if you follow this rule. Even kindergartners will understand.

One more thing. Don't underestimate the importance of relating the problem. There are good reasons for it. What telling does is make students (a) more "with-it" because they've been informed regarding their performance, (b) more manageable because they can "see" the rationale for the procedure, and (c) more aware of their own singing and listening habits. The fact is, relating the problem is an integral part of the teaching-learning process in general, not just the fix-it procedure. But remember, it has to happen as soon as the class stops singing.

Step 3: Demonstrate the Problem (for the Class). Almost in the same breath with telling, you demonstrate for the class. That's the third step. It could be,

---

[1]Bruner, Jerome. *The Process of Education* (Cambridge, MA, Harvard University Press, 1963), p. 33.

however, that you need to know what you'd demonstrate. Basically, you have three choices. You could model:

1. what the class did (the wrong way)
2. what the class should do (the right way)
3. what the class did and what it should do (the wrong way and right way)

Which you use depends on the situation. Sometimes just the error will suffice, and other times the correction. The most explicit demonstration, though, is the comparison where students are shown both ways.

Regardless of which demonstration is used, the fact is that demonstrating is a crucial step in the fixing process. It's where the teacher puts the "right" sound, as well as the "wrong" sound, into the students' ears so they'll know the difference. In short, it's a modeling tactic. (Modeling and demonstrating are often used interchangeably in many texts.) Unless students hear what you want, they'll just approximate what they've been told and give a mediocre performance just good enough to "get by." But when you demonstrate, you make it possible for them to perform up to your standard. That's why demonstrating, or modeling, is so important—it "models" the standard.[2] And thus, improves the response.

Let's look at the verbiage connected with demonstrating. It can be a problem! Want to know what to say just before you do your demonstration? It's easy. Just remember that it's going to be an instructional statement. Here are some examples that cover each demonstrating way:

- "Let's not sing in our chest voice. Here's how harsh it sounds. . . ." (*demonstrating problem*)
- "Your last three notes are still flat, like this . . ." (*demonstrating problem*)
- "Listen and watch as I sing those three notes correctly." (*demonstrating correction*)
- "Let me sing the phrase on one breath like it should be sung. Listen." (*demonstrating correction*)
- "Here's what you sang on 'Jingle all the way . . .' But the right pitches sound like this . . . Listen and watch." (*demonstrating problem/correction*)
- "This is how flat you were. . . . Now listen and watch how it sounds on pitch." (*demonstrating problem/correction*)

All you do is tell the students what you're going to show them—either the right way, wrong way, or both. Notice, though, that I keep saying, "Listen and watch" because you should be using some visual aid to reinforce the correction. When the problem involves wrong pitches, it's just not enough to sing the pitches correctly. What really helps is to use some kind of visual aid, or even some bodily movement, to reinforce the direction of the pitches.

Probably the most common body movement that most teachers fall back on is hand designing. That's where you place the hand about chest high with palms down, fingers closed, and arm parallel with the floor. You raise and lower your arm in approximate conjunction with the steps, skips, and leaps. Here's an illustration.

Let's say the first graders are having a problem with the pick-up interval in

---

[2]Bugelski, B.R. *Some Practical Laws on Learning* (Bloomington, IN: The Phi Delta Kappa Education Foundation, 1977), p. 18.

"*Farmer in the Dell*," i.e., the ascending fourth. After instructing the class to listen and watch, sing, very slowly, the pitches (for "the farmer"), first on "lu" several times, and then with the words while at the same time hand designing the approximate distance of the interval on "the" and "farmer" (or positioning the hand chest-level for the first pitch and raising it about eye-level on the second pitch while singing either "lu" or the words).

This technique makes it possible for the class to see as well as "hear" the correct pitches. Notice the sequence moving from "lu" to the words. It's a little technique that really works in correcting pitches on the spot, probably because it's easier for children to sing pitches with a sustained vowel than with the given words. So keep this strategy in mind. The point is that some kind of visual assistance is helpful when demonstrating for students, even if it's something so simple as stooping down and shooting up or manipulating some visual item up and down. This **oral-visual approach** to demonstrating is one of the secrets to handling your singing problems.

One word of caution, though, with hand designing. Hand design **only** the problem, not the whole phrase or the whole song. There's no need to hand design once the problem has been "designed." It destroys the impact (of the technique) when you do, and it frustrates the students because they can't design more than three or four pitches at a time. Don't forget, hand designing depends upon their listening skill which isn't well developed yet. If you remember nothing else, remember to hand design just the problem spot (maybe a pitch or two after, but no more).

While we're on the subject of intervals, let's mention the ones that cause the most problems in classroom singing. Besides the pick-up of a perfect fourth (P4th), there's the ascending perfect fifth (P5th), the notorious half-step, and those deceiving repeated tones. Of course, large leaps of 6ths, 7ths, and octaves are always a problem! But isolating these intervals and hand designing them will make a difference.

Demonstrating (with visual reinforcement), then, is step three in the fix-it procedure. Use a properly supported head voice; no chest voices in the demonstrations!

Step 4: Drill the Correction (with the Class). Now you're ready to have the class "work on" the correct way. What that means is you initiate a brief mini-drill for students so that they can imitate your demonstration. This is the hands-on part of the procedure, or the place where you reinforce the correct way.

Reinforcing is very important. Unless you drill or reinforce the right response, it's likely the class may never do it right. And the **degree** to which students will be able to sing correctly will depend on how well you "drill" them. Let's talk about what's involved.

First, you've got to tell the class to repeat the demonstrations. Just ask the students to sing what you just sang, or to repeat it with you. (Don't forget the starting pitch.) For example, you could ask:

"Think you can do this with me?"

"Let's sing this with me. Ready."

"Can I hear you do this? Ready."

"With me now. Ready."

"Everyone with me now. Ready."

See how easy? But the key is your tone of voice. You've got to use a pleasant, yet authoritative, tone that leaves no doubt whatsoever in the students' minds that this is what they're supposed to do and what the teacher is expecting to hear or see. An authoritative voice is a "must."

The second thing you tell students is whether they should just sing, or sing and hand design (or whatever else you want them to do, such as pulling up on imaginary puppet strings above your head to correct a flatting pitch). Otherwise, there will be confusion. Some will imitate, and some won't. If you do use some technique (with your singing), then be very clear about students doing it when they drill.

How many times does the class do the drill? The only honest answer I can give you is, generally not more than three times. After that students start getting bored. But listen, there's usually a moment when you know they've "got it," just like Eliza Doolittle in *My Fair Lady*. Trust your own educated judgment here. You'll know when to stop! Just keep in mind that this is where the problem must be corrected, or improved. If it isn't, the whole procedure is a waste.

Step 5: Reinstate the Correction. This is your payback step, or your reward. It's where you return the corrected or improved item back to the phrase it belongs. You see, the formula for fixing a problem is a matter of:

    a. taking problem out of context or phrase;

    b. drilling problem as prescribed in the demonstration; and

    c. throwing it back into the phrase.

Reinstating creates a cycle of taking out and putting back. You've got to test the drilled correction to see if it "took." If so, then you're ready to assess the class by something like the following:

"Excellent! You sang all the right pitches this time in the last phrase. Now do you think you can sing the whole song correctly? Let's try."

Get the idea? It's like putting the problem back in the slot after giving it a "working out." This is the step that makes the whole process worthwhile, especially when the problem gets "fixed."

Concluding Challenge

Although the explanation has taken time, the procedure itself takes only a minute or two. That's because it deals directly with the problem, and moves logically from the part to the whole. The irony of repeating the entire song to "fix" a few notes is like swabbing the whole deck to remove a single spot! So, if you want to handle your problems competently, try this procedure.

But there's one last consideration. Be sure you're clear as to how the fix-it procedure fits in with the verbal bridging. A verbal bridge is a verbal mechanism for assessing and instructing after each response (See "Using Verbal Bridges in Chapter 3.) Here's how the two have a definite "working" relationship. Starting with hearing what's wrong (identifying), you'd then assess the class (relating) and instruct them to listen and watch (demonstrating). What's next is the imitating (or drilling) followed by an assessment that the class "got it" and the instruction to put back (reinstating). Notice the class response, teacher response, class response, etc., pattern. Actually, the fix-it procedure is "superimposed" on the verbal bridging.

So use this fixing approach. You'll be amazed how it structures your teaching when it comes to singing problems—and what rewarding mileage you get from it!

LESS EFFECTIVE	MORE EFFECTIVE
Mr. Art Song's fifth graders were working on their new song. When they finished the first verse, Mr. Art Song yelled "Cut. Let's do that much again. It still wasn't very good." The class groaned. "Do we have to do it over? We don't like this song." Mr. Art Song put his "stop" hand out. "Yes, we do have to do it again. I don't care if you like it or not. Sarah, Jane, stop rolling your eyes. And everyone sit up." Mr. Art Song was disgusted.	The fifth graders in Mr. Art Song's music class were learning a new song. Mr. Art Song winced when he heard a problem. "Let's stop here. We're still not getting that upward scale passage in the second line. You're singing this . . . But it goes like this . . ." He hand designed as he sang. "With me. Do the hand design, too! Good! Again. And again. Now let's go back to the second line. Ready." Mr. Art Song smiled. The class sang it perfectly this time.
Mr. Stan Zuh listened to the fourth graders read the rhythm exercise on the board. "We fell apart on the sixteenth notes, didn't we? We better do it again. Be sure you count 1-e-&-uh for those sixteenth notes. Ready." When the class flubbed again, Mr. Stan Zuh yelled out, "Do it again. And concentrate!" Immediately a small din of "Oh no's!" went up. "Come on. Try it again," Mr. Stan Zuh coaxed. "See if you can get it."	Mr. Stan Zuh asked his fourth graders to clap and count the exercise on the board. But they had problems with the sixteenth notes. "Not so good, was it? You forgot how to count the sixteenth notes. They're counted 1-e-&-uh. With me. Again. Good!" Then he asked them to clap while counting. "Again. Once more. You've got it! Now back to the exercise." Everyone sat up. When they breezed through it, Mr. Stan Zuh shouted, "Great!"

Establishing Pitch and Tempo for Songs _____

Establishing the starting pitch and tempo for a song also works best when you have an organized approach. You've got to have a logical approach if you want students to start on the right pitch, at the right tempo—and together, especially when you're not using a piano. That's when an established procedure is a "must," whether you're in the lower grades or upper grades, or doing a new song or an old song.

The trouble is, not everyone has a set procedure. A lot of teachers just start singing (the song) and then make a motion for students to join in. But that's a no-no in classroom singing. The class needs to start together—and on the right pitch and right tempo. That, along with having a set approach, should be your primary objective where classroom singing is concerned.

Procedure for Establishing Pitch and Tempo

Do you need a procedure for establishing pitch and tempo for your students, or maybe a better way than your own? Take a look at the simple four-step approach below.

- **Step One**: Identify beginning pitch for class
- **Step Two**: Sing instructions to match beginning pitch
- **Step Three**: Cut-off "matched pitch"
- **Step Four**: Sing metric count-off to start singing

Keep in mind this is the procedure you would use right after you demonstrate the song, whether it be for the whole thing or one or two phrases.

Step One: Sound the Beginning Pitch. Do this as soon as you finish the demonstration so that the beginning pitch can be quickly identified by the students. It really doesn't matter what you use—piano, bells, or pitchpipe—or, for that matter, your own voice on "lu." What matters is that students have an opportunity to hear the starting pitch again. (If you use the bells, be sure to tremolo the note; otherwise it will fade as soon as it's struck.)

This first step is really necessary because the students' pitch memory isn't nearly as good as their rhythmic memory. Most of them won't remember the beginning pitch once they've heard the teacher demonstration or piano intro. So you've got to "sound" it again if you want the class to start on the right pitch. Even with that, some still won't be able to get it right. But that's another problem. The point is, repeating the beginning pitch is necessary, at least until pitch memory improves. (See Step Two for when that happens.)

Here's a good way to initiate this first step. **Sing** what you're doing rather than speak it. That's right, sing it on the beginning pitch. In other words, as soon as your demonstration is finished, sing an announcement like the ones below before you actually "lu" or play the pitch. For example, you could sing:

"Here's your (starting) pitch."

"Start on this pitch."

"This is your (starting) pitch."

"Now listen to your (starting) pitch."

"I'll give you your (starting) pitch."

Notice how simple and direct each statement is. The secret is to be precise and only "say" that you're giving the (starting) pitch. Nothing more, nothing less; otherwise, it'll get wordy and confusing. Keep it short-and-sweet so you can get right to the pitch. By the way, the word "starting" (or "beginning") can be optional because the pitch is obvious. In Step One, then, you restate the starting note.

Step Two: Sing Instructions to Match Pitch. As soon as you've "lu-ed" or played the starting pitch, instruct the class to match that pitch. But here's the trick: sing the instruction like you did the announcement for the first step—on the beginning pitch. Like this:

That way, you can prolong the sound of the pitch so that students have more time to "bathe" in it before trying to match it. But, as students' pitch memory improves, you can move directly from the announcement (in Step One) to the instruction (in Step Two) without having to restate the pitch. Singing the announcement on pitch suffices. So Step One and Step Two can be done in the same breath, so to speak, as follows:

Why have students sing the starting pitch on "lu"? For two reasons: (1) the ooo vowel is an open vowel and easier to produce and sustain, in most cases, than some of the other vowels, and (2) most students need time to "find" that first pitch. They can't get it the first time, so having them sustain the pitch on "lu" gives them that extra time. Once pitch memory improves, however, even this step can be omitted. You can go from "Here's your pitch" to "Ready, sing."

Here are several suggestions about implementing this second step. The **first** one has to do with the time allotted for "lu-ing." My advice is: **Allow an appropriate amount of time**. Don't do it in such a hurried, perfunctory manner that it loses its purpose and its value. Give students time to "find" the pitch. Be patient, and make an effort to listen—*really* listen—so you know when it's better. Watch, too. You need to see the "I have it" expressions on students' faces. On the other hand, don't let the "lu-ing" go on so long that the students get silly and start purposely messing up. Have a reasonable expectation and abide by it. The fact is, the lu-ing should last only as long as it takes for most children to match it—no more than five or six seconds. After that it's a lost cause and kids quit trying. So here's the key: have a predetermined expectation. You won't rush or dawdle if you do.

The **second** suggestion when it comes to implementing the "lu-ing" part is to **coordinate the class's response on the "lu."** You can't have everyone coming in one by one; the "lu-ing" must be together, like a choir. That means you need some basic conducting gestures for cuing the class. The two that are absolutely essential are prep breath and hand movement.

Take the **prep breath first**. As soon as you finish instructing students to "Sing (the pitch) on lu," take a deep breath and let your head go back as you inhale. It happens almost automatically, doesn't it? It should feel very natural. Actually, it's the same gesture you use on the podium before giving the down beat (the "prep breath"). So what you do is, take a prep breath right after you give the instruction to sing (the pitch) on "lu." Notice what happens as the head comes back. It bounces slightly when it stops. This stopping point is actually the bottom of the gesture, or what we call the "ictus." To be more precise, then, you've got to have an ictus to your prep breath in order to get students to come in together.

But remember, the prep breath and the ictus need to be obvious and convincing, or else they won't do much good. You've got to bring your head back far enough so that there's a clear-cut ictus that says "Start now." You can't be subtle about it. You've got to execute the prep breath deliberately to get a coordinated response.

The other gesture needed for cuing is **hand motioning**, particularly in two places: (1) on the "lu-ing" entrance and (2) on the "lu-ing" response. Don't do anything fancy, just something basic. For example, a simple downbeat will do just fine when it comes to getting the "lu" started. The good part is, you can do it right with your prep breath. First, extend your hand (about chest level) with the palm up, down, or sideways as you sing the instruction to match the starting pitch. Then, take a prep breath and lift your hand in sync with your head movement—about shoulder level. Feel your whole upper body lifting upwards with your hand. Bring your hand back down immediately and stop. The little bounce on the stop is the "ictus." That's when the students come in.

Here's a list of tips so you can check out your own downbeat pattern:

- Be sure the hand goes up at the same time the head goes back.
- Bring the hand straight up in line with the side of the body to shoulder level.
- Find the most comfortable position for you in placing the palm.
- Keep the fingers slightly bent and separated, and the pointer finger more extended.
- Stop the downward movement about mid-chest with an ictus.

Your downbeat should look more natural and polished if you follow these suggestions, and it should work better for you as well. So practice the downbeat pattern until you look and feel comfortable with it because it's the right way to get the lu-ing started!

The other place where some motioning is needed is **during the lu-ing**. You've got to do more than just scan the group. It really helps, for example, to make a slow sweeping motion with **both hands** in sync while you're scanning. Just bring up the left hand on the downbeat, face both palms upward, and then synchronize the movement. You'll get a better response this way. If you **wiggle your fingers** a little and **nod your head** slightly when the class starts "getting the lu," you'll encourage the students even more. Remember, too, to smile; students need to see that you're pleased.

Let me stop here a minute and comment on some of the funnier gesturings I've seen whenever teachers aren't quite sure how to give a downbeat or get the singing started. Most of them fall into one of two categories: (1) the "Tumbling Tumble Weed" type, or (2) the "Hearty Head Shaker" type.

Take the "Tumbling Tumble Weeders!" What these teachers do is make a big

"come on" gesture over and over again. After a while, the rolling or circling motion starts looking like a tumbling weed. But it isn't because this motion looks so silly and amateurish that I object to it; what really bothers me is that it doesn't do the job. There's no clear-cut downbeat and students don't know when to come in.

Then there's the "Hearty Head Shakers" who look even sillier. Instead of giving a downbeat, they just start singing and nodding as a signal, of course, for the students to join in—and they do, but not all together! They dribble in a few at a time. To make matters worse, some head shakers start doing a tumble weed motion with their nodding. It looks like they're doing the rumba, but even that doesn't help!

Let's mention one other matter before going on for the classroom teachers' sake. It's about matching pitches. The truth is, most classroom teachers feel self-conscious

about their singing, to say nothing about matching pitches! But, if you can hear and speak, you can match pitches. It's true! If not, it's probably because of the following reason(s):

1. having a limited vocal range, and/or
2. using chest voice instead of head voice, and/or
3. singing before listening carefully (to pitch)

I have yet to find one human being with normal speech and hearing—and no shortcomings—who couldn't match pitches. Not one! But should you have any of these shortcomings, here's what you can do.

If you have a limited vocal range (meaning you can only sing a limited number of pitches comfortably—and correctly) find yourself a vocal teacher who can vocalize your voice properly and help expand your range. A fifteen-minute workout two or three times per week will do wonders! Try it and see. That's the best advice I can give you, and the safest as well.

If you sing mostly with chest voice and can't go above B or C on the staff without straining, what you've got to do is learn to use your head voice. I'm talking to you women, of course. The head voice is your higher placed, lighter-sounding voice that all women can produce. You'll be amazed how much more comfortable it feels, how much better you can match pitches, and sing in tune.

What if you don't listen carefully enough before matching the pitch? You may not even know you need to do this. If not, hopefully someone will tell you because the solution requires some self-discipline. You've got to train yourself to take sufficient time to let the pitch "register." You've also got to learn to listen with more intensity. You really need to "hear" the pitch and get it in your head before you can reproduce it. If it doesn't register, you can't match it. It's that simple. The secret is learning to listen more intensely when the pitch is sounded.

Step Three: Cut-off Matched Pitch. When the students finally "settle" on the pitch, you've got to stop the "lu-ing" in order to start the song. No, you just can't yell out "Stop!" "Hold it," or (gasp!) "Cool it!" That's not how it's done. You need a cut-off gesture as described here.

Both your hands are extended outward about chest level with palms up. You've just finished scanning, and you're holding the "settled" lu. Now you need a cut off. Here's what you do for all grade levels: Make a **circular gesture** inward with each hand at the same time. In other words, circle clockwise with the left hand, and counterclockwise with the right hand. Make the circles about the size of a large balloon, which means go up to about eye level and back to your starting point for the actual cutoff. You cut-off by pinching your thumb and pointer finger together as soon as you end the circle or each the place at which you started. That "pinch" or snip is what tells the students to stop. Look at Figure 7.1 for a diagram of the cut-off with both hands.

The cut-off can also be given with **just a nod** when you're at the piano or when

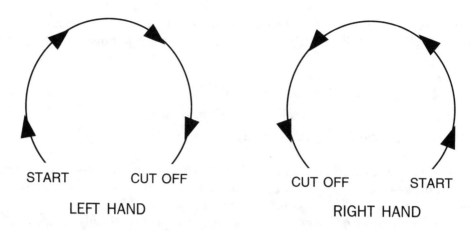

START   CUT OFF   CUT OFF   START

LEFT HAND   RIGHT HAND

Figure 7.1. Conducting Cut-Off With Both Hands at Same Time.

you're using both hands. Music teachers give the cut-off nod a lot, but not many classroom teachers because most don't know how. It's simple, though. All you do is tilt your head backward as soon as the "lu-ing" settles, and then come forward with such a definite stop that there's a little bounce, or an ictus, on the stop. It works even better if you open your mouth slightly and take a prep breath when your head goes back. That way everything comes together on the stop: (1) the movement of the head, (2) the closing of the mouth, and (3) the bounce of the ictus. But whether you use conducting or nodding to cut off, you've got to have that ictus. It's the actual stopping point in both cases.

Talking about cut-offs always reminds me of the student teacher who kept shouting out "whoaaa" every time she wanted the lu-ing, or the singing, to stop. I nearly fell out of my seat the first time I heard it. When I tactfully asked if she thought she was stopping a herd of horses, she got rather huffy. "They stop, don't they?" I agreed that they did, but I said it was like cracking an egg with a sledge hammer. It was too much! I suggested a more musical approach like conducting. She frowned a second, and then said, "I'll see." I can't tell you how happy I was when the "whoaaing" finally stopped! I told her she sounded more like a teacher now. Know what she said to that? "Well, yippee!" I just let it pass.

Step Four: Sing "Ready, Sing." Once the cut-off is given, you can't just assume the class will start singing, because they won't—not unless there's some sort

of signal. I sing "Ready, sing" on the beginning pitch as soon as I give the cut-off. That way I keep the pitch alive after the cut-off and make certain the students don't lose it. But it's got to come *immediately* after the cut-off, and you need to sing it, not speak it. That's the secret.

This means, of course, that you need another pre-breath and another downbeat to bring in the class; in other words, another conducting motion, with a definite ictus resulting from the head or hands coming to a stop after the prep breath. So the sequence following the cut-off is: (1) sing "Ready, sing," (2) take prep breath, and (3) give the downbeat. Students shouldn't have to guess when to come in. That's the whole point of Step Four: to make the signal clear and obvious.

That takes care of the pitch, but what about the tempo? Students also need to know how fast or slow the song goes. The best place to establish tempo is the "Ready, sing." You simply sing the phrase in the desired tempo—no faster, no slower. Decide what tempo you want in your preparation—get it settled beforehand; if you don't, your uncertainty will backfire on you. Important: Whenever you're unsure about something before you teach, that "thing" will elude you completely or stump you totally when you do teach. That's what will happen with tempo. If you're the slightest bit uncertain before class, you'll be completely confused during class. It's one of the weird phenomenons of teaching!

Does this mean you have to have the precise metronomic beat? Of course not! As long as the tempo is appropriate for your own needs and doesn't go too fast or too slow, you're fine. But you still need to have a particular tempo in mind because you've got to sing "Ready" and "sing" in the framework of that tempo—whatever it is. And what if you draw a blank? Just sing the first few bars in your head. Don't worry about pitch, just the tempo. You can do this in a matter of seconds! Don't panic. The important point here is that you've got to establish tempo as well as pitch, and you do it by singing "Ready, sing" in the tempo you desire.

Concluding Challenge

Now you know the four steps for setting pitch and tempo. They'll make the singing experience a more enjoyable event for both you and your students. Because of all the tasks involved in teaching music, establishing the pitch and tempo is one that requires a consistent approach to be effective, so practice this four-step process and try it in your next lesson.

LESS EFFECTIVE	MORE EFFECTIVE
"Let's sing 'Jingle Bells' to open our lesson," Ms. Viv Achi said to her third graders. With that she just started singing without any downbeat cue. But when the students didn't jump in, she started scowling and making a "come on" motion with both hands. It wasn't until the chorus that all the class was singing. "Why do I always have to coax you to begin?" Ms. Viv Achi asked. "When I start singing you start. Understand? Let's try it again." But the same thing happened! "If you're not going to cooperate, we won't sing, and don't give me those blank looks!"	To open the lesson, Ms. Viv Achi asked her third graders to sing 'Jingle Bells.' "Let me give you your starting pitch," she said. Then she tremoled the pitch on a resonator bell and sang, "Here's your pitch, sing it with me on 'lu.' " When Ms. Viv Achi was satisfied the "lu" was on pitch, she gave a cut-off and immediately sang "Ready, sing" on the same pitch and in the correct tempo. Finally, she took a breath and gave the downbeat with a clear-cut ictus. Like clockwork, the class came in together on the first word. Ms. Viv Achi smiled at her class as they continued singing.

Mr. Al Legro had a hard time getting his fifth graders to cut off after they matched the starting pitch. Most of the time, he had to yell out "Cut" or "That's enough" while making a horizontal slicing gesture with his hand. Then when it came to actually singing the song, Mr. Al Legro couldn't get students to start together, even after asking, "Is everyone ready?" What he had to do was tell them, "I'll start singing, then you join in, okay?" Then, Mr. Al Legro would go on and on about the class's inability to follow singing instructions. Any wonder that these fifth graders didn't like to sing?

One of the things Mr. Al Legro enjoyed doing most with his fifth graders was singing. He was pleased that they could follow his conducting gestures, like the cut-off on the "lu-ing." And when it came to starting together after the "Ready, sing," they could even take the downbeat from the head gesture when he was at the piano. In fact, some of the children even took the prep breath with him after the "Ready, sing," which meant they came in perfectly on the downbeat. Mr. Al Legro made sure he always praised the class for following his gesturings so well.

Implementing Prep Procedure for Class Activity

Anyone can introduce an activity. That's easy. But how do you get it started so that it "works"? That's the hard part. It takes more than just a simple instruction, like "Ready, begin" or "Start now," to make sure an activity "will fly." What you need is a simple procedure that can be applied between the announcement of the activity and the actual "doing." You need to prepare the class and let them know what to expect. I use a procedure called a "Prep Procedure" because that's precisely what it is—a get-ready routine to make sure the activity will "go." The procedure has three steps:

- **Step 1**: Teacher demonstration
- **Step 2**: Class imitation
- **Step 3**: Class (starting) position

This procedure comes in the scheme of a lesson **immediately** after the announcement (of the activity) and just before the implementation; more specifically, after the instructional part of the verbal bridge. (If you're not familiar with verbal bridging, go back and read "Using Verbal Bridges" in Chapter 3.) Then look at Figure 7.2 to

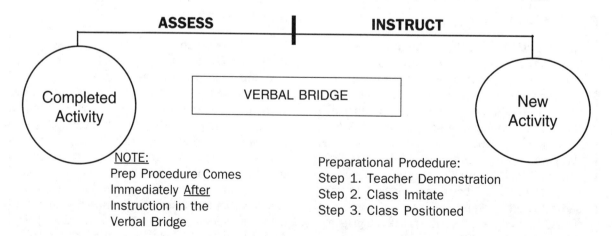

Figure 7.2. Placement of Prep Procedure in Relationship to the Instruction Part of Verbal Bridge.

get a pictorial view of where the **Prep Procedure** comes in relationship to the instructional part of the verbal bridge. The Prep Procedure is such a simple procedure, but, oh, so crucial in assuring the success of an activity.

Step One: Teacher Demonstration

The first step is the demonstration, which is indispensable. It's not enough just to tell students what they will do, you also need to show them as well, especially when it comes to the Prep Procedure. You literally "model" the activity so that the students can see **exactly what you mean** and what you expect.

The problem, however, is getting into the demonstration or knowing what to say right before you do it. Just tell the class to "Listen and watch as I . . ." Or simply say "Like this" after you announce the activity. I prefer the "Listen and watch . . ." statement because it's more specific and it tells the class exactly what it's supposed to do while you're doing the demonstration. Here's a typical example where you could say:

> "Listen and watch as I use big claps on the strong beats, and little claps on the weaker beats."

It instructs students to "watch" for big claps and little claps, and "listen" for strong beats and weak beats. Unfortunately, you can't assume that students will automatically listen and watch. Most won't! That's why you should use the "Listen and watch" comment. It's the most logical and instructive statement you can make right before your demonstration.

Another factor that needs mentioning is the **duration**. How long should a demonstration last or how many times should it be repeated? Doing the demonstration too long is just as frustrating (for the class) as making it too short. Here's a simple rule for deciphering the "right" duration: Limit the demonstration to **five or six seconds**, or else no more than three repetitions, whichever is more appropriate. For instance, a marching demonstration for the steady beat should go no longer than six seconds, whereas a tapping demonstration for the metric rhythm should have no more than three repetitions. Incidentally, I arrived at the five- or six-second limit when I discovered that this was what my teacher intuition dictated most of the time!

Then there's the **execution** factor, or the manner in which you "do" the demonstration. In short, it's got to be done very precisely, with a bit of theatrical flair, a lot of energy, enthusiasm, and enjoyment. In other words, you've got to do the demonstration exactly the way you expect the students to do it. It's got to be a "model" in every sense of the word; otherwise, the class's response won't be up to your expectations. (If you want more information about how to execute the demonstration, read "Demonstrating in Deliberate Manner" in Chapter 5.)

The **first step**, then, in the Prep Procedure is **the demonstration** that must be (a) preceded by appropriate verbiage, (b) presented for the "right" length of time, and (c) executed in a very precise manner.

Step Two: Class Imitation

The next step is to invite the class to "try out" the demonstration, or imitate it, if you will. Here again you need to instruct the class like you did for your demonstration. Only this time it's a matter of telling (or asking) the students to "do" what you just did, in the most straightforward way possible. For example, you might say:

"Now try . . . with me. Ready."

"See if you can do . . . with me now."

"Try it with me this time. Ready."

"Do you think you can . . . with me? Ready."

"Can you do . . . with me? Ready."

"With me. Ready."

Just use something short and sweet, and to the point. But did you notice I added use "Ready" every time because it's one of those little tricks that keeps the process moving!

You should have the class imitate for several reasons. The most obvious is that you need to be sure the students can do the demonstrated activity, that it isn't too hard or too easy for them. A second reason is that you need to be sure the activity is done correctly—just like the demonstration. And third, you need to communicate any special instructions before actually doing the activity, such as which direction to turn, which hand to raise, or on which foot to start. Imitating is like an insurance policy; it "covers" the preparation and assures the readiness.

There's also a marvelous ripple effect that happens as a result of this imitating. With better "prep" comes a better response, and with a better response, a stronger sense of togetherness and with-it-ness. With this sense of unity and achievement comes a more motivated group of students who try harder and give their best. So, the **"prep" step is a powerful instigator** and not just some silly exercise.

You probably want to now know how long the prepping should last. Truth is, there isn't any hard-and-fast rule—with the one obvious exception—it can't go on forever. But I can give you a ballpark estimation, as I did for the teacher demonstration, based on many years of experience with prepping. All you need is just enough time to scan the class once, maybe twice, in order to determine whether or not the students are doing the activity as demonstrated. If so, the experience shouldn't last any longer than ten or twelve seconds. If it does, students will start going bonkers! It's more difficult, however, to estimate how long it will last when the students **don't do it correctly**, especially if they need to do it several times. The best rule of thumb is this: Keep it under thirty seconds—way under; otherwise, you'll lose them.

One more point. You understand, don't you, that it isn't necessary to have music when the class imitates? You can, if you want; but most of the time, you can do without it. What's crucial is the tempo. The imitating must be done *in the tempo* of the music selected for the activity or else the imitating will be for naught. That also means your demonstration must be in tempo. Remember, tempo is the key to a successful imitative experience.

Step Three: Class Positioning (State-of-Readiness)

The third, and last, step is a matter of getting the class in the starting position as soon as they finish the imitative exercise. It puts the clincher on the Prep Procedure. All you've got to do is instruct the students to assume the position that's needed to start the activity, and have them momentarily "freeze" it until the music begins.

Notice that it boils down to giving instructional verbiage again. As always, my advice is to keep it lean and clean, and to the point. Say exactly what you want to happen, and no more. For example, you could say:

"Back to the starting position."

"Hands ready to start."

"Get in starting position."

"Ready to begin?"

"Starting position!"

You don't want a lot of verbiage right here because you want to keep the activity moving and the attention focused. Lean instructions will do that for you.

Here's an example of positioning. Suppose you've planned a wood block activity. You've already done your demonstration and assessed the imitative activity. We'll say they did a good job. Immediately, then, you instruct the class to "Go back to the starting position now," which means cupping the wood block in the left hand, and holding the mallet with the right hand just above the wood block. At that point, both you and the class would remain "fixed" in this starting position until the music began. I like to call this "fixed" starting position a state-of-readiness because the students are with-it at this moment. They haven't dropped back to just a waiting stance. Students will do this, if you let them. But then you get what I call a **yo-yo effect**, or a situation where students are held on-task one minute, and let go the next, an up-and-down focus which is hard on students. Class positioning, on the other hand, keeps the students on-task up to the very moment the activity begins. You don't lose them. So don't forget this position step; it's another of those little tricks that makes the activity go better.

Now let's put the whole procedure together. Take a look at Figure 7.3 to get the continuity.

Step One (Teacher Demonstration)	"Listen and watch me as I . . . . . . (*identification/instruction*) When the music is loud, I'll stand and march. Like this. And when it gets soft, I'll sit and tip this way. Looks like fun, doesn't it?" (*comment*)
Step Two (Class Imitation)	"Think you could do this? (*class nods excitedly*) Let's try. (*instruction*) Pretend the music is loud. (*class stands and marches*) Pretend it's soft. (*class sits and tips*) Loud. Soft. Excellent, class." (*assessment*)
Step Three (Class Positioned)	"Get ready now for the soft beginning. Tipping, hands up. (*instruction*) Very good. (*assessment*) Here's the music. (*teacher returns quickly to front of class and assumes starting position with class*)

Figure 7.3. Overview of Prep Procedure with Verbiage Examples.

Salient Points. Let me mention several significant points about the process now. **First**, notice that each step begins with an instruction. In **Step One**, it was "Listen and watch . . ."; in **Step Two**, "Let's try it"; and in **Step Three**, "Get ready now for . . ." That's because each instruction is a part of the verbal bridge that precedes each step. Notice also that each response ends with an assessment, except for the teacher demonstration, that is, where a comment is more useful than a self-assessment. The point is, verbal bridging is an integral part of the procedure. (See Figure 7.4.) Reread the procedure example in Figure 7.3 and then come back to Figure 7.4. That should help clarify any questions you might have about verbal bridging.

Second, it's not always necessary to have the class standing for the imitative act in Step Two. The class does not need to stand for clapping, tapping, or playing rhythm sticks, especially if they're not going to stand when the activity begins! It just wastes time and energy. But, if students need to do aerobic movements, dance steps, or conducting patterns, then, by all means, get them up. Just give a short, precise command right after the "Let's try it" statement, and add the adverb "quietly." For example:

"Let's try it. Stand up quietly."

"With me this time. Let's stand quietly."

"Can you do . . . with me? Everyone up. Quietly."

"You try it now. Stand quietly please."

"Now your turn. On your feet. Quietly."

Be concise and don't forget to use an assertive tone of voice if you want the class to "hear" you. How you say something is just as important as what you say, especially when it comes to standing up.

The **third** point concerns specific instructions. Remember, one of the purposes of the Prep Procedure is to handle details, like which hand to raise, which direction to turn, or which instrument to tap first. You should give these specifics right after the try-it command (or the stand command, if there is one) and just before the "ready" signal for the actual imitating. Don't overlook these details, which are your responsibility. The activity won't be precise without them.

My **fourth** point has to do with reinforcing the imitative response. You may need to drill a bit in Step Two if the class doesn't "do" the activity well enough on the first try. You need to make sure the class can "do" it before the activity begins, but no more than three tries and no longer than thirty seconds for this entire mini-drill. Thirty seconds is a long time! And don't forget your assessment after the drill; feedback is important after every class response.

The **last item** I want to mention is the teacher's readiness in the third step.

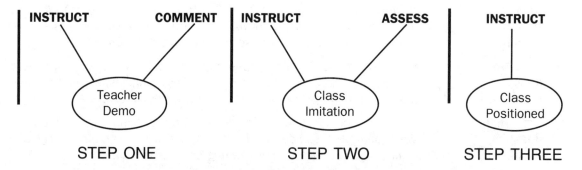

Figure 7.4. How Verbal Bridging Connects the Readiness Procedure.

When you give out the position instruction to " . . . get your tipping hands ready and sit up straight," you need to assume that same stance yourself. Remember, **you're the model**, and when you turn on the music, you need to return as quickly as possible and assume the same readiness position as the class. This state-of-readiness on the teacher's part makes a huge impact on the way the students respond. When the teacher "looks" ready, so do the students because they imitate. It's that simple.

Situation Without Prep Procedure

When this procedure isn't used, the **activity usually starts off with a limp**, kind of sloppy like, or even haphazardly in many cases. What happens many times is that after the teacher announces the activity over-the-shoulder, he/she goes tripping off to the record or CD player without saying another word. Except for the click-click-clicking of heels, everything is quiet. Even the students! I call these silent interludes "Dead Spots."(See "Avoiding Dead Spots in Teaching" in Chapter 2.) The upshot is that the class's attention goes out the window during these dead spots. Students do everything from imitate the teacher, stare out the window, or whisper to a neighbor; and when the teacher says "Get ready," nobody's paying attention, let alone getting in the starting position! But the funniest part is when the teacher turns around and says "Go" and nobody starts doing the activity but the teacher!

Another calamity that happens without the Prep Procedure is that **students either can't do the activity** or they do it very sloppily. So, the teacher gets caught having to do the prepping, or the imitative step, *after* the activity goes down the tube.

This doesn't mean you never have to backtrack with the Prep Procedure. There will be activities that may be right on the fringe of the class's ability, and you will need to go back and drill part, or all, of the activity to bring it up to par. But that's the beauty of the Prep Procedure—it has a built-in drill step! So use it when it's necessary.

Exemplary Examples of Prep Procedure

I'd like to leave you with a textbook-perfect example I saw years ago. I remember how impressed I was. The kindergartners were just beginning to recognize high-low pitches. The teacher planned a game where she played high-and-low pitches on the resonator bells and had the children raise their arms with thumbs up for the high pitches, and lower their arms with thumbs down for the low pitches. Her demonstration was wonderful. She was so precise and enthusiastic, I almost joined in with the kids. Then she said to her children:

> "Let's practice raising and lowering our arms with the thumbs, okay? Here are two pitches. This is the high one (she tremoled the pitch), and this is the low one (again she tremoled). Now, if I played this one (the high pitch), show me what you would do. That's right! You'd raise your arm with thumbs up. And if you heard this pitch? (the low one) Great! Your arms go down with thumbs down. Hands in your lap now."

When everyone was in starting position, she quickly spelled out the details—when to respond, how to answer, what to do in between, etc. A minute later, she said "Ready" and played her first example. I never speak about this procedure without thinking of this teacher. Her children loved her dearly. She was a master teacher!

Concluding Challenge

If you're looking for a time-saving tactic for teaching, the Prep Procedure is it. What this quick process does is get the kinks out of the activity before it's "put into play."

What ought to make it even more appealing is the fact that students can approach an activity in a more confident, and competent, frame of mind. Make the Prep Procedure part of your repertoire of teaching techniques. You'll be delighted how well it readies the students for your activities and adds a touch of finesse to your own teaching.

LESS EFFECTIVE

Ms. Consonance instructed the fourth graders to play the accented beats on the top part of the rhythm sticks, and the unaccented beats on the lower part. "Let's try it." When the music started, she was still fiddling with the CD player. "They sound awful," she thought when she finally turned around. "Like this, like this," she shouted. But only a few listened. "Okay, stop. I'll show you once more how I want you to play. Now you try it." "Hope they do better this time," she said to herself. "They don't listen like they should!"

"Okay, today let's learn how to strum," Mr. Dissonance said. "Pay attention so you know what to do. Go down on the soft side of the thumb and up on the nail. Let's do it—on the C and G₇ chords. Ready." But it was a disaster. Some couldn't get the chords, and others weren't strumming right. "Stop. We better go over everything again. Let's try it a few times before we try singing. That's better. Let's try it once more now." Mr. Dissonance was disgusted that he had to repeat everything. "This isn't a good class," he mumbled under his breath. "They can't do anything right the first time!"

MORE EFFECTIVE

In preparing the fourth-grade class for playing the rhythm sticks, Ms. Consonance demonstrated for the class. "Notice I'm holding the stick in a vertical position, and that I'm playing the accented beats on the top part and the unaccented on the bottom part. Try it with me." She was pleased that everyone was playing the sticks as instructed. "Excellent! Let's do it with music this time. Rhythm sticks up." When the CD player was turned on, she scampered back to the front and got in playing position. "Everyone looks good," she told the class.

When he finished instructing the class how to play the up-and-down strums, Mr. Dissonance said, "Let me show you now." Then he asked the class to try it. "Remember, come down on the soft side of the thumb and up on the nail. Subdivide the beat into eighth notes, okay? And let's use the C and G₇ chords. Good. Practice strumming now. Can you chant one-and-two-and while you strum? Very good. I think we're ready to accompany ourselves on 'Skip to My Lou.' Here's your pitch. Ukeleles in place. Ready." Mr. Dissonance smiled and nodded as the class played and sang on pitch.

Steps for Implementing Instrumental Activities

There's more to do than meets the eye when you use a playing activity in your lesson. There are four separate tasks that need to be engineered during the course of the activity—if you want it to go well, that is. From start-to-finish, these tasks include:

1. Distributing the instruments quickly
2. Keeping the instruments quiet (until ready to play)
3. Giving instructions precisely (for playing correctly)
4. Making the performance musical (during the activity)

Keep in mind, these steps are geared primarily for instrumental activities and can either make or break the activity depending on whether or not they're addressed. It helps to know the steps (or "mechanics").

Problems Without Steps

There are always problems when you don't do the steps, and, unfortunately, most teachers don't even think about some of these details when they plan the activity. That's why there's so much chaos with instruments and why teachers shudder when they think of using the rhythm sticks or the tom-toms.

For example, a lot of teachers don't concern themselves with passing out instruments. They just use a few student helpers. So what happens? There's a lot of dilly-dallying, invariably some giggling and snickering, and, of course, always wasting of time.

Other teachers have a problem when they forget to tell students what to do when they get the instruments. But I'm not always convinced that it's just a matter of forgetting; in some cases, I think it's not knowing any better. I see the same fiasco happening over and over with some teachers. Students start banging, jingling, or shaking the instrument as soon as they're in their hands. And the teacher just keeps on talking. Why he/she doesn't tell them to stop, I'll never know! The point is, this doesn't have to happen. Not if students are told what to do with their instruments as soon as they get them.

Then there are those who **never** give any instructions, so there's no uniformity or sense of togetherness. Everybody does "his or her own thing." It's the situation where students start getting silly and mimicking each other, while others start looking embarrassed because the class sounds so awful! The real tragedy, though, when instructions aren't given, is that you waste time. You have to stop to (a) restore order, (b) improve the playing, and, most times, (c) rekindle the interest. All this takes time! It's a big price to pay for what ought to be an obvious responsibility.

So, yes, you can be sure you'll have problems when you try to do an instrumental activity without these steps. But what's important now is that you recognize the need for these steps and that you start applying them in your own teaching.

Description of Implementing Steps

Let take a closer look at the four steps or "mechanics."

Step One: Distributing Instruments Quickly. The first task is to get the instruments passed out quickly. That's a "must." (See "Passing Out Classroom Instruments" at the beginning of this chapter.) Let me reinforce some points. An important one is that you have options. There's more than one way to distribute the instruments. Let's briefly review these options:

Option 1: Place Under Desk/Chairs (Before School)

Use this option if you have back-to-back classes and no time to get ready in between. When one class gets done, students put the instruments back for the next class. Be sure, however, to tell students not to play the instruments until they're needed; in fact, make it a rule.

Option 2: Appoint Student Helpers (One or more)

Student helpers will work, but only if you give them explicit instructions, i.e., where to start, how to proceed, how many to give, where to put it, etc.; otherwise, they'll waste time. Too, you can use permanent or temporary helpers, as you see fit.

Option 3: Hand Out to Students (Before Activity)

If you have only a few instruments, you might want to hand them out yourself. If so, do it selectively, not randomly. In other words, give instruments to the students who do well in the prep; that way they can be a model for the others. Be sure to tell the class (during the prep) that you're "looking for x numbers of . . . players." Then watch them hop to attention!

Option 4: Call Students Up Front (Before Activity)

Another option if there are only a few instruments is to have students come up front. Again, be selective. Choose the ones who do well in the prep. That's how you can avoid those little "how-to" pow-wows when students come forward. Also, have the instruments laid out up front, ready and waiting. Those in their seats can participate vicariously by pretending. Young children love to pretend! But be more realistic for older students. Use pencils for mallets, circles for drumheads, cardboard replicas for keyboards, etc. Keep everyone involved.

Option 5: Let Students Pick Up/Put Back

Probably the easiest option, once it becomes routine, is to set up a station somewhere in the room where students can pick up and put back the instruments themselves—in an orderly way, of course, and upon your instructions, either as students come into the classroom or after you announce the activity. Students like the responsibility, so try it if you've got space.

Which option you use is up to you. Use the one with which you feel more comfortable. What matters is that you have a system ready when the lesson begins, and that you're ready to do it as quickly and orderly as possible.

Step Two: Keeping Instruments Quiet. The second task is to instruct the students not to play or touch the instruments until it's time. Keep them quiet, in other words. If you use student helpers who have been told where to put the instruments, then all you need to say is "Don't touch!" But if there aren't any desks, and the helpers are supposed to hand the instruments to the students, you'd better be ready to tell the class what to do with them in the passing-out instructions—and be specific. Here are some examples with different instruments.

a. *For mallets or drum sticks*: To put them under their right armpit, on their laps, or to hold them with both hands.

b. *For resonator or diatonic bells*: To put them under the chairs, on their laps, or on the floor in front of them.

c. *For tom-toms or bongo drums*: To put them on the floor in front of them or hold them on their laps; if they have desks, on the desktop.

This isn't childish or demeaning; to the contrary, it's instructive—and expected! Even students realize it's the teacher's responsibility to make the activity work. You save yourself time and energy when you give procedural instructions. You don't have to keep yelling "Stop it" or "Put those instruments down!" a hundred times before the activity actually begins, not if you've done your job of telling students where to put the instruments and saying "Positively no touching!" Let these instructions be the last thing you say before the instruments are passed out—no matter who is doing the honors, you or your helpers. That's the only way you'll keep those instruments quiet!

Step Three: Giving Instructions Precisely (For Playing the Instruments).
The third step is another instruction, only this time it's giving specific *playing*
instructions on (a) **how** to hold the instruments, (b) **where** to strike (or tap) them,
(c) **when** to play them, as well as (d) **what** to play. The quality of the class's response
(in the activity) depends on how thorough and precise you've been. It's a crucial step!

When do these instructions happen? Just **after** the teacher demonstration, and
right **before** the prepping (or imitating) in the Readiness Procedure. If you aren't
familiar with this approach, read "Implementing Prep Procedure for Class Activity"
in this chapter. It's a three-part process including: (1) Teacher Demonstration, (2)
Class Imitation, and (3) Class Positioning (or getting in starting position). The
teacher demonstration occurs either (a) after the announcement, if the teacher
does the passing out or calling forward, or (b) after the helpers distribute the instruments.

The instructions should not be long. Make them short and explicit. If you're a
beginning teacher, take time to think through the instructions and practice saying
them out loud. It's one thing to "think" the instructions, and quite another to say
them. If you're more experienced, think about putting these instructions in an orderly progression, such as one, two, three. Always think in terms of sequence with
instructions; you'll get a better response if you do.

I'm adamant about explicit instructions because the better prepared the students are for the activity, the more confident and comfortable they feel and the better they can concentrate on listening and responding.

The other reason I insist on explicit instructions is that they help create a more
motivated attitude. The more cohesive and coordinated the response, the more
involved, willing, and enthusiastic the students get because they're proud of themselves. Self-satisfaction is a great motivator!

Step Four: Making the Performance Musical. The fourth, and most important step, is to achieve a musical response. For some unknown reason(s), however, when it comes to instrumental activities, some teachers are overly tolerant of (gasp!) non-musical outcomes—or noise. This happens when the "playing" gets too loud, too fast, too slow, or too ragged, and nothing—other than "Fine!—is said.

I'm baffled as to why teachers tolerate such shenanigans. If it's because they don't "see" classroom instruments as real instruments, and think they can't be played as well, they're wrong. Classroom instruments are, indeed, legitimate instruments for classroom use, and can be played in a musical fashion. What I fear most is that these tolerant teachers don't know how to make the playing better.

You achieve a more musical response by having expectations, or standards; in other words, knowing how YOU want the class to sound. That's got to come first, so do it in your planning. After that, it's a matter of being persistent in upholding these expectations, such as making students (a) play softer when they get too loud, (b) slow down when they go too fast, or (c) listen more carefully when they got too sloppy. It's up to you now to make the performance more musical. One more thing. Don't underestimate the students. They can play musically at any age—if you insist upon it. Have them:

- tap, not whack, the rhythm sticks on the steady, on-going beats
- beat, not pound, on the tom-tom for the Swww beats
- ring, not beat to death, the triangles on phrase endings

Don't forget to tell students *why* they need to play *this* way. Let them know you want them to sound better (more musical), and be sure they hear the difference, too, because class response is directly tied to perception. The more they perceive about their own performance, the better they'll respond.

So reach for the stars! Make every instrumental activity a musical experience for students, and don't tolerate mediocrity. Remember, to achieve a musical perfor-

mance when you use instruments: (1) establish your expectations, and (2) uphold these expectations.

Summary of Steps for Instrumental Activities

Doing an activity with instruments is no picnic. If you want some assurance that the activity will "fly," then you need to consider four tasks: (1) distributing the instruments quickly, (2) keeping the instruments quiet (until they're needed), (3) giving out playing instructions, and (4) making the response musical. In short, these are the details, or the "mechanics," that make the activity work.

Concluding Challenge

What happens when you use instrumental activities? Is there any confusion when the instruments are being passed out? Any annoying sounds going on once the instruments are handed out? If so, you don't follow steps one and two. Too bad, because you're making things harder for yourself. And what about the playing instructions? Are they specific? If not, the class's performance isn't all that great most of the time, so you need to get acquainted with the four steps and start using them. Instrumental activities can be exciting musical experiences for your students, but you need to have the expertise in implementing them.

LESS EFFECTIVE

When her demonstration was over, Ms. Slur rushed to get the rhythm sticks on her desk. "I'll get these out myself," she said. But by the time she got to the second row, she couldn't hear herself think! She yelled "Stop it" so many times she felt like a recording. Finally, she had to say, "If you don't keep those rhythm sticks quiet, we won't go on." It never occurred to her that she should have told the class what to do with the sticks before she passed them out. "This class always gets noisy with instruments," she snapped.

Mr. Tie put wood blocks and finger symbols under all the chairs before the lesson. When it was time for the students to play, Mr. Tie gave a quick demonstration and rattled off some instructions about playing instruments. "Wood block players, cup your hand and hit it where it sounds the loudest. Cymbal players, don't clap the cymbals, okay?" Then, he told the class to pick up the instruments and get ready to play. "Okay, start," he shouted over the CD. He couldn't believe his eyes! Nobody was playing the right way. "This is a mess," he said to himself. "They need to be chewed out!"

MORE EFFECTIVE

"We're going to play the melodic rhythm on rhythm sticks," Ms. Slur told her class. "Would my helpers come up and help pass out the instruments?" The two came quickly. "Jim, take these three rows, and, Jane, these three." Immediately, Ms. Slur instructed the class they were to put the rhythm sticks under their right arm until they were needed. "That means I shouldn't hear any sound, should I?" By that time, the instruments were all distributed, and she was ready to demonstrate. "Thank you for listening so well," she said.

As usual, the wood block and finger cymbals were under the chairs when Mr. Tie's class came in. Students knew they weren't to touch the instruments before they were told. It was one of Mr. Tie's rules. When it was time for the playing activity, he first demonstrated for students on each instrument and then gave them specific instructions. "For wood blocks, cup your hand with fingers closed, and put the wood block over the 'cups' so the cup can be a resonator. Then tap from right to left to make a 'clip-clop' sound. Try it." He did the same for cymbals. "In position, ready." Mr. Tie was delighted with the class's response. They were all doing it right!

Class Procedure for Tuning Guitars/Ukeleles _____

If any task can drive you crazy, it's tuning the guitars or ukeleles. You can run around from kid to kid, like a busy bee, and try to "hear" everyone individually; or, you can have some kind of group plan and be more organized and much more efficient. So why do so many teachers flit around trying to do it the first way? The result is always sheer pandemonium. Between students calling out, "Me next, me next," and everybody plinking his/her strings, the tuning gets out of control in a heartbeat, and the teacher starts looking more frantic with every passing moment. None of this confusion needs to happen, though, if you have an organized strategy.

Organized Procedure for Tuning Guitars/Ukeleles

Guitar tuning can be done as a group, but you've got to have a plan of action, or definite procedure. That way, you can walk the class through the process in an organized, step by step manner; otherwise, it won't work.

The four-step procedure is simple and straightforward, and it works—mainly because it's so logical.

- **Step One**: Arrange the classroom setting
- **Step Two**: Conduct the distribution approach
- **Step Three**: Select the participating students
- **Step Four**: Administer the tuning procedure

Step One: Arrange the Classroom Setting. You've got to get the room rearranged before the lesson begins in order to accommodate the instruments. That means making more room between chairs and pushing back desks. **If you don't**, students **will** when they get the ukes or guitars, which means interrupting the whole process. When you do the rearranging ahead of time, you can move quickly and quietly during the lesson without fear of sudden mayhem. Whatever arranging means in your own classroom, be sure it's the first step you take in getting ready to deal with tuning. You'll save a lot of time, and a few headaches as well!

Step Two: Conduct the Distribution Approach. If you have enough ukes and guitars to put one under every chair before the students come in, you've already taken care of your distribution approach. Just be sure students know they're not to touch them. But if you don't use this method, then getting out the instruments, in the most orderly way possible, is your next chore. You don't think this is part of the tuning process? Oh, but it is! You can't start tuning if students don't have instruments, and you can't maintain order if the class goes haywire when you're passing them out. So, yes, it is part of the package. If you don't have enough ukes or guitars for everyone, you have two ways to do the job: (1) select students to come forward, or (2) pass out to students at their seats. If they come forward, you need to have the instruments on the chairs and tell the students where to put them (until needed)—and not to touch them! Ditto, if you choose to pass them out to students yourself. Either way, however, the procedure needs to be done as smoothly and orderly as possible, so that students can be in the proper frame of mind for the tuning procedure. Clear instructions are the key to this chore. (See "Steps for Implementing Instrumental Activities" earlier in this chapter.)

Step Three: Assign the Participating Students. This third step is one of the unique twists of the procedure, a little strategy I stumbled on years ago. It's perfect for tuning (and playing experiences) when there's a limited number of instruments. Actually, it's like a "buddy" system, although kids in the upper grades think it's great when I call it an "understudy" arrangement. Incorporate it during the "Don't touch" mode, like this:

a. Recognize the students who have the ukeleles or guitars. Call them your "leads."

b. Assign each "lead" a buddy or understudy to observe the "leader" with the understanding that the buddy (or understudy) will take the "lead's" place.

c. Make sure that all the buddies (or understudies) imitate or parrot the "lead"; in other words, pretend to be tuning. Be sure also that they listen to all the instructions and take full responsibility for everything the "lead" does.

d. Finally, switch the "lead" and the buddy (or understudy) at some appropriate point so that the buddies (or understudies) can experience tuning with a real instrument. Have the former "lead" tune vicariously.

e. If necessary, use two understudies (but no more). Just switch more often so that everyone has a chance to be "lead" and play the instrument.

What I like most about it is that it keeps the whole class involved through the vicarious "playing," even those left in their seats. I also like the fact that the "leads" become "teachers" for the understudies. As far as the time it takes to do the pairing up, it shouldn't take any longer than a minute or two at the most. After all, how long can it take to say, "Bob, you be John's understudy and, Jane, you understudy with Betsy," etc.? When you've done assigning, you're ready to start the actual tuning process.

Step Four: Administer the Tuning Procedure. Of course, this is the crux of the whole chore. It's where you start the actual job of tuning the ukes and/or guitars. But, as stated earlier, if you don't have an organized way of going about it, you'll end up running from one student to the next—and that's ridiculous. Here's a simple, organized way that lets *you*, not the students, control the task. Do this **after instructing the class**:

a. Play the pitch (on piano or uke/guitar) for the lowest string first, and then give a signal (downbeat with nod) for the class to begin tuning.

b. Have students drop out (or stop tuning) as soon as the string is tuned, while you continue to sound the pitch at 10- to 12-second intervals until everyone has the low string tuned.

c. Have students who can tune quickly and easily help those around them having difficulty.

d. Continue the same process for each string, i.e., sound the pitch every 10 to 12 seconds until everyone has tuned his/her string and dropped out.

e. Repeat the whole process on every string quickly as a fast check, with students listening carefully for in-tuneness of strings.

f. Have everyone play their C major chord individually so that you and the students can obtain the final proof that the strings are in tune.

Be sure to **play the pitch intermittently** every 10 to 12 seconds, not continuously. That's important because it makes students depend on their own tonal memory until the pitch is repeated. Plus, it lets the teacher control the momentum.

Did you notice the little ploy of having **students "drop out" once their strings were in tune**? What that does is allow students who have more difficulty in tuning hear their own instruments better, and gives the one who can tune quickly an opportunity to help these students. In a sense, these helpers become the teachers' assistants! Are you thinking it will take too long to do all the strings this way? It doesn't, because the students get better very quickly in their ability to match pitches, so the procedures move faster than you would think.

Here's one other point: **students are urged to listen for in-tuneness** on the repeat; to make sure there isn't any "fighting" between their strings and the piano, that the two pitches sound like one. Yes, students can do this—don't underestimate them. An organized approach can make it happen. (By the way, playing the C major chord at the end is the final touch. It's worth it all just to see the smile on the students' faces when they hear their chord is in tune!)

Summary of the Tuning Procedure

Tuning ukeleles and/or guitars in the classroom can be nervewracking. That's why you need to consider this classroom-tested procedure. There are only four steps. First, you make sure your room is properly arranged. Second, you pass out the instruments in an orderly way. Third, you assign the understudies or the pairings. And fourth, you administer the tuning procedure by playing the pitches intermittently and having students "drop out" when their strings are in tune.

Concluding Challenge

Are you looking for an organized and orderly way of tuning ukes and/or guitars in class? Or maybe just a better way? I hope you are, because you don't need to have confusion and disorder when you're tuning with students. Give serious thought to the procedures discussed. Do you see how closely related the classroom setting and the distributing of the instruments are to the process? See how you can keep everyone involved by using the "buddy" system? Then all you need to do is get the administering part under control and you're ready to "roll." Try this procedure; it'll give you the sense of orderliness and organization you're looking for when you tune with your students.

LESS EFFECTIVE

"Let's work with tuning the ukelele today," Ms. Bea Intune said to her fourth graders. "Just push those desks back so you have some room. Not so rough! And get the chairs over here. Everyone, go get a ukelele on the shelf." She told them to walk, but they all made a mad dash to get their hands on the instruments. "Leave it in the case. Don't play them. Hear me! Don't play them!" Ms. Bea Intune shouted. She couldn't get them back to their seats to get started tuning. "Take your seats," she hollered, "or we won't do this today." By the time the class got seated, she was beside herself—and disgusted with the students.

Mr. A. Gitar passed out the five ukeleles and told the other fifth graders to watch and listen. Then he proceeded to help students tune them. "Okay, here's the low string pitch. Let me hear it. Bring it up, Jim. No, not like that. Here, let me do it. Lower, Alice. Wait, I'll come over there!" By that time, the class stopped watching. "Keep quiet," he yelled. "I can't even hear the strings!" "Hey, Mr. Gitar, come here. My E string slipped again," Bill called out. "This is going to take all day!" Mr. Gitar said to himself. "I'll never get to the playing part of the lesson!"

MORE EFFECTIVE

Ms. Bea Intune arranged her room before school started. She planned to work on tuning the ukeleles with her fourth graders. When they came in, she instructed them where to sit and how to pick up the instruments on the shelf. "Leave them in the cases, please, until I tell you to take them out. When you get to your seats, put the cases on the right side." Ms. Bea Intune watched as the students moved quickly to pick up their instruments. "I really liked the way you got back to your seats so quickly and quietly," she told them. "We're ready to start now!"

"This is how we're going to tune our ukeleles, class," Mr. A. Gitar said after he passed out the five guitars. "I want the person on your right to be your 'understudy' and imitate what you do as we tune. Everyone else who is not an 'understudy' imitate me." He waited a moment until the students paired themselves. Then he continued. "I'll play the lowest string pitch first, then you'll tune yours. I'll play the pitch again and you'll continue until you have it tuned. When you do, drop out. That way I'll know who's tuned." The class followed Mr. A. Gitar to-a-tee! "Excellent! You got tuned in record time!"

8

Guiding Student Responses

This chapter deals specifically with those skills needed for guiding student response. The fact is, teachers spend a large portion of their time and energy eliciting responses (or feedback) from the class at large as well as from the individual student. It's an indispensable part of teaching, especially in the classroom. For instance, obtaining responses is an excellent way to maintain momentum and to keep students involved throughout the lesson. It's also an ideal way to generate enthusiasm. Students like reciting together and individually, particularly when they receive praise. Then there's also the fact that class (or collective) responses can result in a more efficient way of class time. And, or course, as we all know, student responses provide immediate assessment on the basis of how well they perform.

But whether class or individual responses are elicited as a result of careful planning, or simply by on-the-spot intuitive impulse, teachers need to be competent in carrying out such responses so that the task is done smoothly, effectively, and efficiently.

This implies that teachers need to be familiar with the skills involved. It should come, then, as no surprise that there are some specific, identifiable skills associated with the job of guiding student responses.

Among the more obvious skills to be discussed in this chapter include such chores as: rephrasing questions, repeating responses, requiring focus, and appraising performance.

Obtaining Enough Individual Responses _____

To the class (or group) responses, do you make a conscious effort to get individual responses from students during a lesson? It's just as essential to have individual feedback as class feedback for the sake of obtaining better insight (regarding students), generating more interest, and because one response is often more feasible, or more appropriate, than the other. The point here is that it's essential to provide ample opportunity for individual responses.

Definition of Individual vs. Class Response

"Individual response" means a "reply" given by an individual student. Many of you probably think of it as "feedback." The reason I call it a "reply" is because that word has a broader connotation in terms of a response. For example, it could mean (a) an **answer** to a specific question, (b) a **comment** in a class discussion, or (c) a **recitation** for a class assignment.

On the other hand, the expression "class response" refers to a "reply" given by the whole group—like a choral response, only spoken. Or, to use your word, it's feedback from everyone—at the same time.

Problems Related to Individual Responses

There are several problems here that really concern me, which is why I wanted to deal with this skill. The one that happens most often is having an **imbalance** between class and individual responses. The imbalance goes both ways. Some teachers use **too much class response** and not enough individual response. They seem hesitant to call on students and avoid raised hands. It's like they think they'll lose control if they call on too many students. New teachers seem to have this problem more than the experienced ones, probably because of their insecurity.

But then other teachers do just the opposite. They use **too much individual response**. There's too much "waiting time" for the rest of the class. Occasionally they'll ask for a class response, but not very often. They forget about class involvement and lesson pacing. A lot of teachers, unfortunately, are guilty of this. They take too much time for individual feedback. Often it's because they don't know how to elicit group responses. (See the suggestions given in the section, "Insisting on Confident Class Response," later in this chapter.)

Besides the imbalanced situation, there's the more serious problem of **complete absence of one response or the other**. It doesn't happen that often, but, there **are** teachers who operate this way. There are either all class responses or all one-on-one—and, believe me, it's deadly. The reason I get more upset with this problem is because it's hard to change one's operating style once it gets a foothold, which means these individuals will continue to operate the same way, without any change.

Importance of Individual Responses

It's important, and even crucial, that there's ample opportunity for individual responses in your lessons. It's even more crucial that you don't by-pass them for the more convenient class responses and that there's a balance between the two responses. Why? Because the individual response:

  a. Provides more insight regarding individual students
  b. Generates more attentiveness during lesson presentation

    c. Offers more flexibility in eliciting feedback

    d. Instills more motivation throughout the whole lesson

Provides more insight in regard to the individual student seems so obvious, doesn't it? But don't let the obviousness fool you. It's still the best way I know to find out how a student is "doing" because it's coming straight from the "horse's mouth." There's no way you can "get" as much from the class response, not with everyone talking, or whatever, at the same time! That's what makes the individual response so indispensable—you can zero in!

Too, the individual response **generates more attentiveness** throughout the lesson. Students pay closer attention when they know the teacher is apt to call on them individually. They stay "with it" better and are more alert! Even the classroom itself feels more alive. Notice this with-it-ness the next time you teach using individual feedback.

Individual response also **offers more flexibility** in obtaining feedback. You can go from class response to individual response, from class-to-class responses, or from individual-to-individual responses. In other words, you can "mix and match" your tactics to keep your lesson fresh and stimulating, and your students interested and alert. You have flexibility when you use both class and individual responses and you can be versatile.

Last, but not least, the individual response **instills more motivation**. There's a fine line here between generating interest and instilling motivation. The former is a reference to attentiveness, while the latter, to involvement. Students want to "do" or "try" what their peer(s) did. Thus, motivation is the hidden entity in getting individual feedback.

Guidelines for Individual Responses

There are no so-called "Steps" or "How-to" tips because there's not much to say beyond "just do it"! But I do have three guidelines that have been lifesavers for me through the years. They are:

Guideline No. 1: Be Observant. Keep your eyes and ears open at all times so you can "tell" if it's the right moment or the right occasion for an individual response. It's a matter of being aware or "tuned-in" to the class's state of readiness and receptivity in order to be able to make an intelligent, split-second decision as to whether or not to "go" for an individual response or whether the class response would be better. So being observant is a crucial factor in knowing which response to go for on the spot.

Guideline No. 2: Be Articulate. Be sure you're able to express yourself in a very clear and concise way. Successful handling of an individual response depends to a large extent upon your own speaking ability. For example, you must be able to:

a. formulate specific questions and clear instructions

b. rephrase questions and instructions on the spot

c. frame ad-lib questions and comments for getting students back on track

d. make cut-off comments for off-track or rambling responses

Besides these specific speaking requirements, you also need to demonstrate normal speaking habits, such as using (a) proper projection, (b) appropriate inflection, and (c) dynamic differentiation. (See the section "Using the Teacher Voice" in Chapter 2.) In short, you've got to be competent with speech.

Guideline No. 3: Be Sensitive. Lean heavily on your intuitive reaction to praise when a student answers correctly and to offer kindness when the student falters or fails. Sensitivity plays a big part in the successful handling of individual feedback. You've got to honestly acknowledge the good responses in order to encourage and motivate the students—and then do it because you "sense" the impact on their self-esteem. Moreover, you've got to avoid harsh words on poor responses, so you don't discourage any student. You must be totally conscious of (a) the students' needs and (b) your own response as the teacher. But, you also need to be sensitive to the length of the response, and "feel" when it's time to bring it tactfully to a close or when to give a "jump start" whenever there's a lull. See how many ways you need to be sensitive?

That's it for the three guidelines. True, they may be few in number, but, they're powerful in practice. You can't get any better advice for dealing with feedback on an individual basis than being sure you're (1) observant, (2) competent, and (3) sensitive.

Concluding Challenge

Do you give your students enough opportunity to respond individually in your classes? Do you make sure you maintain an effective balance between class and individual responses? Hopefully, you can give a resounding "yes" to both questions.

But if you're one of those who uses class (or collective) feedback constantly, to the near exclusion of individual response, then you must rethink your approach because you really need to use individual feedback!

It could be you need to be (a) more observant in "seeing" when to use individual vs. class feedback, (b) more competent in expressing yourself, and (c) more sensitive to the climate of the classroom and the needs of the students. If so, then take these guidelines to heart so that you can deal with individual feedback in a more equitable way in the future.

LESS EFFECTIVE	MORE EFFECTIVE
Mr. Jon Cage pointed to the 2/4 on the board. "What do we call these two stacked numbers, class?" Then he circled the top number. "What does this '2' tell us, class? Yes, the beat moves in groups of two. And what if it were a '3' everyone?" Then Mr. Cage called attention to the time signature on p. 26. "What is our time signature here, class? Yes, 4/4. What does the top '4' mean?" Mr. Cage looked up. "How can I get an answer if everyone is talking? I'll ask you again." Mr. Cage was annoyed with the class's lack of attention. He always had to scold them for not listening!	Pointing to the 2/4 on the board, Mr. Jon Cage asked the class what these two numbers were called. "Yes, the time signature. And the other name, class? That's right, meter signature." Pointing to the top number, he asked, "Who can tell me what this number means?" Several hands popped up. "Philip? That's exactly right. The beat moves in groups of two." Then he asked, "What if it were a '3'?" Susan's hand shot up. "That's right!" Turning to p. 26 in the text, Mr. Cage asked the class to point to the time signature. "And what does the top '4' mean? Very good. I like the way everyone is paying attention today."
"Okay, Barry, where does the first phrase end in 'O Susanna'?" Mr. Walt Piston waited then asked again. "Well, how many measures are there in a phrase, Barry?" Mr. Piston scowled at the class because of the loud talking. "Where does the phrase end, Barry? No, on 'knee.'" Looking around, he called on Terry to find the next phrase. "Tell us the word, Terry. No, don't tell her, Mark. Let her find it herself." When the class started getting restless, Mr. Piston warned them they wouldn't be able to play the guitars if the talking didn't stop. "Terry, I'm waiting!"	"Let's analyze the phrases in 'O Susanna' today," Mr. Walt Piston said to his class. "Where does the first phrase end, class? Don't forget that a phrase is 4 bars long." Immediately the class answered. "That's right. On 'knee.' What about the second phrase? Raise your hand, if you know." A dozen hands went up. "Mark? Good for you. On 'see.'" Then Mr. Cage challenged someone to find the next two phrases. "I can," Laura called out. "Excellent, Laura. You got both phrases! Now, everyone, read the words together and snap at the end of each phrase. Ready. That was great! Ready for guitars?"

Using Group Reciting Technique

One of the best group response techniques I know of is the one called "group reciting." It's a marvelous way to vary the kind of responses you use with the class and to keep students on their toes. With group reciting, you can have the class doing such things as (a) repeating after you, (b) reading from the board, or (c) reiterating something from memory—something else, in other words, besides giving short answers. But I'm always amazed that more teachers don't latch on to this technique and make more use of it in their own teaching, especially since it's so easy to instigate and so helpful as a teaching tool.

Description of Group Reciting

Let me describe the group reciting technique a little more, to make sure there isn't any confusion. Besides the short answers, reciting could be something as simple as repeating terms, spellings, or definitions (after the teacher). Or reading some statement, comment, or paragraph together from the chalkboard or the text. Or quoting or reiterating something from memory.

So group reciting can refer to virtually any kind of feedback you want, or any kind you deem necessary at the moment—whether it be reading, repeating, quoting, or whatever. It could be any kind of verbal response.

Situation Regarding Use of Group Reciting

For some reason(s) teachers don't use this group reciting technique very much. Maybe some **think it's too babyish** to ask students to read, repeat, or quote something together, and that students will get embarrassed. But, group reciting is *not* babyish and students **won't** get embarrassed if it's done right.

What the real hang-up could be, however, is that a lot of teachers **have never been introduced** to this idea or shown how it works. That disturbs me more than their thinking it's too babyish because then I know they'll never try it. I get so frustrated when I see teachers missing golden opportunities to use group reciting to their advantage, like when they don't ask the class to repeat (a) the name of the new composer, (b) the definition of a new term, or (c) the spelling of a difficult word, such as S-Y-N-C-O-P-A-T-I-O-N. Then I stop and think that they might not be aware of the group reciting technique, and not have the slightest inclination that they should use it!

Reasons for Using Group Reciting

The reasons why group reciting is such a valuable teaching technique is that it (a) reinforces students' learning, (b) maintains students' involvement, (c) varies the teaching procedures, and (d) helps classroom management.

The most significant reason is that group reciting **reinforces students' learning** right on the spot. Asking the class to repeat verbiage immediately—be it a word, a concept, or a definition—helps to solidify that material. It's one thing to hear information and quite another to speak it. The repeating tactic capitalizes on this theory.

What about reading together? Remember, it's not just reading anything, but rather reading something that's related to the lesson, something used in the lesson, or something written during the lesson. In other words, it's a matter of using the group reading to put the finishing touch on the idea, to stamp it in the minds of the students—especially if the teacher read it first. So, group reading is a reinforcing technique.

And reiterating something from memory? That's another good way to reinforce learning. Ever try to recite with a group without having the material quite memorized? Couldn't do it, could you? The same with the students. They've got to have the definition, the passage, or the words memorized in order to say them with the class. And when they do, they reinforce their own memory.

The second reason is that group reciting **maintains student involvement** throughout the lesson. In other words, it keeps students on their toes. They never know when you're going to ask them to repeat something. They've got to be listening, so that they're ready to parrot-back what you've just said. Now look at it from the teacher's angle. Throwing in some group reciting works wonders when the class starts getting fidgety and losing focus. You can get the attention back by involving everyone on the spot.

A third reason is that group reciting **varies the teaching procedures**. You don't have to be tied down to a humdrum question/answer approach with class responses; rather, you can get a variety of group responses, like imitating, reading, quoting, etc., which means you can be more flexible in the way you teach your classes and get your feedback. Group reciting can give you more options for teaching and more variety for learning.

"A QUARTER NOTE IS..."

Here's the last reason. It **helps class management**. On those occasions when one or two students, or even the whole class, start getting fidgety, fooling around, or buzzing loudly, you can use your group reciting tactics to stop the tomfoolery. It's amazing how quickly you can restore order and regain control of the classroom just by getting some group reciting going! That's almost reason enough, isn't it?

Guidelines for Group Reciting

You don't need specific steps to implement group reciting, just some helpful guidelines to make sure it's done effectively. Basically, you need to know (1) **when** to use group reciting and (2) **how** to implement it. We need to consider each of these guidelines individually. But first let's look at the **what** guideline.

Guideline #1: When to Use Group Reciting. Knowing that learning needs to be reinforced, students need to be involved, procedures varied, and discipline managed, will "tell" you when to use group reciting. This means you would know the time is ripe because:

- learning needed reinforcing
- students required involvement
- procedures needed variation
- discipline needed managing

Guideline #2: How to Implement Group Reciting. I have three suggestions or tips for you under this "how" guideline. You'll execute the reciting more competently if you follow them.

Give Short Directive

Give the class a brief clue, or instructional phrase, that tells them what you want them to do. Make it a short, simple directive, for example:

- "Repeat with me."
- "Repeat."
- "Read it together. Ready."
- "Let's read. Ready."
- "Give me the definition."

See what I mean by brief? These are short and to the point. If you make it any longer, you'll kill the momentum. I'll give you a good example. I was impressed with this one teacher's recap of the Classical Period. But when she got ready to ask the class to read the short paragraph in their texts, she went into this long-winded instruction/explanation that nearly bored the class to death! Instead of a simple, "Read on p. 20. Ready," she went on-and-on-and-on. I saw some kids closing their books and looking at the clock. I felt like doing the same thing!

Give Clear Downbeat

Right after the "Ready," if you use it, give a downbeat so that the class will come in together, especially on the repeating and the quoting. That's a must, because the class will be looking at you. But don't forget the prep breath, or the slight intake of breath, just before the downbeat. Be sure the head goes back slightly and the hand goes up with the breath intake. Then just give the downbeat with an ictus, or slight bounce, on the bottom, so the class knows exactly where to come in. This downbeat is often the difference between success or failure with reciting as a class, so don't forget it.

Give "Repeat" Word

Literally say the word "repeat" or "again" if you want the class to say or read anything more than once. How many times should the class repeat something? I say *no more* than three times. After three times, the kids will tune out. And remember to give the actual "repeat" word.

Guideline #3: What Material for Group Reciting. What kinds of things could you have the class recite? Figure 8.1 shows each kind of reciting and gives specific examples for each.

REPEATING (AFTER TEACHER)	READING (TOGETHER)	REITERATING (MEMORIZED MATERIAL)
• Names	• Definitions	• Definitions
• Places	• Rules	• Rules
• Symbols	• Descriptions	• Names
• Rules	• Handouts	(Lines/Spaces)
• Definitions	• Board Work	• Words in Songs
• Spellings	• Text Paragraphs	• Poem
• Directions	• Words in Songs	• Composers' Names
• Adjectives/Adverbs		• Spellings

Figure 8.1. Examples of Items That Can Be Used in Each Type of Group Reciting.

Concluding Challenge

Do you use the group reciting technique in your teaching? If not, you need to because it's such a valuable teaching tool for dealing with class responses. If you want more variety in your teaching tactics, better control of your classroom, and more class involvement for your students, this is the way to get it. Start your group reciting in your classes and see the difference.

LESS EFFECTIVE	MORE EFFECTIVE
"We call this symbol a 'sharp.' See it here?" Ms. A. Chord pointed to the sharp sign on the board. "A sharp raises a note one-half step. Not a whole step, just a half step." Ms. A. Chord looked around the class. "Remember that. It's important. A sharp raises a note a half step. Like F to F#." To make sure they were listening, she warned, "This information will be on our next test, so you better know it." She pointed to the sharp again.	"Look at this symbol, class. It's called a 'sharp.' " Ms. A. Chord drew another sharp sign on the board. "What do we call this sign, class? Yes, a sharp. Again." She explained that the purpose of the sharp sign was to raise a note a half step. "Let's say that rule together, okay?" Then Ms. A. Chord took a prep breath and gave the downbeat. "Very good, class. Say it again." She could see everyone repeating the rule. "Now you know what this symbol is called. Got it? Let's say the rule one more time. Ready."
Ms. Bea Chord held up a picture of a cloud for her children. "See this cloud? Where do we find clouds? Yes, in the sky. High in the sky. Right?" Ms. Bea Chord pointed to the sky. "Today, children, we're going to learn about high pitches. They sound high. Like this." She played some high pitches on the piano. "Hear these high pitches? See how high they sound? They're high, like the clouds. Understand?"	Holding up a picture of clouds, Ms. Bea Chord asked the class, "What do we call these? Yes, clouds. And where are clouds? Right, in the sky. High in the sky. Can you say that with me? Once more." Then Ms. Bea Chord told the children that there were high pitches, too. She played some examples. "What do we call these pitches, class? Yes, high pitches. What are they? Good. High pitches. So pitches can be high, just like our clouds, can't they?" The children nodded excitedly.

Rephrasing Questions and Instructions

One of the skills you absolutely need when it comes to feedback is being able to rephrase questions as well as instructions, especially for individual responses. Many times students don't comprehend the questions or instructions the first time around for a variety of reasons: some simply don't pay attention, some get confused, and others misinterpret what they hear. What that means, of course, is that you've got to come back immediately and restate (or rephrase) the question or instruction in order to help and encourage the student(s) to answer; otherwise, you won't get any feedback.

I've seen many potentially effective lessons, however, go down the tube all because the teacher wasn't able to rephrase questions and instructions. That's inexcusable! Teachers need to be competent in rephrasing—it's part of the feedback process!

Definition of Rephrasing

What the term "rephrasing" refers to in this context is the technique of restating (a) questions, (b) comments, or (c) instructions. That could mean changing the verbiage, switching the perspective, or varying the emphasis. Actually, what it really boils down to is a simple act of on-the-spot paraphrasing for the purpose of clarifying the meaning.

Problem with Rephrasing

A lot of teachers don't rephrase very well, and some, not at all! That's true. I see plenty of situations where the teacher makes no attempt whatsoever to rephrase when a student doesn't answer, and just stands there waiting. I call that waiting time the deadly "grand pause"; you could cut through it with a knife.

Here's another familiar scenario. Ever notice how uncomfortable students get when they're left hanging without any help? The teacher either repeats the same question over-and-over, like a broken record, or else just stands there hovering like a vulture. Meanwhile, the poor student starts slinking down farther and farther into the seat, and drooping his/her head until the chin looks like it's glued to the chest and there's no more neck.

The sad part is that these aren't isolated situations. As stated earlier, a lot of teachers can't, and don't, rephrase their questions for the students. The result? They lose valuable teaching time (because of the "grand pauses"), create an uncomfortable classroom atmosphere and, most disturbing of all, tear down the students' self-esteem. Teachers pay a high price for their incompetence in rephrasing questions.

Reasons for Rephrasing

I **know** you know that rephrasing is important. But do you really know the specific reasons for needing to rephrase questions? People are more committed to those things that they know have value. That goes for rephrasing, too. So let's look at some of the significant reasons.

Provides an Available Tactic. You don't have to wait to do it, go some place to get it, or rely on someone else to use it. You can rephrase questions and instructions any time you want. It's readily accessible because it comes from your person. Availability, then, is the most obvious reason.

Helps the Struggling Student. Plain and simple, rephrasing does the job to make a successful response possible. By using a different choice of words, shifting the focus, or simply by turning the question around, you give the student a different perspective, and even add information that helps trigger the answer. There isn't a more persuasive reason for rephrasing than this one.

Builds the Self-Esteem. Every time you obtain a successful response by rephrasing, you help build up the students' self-esteem and give them more confidence in themselves. In essence, this is the result of a successful response. Rephrasing is worth it just to see the looks on students' faces when they finally "get" the answer.

Maintains the Ongoing Momentum. The flow of the lesson keeps moving when you rephrase questions and/or instructions. There's more energy in the air when you're at the business of "doing," not waiting; in other words, the lesson keeps moving forward. It doesn't come to a sudden halt because of the long pauses. Rephrasing maintains the momentum; which is another good reason for doing it.

Make sure these reasons sink in so that you'll be more convinced about the merits of rephrasing, and more committed as well. Rephrasing questions, comments, or instructions does, indeed, make it possible to help students build self-esteem and maintain momentum.

Suggestions for Rephrasing

Here are some suggestions for rephrasing. They're just some common-sense tips, but I wish I had known about them when I started teaching. They would have helped me immensely. They'll help you, too, even if you're not just starting out. They'll tell you exactly what needs to happen in order to rephrase effectively. Here's what you do:

Suggestion #1: Exercise Perceptive Insight. This comes first. You've got to notice the student's reaction to the question or the instruction—so you'll know what to do. In other words, you need to "see" (a) **facial expressions**, like blank stares, frowning brows, puzzled looks, etc., and (b) **body language**, like lowering eyes, slouching body, fiddling fingers, etc. All these are clear-cut signs that the student is struggling and that you need to jump in and rephrase. Bottom line? You've got to be very alert and aware when you're asking for individual (or group) feedback.

Suggestion #2: Execute Sensitive Timing. This is the tricky part. You've got to sense how long to wait before you start rephrasing. Jumping in too fast is just as bad as being too slow! So how do you know? Mostly by intuition, by having that gut feeling that says "now." You can help this intuition, though, by keeping your eyes on the students and noting all the "trouble signs." Experience will help you after awhile, but in the final analysis, it'll be up to your intuitiveness. Start "listening" to it.

Suggestion #3: Make Relative Paraphrasing(s). You've got to have the ability to reword the question or instruction. That means you have command of English grammar, know sentence structure, and have a good working vocabulary so that you can use comparative words to express the same thought. On top of that, you need to be quick-witted and articulate in order to state the paraphrased material quickly and clearly. Here are some examples:

ORIGINAL STATEMENT	REPHRASED STATEMENT
Questions:	*Questions:*
• What's the key signature for D Major?	• How many sharps are there for the key of D Major?
• What is the enharmonic of A#?	• What note sounds like A#, but is spelled differently?
• How many beats does a half note get in 4/4?	• If a quarter note gets one beat, what would the half note get?
Instructions:	*Instructions:*
• This time, tap the melodic rhythm instead of the accented beats. Ready?	• Let's tap the rhythm of the melody this time, not the accented beats. Ready?
• Everyone put your finger on the time signature.	• Put your finger on the two stacked numbers after the G Clef.

Do you see that the rephrased statements are nothing more than paraphrasings? They say (or ask) virtually the same thing but with different verbiage.

Suggestion #4: Display Positive Body Language. Here's the proverbial X factor, the one ingredient that can make-or-break the rephrasing process. You've simply got to display positive body language. It doesn't matter that you're perceptive and competent if you give students the appearance of being irritated, impatient, or annoyed. Doing things like shifting weight from foot to foot, or glancing steadily at the clock, or pursing your lips while tilting your head, will intimidate students no matter how good the rephrased question(s) are. You've got to have (a) a pleasant facial expression, (b) encouraging body language, and (c) a calming attitude if you want your rephrasing episode to work. Don't overlook this X factor. Positive body language is a "must." (See Chapter 2 for additional discussions on body language.)

Suggestion #5: Give Objective Appraisal. You don't want to forget the evaluation because the teacher's praise is even more crucial in a rephrasing situation. Students need to hear the teacher say "Good job" or "I'm proud of you" so that they take pride in their achievement. The teacher can bolster the students' confidence and their self-esteem.

Concluding Challenge

I hope you have a better understanding now of how important rephrasing is in getting feedback from unresponsive students, and how essential it is to be competent in rephrasing material, if it's to be done successfully. If you already use rephrasing techniques to your advantage, to you, I say "Bravo!" If not, then why not start preparing yourself right now. Study the suggestions and then put them to work. You'll get more out of students when you rephrase.

LESS EFFECTIVE	MORE EFFECTIVE
"Everyone, look at this chord now," Ms. Carol Ling told her fifth graders. "Keep in mind how we form a chord. Okay, who can tell me the home tone? Susan?" When Susan didn't answer, Ms. Carol Ling repeated the question. "What's the home tone?" Then after two more times of repeating the question in a disgusted manner, she told Susan she couldn't wait any longer. "Pay better attention next time, Susan," Ms. Carol Ling snapped.	"Let's analyze this chord now," Ms. Carol Ling said to the fifth-grade class. "How do we form chords? Jim? Right, taking every other note." Then she asked, "What the home tone? Susan?" After a few seconds, Ms. Carol Ling asked, "What's the name of this chord, Susan? Yes, a C chord. And if it's a C chord, what note must it start on? That's right, C. So what's the home tone? Yes, C. Good for you, Susan. You followed that beautifully."

LESS EFFECTIVE	MORE EFFECTIVE
"This time we'll listen to a small chamber group with a piano, violin, viola, and cello," Mr. Sol Fegging announced to the sixth graders. "Stan, what would we call this group?" Stan slinked down in his seat and put his hand over his eyes. Mr. Sol Fegging stood by the CD player and tapped his fingers. "I'm waiting," he told Stan. After another few seconds, he said disgustedly, "Tell him, class." Stan didn't even look up.	Just before listening to the CD, Mr. Sol Fegging asked, "What would we call a group with four players, in this case, piano, violin, viola, and cello? Stan?" Mr. Sol Fegging could tell Stan was unsure because he immediately slouched down in his seat. "Stan, when we have three people, we call them a what? Yes, a trio. So if we had four people, they would be a what? Yes! A quartet. Good for you, Stan. I knew you'd get the answer." Stan grinned from ear to ear.

Sequencing Series of Questions

Every teacher faces the challenge of having to deal with students (or classes) who aren't able to answer the teacher's questions even after the teacher rephrases them. (See the previous section, "Rephrasing Questions and Instructions.") That's when the teacher needs to throw out a short series of questions to the students—in logical order—to help prod their thinking and get the correct responses. This sequencing of questions in logical order is a crucial skill in getting students (and classes) to respond. Rephrasing isn't always enough; all too often it takes sequencing a series of questions to be successful. That's why you need to be competent in sequencing and ready to use it when you need it.

Explanation of Sequencing

Basically, this is a retrieval tactic for those student (or class) responses that don't come quickly and need prodding. What the teacher does is take a short series of two, maybe three questions, that backtrack to smaller component ideas, and put them in a logical order so that they lead back to (or up to) the original question. Here's an example:

ORIGINAL QUESTION	SERIES OF SEQUENCED QUESTIONS
"Where does the first phrase end, Mary?" (Mary hems and haws, so the teacher starts asking her some questions.)	1. "Remember what we call a phrase, Mary? Yes, a musical sentence."
	2. "And how long is a musical sentence? That's right! Four measures."
	3. "Can you tell me now where the phrase ends, Mary? Good for you! On the word . . . in the fourth measure."

See how the teacher helps the student "think through" the question by asking a logical progression of questions? In essence, what you have, then, is a prodding tactic that uses probing questions in a sequential order.

Problem With Sequencing

Teachers do this sequencing bit, so that's not the problem. The problem is, I don't see a lot of teachers doing it well—or even trying to do it well, in many instances. I see them doing such things as:

a. **Stumbling through questions**, or hemming and hawing. They use a lot of "ers" and "uhms," and pause too often. In other words, they are not being very articulate.

b. **Rattling off too many questions**, or asking a string of questions one after another. They don't wait for the student(s) to answer them.

c. **Not sequencing the questions**, or throwing out questions off the cuff in no particular order. Teachers make no attempt to sequence them.

d. **Sounding too pedantic**, or stating questions in boring one-two-three-ish manner. They use a dull tone of voice without any inflection.

e. **Racing through questions**, or articulating each question so fast that students can't understand what the teacher said.

The bad news is that these antics do happen, and it's the students who get short-changed because of it. The good news is that all of these idiosyncrasies can be overcome with some self-discipline and a little know-how.

But first, I've got a marvelous illustration. I can still clearly "see" what happened. The poor student sat wiggling like a worm trying to answer the teacher's question, and right in front of him was the teacher getting more impatient by the second. I knew she was going to "blow" any time—and she did! She blurted out a string of questions so fast she sounded like a machine gun. Rat-tat-tat-tat-tat! The poor student was stunned. He even stopped wiggling! All he could say when the teacher asked for an answer was, "I forget!" I got so tickled I had to slap a hand over my mouth to keep from giggling. The teacher? She walked off in a huff. Couldn't ask for a better illustration, could you?

Suggestions for Sequencing

How can you become more competent in sequencing a series of questions to help students answer correctly? You can discipline yourself, but it's a matter of knowing *what* to do and *how* to do it if you want to formulate relevant questions. Here are specific suggestions.

Prepare (or Anticipate) Your Questions. Here's the key to getting "good." Initially, you must take time to anticipate problems in your planning and prepare your line of questions beforehand. There's no substitute for preparation in developing the skill to think logically and sequence your thoughts. So begin disciplining yourself. That's the only way you'll get "good" at sequencing a series of questions on the spot, automatically.

Know Your Conceptual Material. This is another "beforehand" suggestion. You simply must have a clear grasp of the sequencing of conceptual material for each element, including melody, rhythm, harmony, and form. There's no way you can sequence your questions without having this "unfolding" knowledge of conceptual ideas firmly entrenched in your mind and at your proverbial fingertips. This is a good place to start if you don't know conceptual sequence.

Consider Students' Experience. We're talking about an "on-the-job" suggestion here. You need to keep in mind the students' backgrounds in terms of their conceptual awareness and skill development, because your questions need to be formulated on the basis of this information. In other words, you've got to take into account what the students know and don't know when you're getting ready to ask your questions.

Make Your Questions Sequential. Here's your "big gun," so to speak. Even though it's a brief series of questions, you've got to structure the questions so that they are sequential. Your first question sets the stage for the second question; the second, for the third, which then leads logically to the original. Just go back to a previously learned idea and work your way back, in logical order, to the original one—in question form, of course. That's the blueprint for making questions sequential.

Keep Your Questions Short. The technique works best if you keep the series of questions short and to the point. Long, drawn-out questions will slow down the intentional fast flow of the process. There's more impact and pizzazz when the questions go one-two-three. Then, too, try to formulate the questions so that the answers are short. That's another way to keep the momentum moving. Let me give you an example.

ORIGINAL QUESTION	*SERIES OF SHORT QUESTIONS WITH SHORT ANSWERS*

ORIGINAL QUESTION

"How can you tell the beat moves in groups of three in this piece, class?" (When no response is forthcoming, the teacher would ask a series of short questions.)

SERIES OF SHORT QUESTIONS WITH SHORT ANSWERS

1. "What's the ongoing beat called, class?" *Answer*: A pulse.
2. "Do all pulses sound the same?" *Answer*: No.
3. "Some sound how?" *Answer*: Stronger. "And others?" *Answer*: Weaker.
4. "So how can we tell the beat moves in three's here?" *Answer*: The strong beat is followed by two weak beats.

Reasons for Sequencing

The reasons for articulating a short series of questions for hesitant and unresponsive students should be obvious to everyone. First of all, it's an **excellent tool for "drawing out" responses** from students who might not have succeeded otherwise. What makes it even more attractive as a response tool is that the teacher can skew the series of questions to fit the individual (or class); be flexible, in other words, with the questioning. That's why it works so well, especially when the teacher is skilled at sequencing the questions.

The other obvious reason for using the sequence is that it's a **marvelous tactic for building self-esteem**. Only the student can tell you what it feels like when he/she is able to answer the question, and in such a way that it doesn't demean the student or tear down his/her confidence. Rather, it is built up, and a sense of pride is instilled in his/her effort.

Concluding Challenge

How would you rate yourself with this sequencing task? Are you good at asking a short series of sequential questions to get an answer? Does it come easily? Or do you hem-and-haw and sort of stammer through the questions? Or maybe you rated yourself "poor" because you can't do it? Now you've got some suggestions to help you. You'll need to follow the suggestions, however, and discipline yourself if you want to get better.

LESS EFFECTIVE

Mr. Percy Cetti worked hard on the dotted quarter note with his third graders. "Okay, who can tell me how many beats the dotted quarter gets? Jim?" After waiting several seconds, Mr. Percy Cetti shook his head. "Okay, Jim, how long is the quarter note? And with the dot?" Jim looked totally confused. "I donno," he finally mumbled.

MORE EFFECTIVE

Mr. Percy Cetti's third graders were working with dotted quarter notes. Before closing the lesson, he asked Jim, "So how many beats does the dotted quarter get?" When Jim's face turned red, he asked him, "Remember what the quarter note gets? Yes, one beat. And what's the rule for dots? Good! Half the value. So the dot here gets what, Jim. Yes, half a beat. So how many beats does a dotted quarter note get? You got it! A beat and a half. Good for you, Jim."

"Don't forget the Da Capo al Fine in this song," Ms. Deb Bussy warned her class. "What does Da Capo al Fine mean, class?" There wasn't a peep from anyone. "Okay, what does, uhm, what does 'Fine' mean? And what did, uhm, we say (pause) 'Da Capo' means? What? Yeah, that's right. And uh, what about 'al'? What does it mean?" But by that time no one was listening. "Pay attention," she yelled!

Ms. Deb Bussy noticed the Da Capo al Fine in the song. "Remember what Da Capo al Fine means, class?" She was surprised at the dead silence. "Well, we said 'Da Capo' was the Italian word for what? (Pointing to her head) Good! The head. And 'Fine' in Italian means? Yes, 'end.' So now we have the head 'blank' end. Remember the little word 'al'? Good! It means 'to.' Now tell me what Da Capo al Fine means. Super! I knew you would remember," she beamed.

Insisting on Confident Class Responses

Do you pay attention to the way your class answers? Do you notice how the responses are voiced? Do you insist on healthy, forthright responses rather than weak, hesitant ones? I'm interested in your expectations with regard to class responses and how insistent you are in getting responses that are strong and confident sounding because confident responses reflect the students' grasp of the material and help build up their self-esteem.

Definition of Confident Responses

When I say confident-sounding, I mean a response that is made in a forthright, or assertive, manner—without any hesitation, without any faltering, and with a projected and self-assured tone of voice. In short, I'm talking about a healthy, secure-sounding response that gives every indication that the class "has it." The word that says it all is "convincing." Thus, a confident response is a convincing response.

It's just the opposite when the response isn't confident. The class hesitates and holds back, and there's fumbling and mumbling of words with no vocal projection and no clarity. The response is feeble-sounding, shaky, and a far cry from convincing.

Reasons for Confident Responses

Confident-sounding responses are crucial not just for the teacher, but for the students as well. Here's why.

First, a confident response **reinforces learning**. Making students answer in a firm, self-assured manner helps stamp the response in the students' minds and solidifies the information. It's that simple: confident responding reinforces.

But not only does it reinforce, confident responding also **builds self-esteem**. Students feel good about themselves when they've contributed in a viable and confident way. They experience a sense of with-it-ness, accomplishment, and even a feeling of camaraderie with the rest of the class. All the things, in other words, that trigger the feeling of self-worth.

Then there's the fact that a confident response **generates enthusiasm** and gets the students more motivated. The better they respond, the more willing and anxious they are to "try" it again. The saying "Success breeds success" is really true—students do get more enthusiastic when they're made to respond in a confident way.

And for the teacher, a confident-sounding response is important because it **demonstrates comprehension** on the class's part and gives the teacher evidence that the class has grasped the information. The fact is, students won't respond in a confident way unless they do understand. That's what makes a confident response so important: it indicates understanding, and that's crucial for teachers.

Are confident-sounding responses important? Absolutely. Do they benefit both teacher and students? Definitely. Keep in mind that they (a) reinforce learning, (b) build self-esteem, (c) generate enthusiasm, and (d) demonstrate the class's comprehension.

Problem with Confident Responses

So what's the problem? In a nutshell, too many teachers don't insist on confident-sounding responses. They take whatever way the class answers and make no attempt to improve it or make it sound more convincing, more articulate, more enthusiastic. They just accept the pitiful responses. Here are some of the common qualities of a pitiful response. They include some (or all) of the following:

- feeble sounding
- half-hearted reciting
- under-breath mumbling
- yelled-out answering
- uncoordinated replying
- hesitant starting
- noticeable faltering
- frequent pausing

Why do teachers accept responses of this ilk? And why do they allow students to get away with it? It's not because they don't notice; most will say they do. It mostly boils down to not knowing **what** to do, or not knowing **how** "to insist." That's the real problem.

Suggestions for Confident Responses

What we're dealing with here is how to get your class to voice a better response, whether it be in regard to a specific question or a short recitation (for a definition, or a rule, or a list, etc.). What do you do when the response is feeble, faltering, and not confident-sounding? Just follow these four simple steps:

- **Step 1**: Give verbal bridge.
- **Step 2**: Take prep breath.
- **Step 3**: Execute downbeat.
- **Step 4**: Repeat response.

Let's look at each step separately, as we assume that the class's response to the question, "What does the top number in the time signature indicate?" is garbled and hesitant. Here's what you would do:

Step 1: Give Verbal Bridge. As soon as you stop the class, verbal bridge their response. In other words, briefly assess and instruct. Make the assessing specific and to the point, like this:

"I didn't hear everyone."

"Only two people knew the answer."

"That was a lot of mumbling."

"Let's not yell out the answer."

"How come you stopped before finishing?"

Notice that I left out the declaratives like "Not so good," or "Pretty poor," and went right to the prime deficiency. You make a stronger impact this way and keep the momentum. Now the instruction. This is tricky because you've got to tell the class exactly what you expect the second time around. For example, you could say:

"Can you say that louder? Ready."

"I need to hear every word this time."

"You need to say it more confidently next time."

"Let's not mumble. Speak distinctly."

"Would you to slow down and speak together?"

"Say it with more conviction this time."

You tell the class precisely what needs to be better next time. Then say "Ready" right after the directive in order to keep it moving and start the repeat together. (See first instruction above.)

Step 2: Take Prep Breath. Next, you take a prep breath *immediately* after the "Ready." That means take in air through a slightly opened mouth and bring back your head at the same time. What you're doing is coordinating the initial breath that everyone does naturally before starting to speak or sing. The secret is taking that prep breath at the same speed you want the students to respond. That's what the prep breath does: it establishes tempo for the class.

Step 3: Execute Downbeat. All you need to do here is give a downbeat following the prep breath to get the class to start together. A downbeat is simply a gesture for saying, "Respond now." You can give it with your head by bringing the head down after the prep breath; this works best with older students, but an actual downbeat is probably clearer for the younger ones. All you do is bring your hand up simultaneously with the prep breath, and then given a downbeat with an ictus, or little "bounce" on the bottom, that "tells" to class to begin. The downbeat is the key here to start the class together the second time.

Step 4: Repeat Response. Have the class repeat the "beefed up" (or corrected) response once or twice, but no more than three times because the class will "tune out" if you do. Just give the simple one-word command "Again" every time you want the class to repeat. Actually, the repeating is like a mini-drill; it helps nail down the improved response. Sometimes, however, you don't need to repeat, so if not, don't. Repeat only when you feel it's necessary to "lock in" the response.

Concluding Challenge

Your expectations with regard to class responses should be established so that you insist on confident-sounding responses when they aren't forthcoming. Use the four simple steps to insist on such responses with your class. Confident-sounding responses are a sign of good teaching.

LESS EFFECTIVE	MORE EFFECTIVE
"All right, class. Let's see how well we remember our tempo terms." Then Ms. Vi Brato scanned the class slowly and asked, "What does 'allegro' mean?" There was a lot of mumbling but finally a few students yelled out the answer. "Okay, some of you remembered. Let's see how you do on this one." Ms. Vi Brato's class always mumbled when it responded. She didn't seem to notice, though.	"Let's review our tempo terms today," Ms. Vi Brato announced. "Think now. What does 'allegro' mean, class?" When the class started mumbling, Ms. Vi Brato stopped immediately. "What's all the mumbling about? I need to hear everyone give the meaning together. And no hesitating. Ready." Then she took a prep breath and gave the downbeat. This time the class answered together, without any hesitation. Ms. Vi Brato nodded approvingly.
Ms. Tessa Tura's fourth-grade class was learning the names of notes above and below the staff. "All these notes use leger lines," Ms. Tessa Tura said. "What did we say a 'leger line' was, class? It's a what?" The class started out strong. But then began to sputter. "Keep going. Don't stop," Ms. Tessa Tura shouted. "Why did you stop? Guess you're not quite sure what a leger line is. Let me give you the definition." The class knew Ms. Tessa Tura would tell them if they didn't get it.	Since Ms. Tessa Tura had been working on the leger line notes above and below the staff, she asked a review question. "Remember the definition for 'leger line'?" Students nodded their heads 'yes.' "A leger line is . . . together, class." When the definition fizzled out, Ms. Tessa Tura said, "I'm surprised you forgot and couldn't finish. Take a minute to review the definition to yourself, then let's try to get through it this time. Ready." The class started on the downbeat and recited the definition perfectly. "You got it that time!"

Requiring Focused Individual Responses

One of the hazards of getting feedback from individual students is that students often ramble, or beat around the bush, and take up a lot of class time "running off at the mouth." You mustn't let this happen though. It's your responsibility, as a teacher, to keep the individual response focused, or on track, as we say. After all, there are other students to consider and pacing to maintain, not to mention the effect on classroom morale when one student "hogs" the show! Make no mistake! Knowing how to keep individual responses on track is a necessary part of guiding feedback in the classroom—a part that every teacher, including you, needs to know about. So if you need more information on the subject, keep on reading.

Definition of Focused Responses

Even though there's a general consensus among teachers as to what a "focused response" means, and a catchy on-track phrase to convey that consensus, most of us would probably be hard put to come up with a definition. As teachers, however, it's important that we do have a clear interpretation.

So what do we mean by a "focused response"? It is basically any comeback or reply that doesn't stray from the intent of the question or comment; in sort, any reply that's on target. What it doesn't do is "beat around the bush" or ramble.

Now think of the definition in terms of the individual student. That makes it a focused **individual** response, or a nuts-and-bolts answer that keeps to the point.

Reasons for Focused Responses

You need to insist on focused responses with individual students for lots of reasons. By making the student stay on track, you (a) keep the lesson moving, (b) obtain the intended reply, (c) control the classroom discipline, and (d) avoid the negative vibes. Let's take a closer look at each reason.

Keeps the Lesson Moving. The consequence here is obvious. When you keep the student on track and don't allow rambling, you can move more quickly to the next step and thus keep the flow of the lesson. You don't have to wait impatiently or fume inwardly. When the student keeps to the point, you move the lesson forward and maintain the momentum.

Obtain the Intended Reply. No doubt about it, the more insistent you are that the student stay on target and not wander, the more likely it is you'll get the response you envisioned. That's the whole purpose for requiring focused responses: to draw out the "right" information. Rambling, off-track answering rarely, if ever, results in a substantive response, much less one that's precise and to the point. So remember, a focused response is generally the "right" response.

Control of Classroom Discipline. This happens indirectly, as a result of the lesson being able to move forward more easily (when responses are on track). The upshot is that students don't have time to get bored or restless, and start whispering, fidgeting, or giggling. The focused answering puts a lid on these antics because there's not as much slack time. Students have to pay close attention, which means you have control of the discipline in your classroom.

Avoids the Negative Vibes. You don't have to put up with rolling eyes and pouting looks from other students when you insist on focused responses. You can sidestep all these childish displays and curb the negative vibes your class will vent whenever a student starts rambling. The focused response is your "tool" for dealing with this situation. You avoid the hassle of noses getting out of joint and feelings getting snubbed when responses are focused and on track.

Problem Regarding Focused Responses

The problem is obvious: too many teachers let their students ramble when they answer and don't even lift a finger to get the student back on track. But what is puzzling is why they take on that resigned-like attitude of having to "hear the student out," even when it's clear that the kid is "beating around the bush."

Here's a perfect illustration of this attitude. I was observing a sixth-grade music class, with the lesson being on shifting meters. As part of the discussion, the teacher asked, "Who could tell me how we can tell when the meter moves from 2/4 to 3/4? Anyone?" She called on the big kid in front who was flapping his raised hand right under her nose. I knew it was going to be a snow-job when he started out with, "Well, uh, when I play my drum set, I, uhm . . ." I was right! He went on forever. Meanwhile, Ms. X stood listening and nodding intently with her arms folded, as though the student was saying something earth-shakingly important or else answering the question magnificently—but he wasn't. He was just running his mouth, and Ms. X was letting him! (You ought to have seen the class's reaction!)

But not only do teachers let students "shoot the bull," they also let them get off track onto another tangent and lose the point—without helping them to get back or even telling them they're "off." What a colossal waste of time—for the teacher as well as the students.

Suggestions for Focused Responses

There's only one way you can deal with focused responses as a teacher: verbally. You can't get it by drawing an illustration, writing a formula, or reading an example. It won't help. It's a matter of **informing** students or **telling** them.

Knowing what to say is the key, which means you need to know the kinds of comments you would make to obtain a more focused response. Actually, most comments fall into one of three categories: (a) **an assessment**—making an evaluative remark, (b) **an instruction**—telling (students) what to do, or (c) **an observation**—giving a general comment about the response. Here are some examples for each category.

1. **Assessments** (evaluative statements)

   - "That's a good idea/thought, but we need to . . ."
   - "You've got an interesting point, but go back to . . ."

- "I like your idea, but let's get back to . . ."
- "Good for you! But what about . . ."
- "I never thought of that! For now though, go back to . . ."

2. **Instructions** (directive statements)

- "Let's come back to . . ."
- "We need to keep on this idea/thought/topic"
- "Can you be more specific about . . ."
- "Don't get off on that topic."
- "Talk more about . . . instead of . . ."
- "Keep on the idea about . . . not . . ."
- "Let's save that discussion for later."

3. **Observations** (speculative statements)

- "I see your point. But what about . . ."
- "You could look at it that way. For now, though, . . ."
- "That's true too! But stay with . . ."
- "There's another thought! But go back to . . ."
- "I'll have to think about that one. Right now, talk more about . . ."

See the kind of comments you could make and how they basically fall into one of these three categories? Understand though, there's no set rule for using these comments or these categories. They are only examples, not hard-and-fast scripts. The best advice I can give you: make comments relative to the given response.

By the way, there is one other suggestion that concerns the **delivery of your comments**. Be sure you use the appropriate inflection and projection; in other words, say it with conviction. Use dynamic levels, too; speak louder or softer at different times. Last, keep a pleasant facial expression. Students will respond better if you aren't scowling at them. Let me leave you with this thought: *How you sound and how you look affects the overall success of your comments.*

Concluding Challenge

How good are you at getting focused responses? Do you make sure your students stay on track? Do you know the kinds of comments to keep the students from rambling? Or, are you guilty (gasp!) of letting students beat around the bush? If you put yourself in this latter group, take note of the comments you can use. For you others, it might just be a matter of tightening-the-reins and being even more insistent on focused responses with your students.

LESS EFFECTIVE	MORE EFFECTIVE
Ms. B. A. Clef was reviewing with her fourth graders. "What do we call the space between the bar lines? Jim?" Jim sat up slowly. "Well, it's the space where the notes go. Like when you write a song and you have to use a lot of bar lines. That means you got a lot of spaces and . . ." Ms. B. A. Clef just kept waiting. Some of the guys in the back started to snicker, while someone dropped a book. "Let's be quiet and give Jim a chance to think." With that the whole class let out a groan.	In reviewing for a test with her fourth graders, Ms. B. A. Clef began asking questions. "Jim, what is the name for the space between two bar lines?" Jim frowned a bit. "Let's see. If it's between two bar lines that means it's gotta have four beats. I know the first measure only has . . ." Ms. B. A. Clef broke in and said to Jim, "You're not answering the question. All it requires is one word." Jim shook his head, "I'm not sure." With that, Ms. B. A. Clef asked Susan who rattled off "a measure" without hesitating. "Good, Susan. Now let's go to the next definition."
"Good job conducting the 3/4 waltz," Mr. C. A. Staff said to his sixth graders. "Now who can tell me what the top number '3' means? How about you, Matt?" "It's like when, you know, you count 1-2-3 and you can like waltz to it." Mr. C. A. Staff kept listening and saying "uh huh." Matt went on, "and you know it's a three-beater because you gotta conduct it in three's." Another "uh huh" by Mr. C. A. Staff. "Put your hands down. Matt's not finished yet." A bunch of loud sighs and "aw man" comments went up. "Shhhh. That's enough," he warned.	After the class conducted the 3/4 waltz, Mr. C. A. Staff praised his sixth-grade class. "Saw some good conductors," he said. "I need to have someone tell us what the top '3' means. Matt?" Matt sat up quickly. "It kinda means a waltz time, like we conducted. There's three beats going and . . ." Mr. C. A. Staff flagged Matt to stop. "Just say 'the three means . . .' Don't beat around the bush," he instructed Matt. When Matt didn't answer, Mr. C. A. Staff told him to listen, and quickly asked Jane who rattled off the answer.

Repeating Students' Answers

A very important part of handling student responses is repeating the answers—not just the ones from individuals, but from the class as well. Students don't always speak loudly or clearly enough when they answer, or pay close enough attention all the time. In addition, some students just don't "get it" when another student answers. So it helps when the teacher parrots, or repeats, what the student said. It reinforces the answer, even solidifies it, in some cases. But here's the implication. You need to be good at repeating, and how **how** to repeat and **when** to repeat because repeating isn't always necessary.

Definition of Repeating Answers

You probably think "repeating" means spewing back **verbatim** what the student says, and it does, but that's only part of what it means. There are other connotations as well.

It also means **an abbreviated reiteration** of the student's answer. In other words, repeating (a) only a portion of the answer, and/or (b) just the affirmative or negative declarations, like "yes" or "no." In the former, it's a matter of repeating only the pertinent part(s) and omitting the extraneous, but still using the student's same words. Here's an example of repeating a portion:

Teacher: "How do we construct a chord from the root? Robert?"
Student: "By having a third and fifth above the root. Like taking every other tone above the root."
Teacher: "Good. By taking every other tone above the root."

But then repeating answers also infers **a paraphrased reiteration** or an accurate facsimile of what the student said. In short, a translation. It's the kind of "repeating" you would use when the response is long—too long to repeat verbatim or to abbreviate. While you won't repeat in this sense as much as the others, you still need to have this option available and be aware of the fact that paraphrasing is one other way you can repeat answers.

Reasons for Repeating Answers

There are at least four good reasons why you need to repeat students' answers and why it should be done automatically most of the time, especially when the answers are correct. Repeating answers (a) provides instant gratification, (b) gives immediate reinforcement, (c) presents audible restatement, and (d) sustains with-it attitude.

Provides Instant Gratification. Everyone likes to be recognized and know they've "done good." Students are no exception! Repeating their answers, especially when they're correct, does just that. It makes the students feel good about themselves, and raises their self-esteem and feeling of worth. There's also a momentary sense of pride and accomplishment that wells up inside when answers are reaffirmed by the teacher. To put it simply, there's instant gratification for the students.

Registers Immediate Reinforcement. Repeating the students' answers has the same effect as pounding in the last nail or giving the last "Amen." It solidifies the answer or stamps it in, if you will, for the rest of the class, and even reinforces it by virtue of the fact that the answer is repeated with conviction and appropriate emphasis. That's why students "hear" the teacher's repetition better and why it registers better than the student responses.

Presents Audible Restatement. All too often, students don't speak loudly enough or clearly enough when they answer, which means the class isn't always able to hear the answers. But because the teacher projects his/her speaking voice more than the students, the whole class has an opportunity to hear the response. Fact is, many students depend upon the teacher's repeating to know what someone has said. Making sure student responses are heard is no small matter in the classroom.

Sustains With-It Attitude. Repeating answers does wonders to keep students focused and attentive. Being able to hear what their classmates say via the teacher's repeating, and being able to follow the flow of the lesson as a result, are crucial factors in sustaining the students' with-it-ness and keeping them focused. In essence, repeating answers helps to keep students better informed throughout the lesson, and more involved, either directly or indirectly. So while it's a good way to keep control of students, it's an even better way to sustain students' with-it-ness.

Problem with Repeating Answers

What happens in regard to repeating responses is that many **teachers don't do it**. They skip it and go right on, mostly because they assume everyone can hear what's been said or else think that the repeating isn't really necessary. That might well be true in some instances, but not all the time! These teachers don't "see" the value of repeating answers or realize they need to do this.

Most of the time, however, the problem is that **teachers aren't consistent** about repeating. There's no commitment to doing it on a regular basis. Oh, they might do it occasionally when repeating an answer is an absolute "must," but that's about it. In general, they go from one response to another, and carry on as though they and the student are the only ones involved in the answering, as if it's a private conversation and no one else matters. And if you ask them why they don't repeat more, they'll just nonchalantly say they "didn't think of it!"

Guidelines for Repeating Answers

Here are a few guidelines to help you implement this tactic and perhaps feel more comfortable with it. Hopefully, the guidelines will answer any questions you still might have after reading this discussion. Consider the following then:

Use Repeating with Both Individual and Class Responses. While it's more common to repeat after individual responses, don't forget to use the same technique on class responses. It's just as effective with the group as it is with an individual because it serves the same purpose—namely, to reinforce the collective answer and to give the class some "strokes." Would you repeat for every individual or class response? Goodness, no! That would be foolish.

Use Repeating on Both Right and Wrong Responses. It's obvious to see how repeating can work on "right" answers, but on wrong answers? Yes, it works just as effectively, and maybe more. What you need to do, however, on the wrong responses is repeat it in a questioning tone-of-voice to cast doubts on the answer, and let the student know the answer isn't correct. Don't come down hard, like "No, that's not right" or "That's the wrong answer." Rather, use repeating in both instances but for different reasons: **to reinforce** the right answers and **to alter** the wrong ones.

Use Repeating on Most Appropriate Occasions. Most teachers ask, "Do I repeat after **every** response?" Absolutely not. You need to exercise some common sense. For example, you **don't need to repeat when** (1) the response is loud enough and generates its own reinforcement, (2) the student is in an intentionally fast-paced answering session where you don't want to interrupt the flow, or (3) you intuitively feel it isn't necessary and that it would be redundant at that time to repeat. That's an illusive reason, I know, but you know what I mean if you've ever taught. In general, though, there will be more situations needing your repetition than not. Keep that in mind.

Use Repeating with Automatic Ease. This might seem like a contradiction with the above guideline, but it's not. What I mean here is that you need to be skilled and smooth in repeating the answer when it is needed. There mustn't be any awkward hesitating or fumbling of words in the process. Competency is what I'm talking about here: being able to repeat the answer without blinking an eye or skipping a breath.

Use Affirmative Acclamations on Right Answers. Here's a little tip you might find helpful, especially on the "right" responses. Begin the repeating with a simple "Yes!" or "That's right" or "Right!" Then just continue on and repeat, abbreviate, or paraphrase the response, whichever is most appropriate. Say these affirmative expressions like you really mean it, with enthusiasm and inflection. It needs to be genuine-sounding to really make an impact and be gratifying for the student. You can use any expression you want, just don't make it too long (one or two words, three words at the most).

Use Appropriate Inflection and Expressions. As a reminder, it is important to use appropriate inflection and facial expressions with your repeating. Sometimes you can use the same inflection as the students, and catch the students' same expression. Other times, you will need to add the inflection and expression in order to give the proper emphasis and make a stronger impact on the class.

Concluding Challenge

Hopefully, you already repeat answers as part of your teaching style, and that you do sense when it's necessary and when it's not. But, if you can't say this about yourself, read this section carefully, especially the reasons for using this tactic and the suggestions. You can add another effective dimension to your teaching just by repeating answers. So, start with the correct responses and see what a difference it makes.

LESS EFFECTIVE	MORE EFFECTIVE
"Let's have a review of key signatures, okay? I'll ask the question and call on someone." Walking to the front of the class, Mr. Bart Tock asked Jeff, "What key has two sharps? Uh huh." "What key has one flat? Susan?" He leaned forward to hear her. "Okay, and what key has three sharps?" Before he could call on someone, Mr. Bart Tock had to tell Charles to turn around, and ask Andy to stop giggling! "I need your cooperation. Otherwise, we'll have a written quiz!" he scolded. It was obvious he was annoyed.	Mr. Bart Tock wanted to review key signatures in his fifth-grade class. "Let me ask the question and then call on someone," he told the class. "Jeff, what's the name of the key with two sharps? Good! D Major," he repeated. "Susan, what key has just one flat? That's right! F Major. Everybody get that themselves?" Hands went up all over. "Good. One more. Two flats is the key of what?" Lots of hands went up. "Jane? Super. B-Flat Major." Mr. Bart Tock praised the class for being so attentive. He felt pleased.
Before singing the round called "Kookabura," Mr. E. Bear asked, "Who can tell what we mean by a 'round?' Mary? Your hand went up first." Mary smiled. "It's like a song that goes on and on. Two groups sing it, only the second group waits until the first group gets through the first line. And then each group keeps going back to the beginning." Mr. E. Bear nodded and said, "Everyone got that?"	"I need someone to tell me what a 'round' is before we sing 'Kookabura,' " Mr. E. Bear said to his fourth graders. "Mary? How about you?" Mary sat up. "It's a song sung with two groups. One group starts and another one comes in after the first line. They both keep going back to the beginning." Mr. E. Bear smiled. "Good. So it's a song that keeps going back to the beginning."

Projecting Appropriate Expressions/Body Language

The teacher's facial expressions and body language are crucial when dealing with student responses, whether it's to sequence a series of questions, repeat the students' responses, or to insist on confident-sounding answers. It's not enough to just go through the motions of any of these tasks; they won't "work" or be nearly as effective without the "right" facial expression and body language. I'd even go so far as to say that they *can't* work because expression and presence are part-and-parcel of every task associated with student responses. That's why you need to take a serious look at these two aspects and not underestimate their impact on influencing successful student response.

Definition of Projecting Expression/Body Language

Generally speaking, it's assuming the kind of expressions and stances that encourage and inspire students to respond more easily and more readily. The kind, in other words, that don't intimidate and make the students anxious.

What constitutes an "appropriate" facial expression? It's easier to tell what doesn't than what does. So let's start with what's **not** appropriate. Scowling, frowning, glowering, and grimacing are all unacceptable; so are impatient, disgusted, angry, and irked expressions, as well as sneering and smirking. They have no place in the repertoire of facial expressions for teachers, and especially not with student responses.

So, what **is** an "appropriate" expression? It is a pleasant, calm, and encouraging look that puts the student(s) at ease, and makes him/her feel comfortable and appreciated. In that sense, it also needs to be a warm, understanding expression.

"Appropriate" body language refers to a stance or posture that is calm and com-

posed, without any distracting or intimidating movements, like pacing, tapping, or rocking. There are no distracting or intimidating poses, such as the folded-arms-and-fixed-stare stance, or the hands-on-hips-and-eyes-on-clock pose, or the lean-back-and-wait stance. Appropriate body language has none of these traits. Instead, it's a calm, unassuming posture that sets the student at ease.

Importance of Appropriate Expressions/Body Language

Keep in mind we're talking about "appropriate" expressions and posturings for all the tactics you would use in handling student responses, like repeating questions, rephrasing inquiries, reciting together, etc. Make no mistake—your facial expressions and body posturings are crucial factors where student feedback is concerned. They can:

Relieve the Intimidation Element. When expressions are pleasant looking and body posturings are composed, students don't get as frightened or as alarmed when they respond. In short, they aren't intimidated. Appropriate expressions and posturings help relieve the intimidation.

Encourage the Responding Student. Facial expressions that convey a pleasant, expectant look "spur" the students on. What they do is bolster the students' confidence—and yes—even their willingness. Likewise, a teacher's calm, patient-looking stance gives students the assurance that the teacher has faith in their ability to "come through." These "signs" become a source of encouragement.

Create a Comfortable Climate. Another rewarding facet of projecting pleasant expressions and composed posturings is a more relaxed feeling in the air. The atmosphere is not as tense or as strained as when the teacher is frowning and swaying, or else tapping a pencil and looking at the clock. The climate is much more comfortable, unstressful, and reassuring.

Enable the Responding Student. Because the students are more encouraged and more comfortable in the setting, they are able to respond better. There's a whole different attitude! Students feel like the teacher is "on their side" and encouraging them. They have more "breathing space" around them, so they feel more capable of responding and more confident in their own ability.

See the impact appropriate expressions and posturings have on the feedback process? They can relieve the intimidation, encourage the students, create a climate, and enable those who respond.

Problem with Expressions and Body Language

What most teachers are guilty of is forgetting about facial expressions and body posturings when dealing with feedback.

What a lot of teachers do in the course of getting answers, or repeating responses, or sequencing questions is they keep frowning, scowling, or pursing their lips—and then start tapping their fingers, rocking to-and-fro, or looking at the clock while waiting for the students' answers. So the situation is not just boring, in most cases, but also intimidating!

Here's an example. Mr. X was truly a marvelous fellow. But when he got to asking questions and getting answers, he had a habit of raising an eyebrow and pulling his mouth to the right while waiting on the student. If he had to wait any longer than five or six seconds, he'd take a few steps in the student's direction, lower his head until his chin hit his chest, and put both hands out, palms up, as if he were saying, "So what's the hold-up?" On top of that he'd stare at the poor student. Talk about intimidating! Know what I did? I videotaped him. He was flabbergasted. Did he change? Yes, he did, and his students stopped cowering. He got rid of that silly smirk!

Suggestions for Expressions and Body Language

This is a touchy area to deal with because it's so personal. I have no intention of dictating any specific kind of expressions. I simply want to show you some of the things you can do to change expressions, and some bodily posturings and gesturings you might want to avoid.

    a. **Facial Expressions**

       • **Lift eyebrows** like you were surprised, or as if you were pulling up on puppet strings. Raised eyebrows give the face a bright, with-it look.

- **Smile slightly** as though you were thinking of something pleasant. Not ear-to-ear—just a slight pulling back of each corner to get a pleasant look.
- **Tilt head** ever so slightly (either way) to give the impression that you're really listening. If you tilt too much, you'll look silly and give an impatient expression instead.
- **Nod head** almost imperceptibly and slowly while student is answering to give a more visible sign of encouragement. Nodding too much will make the students nervous.
- **Display looks** on your face that reflect your thoughts while student is responding. Like your "that's great" look, or "yes indeed" look, or "yeeees look." Let your face do the talking. That way you'll adjust your own features.

b. **Body Posturings**

- **Avoid** the following stances or posturings while listening to or waiting for student feedback:

1. eyes fixed on clock	5. chin cupped in hand
2. arms folded on chest	6. chin buried in chest
3. hands on hips	7. hands behind back
4. finger pointed at student	8. head back, eyes on ceiling

- **Avoid** the following body gesturing or movements while student is answering:

1. tapping foot, finger, pencil	5. stepping up and back
2. swaying side to side	6. rattling change in pocket
3. shaking head up and down	7. flipping pages in book
4. rocking back and forth	8. swinging legs while sitting

The key here is self-awareness. You need to be aware of doing or **not** doing these kinds of things in order that **your** expressions and posturing can be an asset to you, especially where student responses are concerned. The only other advice I can give you is to get some feedback yourself. Videotape yourself or get a peer evaluation, and see how **your** expressions and posturings stack up.

Concluding Challenge

It's back to you again. Do you use "appropriate" facial expressions and bodily posturings? Do you know that your expressions and posturings need to encourage students when they respond? And create a comfortable, non-threatening climate in the classroom? If so, then most likely you are using appropriate expressions and stances. But, if not, then it's time to "get with it" and start concentrating on these two facets in your feedback with students. They make a difference.

LESS EFFECTIVE	MORE EFFECTIVE
Ms. Eunice Son made her way to the board. "Now who can tell me the tones in a G major scale?" she asked. Folding her arms like an Indian chief, she scanned the room and called on Gina. "How about you, Gina?" Gina looked at Ms. Eunice Son's frowning face and gulped. "Why does she always look so mad?" Gina wondered. She was so scared she couldn't even think.	"Who can name the notes in the G major scale?" Ms. Eunice Son asked as she walked to her desk. Raising her hand (to remind the class) and smiling just a bit, she scanned the room. "Gina, do you think you can? Try it." Ms. Eunice Son dotted the notes in the air and smiled each time Gina called out a note. "This is fun," Gina said to herself. "Ms. Eunice Son makes it easy!"
When the activity ended, Ms. Polly Tones turned off the tape and asked the class, "Okay, so what three directions can a melody go?" When no one answered, she pursed her lips tightly and scowled at the class. "Michael? You certainly know, don't you?" Then she plunked her left hand on her hip, and tapped her fingers on her desk with the other hand. Michael got flustered when he looked up at Ms. Polly Tones. She scared everybody when she scowled like that. "Well, I'm waiting." But Michael couldn't answer.	Ms. Polly Tones' third graders sat down quietly after moving to upward and downward passages in the music. "So besides going up and down, what other direction can a melody go?" she asked. Waiting for hands to go up, Ms. Polly Tones made a slow sweeping gesture with palms up while looking expectantly. "Michael? Can you tell us what other direction?" She smiled at Michael and pointed to the bulletin board that illustrated the three directions. Michael's face brightened. "Across. A melody can go across too," he blurted out with confidence. He smiled back at Ms. Polly Tones. "That's exactly right," she said.

Obtaining Group Response in Summary

If there's one point in the lesson where you need to "get" feedback from the students, it's in the summarizing part. Not just from one or two students, but from the whole class. You need to have everybody involved in the summary. That way you give every student an opportunity to articulate the answer and, at the same time, keep everyone with you right to the end. That means, of course, you need to know how to formulate questions geared for a group response and how to "conduct" a class-oriented summary as opposed to an individualized one.

Definition of Group Responses in Summary

Just so you don't think that the phrase "group response" is just a figure of speech, let me tell you right now, it's not! I mean it literally—getting the whole class to respond (or answer) together, as a group.

Collective responses work very well in a summary. Do I mean **all** the time? No, not all the time, although I'd say a good portion of the time. That way you can get **everybody** to think through the lesson with you and keep them on task. Yes, individual responses can be used as well; in fact, there are times when you have to get individual feedback because it's the only way "to go." All I'm saying is the bulk of your summarizing responses should come from the group (or class) so that the whole class, not just a few students, can be involved.

Significance of Group Responses in Summary

Even though you've already read some of the reasons, don't skip this section. I want you to see some of the ramifications of group responses and know the "why" of going for a group response (in summarizing). Otherwise, you won't be "sold" on it or committed to using it. A group response accomplishes the following:

Keeps Everyone On-Task in Summary. By having everyone respond, you keep the **whole class** involved, not just two, three, or four people. More than that, you keep everyone focused and on-task. Until the end. There's no opportunity for anyone's thoughts to wander because the questions are aimed at everyone. That means **everyone** (in the class) is responsible for summarizing. As the saying goes, everyone is "on the hot seat."

Gives Everyone Opportunity to Recite. The point here is that with a group response everyone has a chance to articulate the answer and actually "say" the answer, not just **think it** or **listen to it** while someone else responds. In other words everyone gets to reinforce the information by having an opportunity to speak it. That's the real beauty of group response. Everyone gets a "shot" at answering and, more important, reinforcing.

Lets Everyone Experience the Review. When you let the whole class answer the summarizing questions, you give everyone an opportunity to **actively participate** in the entire review and think through the lesson in a logical, reinforcing manner to get a clearer overview of the lesson. With group responses, the whole class experiences a more rewarding review.

Sustains Everyone's Interest to the End. Involving the whole class (in the summarizing part of the lesson) is an excellent way to keep interest high right to the end. You avoid that turn-off attitude the class gets at the close of a lesson, especially when they know that it's time for individuals to "get called on." You can sustain the interest and enthusiasm right through the review just by having the whole class answering the questions. Students like group response when they review!

Problem with Group Responses in Summary

The most noticeable problem with group responses in summarizing the lesson is that most teachers "go" for individual responses instead. In other words, they start directing their questions to specific students for the whole review! So it's "John, what does . . . mean?" Then, "Susan, how many . . . do we have?" Followed by, "Sean, where do we find . . .?"

Individual responses are fine as long as they don't constitute your entire feedback approach in the review, because then you leave the rest of the class just sitting there "picking their nails" and getting bored. Students start "tuning out" when the summarizing turns into a one-on-one affair. They lose interest and stop paying attention, which usually means the lesson comes to a slow halt. And you know what? Some teachers can't even figure out why!

I'll give you an example. Every time I observed this one teacher doing the summary, I noticed she never used group responses. She always called on individuals instead. But she had a little trick she'd always use to get the class to listen; the only thing is, it didn't work! Just before the student answered, she'd yell out, "Now listen to (student's name). See what he/she says." As if the student was going to say something profound, but didn't! The class just tuned out her—and the student as well. Pity was, the teacher never realized the lesson was over at that point!

Be sure you understand the problem. It's not individual responses per se. It's the exclusive use of this approach, especially in the summary of a lesson, that becomes the problem because it excludes group responses which make for a more sensible way to summarize a lesson with a class.

Suggestions for Group Responses in Summary

Here are some suggestions for you in regard to formulating the questions for group responses and for eliciting the response. Yes, there is a technique for asking group-oriented questions, and yes, it does take skill to "conduct" group responses. Here's what you need to do:

Indicate Group Response. First of all, you need to inform the class that you want everyone to answer. You can do this by (a) telling or (b) by gesturing. It doesn't matter, just as long as it's clear. The point is, students need to be informed. Here are some examples of what to say:

- "Everyone. What is . . ."
- "The whole class, tell me . . ."
- "I want everyone to give me . . ."
- "Let's have everybody . . ."
- "Can I have everyone this time?"
- "What is such-and-such? Everyone."

Get the idea? Notice the last example tacks on the "everybody" after the question, while in the other examples, it's part of the question or instruction. Both ways are acceptable. As for the gesturing, you could use a sweeping motion with your hand(s), or nod your head, or point at the class with both fingers. Students will get the point.

Ask Short-Answer Questions. This task is really the key to using group responses. You've got to ask questions that require either (a) one or two words or (b) a short sentence or phrase. Basically, it's a matter of phrasing your questions so that the answer flows directly from the "What" kind of question or from questions formulated for short answers, like in the following examples:

- "A quarter note gets how many beats in 4/4?" (*one*)
- "What do we call the space between bar lines?" (*measure*)
- "Pianissimo means what?" (*very soft*)
- "What key has two flats?" (*B-flat major*)
- "The rhythm of the melody is called what?" (*melodic rhythm*)
- "Three-part form is called what?" (*Ternary or ABA Form*)

Your thinking must be so attuned to getting a one- or two-word answer that you automatically phrase questions to obtain such answers. Notice that the "what" can come first or last. It doesn't matter, as long as it results in a short answer.

Start Group Response. Once you ask the question, you need to know **how** to get the class to answer all together. But you need more than know-how; you need skill as well. Specifically, you need (a) **a prep breath** and (b) **a downbeat** with an ictus. Take one of the questions above for a frame of reference. After you ask the question, take a breath like you would if you were bringing in a choral group. Breath in through your mouth, and let your head go back at the same time. Now you're in position for the downbeat. By the way, that prep breath corresponds to the breath the students take when they answer. Next, bring your head down (the same speed it went up) and stop where you normally do. There should be an ever-so-slight bounce on the stop. That's the ictus. That's where the class comes in. And they will, if you do it right. Practice!

Conduct Group Response. Now that you've got the class started, you need to coordinate the response. By that I mean get the class to answer together in tempo so that the response isn't ragged. All you need to do is "conduct" the response with your head. Since the answers are short, most of the time this will amount to two or three nods. Four at the most. Try it on the pianissimo question. You'll do a nod-nod for "very soft." See that? Try the last two questions. See how you can keep the class together. It really works, especially on the short answers.

Concluding Challenge

How much do you use group responses when you summarize a lesson? Or do you fall back on individual responses? Hopefully, you'll be convinced to try the group technique after reading this discussion. If so, don't overlook the suggestions. They're sequenced so you should be able to follow the procedure easily. You really do need to use more group responses in your summarizing. You'll see the difference if you try it.

LESS EFFECTIVE

Mr. Basil Drum was just completing a unit on brass instruments with the fourth graders. "Let's review what we've learned about the brass family today," Mr. Basil Drum said. "John, which instrument has a slide? Yes, a trombone. Everyone hear that? Sharon, how is sound produced on brass instruments? Good, by buzzing lips. Is everyone listening? I don't think so. And which instrument has rotating valves? Jerry? Wait a minute, Jerry. No one's paying attention." Mr. Basil Drum was upset with the class.

"Let's summarize what we learned about melodic movement today," Mr. Woody Block announced. "Joe, tell us one way a melody can move. Okay, by steps. What does that mean? Bill? Uh huh. Moving scalewise. Why aren't we listening?" Mr. Woody Block yelled. "Steve, give me another direction." But he had to stop again. "This class never listens to anyone!" he told them.

MORE EFFECTIVE

"Before we leave today, let's review what we've learned about brass instruments," Mr. Basil Drum said to his fourth graders. "Which instrument doesn't have keys? Everyone. Good, the trombone!" And nodding at the class, he asked, "And how is sound produced on brass instruments?" The class answered again. "Great, by buzzing lips. And who can tell me which instrument has rotary valves? Jim? Exactly right. The French horn. Everyone this time, which is the lowest sounding instrument? Yes, the tuba! Good review, class. I'm proud of you."

Mr. Woody Block was ready to summarize the lesson on melodic movement. "Okay, tell me the three directions melodies can move, class. Great! Step, skip, repeated tones. And what does stepwise mean? Everyone. Yes, scalewise movement." Gesturing a sweeping motion, he asked, "And skipwise movement? Right! Every other note. Good job, class."

Distinguishing Confused Vs. Unprepared Students

Probably the most discerning task you've got to deal with when it comes to student responses is distinguishing between those who are genuinely confused and those who are flagrantly unprepared. It's a matter of being able to discern on the spot who needs some mental prodding and who needs by-passing. Yes, this is a difficult decision. It takes every ounce of perceptivity a teacher has! But distinguishing between the two responses is important if you want to facilitate learning for those who are honestly confused and maintain momentum by by-passing those who aren't.

Definition of Distinguishing

Briefly, "distinguishing" means that the teacher is able to **differentiate** between the two, or **discern** which student is really confused and which one is simply unprepared. Or, you could just say it's a matter of identifying, or recognizing, one or the other.

What I really want to get at is the distinction between "confused" vs. unprepared. There's a fine line here. That's why it's so difficult to tell the difference at times. It has to do with body language and tone of voice. In general, **the "confused" student** assumes a more timid posture, like lowering the head, slumping the shoulders, or slouching in the seat. Girls tend to put their hands on or near their mouths, while the boys start tapping a foot, finger, or a pencil. In other words, the body language is more nervous and self-conscious looking. But the tone of voice is the giveaway. Confused students almost always answer in that uncertain, questioning tone of voice where the end of the sentence goes up and nothing is said with conviction. That's how you can "tell" a genuinely confused kid.

And the kid who's "**unprepared**?" The body language is definitely more aggressive in these situations, almost defiant at times. For example, sometimes the student will (a) shrug a shoulder flippantly, (b) shake his/her head vigorously, or (c) make a face intentionally. And look for a smirk with the gesture—they seem to go hand-in-hand, especially with the guys. The tone of voice is sometimes a "who cares" tone, sometimes a belligerent "make me" tone, and other times a "how should I know" tone. In short, the unprepared student will usually be more defensive and outwardly aggressive.

Of course, there will be exceptions where the confused student will act defensive, and the kid who's unprepared will be real laid back. In general, however, you'll find that students run pretty much true-to-form when it comes to their particular situation. That's why it's important to have a clear mental picture of each group so that you can easily distinguish between the two.

Significance of Distinguishing

It is very important that you be able to differentiate between confused and unprepared students, especially since feedback is such an integral and ongoing part of the teaching-learning process. By discerning the difference you (a) promote the learning process, (b) nurture the students' self-esteem, (c) maintain the class momentum, and (d) convey the teacher's with-it-ness.

Promotes the Learning Process (for Confused Students). By virtue of the fact that you discern confusion, rather than inattentiveness or lack of readiness, you can "stay" with the student until he/she reaches the answer. By asking a series of questions, rephrasing the question, or simply restating the question with more emphasis on certain words, you keep the learning process alive for the student who is genuinely, and momentarily, confused. That's a mighty important reason!

Nurtures the Student's Self Esteem (for Confused Student). Obviously, this is one of the rewarding outcomes of helping the student because it's so vital to the student. It's not just getting the "right" answer that's important; it also helps build the student's self-esteem, self-confidence, and sense of pride in one's self. These attributes are crucial in the students' scheme of learning, so anything a teacher can "do" to nurture self-esteem is worth doing. That goes for recognizing the difference as well.

Maintains the Class Momentum. This happens as a result of the teacher's discernment that the student isn't on task at the moment or isn't paying attention. Taking class time to "help" the students who fall into this category is not only unfair to those who do stay with it, but also time-consuming as well. Here's where a reprimand becomes the more appropriate route because then the teacher can keep the lesson moving and not get bogged down by those students who simply aren't ready. Being able to "spot" these students is one sure way to maintain your momentum.

Conveys the Teacher's With-it-ness. We always talk about the students' with-it-ness, but think about **your** own with-it-ness—particularly with regard to distinguishing the difference between students' readiness and confusion. It's good for students to see that you can tell the difference. In fact, they should **know** that you can sniff them out. After all, being perceptive is part of being a teacher. So when you do make these judgment calls, you are actually demonstrating your own with-it-ness to the students. More than that, you are nurturing the students' respect for you as a teacher. This reason alone should make differentiating a "must."

Problem with Distinguishing

The problem is that it's not always so easy to tell the difference, but it is possible, especially if you keep the general traits in mind. Students will usually give themselves away by their body language and tone of voice. But the problem isn't just that it's difficult to ascertain the difference; it's also the fact that a lot of teachers don't even think of making a distinction. Every student who hems-and-haws and ers-and-ahs is thrown into the same heap. Some think that all these students are mixed up and need their help. But then there are other teachers who think all the students are trying to con them, so they bypass—and even ignore—the student. Either way, the students get the short end of the stick.

Suggestions for Distinguishing

Basically, there are three suggestions for you. They'll help you "tell" the difference if you follow them.

Know the Characteristics. First, you must know what to expect from the students. I'm talking about (a) the body language and (b) the tone of voice. Unless you know what to look for, you won't be able to differentiate between the student who needs help and the student who needs reprimand. You can't act upon something you don't know, so go back to the **Explanation** section and study the characteristics of each group. You'll be amazed at how much you "see" when you know what you're looking for when the student responds. That's your first job then; get those characteristics firmly in mind.

Exercise Your Perceptivity. Once you know what to expect and how the students will probably act, you can let your learned eye and your intuition work together. (By the way, that's an unbeatable combination!) Now you're ready to "take in" what you see and act upon it. Not only will your trained eyes and ears tell you what's happening, but so will your intuition. You'll feel better equipped, and even more confident, in sizing up the student. You'll **know** when you should take the time to help the one who is truly in a quandary, or else bypass the one who's not prepared, or reprimand, if needed. In other words, you'll be able to put your perceptivity to work and let your intuition—as well as your sensitivity—lend their support. Above all, you'll need to be sensitive and tactful in this situation, even with the unprepared. The point is, now you're ready to act.

Deal with Students. In the case of **the confused student** you need to be ready to help these individuals. You could do any (or all) of the following:

- Ask a short series of questions.
- Rephrase the original question.
- Replace a particular word or words.
- Emphasize certain words in the question.

This means of course that you must be able to do all the above tactics automatically and competently. If you need to, go back and read up on some of these tasks. They're all in this chapter. If you're going to help that confused student, these are the kinds of things you'll need to do on the spot.

And what about **the unprepared student**? You can do several things. You can (a) reprimand the student, (b) move on to another student, or else (c) indicate you'll come back. Let me give you reprimanding examples. You could say:

- "You'll need to pay closer attention next time."
- "I don't think you're ready to answer, are you?"
- "You weren't paying attention!"
- "You'll need to get your thoughts together better."
- "That's not what we've been talking about!"

Any of these comments will send the message to the student that he/she is **not prepared**. Make the comment or just move on to the next student. Sometimes, however, you won't even feel the need to reprimand. A slight shake of the head will do it. Then just move on like the second option indicates. If you use the third option, which gives the student opportunity to redeem himself, just tell him/her exactly what you'll do.

- "I'll come back for the correct answer."
- "You think about that more. I'll come back."
- "I need to come back to you later."
- "I'll get back to you after . . ."

See how simple and straightforward the comment can be? This really is the most tactful way of handling the situation. Trouble is, you may not always have time to do it this way.

The three suggestions tell you precisely what to do before and during the time you need to differentiate. You've got to learn the characteristics, exercise your perceptivity, and then deal with students—in that order.

Concluding Challenge

Do you know when a student is genuinely befuddled? And when he/she simply isn't ready? If you don't, take time to read and study this discussion. Maybe you don't know how students act in these situations, or maybe you don't know what to say or do, even if you do notice. The suggestions will help you.

LESS EFFECTIVE	MORE EFFECTIVE
Ms. May Zur told her third graders she wanted to ask some review questions. "Tim, what do we call a phrase that sounds exactly like the first phrase?" Tim squirmed a bit and slid down in his seat, "Ah, it's ah; I uhm, I don't know," Tim said very softly. Ms. May Zur shook her head. "You'd better listen next time, Tim," she snapped. Tim's face turned red like a beet and he slouched down even more.	When Ms. May Zur was ready to summarize the lesson, she said she would ask some questions. "Let me start with Tim," she said. "Tim, if another phrase sounds like the first phrase, what would we call that phrase?" Tim dropped his eyes and slid down in his seat. Immediately, Ms. May Zur rephrased the question. "If the phrase sounded exactly like the first phrase, it would be a what, Tim? Yes! A 'like' phrase." Tim's face brightened up like the sun.

"Okay, who can tell me how to construct a chord," Mr. Al Feena asked his sixth graders. "Jack?" Jack sort of smirked and started saying something like, "Well, you take a note and go above it and . . . then you look for the key signature." Mr. Al Feena stopped Jack at that point. "I think you're a little confused. I'll explain it to you." By the time he finished explaining, the rest of the class was bored to tears! And the class was over.

"I need someone to tell me how a chord is constructed," Mr. Al Feena said to his sixth graders. "How about you, Jack?" Jack leaned forward, flipped his hair back and began explaining. "Okay. Uh, you get the first note and, uh, go to the next one. Like up a couple of notes. Uhm then . . ." Mr. Al Feena held up a hand. "Wait a minute, Jack. You need to think about this more. I'll come back to you." Mr. Al Feena went on to the next question in order to keep the class moving.

Insisting on Raised Hand for Responses

When it comes to getting student feedback, you need to insist that students raise their hands before they answer so that you don't have chaos every time you want feedback. You simply can't have everyone shouting out the answer. If you aren't adamant, students will start calling out again. Make no mistake about it! Raising hands is an important and an essential part of the feedback process.

Definition of Insisting on Raised Hands

"Raised hands" means that students are expected to lift their hands above their heads, in anticipation of being called upon by the teacher. Everyone probably has the same interpretation, but there are a few ins-and-outs that need to be mentioned to get the complete picture.

One of these details is the "when" factor. Do you need to ask for raised hands on every occasion? In other words, can there be some exceptions? Absolutely; it's just a matter of letting students know the normal procedure is suspended and that they can answer **without** raising their hands. There are many times when the spontaneity of speaking out is much more suitable, so forget the hands, but then go right back to it.

Another aspect that needs mentioning is the "consistency" angle. That's what being insistent means in this case. It's being adamant about students raising their hands and resistant in recognizing those who don't. The consistency factor is part-and-parcel of being insistent.

Those are the two ins-and-outs that need to be understood in this task. There can be exceptions, but most of the time you must be consistent with the procedure. That's important in "getting" the complete picture.

Reasons for Insisting on Raised Hands

There are two obvious, but **very important**, reasons why you need to have students raise their hands in order to respond. One is to keep an orderly learning environment. The second is to insure a smooth flowing lesson.

Take the reason that raising hands **promotes a healthier learning environment**. You don't have kids shouting out the answer at the same time or yelling "I know, I know" in your face or calling out different answers at the same time so that you can't hear one answer from the other! You don't have that constant upheaval and disruption. Instead, you have a calm, orderly, and manageable situation where everyone can hear everyone else and the business of learning can go on without confusion and frustration—on both the teacher's and the students' part. An orderly approach to feedback is crucial to the learning process, especially in the confines of a classroom, mainly because it establishes an organized learning environment. That's the bottom line. Learning must be an orderly process, and raising of hands contributes in a large way towards this goal.

The second reason raising hands is so important is because it **insures a smoother flowing lesson**. When the feedback is handled in this orderly and organized manner, the lesson automatically moves forward smoothly and easily, without any start and stops for sudden outbursts, scrambled jabber, or screaming urchins! You can maintain the flow of the lesson and keep the momentum moving. All because there's less interruptions in obtaining the feedback. It's that simple.

But wait. There's one other reason I want to mention before going on, which is a direct outcome from the reason above. You probably already know it: raising hands also **makes for better behaved students**. When the lesson moves forward smoothly and steadily, the students stay with-it better and feel less prone to "monkey" around. Remember: the smoother the flow (of the lesson), the better the behavior (of the students). Classroom discipline improves dramatically when you insist on raised hands.

The raising of hands is no small matter in the process of teaching and learning. It's not just an inconsequential detail or some idiosyncratic method on the part of the teacher. It might well be a detail, but it's an absolutely essential detail in the handling of student feedback. So don't underestimate it and, above all, don't neglect this so-called "detail" in your own teaching.

Problem with Insisting on Raised Hands

What happens so much of the time is that **teachers aren't always consistent** in having students raise their hands. The teacher might go "bananas" in demanding that every hand be raised, and the next time, forget all about it. The upshot is that the kids aren't consistent either. In fact, a lot of the time they just don't know what they're supposed to do. That's when you get the "mix" of dutifully raised hands and rudely shouted answers—and a teacher who blasts the class for not "obeying" the rule(s). You really confuse a class when you do this. Unfortunately, however, being inconsistent is the biggest problem teachers have when it comes to raising hands.

Let's briefly comment on the less common problem of some **teachers being overly consistent**, to the extent that the students can't say "moo" or "boo" without raising their hands. The classroom environment is so rigid and lifeless that there's no joy and excitement left, and no spontaneity in the students' feedback. Obviously, this is not the intended reaction. The raising of hands should be for the purpose of *helping* the learning process, not hindering it.

Suggestions for Raising Hands

Here is a list of suggestions or guidelines you'll find helpful.

Instructing Raised Hands Immediately. You need to know *when* to give this instruction and *what* exactly to say. As for the *when* part, you have two choices: (1) **right before** the question or (2) **right after** the question.

- **Before**: "Raise your hand. What does 2/4 mean?" **or** "Hands up. Who knows what presto means?"

- **After**: "Did the melody move by steps or skips? Raise hands." **or** "How many measures long is a phrase? Hands, please."

But there's a silent way too, where all you do is lift your hand while you're asking the question. That way you can "tell" the class without having to say a word. This is especially effective when raising hands is an established routine and you don't want to sound like a broken record. Try it. It works like a charm. And the **what** part? That's easy. Just tell students to raise their hands. For example:

- "Raise your hands."
- "Hands up."
- "Hands, please."
- "Can I see hands?"
- "Remember hands, please."

The shorter, the better; you don't want a long, drawn-out instruction.

Acknowledging Raised Hands Only. One of the best ways to get the point across that you expect raised hands is to recognize only those who do raise their hands. That way, you won't have to keep harping on the offenders. It doesn't take students very long to "get the message" and figure out they don't get called on because they don't raise their hands.

Cuing Selected Students Clearly. You need to know all the possible ways you can cue in the student so that you won't destroy the mood of the moment or interrupt the flow of the lesson, besides calling out the name. For example, you could also give cues by:

- nodding your head
- raising your eyebrows
- nodding and raising eyebrows
- pointing your finger
- tapping student's shoulder or desk,
- smiling and nodding at student

Try to do all of these cuing tactics. That way, you can be more competent in acknowledging raised hands and maintaining the smooth flow of the lesson.

Reminding Whole Class Frequently. Don't think that students are going to remember raising their hands just because you told them how it was "going to be" one day, or because you put it on the class rules list. They won't. You'll have to remind students almost daily to raise hands, so use the little tactic mentioned earlier: raise your own hand while you're asking the question. It's an obvious reminder to raise their hands as well. And if you can remember, try to **mirror** the class's hand. In other words, raise your left hand, not your right. That helps even more!

Praising Raised Hands Immediately. You'll get better results from students if you praise them immediately for raising their hands. That lets them know you recognize their effort to remember and also keep the "rule." You could praise the whole class before calling on the individual, or you could wait and praise the student after he/she has answered. It'll depend on the situation at the moment. Here are some examples of praise:

- "I'm really pleased to see all the raised hands."
- "Great. Everyone remembered to raise hands!"
- "I see everyone's hand up. Very good, class."
- "I appreciate your raised hand, Mary."
- "Thank you for raising your hand to answer, Bill."

All it takes is a simple word of praise to make students want to cooperate next time as well. That old saying is true. You **can** catch more with honey than with tar.

Recognizing Shy Students Tactfully. Because you'll always have those students who don't answer as often as others, you'll need to be very careful how you handle them. **First**, be sure you do acknowledge them. Don't let their effort go unheeded. Call on them. Shy students are often a bit paranoid. They'll think you don't like them if you don't call on them. **Second**, be sure to use reassuring body language, like nodding with a smile or raising eyebrows with a smile, etc. And **third**, praise the student immediately after responding for (1) raising his/her hand and (2) answering the question correctly. You'll encourage the student tremendously if you follow these simple rules.

Concluding Challenge

Insist upon students raising their hands in your classes and recognize the importance of establishing such a practice. Read, and even reread, this discussion to note the significant reasons and then to study the suggested guidelines. I leave it in your hands now.

LESS EFFECTIVE	MORE EFFECTIVE
"Before we pretend to be birds high in the sky, let's talk about high things," Ms. Sandy Blocks said to her kindergartners. "Who can tell me something else that's high in the sky?" Ten children popped up shouting, "I know, I know." And Billy kept yelling, "an airplane, an airplane." Ms. Sandy Blocks "shhhed" Billy and motioned for the "I knowers" to stop. But they didn't. "I can't hear anyone," she yelled. "And stop that 'I know' stuff." Ms Sandy Blocks was getting miffed.	Ms. Sandy Blocks told her kindergartners they were going to be birds in the sky. The children "oohed" excitedly. "But first, let's talk about high things, like birds." Raising her left arm, Ms. Sandy Blocks asked, "What things are high in the sky?" Hands flew up all around her. She smiled and nodded at Julie. "Yes, a star. Thank you for raising your hand. Anything else?" she asked. She pointed to Tom while still holding her hand up. "Good! An airplane. And thank you for the raised hand." She smiled warmly at the children.

Ms. Melody Bells wrote "Drum Roll Symphony" on the board. "Who wrote this work?" she asked her sixth graders. Everybody tried to tell her at the same time, except John and Erik. They kept shouting "I got it. I got it!" Ms. Melody Bells shook her head disgustedly. "I won't call on anyone if this noise doesn't stop. You know you're supposed to wait until I call on you," she snapped. Students looked at each other. "But we didn't know," Mark said. "You didn't tell us."

Directing the class's attention to the board, Ms. Melody Bells pointed to the name of the work the sixth graders listened to last week. "Raise your hand if you remember who wrote the 'Drum Roll Symphony'." She raised her own hand while asking the question. "Tim? Excellent. Joseph Haydn. I appreciated your raised hand too." Smiling, she asked, "What is a symphony? Cindy? Bravo. A large orchestral work with four movements." Then she praised the students for raising their hands.

9

Managing Classroom Behavior

The spotlight is on classroom management in this chapter. Is there any other responsibility in teaching that strikes as much fear and anxiety among teachers as keeping order in the classroom? I don't think so. After years of teaching, I'm convinced that discipline is a primary concern for practically **every** teacher—whether experienced or not-so-experienced—who steps foot into the classroom today.

Discipline is a major problem today in the classroom, where students misbehave in distracting ways. Teachers need all the know-how and skill they can muster to handle the discipline and keep control of the classroom. These "given" conditions are the ones that cause all the anxiety when it comes to discipline.

Most teachers **want** some kind of discipline system, or approach, as C. M. Charles contends, so that they can (a) prevent student misbehavior, (b) provide positive control, (c) nurture better behavior, and (d) gain parental support.[1] So, an

---

[1]Charles, C. M. *Building Classroom Discipline*, 3rd Edition (New York: Longman Publishing Co., 1989), p. 168.

approach, or such a "system," if you will, is such suggested in this chapter, which can help you achieve these goals. Basically, it focuses on three so-called "control" factors, including: (1) personal tools, (2) preventive techniques, and (3) corrective measures.

Keeping order is an actual part of the teaching-learning process.[2] It's an integral part—even indispensable! It's like this. You may well be organized to-a-tee, prepared to-the-max, skilled to-the-nth degree, and articulate to-the-hilt, but, if you can't keep order and manage behavior, all these wonderful qualities don't mean anything. You've got to have control of your class before you can teach; if you don't have control, you can't teach. It's that simple.

If you're serious about getting a better "handle" on managing behavior in your classroom, read this chapter to find many practical suggestions that can help you immediately. Whatever you do, though, don't make light of any of the suggestions, especially the ones under personal tools, because they have the most impact when executed the proper way.

Definition of Managing Behavior

Because so many terms and expressions are used in conjunction with discipline, let's be sure the meaning of "managing behavior" is clear. Actually, the definition fits several other familiar expressions as well, like controlling behavior, guiding discipline, or keeping order.

What the expression "managing behavior" and all the similar ones mentioned, refer to is a **handling** of misbehavior in the classroom. It means dealing with misbehavior in such a way as to eliminate inappropriate behavior and promote appropriate behavior; to establish positive control; and create an effective classroom climate.

You could also think of "managing behavior" and all the other expressions as the job of "conducting" class conduct. It's where the teacher stops the out-of-tune behavior and encourages the in-tune behavior, and then nurtures the positive response of the entire group.

Knowing the meaning, however, has little value unless you know the purpose of the task. In other words, you need to know what's so important about managing behavior or handling discipline. The answer is clear to those who have been in the classroom. But for those who haven't or for those who haven't been there as long, let me answer as clearly as I know how. Plain and simple, the reason for keeping order and managing discipline is to create a conducive environment for teaching and learning—one that has a low potential for trouble.[3] There's freedom to teach and learn without disruption or interference—that's the sole purpose for managing classroom behavior.

Now that we have a consensus of understanding as to the **meaning** of the phrase "managing behavior" and the **purpose** of such a task, let's discuss the three-pronged approach for handling discipline, as mentioned earlier.

Three-Pronged Discipline Approach

After years of teaching and preparing teachers to teach, it became clear to me at a particular point in my experience that practically every "do" or "don't" that can be said about handling discipline falls into one of the following three categories:

---

[2]Heck, Shirley and William C. Ray. *The Complex Roles of a Teacher* (New York: Teachers College Press, 1984), p. 67.

[3]Good, Thomas L. and Jere E. Brophy. *Looking in Classrooms* (New York: Harper & Row, 1978), p. 166.

1. Personal Tools
2. Preventive Techniques
3. Corrective Measures

Let's talk about this three-pronged approach. More needs to be said about it.

Take **personal tools** first. A good number of tactics used for controlling discipline comes from the teacher's own person, such as (1) bodily proximity, (2) physical mobility, (3) facial expressions, (4) body gesturings, and (5) verbal commenting. They're the tools the teacher carries with him/her, the ones that he/she can call upon in a moment's notice. That's why these personal ploys play such an important role in managing classroom discipline. The next time you talk about the do's and don'ts of handling discipline, notice how many of the suggestions have to do with these five tactics. The truth is, so much of classroom disciplining is done simply with the help of one's own personal tools. They often have the greatest impact on the management of misbehavior.

Next there's the **preventive techniques**. Teachers also rely a lot on tactics that come under the heading of "preventive efforts." Teachers have learned that preventing misbehavior—rather than correcting it after it begins—is a much better approach for everyone concerned, which accounts for all those things teachers do to purposely ward off any misbehavior—or to **stop it** from happening in the first place,[4] or simply to **avoid it** in order to promote the preferred behavior. I'm talking about such tactics as (1) being well prepared, (2) establishing effective guidelines, (3) taking authoritative charge, (4) providing behavioral model, (5) keeping organized classroom, (6) finding out behavioral causes, and (7) establishing good rapport. These are some of the more obvious measures you can take to actually "reduce the likelihood of misbehavior" in your classroom,[5] and are an important segment of the teacher's classroom management tactics.

Corrective measures is the third category. Despite all your well-meaning efforts to prevent and avoid misbehavior, it's still going to happen. Students are still going to break the rules and challenge your authority, no matter how many preventive gimmicks you use. This means you've got to have ways **to stop the misbehavior** on the spot and **rechannel it** in a positive direction.[6] What we're talking about, then, is another category of indispensable tactics because you've got to be **ready to react** to these violations when they occur. In short, you've got to have some corrective techniques at your fingertips.

Unfortunately, corrective discipline is often seen as the only kind of disciplining. Too many teachers think that managing misbehavior is solely a matter of scowling, frowning, pointing a finger, etc., in the direction of the erring student. That simply isn't so. Like C. M. Charles says, corrective disciplining isn't like that at all. It's not intimidating, punishing, or traumatic. It's just the opposite. It's a positive way of handling misbehavior.[7] Moreover, it's firm, yet fair, and it doesn't destroy the student's self-esteem or take away his/her dignity.

Examples of such corrective techniques include: (1) abiding by established rules (established by teacher and students), (2) applying the determined consequences, (3) seeing student after class, (4) stopping undesired behavior, (5) suggesting desired behavior, (6) applying powerful reinforcement, and (7) explaining classroom rights to

---

[4]Charles, C. M. *Building Classroom Discipline*, pp. 171–172.
[5]Charles, C. M. *Building Classroom Discipline*, p. 172.
[6]*Ibid.*, p. 174.
[7]*Ibid.*, p. 174.

PERSONAL TOOLS	PREVENTIVE TECHNIQUES	CORRECTIVE MEASURES
• Bodily Proximity	• Establish Positive Climate	• Apply Consequences
• Physical Mobility	–Focus on Relationship	• Stop Undesired Behavior
• Facial Expressions	Skills	–Hand Signals
• Bodily Gesturings	–Maintain Organized	–Humorous Remarks
• Verbal Commenting	Environment	–Seat Changing
–Reactional	• Be Well Prepared	–Touching/Tapping
–Singular Negative	• Adhere to Classroom	–Calling on Student
–Humorous	Routines	–Seeing After Class
–Situational	• Set Up Guidelines	–Making Comments
	• Reinforce Good Behavior	–Removing Object
	• Assume Model Behavior	• Apply Reinforcement
	• Get to Know Individual	• Explain Classroom Rights
	Students	• Apply Personal Tool
	• Find Out Misbehavior	
	Causes	
	• Communicate in	
	Appropriate Manner	

Figure 9.1. Three-Pronged Discipline Approach.

the students. This is a tough list of tactics, but these are the kinds of things you've got to do in order to stop disruptive behavior when it occurs.

Do you have a clearer idea now of the three categories of behavior needed for managing discipline? Do you see that just about every suggestion you have regarding discipline can be considered (1) a personal tool, (2) a preventive technique, and (3) a corrective measure? Test it out. Suggest some tactics. And see if they don't fit under one of these categories. Hopefully, this approach will make it easier for you to deal with discipline because of the clear-cut categories. (See Figure 9.1)

Let's look closely at each category individually for some specific suggestions and examples.

Personal Tools

You possess invaluable ammunition for controlling classroom discipline on your own person. Your own personal "tools" are perhaps the most effective weapons you have for dealing with discipline. A lot of teachers don't know this nor does every teacher "see" his/her personal maneuvers as potential tools for disciplining. But they are! Expressions, gesturings, and "verbiaging" make up an impressive category of tactics that have a definite—and, in many instances, the most powerful—impact on classroom discipline.

So, to be certain that there's a clear understanding of all the "tools" involved in this first category and how each one contributes to controlling discipline, let's examine each tool carefully and look at some suggestions for implementing these tools. Consider, then, the following personal strategies for managing classroom behavior:

Physical Proximity. This "tool" simply refers to the act of moving nearer to the misbehaving student(s). Position or station yourself so that you are standing (or sitting) in close range of the student(s), close enough to be seen, that is, or "felt." In most cases, there isn't any need to say anything. The brief eye contact and close physical presence will be enough to make the student(s) stop almost immediately[8] and go back to the "right" behavior. How long should you stand near the student?

---

[8]Charles, C. M. *Building Classroom Discipline*, p. 92.

It's hard to say. Every situation is different. Sometimes you'll need to stay put for a couple of minutes; other times, for only a split second. It depends upon the student(s). But your intuition will "tell" you. Here are some other guidelines for implementing proximity:

- **Arrange the classroom** so that there is walk space between tables or desks.
- **Seat misbehaving student near you**, if accessible walk space isn't possible.
- **Keep close eye on those** students who are prone to misbehave.
- **Establish eye contact** with misbehaving student(s) while in route or when in position.
- **Move around the room** intermittently while teaching to be near everyone at one time or another.
- **Position yourself** in the most advantageous spot—in front, to the side, in back, or in between student(s).
- **Remain as long as you think necessary**, or as long as it takes for the student(s) to settle down.
- **Give some gesture** or expression to let student(s) know that you appreciate his/her stopping disturbance, such as:

  - signaling okay
  - giving thumbs up
  - patting back
  - patting shoulder
  - touching head
  - nodding head
  - mouthing "Thank you"
  - tapping hand

- **Avoid saying anything** to the student(s) unless absolutely necessary—let your presence do the "talking."

Make no mistake about physical proximity—it is probably the most controlling personal tool you have, from a positional point-of-view. A standing position always projects more authority than a sitting one because you're literally looking down on the student—from a close distance. That alone makes proximity a formidable tool. Use it wisely, though. Don't overkill it; if you do, it'll lose its impact.

Physical Mobility. Another effective "tool" you have at your disposal is moving about as you teach—or exercising mobility. I don't mean that silly back-and-forth pacing where you look like a caged lion. That's not mobility; that's hyperactivity! Nor am I talking about those deliberate premeditated trekkings you take from point A to point B. That's not the right idea either. Mobility is more loosely structured than that. Sometimes it's nothing more than (a) **taking a few steps** forward, backward, or sideways, while other times it's a matter of (b) **taking a meandering stroll** up and down the aisles, between the desks, or around the room, without any specific destination in mind. It's just to circulate aimlessly and leisurely in order to keep tabs on everyone, not just those in the front rows. That's why mobility is such an important "tool" for disciplining. It's an unobtrusive way to keep an eye on students.

It's unfortunate, though, that some teachers underestimate the significance of their own mobility and stay glued to one spot, while others have the mistaken idea that mobility means pacing back and forth. Maybe this discussion will open some eyes and convince those who need convincing to start being more mobile. Here are some guidelines so that you can be as effective as possible. Mobility needs to be implemented in the following ways:

- **Intermittently**, not all the time; only off and on as you "feel the need."
- **Unobtrusively**, like the movement was part of the procedures; not out of the ordinary.
- **Slowly** and **calmly**, in a leisurely and non-threatening manner.
- **Aimlessly** with no particular destination in mind; like a meandering effect on the longer strolls.
- **Smoothly** and **lingeringly** when taking steps forward, backward, or sideways; not spastically or nervously.
- **Alternatingly** when it comes to the routes you take on longer strolls; go different direction each time.
- **Intuitively**, not in a planned manner; move around or step off as the spirit moves you; extemporaneously, in other words. Keep the students guessing.

When implemented as indicated above, teacher mobility becomes a strong weapon (in your arsenal of personal tools) to combat discipline. You can't do without it if you're going to keep your eye on everyone, so take the guidelines to heart and start applying them to your own mobility efforts. You'll notice a difference when students are more responsive to your movements.

Personal Appearance. One of the personal tools we teachers don't often think of as a discipline agent is our own personal appearance. We're all concerned about looking good, but then we stop short of recognizing the implication(s) of a good appearance when it comes to discipline. As teachers, however, we need to know that everything about our outward appearance makes an **authoritative impression** on students. Everything! That includes (a) our grooming, (b) our clothing, (c) our posture, and (d) our carriage. That's all part of our so-called "personal appearance." To put it another way, our appearance speaks volumes to the students in terms of our **authoritative stature**. It either elevates it or diminishes it. Appearance has that much leverage where discipline is concerned. With that thought in mind, let's examine the various facets of our appearance as mentioned above in order to establish the proper expectations and offer some suggestions.

Grooming

Being well-groomed is an integral part of "looking good." It's giving the appearance of being "together" as a person and having respect for one's self. Specifically, it means that the teacher has given special attention to his/her (a) hair, (b) skin, (c) nails, and (d) makeup or beard. All these parts of one's self are made to look neat, clean, and attractive, and contribute in a large measure to the teacher's overall appearance of "looking good." In a more practical sense, it means attending to the following kinds of chores:

- Keep hair neat and clean
- Style hair attractively
- Maintain clean, healthy skin
- Take care of skin properly
- Keep fingernails neat, clean, and well manicured
- Select appropriate makeup
- Apply makeup attractively

- Keep face clean-shaven
- Trim moustache/beard neatly
- Maintain clean, healthy, well-brushed teeth

To be well-groomed, then, is a matter of giving personal attention to yourself. The fact is, your grooming can be a positive factor in establishing your authority in the classroom. It goes hand-in-hand with being disciplined as a person.

Clothing

Another obvious facet of the teacher's personal appearance is clothing. There's a lot of truth to the saying, "Clothes make the man," especially when it comes to discipline. Clothes *do* make a difference. Teachers need to look well dressed in order to command respect. They need to look like they're "put together" properly and attractively, so that they feel confident in their attire. In terms of the actual clothing, that means teachers need to dress in such a way that their attire can be described as:

- **stylish**—not out of date, frumpish, or too-far-out; always in vogue and in good taste.
- **coordinated**—separates matched according to color, pattern, or fabric. Accessories (belts, scarves, jewelry) used for accentuating.
- **fitted**—not too tight, too baggy, too long, or too short; appropriately sized for one's physical frame.
- **well-made**—not skimpy or poorly made, but having a look of quality and good workmanship.

When it comes to managing discipline, being well-dressed goes a long way in establishing your authority and making an impact on the class. Don't let today's philosophy of "anything goes" influence how you dress. Even in this day and age, it makes a difference when you're well dressed.

Body Posture

Consider your posture, that is, the way you hold yourself. Posture *does* have a bearing on managing discipline. Good posture gives the impression that the teacher is strong and determined. Poor posture, like drooping shoulders, makes the teacher look weak and timid.[9] The fact is, students learn to read body language quickly and react to the teacher accordingly. That's why good posture plays such a key role in managing behavior. Good posture is achieved when you do the following:

- Keep shoulders back and avoid slumping or drooping shoulders.
- Hold head up and look straight ahead, rather than look down.
- Draw whole body up (like a puppet on a string) and stand tall; avoid slouching.
- Pull in stomach and raise up the chest; avoid letting chest cave in.
- Sit up straight in chair with feet on floor; avoid sliding down in chair and slumping shoulders.

---

[9]Charles, C. M. *Building Classroom Discipline*, p. 92.

The bottom line is, you've got to maintain good posture as a teacher not just because it looks so much better than poor posture, important as that is, but more so because good posture is essential in managing discipline. It gives you that "edge" you need. So take a look at your posture, and see if it needs some shoring up. If it does, get it in shape.

Body Carriage

I purposely separated body posture and body carriage because there is a distinction and you need to be aware of it. Posture has to do with your stance—how you hold yourself. Carriage, on the other hand, deals with your movement; that is, how you navigate your body—whether your posture is good or bad. Your carriage might be lethargic-looking because of droopy shoulders, timid-looking due to a downcast head, or agitated-looking as a result of a leaning forward rather than standing straight. But when your head and body are held high, your carriage tends to be more regal-looking and more vigorous-looking when the shoulders are back and the stomach is in. Your carriage has a certain "look" to it depending upon your posture. That's the link between the two traits—the way the body is held.

So what's the key to good carriage? Just follow the same suggestions for good posture because good carriage depends totally upon having good posture. (See "Body Posture.") As for the impact on managing misbehavior, body carriage is dynamite! Think about it. What would you do if you saw a teacher with a determined-looking carriage making a bee-line drive in your direction as a result of seeing you do . . .? You'd stop doing it in a heartbeat, wouldn't you? Remember, a confident carriage is powerful stuff when you're handling discipline.

Summary of Personal Appearance

Your outward appearance is vitally important in dealing with discipline. That means everything about you—your grooming, your clothing, your posture, and your carriage—makes an impression on students. You might think these are incidental aspects, even after reading about them, but they aren't! They have everything to do with making your outward self a viable and convincing force in the managing of classroom behavior.

Facial Expressions. Facial expressions are the most personable personal tool you've got. They're the whole bevy of "looks" you are capable of mustering up for the purpose of (a) "saying" something without having to speak, or (b) reinforcing something you are saying. What's so important about facial expressions where managing behavior is concerned is that students can read teacher "looks" about as quickly as they can decipher body language, which means you can encourage good behavior just by looking pleased, impressed, or elated—and stop bad behavior just by looking annoyed, disgusted, or disappointed.[10] Facial expressions are that persuasive.

But the truth is, a lot of teachers don't feel comfortable using facial expressions. Not only do they miss out on communicating more effectively, but they also miss out on disciplining more efficiently—and more personally. Thus, every teacher needs a repertoire of facial expressions, especially for discipline purposes.

Repertoire of Expressions

As a teacher, you do, indeed, need a list or collection of "looks" that can be communicated in a twinkling of an eye. Here is a list of examples. Your repertoire should include faces, or "looks," that indicate you are:

---

[10]Charles, C. M. *Building Classroom Discipline*, p. 93.

- pleased
- excited
- surprised
- encouraged
- concerned
- amused

- concerned
- puzzled
- annoyed
- disappointed
- disgusted
- relieved

Obviously, the list could go on-and-on, but you get the idea. There's a catch, though; you need to know *how* you look when you don these faces, so practice in front of a mirror and make sure your face is clearly conveying the emotion you intended. Don't fall into the trap of thinking you look so-and-so when, in fact, you don't. Know how you're "looking" when you put on one of your faces. Then, too, some of you may need to expand your repertoire. If so, do it. You've got to have a varied repertoire of "working" faces when you're dealing with discipline, even a very specific face or "look" at times.

Repertoire of Specific Looks

Let's go a step further with facial expressions. I found out years ago in my own teaching that it really helped to have specific "looks" in place, expressions that clearly communicated a particular feeling or thought. What I did was mentally attach the comment I would normally make to the "look" I was giving. It worked magnificently. Like mental telepathy, students knew exactly what I was thinking when I gave my "look." All you need to do is identify your thought and let your face do the "talking." Here's a sampling of the specific "looks" you could use according to the intended thought. You could have a:

- "I'm surprised at you" look
- "Cut it out" look
- "Are you doing that again?" look
- "Can I help you?" look
- "What's going on there?" look
- "Okay, I'll wait" look
- "Yes, that's right!" look
- "Good, I like that" look
- "I'm proud of you" look
- "Keep going" look
- "Excellent job!" look
- "I understand" look

Attach a specific thought to your expression or "look" and then call the "look" by that intended thought. It's a marvelous technique, particularly in discipline situations, because many times you won't even have to say a word. Just give your "look." But again, practice in front of a mirror to be sure your face is really communicating the idea. If it isn't, the expression won't work.

One final point. I did not go into the contributing facets of one's facial expressions, like the eyes, the eyebrows, the mouth, etc., mainly because this information has already been covered elsewhere in the book. (See the section "Using Facial

Expressions" in Chapter 2.) Also, the focus of this chapter's discussion has been on promoting facial expressions as a disciplining technique. However, knowing how to manipulate one's facial features must come first, like: raising eyebrows, squinting eyes, widening eyes, pursing lips, rolling in lips, tilting head, etc.[11] My suggestion is to explore your features initially, if you haven't already. Find out all the ways you can alter each feature. Once you've done this, you'll be ready to start on your repertoire of facial expressions.

Summary of Facial Expressions

Having a repertoire of facial expressions that clearly communicates your feelings or your thoughts without having to speak is a "must," especially when it comes to discipline, because students read the teacher's facial expression very well. You can help maintain discipline many times just by giving the student(s) a specific "look" to convey your sentiments. Don't lose out on one of your most valuable personal assets as a teacher. Facial expressions are a lifesaver in keeping order.

Verbalizing Efforts. Talk about an awesome personal tool! This is it. Your words are the strongest weapon you have, and potentially the most dangerous. Words can penetrate and hurt, and, worst of all, they can linger; but they can also encourage, strengthen, and soothe. It's up to you. You're the one who has to exercise the wisdom to temper your words and use them in a positive way when you're dealing with discipline. Be sure you understand that before you go spouting off to some poor student. It's an imperative prerequisite.

The obvious question is, what do you say when something happens? That is, what do you say to the student(s)? You could say lots of things, rant-and-rave until you turn blue, or pontificate on the fallacy of wrong doing until the cows come home—none of which are very practical. You need to say something that's **short, concise**, and **to the point**—and then move on. That's the secret to good verbiage when you're involved with discipline. So here's what you do: confine your verbiage

---

[11]Madsen, Charles H. and Clifford K. Madsen. *Teaching Discipline*, 2d ed. (Boston: Allyn and Bacon, 1974), p. 182.

to (a) calling out name(s) and/or (b) making brief comments. Let's discuss each one individually.

Call Out Name

One of the quickest ways to get a student's attention is to call out his/her name. But you need to consider three stipulations to make sure you do it properly. First, you've got to **use** an **authoritative voice**, or a voice that's properly projected, strongly inflected, and noticeably punctuated. Calling out a name with authority almost stops the student in his or her tracks.

The second stipulation is, you need to **establish eye contact** as soon as you call out the name(s). That brief meeting of the eyes is what clinches the impact; it makes the calling out of one's name even more personal. So don't just call out the name and look off yonder—get the student's eye and hold it for a second or two. It stops the student cold!

The third stipulation is that you must **learn the correct name(s)** of every student before attempting to call out. Nothing is more embarrassing for the teacher—and more amusing to the students—than the bloopers that happen with names.

Make (Brief) Comments

Here's where all the "action" is when it comes to your verbal tool. You can do more than call out a name—you can make comments regarding the misbehavior. But, what kind of comments? It's very difficult to know what should be said each time there's a problem, and even more difficult to avoid being rude, wordy, or redundant when you're not sure.

Being wordy always reminds me of the teacher who turned every discipline situation into a sermonette. As I recall, the lesson was going swimmingly; that is, until some smart-alec thought it would be cute to make his desk squeak by rocking it. I was impressed how quickly she spotted him. "We don't need any of that, thank you," she began. "What if everyone did that? It would get so noisy that blah-blah-blah,

blah, etc." A couple of minutes later she was still going on about the "Episode of the squeaky desk." It was too much flap for the deed!

I'd like to share with you some suggestions as to what kind of comments you can make. They're comments for stopping misbehavior quickly, so they're short and to the point. It really helps if you think of comments falling into four types, and then using the one that fits the best at the moment. Here are the four types of comments with specific examples. Your comment could be:

1. **A situational direction** or a statement that makes reference to the specific misdemeanor, such as the following:

   - "Stop that whispering, please."
   - "Put that comb away, if you will."
   - "Take the gum out of your mouth right now."
   - "I'd appreciate it if you'd quit tapping that pencil."
   - "That talking needs to stop back there, you two."

2. **A cease request** or a command that simply asks the student(s) to stop the inappropriate behavior, such as:

   - "Quit that right now."
   - "Cut it out. Now!"
   - "Stop it before I come back."
   - "That's enough of that."
   - "Let's have no more of that!"

3. **A humorous statement** or a funny one-liner to which students can relate and that fits the moment, like:

   - "So now you're going to try your hand at talking, huh?"
   - "I didn't know you're a heavyweight boxer, Jack."
   - "Well, aren't you the world's best bubble gum chewer!"
   - "Are we interrupting your conversation?"
   - "We got some highly classified information being passed back-and-forth, girls?"

4. **A reactional remark** or a comment that makes reference to your response, or feeling, towards the misbehavior, such as:

   - "I'm annoyed with all this running back and forth."
   - "This talking is giving me a headache."
   - "I'm disappointed in your hallway behavior, boys."
   - "I dislike that kind of talk in this class."
   - "That pencil tapping is driving me batty!"

See how you can really focus your comments and keep them streamlined? You don't have to ramble or get off-track, not if you have these types established in your mind. Your intuition and the circumstance will automatically give you the "right" comment at the moment. By the way, your comment could be a combination, such as situational/case, or situational/reactional.

Here's one more piece of advice. Knowing what to say isn't enough—it's **how** you say it that counts. Your comment might well be the best thing you could have said, but, if it's not delivered in an appealing and effective manner, it won't do the job! You've got to use all your speech skills including:

- inflection (highs-lows)
- dynamic differentiation (loud-softs)
- tempo variation (fast-slow)
- vocal modulation (proper voice placement)

- projection
- intentional hesitation
- conviction
- sincerity
- eye contact

Summary of Verbalizing Efforts

Of all your personal tools, it's your verbal tool that potentially packs the most power. Basically, you have three options. You can: (1) call out student's name, (2) make a brief comment, or (3) use a combination of call out and comment. The heavy-duty one, however, is the commenting category. To be most effective, your comments should be precise and to the point, not rambling and repetitive. You'll find it helpful if you frame your comments within the context of four categories, namely, situational directives, cease requests, humorous statements, or reactional remarks—or any combination of categories. Try it; you'll be pleasantly surprised how well it works in regard to disciplining.

Bodily Gestures. Last, but not the least, of your personal tools is the gesturing—all those head, hand, and body signals that clearly communicate your thoughts without having to say a word. Experienced teachers know that gesturing can discourage behavior, as well as encourage it—quietly and without any embarrassment.[12] That's the beauty of gesturing. It's discreet.

You can also use gesturing as a preventive technique. It helps maintain the students' attention and keeps them from misbehaving as much. Any wonder why gesturing is such a valuable personal tool for disciplining? However, gesturing isn't perceived as a teacher skill—or even as a disciplining tool—by a lot of teachers. But make no mistake: gesturing *does* require skill and is a very effective tool for disciplining. Thus, you need to cultivate a repertoire of gesturings, just like you did for facial expressions.

Repertoire of Gestures

You've got to systematically cultivate a repertoire of gestures if you're going to be good at gesturing. Effective gesturing doesn't just happen. Sure, you can flip a hand here, nod your head there, and shake your finger everywhere, but that hardly constitutes having a variety of appropriate gestures. If you leave gesturing to chance, or depend on doing "what comes naturally," you'll never cultivate a repertoire of gestures that "work" for you.

The list of gesturings you could use is practically endless, but you don't need every gesture ever invented. That would be ridiculous. A **good rule** for selecting your gestures, at least initially, is this: To look most natural (and feel most comfortable), select movements (or poses) that most closely resemble the ones already established in your social life. If you follow this rule, you won't feel so uncomfortable because the gesturing will be close to what you already do. Only now you'll be more precise and deliberate; and those gestures that "aren't you," so to speak, you don't do!

---

[12]Charles, C. M. *Building Classroom Discipline*, p. 93.

Here's a sample repertoire. You'll notice that it includes a variety of gestures using the head, shoulders, arms, hands, and fingers. Keep in mind this is only a sample list, not a complete list, and that some of these gestures might not be "your thing."

- shaking head
- nodding head (up/down)
- tilting head with pursed lips
- lifting both shoulders
- lifting right or left shoulder
- shrugging shoulders
- raising arms
- folding arms
- extending arms with palms up
- holding arms behind back
- hands(s) on hip(s)

- hands out with palms up
- hands folded
- hands on desk, piano, etc.
- thumbs up
- palms up with fingers flexing[13]
- index finger on cheeks
- finger on student's hand/head
- shaking finger
- finger to lips
- signaling OK[14]
- pointing finger

A word about how gesturings should be executed. What was said earlier in regard to facial expressions holds with gesturing as well. It isn't so much what you do, gesture-wise, as *how* you do it. The gesture may fit the occasion, to-a-tee, but if it's not executed "right," it won't work. Period. Here's what I mean by "right." It's doing the gesture with:

- definitive actions (or well-defined motions)
- theatrical flair (or appealing showmanship)

---

[13]Charles, C. M. *Building Classroom Discipline*, p. 93.
[14]Madsen and Madsen, *Teaching Discipline*, p. 182.

- convincing manner (or authoritative air)
- deliberate attitude (or purposeful progress)
- natural ease (or automatic response)

Gesturing must project all of these qualities in order to be effective.

Combination of Personal Tools. Each personal tool is really a discipline weapon in its own right. But, rarely is one tool used by itself. What usually happens is that teachers use a **combination of these tools**. It's almost impossible to make a gesture without any facial expression, or rattle off a comment without gesturing. Try it. You'll see. The most commonly used combinations include:

- Expression + Gesture
- Name + Expression + Gesture
- Comment + Expression + Gesture
- Name + Expression + Comment
- Name +Expression + Comment + Gesture

If this combining of personal tools is a new concept for you, take time to test out each combination. When you do, you'll see that everything happens together—in a split second—with the exception of the name; calling the name usually comes first. Role play and see which combination(s) suit(s) you best. Then use it.

Summary of Personal Tools

This concludes the discussion on the first category of disciplinary tactics in the three-pronged approach. Using your personal tools is a major factor in keeping order in the classroom, a point that can't be stressed enough. Such tactics as physical proximity, teacher mobility, physical appearance, facial expressions, verbal input, and body gesturings have a profound effect on the student's behavior. The extent to which you can execute these personal facets in a competent and skillful manner, the more leverage and control you will have in managing behavior.

In the final analysis, keeping order in the classroom boils down to how well you can execute your own "tools." You will be only as effective in managing discipline as your personal tools, so give these tools your utmost consideration.

Preventive Techniques

Another category of tactics that plays a crucial role in managing classroom behavior is the preventive measures. Prevention is the key to behavior management, and teachers who are good at preventing problems (before they occur) are usually good at disciplining as well.[15]

The term "preventive techniques" refers to, of course, any act or deed that has the potential of **reducing** the occurrence of behavior problems[16] or the potential of **avoiding** them! Here's why preventive deeds are so important. Discipline problems create stress and cause tension between teacher and student(s). Plus, they invariably interrupt the learning process—and the teaching process as well. They even put a damper on the class's enthusiasm.[17]

By taking steps, however, to avoid these situations, you enhance the learning environment by (a) reducing the stress level in the classroom, (b) insuring the smooth flow of the lesson, and (c) establishing a better rapport with the students. See why preventive measures need to be a necessary course of action in your own teaching? In the long run, they'll save you time and energy. In the short run, you'll experience more success as a teacher. The obvious question now is, what kinds of deeds fall under the heading of "preventive techniques"? What do you need to do in order to avoid discipline problems? The answer: a whole lot of common-sense things, like the ones mentioned below:

- Establish Positive Climate
    - focus on relationship skills
    - maintain organized environment
- Be well prepared
- Adhere to classroom routines
- Set up guidelines
- Reinforce good behavior
- Assume model behavior
- Get to know individual students
- Find out misbehavior causes
- Communicate in appropriate manner

This isn't a complete list by any means, nor a prioritized one either. But at least it gives you an idea of the kind of tasks included in the preventive category.

Establish Positive Climate. You've got to create, and maintain, the kind of atmosphere in the classroom that fosters good behavior and encourages it. Without a **positive aura** where students "know" they're expected to behave, it's virtually impossible to have control of the discipline. How do you establish an environment that's warm, pleasant, and supportive, instead of one that's cold, unfriendly, and threatening?[18] By following through on two important practices.

---

[15]Osborn, D. Keith and Janie D., *Discipline and Classroom Management* (Athens, GA: Daye Press, 1989), p. 179.

[16]Charles, C. M. *Building Classroom Discipline*, p. 154.

[17]*Ibid.*, p. 153.

[18]*Ibid.*, p. 154.

Focus on Relationship Traits

Concentrate on those skills that allow you to interact comfortably as a human being from the standpoint of your own reaction (a) toward the students and (b) with the students. C. M. Charles says that to react better toward students, you need to cultivate such personal skills as:

- **Demonstrating friendly disposition** or calling student(s) by name; speaking gently; and showing interest in student by asking about family, hobbies, skills, etc.

- **Exhibiting positive outlook** or looking on the bright side; identifying the solutions, not complaining about the hurdles; and saying only positive things about others, not negative gossip or rumors, etc.

- **Displaying attentive attitude** or focusing in on other's conversation; showing genuine interest in the discussion; and accepting other's conversation without expressing a value judgment, etc.

- **Exercising complimenting spirit** or calling attention to one's positive points, not negative points; delivering comment in a sincere tone of voice; and making honest compliments and appraisals, etc.[19]

So, in order to create a climate that encourages desirable behavior and discourages undesirable behavior, you've got to hone your own skills first so that you have the ability to act comfortably—**towards the students**. But that's not enough. You also need to focus on those skills that make it possible to interact easily with students. There's a difference here. The foregoing skill focuses on **reacting** to the students, while this one, focuses on **interacting** with them. Here are some tips from C. M. Charles again. If you want to interact better with students, he suggests[20]:

- **Giving adequate attention** or spreading your attention around to every student, not just to the troublemakers and the high achievers; speaking to as

[19]Charles, C. M. *Building Classroom Discipline*, p. 155–156.
[20]*Ibid.*, p. 156–157.

many students as possible when they come in; addressing individuals frequently, but briefly. (Improves students' sense of self-worth.)

- **Giving sufficient reinforcement** or providing verbal recognition in hopes that behavior will be repeated; expressing praise, encouragement, or suggestions in order that behavior and productivity will improve; recognizing both class and individual performances; and reinforcing more frequently and more briefly. (Builds students' self-esteem.)

- **Giving willing assistance** or displaying pleasant readiness to help at all times; attending to student(s)' request immediately without putting off; and maintaining patient, understanding attitude toward student(s). (Leads to respectful admiration of teacher.)

- **Providing necessary model** or demonstrating courtesy and good manners as often as possible; staying with modeling despite the lack of administrative and parental support (in many cases); exercising perseverance and patience even when students seem oblivious to teacher's modeling; and keeping foremost in mind that teacher is "the" model for the class.

Maintain Organized Environment

The second way to establish a good classroom climate is to keep an organized learning environment (classroom). A neat, clean, well-organized classroom "says" loud and clear that you are an orderly person, and that you expect students to act in a well-behaved manner in accordance with the orderly environment. Most of the time, the class lives up to the challenge and behaves in an orderly manner—even the troublemakers!

Let's quickly identify some of the characteristics of an organized classroom. They include:

- neatly arranged chairs/desks
- orderly shelved books
- properly organized instruments
- carefully ordered teacher desk
- obviously picked-up floor
- attractively arranged room
- neatly filed materials
- cleanly washed chalkboard
- attractively displayed materials
- appealing decorated room

To establish a positive climate, then, you need to concentrate on two tasks: (1) refining your relationship skills, and (2) maintaining an organized environment. The right "tone" in the classroom is a strong influence in promoting good behavior and discouraging bad behavior.

Be Well Prepared. If I had to choose the single most important tactic in preventing discipline problems, it would have to be teacher preparation. When the teacher is "ready to go" and the students are immediately involved, there's less opportunity for any shenanigans. That's always the case when the lesson starts out with a "bang."

Another reason why there's less discipline problems when you're well prepared is that you've taken the time and effort to (1) plan interesting and appropriate activities, and (2) select appealing and clear-cut music. This means students generally will be more attentive and stay on-task better, and be less apt to get frustrated and bored, and start to misbehave.[21] Thorough preparation thwarts misbehavior *every time*. It can do the job of preventing problems almost singlehandedly. Here are some suggestions for being well-prepared. Incorporate them into your lessons:

- Use a variety of music.
- Select at least two different activities (per lesson).
- Vary the size and types of groups.
- Include listening as well as performing.
- Talk about the composer and/or historical perspective of the music.
- Sequence the presentation of musical elements.
- Provide opportunities for both group and individual responses.[22]

Adhere to Classroom Routines. Your daily chores, or everyday routines, are far more important in preventing discipline problems than most teachers think.[23] When routines are well established and well managed, students are less inclined to fool around because there isn't any wasting of time. Students know what to do, and they just do it—without misbehaving. To put it simply, established routines help prevent many discipline problems. Let's identify some of these routines and discuss them. The more common ones include:

---

[21]Osborne, D. Keith and Janie D. *Discipline and Classroom Management*, p. 147.
[22]Elrod, Wilburn. "Don't Get Tangled in Discipline Problems," *Music Educators Journal*, December, 1976, p. 48.
[23]Charles, C. M. *Building Classroom Discipline*, p. 159.

Opening and Closing Routines

You need to establish a routine procedure for entering the classroom and getting started. Too much time is wasted when students meander in and continue talking. One routine might be to have students (1) march in quietly to a recording, (2) take seats immediately, and (3) begin lesson quickly after class is seated.

You may have your own routine. That's okay because routines can vary. What counts is that the class, or the lesson, gets started on time.[24]

You also need a routine for closing the class or the lesson. Leaving row by row, lining up quietly in front of the classroom door, or selecting the best behaved row to leave first are all feasible options. If you use lining up, you'll need a rule about keeping hands to one's self; otherwise, you'll have a problem now and them.

Passing Out Instruments/Books

Have a routine set up when you pass out instruments or books; otherwise, you'll have bedlam! There are three routines you can use: (1) place the instruments under the chairs and have students put them back for next class, (2) have each student pick up the instrument from a conveniently located shelf to avoid a long line, or (3) select several students to pass out the instruments to the others (but be sure to give these "helpers" specific instructions, or else you'll have chaos). It doesn't matter which of the routines you use, just as long as you have one to avoid such antics as students grabbing for instruments, playing the instrument while you're talking, or fighting over an instrument.

One more suggestion: make a stipulation in the routine, "no playing until instructed." Have the students put their instruments (1) on the floor, (2) in the pencil tray, or (3) in their laps when they get it. They should do this automatically if it's part of the routine.

Raising-Hand Routine

You simply must have a routine for obtaining answers from students, besides letting them shout out or go "oooh, oooh, oooh" in your face. You can't let students do this! It leads to rowdiness, silliness, and, worst of all, rudeness. You've got to have a raising-hands routine (without the "ooohs"), where students know the only way you'll acknowledge them is if they raise their hands. You save yourself a lot of headaches by having a hand-raising routine.

Standing and Sitting Routine

Here's another situation where a routine procedure is crucial, especially because so many activities in music require standing. Unless you have some way of getting students up or down quickly and quietly, you'll have a maddening uproar and a few antics every time! All you need to do is "conduct" the standing up by raising both hands, palms up, in tempo with the class's standing; and lowering both hands, palms down, in tempo with class, when they're sitting down. You've got to instruct the class briefly beforehand by saying, "Stand up quietly," or "Sit down quietly," followed by a prep breath. Then just "conduct" the standing or sitting as indicated. (See the section "Getting Class to Stand/Sit in Orderly Way" in Chapter 6.) You desperately need a routine for standing and sitting to avoid confusion.

Set Up Rules (or Guidelines). There's nothing like rules to help you manage behavior in the classroom! In fact, rules, or guidelines, are essential in the scheme

---

[24]Charles, C. M. *Building Classroom Discipline*, p. 159.

of disciplining. They make it clear to the students that certain behaviors are unacceptable, while others are more acceptable. Rules, or guidelines, are also the ideal means for keeping the unacceptable behavior from happening in the first place and encouraging the "right" behavior because the rules are posted as a constant reminder to the students. They're out in the open.

Some of you, I know, don't take kindly to rules. You have the notion that rules stifle initiative, creativity, and self-direction.[25] Not true! Rules, in fact, stimulate initiative and creativity, and allow for even more independence in that they help maintain a more conducive learning environment, with less stress and less disruption. You might want to read what Glasser says about rules in his writings on discipline.

In order for rules, or guidelines, to be successful, however, you need to exercise some know-how in setting up the rules. Here's a list of so-called "rules" for making your own rules. You need to:

- **Involve the class consistently** in making rules. Rules should be established by teacher and students together.
- **Keep the rules short** and to the point. Rules should not be long, drawn-out statements, but rather short one-liners, such as:
  - Raise hand to talk.
  - Listen carefully to instructions.
  - Take seat quickly.
  - Be on time for school.
- **Limit the rules** carefully. Rules should not be lengthy. Keep the list to four, and not more than six, so they can be remembered easily.
- **Phrase the rules positively** whenever possible. Rules need to be stated as "do's" not "don'ts" in order to give students a positive attitude toward the rules. For example, say "Sit quietly until the bell rings," instead of "Don't talk until the bell rings."[26]

---

[25]Charles, C. M. *Building Classroom Discipline*, p. 122.
[26]Madsen and Madsen, *Teaching Discipline*, p. 181.

- **Adapt the rules to age and ability** of the class. Rules must be age-level appropriate, as well as ability-level appropriate; students must be able to understand the rules and have the capability of doing them.[27]
- **Evaluate the rules constantly.** Rules that are no longer necessary should be replaced with another "necessary" rule, or else discarded in order to keep rules current.
- **Post the rules conspicuously** in the room. Rules need to be displayed where they can be in view at all times by every student as a constant reminder of the rules.
- **Review the rules regularly.** Rules need to be reviewed periodically with the students in a brief, not long-winded, manner to keep rules in their minds.

Most of you already follow these "rules." But in case you hadn't thought of one (or more) of these as listed, begin right now to apply them, so that your rules can work effectively.

Reinforce Good Behavior. Another good way to ward off misbehaving deeds is to start reinforcing the good behavior by praising the student(s). Instead of concentrating so much on the bad behavior, begin focusing on the good behavior. You'll be absolutely amazed how much impact this little strategy has on students, not just for those who receive the praise, but more so for those who don't, including the chronic misbehavers. That's because after a while, students begin to notice who's getting the recognition and who's not—and why. What happens? More students start displaying good behavior, and fewer students, bad behavior. It doesn't happen overnight, however; it takes time. But it **does** work. Try it and see. You can start reinforcing immediately. Here are some pointers you might find helpful:

Be Specific and to the Point

Don't make it a lengthy discourse. Keep it short and concise. Only three items need to be mentioned: (1) the praise phrase, (2) the good deed, and (3) the student's name. Like this:

- "Good for you, Mary. You raised your hand to speak."
- "Bravo, Tom. You walked to your seat that time."
- "Thank you for not talking, John."
- "You've been on time every day this week, Bob. Great!"

Refer to Student's Name

Notice that the student's name was one of the three items to be mentioned in a praise statement. Including the name makes the praise more personal and meaningful. (See the examples in the "Be specific" guideline above.)

Look at Student Directly

Be sure you establish eye contact while praising the student and your body is turned in his/her direction. Give every outward indication that your complete attention at that moment is focused on the student. It might be only for a second or two, but that's long enough to make the student feel special.

[27]Charles, C. M. *Building Classroom Discipline*, p. 122.

Deliver the Praise Convincingly

You've got to give the praise with conviction in an enthusiastic "I mean it" tone of voice. It doesn't matter one iota if you are specific, mention the student's name, and establish eye contact; if you don't sound convincing, it's all for naught.

Provide Model Behavior. Modeling, on a daily basis, the kind of behavior you want to see in your students is another effective way of curtailing misbehavior. But don't expect any drastic conversions to sainthood or any sudden utopia to blossom forth without any wrongdoings. That's not the way modeling works. Modeling makes its impact over a longer period of time, similar to reinforcing.

The key is "practicing what you preach." Students need to see you doing the things you tell them to do, and not doing the things you ask them **not** to do. Modeling starts to pay off when students start to "think twice" before doing something naughty. And don't think students won't notice when you goof—they will and they'll tell you in a flash. So take your modeling very seriously because students are watching, especially the ones who misbehave.

Get to Know Your Students. The better you get to know your students, the better they'll respond. Students tend to be more positive when the teaching is more personalized.[28] I don't mean hanging out with students or trying to be one of them. Getting buddy-buddy is not the way to do it. There are other, more professional ways by which you can get to know your students better:

Learn Students' Names

Make a seating chart or make up a system to help "trigger" the name. The quicker you learn the names, the better.

Note Personal Characteristics

Make a mental note, for example, of the shy, sensitive, or aggressive students. Observe students closely. Get to **know** your students.

Identify Special Interest

Ask about students' hobbies, talents, interests, etc. Take an interest in their likes and dislikes. Gather information informally—on the playground, during recess, in the cafeteria, etc., and be a good listener.[29]

Make Brief Conversations

Engage students in brief conversations at opportune times using garnered information. Make an effort to get around to everyone before coming back to a student.

Be Genuinely Friendly

Smile at students, put on a pleasant face, and acknowledge their comments and gestures. Let them know you're approachable, and that they can talk to you.

Find out Misbehaving Causes. One helpful way to prevent chronic misbehavior from continuing is to research the cause. You can't have continual disruptions

---

[28]Elrod, Wilburn. "Don't Get Tangled in Discipline Problem," p. 50.
[29]*Ibid.*, p. 49.

in the classroom, and you can't let one student usurp all your time and energy. You may have struggled for solutions on your own, but there comes a time when you need to reach out for help.

The good news is, there are numerous sources within the school environment to get background on the student. You could:

- Consult school records in the office.
- Make an appointment with the guidance counselor.
- Talk with the student's previous teacher.
- Visit with the school psychologist.
- Confer with the parents.

Once you obtain helpful information from one, or more, of these sources, you're better equipped to deal with the problem. While action of this sort is reserved for your most difficult cases, it nevertheless, must be included in this discussion; not only to give hope and help, but to cover all bases where discipline problems are concerned.

Communicate in Appropriate Manner. Sometimes it's just a matter of communicating, or relating, to students in the "right" way in order to avoid having discipline problems. It's not easy to know if this is the proper solution, but you don't lose anything by trying and you have everything to gain if it works.

C. M. Charles suggests these special ways to relate with the student(s) in order to establish a more positive attitude on the student's part.[30] Let me give you these three ways with some brief comments.

Give Constant, Positive Attention

Some students simply require more attention and more stroking than others. When they don't get it, they find any and every way to get it. With students like this, it's best for all concerned to give the constant attention. Of course, you'll have to figure out how to juggle your attention between this student and the rest of the class. That's the trick! But if more attention and more strokes do the trick, then figure it out!

Display Constant Willingness to Help

Then, too, some students just want to know they can come to you for help any time; that you won't refuse it, but be happy to help. For some reason, that willing attitude is terribly important to some students. If that should be the case, then just resign yourself to being "ready and willing," especially if it means you can ward off any problems. An open and willing attitude seems to be the key with these students.

Encourage Constant Progress

For others, it's a matter of your giving ongoing encouragement with regard to their progress and overcoming any physical or emotional obstacles. These are the students who have a strong need to be reminded "You can do it" over and over, and given the confidence and motivation to overcome any handicap; otherwise, they tend

---

[30]Charles, C. M. *Building Classroom Discipline*, pp. 162–163.

to misbehave. My advice is, go ahead and be their private cheerleader if it keeps them in line. It takes less time to do the cheering than it does the disciplining.

Summary of Preventive Techniques

That does it for the Preventive Techniques. As you can see, you have a number of ways to keep discipline problems to a minimum, or else avoid them entirely. You'll have to be the one, though, to decide which ones to exercise. Each of you should see the wisdom, however, in making the first four suggestions a top priority. Establishing a good classroom climate, being well prepared, adhering to classroom routines, and setting up guidelines should become your strong allies in discouraging, and even preventing, discipline problems in your classroom.

Corrective Measures

The third category of strategies in the three-pronged approach is corrective measures. You must have corrective tactics ready and waiting, even if you have a zillion preventive strategies in the works. Kids are still going to misbehave and break the rules, no matter how many precautions you take. You need to stop them—*immediately*.

So **corrective measures** are ways (or means) to deal with these misbehaviors on the spot or, more specifically, to bring them to a halt in the most positive, nondisruptive way possible. Certainly not with scowling looks, sharp words, or punishing tactics; that's not what "enlightened" correction is all about.[31]

The whole purpose of correction is to refocus, or rechannel, the errant behavior—calmly and without intimidation—such that the behavior is changed in a positive way. With the appropriate reinforcement and praise, both teacher and students can get back to the business of teaching and learning without further ado. You can see why corrective measures are so important: they not only halt the undesirable behavior, but also improve the classroom environment.

Let's take a look at some of these corrective measures now. No doubt, you have some of your own; if so, fine. Hopefully, you can find other ideas here that you might want to add. Corrective measures can include:

- applying established consequences
- stopping undesired behavior

  - silent signals   - removing object
  - humor tactics   - ignoring tactic
  - seating changes   - seeing after class
  - touch/tap gesture   - calling on student
  - make requests   - changing activity

- redirecting bad behavior
- reinforcing good behavior
- explaining classroom rights
- applying personal tools

Apply Established Consequences. Once you've established your consequences, it's a simple cut-and-dry matter of carrying out the "results" when students

---

[31]Charles, C. M. *Building Classroom Discipline*, p. 174.

violate the rules. There's no need for any discussion, just say, "Robert, since you've decided to keep talking while I'm talking, you'll have to . . ." Make sure your consequences are (1) feasible, or possible to implement, (2) relevant, or impinging on the students, and (3) reasonable, or fair, not extreme, and accomplishable. Here's another guideline: Be sure to explain the consequences beforehand—that this is what happens if they "choose" to break the rule(s). (The word "choose" puts the onus on the student, not the teacher.)

Here's a list of some reasonable and relevant consequences. See if you can use any of them:

- loss of special privilege
- lowering of daily grade
- send to principal's or counselor's office
- reporting for detention
- staying after school
- dismissal from school
- loss of preferred activity
- getting extra assignment
- getting classroom chore
- receiving discipline points

This isn't an exhaustive list by any means, but at least it gives you a better idea, or even a new idea, or two. Note that all of these consequences are enforceable, or feasible. That's an important criterion.

Now let's talk about how consequences should be applied. The way they're carried out has everything to do with the success or failure of the consequences. Here are some specific suggestions that need to be taken seriously. You need to apply the consequence:

- immediately after
- not hesitating
- with firmness
- in matter-of-fact way
- without favoritism
- without altering
- with consistency
- on first offense (unless otherwise indicated)
- with positive tone of voice

These are all self-explanatory. But let me say a word about applying consequences on the "first offense." Some teachers like to **give one warning** before "inflicting" the consequence. If you want to do this, make it a standing rule that everyone understands. Then follow the rule to-a-tee.

Here's another guideline. When no consequence has been established for the misdeed, **give the student a choice**. Don't back the student in a corner because he/she will come out fighting and it'll make the situation worse. So use a "stop-or-do-this" approach, like this:

- "Either stop talking or I'll ask you to leave the room."
- "Put that comic book away, or else you'll get a zero today."
- "If you can't keep your hands to yourself, I'll have to move your seat."
- "You're going to lose your computer time, if I see you hitting Jack once more."

This should give you some help in carrying out your consequences. Established consequences play a large role in correcting misbehavior. They're probably your best bet when it comes to correcting misbehavior. The only hang-up is that you can't have a consequence for everything. It isn't possible. That's why the guideline on giving students a choice is so important. You'll handle a lot of problems this way. Other than that, established consequences do the job.

Stop Undesired Behavior. What do you do about all those discipline problems that don't have consequences attached, besides giving them a way out? (As discussed in the above consequence section.) You can do lots of things—and you'll need to, because the problem has to stop. Right now! Here are some of the tactics you can use to "put out" the discipline quickly and, in many cases, quietly.

Silent Signals

Learn to use your head and your hands to communicate with students. You can point a finger, shake a finger, dot the air, shake your head, shake your head and finger together, etc. Of course, that means catching the student's eye first. You can stop a lot of nonsense this way, without even saying a word.[32]

Humor Tactics

You don't always have to be sober looking or tough sounding to stop a problem. You can be humorous, too. You can make a face at the student, crack a one-liner, or do a silly gesture. It gets the message across and, at the same time, establishes a closer bond between teacher and student because of sharing that one brief hilarious moment. So don't be afraid of using humor on occasions. It's a refreshing change of pace for both you and the students.

Seating Changes

Sometimes the best, and the only solution, is to move one student away from another, particularly when the problem involves two (or more) students in close proximity. It doesn't matter whether the problem is giggling, passing notes, punching, talking, etc. The point is, someone has to be moved if the problem's going to stop. You will know from your gut reaction and trained eye. And you better have a spot picked out, though, before the student is moved.

Touching/Tapping Tactic

There are times when just a touch on the shoulder, a tap on the head, or a tap on the hand takes care of the problem. It's even more effective when you put your hand on the student's when he/she is tapping a pencil, clicking a pen, or rattling a trinket. It's best to confine this tactic to the lower grades, though, and you don't want to use touching too much either. Use it sparingly so that it really "shocks" the student into stopping! By the way, tap one or two times, and no more. Three starts getting friendly!

Making Request

You don't always need to address the misbehaving student directly; you can address the whole class. The guilty student will "hear" you. It's a good tactic to use

---

[32]Charles, C. M. *Building Classroom Discipline*, p. 173.

when you can put your finger on what's causing the problem, like the students being overtired, the room being too hot, or the assignment being too difficult. That way you could say something like:

> "I know this is a hard song to learn, but I'd really appreciate it if everyone would stay with me just a few minutes longer."

The reason this works is because there's understanding, compassion, and respect all rolled into one in this request—and the students sense it. So make a group request every now and then.

Removing Objects

What causes a problem in many cases is some non-school object, such as a comic book, play toy, rubber band, or cosmetic item. Invariably students get distracted by these items and start fidgeting, fighting, or giggling. What you do is, ask the student to put it away. If he/she doesn't, simply (a) walk over calmly, (b) remove object respectfully, and (c) place on your desk. When the class is over, return the object. Removing the cause, in this case, usually stops the problem.[33]

Ignoring Tactic

Ignoring a problem really works, but you've got to know when to use it and when not to. You really don't have to do something about every little thing that happens. Sometimes the best thing you could do is "not see" something and keep right on going, like nothing ever happened. If that's not the right decision, you'll find out soon enough.[34] Most of the time, however, ignoring works when it's used at the right time because it overlooks the very mechanism (bad behavior) the student is using to get the attention. Used at the right time, ignoring is a powerful tool.

---

[33]Charles, C. M. *Building Classroom Discipline*, p. 173.
[34]Callahan, Joseph and Leonard H. Clark. *Teaching in the Elementary School* (New York: MacMillan Publishing Co., 1977), p. 120.

Seeing After Class

One of the quickest ways to get a student to quit doing something is to say the magic words, "See me after class." Be ready for the big "Ooooooo" from the rest of the class, though. You'll probably have to say, "That's enough!" But whatever you do, don't pause after you say "see me" because then the student will feel disposed to give you some "lip." Just say "See me . . ." in a calm tone of voice and move on. Don't wait. The sheer anticipation of "seeing you" will take the wind out of the student's sail. The problem will stop right then and there. As to the conference with the student, follow four steps: (1) give teacher's reaction, (2) obtain student's reason, (3) arrive at an acceptable solution, and (4) elicit student's cooperation in the future.

Calling on Student

You can stop the misbehaving student in a minute if you call on him/her to perform or recite next—and then watch how fast his/her jets cool down. The student is usually in left field and doesn't have the foggiest notion which page the class is on and what the instructions were. But no matter. Just repeat the instructions quickly, and let the student do his/her thing. The response will most likely be awful, but at least the student isn't misbehaving anymore. Listen: If students know there's a good chance of getting called on if you "fool around," there will be less fooling around. So keep your eyes open, and call on that student next time. It'll stop him/her cold!

Changing Activity

You'll notice that most times it's the students having the difficulties who cause the problems. You've got to keep an eye out for these students and try to help them. But there are times when the activity has to be modified—or quickly restructured—right in midstream so that you can get back the excitement and reduce the stress that comes from an activity that's a little too tough. Again, it's a matter of being perceptive and sensing when an activity needs to be beefed up or whittled down. If you can't sense this, you're in for a lot of discipline problems. You need to be ready to change, or even switch, an activity if problems start popping up here and there.

Redirect Bad Behavior. As important as stopping the bad behavior is, it's even more important to re-channel the misbehavior in a positive direction. You need to help students who misbehave decide what they should do instead—and why. You could give them some choices if they seem to have difficulty coming up with their own ideas. A large part of corrective discipline is devoted to learning good behavior, not just stopping the bad, because the more students learn about good behavior, the less they'll entertain bad behavior. Take time, then, to redirect the misbehavior in your classroom.

Reinforce Good Behavior. Along with stopping the bad behavior and redirecting bad behavior, it's also important to reinforce the good behavior. Recognize good behavior in a quiet, low-key way using simple, yet meaningful, gestures such as nods, signals, smiles, taps, pats, etc., and simple words and phrases like "Great," "Very good," or "That was good!" It is best to compliment the whole class rather than individuals when giving verbal praise, so that you don't embarrass anyone.[35] The ones who misbehave will notice the reinforcing, and it will make an impact. Remember, reinforcing the good must go on simultaneously with stopping the bad.

---

[35]Charles, C. M. *Building Classroom Discipline*, p. 173.

Explain Classroom Rights. An integral part of correcting misbehavior is being sure that students understand classroom rights, those basic expectations that both teacher and students are entitled to experience. Teachers need to explain these rights to the students, and then reassert them whenever students begin to misbehave. Here are several examples of teachers' and students' rights.

Students' Rights

- The right to a well-ordered, peaceful, non-threatening learning environment, conducive to learning.
- The right to have a caring, well-prepared, competent teacher who limits disruptive behavior.
- The right to choose one's own behavior with full understanding of the consequences.[36]

Teachers' Rights

- The right to expect behavior from students that contributes to their maximum growth.
- The right to teach in a classroom climate that is free from disruptions.
- The right to teach in ways that meet the learning and behavioral needs of the students.[37]

Students need to be made keenly aware of these classroom rights, which can have a tremendous influence on the students' behavior. These rights can make students think before misbehaving. By stressing these rights, then, teachers can expe-

---

[36]Charles, C. M. *Building Classroom Discipline*, p. 171.
[37]*Ibid.*

rience the freedom to teach in accordance with their abilities, and students, the freedom to learn in accordance with their potential.

Apply Personal Tools. Enough has been said about personal tools and the significant role they play in the managing of discipline, but very little has been said about the impact of personal tools on redirecting behavior and encouraging good behavior. The fact is, though, personal tools are just what the doctor ordered! Think about it. One look is worth a thousand words, as the saying goes, which means facial expressions have great power to encourage good behavior. And what better way to offer encouragement than through gesturing? Words of praise are always uplifting. So let's not forget that personal tools are your strong allies in correcting misbehavior and encouraging good behavior.

Summary of Corrective Measures

This is the third and last category of the three-pronged discipline approach. The focus has been on corrective measures, strategies that can bring disruptive behavior to a halt for the purpose of redirecting that behavior to a more positive behavior. To accomplish this task, you need a repertoire of strategies in order to deal with the misbehavers. The fact is, students will break your rules no matter how many preventive techniques you use. That means doing such things as: applying established guidelines, stopping undesired behavior, redirecting bad behavior, reinforcing good behavior, etc.

If you don't have any corrective measures for your own teaching, consider any one, or all, of these strategies. They'll do the job of discouraging bad behavior and encouraging good behavior.

Additional References

Axelrod, S. *Behavior Modification for the Classroom Teacher.* New York: McGraw-Hill, 1977.

Brophy, J., and Evertson, C. *Learning from Teaching: A Developmental Perspective.* Boston: Allyn and Bacon, 1976.

Canter, L. *Assertive Discipline: A Take-Charge Approach for Today's Educator.* Seal Beach, CA: Canter and Associates, 1976.

Charles, C. *Elementary Classroom Management.* New York: Longman, 1983.

Chernow, Carol, and Chernow, Fred B. *Classroom Discipline Survival Guide: For Middle School/ Junior High Teachers.* West Nyack, NY: The Center for Applied Research in Education, 1989.

Coloroso, B. *Discipline: Winning at Teaching.* Boulder, CO: Kids, Inc., 1983.

Dreikurs, R. *Psychology in the Classroom*, 2nd Edition. New York: Harper and Row, 1968.

Dreikurs, R., and Gray, L. *A New Approach to Discipline: Logical Consequences.* New York: Hawthorn Books, Inc., 1968.

Dreikurs, R., Grunwald, B., and Pepper, F. *Maintaining Sanity in the Classroom.* New York: Harper and Row, 1982.

Emmer, E., et al. *Classroom Management for Secondary Teachers.* Englewood Cliffs, NJ: Prentice Hall, 1984.

Evertson, C., et al. *Classroom Management for Elementary Teachers.* Englewood Cliffs, NJ: Prentice Hall, 1989.

Ginott, H. G. *Teacher & Child.* New York: Avon Books, 1972.

Glasser, W. *Schools Without Failure.* New York: Harper & Row, 1969.

Glasser, W. *Control Theory in the Classroom.* New York: Perennial Library, 1985.

Good, T. L., Biddle, B. J., and Brophy, J. E. *Teachers Make a Difference.* New York: Holt, Rinehart and Winston, 1975.

Good, T. L., and Brophy, J. E. *Looking in Classrooms.* New York: Harper & Row, Publishers, 1973.

Hart, J. *Teachers and Teaching.* New York: Macmillan, 1936.

Jackson, P. *Life in Classrooms*. New York: Holt, Rinehart and Winston, 1968.

Johnson, D., Johnson, R., Holubec, E., and Roy, P. *Circles of Learning: Cooperation in the Classroom*. Alexandria, VA: Association for Supervision and Curriculum Development, 1984.

Jones, F. *Positive Classroom Discipline*. New York: McGraw-Hill, 1987.

Jones, V., & Jones, L. *Comprehensive Classroom Management*. Boston: Allyn and Bacon, 1986.

Wallen, C., & Wallen, L. *Effective Classroom Management*. Boston: Allyn and Bacon, 1978.

Wickman, E. K. *Teachers and Behavior Problems*. New York: The Commonwealth Fund, 1938.

10

Preparing Lesson Plans

This chapter is devoted to preparing lesson plans because I feel so strongly about being "ready" to teach (besides being competent, that is), and because I'm adamant about teachers having a planning document, or lesson plan, to follow. No matter which end of the teaching spectrum you're at—the experienced end or the not-so-experienced—you still need to plan, whether it be a detailed written plan, a sketchy mental outline, or anything in between. Lesson planning is the key to effective teaching!

The chapter will present and explain in detail a lesson plan model for the elementary classroom teacher who is responsible for teaching music in his/her own classroom. Examples are included for both lower and upper elementary grades, guidelines are given for planning a mini (not a full) lesson and for using music for extrinsic, as well as intrinsic, reasons, and getting help from a variety of sources.

The chapter also includes a suggested lesson plan for the general music teacher, along with several examples.

Lesson Planning for Elementary Classroom Teachers _____

You think you can't teach a music lesson, right? You feel that the music teacher is the only one who can do the job, correct? But that's not true. You **can** teach a music lesson, and you can teach it effectively with the knowledge and skill you have right now. What you need is a practical plan of action, or a lesson plan you feel comfortable using. First, here are several guidelines for planning a music lesson.

Guideline #1

Make the lesson a "mini" lesson. It should be no more than ten minutes for grades K-2, and no longer than twenty minutes for grades 3-6, because children in the early grades have a short attention span. They have enough after ten minutes, even if the lesson is appealing. They'll start fidgeting, whispering, and looking around. It's nothing personal; they're just ready to move on. Twenty minutes in the upper grades are appropriate because there are too many curricular demands on the teacher, and not enough teaching time. The mini-lesson is usually a necessity, but is still adequate if you're properly prepared.

Guideline #2

Focus on intrinsic, not extrinsic, reasons. It's not enough to use music for only extrinsic or non-musical reasons, or for the sole purpose of (a) changing the pace, (b) relaxing the students, (c) varying the curriculum, or (d) improving the mood. True, these are good reasons, but they're not primary reasons for "doing" music. That's why you need to focus more on the intrinsic or the musical reason(s), the most important one being that **music nurtures the aesthetic nature**. That's the primary reason for music.

Guideline #3

Plan purposely for fun experiences. There should be times when you should have no other goal for music than to "have fun." This isn't a contradiction of the previous guideline, not if your goal is intentional. After all, music **is** a fun experience, and on occasions students should have opportunities to experience music for the sheer enjoyment of it. This can happen when young children sing a favorite action song or do a fun dramatization, or when older students accompany themselves on guitars or autoharps or chant their favorite rap. These experiences are enjoyable and refreshing, a change from the normal routine.

Guideline #4

Prepare fewer materials/activities. Remember, the mini-lesson is a shorter lesson, so you don't need as many materials or activities. Two recordings (or two songs) will do it, one for each concept (if you have two concepts) and then one (or two) activities for each concept (or for each musical selection). This formula works for both upper and lower grade levels. (See the lesson plan model later in this chapter.) So don't get all in knots over the amount of material or activities you need. Just get one or two selections that clearly demonstrate the concept of the day and a couple of good activities, and you're all set. More than that would be too much for a mini-lesson, or too frustrating, to be more accurate. Fewer is better in this case; just be sure they're age-level appropriate.

Guideline #5

Obtain conceptual information from available sources. There's no need to get alarmed about conceptual material either. You can turn to several accessible sources: (1) the music teacher, (2) the professional literature (such as texts and journals), or (3) the teacher's edition of the basic music series your school uses. Let me also say that the first two or three foundational concepts (or smaller ideas) under melody, rhythm, harmony, or form are within the grasp of every classroom teacher. These foundational concepts (or ideas) will also give you more than enough teaching material for one year. What you've got to keep in mind, however, is that the concepts must be presented in a logical, or sequential, order. See Figure 10.1 for this sequential ordering.

Guideline #6

Apply the necessary teaching skills and competencies in implementing the lesson plan.

a. Use appropriate facial expressions, eye contact, teacher voice, and overt gesturings.

b. Maintain a smooth, ongoing momentum or pace throughout the lesson.

c. Provide accurate and honest assessment after each class/individual response.

d. Obtain class/individual responses in a tactful, competent manner.

e. Begin singing on the right pitch, which means:

- Sound the initial pitch (consult text or seek help).

- Ask the class to "match" the pitch with you if you can't match pitches. Remove focus from yourself.

- **Or**, ask individual students to sing the pitch while you tremolo (pitch) on bells.

- **Or**, simply use the recording until you gain confidence.

- **Or**, transpose song to a higher or lower key if song is pitched too high or too low.

f. Think through the steps (or "mechanics") of each activity.

g. Achieve musically performed activities.

These are some of the basic skills and competencies to keep in mind as you get ready to implement your lesson plan. Now let's take a look at a suggested lesson plan that will help you prepare your next mini-lesson.

Suggested Lesson Plan Format for Music (For Elementary Classroom Teachers)

NOTE: Lesson plan model based on *TEN-MINUTE* music experience using *ONE* musical selection to teach *ONE* musical concept with *TWO* activities. (Extra activity included for example.)

I. CONCEPT

State the specific concept to be taught. Refer to the smaller idea of the larger concept, e.g., "Some songs/or recordings have a steady, fast beat," not just to rhythm. (Use the complete sentence form of the concept.)

II. BEHAVIORAL OBJECTIVE

Follow this statement that indicates: (1) time limits, (2) grade level, (3) terminal behavior, (4) musical concept, (5) anticipated criterion, and (6) musical activities.

RHYTHM

Pulse

-Most songs/recordings have a steady, ongoing beat.

-In some songs/recordings the beat is fast/slow.

-In some songs/recordings the beat gets faster/slower. (TWO CONCEPTS)

Accented Beats

-Within the ongoing beat, there are stronger beats called "accented beats" (S) and weaker beats (s).

-Stronger beats may be followed by:

a. Three weaker beats $/\ /\ /\ /$

b. Two weaker beats $/\ /\ /$

c. One weaker beat $/\ /$

Melodic Rhythm

-Melodies have their own sound apart from the ongoing beat.

-The rhythm of the melody can be identified by long and short sounds

L s L L.

-The long and short sound can be converted into eighths, quarters, half notes:

♪♪ eighth-eighth
s s

♩-quarter
L

♩-half-note
Lon-ger

MELODY

Hi-Lo

*-Some recordings sound in the high pitched range; some sound in the low pitched range. (TWO CONCEPTS)

-Some songs have high pitches; some have low pitches.

-Many songs have high and low pitches in the melody.

Melodic Direction

-Some songs have upward passages; some have downward passages.

-Some songs have both upward and downward passages.

-Some songs have passages that move across or straight ahead.

Melodic Movement

-In some songs the upward/downward passages move in steps (line-space-line movement).

-In some songs the upward/downward passages move in skips (line-line-line or space-space-space movement).

-Still in other songs, there are repeated tones. (See ACROSS under Direction.)

*Best to use ORCHESTRAL RECORDINGS initially that have longer sections where the range remains high or low.

FORM

Song Phrases

-Songs are divided by musical sentences called phrases.

-Phrases are identified by definite pauses at the end.

-Phrases having the same tones and rhythm are called "like phrases."

-Like phrases are "a" phrases while different phrases are "b."

Large Form

-Recordings usually have a main theme (MT) that repeats.

-Main theme followed by a different theme is known as A B Form or Two-Part Form.

-Main theme followed by B theme and a repetition of the main theme or A theme is known as A B A Form or Three-Part Form.

-Main theme, or A theme, followed by B theme with a repeat of A theme, followed by C theme with another repeat of A theme is known as ABACA Form or Rondo Form.

DYNAMICS

Loud-Soft

-Some songs/recordings are loud.

-Some songs/recordings are soft.

-Some songs/recordings are loud and soft.

-Some songs/recordings get suddenly loud or suddenly soft. (TWO CONCEPTS)

-Some songs/recordings get gradually loud or soft. (TWO CONCEPTS)

-some songs/recordings may have dynamic markings below the staff, such as

•piano (p) - soft

•mezzo piano (mp) -medium soft

•pianissimo (pp) - very soft

•forte (f) - loud

•mezzo forte - medium loud

•fortissimo - very loud

Figure 10.1. Sequential Order of Musical Concepts for Rhythm, Melody, Form and Dynamics

By the end of (*1*) ten minutes, the (*2*) first-grade children will be able to (*3*) recognize the (*4*) fast, steady beat (*5*) without difficulty as a result of (*6*) **marching** to the beat, **playing** rhythm sticks, and **chanting** "beat" while line designing the beat.

III. MATERIALS

Indicate what book, recording, instruments, equipment, and visual aids you will be using to teach your lesson.

IV. PROCEDURES (*Need to include the following steps*)

A. Prologue
B. Motivational Idea (*relate concept to something* **FAMILIAR** *in students' environment*)
C. Activity #1: Marching

  1. Teacher Demo
    Verbal Bridge
  2. Class Prep
    Verbal Bridge
  3. Class Perform
    Verbal Bridge

D. Activity #2: Playing Rhythm Sticks
E. Summary

Explanation of Lesson Plan

In order for you to have a clear understanding of this lesson plan, let's take a few minutes to discuss each of the four steps.

Concept. Stating the concept(s) is an important first step, especially for the classroom teacher, because it helps solidify the concept(s) in the teacher's mind and, in some cases, even clarify it by virtue of seeing it written down. That's because the conceptual material in music may not be as firmly established as the material in other subject areas. Then, too, solidifying the concept(s) at the outset is a good way to keep yourself focused throughout the planning. You've got to get the concept(s) nailed down before you do anything else.

There can be more than one concept, such as when you have a review concept and a new concept in one lesson, two review concepts, or maybe even two new concepts on rare occasions. You would label your concepts, then, like this:

I. Concepts (Review and New)

A. *Review*: Stronger sounding beats are called "accented" beats.
B. *New*: Some passages in a melody can go in an upward ($\nearrow$) direction.

OR

I. Concepts (Review Concepts)

A. *Review #1:* In some recordings, the music gets suddenly loud and then soft.
B. *Review #2:* Some songs can have an "A B A" phrase form, with only one contrasting phrase.

One more point about concepts. As stated earlier, they need to be presented in a sequential order, meaning that you would start with the most basic idea and proceed to the next logical one, and the next, etc., so that each new concept is based on the previous one. What this means for you is that you need to **know the sequential progression** of concepts for each of the smaller ideas under melody, rhythm, harmony, and form; **not every** concept, but at least the first two or three. You'll feel more confident about teaching music if you do. Figure 10.1 gives a sequenced listing. Try to memorize these sequences if you don't have a music teacher in your building to help you. Go to summer workshops and even consult one of the basic music series, such as *World of Music; Spectrum of Music;* or the *Music Book*, if you want more help. The bottom line is, you've got to have a "handle" on sequential concepts to deal meaningfully with music.

Behavioral Objectives. The behavorial objective step is your blueprint for the mini-lesson. In one fell swoop, it tells the intended outcome in terms of what the students will be able to do. In other words, the objectives are stated in terms of the student's **observable musical behavior**. Whether your objectives are written down or simply thought out, you need to account for six pieces of vital information:

1. **Time limit**: Indicates how long the mini-lesson will last, such as ten minutes, fifteen minutes, or twenty minutes.

2. **Grade level**: Designates the specific grade involved, such as kindergarten, second grade, or sixth grade.

3. **Terminal behavior**: Identifies the particular behavior you would like students to demonstrate by the end of the mini-lesson. For example:

   - identify
   - differentiate
   - recognize
   - list or name
   - construct
   - perform

4. **Musical concept**: Designates specific conceptual idea to be highlighted (or focused upon) in the mini-lesson, such as:

   - high-low pitches
   - upward passages
   - long/short melodic sounds
   - like/contrasting phrases
   - ABA form
   - I, V7, chord construction

5. **Response criterion**: Specifies the word or phrase that indicates HOW WELL you expect the students to do the terminal behavior, such as:

   - accurately
   - correctly
   - easily
   - with 100% accuracy
   - without error
   - without difficulty

6. **Musical activities**: Identifies the particular musical experiences students will participate in to learn or reinforce the concept, such as:

   - singing
   - playing
   - moving
   - listening
   - notating
   - dramatizing
   - composing
   - analyzing
   - reading

Look at the example on the "Suggested Lesson Plan Format for Music." Once you've determined your objective(s), you've done the "legwork" for the lesson; you've thought it through, in other words. All you need to do is select the materials and teach it. So don't think that objectives are just an academic ritual. They're not! They're the groundwork for your lesson. Here are a few more examples:

- By the end of (*1*) fifteen minutes, the (*2*) second graders will be able (*3*) to recognize the (*4*) repeated passages in familiar songs, like "Farmer in the Dell," (*5*) with ease as a result of (*6*) **air dotting** the repeated passages, **singing** passages on "lu" instead of words, and **playing** passages on resonator bells.
- By the end of (*1*) twenty minutes, the (*2*) fifth-grade class will be able (*3*) to identify the (*4*) A B A B phrase form in selected songs (*5*) with 100% accuracy as a result of (*6*) **singing** the "A" phrases and **conducting** the "B" phrases, **analyzing** and **marking** other examples, and **clapping** the melodic rhythm on "A" phrases and **tapping** laps on "B" phrases.

The last thing about objectives is: Use a separate objective for each concept. If you're only dealing with one concept with two or three activities, then you'll only need **one** objective. But, if you plan to review a concept with an activity or two, and also introduce a concept with one or two activities, you'll need **two** objectives—even when you review two different concepts. That's an important detail in your planning.

Materials/Equipment. This step of the lesson is especially helpful when you have a lot of materials and equipment for the lesson. It could be an optional part of the lesson if you're using only one text, or one recording or CD. But let's say your mini-lesson calls for the music series book, a few recordings or CDs, and an overhead projector. Then categorize your items according to music, instruments, and equipment, like this:

III. Materials

    A. *Music*

        1. Recordings: *Adv of Music*, Gr 3, vol. 2, side 1
          World of Music, Rec 12, side 2

        2. Songs: *The Music Book*, Gr 3, p. 15, 42

    B. *Instruments*

        1. Rhythm sticks   3. Soprano metalaphones
        2. Alto xylophones   4. Piano

    C. *Equipment*

        1. Overhead projector/screen
        2. Record/CD player
        3. Music stands

With this outline, you only need one glance to see what's needed. It's a time-saving tactic, particularly when you're using more materials and equipment than usual. If you don't need this materials step, then, by all means, discard it and go to the procedures.

Procedures. This is the most crucial part of the lesson plan. It's the "heart" of the document where you fill out the behavioral objective(s).

IV. Procedures

A. *Prologue*

The prologue is really a verbal bridge, or a two-part opening statement consisting of (1) an **assessment** of whatever went on immediately before the prologue began, and (2) an **instruction** to get ready for the about-to-begin music lesson. The beauty of this verbal bridging prologue is that it can fit anywhere in the classroom schedule, whether it be at the regularly scheduled time or at any other rearranged time. It's a marvelous transitional tool from one event to the next, as well as a logical introductory device. Here are some examples:

• **Lower Elementary**

"Everyone got seated so quickly and quietly. Very good!" (ASSESS-MENT) "Let's sit up straight now and get ready for our music lesson on . . ." (INSTRUCTION) (concept)

• **Upper Elementary**

"You did some excellent work on those short stories, class. Good for you!" (ASSESSMENT) "Put them away for now, so we can go to our music lesson on . . ." (INSTRUCTION) (concept)

See how you can "close" the previous activity and "bring in" the new one with this kind of a prologue? It takes away all the fears of wondering how to "get into" the music lesson. So use the Prologue as your introduction.

B. *Motivational Idea* (for new concept)

You can move right into your motivational idea after the prologue, if you're **introducing a new concept**, that is. What you need to do is relate the new idea to something familiar in the students' environment to make it easier for them to understand. That's what the motivational idea refers to in this case, some familiar person, place, or thing in one's surroundings that is "like" the new concept in some way. For example, you might refer to a steam engine train with its CHOO-choo-choo sound to clarify the new concept of meter in 3's. By doing so, you give students an idea of what the new concept is "like" and help them create a mental picture so that they have a better expectation of how the concept will sound.

You get into this step by tacking on one simple instruction in the prologue, such as: "Let's talk about so-and-so." That's all you need to say. I'll use the prologue examples:

• "Everyone got seated so quickly and quietly. Very good!" (ASSESS-MENT) "Sit up straight now and get ready for our music lesson on . . . Let's talk about (new concept) . . ." (INSTRUCTION) (new concept)

• "You did some excellent work on those short stories, class. Good for you!" (ASSESSMENT) "Put them away now so we can move on to our music lesson on (new concept) . . . Let's talk about (new concept) . . ." (INSTRUCTION)

Would you use the motivational idea with **review concepts**? Maybe as a reminder in the following lesson, but after that, no, because the impact is gone. You made the point when you introduced the concept, so there's no need to keep rehashing it. It gets old, even on the second time around. In place of the "Let's talk about . . ." when you're dealing with a review concept, simply replace it with "Let's review such-and-such," and go right on.

In the Motivational Idea step, you get the students involved in responding to the motivational idea. You have them (a) dramatize, (b) imitate, (c) answer questions, (d) recite, or even (e) move creatively. The point is, get students **doing** or **being**, or **talking about the motivational idea** so they can understand the concept better.

- **Verbal Bridge**: Remember, verbal bridging is the mechanism that gets you from one response to the next smoothly and easily. So after the students respond to the motivational idea, you need to "verbal bridge" it. Make the first part of the verbal bridge a combination assessment/comment where you assess the class's response (to the motivational idea) and then **relate** the **motivational idea to the music** using such comments as:
- Did you know that **melodies** have upward passages like our escalators?
- We have **musical sentences** in music just like these English sentences.
- I'll bet you didn't know that the **steady beat** in music has stronger beats and weaker beats, did you?

Then make the instructional second part straightforward, such as, "Listen and watch as I do such-and-such." Having said that, you're right into the first activity. Here's what the whole verbal bridge would sound like:

a. "I like the way everybody's hands twinkled like stars high in the sky." (ASSESSMENT) "Did you know music has high pitches just like our high stars?" (COMMENT) "Listen and watch as I play my finger cymbals up high, like this." (INSTRUCTION)

b. "That was an excellent discussion on like and contrasting designs, class." (ASSESSMENT) "What you need to know is that melodic phrases can be alike and contrasting just like these designs." (COMMENT) "Listen and watch as I tap out the melodic rhythm on like phrases, and sing and conduct the beat on the contrasting phrases. Like this." (INSTRUCTION)

C. *Activity #1*

The activity unfolds in three parts: (1) the teacher's demonstration, (2) the class preparation, and (3) the class performance. After each, there's the verbal bridge. Let's take a look at each part.

1. **Teacher Demonstration**: Notice how nicely the "listen and watch" directive from the motivational verbal bridge leads right into the demonstration. As soon as you start the "doing" you are in the throes of activity one. Be sure the demonstration is done in a very precise and overt way, with a bit of flair. Remember, you're the model for the students. But keep it short—no more than three times or not longer then 8-10 seconds. If some students jump in while you're doing your demonstration, let them; they can be your helpers.

   - **Verbal Bridge**: Because this is a teacher response, you make a relevant comment followed by an instruction for students to "try" the activity with you. It automatically starts the class prep. Take a look at the examples.

"Think you could do this?" (COMMENT) "Try it." (INSTRUCTION)
"See how I did it? With me."
"It's a fun activity. Let's try it."
"Now it's your turn. With me."

The rule is: Keep the verbal bridge short and sweet before the prep.

2. **Class Prep**: This is the step where the class gets to "practice" the activity. For you, the teacher, it's a preventive tactic to make sure everyone can "do" the activity before doing it for "real," or **with** the music. You don't really need to use music in the prep, but you've got to have the "right" tempo if you don't. That's a "must." Otherwise, the prep is a waste of time. The prep should last long enough for you to see that the class can do it, or no more than three or four times and no longer than 8-10 seconds. Don't forget to stop the class together with an "And stop" command to keep control.

   • Now you're ready to **assess** the class's prep response, and **instruct** the class to get into ready position to start. So your verbal bridge would go like this: "Super! I saw everyone doing such-and-such." (ASSESSMENT) "Clapping hands up," or "rhythm sticks in place," or "pointer finger on first note. Ready." (READINESS INSTRUCTION)

   Do you see that once again the verbal bridge leads you right into the next step? Without any confusion? That's the class performance. By the way, if the prepping doesn't go well, you simply instruct the class to repeat it and not to go on. Remember, the instruction after the prep is a readiness command. You get students in starting position immediately. (See the section "Implementing Prep Procedure" in Chapter 7.)

3. **Class Performance**: This is the actual performance of the activity with music. The success of the activity will be dependent not only on the prep, but also on the appeal of the activity. Keep that in mind when you select your activities. Here's another hint. Always try out an activity yourself before using it. If **you** have any difficulty or uncertainty with it, you can bet the students will too, even if they've been prepped. You'll need to watch carefully as the class is doing the activity—I mean *really* watch, so you can assess honestly and so that the experience is a meaningful one for the students.

   • **Verbal Bridge**: Here's the big one! You know what to do now. First, you **assess** what the class did. In other words, you decide whether or not they performed up to your criterion level. Either the class did **or didn't**; in either case, you tell the students so **they** know too. Then you **instruct** them to either (a) repeat the activity or (b) go on to the next one. If you do the latter, you'll give another "listen and watch" in the same breath, which means you're moving right into the second activity. Here's an typical example:

   "Excellent! I saw everyone conducting the 3/4 meter with the right pattern. You looked good!" (ASSESSMENT) "This time let's see if you can step-snap-snap to the meter in 3's. Like this. Listen and watch." (INSTRUCTION)

D. *Activity #2*

Once the demonstration starts, you are into the second activity, which means you just follow the same steps you did for the first activity. In other words, repeat the procedure, but with the new activity and possibly with another musical selection, if you so choose. For example:

1. Teacher Demonstration

    Verbal Bridge: Make relevant comment/instruct "try it"

2. Class Prep

    Verbal Bridge: Assess the prep/instruct the readiness

3. Class Perform

    Verbal Bridge: Assess the performance/instruct the summary

The only change in procedures for the second activity is that you'll need to instruct the students to engage in a summarizing of the lesson instead of going on to another activity. This occurs after the class response, so that last verbal bridge would go like this:

"Bravo for you! The whole class stepped-and-snapped to the 3/4 meter in 'Les Patineuss' perfectly." (ASSESSMENT) "Let's review what we've done today, okay?" (INSTRUCTION)

E. *Summary*

This part of the lesson should come from the children, not the teacher. In other words, the summary should not be the proverbial "today we have learned" lecture or the teacher's blow-by-blow recap of what the class did today. These are meaningless to the students, who will "tune out" when you do this.

Conduct the summary by asking the class—either individually or collectively—a series of short-answer questions, like this:

"Today we heard that our beats in music can sound how?" (TEACHER ACTION) "Yes, strong. And if some beats are strong, how do other beats sound, class? (TEACHER ACTION) Very good. They sound weak," etc.

Notice that the questions require specific, not rambling responses. This is an important aspect in asking questions—phrasing them so that they require only one- or two-word answers, rather than open-ended responses. Notice also that actions can give students clues as well. Make no mistake—phrasing questions properly doesn't happen naturally. You'll need to "work" at it, and self-groom yourself in the art of summarizing a lesson via short-answer questions.

Here's one other point. Bring back the motivational idea in your summarizing. That's essential in "tying" the lesson together. For example, you could say:

"Today, we learned that our strong and weak beats sound just like a . . ." (TEACHER ACTION) (choo-choo)

"Yes! Like a choo-choo train . . ." etc.

That brings the lesson together and, of course, you'd continue the summary.

Finally, when you finish summarizing, end the lesson with one last verbal bridge where you **assess** the students for their response (in the summarizing) and then **instruct** them as to what they will be doing in the lesson (followed by the dismissal instructions, of course). It's a nice "closing" touch to the lesson. Here's an example:

"Good job answering the questions, class. You remembered everything." (ASSESSMENT) "Next time, we'll work on rhythmic patterns in other songs, okay? Now let's line up quietly to leave." (INSTRUCTION)

You can see now that it's possible to do a music lesson with your class if you have a **practical lesson plan** to follow. Hopefully, you'll be inspired, as well as challenged, to deal with music again, or maybe more often, as a result of reading this discussion and studying the format. To help you further, I've included two sample lesson plans, for lower and upper elementary respectively, with full scripts. Verbiage is a problem for many teachers, so take time to study these lesson plans carefully. With the help of a good lesson plan, you **can** teach a mini-music lesson.

*Sample of Lesson Plan
for Mini Music Lesson
(Lower Elementary)*

I. *New Concept*

In most songs and recordings, the ongoing beat is steady and unchanging.

II. *Behavioral Objective*

By the end of ten minutes, the first-grade children will be able to identify the steady, ongoing beat without difficulty as a result of participating in: (1) **tapping the beat with fingers on lap,** (2) playing rhythm sticks while chanting "beat, beat," and (3) **marching** in place while beating drum.

III. *Materials*

A. Books: *World of Music*, Book 1, p. 32

B. Instruments: Rhythm Sticks
                 Tub Drums
                 Piano

C. Equipment: Record Player
                 Chalkboard

IV. *Procedures*

A. *Prologue*: "I'm so proud of each of you! You did your reading so well this morning." (*assessment*) "Let's put our books away quietly and sit up straight." (*pause*) "We're going to have a music lesson about steady beats. But first let's talk about steady beats." (*instruction*)

B. *Motivation* (Questions/Imitation)

1. "What kind of clock is this?" (Hold up a picture of grandfather clock) "Yes, Michael, a grandfather clock!"

2. "And what is this gold ticker called? Almost, Jay, it's a pendulum." (Say slowly) "What's it called, class?" (Pen-du-lum. Again, pen-du-lum)

3. "Let's be a pendulum. Hands like this. Tick that way, and say tick-tock. Ready." (Class tick-tocks) "See how steady our pendulum ticks? It keeps on going, doesn't it?"

4. "Well, our beat in music is steady too. And keeps on going just like the pendulum." (*comment*) Listen and watch me as I tip the beat to our song/recording." (*instruction*)

C. *Activity #1*

1. *Teacher demonstrates* tapping with or without recording—in tempo.

2. *Class imitates* (this is a prep for activity—briefly).

3. "Good, everyone can tap correctly." (*assessment*) "Let's tap with the record now. Tapping hand up." (*instruction*) "Ready."

4. *Class response*

5. "Wonderful! I saw everyone tapping to the beat correctly. This time let's tap our laps. Like this. Ready. Yes, we tapped our beat on our laps

so well, too." (*assessment*) "Now let's play our rhythm sticks." "Listen and watch." (*instruction*)

D. *Activity #2*

1. *Teacher demonstrates* playing rhythm sticks and chanting—in tempo.

2. *Class imitates* (prep for activity—briefly).

3. "Good! We can all play and chant easily." (*assessment*) "Let's tap with the record. Sticks up." (*instruction*) "Ready."

4. *Class response*

5. "You all tapped and chanted perfectly to the beat. Super." (*assessment*) "Know what we're going to do now? We're going to march and play our big brass drum. Watch me." (*instruction*)

E. *Activity #3* (optional)

1. *Teacher demonstrates* marching and playing bass drum—in tempo.

2. *Class imitates* (prep for activity—briefly).

3. "Great! You can all march easily and beat your bass drum." (*assessment*) "Now with the music. Marching feet in place." (*instruction*) "Ready."

4. *Class response*

5. "I'm so proud of you, class. We marched to our steady beat and played our bass drum without missing a beat." (*assessment*) "Let's review what we've learned today." (*instruction*)

F. *Summary*

1. "Just like our grandfather clock, we discovered that our music has a steady what?" (teacher imitates pendulum) "Yes, a steady beat."

2. "And what were we tapping to when we tapped our fingers and laps? Good, Billy, our steady beat."

3. "And what were we tapping with our stick (imitate playing) and marching to with our feet?" (imitate marching) "Yes, class, the steady beat."

4. "In our next lesson, we'll listen to other familiar songs with a steady beat."

Sample Lesson Plan
for Music Mini-Lesson
(Upper Elementary)

I. *New Concept*

In some songs and recordings, the steady ongoing beat gets suddenly faster.

II. *Behavioral Objective*

By the end of ten minutes, the sixth-grade class will be able to recognize the suddenly fast beat with 100% accuracy as a result of participating in: (1) **standing/sitting** while conducting, (2) **raising up** "Suddenly Fast" card while pulsating the beat, and (3) **playing** steady and suddenly fast beats on rhythm sticks at different levels.

III. *Materials*

A. Books: *World of Music, Book 6, p. 34*

B. Instruments: Rhythm Sticks
Piano
Autoharps

C. Equipment: Record Player
Chalkboard

D. Recording: "Hungarian Dance No. 5." *Bowmar Orchestral Library* (BOL #62)

IV. *Procedures*

A. *Prologue*: "You've worked very well on your compositions, class. We should have some good papers forthcoming." (*assessment*) "Put away your writing for now and let's have a music lesson on the concept of suddenly fast beats. Let's talk about this concept first." (*instruction*)

B. *Motivation* (Question/Answer/Discussion)

1. "Let's suppose you're driving in the rain and you need to put on your windshield wipers. Say you put them on normal speed first, but then the rain starts coming down fast. So you turn the switch and what happens immediately with the wipers? Sure, they immediately get fast!"

2. "Let's imitate this effect with our hands, like this, and say swish-swish. Great! See how the swishing gets suddenly faster just by turning the switch?"

3. "The same phenomenon happens with the speed when you turn the dial on a blender or beater. It gets suddenly faster if you turn up the dial, doesn't it?"

4. "Well, our beat in music does the same thing. It can get suddenly fast too." (*comment*) "Listen and watch me."

C. *Activity #1*

1. Teacher demonstrates standing/sitting with or without recording—in tempo.

2. *Class imitates* (this is prep for activity—do briefly).

3. *Class response* (to the recording—the activity proper).

4. "Great. I really liked the way everyone stood up so promptly on the suddenly fast part and sat back down when it returned to the regular tempo. That means you were really listening." (*assessment*) "This next time, let's hold up our Suddenly Fast cards. Watch me." (*instruction*)

D. *Activity #2*

1. *Teacher demonstrates* holding up "Suddenly Fast" card with or without recording—in tempo.

2. *Class imitates* (prep for activity—briefly).

3. *Class response* (to recording—the activity proper).

4. "I'm impressed with how well everyone raised their cards on the suddenly fast parts. Wonderful! You responded perfectly!" (*assessment*) "Now, this last time, we're going to play the rhythm sticks like this— when it goes fast we'll tap up here—and when it slows down, we'll tap here. Watch me." (*instruction*)

E. *Activity #3* (optional)

1. *Teacher demonstrates* playing rhythm sticks with or without recording—in tempo.

2. *Class imitates* (prep for activity—briefly).

3. *Class response* (to recording—the activity proper).

4. "Not quite, class. Let's try it again. I didn't see everyone lifting the sticks up on the suddenly fast part. Yes, now you've got it!" (*assessment*) "Now with the record once again. Ready." (*instruction*) "Great, I saw everyone playing correctly that time." (*assessment*) "Let's review what we learned today." (*instruction*)

F. *Summary*

1. "So what did we discover about our steady beat today? That it can get what?" (teacher imitates windshield wipers) "Yes, it can get suddenly fast."

2. "Just like turning a dial up—the machine gets suddenly what? Yes, it gets suddenly faster, doesn't it?"

3. "In our next lesson, we'll listen to other recordings that get suddenly slower. Now, take your math books out."

Lesson Planning for General Music Teachers

Lesson planning is crucial for the music teacher as well. Most of you, no doubt, have your own lesson plan format. That's fine. My intention for presenting a sample format is to provide another perspective in regard to lesson planning to keep your own thinking fresh and to offer some assistance to those who genuinely want it.

Suggested Lesson Plan Format for General Music Teachers

I. CONCEPTS

Usually two (sometimes three) in a regular lesson. Can be stated as an idea or as a complete sentence (e.g., accented beats, or stronger sounding beats are called "accented beats").

II. BEHAVIORAL OBJECTIVES

Must be an objective for each concept that indicates what students will be able to do by the end of the lesson.

III. MATERIALS

Should include every item needed for teaching the lesson. Categorize the items, if necessary, according to music, instruments, and equipment.

IV. PROCEDURES (*Need to include the following steps*)

A. *Opening Activity (Start lesson with a familiar, well-liked activity for interest-getting purpose. Need not be related to lesson material. Must be brief.)*

B. *Review Concept*

C. *New Concept (Introduce a new musical idea through a motivational idea. New concept not possible at every level. Suggested steps include the following.)*

1. Motivational Idea

2. Verbal Bridge

3. Focusing Selection (first, more obvious selection)

　a. Activity #1: Verbal Bridge

　　• Teacher Demonstration

　　• Class Preparation

　　• Class Performance

　b. Activity #2: Verbal Bridge

　(same as above)

4. Reinforcing Selection (second, less obvious selection)

　a. Activity #1: Verbal Bridge

　(same as above)

　b. Activity #2: Verbal Bridge

　(same as above)

5. Summarizing New Concept

D. *Closing Activity (End lesson with same or different activity than opening. Purpose is to leave students with pleasurable music experience.)*

Explanation of Lesson Plan

Concepts. Cite each conceptual idea you plan to teach. Label the concepts as being "new" or "old" as shown on the sample lesson plan. State the concept either as an abbreviated idea or a complete sentence, like the following examples:

- Upward melodic direction **or** Some passages in the melody go in an upward direction.
- I-V accompaniment chords **or** Many songs can be accompanied with only the I and V chords.
- Phrase identification **or** Phrases in music can be identified by rest signs, long notes, or punctuation marks.

Behavioral Objectives. Include an objective, or short-term goal, for each concept. When there's more than one concept involved, use a preface statement, like:

By the end of . . . minutes, the . . . grade class will be able to . . .

Be sure the behavioral objective includes six pieces of information: (1) time limit, (2) grade level, (3) terminal verb, (4) conceptual idea, (5) criterion indicator, and (6) musical activities. See the description for each of these items and the sample lesson plan with items numbered in the earlier discussion on behavioral objectives.

Materials. Indicate everything you need to teach the lesson. If you have just a few materials or instruments, simply list them neatly so you can see them at a glance. But if you need music, instruments, and some equipment, then use a categorized list, such as:

A. *Music and Materials*
   1. Textbooks or music
   2. Visual aids
B. *Instruments*
   1. Rhythm sticks   3. Maracas
   2. Autoharps   4. Electric pianos
C. *Equipment*
   1. CD or cassette player
   2. Overhead projector

Even if you don't need a full-blown lesson plan like the one in the sample, you still have to write your materials somewhere. The point is, you need a convenient, easy-to-read list regardless of what kind of lesson plan you use. So list your materials; it'll save you time. I kid you not!

Procedures

A. **Opening Activity**: This is simply a brief attention-getting device. It's an interest-grabbing ploy where you get everybody's mind focused on music and away from everything else. So the activity **should not be related to the**

lesson. It's just for enjoyment, such as doing an action song, singing a round, or chanting a rap. You'll be smart to get a repertoire of students' "favorites," in fact. Keep it short, though, no longer than five minutes. Just long enough to get the class's mind on music. Then use a **verbal bridge**, like this:

> "Good job! You did such-and-such exceptionally well today." (*assessment*) "Let's go on now and work some more on our high and low pitches, okay? Today, we're going to stretch up on the high pitches (teacher stretches) and squat on the low ones (teacher squats). I'll do it with the music. Watch me. And listen." (*instruction*)

B. **Old Concept**: Most of your lessons will be review or reinforcing lessons in that the concept(s) and skill(s) will have been **previously introduced**. When there's a new concept, part of the lesson is devoted to reinforcing the "old," and part to introducing the "new."

Activity #1: Notice how the instructional part of the verbal bridge (at the end of the motivational idea) sets you up for the teacher demonstration. The activity officially begins with the demonstration, so do the **demonstration** precisely, with a little flair, and then **prep** the class by having everyone "try" the activity with you. Music is optional in the prep. Just be sure you get the "right" tempo if you don't use music. Keep the prep short. Good rule is: Three times or no longer than 8-10 seconds. Get students in starting position immediately after the prep so they're ready when the music begins. Then let the students **perform**, or "do," the activity with the music. After that? The verbal bridge, of course.

Verbal Bridge: Assess the activity (acceptable or unacceptable) and instruct class to either (a) go on to the next activity, or the summarizing, or (b) repeat the activity.

Activity #2: The second activity is tentative in a lesson with a new concept because there may not be time. If you do have a second activity, follow the same procedure as in the first activity. The **verbal bridge** should take you right into the summary.

Summary: This is really a closing tactic where you bring the activity to a smooth end before going on to something else. Get the class involved, and ask short-answer questions. Don't end up "telling" the class what they learned. Then "verbal bridge" it to the new concept.

C. **New Concept**: Once again, the preceding verbal bridge (after the summary) should do the job of leading you right to the motivational idea.

Motivational Idea: To help students get a "handle" on the new concept, relate the new concept to something familiar in their surroundings. Involve the class by letting them imitate, dramatize, or answer questions. (The sample lesson used a basketball to emphasize accented/unaccented beats.) Then close the motivational step with a verbal bridge.

Verbal Bridge: See the sample lesson plan.

Focusing Selection: The first selection must be a very clear-cut, obvious example of the concept; thus, the name "focusing." If there's time, you could do several activities with the focusing selection, as the sample plan shows.

Activities #1 and #2: Notice that the presenting formula is the same for every activity: namely, the teacher demonstration, class prep, and then class performance. The procedure does not take away from the creativeness of the lesson because different music and different activities add the variety. And as always, it's the verbal bridges that connect one activity with the next.

Reinforcing Selection: Once you get past that first focusing selection, every musical example after that becomes a "reinforcing" selection. These reinforcing selections become less and less obvious and more subtle, as time goes by. Once again, the last verbal bridge (of the focusing activities) sets the stage for the reinforcing activities.

Activities #1 (and #2): There may not be time for two reinforcing activities. But whether there's one or two, the presenting formula stays the same. See the sample plan for the verbal bridging into the summarizing.

Summarizing: See the sample lesson plan.

With the sample lesson plan and the accompanying explanations, you should have a clear idea of the overall scheme of the lesson plan and the significant role the verbal bridging plays in this plan.

One point needs to be clarified, however. Be sure you understand that this lesson plan is the one you would use to introduce a **new concept**. Most of the time you will be dealing with two (maybe three) **review concepts**, in which case, the new concept section (in the lesson plan) would be replaced with the second reinforcing concept.

Concluding Challenge

When all is said and done, the fact is that good teaching starts with good planning—and good planning, in turn, depends largely upon having a practical, easy-to-use planning document (a workable lesson plan). Some of you might still be looking for a planning model; while others might just want some fresh ideas for your own lesson plan. This chapter will help meet both needs.

*Sample Lesson Plan
for General Music Teachers
(Lower Elementary)*

I. *CONCEPTS*

   A. Old Concept: Most songs and recordings have high and low sounding pitches.

   B. New Concept: Stronger beats are called "accented beats" and are followed by weaker beats called "unaccented beats."

II. *BEHAVIORAL OBJECTIVES*

By the end of twenty minutes, the first-grade class should be able to:

   A. Recognize high-low pitches in a familiar song, as a result of participating in (1) **stretching and squatting** on high-low pitches, and (2) **playing** finger cymbals and drums.

   B. Identify accented and unaccented beats easily, as a result of engaging in (1) Indian **dancing**, (2) **playing** drums, and (3) **clapping and tapping** on accented/unaccented beats while chanting S w w w.

III. *MATERIALS*

   A. Music (Songs and Recordings)

      1. "Do a Little Dance," *The Feel of Music*, Gr. 3, vol. 1.

      2. "Hop Up, My Ladies," *Spectrum of Music*, p. 78.

      3. "Dagger Dance," *Adventures of Music*, Gr. 3, vol. 1.

      4. "London Bridge"

   B. Instruments

      1. Drum heads with mallets

      2. Finger cymbals

IV. *PROCEDURE*

   A. *Opening Activity*: Dancing movement with "Do a Little Dance" by Hap Palmer (dancing in place)

   B. *Old Concept*: High/Low Pitches

      1. *Reinforcing Selection*: "Hop Up, My Ladies," *Spect. Mus*, p. 78

         a. *Activity #1*: Stretching/Squatting

            • Teacher demo (modeling activity for students)

            • Class prep (imitating teacher demo, "trying out")

            • Class perform (doing activity WITH the music)

         b. *Verbal Bridge*: "Very good, class. I saw everyone stretching way up high on those high pitches and squatting down quickly on all the low pitches. You were really listening." (*assessment*) "I wonder! Do you think you can pretend to play finger cymbals on the high pitches and drum on the low pitches this time? Like this? Watch me." (*instruction*)

    c. *Activity #2*: Playing finger cymbals and drums

  2. *Summarizing* (or Closing) Review Concept

"Bravo for you, class! You 'played' your cymbals on all the high pitches and tapped out all the low pitches on your pretend drums. Good job." (*assessment*) "Let's put our high-low pitches away for today, and learn about a brand new idea called 'accented beats.' But first, let's talk about accented beats." (*instruction*)

C. *New Concept*: Accented Beats Followed by Unaccented Beats

  1. *Motivational Idea*: Teacher demonstrates how basketball sounds when it bounces, i.e., stronger on first bounce, weaker on second, third, etc., beats.

  2. *Verbal Bridge*: "Did you know that beats in music sound just like a bouncing basketball? That's right. Some beats are stronger sounding. And the following ones sound weaker." (*comment*) "Listen and watch me do an Indian dance with stronger, or accented steps, and weaker steps, which would be the unaccented beats."

  3. *Focusing Selection*: "Dagger Dance," *Adventures of Music*, Gr. 3, vol. 1, side 1

    a. *Activity #1*: Doing Indian Dance

- Teacher demo

- Class prep

- Class perform

    b. *Verbal Bridge*: "What good Indian dancers you are! Everyone stepped hard on the accented beat and softer on the unaccented beats. It sounded just like a real Indian celebration." (*assessment*) "This time let's be the Indian braves who play the drums. Like this. Watch me. And listen." (*instruction*)

    c. *Activity #2*: (Follow same procedure as in Activity #1)

    d. *Verbal Bridge*: "Excellent! I could really hear the S w w w beats, or the accented-unaccented beats. You're good Indian drummers." (*assessment*) "Now let's see if we can hear the accented-unaccented beats in 'London Bridge.' We're going to clap-and-tap this time. Like this. Everyone listening and watching?" (*instruction*)

  4. *Reinforcing Selection*: "London Bridge"

    a. *Activity #1*: Clapping and Tapping

- Teacher demo

- Class prep

- Class perform

    b. *Verbal Bridge*: "Very good! You clapped and tapped the accented and unaccented beats perfectly. I'm proud of you." (*assessment*) "We don't have time for another activity today, so let's review our new concept before we leave, okay?" (*instruction*)

5. *Summarizing* (or Closing) New Concept

    a. *Summary*: "Today, boys and girls, we learned that some beats sound like the first bounce of this basketball" (teacher bounces basketball). "Some beats sound like the first bounce. So they sound how? Yes! Stronger. And do you remember what new name we gave these stronger beats? Very good. Accented beats. And if the beat isn't accented, or it's like the weaker bounce, we call it what? Right! An unaccented beat."

    b. *Verbal Bridge*: "Well, you just remembered everything about our new accented and unaccented beats, didn't you? Super! You worked hard today." (*assessment*) "How about if we close with our 'Do a Little Dance' before we go."

D. *Closing Activity*: Dancing movement with "Do a Little Dance" by Hap Palmer (dancing in place)

    a. *Verbal Bridge*: "You really like doing those dance steps, don't you? Good job." (*assessment*) "Next time, we'll work more on our accented and unaccented beats and find more songs with high and low pitches. Right now, let's sit up and get ready to leave." (*instruction*)